I0053031

SMEs AND ECONOMIC INTEGRATION IN SOUTHEAST ASIA

The **ISEAS – Yusof Ishak Institute** (formerly Institute of Southeast Asian Studies) is an autonomous organization established in 1968. It is a regional centre dedicated to the study of socio-political, security, and economic trends and developments in Southeast Asia and its wider geostrategic and economic environment. The Institute's research programmes are grouped under Regional Economic Studies (RES), Regional Strategic and Political Studies (RSPS), and Regional Social and Cultural Studies (RSCS). The Institute is also home to the ASEAN Studies Centre (ASC), the Nalanda-Sriwijaya Centre (NSC), and the Singapore APEC Study Centre.

ISEAS Publishing, an established academic press, has issued more than 2,000 books and journals. It is the largest scholarly publisher of research about Southeast Asia from within the region. ISEAS Publishing works with many other academic and trade publishers and distributors to disseminate important research and analyses from and about Southeast Asia to the rest of the world.

SMEs AND ECONOMIC INTEGRATION IN SOUTHEAST ASIA

EDITED BY
**CASSEY LEE,
DIONISIUS NARJOKO
AND SOTHEA OUM**

ISEAS YUSOF ISHAK
INSTITUTE

ERIA
Economic Research Institute
for ASEAN and East Asia

First published in Singapore in 2019 by
ISEAS Publishing
30 Heng Mui Keng Terrace
Singapore 119614

E-mail: publish@iseas.edu.sg
Website: <http://bookshop.iseas.edu.sg>

All rights reserved. No part of this publication may be reproduced, stored in a retrieval system, or transmitted in any form or by any means, electronic, mechanical, photocopying, recording or otherwise, without the prior permission of the ISEAS – Yusof Ishak Institute.

© 2019 ISEAS – Yusof Ishak Institute, Singapore

The responsibility for facts and opinions in this publication rests exclusively with the authors and their interpretations do not necessarily reflect the views or the policy of the publisher or its supporters.

ISEAS Library Cataloguing-in-Publication Data

SMEs and Economic Integration in Southeast Asia / edited by Cassey Lee, Dionisius Narjoko and Sothea Oum.
1. Small business—Southeast Asia.
2. Southeast Asia—Economic integration.
3. East Asia—Economic integration.
4. Corporations, Asian—Southeast Asia.
5. Corporations, Japanese—Southeast Asia.
6. Corporations, Chinese—Southeast Asia.
7. Taiwan—Foreign economic relations—Southeast Asia.
8. Southeast Asia—Foreign economic relations—Taiwan.
I. Lee, Cassey.
II. Narjoko, Dionisius.
III. Oum, Sothea.
IV. Title: Small and Medium Enterprises and Economic Integration in Southeast Asia
HD2346 A9S63   2019

ISBN 978-981-4818-78-0 (soft cover)
ISBN 978-981-4818-79-7 (E-book PDF)

Typeset by International Typesetters Pte Ltd
Printed in Singapore by Mainland Press Pte Ltd

CONTENTS

List of Tables   vii

List of Figures   xvii

About the Contributors   xxi

1. Introduction   1
   Cassey Lee, Dionisius Narjoko and Sothea Oum

PART 1: COUNTRY STUDIES

2. SME Participation in ASEAN and East Asian Integration: 9
   Case of Cambodia
   Shandre M. Thangavelu, Sothea Oum and Samsen Neak

3. Indonesian Small and Medium Enterprise Participation in   34
   ASEAN Economic Integration
   Titik Anas

4. Lao SME Participation in Regional Economic Integration   97
   Phouphet Kyophilavong

5. Government Policies, Regional Trading Agreements and   142
   Economic Performance of National Electronic Components
   Small and Medium-sized Enterprises in Malaysia
   Rajah Rasiah and Govindamal Thangiah

6. Myanmar SMEs' Participation in ASEAN and East Asian   170
    Regional Economic Integration: With a Focus on Food and
    Apparel Manufacturing
    Thomas Bernhardt, S. Kanay De and Giles Dickenson-Jones

7. Philippine SME Participation in ASEAN and East Asian   287
    Regional Economic Integration
    Rafaelita M. Aldaba

8. Thailand's SME Participation in ASEAN and East Asian   355
    Regional Economic Integration
    Teerawat Charoenrat and Charles Harvie

9. Vietnam SMEs' Participation in Regional Economic   435
    Integration: Survey Results of Three Manufacturing
    Sectors
    Nguyen Dinh Chuc, Nguyen Ngoc Anh and Nguyen Thi Kim Thai

PART 2: MULTINATIONAL ENTERPRISE STUDIES

10. Use of Preference at Export Platform: Evidence from Export   491
    to China by Japanese Affiliates in ASEAN
    Kazunobu Hayakawa and Toshiyuki Matsuura

11. South Korean Multinational Enterprises and Vietnam SMEs'   514
    Participation in Global Production Networks in the Context
    of Increased ASEAN and East Asian Regional Economic
    Integration
    *Nguyen Ngoc Anh, Nguyen Thi Tuong Anh, Nguyen Ngoc Minh
    and Nguyen Thi Phuong Mai*

12. The Evolution of Taiwan's Economic Links with ASEAN   550
    Shin-Horng Chen, Pei-Chang Wen and Meng-Chun Liu

13. Chinese Multinational Firms in Southeast Asia: A Study of   578
    Chery in Malaysia
    Zhang Miao

Index   613

LIST OF TABLES

1.1	Sample Distribution by Industry and Country	3
2.1	Key Indicators of Cambodia's Economic Structure	10
2.2	Characteristics of Industrial Sector in Cambodia	13
2.3	Distribution of Firms by Size and Industry in Cambodia	14
2.4	Sample Distribution by Size and Industry	16
2.5	Characteristics of the Surveyed SMEs	17
2.6	Summary Statistics of Variables	27
2.7	Characteristics of SMEs' Utilization of FTAs	28
3.1	Employee Productivity by Enterprise Scale (in million rupiah)	41
3.2	Comparison of MSMEs' Contribution to Economy across ASEAN Members	42
3.3	SME Policy Initiatives in Indonesia, 1969–2000	45
3.4	SME Policy Initiatives in Indonesia Since 2008	47
3.5	ASEAN SME Policy Index	52
3.6	Profile of the Sample	56
3.7	Sales Distribution and Product Type	59
3.8	Overall Sales and Destination	62
3.9	Distribution of Sales Based on Output	63

3.10 Distribution of Sales Activities Based on Destination   63

3.11 Production and Input Characteristics   64

3.12 Employment Profile   66

3.13 Workforce and Salaries, 2014   67

3.14 Training Expenditures   68

3.15 Innovation Activities and Expenditure, 2012–14   69

3.16 Use of Internet-related Services   72

3.17 Business Relations with Firms in ASEAN   73

3.18 Distribution of Respondents by Exporting/Importing   74
      Activities

3.19 Perception of Respondents on Impact of AEC on Businesses   76

3.20 AEC Key Changes Affecting Businesses   77

3.21 Cross Tabulation of Export-Import Activities and Business   78
      Relations

3.22 Cross Tabulation of Foreign Ownership and Business   79
      Relations for Actively Trading Firms

3.23 Cross Tabulation of Usage of FTA Forms and Awareness of   80
      AEC for Actively Exporting Firms

3.24 Government Support and Business Relations in ASEAN   81

3.25 Perception of Respondents: How FTAs Will Affect Their   82
      Businesses

3.26 Description of Variables   83

3.27 Probit Model for Export   84

3.28 Probit Model for Import   85

3.29 Probit Model for FTA   86

3.30 Percentage of Respondents Who Received Government   88
      Support

4.1   Macroeconomic Situation in Laos   99

4.2   Definition of SMEs   105

4.3   SMEs' Contribution   106

4.4   SMEs by Activities   106

4.5   External and Internal Constraints of Enterprises   107

4.6   Determinants of Preferential Tariff Utilization   117

4.7   Factor Determinants of SMEs Exporting Using the Logit   120
      Model

5.1   Employment by SMEs and Large Enterprises in Malaysia,   145
      2009–13 (millions)

5.2   SME Development Programmes, 2014   146

5.3   Incubators in Malaysia, 2010   151

5.4   Electronic Components Firms by Size, Malaysia, 2014   156

5.5   National Electronic Components Firms by Industry   156
      Breakdown, Malaysia, 2014

5.6   Descriptive Statistics of Variables   157

5.7   Bivariate Association Between Industry, Firm Size and   160
      RTAs

5.8   Mean Values of Key Variables by Industry, National   162
      Electronic Components Firms

5.9   Economic Characteristics of Electronic Components Firms   163
      by Firm Size and RTAs

5.10 Fitted Estimates of Variables that have an Impact on IHRD   164

5.11 Fitted Estimates of Variables that have an Impact on XS   165

5.12 Fitted Estimates of Variables that have an Impact on XSa   166

6.1   Key Macroeconomic Indicators for Myanmar   171

6.2   Myanmar Government Revenues, Expenditures and Deficit   172
      (% of GDP)

6.3   International Transactions: Myanmar's Current Account   173

6.4   Myanmar's Bilateral Exports to ASEAN and East Asian   183
      Countries (USD thousand)

6.5   Myanar's Top-20 Export Products to ASEAN   184

6.6   Myanmar's Bilateral Imports from ASEAN and East Asian   186
      Countries (USD thousand)

6.7   Myanmar's Top-20 Import Products from ASEAN   187

6.8   Myanmar's Free Trade Agreements   189

6.9   Intra- and Extra-ASEAN FDI Inflows (USD million)   192

6.10 Approved FDI of ASEAN and East Asian Countries in   193
      Myanmar (USD million)

6.11 New SME Definition in Myanmar According to the 2015   197
      SME Law

6.12 Survey Sample Characteristics   201

6.13 Selected Firm Characteristics by Industry   204

6.14 Informality Among Myanmar Firms   207

6.15 Age Distribution of Survey Firms   209

6.16 Domestic vs. Foreign Ownership According to Firm Size   211

6.17 Share of Foreign-invested Firms by Firm Size and Industry   212

6.18 Innovation and Use of Technology among Myanmar Firms   213

6.19 Percentage of ICT Usage by Size   213

6.20 ICT Usage Score by Firm Size, Ownership and Industry   214

6.21 Introduction of a New Product and/or Service by Firm Size   217
      and Ownership, 2012–14

6.22 Share of Firms Having Introduced a New Product or New   218
      Service, 2012–14

6.23 Access to Finance for Myanmar Firms   219

6.24 Access to Bank Loans for Myanmar Firms   220

6.25 Workforce Characteristics of Myanmar Companies   222

6.26 Education Level of Founders/Owners of Family-run   223
      Businesses

6.27 Share of Firms Employing Foreign Staff in Different Occupations 225

6.28 Countries of Origin of Foreign Investors in Myanmar by Sector and Firm Size 228

6.29 SME Participation in International Trade for Selected ASEAN Countries 233

6.30 Source of Inputs by Industry and Firm Size 237

6.31 Share of Firms with ASEAN Business Relations by Firm Size and Foreign Ownership 239

6.32 Business Relationships with ASEAN Countries 239

6.33 Exporting Firms by Industry, Firm Size and Export Markets 241

6.34 Myanmar's Major Export Destinations by Industry 242

6.35 Myanmar's Major Export Destinations by Firm Size 244

6.36 Sources of Foreign Inputs by Sector and Country of Origin 246

7.1 Manufacturing Structure and Growth Performance 291

7.2 Number of Establishments by Industry and Employment Size, 2013 295

7.3 Total Employment by Industry and Size, 2013 296

7.4 Total Number of Manufacturing Enterprises and Employees 297

7.5 Tariff Profile by FTA 300

7.6 Profile of the Sample Firms 303

7.7 Sales Activities 306

7.8 Production Activities 309

7.9 Employment Profile 311

7.10 Innovation Activities 312

7.11 Use of Internet-related Services 315

7.12 ASEAN Economic Community 2015 316

7.13 Perceptions on the Impact of AEC on Businesses (%) 318

7.14 FTAs   322

7.15 Perceptions on the Impact of FTAs on Businesses   325

7.16(a) Characteristics of FTA Users   327

7.16(b) Characteristics of FTA Users   328

7.17 Awareness and Perceptions on the Impact of AEC   333

7.18 Firm Size and Perceptions on the Impact of AEC   335

7.19 Export Activity and Perceptions on the Impact of AEC   337

7.20 FTA Use and Perceptions on the Impact of AEC   338

7.21 Risk Preference and Perceptions on the Impact of AEC   339

7.22 Hiring of Foreign Workers and Perceptions on the Impact   340
      of AEC

7.23 Introduction of New Products and Perceptions on the   341
      Impact of AEC

7.24 Selected Firm Characteristics and Perceptions on the Impact   342
      of AEC

7.25 Characteristics of the Firm Respondents   344

7.26 Definition of Variables   345

7.27 Regression Results   347

8.1   Contribution of Manufacturing SMEs to the Thai Economy,   356
      2007–12

8.2   Summary: Definitions of Thai SMEs by Sector   359

8.3   Number and Percentage of SMEs and Enterprises by Size,   361
      2007–12

8.4   Number and Percentage of SMEs by Sector, 2007–12   363

8.5   Number and Percentage of SME Employment and   365
      Enterprises by Size, 2007–12

8.6   SME Employment by Number and Percentage, Classified by   366
      Sector, 2006–12

8.7   GDP Classified by Size of Enterprise, 2007–12   368

8.8 GDP of SMEs in Aggregate, Classified by Economic   370
     Activity, 2007–12

8.9 Value and Percentage of Exports, Classified by Size of   372
     Enterprise, 2009–12

8.10 Value and Percentage of SME Exports, Classified by   374
     Country, 2007–12

8.11 Thailand's Merchandise Trade Value by Country and   376
     Trade Group, 1995–2013 (million baht)

8.12 Results of the First SME Promotion Plan, 2002–6   383

8.13 Number and Percentage of Interviewed Firms,   388
     Classified by Size, Sub-manufacturing Sector and
     Type of Ownerships

8.14 Number and Percentage of Manufacturing Firms,   389
     Classified by Firm Size and Sector

8.15 Number and Percentage of Ownership Type, Classified by   391
     Firm Size and Sector

8.16 Number and Percentage of Type of Family Business and   393
     Ownership of the Parent Company, Classified by Firm Size
     and Sector

8.17 Highest Academic Qualification of the Founder or Family   396
     Relative Running the Firms in the Sample, Classified by
     Firm Size and Sector

8.18 Number and Percentage of Exporting and Non-Exporting   398
     Enterprises, Classified by Firm Size and Sector

8.19 Number and Percentage of Firms in the Sample Conducting   400
     Production Only In-house, Through Outsourcing or Using
     Both of These, Classified by Firm Size and Sector

8.20 Number and Percentage of Firms that Spent on Worker   403
     Training and Hired Foreign Workers, Classified by Firm
     Size and Sector

8.21 Number and Percentage of Firms in the Sample that Spent   405
     on In-house R&D and Outsourcing R&D Activities,
     Classified by Firm Size and Sector

8.22 Number and Percentage of Firms in the Sample that had   406
      Acquired Machinery Equipment, Software and External
      Knowledge, Classified by Firm Size and Sector

8.23 Number and Percentage of Firms in the Sample that   409
      Introduced New or Significantly Improved Goods and
      Services, Classified by Firm Size and Sector

8.24 Number and Percentage of Firms in the Sample that   410
      Introduced Innovation and Technology, Classified by Firm
      Size and Sector

8.25 Number and Percentage of Sample Firms Using Internet-   412
      related Services, Classified by Firm Size and Sector

8.26 Number and Percentage of Firms Having Business   415
      Relations with Firms in Other ASEAN Countries,
      Awareness of the ASEAN SME Policy Blueprint/Strategic
      Action Plan and Awareness of the AEC, Classified by Firm
      Size and Sector

8.27 Maximum Likelihood Estimates for Parameters of Probit   423
      and Logit Models for Aggregate Manufacturing Firms

8.28 Maximum Likelihood Estimates for Parameters of Probit   424
      and Logit Models for Large Manufacturing Firms

8.29 Maximum Likelihood Estimates for Parameters of Probit   425
      and Logit Models for Small Manufacturing Firms

8.30 A Summary of the Main Findings from This Study: 427
      Statistically Significant Factors Impacting the Export
      Participation of the Sample of Thai Firms

9.1   Vietnam's Definition of SMEs   438

9.2   SMEs in Vietnam, 2000–12   440

9.3   SMEs by Ownership (%)   442

9.4   Export Turnover and Three Major Markets of Vietnam's   447
      Textile and Garment Industry, 2011–13

9.5   Basic Information of the Sample   456

9.6   Sales Activities   459

9.7 Production Activities — 462

9.8 Human Resources — 464

9.9 Innovation Activities — 466

9.10 International Trade Participation — 467

9.11 Awareness of the ASEAN Economic Community and Its Policies — 468

9.12 Influence of the ASEAN Economic Community, by Sector (%) — 470

9.13 Influence of the ASEAN Economic Community, by Size (%) — 471

9.14 Awareness of FTAs — 473

9.15 Impact of FTAs on the Enterprises (%) — 474

9.16 Government Support — 475

9.17 Average Value of SME Characteristics — 479

9.18 Comparison Between Participating and Non-participating Enterprises — 479

9.19 Determinants of SMEs to Participate in Production Networks — 481

10.1 Affiliate-level Share of Sales and Procurement According to Parent's Size: Average in Japanese Affiliates in ASEAN, 2013 — 498

10.2 Affiliate-level Shares of Originating Inputs According to Parent's Size: Average in Japanese Affiliates in ASEAN, 2013 — 499

10.3 Export and ACFTA Use by Japanese Affiliates, 2013 — 500

10.4 Problems Encountered when Japanese Affiliates in ASEAN Export under FTA Schemes — 501

10.5 Basic Statistics — 502

10.6 Significant Factors in Export and FTA Utilization — 503

10.7 Results in Industry Dummy and Export Country Dummy — 504

10.8 Decomposition of Originating Inputs   506

10.9 Correlation with Parent's Size   507

11.1 Key Investors in Vietnam (as of February 2016)   520

11.2 Vietnamese SMEs' Participation in Global Production   525
      Networks

11.3 Top Ten Largest Exporters of Apparel Worldwide, 2014   526

12.1 Taiwan's Outward Investment to ASEAN   554

12.2 Major Sectors of Taiwan's Direct Investment in the ASEAN   555
      Members

12.3 Taiwan's Export to Different Parts of the World, 2001–15   557

12.4 Taiwan's Export to the ASEAN Members, 2001–15   558

12.5 Taiwan's Import from Different Parts of the World, 2001–15   560

12.6 Taiwan's Import from the ASEAN Members, 2001–15   561

12.7 A Snapshot of Taiwan's Trade in the Textile and Apparel   563
      Industry, 2015

12.8 Structural Changes of Taiwan's Export in the Textile and   563
      Apparel Industry

12.9 The "Trade-Investment-Service-IP Nexus" of the Textile   568
      and Apparel Industry: A Taiwanese Perspective

13.1 China's Outward FDI Flows, 2005–13 (USD million)   586

13.2 China's Investments in ASEAN by Sector, until 2014   588
      (USD million)

13.3 Accumulated Investments in the Manufacturing Sector: 589
      China to ASEAN, 2005–14 (USD million)

13.4 Policy Support Framework: China's "Going-out" Policy   592

13.5 ACFTA Legal Framework, 2002–9   595

13.6 Duties and Local Taxes for Automobiles in Malaysia, 2015   603

LIST OF FIGURES

2.1	Characteristics of Cambodia's Economy (% of GDP)	11
2.2	SMEs' Awareness of ASEAN	18
2.3	Relations with Other Firms in ASEAN	19
2.4	Imports and Exports	21
2.5	Perception of the Impact of AEC on SMEs	22
2.6	Key Changes of AEC: Perceived Impact on SMEs	23
2.7	Use of FTAs and Custom Forms by SMEs	24
2.8	Reasons for Not Using FTAs and Custom Forms by SMEs	25
3.1	Contribution of MSMEs to the Economy	38
3.2	GDP Distribution and Growth, 2013 (%)	39
3.3	MSMEs' Contribution to Employment, 2008–14	40
3.4	Enterprise Establishment Growth, 2008–14	40
3.5	Distribution of SMEs across ASEAN (%)	43
3.6	Distribution of Survey Sample	55
3.7	Academic Qualifications of Workers	68
3.8	Introduction of Product Innovation, 2012–14	71
3.9	Share of New and Improved Products in Sales (%)	71
3.10	Proportion of Respondents that Introduced Process Innovation, 2012–14	71

3.11 Firms' Awareness of AEC and ASEAN SMEs Policy   75
     Blueprint

3.12 Reasons for Not Utilizing FTA Forms   80

4.1 Awareness of AFTA and WTO   110
     (ES2007, ES2009, ES2011, ES2013)

4.2 Awareness of AEC, AFTA and WTO   110

4.3 Perceptions of How AEC Will Affect Businesses   111

4.4 Overall Effects of AFTA   112

4.5 Overall Effects of WTO   113

5.1 Average Annual Value Added Growth of SMEs and GDP   144
     in Malaysia, 2006–14 (%)

5.2 SMEs' Value-added Share of GDP in Malaysia, 2005–13 (%) 145

5.3 Sources of Venture Capital Funds   150

6.1 Myanmar's Exports and Imports in USD Million (left axis) 177
     and as Share of GDP (right axis), 1995–2013

6.2 Share of ASEAN in Member States' Total Exports and   179
     Imports, 2013

6.3 Growth Rates of Exports to and Imports from ASEAN,   180
     2005–13 (%)

6.4 Per Capita Exports to and Imports from ASEAN, 2013 (USD) 181

6.5 Share of Myanmar in Total Intra-ASEAN Exports, 2013   182

6.6 Intra- and Extra-ASEAN FDI Inflows, 2014   191

6.7 Share of Myanmar in Intra-ASEAN FDI Inflows, 2014   194

6.8 Legal Status of Myanmar Companies   210

6.9 Innovation and Technology Efforts, Classified by Firm Size 216
     and Sector, 2012–14

6.10 Percentage of Firms Reporting Expenditures on Worker 224
     Training

6.11 Share of Firms Employing Foreign Staff in Different   227
     Occupations, Classified by Firm Size and Sector

6.12 Percentage of SMEs Exporting Directly or Indirectly   234
     (at least 1% of sales)

6.13 Main Marketing Channels (%)   235

6.14 Percentage of SMEs Using Material Inputs and/or Supplies   236
     of Foreign Origin

6.15 Awareness of AEC and ASEAN Blueprint for SME   248
     Development by Industry and Firm Size

6.16 Firms' Responses to the Question: "How Has AEC Affected   249
     or Will Affect Your Business?"

6.17 Firms' Responses to the Question: "What are Key Changes   251
     due to AEC that Affect Your Business?"

6.18 Usage of FTAs and Reasons for Not Using Any FTA   254

6.19 Reported Usage of Different FTAs and Trade Preference   255
     Schemes

6.20 Perceived Impact of FTAs on Businesses   257

6.21 Extent and Nature of Government Support by Firm Size,   259
     2012–14

7.1 Quarterly Industry Growth, 2009–14   290

7.2 Distribution by Manufacturing Sector   302

7.3 FTA Use   323

8.1 Business Relations with Firms in Other ASEAN Countries,   417
     Awareness of the ASEAN SME Policy Blueprint/Strategic
     Action Plan, and Awareness of the AEC

8.2 How Has the AEC Affected or Will Affect the Businesses of   418
     Sample Firms, Classified by Firm Size

8.3 How Has the AEC Affected or Will Affect the Businesses of   419
     Sample Firms, Classified by Sector

9.1 Share of SMEs in Total Number of Enterprises   439

9.2 Total Employment of Enterprises: SMEs vs. Large   441
     Enterprises

9.3 Share of SMEs in Total Revenue   443

9.4   State Budget Contribution: SMEs vs. Large Enterprises   444

9.5   Revenue of the Food and Beverage Industry (billion VND)   450

9.6   Vietnam's Wood Product Exporting Markets, 2009 and 2013   452

9.7   The Survey Sample   454

11.1   Vietnam–South Korea Bilateral Trade Flows (USD billion)   519

11.2   South Korean FDI Inflows into Vietnam, 2005–15   521

11.3   Vietnam's Key Exports: Electronics a Rising Sector   532
       (USD million)

12.1   Taiwan's Export to ASEAN, 2001–15   556

12.2   Taiwan's Import from ASEAN, 2001–15   559

12.3   International Division of Labour in the Textile and Apparel   565
       Industry Since 1990s: A Value Chain's Perspective

12.4   Taiwan's Textile and Apparel Industry and Its Relationships   566
       with the Global Value Chains

13.1   Analytic Framework   583

13.2   China's Outward FDI Stock in ASEAN by Country, 2013   587
       (USD million)

13.3   ASEAN's FTA Network   598

ABOUT THE CONTRIBUTORS

Rafaelita M. Aldaba, Assistant Secretary, Department of Trade and Industry (DTI), Philippines

Titik Anas, Managing Director, Presisi Indonesia

Nguyen Ngoc Anh, Chief Economist, Development and Policies Research Center (DEPOCEN, Vietnam); and Affiliate Professor, IPAG Business School (France)

Nguyen Thi Tuong Anh, Vice Dean, Faculty of International Economics, Foreign Trade University, Hanoi; and affiliated member, Development and Policies Research Center (DEPOCEN, Vietnam)

Thomas Bernhardt, Researcher and Policy Analyst, Centre for Economic and Social Development (CESD) Myanmar

Teerawat Charoenrat, Director, Centre for Entrepreneurship, Innovation and SME Development (CEISDA) in the ASEAN Region, Faculty of Business Administration, Nong Khai Campus, Khon Kaen University, Thailand

Shin-Horng Chen, Director, International Division, Chung-Hua Institution for Economic Research

Nguyen Dinh Chuc, Deputy Director, Institute of Regional Sustainable Development, Vietnam

S Kanay De, Centre for Economic and Social Development (CESD) Myanmar

Giles Dickenson-Jones, Centre for Economic and Social Development (CESD) Myanmar

Charles Harvie, Associate Professor and co-Director, Centre for Contemporary Australasian Business and Economic Studies, School of Accounting, Economics and Finance, Faculty of Business, University of Wollongong, Australia

Kazunobu Hayakawa, Overseas Research Fellow, Institute of Developing Economies, Japan

Phouphet Kyophilavong, Associate Professor and Vice Dean, Faculty of Economics and Business Management, National University of Laos

Cassey Lee, Senior Fellow, ISEAS – Yusof Ishak Institute, Singapore

Meng-Chun Liu, Deputy, Director, International Division, Chung-Hua Institution for Economic Research

Nguyen Thi Phuong Mai, Deputy Director, Development and Policies Research Center (DEPOCEN, Vietnam)

Toshiyuki Matsuura, Associate Professor, Keio Economic Observatory, Keio University, Japan

Nguyen Ngoc Minh, Senior Researcher, Development and Policies Research Center (DEPOCEN, Vietnam)

Dionisius Narjoko, Senior Economist, Economic Research Institute for ASEAN and East Asia (ERIA)

Samsen Neak, Head of Market Research Unit, Nuppun Institute for Economic Research

Sothea Oum, Research Fellow, Asia Growth Research Centre, University of Adelaide

Rajah Rasiah, Distinguished Professor of Economics, Asia-Europe Institute, University of Malaya

Nguyen Thi Kim Thai, Vietnam Academy of Social Sciences

Shandre M. Thangavelu, Regional Director, Southeast Asia, Centre for International Economic Studies, University of Adelaide

Govindamal Thangiah, Department of Development Studies, University of Malaya

Pei-Chang Wen, Research Fellow, International Division, Chung-Hua Institution for Economic Research

Zhang Miao, Associate Professor, Institute of Malaysia Studies, Research School for Southeast Asian Studies, Xiamen University; China Research Fellow, Institute of China Studies, University of Malaya, Malaysia

1

INTRODUCTION

Cassey Lee, Dionisius Narjoko, and Sothea Oum

The economic importance of small and medium-sized enterprises (SMEs) is widely recognized and acknowledged by researchers and policymakers in Southeast Asia. This is not surprising as SMEs typically account for about 97–99 per cent of total enterprises and 60–80 per cent of total employment in Southeast Asian countries (Lee and Zhang 2016). Such statistics notwithstanding, SMEs are often viewed as being disadvantaged compared to large firms because they lack economies of scale and face resource constraints (Harvie 2015). In the theoretical and empirical trade literature on heterogeneous firms, these disadvantages translate into low productivity which affects SMEs' exporting behaviour. For countries in Southeast Asia, this is a serious problem given the fact that many, if not all, countries in the region are committed to achieving greater intra- and inter-regional economic integration. This is to be achieved via the formation of the ASEAN Economic Community (AEC) as well as participation in bilateral and regional free trade agreements (FTAs). The question that follows then is this — can manufacturing SMEs participate effectively in economic integration given the disadvantages they experienced? It was with this question in mind that the Economic Research Institute for ASEAN and East Asia (ERIA) and ISEAS – Yusof Ishak Institute (ISEAS) collaborated to undertake a research project to better understand the current state of manufacturing SMEs' participation in economic integration. This book is a collection of the research papers from the project.

The chapters in this book are organized into two sections. The first part covers country papers. The countries included are Cambodia, Indonesia, Laos, Malaysia, Myanmar, Philippines, Thailand and Vietnam. These are based on primary data collected in the research project. The second part covers linkages between multinational enterprises (MNEs) and SMEs in Southeast Asia. Chapters in this category rely on secondary data and fieldwork interviews with MNEs operating in the region.

For the country studies, several methodological challenges were encountered right from the inception of the project. These affected the sampling approach to be adopted for the surveys. First, due to financial constraints, the project could only cover 200–300 firms per country. Due to this relatively small sample size, it made sense to focus mainly on a few key industries. The main criteria for the choice of these industries was the importance of these industries to the country (see Table 1.1).

A second methodological problem relates to the lack of a single definition of SMEs amongst Southeast Asian countries. To overcome this problem, a single definition (based on OECD discussion notes) was used to guide the sampling of firms by firm size.[1] A third methodological decision was to include large-sized firms in the surveys. This was important in order to compare between SMEs and large firms and identify factors that uniquely affect SMEs' participation in economic integration. The guide for sample size distribution given to country researchers is as follows:

- 30–40 per cent of sample: firms with 11–49 workers
- 40–50 per cent of sample: firms with 50–249 workers
- 20 per cent of sample: firms with 250 or more workers

Finally, the questionnaire used for the survey comprised of 40 questions organized into ten key sections: (1) general information, (2) sales and exports, (3) production and inputs, (4) employment and human resource, (5) technology and innovation, (6) ASEAN Economic Community, (7) utilization of free trade agreements, (8) government

TABLE 1.1
Sample Distribution by Industy and Country

Industry	Indonesia	Thailand	Cambodia	Vietnam	Myanmar	Philippines	Total
Food products	52	95	22	48	89	11	317
Beverages	20	0	10	0	0	2	32
Tobacco products	0	0	1	0	0	0	1
Textiles	1	10	2	82	0	4	99
Wearing apparel	70	0	80	0	102	23	275
Leather products	14	21	7	0	0	2	44
Wood products ecl. furniture	15	0	1	78	2	1	97
Paper products	0	0	0	0	1	3	4
Printing and recorded media	0	0	6	0	0	3	9
Coke and refined petroleum products	0	0	0	0	0	0	0
Chemicals and chemical products	0	0	0	0	0	13	13
Pharmaceutical products	0	0	0	0	0	0	0
Rubber and plastics products	0	104	2	0	0	18	124
Non-metallic mineral products	0	0	0	0	0	1	1
Basic metals	0	0	1	0	0	4	5
Fabricated metal products	0	9	30	0	0	16	55
Computer, electronic and optical products	3	0	2	0	0	9	14
Electrical equipment	4	0	0	0	0	3	7
Machinery and equipment n.e.c.	0	33	0	0	0	4	37
Motor vehicles	1	0	1	0	0	14	16
Other transport equipment	0	0	3	0	0	1	4
Furniture	20	29	10	0	0	5	64
Other manufacturing	0	0	20	0	3	67	90
Repair & installation of machinery/equipment	0	0	1	0	0	1	2
Total	200	301	199	208	197	205	1,310

Source: ERIA–ISEAS Project.

support, (9) other comments, and (10) risk preferences. The questionnaire was designed to generate data that could be used to econometrically test the determinants of participation in regional integration. From the onset of the project, the project coordinators made no effort to impose standardized econometric specifications. This encouraged the country chapter writers to experiment with a variety of specifications which include determinants of: (i) export participation, (ii) import participation, (iii) FTA utilization, and (iv) production network participation.

What are the general findings of the country chapters? Overall, there is still a low level of awareness of AEC amongst SMEs, especially in some of the less developed ASEAN member countries. In these countries, there is significant uncertainty amongst SMEs about how the AEC will impact their businesses. The uneven progress in the implementation of the National Single Window — which affects customs procedures — is also reflected in the findings of this study. An important facilitator of SME internationalization is FTA. The relatively low utilization rate of FTAs amongst SMEs, especially in the less developed Southeast Asian countries, indicates that the barriers to using FTAs remain real and substantial. Government support for SME development — including those aimed at encouraging SMEs to export — remain uneven across ASEAN member countries. As ASEAN moves towards another vision of a more integrated community by 2025, more attention needs to be paid to SME development to ensure that the fruits of regional integration can be equitably shared.

Several key findings emerge in the studies on MNEs in the region. In the study on Japanese MNEs operating in ASEAN countries, large firms are more likely to use FTA schemes in exporting compared to SMEs. The key obstacle to FTA utilization is the need to obtain certificates of origins. The study on South Korean MNEs in Vietnam highlights the difficulties faced by domestic SMEs in integrating into the global production networks. Significant government support is needed to bring this about. The role of government is also highlighted in the study on Taiwanese MNEs in ASEAN countries. In particular, the study argues that whilst the second unbundling of production opens up opportunities for SMEs to participate in the global production networks, obstacles exist but these can be overcome by industrial policies aimed at anchoring flagship MNEs and by strengthening the local industrial base and linkages along the value chain/supply chain. The study on Cherry, the Chinese automotive MNE in Malaysia, demonstrates that premature entry of MNEs could feature very limited linkages between MNEs and domestic SMEs. This problem has been compounded by government policies that favour domestically-owned automotive firms.

The studies in this volume collectively demonstrate that the participation of SMEs in regional integration is a challenging problem. It is hoped that this book will provide insights to scholars and policymakers in the Southeast Asia region and beyond on how to enhance SMEs' participation in regional and global economy in the future.

NOTE

1. See the entry for SMEs at <https://stats.oecd.org/glossary>.

REFERENCES

Harvie, Charles. "SMEs, Trade and Development in South-east Asia". Paper presented at the Conference on 50 Years of Trade Impact for Good, October 2015.

Lee, Cassey and Bernadine Zhang. "SMEs, Competition Law and Growth". In *Competition Law, Regulation & SMEs in the Asia-Pacific: Understanding the Small Business Perspective*, edited by Michael T. Schaper and Cassey Lee. Singapore: ISEAS – Yusof Ishak Institute, 2016.

PART 1

Country Studies

2

SME PARTICIPATION IN ASEAN AND EAST ASIAN INTEGRATION
Case of Cambodia

Shandre M. Thangavelu, Sothea Oum, and Samsen Neak

1. Introduction

Since the 1990s, the Cambodian economy has experienced rapid growth through its openness and market-based policies to support trade and investment. The economy grew at the rate of 7 per cent per annum from 1994–2013, one of the fastest growing economies in ASEAN and Asia. This is probably because of its low base after being ravaged with tremendous political conflicts before 1993.

The Cambodian economy is still an agrarian economy but it is structurally shifting rapidly towards the manufacturing and services sector. The agricultural sector is still dominant in the economy and it is mainly focused on rice production. However, the output share of this sector has fallen over the years to around 30 per cent of GDP in 2014 from 50 per cent in the 1990s. In contrast, the manufacturing sector has grown rapidly in recent years, by about 15 per

TABLE 2.1
Key Indicators of Cambodia's Economic Structure

	1990	1995	2000	2005	2010	2014
Real GDP growth rate (%)	1.2	6.5	8.4	13.3	6.0	7.1
as % of GDP						
Agriculture	**52.3**	**44.6**	**35.9**	**29.4**	**27.3**	**22.6**
Industry	**15.0**	**15.1**	**21.8**	**26.8**	**26.5**	**30.7**
Mining	1.1	0.3	0.2	0.4	0.6	1.1
Manufacturing	7.1	8.9	16.0	19.6	20.3	22.5
Electricity, gas, and water	0.2	0.4	0.4	0.5	0.6	0.6
Construction	6.6	5.6	5.2	6.4	4.9	6.5
Services	**31.4**	**36.0**	**37.1**	**38.5**	**39.0**	**39.5**
Trade	11.0	15.8	14.4	13.0	13.9	14.2
Transport & communications	2.6	6.4	6.6	6.8	6.5	6.4
Finance	6.5	6.7	7.3	8.7	7.7	8.6
Public administration	4.5	2.7	2.7	1.5	1.3	1.1
Other industries	6.7	4.3	6.1	8.5	9.7	9.2
Less imputed bank service charges		0.8	1.1	1.0	1.4	1.6
Taxes less subsidies on production and imports	1.5	5.2	6.2	6.2	8.6	8.8
Total	100	100	100	100	100	100

Source: ADB Statistical Database System.

cent per annum, accounting for 27 per cent of GDP from about 15 per cent during the same period. However, it is dominated to some extend by just one industry — the garments and clothing industry — that accounts for more than half of the manufacturing output and most of Cambodian export.

Compared to the neighbouring country of Thailand, the large agricultural processing and home goods manufacturing, that are typically observed in low-income economies, are largely absent in Cambodian manufacturing due to Cambodia's proximity to large industrialized neighbours who can produce these goods more efficiently. Further, the Cambodian economy is dominated by a large service sector, mainly in tourism, restaurants and transport services.

FIGURE 2.1
Characteristics of Cambodia's Economy (% of GDP)

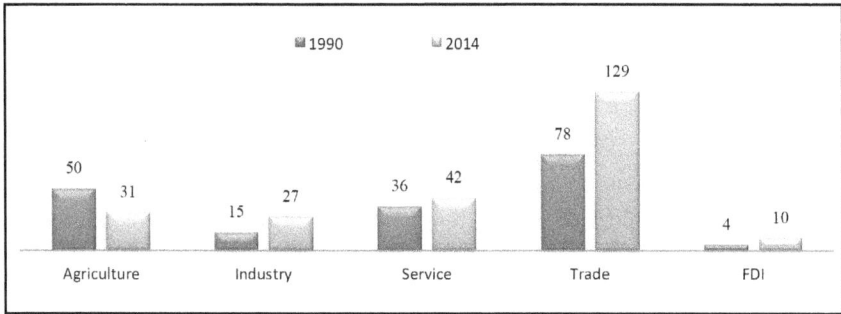

Source: ADB Statistical Database System.

The impact of economic liberalization of the 1990s as well as the granted most favoured nation (MFS) and generalized system of preferences (GSP) status are reflected in the high export and import shares of GDP for the Cambodian economy. The trade share of 129 per cent in 2014 was increased from 78 per cent in 1990, whereas foreign direct investment (FDI) increased from 4 to 10 per cent of GDP during the same period. Exports are narrowly concentrated in merchandise trade with 80 per cent of merchandise exports being garments. The other export commodities include timber, rubber, rice, fish and footwear.

This makes Cambodia susceptible to both internal and global shocks. For example, failure of the rice crop due to adverse weather conditions can cause severe food shortages. In fact, it has been seen that the global slowdown has greatly decreased the demand for tourism and exports of garments as these activities are highly dependent on the developed economies. The global financial crisis revealed the need for the Cambodian economy to structurally adjust to more competitive industries away from the traditional sectors such as garment manufacturing, tourism, and construction sectors.

The need to diversify the domestic industries and link to global production value chains, and increase the competiveness of domestic industries to export market is now becoming an important development strategy. The new strategy for industrial development is needed to avoid the "lower/middle-income trap" by developing human capital, technology, and infrastructure.

Recognizing the role of the private sector, the government has given priority to strengthen governance and capacity of public institutions in order to improve the efficiency of public service delivery and investment climate in its latest "Rectangular Strategy Phase III" report. The strategy aims to attract investment through reducing the cost of doing business and lowering entry barriers, reviewing and reforming incentive system, strengthening business confidence and predictability of government decision making and inter-agency coordination, improving trade facilitation, and cross-border transport processes.

The strategy also put emphasis on the development of industry and small and medium-sized enterprises (SMEs) through promotion of innovation and technology, increased access to finance, strengthening and expanding related support services, enhancing SMEs' capacity to link with large enterprises and form a cluster while promoting entrepreneurship, productivity and specialization, and integrating SMEs into regional and global production networks.

Increasingly, ASEAN and Asia are important for the sustained growth of Cambodia, especially investment opportunities and expansion of export markets through industrial and trade linkages. However, little is known about the extent to which Cambodia's SMEs can actively participate and benefit from these regional trade and investment liberalization.

The purpose of this chapter is to provide basic understanding of the status of the participation of Cambodia's SMEs in the regional economic integration in ASEAN and East Asia, identify the enabling factors, obstacles, and policy recommendations to promote their active participation in regional trade, production networks and investment activities.

The rest of the chapter is organized as follows. Section 2 provides an overview of SMEs and development policy. Section 3 discusses the survey results and analyses the findings. Section 4 concludes the chapter with some policy recommendations to promote active participation of SMEs in regional trade and production networks.

2. Characteristics of SMEs and Development Policy

The industry in Cambodia is dominated by micro firms. Out of 505,134 firms, micro firms (who employed less than 10 workers) have a share of nearly 97 per cent. The share of medium-size (defined as having 51–100 workers) and large firms (more than 100 workers) are pretty small, accounting for only 0.16 per cent and 0.15 per cent of total firms respectively. However, in terms of job creation, large firms provide 27 per cent of jobs in the industrial sector while micro firms account for more than 58 per cent of the total employment.

TABLE 2.2
Characteristics of Industrial Sector in Cambodia

	Micro (1–10 workers)	Small (11–50 workers)	Medium (51–100 workers)	Large (>100 workers)
Total number of enterprises	493,544	10,009	800	781
– Total share	97.71%	1.98%	0.16%	0.15%
Total labour force	975,980	191,792	53,879	451,739
– Total share	58.32%	11.46%	3.22%	27.00%
Total production (million US$)	5,800	1,290	735	4,570
– Total share	46.79%	10.41%	5.93%	36.87%

Source: Cambodia 2011 Economic Census.

In terms of distribution by industry, the majority of firms are concentrated in trade, followed by hotel and restaurants, food, beverages and tobacco, and other services. The Cambodian manufacturing industry remains weak as reflected by its simple structure, narrow base and low level of sophistication, lack of supporting industries, underdeveloped linkages between SMEs and large-scale enterprises, low productivity, while mostly concentrated in garment and food processing industries. Most production activities are family-based with a lack of entrepreneurship and inadequate use of technology, thus limiting their ability to compete in international markets.

To improve industrial development and use manufacturing as the main driver of the economy to achieve its long-term vision of reaching middle-income status by 2030, the government formulated Industrial Development Policy (IDP) 2015–2025. One of the policy objectives is to promote manufacturing and agro-processing by attracting FDI and enhancing the capacity of SMEs, for both export orientation

TABLE 2.3
Distribution of Firms by Size and Industry in Cambodia

	Micro	Small	Medium	Large	Total	% of Total
Mining	71.5%	24.6%	3.4%	0.6%	179	0.04%
Food, Beverages and Tobacco	98.9%	1.0%	0.1%	0.1%	32,108	6.36%
Textile, Wearing Apparel and Footwear	97.2%	1.2%	0.3%	1.4%	25,155	4.98%
Wood, Paper and Publishing	94.5%	3.8%	0.7%	1.0%	2,274	0.45%
Rubber Manufacturing	66.3%	24.8%	4.5%	4.5%	202	0.04%
Non-Metallic Manufacturing	85.8%	13.1%	0.9%	0.2%	2,826	0.56%
Basic Metal and Metal Products	97.9%	1.9%	0.2%	0.0%	4,766	0.94%
Other Manufacturing	98.1%	1.4%	0.3%	0.2%	4,085	0.81%
Electricity, Gas and Water	96.5%	3.1%	0.2%	0.2%	5,068	1.00%
Construction	77.1%	19.1%	2.1%	1.6%	188	0.04%
Trade	99.6%	0.4%	0.0%	0.0%	292,350	57.88%
Transport and Communications	94.7%	4.2%	0.6%	0.5%	6,268	1.24%
Hotel & Restaurants	97.0%	2.8%	0.1%	0.1%	69,662	13.79%
Finance	83.6%	13.9%	1.8%	0.8%	3,584	0.71%
Real Estate and Business	94.6%	4.7%	0.3%	0.3%	7,100	1.41%
Public Administration	73.1%	24.0%	2.0%	0.9%	14,759	2.92%
Other Services	97.5%	2.1%	0.2%	0.2%	34,560	6.84%
Total	493,544	10,009	800	781	505,134	
% of total	97.71%	1.98%	0.16%	0.15%	100%	

Source: Cambodia 2011 Economic Census.

and import substitution industries. The policy is also aimed at integrating Cambodia's manufacturing sector into regional and global production networks to benefit from economies of scale and industrial fragmentation.

One of the four pillars of IDP is to focus on developing and modernizing SMEs by way of expanding and strengthening the manufacturing base, modernizing and officially registering enterprises, promoting technology development, and transferring and strengthening industrial linkages between domestic and foreign enterprises, specifically in the agro-industrial sector.

Apart from its long-term objectives, the Cambodian government has also developed immediate measures and actions to address key constraints. This include measures to lower electricity prices by 5 per cent (from \$0.172/kWh to \$0.164/kWh); reduce transportation and logistics costs by developing and implementing a master plan for transport and logistics covering Poipet/Thailand–Phnom Penh–Sihanouk Ville–Bavet/Vietnam; increase the supply of skilled labour to meet market needs; and develop port city Sihanouk Ville as a multi-purpose economic zone.

In addition to this broader policy framework, the government has also developed policies specifically to support SMEs in Cambodia. The Cambodia's SME Promotion 2015 was developed by the Ministry of Industry and Handicrafts. It is the second SME promotion policy following the SME Development Framework 2005. The policy aims at addressing five key areas to deal with the key challenges faced by SMEs: (i) facilitation of SMEs' efficient and effective business operations; (ii) creation of linkages to global market; (iii) providing technical assistance for promoting technology adoption, innovation and R&D, and development of work skills qualification; (iv) technical assistance for access to finance; and (iv) assistance for human resource development.

The policy has set measures and actions with clear timeframe for implementation. There are 13 action plans the government is expected to implement. This include issues and constraints regarding definition, registration, start-up, technology and skills upgrading, tax incentive, investment promotion, access to finance, clustering and linkages with FDI large industries, internationalization, business development services, women entrepreneurship, employment and labour condition, and access to information.

3. SME Participation in Regional Integration: Results of the Survey

3.1. Sample Distribution

The study uses a questionnaire survey to understand the impact of trade policy on SMEs. The survey covers 201 firms and the results are provided in Table 2.4. The sample survey consists of both micro (68), small (29), medium (12) and large enterprises (92). It also covers key industries in Cambodia: food, beverages and tobacco; and textile, wearing apparel and footwear. The results show that there is a lack of medium-sized firms in Cambodia to create the backward and forward linkages in the economy with the multinational companies. The medium-sized firms are also important for the economy to effectively participate in the export market and regional and global production value chains.

TABLE 2.4
Sample Distribution by Size and Industry

	Micro	Small	Medium	Large	Total	
Other Manufacturing	51	12	5	9	77	38%
Food, Beverages & Tobacco	10	17	4	4	35	17%
Textile, Wearing Apparel & Footwear	7	0	3	79	89	44%
Total	68	29	12	92	201	
	33.8%	14.4%	6.0%	45.8%		

3.2. Characteristics of the Surveyed SMEs

The sample characteristics of firms by size and industry are given in Table 2.5. It is quite clear that SMEs are older, domestically-owned and family-based as compared to large firms. The average age of the SMEs is more than eight years. More than 80 per cent of the SMEs in the survey are domestically-owned and run by family members.

TABLE 2.5
Characteristics of the Surveyed SMEs

Characteristics	All			SMEs			Large Firms		
	N	Mean	S.D	N	Mean	S.D	N	Mean	S.D
Age (year)	196	8.34	5.79	107	9.16	6.51	89	7.35	4.64
Employment (persons)	201	623.43	1,169.24	109	17.08	19.02	92	1,341.83	1,429.02
Ownership (%)									
Foreign	100	99.10	5.34	12	96.67	11.55	88	99.43	3.82
Family-owned	93	1.00	0.00	90	1.00	0.00	3	1.00	0.00
Sale growth (%)	178	19.26	56.45	101	20.41	51.15	77	17.76	63.04
Profit (% of sale)									
2013	178	12.03	48.74	101	11.01	63.75	77	13.38	13.47
2014	178	15.17	50.80	101	16.80	64.74	77	13.02	22.08
Cost Structure (%)									
Raw materials	195	49.37	24.87	108	41.62	25.80	87	59.00	19.94
Intermediate	193	12.37	19.57	106	19.53	22.04	87	3.65	11.03
Utilities	195	5.61	7.39	108	7.35	8.65	87	3.46	4.65
Interest	195	0.43	1.65	108	0.64	2.04	87	0.18	0.93
Wage/Salary	195	31.48	18.14	108	29.88	18.58	87	33.47	17.49
Employees by Education (%)									
a. No formal education	201	5.76	14.94	109	6.96	18.92	92	4.33	7.88
b. Primary	201	52.26	30.15	109	52.53	33.81	92	51.93	25.32
c. Secondary school	201	32.73	27.32	109	32.43	31.37	92	33.09	21.73
d. Vocational/Diploma	201	2.11	6.52	109	0.64	3.24	92	3.85	8.68
e. University degree	201	6.88	14.60	109	6.84	19.20	92	6.93	5.55
Sale Destination (%)									
Domestic	101	95.09	16.70	15	86.00	26.94	86	96.68	13.84
Export	100	91.99	21.94	16	72.19	36.10	84	95.76	15.76

Source: ERIA–ISEAS SME Survey 2015.

It is also interesting to observe that SMEs reported higher sales and profit growth rates in 2014 than foreign firms. Foreign firms used more raw materials but paid less utilities and interests than SMEs. On average, SMEs employed more workers with lower levels of education than large firms. While most SMEs sold a large proportion of their products domestically, larger SMEs tended to engage more in exporting their products.

3.3. Awareness of the Surveyed SMEs on ASEAN

The survey also collected information on whether SMEs are aware of ASEAN and its activities (see Figure 2.2). On average, about 66 per cent of the surveyed firms are aware of ASEAN. As expected, large firms are more aware of ASEAN and its activities. About 59 per cent of SMEs indicated that they are quite aware of ASEAN and its activities as compared with 75 per cent of the large firms, which are largely dominated by the textile, wearing apparel and footwear industry.

FIGURE 2.2
SMEs' Awareness of ASEAN

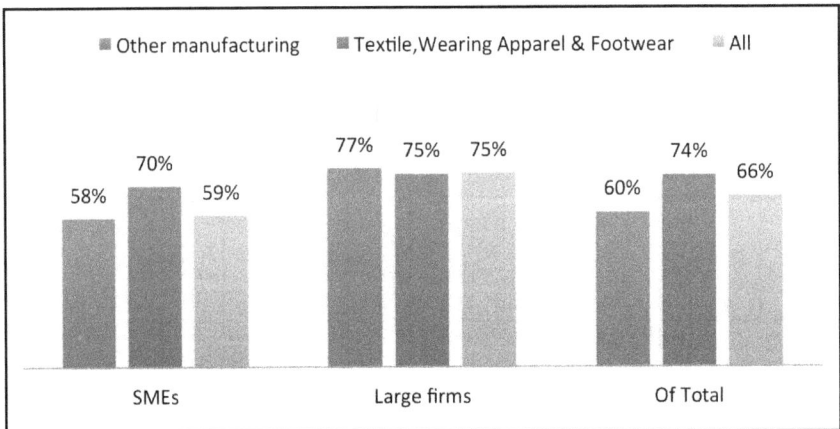

Source: ERIA–ISEAS SME Survey 2015.

3.4. Relations with Other Firms in ASEAN and East Asia

Figure 2.3 shows the firms that have business relations with other firms in ASEAN, by size and industry. While about half of large firms

FIGURE 2.3
Relations with Other Firms in ASEAN

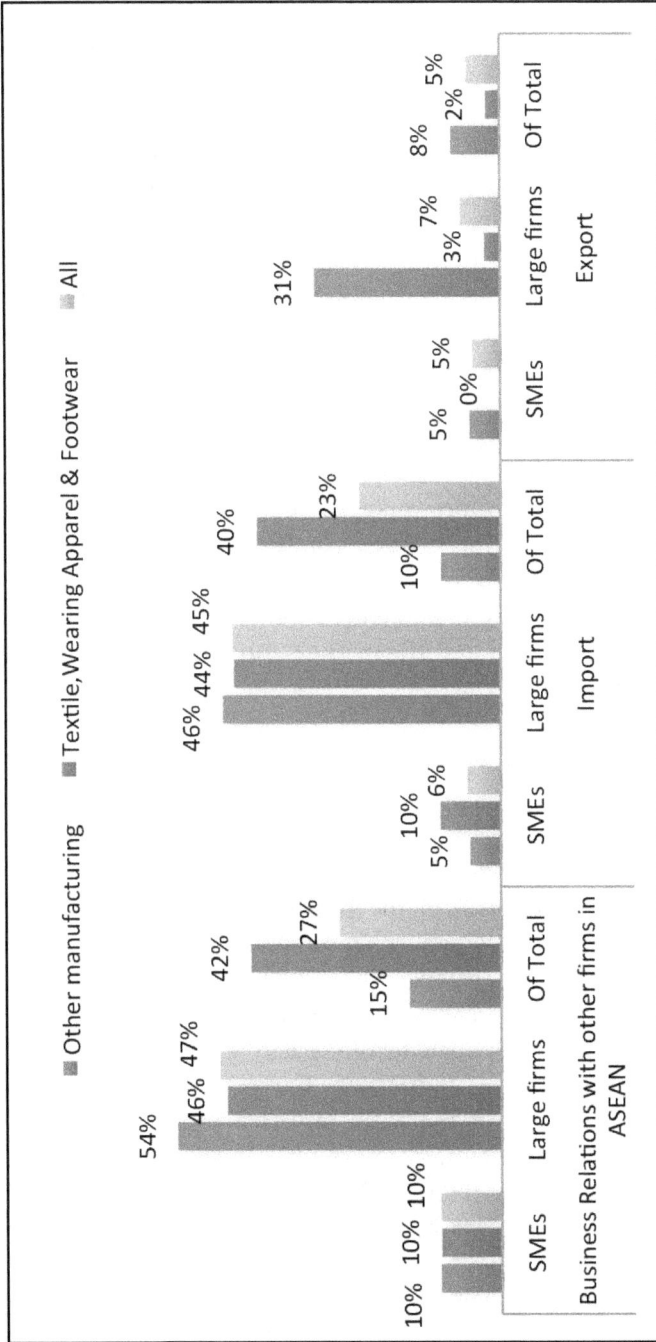

■ Other manufacturing   ■ Textile, Wearing Apparel & Footwear   ■ All

Source: ERIA–ISEAS SME Survey 2015.

have business relations with other firms in ASEAN as compared with only 10 per cent of SMEs, it is interesting to note that these relations are mostly stronger through imports than exports.

It is quite clear that while large firms from both textile, wearing apparel and footwear, and other manufacturing industries have stronger import linkages, the export linkage is weaker for the textile, wearing apparel and footwear industry than that of other manufacturing industries.

The trade linkages of Cambodian firms with other firms become clearer when we expand it to East Asia as shown in Figure 2.4. Firms' import linkages with East Asia are stronger than with ASEAN across firm size and industry, in particular, the textile, wearing apparel and footwear industry as compared with SMEs from other manufacturing industries.

The stronger import linkages with ASEAN and East Asia than that of the export imply that Cambodian firms take advantages of sourcing for cheaper intermediate inputs through ASEAN and East Asian preferential trade agreements and then export the final products to the traditional US and EU markets through GSP and Everything But Arms (EBA) arrangements.

3.5. Impact of AEC on SMEs

For the perception of the impact of the ASEAN Economic Community (AEC), on average, firms believe that AEC would decrease their domestic and export sales and profitability, and face more competition in local and foreign markets. On the positive side, they think AEC would decrease import costs and enhance accessibility to intermediate inputs (see Figure 2.5).

However, the perceived impacts are different between SMEs and large firms, and between textile, wearing apparel and footwear and other manufacturing industries. Large firms and those in textile, wearing apparel and footwear industry reported increases in their domestic and export sales, lower import costs, and greater access to intermediate inputs than SMEs and other manufacturing industries, while sharing concerns about more competition in local and foreign markets.

The impacts of AEC on the SMEs are also seen through different channels as shown in Figure 2.6. Across most firms (irrespective of

FIGURE 2.4
Imports and Exports

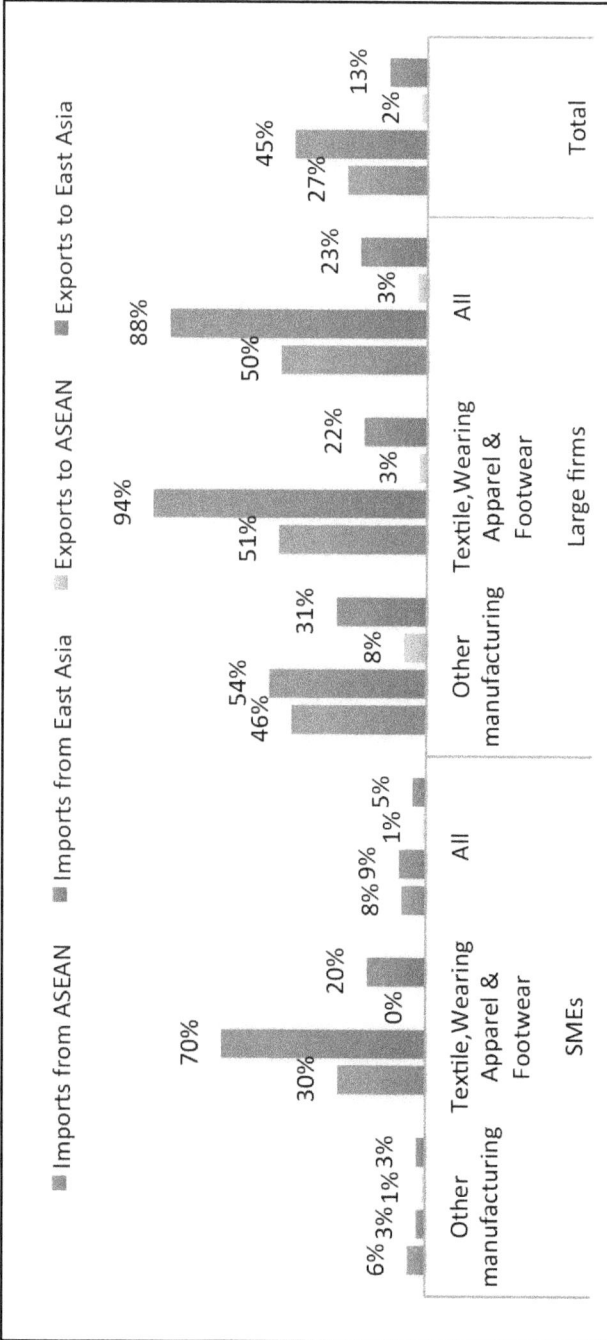

FIGURE 2.5
Perception of the Impact of AEC on SMEs
(Increase = 1, No change = 2, Decrease = 3)

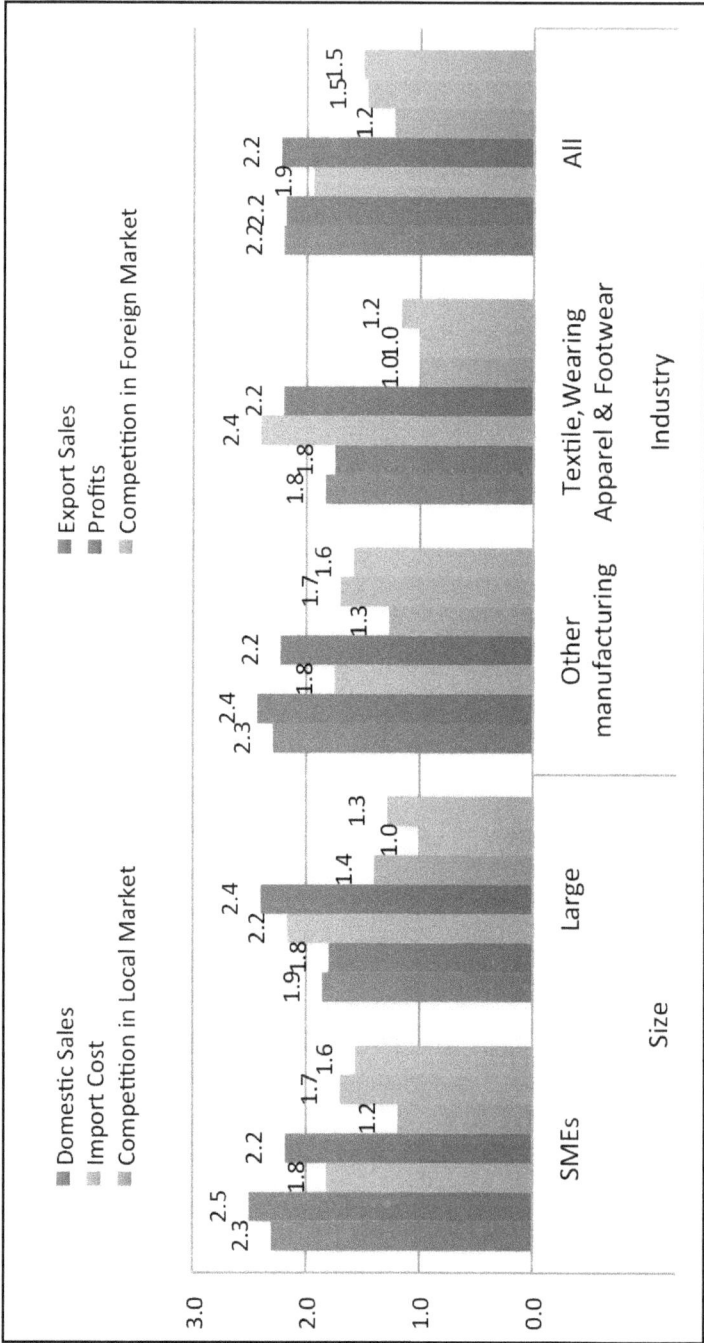

FIGURE 2.6
Key Changes of AEC: Perceived Impacts on SMEs
(Increase = 1, No change = 2, Decrease = 3)

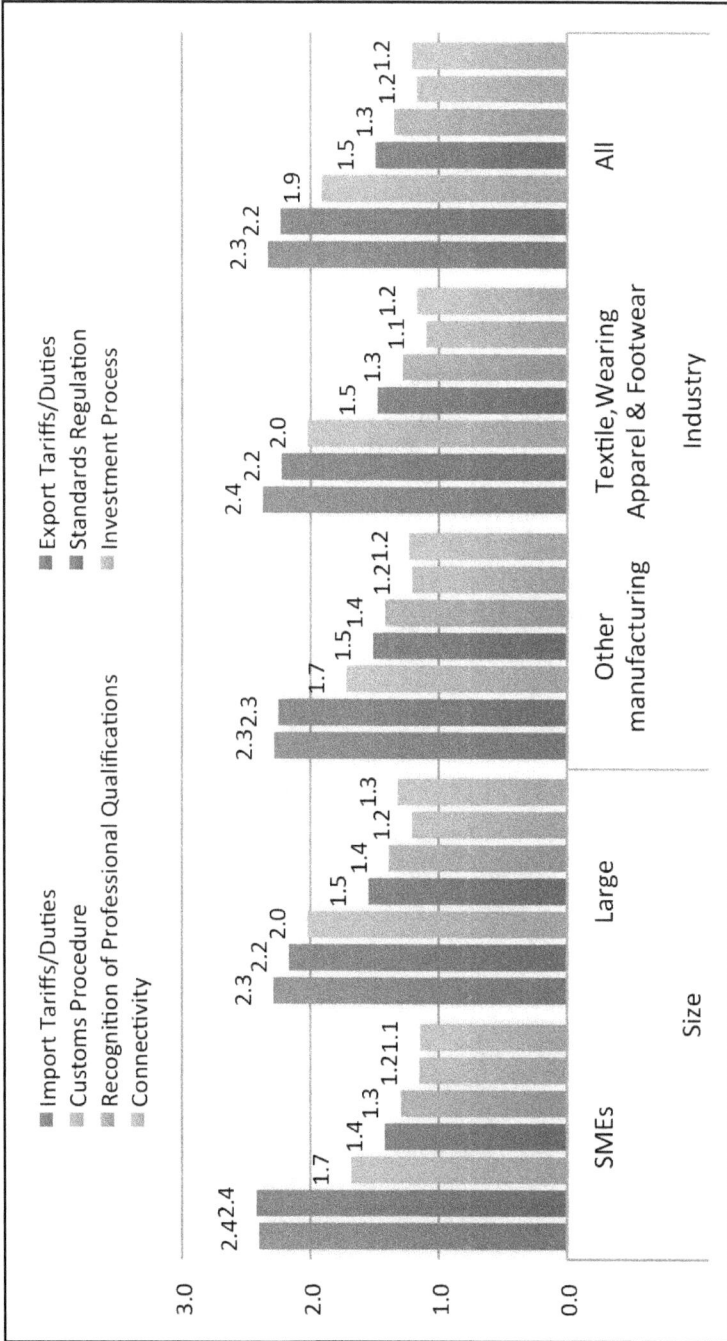

size and industry), they reported reduction in import and export tariffs/duties, increase in custom procedures, standards and regulations, recognition of professional qualifications, investment process, and connectivity.

These results are consistent with other studies, which suggest that while tariff barriers have been eliminated, there are increasing trends of non-tariff and technical measures being potential barriers to trade and investment in the region.

3.6. FTAs' Utilization by SMEs

The utilization of free trade agreements (FTAs) and usage of custom forms by various FTAs are reported in Figure 2.7. Large-sized firms tend to use FTAs more frequently (84 per cent) as compared to SMEs (less than 13 per cent). In particular, they tend to use GSP and most favoured nation (MFN) forms more frequently, consistent with the previous results on the access to US and EU markets. We also observe that the textile, wearing apparel and footwear industry has a higher utilization rate of FTAs (over 88 per cent) as compared to other industries in the sample.

FIGURE 2.7
Use of FTAs and Customs Forms by SMEs

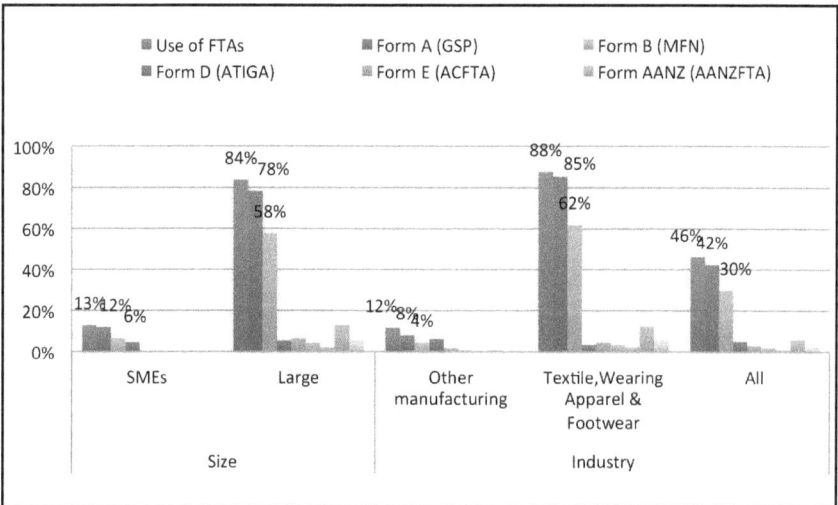

The survey also examines the reasons for not using FTAs (see Figure 2.8). It is clear that most firms reported a lack of knowledge/ not knowing how to use the forms as the key reason for not using FTAs. It is also interesting to observe that large-sized firms reported the small trade value and tariff preference of the FTAs and difficulty in fulfilling the requirements of rules of origin as critical factors for not using the FTAs. However, these are responses for only 10 per cent of the firms in the sample.

FIGURE 2.8
Reasons for Not Using FTAs and Custom Forms by SMEs

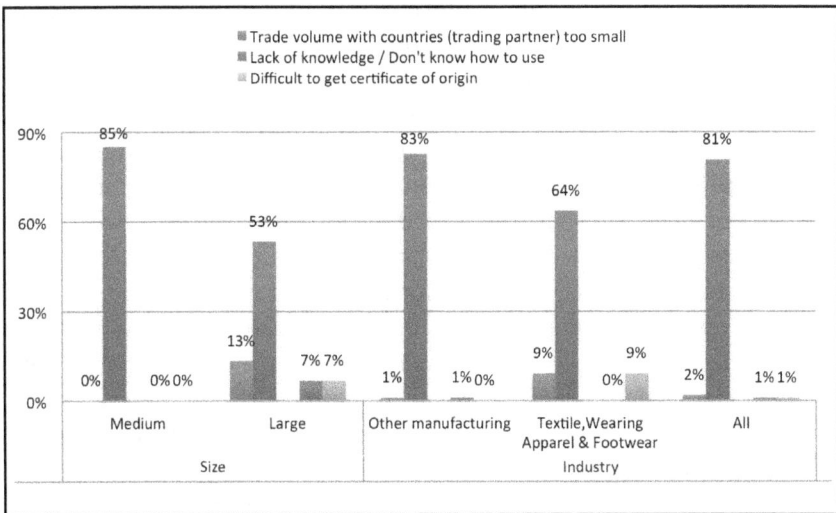

3.7. Characteristics of SMEs' Utilization of FTAs

In identifying the different characteristics of SMEs' utilization of FTAs, we rely on existing literature that shows that size, technological ability, experience in multiple foreign markets are important determinants of their participation in regional trade and investment (Hayakawa 2015; Wignaraja 2014; and Prashantham 2008). The level of firms' productivity and technology capability (Guadalupe et al. 2010 and Intarakumnerd 2011) that influence their cross-border activities can be resource-based or capability-related. These include: access to skilled labour (Hall and

Khan 2002; Dewar and Dutton 1986), utilization of information and communication technology (ICT) (Spiezia 2011 and Machikita et al. 2010), and business networks (Abebe and Angriawan 2011 and Lee et al. 2010).

The determinants of SMEs participation in ASEAN and East Asia through the utilization of FTAs can be examined by way of statistical regression. The statistical model in its general form is given as follows:

$$FTA_i = \alpha_0 + \beta_i X_i + \varepsilon_i \qquad (2.1)$$

where FTA_i is a discrete choice variable for each firm's utilization of FTAs. i represents firm i. X_i is a set of explanatory variables that captures firm characteristic determinants and ε_i is an error term. Estimations also controlled for include dummy variables for industries. The industry dummy variables identify whether firms are in textile, wearing apparel and footwear industry or other industries.

Firm size is determined by the number of employees. Age of the firm is defined as the number of years the plant has been in commercial production. Labour productivity is the ratio between total sales over the number of employees. These variables are in logarithm form. For firm ownership, we assign value 1 for firms with more than 50 per cent of shares owned by foreigners and 0 for local firms. Business network is given value 1 if the firm is a member of business association and 0 otherwise. Skill intensity variable is defined as the percentage of employees with tertiary or vocational education. The utilization of ICT is measured by the average number of ICT usage by type (i.e. email, website, online sales, online marketing, and online payment). A firm's technological capability is indexed by the average of business process or organizational innovation, production process innovation, and product innovation. The last two variables are the total number of import and export markets for each firm.

The summary of statistics is shown in Table 2.6. The summary statistics suggest that mean values of FTA utilization and others for SMEs are significantly lower than that of large firms, except age and labour productivity.

In order to confirm the different characteristics of firms with respect to utilization of FTAs, we conduct two separate regressions. The first is the Probit Model to capture the different characteristics between

TABLE 2.6
Summary Statistics of Variables

Variables	SMEs				Large Firms			
	Mean	Std.	Min	Max	Mean	Std.	Min	Max
(1) FTA Utilization	0.1	0.3	0.0	1.0	0.8	0.4	0.0	1.0
(2) Multiple Utilization of FTAs	0.5	1.1	0.0	4.0	2.7	1.3	0.0	8.0
(3) Age	1.9	0.8	0.0	3.4	1.8	0.7	0.0	3.1
(4) Size	2.4	0.9	0.5	4.5	6.7	1.0	4.6	8.9
(5) Foreign Ownership	0.3	0.5	0.0	1.0	1.0	0.2	0.0	1.0
(6) Member of Business Association	0.2	0.4	0.0	1.0	0.9	0.3	0.0	1.0
(7) Labour Productivity	9.5	1.7	6.8	16.0	9.1	1.0	6.3	13.5
(8) Skill Intensity	7.5	20.6	0.0	100.0	10.8	11.0	0.1	90.0
(9) ICT Utilization Index	0.1	0.2	0.0	1.0	0.2	0.1	0.0	0.8
(10) Technological Capability Index	0.4	0.4	0.0	1.0	0.5	0.3	0.0	1.0
(11) Multiple Export Markets	0.2	0.6	0.0	4.0	1.3	0.7	0.0	4.0
(12) Multiple Import Markets	0.2	0.5	0.0	2.0	1.8	0.9	0.0	4.0

FTAs utilized firms and the non-users. The second model is Ordered Probit regression to distinguish between non-FTA user firms and multiple FTAs user firms. The results are shown in Table 2.7.

Table 2.6 reports the results of estimation of Equation (2.1). It shows the final specifications that give the best results. The Wald test of overall significance in all specifications passes at the 1 per cent level. The table reports robust standard errors for the reason of heteroscedastic variance.

Results from the regression indicate that compared to non-user firms, the FTA-utilized firms appear to be bigger in size, have higher labour

TABLE 2.7
Characteristics of SMEs' Utilization of FTAs

Independent Variable	Dependent Variable	
	FTA Utilization	Multiple Utilization of FTAs
Age	−0.218	−0.328*
	(0.229)	(0.189)
Size	0.573***	0.399***
	(0.0953)	(0.0917)
Foreign Ownership	−0.174	−0.659
	(0.391)	(0.542)
Dummy Var. for Garment Sector	1.038***	1.002***
	(0.309)	(0.260)
Member of Business Association (Network)	0.761**	1.185***
	(0.331)	(0.320)
Labour Productivity	0.506***	0.388***
	(0.107)	(0.0935)
Skill Intensity	1.735**	3.024**
	(0.833)	(1.202)
ICT Utilization Index	0.538	1.165***
	(0.399)	(0.366)
Technological Capability Index	0.0130*	0.0147**
	(0.00699)	(0.00577)
Multiple Export Markets	2.240***	0.456***
	(0.410)	(0.175)
Multiple Import Markets	0.0375	0.00588
	(0.297)	(0.194)
Observations	180	154

Note: 1. Robust z statistics in parentheses.
2. ***significant at 1 per cent; **significant at 5 per cent; *significant at 10 per cent.

productivity, and experiences with multiple export markets, with robust findings and statistically significant at 1 per cent level. These findings are in accord with the literature. They are also members of business association and have higher skill intensity, statistically significant at 5 per cent level, and technological capability, statistically significant at 10 per cent level. Age, foreign ownership, ICT, and experiences with multiple import markets are not significant factors for firms' FTA utilization.

Similarly, multiple FTAs-utilized firms are bigger in size with higher labour productivity, are members of business association, active users of ICT, and have more experiences with multiple export markets at a robust and statistically significant level of 1 per cent. Skill intensity and technological capability are statistically significant at 5 per cent level, and younger age is statistically significant at 10 per cent level. Foreign ownership and experiences with multiple import markets are not significant.

4. Summary and Policy Recommendations

The results from the questionnaire survey show that, on average, more than half of the surveyed firms are aware of ASEAN, and the larger firms tend to use FTAs more frequently as compared to SMEs. Lack of knowledge and not knowing how to use the forms are reported as the key reasons for not using FTAs. The stronger import linkages with ASEAN and East Asia than that of the export linkages suggest that Cambodia's firms take advantages of sourcing for cheaper intermediate inputs from ASEAN and East Asia and then export the final products to the traditional US and EU markets through GSP and Everything But Arms (EBA) arrangements.

The surveyed firms hold the perception that AEC would decrease their domestic and export sales and profitability, and face more competition in local and foreign markets. On the positive side, they think AEC would decrease import costs and enhance accessibility to intermediate inputs. The impacts are through the reduction of import and export tariffs/duties, increase in custom procedures, standards and regulations, recognition of professional qualifications, investment process, and connectivity.

Empirical results indicate that compared to non-user firms, the active users of FTAs appear to be bigger in size, have higher labour productivity, and have experiences with multiple export markets. They are also members of business association, and have higher skill intensity and technological capability. Exploiting scale, higher labour productivity, business networks, active use of ICT, and more experiences with multiple export markets, skilled human capital and technological capability become more important for firms to participate and use multiple FTAs to benefit from regional integration.

There are several challenges facing the Cambodian economy in its next stage of growth. The key ones are: (1) improve the educational attainment of new labour market entrants to ensure quality primary education for all and to significantly increase the share of people with quality secondary and higher education; (2) increase the productivity of the existing undereducated and unskilled labour force through new continuous learning paths; (3) break the vicious cycle of systematic under-investment in education and skills building; and (4) reduce the large skill gaps and mismatches in the context of economic diversification by building the institutions to manage structural transformations and to ensure the linkage between the education system and industrial policy goals, as well as pursuing an industrial policy that actively focuses on upgrading the skills of domestic workers.

There is a need to improve the educational level of the workforce as currently the average educational attainment is at the primary and lower education levels. There is a strong need to improve the educational attainment to secondary and higher education levels, which will be critical for greater access and participation in the regional production value chains. In this respect, the government needs to improve the quality of education and also the training and re-tooling of the workers in the labour force.

The training of the workforce in terms of technical and vocational education and training (TVET) should be progressive and accumulative throughout the career path of the workers. The certification of the various training programmes at the national level is vital for the recognition of the training certificates and to signal to the private sector the competence of the workforce. Thus, proper quality assurance, accreditation and recognition systems need to be introduced. An endorsement by the private sector and businesses would increase the returns for training and further motivate workers to acquire more skills and training. A public–private partnership (PPP) framework could also play an important role in endorsing the formal and informal training framework that includes public and private educational institutes. Part-time studies should also be considered to ensure compatibility with work.

There is a strong need for an industrial policy that will align the industrial transition with skills development and productivity growth in the Cambodian economy. Upgrading of skills and the absorptive capacity could be effectively strengthened by requiring multinational corporations (MNCs) to hire a certain share of local workers for middle and upper management positions. The current industrial strategy of very liberal economic policies and pushing to higher end industries might create intensified skill mismatches and shortages.

To support transition towards industry and manufacturing, more technical skills, such as basic science, technology, engineering and mathematics (STEM), should be introduced at the early stages of education. A different technical pathway in secondary schools could help build these skills in order to create a more skills-based workforce that meets the needs of the industry at the early stages of development. It could be built on the successful examples of the National Technical High Schools and Machinery Technical High Schools in Korea in the 1960s.

The government needs to invest in "absorptive capacity" of the economy such as key infrastructure, science parks, ports, telecommunication infrastructure, airports, and roads that connect urban and rural sectors. The provision of infrastructure is an important component of an innovation system that supports the amalgamation of key local and foreign industries.

It is important to develop a strong SME sector in Cambodia. SMEs will play an important role and conduit in creating linkages to the MNCs and hence create direct and indirect access to the technologies of the MNCs.

REFERENCES

Abebe, Michael A. and Arifin Angriawan. "The Internationalisation of Small and Medium-sized Enterprises (SMEs): a Multi-level Integrative Framework". *International Journal of Entrepreneurship and Innovation Management* 13, no. 3/4 (2011): 377–97.

Asian Development Bank. Statistical Database System, 2015.

Dewar, Robert D. and Jane E. Dutton. "The Adoption of Radical and Incremental Innovations: An Empirical Analysis". *Management Science* 32, no. 11 (1986): 1422–33.

Government of the Republic of Korea, Ministry of Strategy and Finance, and Korea Development Institute. *Policy Agenda for Cambodia in Developing Industrial Skills, Industrial Complex, and Agro-processing Industry*. Korea Development Institute, Korea, 2013.

Guadalupe, Maria, Olga Kuzmina, and Catherine Thomas. "Innovation and Foreign Ownership". NBER Working Paper Series No. 16573 (2010).

Hall, Bronwyn and Beethika Khan. "Adoption of New Technology", November 2002. Available at <http://elsa.berkeley.edu/~bhhall/papers/HallKhan03%20diffusion.pdf>.

Hang Chuon, Naron. "Securing Cambodia's Future: Indicators, Prospects, and Policy Priorities". Presented at the 2013 Cambodia Outlook Conference, Hotel Inter-Continental, 2013.

Hay Sovuthea. "Industrial Skill Training in Cambodia". *Policy Agenda for Cambodia on Developing Skilled Human Resources and Establishing Complex*. Korea Development Institute, Korea, 2012.

Hayakawa, Kazunobu. "Does Firm Size Matter in Exporting and Using FTA Schemes?" *Journal of International Trade and Economic Development* 24, no. 7 (2015): 883–905. [Peer Reviewed Journal]

Hong Choeun. "Skill Need Assessment: Current Situation in Cambodia". *Policy Agenda for Cambodia on Developing Skilled Human Resources and Establishing Complex*. Korea Development Institute, Korea, 2012.

Intarakumnerd, Patarapong. "How to Enhance Innovation Capability with Internal and External Sources". ERIA Research Project Report 2010, no. 9 (2011).

Keller, Wolfgang. "International Trade, Foreign Direct Investment, and Technology Spillovers". NBER Working Paper No. 15442 (2009).

Lee, Sungjoo, Gwangman Park, Byungun Yoon, and Jinwoo Park. "Open Innovation in SMEs: An Intermediated Network Model". *Research Policy* 39, no. 2 (2010): 290–300.

Machikita, Tomohiro, Masatsugu Tsuji, and Yasushi Ueki. "How ICTs Raise Manufacturing Performance: Firm-level Evidence in Southeast Asia". ERIA Discussion Paper 2010–07 (2010).

Ministry of Education, Youth, and Sport. "Higher Education Quality and Capacity Improvement Project (HEQCIP)". Finance Policy, 2013.

Prashantham, S. *The Internationalization of Small Firms: A Strategic Entrepreneurship Perspective*. London and New York: Routledge, Taylor & Francis Group, 2008.

Royal Government of Cambodia. *Financial Sector Development Strategy 2011–2020*. Adopted by the Council of Ministers in the Plenary Session on 25 November 2011*a*.

———. "National Strategic Development Program Update 2009–2013". Cambodia, 2011*b*.

————. "The Rectangular Strategy for Growth, Employment, Equity and Efficiency in Cambodia". Address by Samdech Hun Sen, Prime Minister, Royal Government of Cambodia, First Cabinet Meeting of the Third Legislature of the National Assembly at the Office of the Council of Ministers. Phnom Penh, July 2004.

Spiezia, Vincenzo. "Are ICT Users More Innovative? An Analysis of ICT-Enabled Innovation in OECD Firms". *OECD Journal: Economic Studies* 1 (2011).

Supreme National Economic Council (SNEC). "Diversifying the Cambodian Economy: The Role of Industrial Development". SNEC Working Paper, February 2011.

UNDP Cambodia. *Industry-Agriculture Linkages: Implications for the Rice Policy.* Discussion Paper no. 9 (2013*a*).

————. *Toward Realizing Industrial Development in Cambodia: An Academic Perspective.* Discussion Paper no. 10 (2013*b*).

————. *Human Capital Implications of Future Economic Growth in Cambodia: Elements of a Suggested Roadmap.* Discussion Paper no. 8 (2011).

————. *Cambodia Country Competitiveness: Driving Economic Growth and Poverty Reduction.* Discussion Paper no. 7 (2009).

Wignaraja, Ganeshan. "The Determinants of FTA Use in Southeast Asia: A Firm-Level Analysis". *Journal of Asian Economics* 35 (December 2014): 32–45.

3

INDONESIAN SMALL AND MEDIUM ENTERPRISE PARTICIPATION IN ASEAN ECONOMIC INTEGRATION

Titik Anas[1]

1. Introduction

1.1. Background and Objective

Small and medium-sized enterprises (SMEs) are important in the economic development of ASEAN countries. In Pillar 3 (establishing an equitable economic development) of the ASEAN Economic Community (AEC) Blueprint, SME development is one of the important components. ASEAN established the 2004–2014 SME Blueprint, which set the policies to develop competitive ASEAN SMEs. The blueprint was followed by the 2010–2015 ASEAN Strategic Action Plan SME Development, which outlined specific activities to implement ASEAN SME policies.

SMEs should take advantage of the establishment of the AEC. Easy access to ASEAN markets generates wider selling potential and more options to outsource production inputs. The latter encourages bigger firms to get input materials from SMEs. In more advanced settings, inter-connected production stages that are shared among firms will create mutual benefits among related parties. This will accelerate economic growth.

This chapter aims to examine the extent and nature of SME participation in ASEAN economic integration. More specifically, it attempts to provide a description of the current state of SMEs in Indonesia and survey SMEs on their perceptions on the ways in which they can benefit from this integration.

This chapter is based on a survey of 200 SMEs in Indonesia. The survey gathered information on the perceptions of SMEs on the impacts of ASEAN regionalism on their business activities. The field survey covered firms in the manufacturing sector with more than 10 employees/workers in 9 out of 22 main industries in which SMEs have significant presence. These industries include: (1) manufacturing of food products; (2) manufacturing of beverages; (3) manufacturing of wearing apparel; (4) manufacturing of leather and related products (focus on footwear); (5) manufacturing of wood and products of wood and cork; (6) manufacturing of furniture; (7) manufacturing of electrical products; (8) manufacturing of computers, electronics, and optical; and (9) manufacturing of motor vehicles, trailers, and semi-trailers. Some of the interviewed firms have trading activities with firms from other ASEAN countries while some do not. The survey provides some insights on the trading activities of Indonesian SMEs in ASEAN. It also provides information on factors that enhance their trading activities in ASEAN as well as their engagement in the emerging production networks around the region.

1.2. Literature Review

There have been numerous studies on SME developments in Asia and ASEAN regions, including Indonesia, hitherto. Some of them focused on SMEs' participation in global production networks (Wignaraja 2013*a*, 2013*b*; Wignaraja 2012; Harvie 2010*a*; Harvie, Narjoko and Oum 2010; Machmud and Siregar 2010), while others were on the developments of SMEs amid free trade arrangements in their region (Abonyi 2015; Tambunan and Chandra 2014; Aldaba 2013). A recent study by Prassetya and Intal (2015) revealed that particular sectors faced trading barriers due to standards and conformance, which were quite difficult for SMEs to comply as they lacked knowledge and capabilities.

Production networks could mean interconnections between businesses that end with the production of final goods. Large firms have greater tendency to be leading players of production networks in ASEAN, while SMEs usually only get the spillovers (Wignaraja 2013*a*; 2012). Hence, it is most important to study factors that can further develop SMEs in order for them to join the production networks. In reality, many SMEs have tried to join the production network, but only a few have been successful (Harvie 2010*a*). Globalization and regional integrations can be considered as business prospects for some firms but may become potential risks for others (Harvie 2010*b*). The improvement of SMEs is a key factor to improve the overall economic performance of any country.

The higher the development stage of the economy in which a firm is located, the bigger the chance of its involvement in a production network. Wignaraja (2012) found that among ASEAN countries, Malaysia and Thailand are the most involved countries in production networks due to their level of economic development. Hence, the government plays a central role in encouraging SMEs to join production networks. This is achieved by implementing policies that create a supportive business environment, reduce bureaucratic impediments and facilitate integrated SME institutional support services (Wignaraja 2013*b*).

ASEAN has made commitments to improve economic activities among its member countries. The SME-related provisions in the AEC Blueprint are proofs of this commitment. According to Prassetya and Intal (2015), some of the key challenges in developing SMEs in ASEAN countries include technical capacity, physical infrastructure, governance and some country-specific as well as sector-specific issues. Other researchers have also identified a number of factors that could encourage SMEs to enter global or regional production networks. Statistical analyses in their studies suggested that firm size, productivity, foreign ownership, financial characteristics, innovation efforts, and managerial approach are among the factors (Harvie, Narjoko and Oum 2010*a*, 2010*b*). Additionally, labour, education level, technological involvement and access to financial system could also positively contribute to participation in production networks (Wignaraja 2013; 2012). For Indonesian SMEs, Machmud and Siregar (2010) concluded that bigger firm size, modern business conduct and openness to international market are the most important factors determining participation in production networks.

2. Indonesia's SMEs and Comparisons to Other ASEAN Countries

As a way of background, it is important to highlight the differences between Indonesia's SMEs definition and those used in other countries in the region. In Indonesia, three different definitions of Micro, Small and Medium Enterprises (MSMEs) coexist based on: (i) the number of workers (Board of Statistics definition); (ii) sales; and (iii) assets (Law No. 20/2008 definition).

A micro enterprise is defined as an enterprise with less than 5 employees or with assets of maximum IDR 50 million (US$5,500) or with sales of maximum IDR 300 million (US$33,000). A small enterprise is defined as a firm with 5–19 employees or with assets of IDR 50 to 500 million or with sales of greater than IDR 300 million to IDR 2.5 billion. A medium enterprise is a firm with 20–99 employees or with assets of IDR 500 million to IDR 5 billion or with sales of IDR 2.5 to 50 billion (see Appendix 3.1 for SMEs definition in other countries).

By definition, Indonesia's MSMEs are relatively smaller in size compared to other MSMEs in the region. By way of comparison, Malaysia's micro enterprises are firms with sales up to US$91,645, more than ten times the size of micro enterprises in Indonesia. Singapore's SMEs are enterprises with annual sales turnover of not more than US$73.53 million.

Also, it is important to highlight that when we discuss SMEs, it often includes micro enterprises. In fact, Indonesia's government SMEs policy put greater priorities on micro enterprises. The term MSMEs is often used in addition to SMEs as the number of micro enterprises is relatively large. This chapter will also often mention micro enterprises when discussing SMEs.

The contribution of MSMEs to the Indonesian economy is quite large. Figure 3.1 shows the contribution of MSMEs with regard to GDP, employment, exports and number of enterprises. MSMEs contributed about 57.6 per cent of GDP in 2013, 30.3 per cent of which were from micro enterprises, 12.8 per cent from small enterprises and 14.5 per cent from the medium-scale enterprises. MSMEs absorbed 96.7 per cent of total employment in 2014, 87 per cent of which (about 105 million workers) were in micro enterprises. In terms of the number of enterprises, MSMEs made up about 99 per cent. It is important to highlight that 98.74 per cent were micro enterprises. Large firms largely drove exports, 84.32 per

FIGURE 3.1
Contribution of MSMEs to the Economy

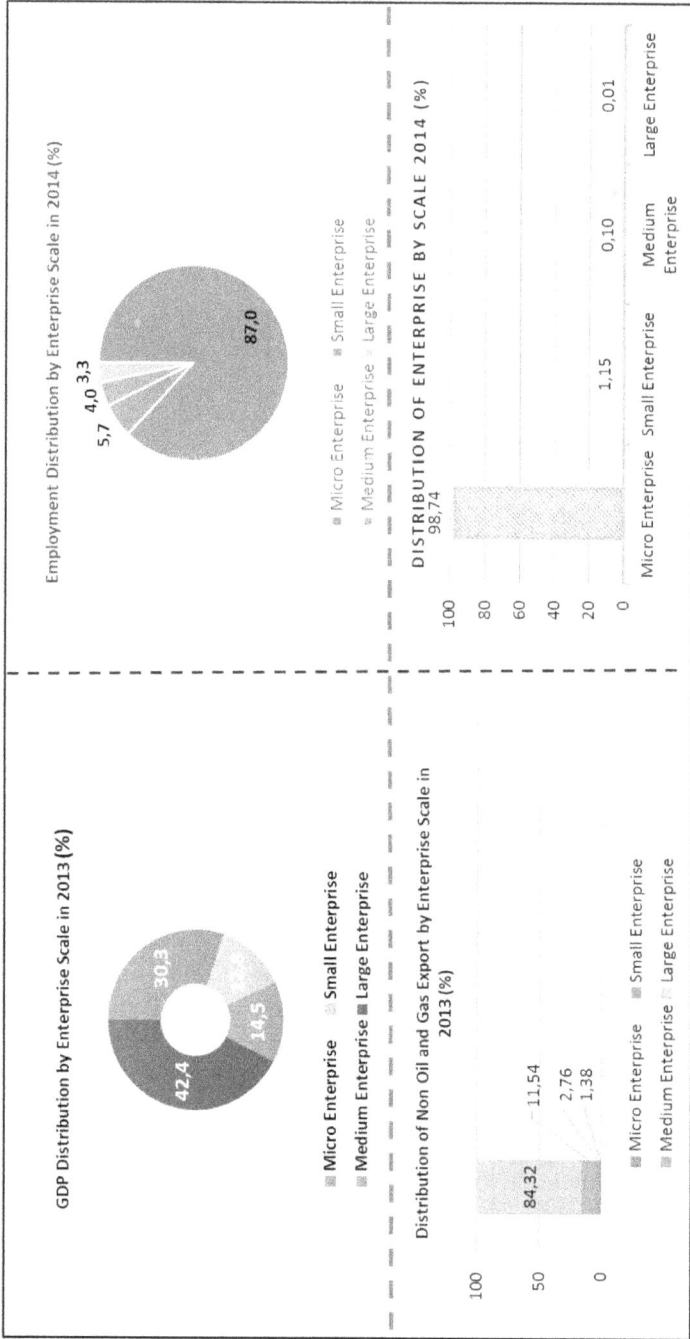

GDP Distribution by Enterprise Scale in 2013 (%)

30,3

14,5

42,4

■ Micro Enterprise   ■ Small Enterprise
■ Medium Enterprise ■ Large Enterprise

Distribution of Non Oil and Gas Export by Enterprise Scale in 2013 (%)

100

50

84,32

11,54

2,76

1,38

0

■ Micro Enterprise   ■ Small Enterprise
■ Medium Enterprise ■ Large Enterprise

Employment Distribution by Enterprise Scale in 2014 (%)

5,7 4,0 3,3

87,0

■ Micro Enterprise   ■ Small Enterprise
■ Medium Enterprise ■ Large Enterprise

DISTRIBUTION OF ENTERPRISE BY SCALE 2014 (%)

100

80

60

40

20

0

98,74

1,15   0,10   0,01

Micro Enterprise   Small Enterprise   Medium   Large Enterprise
                                       Enterprise

Source: SMEs Statistic, Ministry of Cooperatives and SME.

cent of exports were from large enterprises (LEs), and 11.54 per cent from medium enterprises. Small and micro firms contributed about 4 per cent.

The contribution of MSMEs to GDP declined in recent times (see Figure 3.2). During the period 2008–13, the MSMEs' contribution to GDP declined from 58.3 per cent to 57.6 per cent. The decline is due to the decrease in the growth of micro enterprises, from 32.8 per cent in 2008 to 30 per cent in 2013.

FIGURE 3.2
GDP Distribution and Growth, 2013 (%)

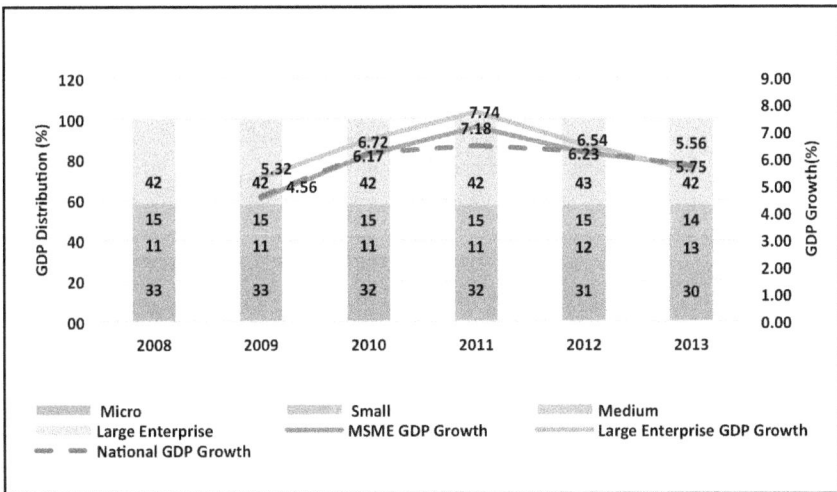

Source: SMEs Statistic, Ministry of Cooperatives and SME.

MSMEs' contribution to employment increased from 94 million in 2008 to 123.2 million in 2014 (see Figure 3.3). However, employment growth in MSMEs was about 4.63 per cent, which was lower than the national employment growth of 4.72 per cent. In contrast, employment growth in LEs was at 7.47 per cent.

Business entities in MSMEs categories increased during 2008–14, from 51.4 million in 2008 to 59.3 million in 2014 (see Figure 3.4). Micro enterprises increased by 2.3 per cent per annum while medium enterprises increased by 6.2 per cent.

FIGURE 3.3
MSMEs' Contribution to Employment, 2008–14

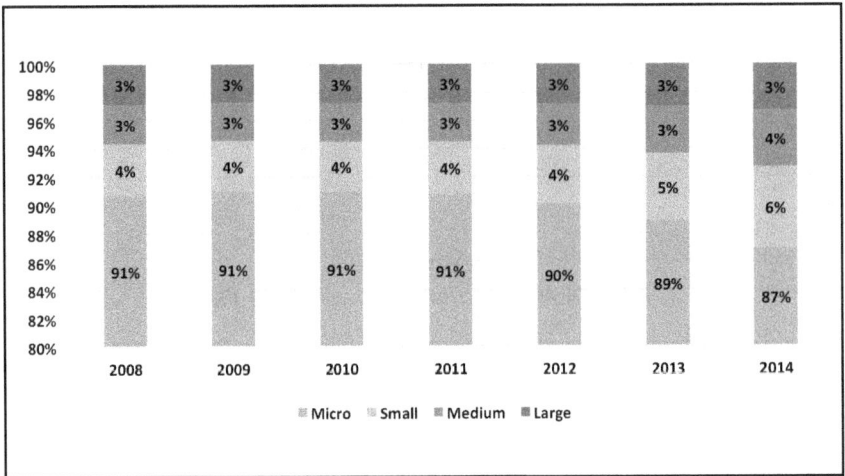

Source: SMEs Statistic, Ministry of Cooperatives and SME.

FIGURE 3.4
Enterprise Establishment Growth, 2008–14

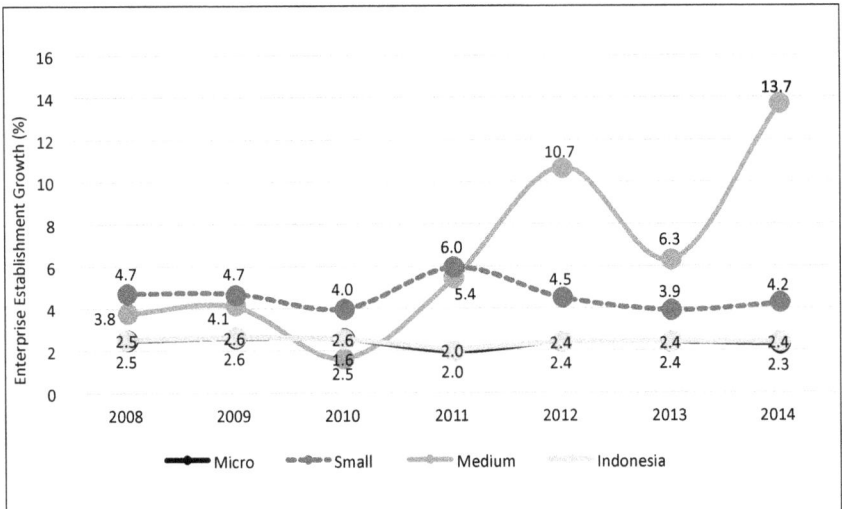

Source: SMEs Statistic, Ministry of Cooperatives and SME.

In terms of productivity, MSMEs exhibit much lower productivity than LEs. During the period 2006–9, MSMEs' productivity was about 4 per cent of LEs'. Micro enterprises showed a significantly lower productivity compared to LEs. For the later period, 2010–13, the productivity of MSMEs remained at 4 per cent of LEs (see Table 3.1).

TABLE 3.1
Employee Productivity by Enterprise Scale (in million rupiah)

Indicator	2006–2009	2010–2013
MSME	12.2	13.3
Micro	7.4	7.8
Small	62	64.7
Medium	104.5	112.4
Large	309.9	334.8
Ratio: Large/MSME	25.3	25.1

Source: SMEs Statistic, Ministry of Cooperatives and SME.

Indonesia's MSMEs are relatively larger compared to other ASEAN countries. Indonesia's MSMEs contributed about 57.6 per cent to GDP while SMEs in other countries contributed less. Similarly, Indonesia's MSMEs contributed more to employment than other countries (see Table 3.2). However, in terms of exports, Indonesia's MSMEs contributed less than Thailand's and Malaysia's SMEs. SMEs in Thailand contributed about 25.5 per cent to total exports, while Malaysia's SMEs contributed about 19 per cent, in contrast to Indonesia's SMEs' contribution to export of 15.7 per cent.

The salient differences between Indonesia's MSMEs compared to other ASEAN SMEs are on their sectoral distributions (see Figure 3.5). Indonesia's MSMEs are mainly in primary sectors (about 48.9 per cent). MSMEs in trade and industries are about 28.8 per cent and

TABLE 3.2
Comparison of MSMEs' Contribution to Economy across ASEAN Members

Country	Enterprise Unit		Employment		MSME Contribution to GDP		Export	
	Share (%)	Year	Share (%)	Year	Share (%)	Year	Share (%)	Year
Brunei Darussalam	98.2	2010	59	2010	24	2010	n/a	n/a
Cambodia	99.8	2014	71.8	2014	n/a	n/a	n/a	n/a
Indonesia	99.9	2013	96.9	2013	57.6	2013	15.7	2013
Lao PDR	99.8	2013	82.9	2013	n/a	n/a	n/a	n/a
Malaysia	97.3	2011	57.5	2013	33.1	2013	19	2010
Myanmar	87.4	2014	n/a	n/a	n/a	n/a	n/a	n/a
Philippines	99.6	2012	64.9	2012	36	2006	10	2010
Singapore	99.4	2012	68	2012	45	2012	n/a	n/a
Thailand	97.2	2013	81	2013	37.4	2013	25.5	2013
Vietnam	97.7	2012	46.8	2012	n/a	n/a	n/a	n/a

Souce: Asian Development Bank & SMEs Statistic, Ministry of Cooperatives and SME

FIGURE 3.5
Distribution of SMEs across ASEAN (%)

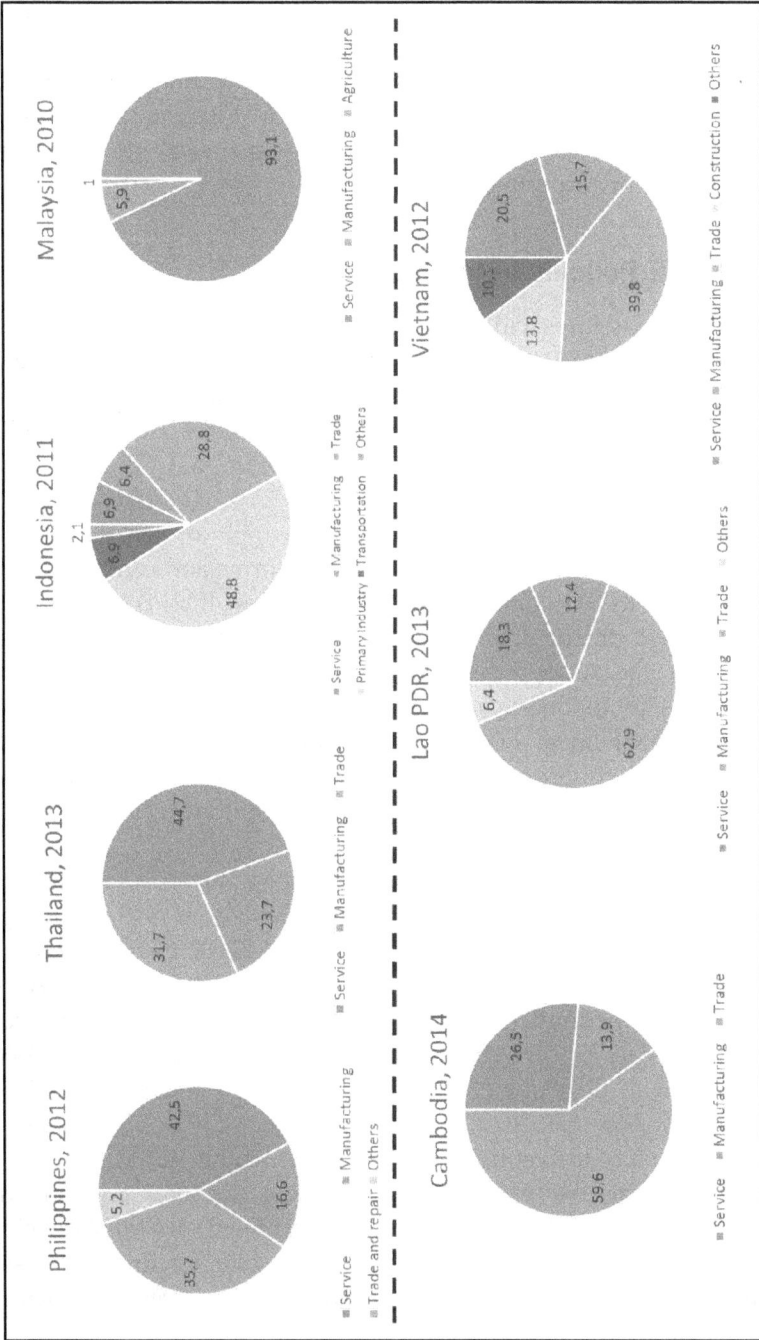

Source: ADB, *Asia SME Finance Monitor 2014* (Philippines: Asian Development Bank, 2015).

6.4 per cent respectively. In contrast, SMEs in other ASEAN countries are mostly in trade, services and manufacturing sectors. More than 40 per cent of SMEs in Malaysia, Thailand and Philippines are in the services sector. In Cambodia, Laos and Vietnam, SMEs are mainly in the trade sector, with shares of 59.6 per cent, 62.9 per cent and 39.8 per cent respectively.

3.   SME Policies in Indonesia

SMEs are strategically important in Indonesia's economy. The development of SMEs is always a top priority of Indonesia's government. The policies tend to be framed in social welfare approach. Hill (2001) outlined Indonesia's SME development policies from the 1970s and suggested that the policies during the 1970s to 1998 were ineffective due to limited resources allocated to SME programmes and a lack of clear policy rationale as well as being supply-driven. Hill also noted that the government rarely engaged large firms and commercial services to support its SME development programmes. Table 3.3 lists Indonesia's SME development policies during 1970 to 2000.

After the Asian Financial Crisis, SMEs continued to be the top priorities in Indonesia's government policies. The policies continued to be framed in a social welfare approach with excessive protection reflected in the policies, such as partnerships with SMEs, business sectors reserved for SMEs and other programmes which shielded SMEs from competition.

In 2008, the Law No. 20/2008 regarding micro, small and medium enterprises was enacted to replace the Law No. 9/1995 regarding small enterprises which lay the foundation of MSME development policies after 2008. In contrast to the Law No. 9/1995, the new law covers micro and medium enterprises in addition to small enterprises. The law continues to carry the mandate for the development of MSMEs as the agent of development, equity distribution and poverty alleviation (Article 5, Law No. 20/2008). Table 3.4 lists MSMEs policies since 2008.

The role of the central and local governments in SMEs development is defined in Law No. 23/2014 regarding the local government. The law re-emphasized the focus of the government on SMEs' development in empowerment and upgrading. In particular for financial assistance, the government enacted the Law No. 1/2013 concerning microfinance institutions.

TABLE 3.3
SME Policy Initiatives in Indonesia, 1969–2000

Technology Initiatives

1969	Establishment of MIDC (Metal Industry Development Center).
1974	Establishment of BIPIK (Small Industries Development Program).
1979	As part of BIPIK, LIK (Small-Scale Industry Areas), and PIK (Small Industry Estates) were established and technical assistance to SMEs was intensified through the UPT (Technical Service Units), staffed by TPL (Extension Field Officers).
1994	BIPIK was replaced by PIKIM (Small-scale Enterprises Development Project).

Marketing Initiatives

1979	A reservation scheme was introduced to protect certain markets for SMEs.
1999	The anti-monopoly law included explicit provisions in support of SMEs.

Finance Initiatives

1971	PT ASKRINDO was established as a state-owned credit insurance company.
1973	KIK (Small Investment Credits) and KMKP (Working Capital Credits) were introduced to provide subsidized credit for SMEs.
1973	PT BAHANA, a state-owned venture capital company, was established.
1974	KK (Small Credits), administered by Bank Rakyat Indonesia, was launched; subsequently (in 1984) it was changed to the KUPEDES (General Rural Saving Program) scheme, aimed at promoting small businesses.
1989	SME loans from state-owned enterprises were mandated.
1990	The subsidized credit programmes (KIK, KMKP) were abolished and the unsubsidized KUK (Small Business Credits) was introduced.
1999	Direct credit programmes were transferred from the Central Bank to PT PNM (a state-owned corporation for SMEs) and Bank Ekspor Indonesia.
2000	All government credit programmes for SMEs were to be abolished.

TABLE 3.3 (*continued*)

General Initiatives

1978	A Directorate General for Small-scale Industry was established in the Ministry of Industry.
1984	The *Bapak Angkat* ("foster parent") scheme was introduced to support SMEs. Later (in 1991) it was extended nationally.
1991	SENTRAs (groups of SMEs) in industrial clusters were organized under the KOPINKRA (Small-scale Handicraft Cooperatives).
1993	The Ministry of Cooperatives was assigned responsibility for small business development.
1995	The Basic Law for Promoting Small-scale Enterprises was enacted.
1997	The *Bapak Angkat* programme was changed to a Partnership (*Kemitraan*) programme.
1998	The Ministry of Cooperatives and Small Business added medium-scale business to its responsibilities.
1998	Under Minister Adi Sasono, the promotion of SMEs as part of the People's Economy (*Ekonomi Rakyat*) became a national slogan.

Source: Based on Thee Kian Wie, "Indonesia", in *Industrial Structures and the Development of Small and Medium Enterprise Linkages: Examples from East Asia*, edited by Saha Dhevan Meyanathan, EDI Seminar Series (Washington D.C.: World Bank, 1994), p. 121, and Mitsuhiro Hayashi, "Support Mechanisms for the Development of SMEs in Indonesia, with Special Reference to Inter-firm Linkages", unpublished paper, Australian National University, Canberra, 2000.

Source: Hill (2001).

TABLE 3.4
SME Policy Initiatives in Indonesia Since 2008

General Initiatives

2008 Law No. 20/2008 concerning micro, small, and medium enterprises.
> The regulation replaced Law No. 9/1995 concerning small enterprises.
> Define micro, small, and medium enterprises.
> Central and local governments facilitate MSMEs through financing, facilities and infrastructure, business information, partnerships, business licences, business opportunities, trade promotion, and institutional support.

2009 Government Regulation No. 24/2009 concerning industrial parks. Industrial park companies are obliged to provide land for activities to MSMEs.

2013 Law No. 1/2013 concerning microfinance institutions was launched.
> Microfinance institutions aim to: (1) increase access to micro-scale funding; (2) increase economic and productivity empowerment of society; and (3) increase incomes and welfare, particularly the poor and/or low income.
> Microfinance institutions have to be owned by the locals, and monitored by OJK (financial services authority).

2013 Government Regulation No. 17/2013 regarding the implementation of Law No. 20/2008 was enacted.
> Regulate MSME development, including facilitation.
> This regulation replaced government regulation concerning partnerships.
> KPPU monitors partnerships between large enterprises and MSMEs.
> Free licensing for micro enterprises and reduced fee for small enterprises.
> Transfer the role of government in MSME development from central to local.
> Coordinate between stakeholders at least once a year.
> Transfer of data from local to central government.

2014 Government Regulation No. 98/2014 concerning licensing for micro and small enterprises.
> Regulate IUMK (*ijin usaha mikro kecil*/licences for micro and small enterprises).
> IUMK is issued as a single sheet of paper.
> IUMK is free of charge or reduced in fee.
> IUMK is issued by the subdistrict head through a delegation from the regent/mayor. IUMK may also delegate to the urban village head/ village head, depending on the characteristics of the region.
> Urban village head/village head collects data on the micro and small enterprises in their region and reports to the subdistrict head periodically.

TABLE 3.4   (*continued*)

General Initiatives

2014   Law No. 23/2014 concerning the local government.
> MSME empowerment implemented through data collection, partnerships, ease of licensing, institutional strengthening and coordination with the stakeholders in central, provincial, and local levels.
> MSME upgrading: the central government focused on upgrading medium enterprises into large enterprises; the provincial level focused on upgrading small enterprises into medium enterprises; while the district/municipal level focused on upgrading micro enterprises into small enterprises.

Technology Initiatives

2012   Minister of Research and Technology Regulation No. 1/2012 concerning research and development technical assistance for business entities.

2013   Presidential Regulation No. 27/2013 concerning development of entrepreneurial incubator.
> Entrepreneurial incubator is an intermediary institution that performs the incubation process for businesses, particularly start-up companies.
> The incubator may be established by the central government, local government, business entity, and/or community.
> Activities include providing working space, guidance and consultancy, supporting research and development efforts as well as providing access to technology, training and skills development, access to funding, business networks and cooperation, and managing of intellectual property rights.
> The coordinating agency is under the Coordinating Ministry for Economic Affairs.

Technology Initiatives

2014   Minister of Industrial Regulation No. 11/2014 concerning reorganization of small and medium enterprise machinery and/or equipment.

Marketing Initiatives

2008   Minister of Trade Regulation No. 53/2008 concerning development and arrangement of traditional markets, shopping centres, and modern markets. The regulation focuses on the partnership between MSMEs and shopping centres/modern markets, including provisions of area and product marketing/MSMEs as the supplier.

2010   Presidential Regulation No. 54/2010 concerning procurement of goods/services for the government. Government procurement needs to expand to include opportunities for micro and small enterprises as well as small cooperatives.

TABLE 3.4 (*continued*)

Marketing Initiatives

2013   Minister of Trade Regulation No. 53/2008 replaced by Minister of Trade Regulation No. 70/2013. Partnerships in MSMEs development conducted through product marketing, provisions of area, and MSMEs as the supplier.

2014   Presidential Regulation No. 39/2014 concerning investment reservation list.
       > 93 business activities reserved for MSMEs and cooperatives.
       > 51 business activities opened for investment which required partnerships with MSMEs and cooperatives.

2014   Asephi (*Asosiasi Eksportir dan Produsen Handicraft Indonesia*/ Indonesia Handicraft Producers and Exporters Association) established INACRAFT Mall (<http://inacraft-mall.com/>) as an online market place for SME products.

Finance Initiatives

2009   Law No. 2/2009 concerning LPEI (*Lembaga Pembiayaan Ekspor Indonesia*/Indonesia Export Funding Agency). One of the focus is to encourage MSMEs and cooperatives to develop export-oriented products by providing funding. LPEI may also provide assistance and consultancy for MSMEs.

2015   Bank Central Regulation No. 17/12/PBI/2015. In 2018 banks have to allocate a minimum of 20 per cent of their total lending to SMEs.

2015   Economic package: The government subsidized KUR, reducing the interest rate from 22 per cent to 12 per cent. The government through LPEI also increases support for export-oriented SMEs through loans or by providing loans with interest rates lower than that obtained from commercial institutions.

Subsequently, the government also established LPEI (Indonesia Export Funding Agency) to facilitate exports. In its mandate, export financing for SMEs are included as outlined in the reform package which the government introduced in 2015.

Regarding SMEs protection, in 2014 the goverment enacted Presidential Regulation No. 39 / 2014 concerning investment reservation list. According to this regulation, 93 business activities were reserved for MSMEs as well as cooperatives. In addition there were 51 business activities open for investment which required partnerships with MSMEs and cooperatives.

ERIA (2014) evaluated SME policies across ASEAN member countries including Indonesia, based on eight factors. They are institutional framework; access to support services; cheaper and faster business registration; access to finance; technology and technology transfer; international market expansion; promotion of entrepreneurial education; and more effective representation of SMEs' interest. The evaluation is presented as an index value starting from 1 (poor) to 6 (good). Indonesia scored 4.1 out of 6.0.

For institutional framework, Indonesia scored 4.4 out of 6.0. This is the result of having a clear SME definition and institutions for SMEs development. In Indonesia, the definition of SME is stated in the Law No. 20/2008. The coordination of SMEs policy formulation and implementation is under the Ministry of Cooperatives and SMEs (MoCSME). Indonesia also states its SMEs development stategies in its National Medium Development Plan with detailed strategies outlined in strategic plans of the respective implementing ministries and agencies.

Regarding access to support services, Indonesia scored 4.0 out of 6.0. To support SMEs, the government action plan includes business incubators, business development services (BDS) and centres for integrated commercial services called PLUT (*Pusat Layanan Usaha Terpadu*). There are 1,096 BDS located in almost all regencies throughout the country. However, these centres are no longer in operation. Also SMEs were unable to access e-commerce sites such as the online portal for SMEs.

The government supports start-up companies through cheaper and faster business registration and financial assistance. Based on regulation, it takes only three days to obtain a company registration certificate and the process is free of charge. The government also established the KPPT (a one-stop licencing office) so that firms no longer have to visit different local agencies to obtain a business permit. However, in practice, business registration certificate is issued in 3–7 days. Meanwhile the performance of the KPPT varies across the local government. In terms of financial assistance for start-up companies, the government introduced working capital assistance for new entrepreneurs. This assistance is under the Government's Social Assistance Program, which targeted new graduates from vocational schools, academies, and universities who are unemployed. Working capital assistance gives up to IDR 25 million (US$2,500), and the receiver is not required to pay back the grant/loan. Until 2014, around 2,160 graduates participated in the programme. Hence, in the aspect of cheaper and faster business registration and better legislation and regulation, Indonesia scored 4.4 out of 6.0.

For access to finance, Indonesia scored 4.3 out of 6.0. Although Indonesia has a good banking system, only a small number of SMEs have access to financial assistance from the banks and non-bank financial institutions are limited. In addition, Indonesia's SMEs are not able to acess capital from the capital markets.

Related to technology and technology transfer, every ministry has its own plan and there is no system to syncronize all the existing regulations. Moreover, most of the initiatives are still in the early stages, for example the development of science parks. Infrastructure necessary for technological development are insuffucient, such as broadband internet and protection of intellectual property. Hence for technology and technology transfer, Indonesia scored only 3.8 out of 6.0.

In the aspect of international market expansion, the score for Indonesia is 4.2 out of 6.0. This is because of the overlapping policies and lack of coordination across relevant SME ministries/agencies. In addition, lack of resources and capacity and Indonesian Trade Promotion Centre (ITPC) also contributed to the low capacity of market expansion. Although there exists an internal monitoring and evaluation process, it is unclear whether there has been a significant number of participating SMEs which have started to export. The government also allocated financial assistance for SMEs to export under the LPEI. In 2011, the share of export credit that is allocated to SMEs is only 8.47 per cent (ERIA 2014). Limited region coverage (LPEI is available only in five cities, which are Jakarta, Medan, Surabaya, Makassar, and Solo) and lack of funding source have impeded export credit distribution.

TABLE 3.5
ASEAN SME Policy Index

No.	Indicators	BRN	CAM	IND	LAO	MMR	MYS	PHL	SGP	THA	VNM	ASEAN
1	Institutional Framework	2.6	2.6	4.4	2.6	2.9	4.6	3.7	5.4	3.9	3.8	3.7
2	Access to Support Services	3.3	2.4	4.0	2.3	2.7	4.8	3.8	5.4	3.8	3.6	3.6
3	Cheaper and Faster Business Registration	3.1	2.1	4.4	2.7	2.9	4.8	3.0	5.0	4.2	4.1	3.6
4	Access to Finance	3.0	2.5	4.3	2.5	2.1	4.6	3.6	5.6	4.3	3.4	3.6
5	Technology and Technology Transfer	3.2	1.9	3.8	2.0	2.4	4.9	3.6	5.6	4.3	3.6	3.5
6	International Market Expansion	3.2	3.3	4.2	3.1	3.3	5.0	4.4	6.0	4.7	4.0	4.1
7	Promotion of Entrepreneurial Education	3.0	2.1	3.9	2.3	2.9	4.2	3.7	5.0	3.1	2.9	3.3
8	More Effective Representation of SMEs' Interest	2.3	2.5	3.0	3.0	4.5	5.7	4.7	5.0	4.4	4.0	3.8

Source: ERIA (2014).

In terms of promotion of entrepreneurial education, Indonesia scored 3.9 out of 6.0. Entrepreneurship education has not been a major feature in Indonesia's education curriculum. Whereas in the aspect of more effective representation of SMEs' interest, Indonesia scored the lowest of the eight aspects evaluated with a score of 3.0 out of 6.0.

Compared to other countries in ASEAN, SMEs in Indonesia are less competitive due to their low productivity and innovation. Ineffective SMEs government policies contributed to this outcome. A continued increase in minimum wages is not accompanied by a significant increase in output, as skills upgrading is not part of SMEs development. In addition, the low productivity is also associated with inefficient business operation. The company culture has also been the main weakness hindering innovation. While the training for workers is often provided at big companies, it barely happens in SMEs. There is a perception that training only results in additional burden in the form of significant cost while it is assumed not to add any value to the business.

Access to finance is also a major obstacle for SMEs in Indonesia. While other ASEAN countries have provided alternative ways with less costly requirements to obtain credit, the banking sector is still the main source of external funding in Indonesia. The government of Indonesia has addressed the problem of high interest rate by providing small business credit (KUR). However, the prudential practices in the banking sector require collateral or at least a decent financial history of business criteria to be considered for a credit. With the absence or limited alternative source of funding, for example from venture capital, angel investors, or crowd-funding institutions, start-up businesses find it very difficult to obtain external funds.

Moreover, doing business in Indonesia is considered costly and requires a lot of time. The World Bank's Doing Business 2016 Report found that to start a business in Indonesia, one needs to spend 46 days for 13 procedures, and the cost of which is also considerably high compared to other countries. Hence, most of the SMEs, especially micro and small enterprises choose to stay as informal businesses, without knowing that there are a lot of benefits that could be obtained if they switch to formal legal entities. Another important factor that provides "incentives" for SMEs to stay informal is that the business owners do not need to worry about cumbersome tax administration.

In addition, SMEs in Indonesia have difficulty or are unable to find the right market for their products. The government has developed and implemented a number of programmes to improve access to market for SMEs. For example, the Ministry of Trade has a number of programmes, such as establishing a local trade forum which is aimed at facilitating SMEs across the regions, partnering SMEs with modern retail businesses to promote their products, and supporting the implementation of online sales system through e-catalogue and e-marketing. However, the programme has had limited impact as the scale of the programme is relatively small. It is also found that technical ministries have overlapping SMEs' programmes among them. Indeed, the government of Indonesia has no grand strategy to develop and no political will to improve the competitiveness of SMEs.

4. Survey Results

4.1. Characteristics of Survey Sample

In the survey conducted for this study, a total of 1,000 SMEs were contacted directly by phone, letters and emails as well as via business associations and the local governments. The successful interviews involved 200 firms in three major locations, namely, the Jakarta greater area, Bandung greater area, and Surabaya greater area. The survey involved interviews with owners or managers of small enterprises (11–49 workers), medium enterprises (50–249 workers), and large enterprises (more than 250 workers). In terms of firms interviewed by industry, there are 52 firms in food products, 20 firms in beverages, 71 firms in wearing apparel, 14 firms in leather and related products, 14 firms in wood products, 21 firms in furniture, 3 firms in computers, electronics, and optical, 4 firms in electrical products, and 1 firm in motor vehicles, trailers, and semi-trailers (see Figure 3.6).

Majority of the respondents (51 per cent) are small enterprises, the remaining 30.5 per cent are medium enterprises and 18.5 per cent are large enterprises. A large number of the respondents (46.5 per cent) are firms that have been in the business for at least 15 years, the remaining 24.5 per cent have been in business for 5 years or less, and 29 per cent have been in business for 6–14 years. Majority of the firms (55.5 per cent) are sole proprietorship, the remaining are either private limited (34 per cent), or partnership (7 per cent). More than 90 per cent of the sample are 100 per cent locally owned, the other 4 per cent are 100 per cent foreign owned, and 5 per cent are joint ventures. Table 3.6 presents the full sample characteristics.

FIGURE 3.6
Distribution of Survey Sample

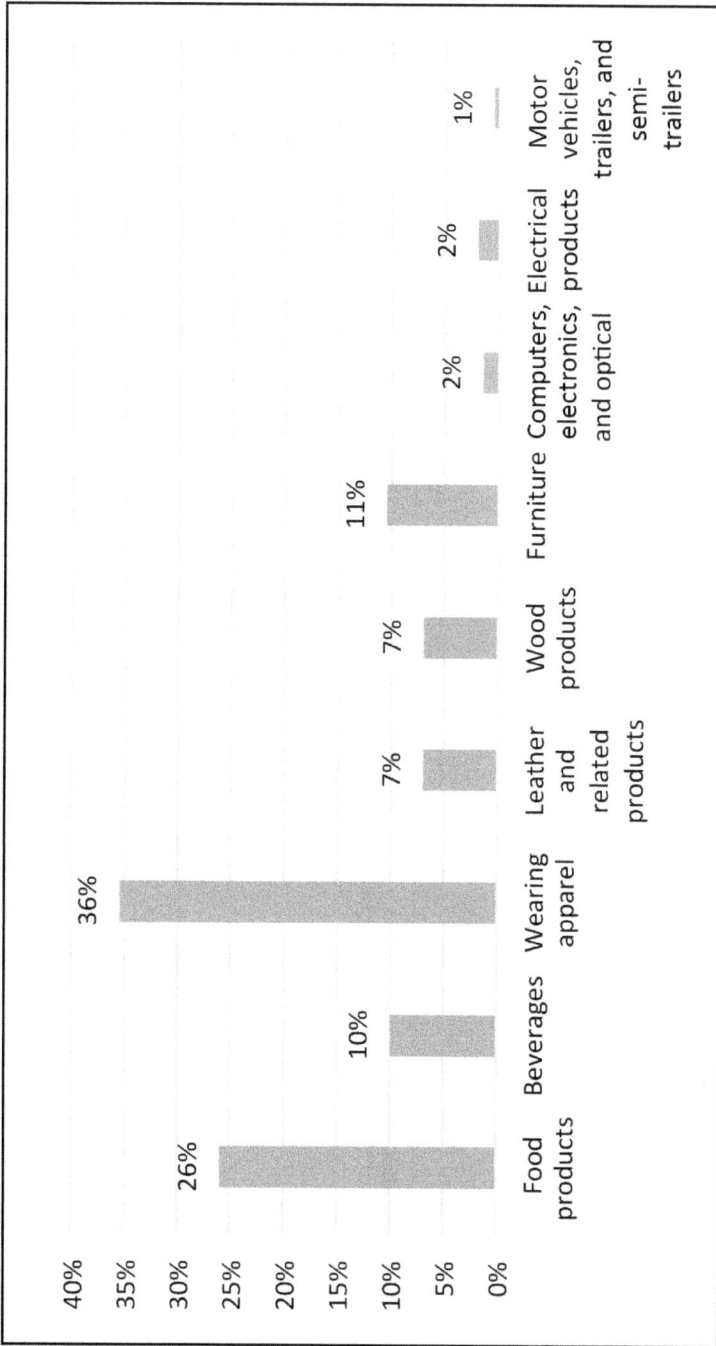

TABLE 3.6
Profile of the Sample

	Full Sample		SMEs		LEs	
Employment Size	**Number**	**Share**	**Number**	**Share**	**Number**	**Share**
Small	102	51.00%	102	63%		
Medium	61	30.50%	61	37%		
Large	37	18.50%			37	100%
Total	**200**	**100.00%**	**163**	**100%**	**37**	**100%**
Year of Establishment	**Number**	**Share**	**Number**	**Share**	**Number**	**Share**
<= 5 years	49	24.50%	47	29%	2	5%
6–10 years	27	13.50%	24	15%	3	8%
11–15 years	31	15.50%	30	18%	1	3%
> 15 years	93	46.50%	62	38%	31	84%
Total	**200**	**100.00%**	**163**	**100%**	**37**	**100%**
Legal Organization	**Number**	**Share**	**Number**	**Share**	**Number**	**Share**
Single Proprietorship	111	55.50%	109	66.87%	2	5.41%
Partnership	14	7.00%	13	7.98%	1	2.70%
Private Limited	68	34.00%	39	23.93%	29	78.38%
Public Limited	4	2.00%			4	10.81%
Cooperative	2	1.00%	1	0.61%	1	2.70%
State-owned enterprise	1	0.50%	1	0.61%		
Total	**200**	**100.00%**	**163**	**100.00%**	**37**	**100.00%**

Ownership Structure	Number	Share	Number	Share	Number	Share
Local	182	91.00%	156	95.71%	26	70.27%
Foreign	8	4.00%	5	3.07%	3	8.11%
Both	10	5.00%	2	1.23%	8	21.62%
Total	200	100.00%	163	100.00%	37	100.00%
Family Business	**Number**	**Share**	**Number**	**Share**	**Number**	**Share**
Yes	113	56.50%	96	58.90%	17	45.95%
No	87	43.50%	67	41.10%	20	54.05%
Total	200	100.00%	163	100.00%	37	100%
Managed by Founder/Family Member	**Number**	**Share**	**Number**	**Share**	**Number**	**Share**
Yes	111	98.23%	95	98.96%	16	94%
No	2	1.77%	1	1.04%	1	6%
Total	113	100.00%	96	100%	17	100%
Highest Academic Qualification of Founder/Family Member	**Number**	**Share**	**Number**	**Share**	**Number**	**Share**
No formal education	3	3.0%	3	3.0%		
Primary	3	3.0%	3	3.0%		
Secondary/High School	24	22.0%	22	23.0%	3	17.7%
Vocational/Diploma	11	10.0%	11	12.0%		
University	70	63.0%	56	59.0%	14	82.4%
Total	111	100.0%	95	100.0%	17	100.0%

TABLE 3.6 *(continued)*

	Full Sample		SMEs		LEs	
	2013	2014	2013	2014	2013	2014
Total Fixed Assets						
Mean (billion rupiah)	696	715	315	315	2,380	2,480
Parent Company	Number	Share	Number	Share	Number	Share
Yes	76	38.0%	56	34.4%	20	54.1%
No	124	62.0%	107	65.6%	17	46.0%
Total	200	100.0%	163	100.0%	37	100.0%
Size of Parent Company	Number	Share	Number	Share	Number	Share
11–49 full-time workers	28	36.8%	28	50.0%		
50–249 full-time workers	20	26.3%	19	33.9%	1	5.0%
More than 250 full-time workers	28	36.8%	9	16.1%	19	95.0%
Total	76	100.0%	56	100.0%	20	100.0%
Ownership of Parent Company	Number	Share	Number	Share	Number	Share
Local	64	84.2%	52	92.9%	12	60.0%
Foreign	12	15.8%	4	7.1%	8	40.0%
Total	76	100.0%	56	100.0%	20	100.0%
Membership	Number	Share	Number	Share	Number	Share
Yes	88	44.0%	63	38.7%	25	67.6%
No	112	56.0%	100	61.4%	12	32.4%
Total	200	100.0%	163	100.0%	37	100.0%

Table 3.6 also shows that 56.5 per cent of the sample are family-run businesses. Most of these family businesses (98.2 per cent) are managed by the founder or family member with 63 per cent of them being university graduates, 10 per cent hold diploma certificates, 22 per cent are secondary/high school graduates while the remaining are primary school graduates at the most. The proportion of family-run business is higher in SMEs than LEs. Table 3.6 also shows that only 38 per cent of the respondents are a subsidiary of larger companies.

Sales, Production Costs, Employment, and Innovation[2]

The average sales of the interviewed firms were IDR 450 billion in 2013, with an increase of 10 per cent in 2014. The average sales of the SMEs were IDR 21.9 billion in 2013 with 3 per cent increase in 2014. In contrast, the average sales of LEs increased by 10 per cent during the same time period. Among the 200 samples, 33 per cent of the firms export their products, with average export sales of 11.6 per cent. Export share of SMEs is lower at about 8.2 per cent. In constrast, export share of LEs is 26.1 per cent. Table 3.7 summarizes the interview results regarding sales.

TABLE 3.7
Sales Distribution and Product Type

	Total Sample		SMEs		LEs	
	No. of Firms	% of Total	No. of Firms	% of Total	No. of Firms	% of Total
a. Parent Companies						
Intermediate	1	0.5%	1	0.6%		
Final	6	3.0%	4	2.5%	2	5.4%
Both	1	0.5%			1	2.7%
No	192	96.0%	158	96.9%	34	91.9%
Total	**200**	**100%**	**163**	**100%**	**37**	**100%**
b. Sister Companies						
Intermediate	3	1.5%	2	1.2%	1	2.7%
Final	8	4.0%	6	3.7%	2	5.4%
Both	1	0.5%			1	2.7%
No	188	94.0%	155	95.1%	33	89.2%
Total	**200**	**100%**	**163**	**100%**	**37**	**100%**

TABLE 3.7 (*continued*)

	Total Sample		SMEs		LEs	
	No. of Firms	% of Total	No. of Firms	% of Total	No. of Firms	% of Total
c. Subsidiary Companies						
Intermediate	4	2.0%	2	1.2%	2	5.4%
Final	4	2.0%	2	1.2%	2	5.4%
Both	1	0.5%			1	2.7%
No	191	95.5%	159	97.5%	32	86.5%
Total	**200**	**100%**	**163**	**100%**	**37**	**100%**
d. Other Companies						
Intermediate	19	9.5%	18	11.0%	1	2.7%
Final	86	43.0%	65	39.9%	21	56.8%
Both	8	4.0%	6	3.7%	2	5.4%
No	87	43.5%	74	45.4%	13	35.1%
Total	**200**	**100%**	**163**	**100%**	**37**	**100%**
e. State-owned Enterprises						
Intermediate	2	1.0%	2	1.2%		
Final	13	6.5%	9	5.5%	4	10.8%
Both						
No	185	92.5%	152	93.3%	33	89.2%
Total	**200**	**100%**	**163**	**100%**	**37**	**100%**
f. Directly to Consumers						
Intermediate						
Final	154	77.0%	127	77.9%	27	73.0%
Both						
No	46	23.0%	36	22.1%	10	27.0%
Total	**200**	**100%**	**163**	**100%**	**37**	**100%**

For intermediate output, 0.5 per cent of the respondents sell their products to the parent companies, 1.5 per cent to sister companies, 2 per cent to subsidiary companies, 1 per cent to state-owned companies and 9.5 per cent to other companies. Regarding final goods, 77 per cent of respondents sell them directly to consumers, 43 per cent to other companies, 7 per cent to state-owned companies, 4 per cent to sister companies, 3 per cent to parent companies, and 2 per cent to subsidiary companies. In addition, there are also companies that sell their products both in intermediate and final goods of which 0.5 per cent of the total sample sell them to parent companies, 0.5 per cent to sister companies, 0.5 per cent to subsidiary companies, and 4 per cent to other companies.

Regarding their products as intermediate input, 11 per cent of SMEs sell them to other companies, 0.6 per cent to parent companies, 1.2 per cent to sister companies, 1.2 per cent to subsidiary companies, and 1.2 per cent to state-owned companies. With final goods, they sell their products mostly directly to consumers and other companies — i.e., 78 per cent directly to consumers, 40 per cent to other companies, 5.5 per cent to state-owned companies, 3.7 per cent to sister companies, 2.5 per cent to parent companies and 1.2 per cent to subsidiary companies. About 4 per cent of these SMEs also sell their products both as intermediate and final goods to other companies.

The survey results show that in terms of their products as intermediate output, 5.4 per cent of LEs sell them to subsidiary companies, and 2.7 per cent each to sister companies and other companies. In this group, 73 per cent sell their products as final goods directly to consumers, 57 per cent to other companies, 10.8 per cent to state-owned companies, 5.4 per cent each to parent companies, sister companies, and subsidiary companies.

In summary, 77 per cent of the respondents sell their products directly to customers, 57 per cent to other unrelated companies, 8 per cent to state-owned companies, 6 per cent to sister companies, 5 per cent to subsidiary companies, and 4 per cent to parent companies (see Table 3.8). With regard to the type of output sold, 83 per cent of respondents sell only final goods, 4 per cent only intermediate goods, and 13 per cent both final and intermediate goods (see Table 3.9). Regarding goods destination, it can be concluded that 54 per cent of respondents send to only one destination, while 46 per cent distributed the products to multiple destinations (see Table 3.10).

TABLE 3.8
Overall Sales and Destination

	Parent Company	Sister Company	Subsidiary Company	Other Companies	State-owned Enterprises	Directly to Consumers	Total	Share
Intermediate	1	3	4	19	2		29	15%
Final	6	8	4	86	13	154	271	136%
Both	1	1	1	8			11	6%
Total	8	12	9	113	15	154	311	156%
Share to Total Respondents	4%	6%	5%	57%	8%	77%	156%	

Note: One firm can have multiple outputs and sales to different types of buyers.

TABLE 3.9
Distribution of Sales Based on Output

Output	Overall		SMEs		LEs	
	Number of Firms	Share	Number of Firms	Share	Number of Firms	Share
Intermediate	8	4%	8	5%		
Final	166	83%	135	83%	31	84%
Both	26	13%	20	12%	6	16%
Total	200	100%	163	100%	37	100%

TABLE 3.10
Distribution of Sales Activities Based on Destination

Destination	Overall		SMEs		LEs	
	Number of Firms	Share	Number of Firms	Share	Number of Firms	Share
Single Destination	108	54%	92	56%	16	43%
Multiple Destinations	92	46%	71	44%	21	57%
Total	200	100%	163	100%	37	100%

The respondents' production process and input characteristics are summarized in Table 3.11. About 69.5 per cent of the respondents have their production process completely in-house, while 22.5 per cent have theirs both in-house and outsourced and the remaining 8 per cent completely outsourced. Similarly, 69 per cent of SME respondents have their production completely in-house, 22 per cent both in-house and outsourced, and the remaining 9 per cent completely outsourced. Among LEs, 70 per cent have processed their production in-house, 24 per cent both in-house and outsourced, and 5 per cent completely outsourced.

TABLE 3.11
Production and Input Characteristics

Production Activities	Overall Sample		SMEs		LEs	
	2014		2014		2014	
Production	**Number**	**%**	**Number**	**%**	**Number**	**%**
Completely in-house	139	69.5%	113	69%	26	70%
Completely outsourced	16	8%	14	9%	2	5%
Foreign outsourced	1		1		0	
Domestic outsourced	15		13		2	
Both in-house and outsourced	45	22.5%	36	22%	9	24%
Foreign outsourced	9		6		1	
Domestic outsourced	36		30		8	
Total	200		163		37	
Production Cost	**2013**	**2014**	**2013**	**2014**	**2013**	**2014**
(billion rupiah)	179	216	9	9	929	1,130
% Breakdown						
Raw materials	44.4	44.7	45.0	45.4	41.8	41.7
Intermediate inputs	12.1	12.1	11.8	11.8	13.7	13.4
Utilities (water, gas, and electricity)	11.1	11.4	11.4	11.7	9.7	10.0
Interest payments	3.0	3.0	2.6	2.5	5.0	5.0
Salaries and wages	29.1	28.8	29.0	28.6	29.7	29.8
Total	100	100	100	100	100	100
Sources of Inputs (2014)	**Number**	**%**	**Number**	**%**	**Number**	**%**
Local	153	77%	139	85%	14	38%
Majority Local (> 50% and < 100%)	26	13%	15	9%	11	30%
Local (Half) (50%)	5	3%	2	1%	3	8%
Local (Minority) (11–49%)	7	4%	4	2%	3	8%
Partially Local	2	1%	1	1%	1	3%
Foreign	7	4%	2	1%	5	14%
Local Source (% of Total Inputs)	89		94		68	

The average production cost was about IDR 179 billion in 2013, which increased by 21 per cent in 2014. Among the SMEs, however, the average cost only increased by 3 per cent, from IDR 8.9 billion to IDR 9.17 billion. In contrast, production cost in LEs increased by 22 per cent from IDR 929 billion in 2013 to IDR 1,130 billion in 2014. The largest component of cost is raw materials, i.e., about 44.4 per cent of total cost in 2013, which is followed by salaries and wages (about 29.1 per cent), and intermediate inputs (about 12.1 per cent). The pattern is similar between SMEs and LEs in which raw materials and salaries are the major parts of the production cost.

Local market is the major input source. The survey shows that SMEs and LEs differ in procurement. The majority of SMEs sourced all their inputs from the local market, i.e., about 85 per cent, while the other 10 per cent of respondents sourced more than 50 per cent of their inputs locally, and the remaining 5 per cent of respondents obtained all or most of their inputs from foreign markets. In contrast, only 38 per cent of LEs sourced all their inputs from the local market, the other 38 per cent obtained more than 50 per cent of their inputs from the local market, and 32 per cent sourced all or most of their inputs from abroad.

The characteristics of employment are also slightly different between SMEs and LEs (see Table 3.12), where the proportion of full-time workers is higher in LEs than SMEs. Shares of full-time workers to total number of workers in SMEs and LEs are 79 per cent and 91 per cent respectively. SMEs employ fewer female workers than LEs. The shares of female workers in SMEs and LEs are about 27 per cent and 46 per cent respectively. Foreign workers are very limited, only 2 per cent in 2013 and it declined to 1 per cent in 2014.

With regard to job position and distribution of salaries, the survey shows that a large number of workers (47 per cent) are plant and machine operators and assemblers, 18 per cent are supervisors and clerks, 15 per cent are engineers and technicians, 13 per cent are service and sales workers, 5 per cent are managers and professionals, and 1 per cent are in other positions (see Table 3.13). Although the managers and professionals made up only 5 per cent of the total number of workers, the share of their salaries to total salaries is about 44.1 per cent. The share of plant and machine operators and assemblers to total workers is similar between SMEs and LEs. However, the salaries distribution is greater in the LEs than in SMEs.

The labour force in the survey is dominated by secondary/high school graduates, i.e., about 54 per cent (see Figure 3.7). Among the

TABLE 3.12
Employment Profile

Employment Profile	Overall Sample 2013 Number of Workers	Overall Sample 2013 % of total	Overall Sample 2014 Number of Workers	Overall Sample 2014 % of total	SMEs 2013 Number of Workers	SMEs 2013 % of total	SMEs 2014 Number of Workers	SMEs 2014 % of total	LEs 2013 Number of Workers	LEs 2013 % of total	LEs 2014 Number of Workers	LEs 2014 % of total
Full-time Workers	573	90%	587	90%	37	79%	38	79%	2,935	91%	3,006	91%
Part-time Workers	61	10%	62	10%	10	21%	10	21%	285	9%	288	9%
Composition of Female Employees (%)	31%		30%		27%		26%		46%		46%	
Composition of Foreign Employees (%)	2%		1%		2%		1%		1%		1%	

TABLE 3.13
Workforce and Salaries, 2014

Workforce	Overall			SMEs			LEs		
	Number of Workers	% to Total Workers	% of Total Salaries	Number of Workers	% to Total Workers	% of Total Salaries	Number of Workers	% to Total Workers	% of Total Salaries
Managers and professionals	28	5%	44%	2	5%	69%	139	5%	24%
Engineers and technicians	90	15%	12%	1	3%	0%	485	16%	22%
Supervisors and clerks	108	18%	13%	3	8%	12%	569	19%	14%
Plant and machine operators and assemblers	278	47%	14%	20	50%	3%	1,414	47%	24%
Service and sales workers	75	13%	14%	14	35%	17%	342	11%	12%
Others	8	1%	3%				57	2%	4%

FIGURE 3.7
Academic Qualifications of Workers

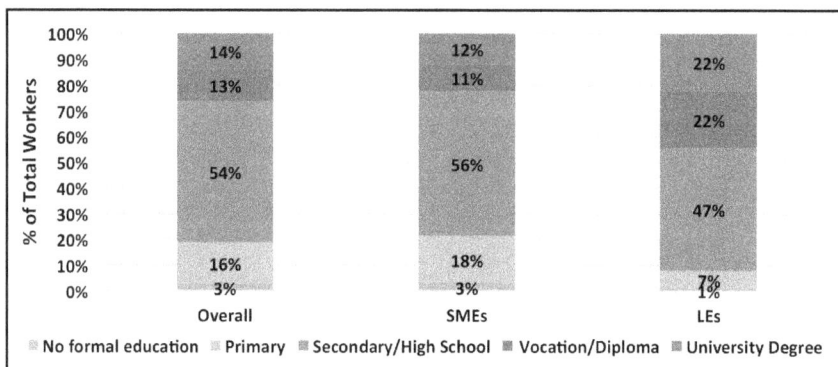

SMEs, the proportion of workers with secondary/high school education and below is higher than in LEs. In SMEs, the share of workers with secondary/high school education is 56 per cent, 18 per cent have primary education, 11 per cent with vocation/diploma certificates, 12 per cent have university degrees, and 3 per cent have no formal education. The share of workers in LEs with primary or no formal education is only 8 per cent, while 47 per cent have secondary/high school education, 22 per cent have vocation/diploma certificates, and 22 per cent have university degrees.

The average training expenditure in 2013 was around IDR 400 million (see Table 3.14). For SMEs, the average training expenditure was less than IDR 400 million, while training expenditure of LEs was more than IDR 600 million.

TABLE 3.14
Training Expenditures

	Overall Sample		SMEs		LEs	
	2013	2014	2013	2014	2013	2014
Training Expenditures (million rupiah)	417	421	373	377	612	617

Table 3.15 shows innovation activities and expenditure of the respondents in 2012–14. Overall, 24 per cent of total respondents managed their research and development (R&D) activities in-house,

TABLE 3.15
Innovation Activities and Expenditure, 2012–14

Innovation Activities	Overall Sample			SMEs			LEs		
	Number of Firms	% of Total	Average Expenditure (IDR million)	Number of Firms	% of Total	Average Expenditure (IDR million)	Number of Firms	% of Total	Average Expenditure (IDR million)
In-house R&D activities	48	24%	75,300	32	20%	52	16	43%	407,000
Outsourcing of R&D activities	27	14%	123	16	10%	19	11	30%	583
Acquisition of machinery, equipment and software	59	30%	165,000	45	28%	99	14	38%	893,000
Acquisition of external knowledge	13	7%	1,790	10	6%	13	3	8%	9,610

while 14 per cent outsourced them. For in-house R&D, the average expenditure was IDR 75.3 billion, while average cost for outsourcing R&D was IDR 123 million. Other than R&D, to support innovation activities, 30 per cent of the respondents obtained machinery, equipment, and software with average expenditure of IDR 165 billion, and 7 per cent acquired knowledge from external resources with average expenditure of IDR 1.8 billion. The proportion of SMEs that carried out innovation activities is lower than LEs.

For SMEs, the proportion of respondents that is involved in in-house R&D is 20 per cent, outsourced R&D is 10 per cent, acquisition of machinery, equipment and software is 28 per cent, and acquisition of external knowledge is 6 per cent. For LEs, the proportion are 43 per cent, 30 per cent, 38 per cent, and 8 per cent for the four innovation activities respectively.

Figure 3.8 shows whether firms introduced product innovation. Overall, 59 per cent of respondents introduced new or significantly improved goods and 29 per cent introduced new or significantly improved services. For SME respondents, 56 per cent introduced new or significantly improved goods and 31 per cent introduced new or significantly improved services, whereas 70 per cent of LEs introduced new or significantly improved goods and only 22 per cent launched new or significantly improved services.

Did innovation contribute to sales? The survey shows the average share of innovation products that are new to the market is 14 per cent of total sales while the share of innovation products that are new to the firm is 11 per cent of total sales (see Figure 3.9). The contribution of new innovation to sales is slightly lower in SMEs, in which the share of innovation products that are new to the firm and to the market respectively are 11 per cent and 13 per cent of total sales respectively.

The survey result also shows process innovation, such as innovation in the methods of manufacturing or producing goods or services; logistics, delivery or distribution methods; and new supporting activities (see Figure 3.10). Overall, 44 per cent of respondents started innovation on the manufacturing method, 42 per cent introduced innovation on the logistic process, and 52 per cent brought innovation to the firms' supporting activities.

FIGURE 3.8
Introduction of Product Innovation, 2012–14

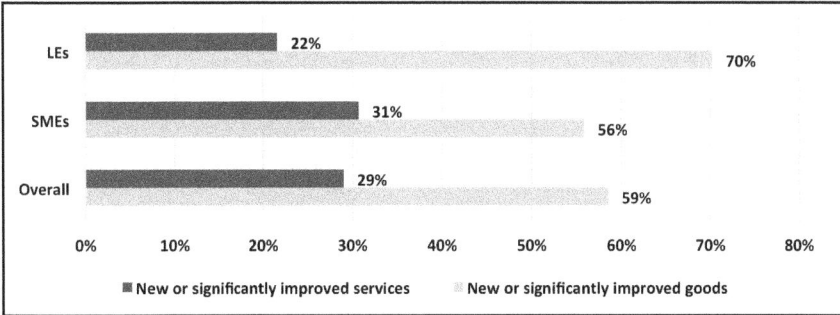

LEs: 22% | 70%
SMEs: 31% | 56%
Overall: 29% | 59%

■ New or significantly improved services   New or significantly improved goods

FIGURE 3.9
Share of New and Improved Products in Sales (%)

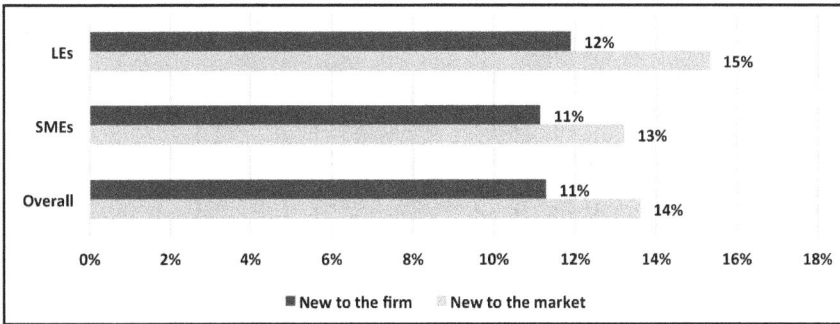

LEs: 12% | 15%
SMEs: 11% | 13%
Overall: 11% | 14%

■ New to the firm   New to the market

FIGURE 3.10
Proportion of Respondents that Introduced Process Innovation, 2012–14

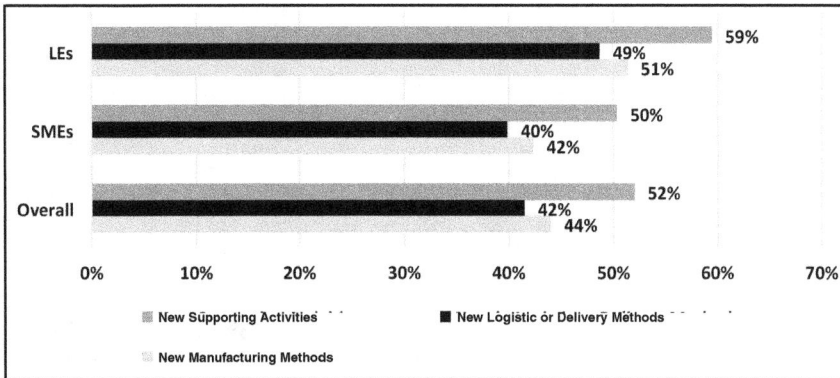

LEs: 59% | 49% | 51%
SMEs: 50% | 40% | 42%
Overall: 52% | 42% | 44%

New Supporting Activities   ■ New Logistic or Delivery Methods
New Manufacturing Methods

The total expenditure for innovation activities spent by all respondents in 2012–14 was IDR 48 trillion, which made the annual total expenditure for innovation at IDR 16 trillion. The respondents' share of revenue from new products to total sales in 2014 was 25 per cent or about IDR 25 trillion.

The survey also shows that majority of the respondents are connected to the internet. As shown in Table 3.16, 64 per cent of total respondents

TABLE 3.16
Use of Internet-related Services

Internet Services	Overall Sample		SMEs		LEs	
a. Email	Number	Share	Number	Share	Number	Share
Yes	128	64%	99	61%	29	78%
No	72	36%	64	39%	8	22%
b. Company website	Number	Share	Number	Share	Number	Share
Yes	89	45%	67	41%	22	59%
No	111	56%	96	59%	15	41%
c. Online sales	Number	Share	Number	Share	Number	Share
Yes	49	25%	38	23%	11	30%
No	151	76%	125	77%	26	70%
d. Online purchase/ procurement	Number	Share	Number	Share	Number	Share
Yes	34	17%	26	16%	8	22%
No	166	83%	137	84%	29	78%
e. Online marketing	Number	Share	Number	Share	Number	Share
Yes	76	38%	59	36%	17	46%
No	124	62%	104	64%	20	54%
f. Online payment	Number	Share	Number	Share	Number	Share
Yes	57	29%	44	27%	13	35%
No	143	72%	119	73%	24	65%

use emails for communication; for SMEs, this is 61 per cent, slightly lower than LEs, which is about 78 per cent. Although not in the majority, 45 per cent of respondents have company websites, 41 per cent of which are SMEs and 59 per cent are LEs. Online services for marketing are also used by 38 per cent of the respondents. Utilization of other internet-related services, such as online sales, online purchase, and online payment, is below 30 per cent.

4.2. ASEAN Economic Community

The main part of the survey is to assess firms' engagement in ASEAN. As indicated in Table 3.17, only 19 per cent of our respondents have business relations with other firms in ASEAN, with more than half of them engaged in exports. For SMEs, only 16 per cent of them are engaged in businesses with other firms in ASEAN, mostly in exports. Meanwhile, 30 per cent of LEs have business relations with ASEAN partners, of which 55 per cent export to and 27 per cent import from ASEAN.

TABLE 3.17
Business Relations with Firms in ASEAN

	Overall Sample		SMEs		LEs	
Business Relations with Firms in ASEAN	**Number**	**Share**	**Number**	**Share**	**Number**	**Share**
Yes	37	19%	26	16%	11	30%
No	163	82%	137	84%	26	70%
Business Relations According to Activity	**Number**	**Share**	**Number**	**Share**	**Number**	**Share**
Import	7	19%	4	15%	3	27%
Export	21	57%	15	58%	6	55%
Investment	1	3%	1	4%		
Import and Export	5	14%	3	12%	2	18%
Export and Invest	1	3%	1	4%		
Others	2	5%	2	8%		

Table 3.18 shows the distribution of respondents by exporting/ importing activities in which 33 per cent of them deal with exports with less than 50 per cent exported to ASEAN. For SMEs, only 26 per cent of respondents are engaged in exports of which 48 per cent are exported to ASEAN. In contrast, the share of LEs exports is 62 per cent. Meanwhile, 24 per cent of respondents deal with imports but only 27 per cent of them are imported from ASEAN countries.

TABLE 3.18
Distribution of Respondents by Exporting/Importing Activities

	Overall		SMEs		LEs	
	Number of Firms	Share (%)	Number of Firms	Share (%)	Number of Firms	Share (%)
Exporting	**65**	**33%**	**42**	**26%**	**23**	**62%**
Exporting to ASEAN	30	46%	20	48%	10	43%
Have relations with firms in ASEAN in exporting activities	27	90%	19	95%	8	80%
Importing	**48**	**24%**	**25**	**15%**	**23**	**62%**
Importing from ASEAN	13	27%	8	32%	5	22%
Have relations with firms in ASEAN in importing activities	12	92%	7	88%	5	100%

We also asked whether respondents know about AEC and ASEAN SMEs Policy Blueprint (see Figure 3.11). It turned out that 79 per cent of respondents are aware of AEC. However, only 18 per cent of them know about the ASEAN Blueprint for SMEs. The proportion of LEs that are aware of AEC (86 per cent) and ASEAN SMEs Policy Blueprint (27 per cent) are higher than the corresponding figures for SMEs (77 per cent and 15 per cent, respectively). This shows that LEs know about AEC and the ASEAN Blueprint for SMEs better than SMEs.

FIGURE 3.11
Firms' Awareness of AEC and ASEAN SMEs Policy Blueprint

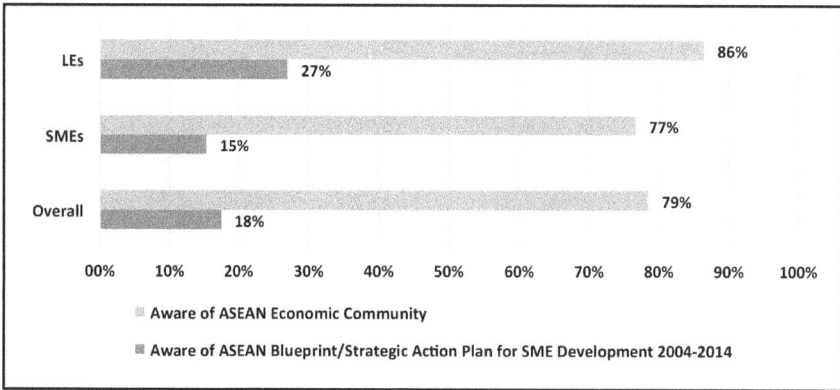

Note: The data on awareness may be overestimated since the definition of awareness in the survey is whether the respondents are aware of AEC and ASEAN Blueprint/Strategic Action Plan for SME Development 2004–2014.

How do respondents perceive the impact of AEC on their businesses? As shown in Table 3.19, with regard to domestic sales, 39 per cent of the respondents think AEC will increase domestic sales, 31 per cent believe AEC indicates no change, 15 per cent perceive AEC will result in a decrease in sales, while 15 per cent do not know or have no opinion. In terms of export sales, 39 per cent of respondents expect their exports to increase and 22.5 per cent believe there will be no change. Only 3 per cent of respondents predict their exports will decrease and 35.5 per cent expressed no opinion.

A large number of respondents, about 42.5 per cent, have no idea on how AEC will impact their import cost. Concerning their profits, 45 per cent of the respondents feel optimistic that their profits will increase, 27 per cent indicate no change, 13 per cent signal that there will be a decline, and 15 per cent do not know or expressed no opinion.

On competition in the local market, 63 per cent of the respondents think AEC will encourage competition, 26 per cent believe there will be no change, and 8 per cent have no idea on how AEC will impact local market competition.

TABLE 3.19
Perception of Respondents on Impact of AEC on Businesses

AEC Impact	Overall Sample (% of Firms)				SMEs (% of Firms)				LEs (% of Firms)			
	A	B	C	D	A	B	C	D	A	B	C	D
Domestic sales	39.0	31.0	15.0	15.0	39.3	30.7	15.3	15.0	37.8	32.4	13.5	16.0
Export sales	39.0	22.5	3.0	35.5	37.4	19.0	2.5	41.1	46.0	37.8	5.4	10.8
Import cost	13.0	23.5	21.0	42.5	11.0	19.6	20.3	49.0	21.6	40.5	24.3	13.5
Profits	45.0	27.0	13.0	15.0	41.1	27.6	14.1	17.2	62.2	24.3	8.1	5.4
Competition in local market	63.0	26.0	3.0	8.0	63.8	24.5	3.1	8.6	59.5	32.4	2.7	5.4
Competition in foreign market	46.5	20.0	0.0	33.5	42.9	19.0	0.0	38.0	62.2	24.3	0.0	13.5
Greater access to intermediate outputs	41.0	31.5	1.5	26.0	39.9	30.7	1.8	27.6	46.0	35.1	0.0	18.9

Note: A: increase; B: no change; C: decrease; D: do not know/no opinion.

On competition in foreign market, 46.5 per cent of the respondents believe AEC will increase competition, 20 per cent expect no change, while 33.5 per cent have no idea on how AEC will impact foreign market competition.

On better access to intermediate outputs, 41 per cent of the respondents think that AEC will increase access to intermediate outputs, 31.5 per cent believe there will be no change, 1.5 per cent expect access to decrease, while 26 per cent have no idea.

When we compare the responses from LEs and SMEs, it seems that LEs have relatively better ideas on how AEC will affect their businesses.

How will AEC affect the respondents' businesses? As summarized in Table 3.20, 42 per cent of the respondents think that import tariffs/duties will be better (lower), 15 per cent state no change, 7 per cent expect the import tariffs/duties to be worse (higher), and 36 per cent expressed no opinion. For export tariffs/duties, 47.5 per cent of the respondents feel that it will be better (lower), 16 per cent foresee no change, 3 per cent feel it will be worse (higher), and 33.5 per cent expressed no opinion. With regard to customs procedure, 42 per cent of

TABLE 3.20
AEC Key Changes Affecting Businesses

AEC Key Changes Affecting Businesses	Overall Sample (% of Firms)				SMEs (% of Firms)				LEs (% of Firms)			
	A	B	C	D	A	B	C	D	A	B	C	D
Import tariffs/duties	42.0	15.0	7.0	36.0	39.3	14.1	6.1	40.5	54.1	18.9	10.8	16.2
Export tariffs/duties	47.5	16.0	3.0	33.5	44.8	13.5	3.7	38.0	59.5	27.0	0.0	13.5
Customs procedure	42.0	21.0	8.0	29.0	41.1	18.4	7.4	33.1	46.0	32.4	10.8	10.8
Standards of regulation	49.5	21.5	6.5	22.5	47.9	19.6	5.5	27.0	56.8	29.7	10.8	2.7
Recognition of professional qualifications	46.0	15.5	8.5	30.0	41.7	14.1	9.8	34.4	64.9	21.6	2.7	10.8
Investment process in ASEAN countries	47.5	13.5	1.0	38.0	44.2	11.0	1.2	43.6	62.2	24.3	0.0	13.5
Connectivity in terms of transport and communication services	63.0	12.5	1.5	23.0	61.4	9.8	1.2	27.6	70.3	24.3	2.7	2.7

Note: A: better; B: no change; C: worse; D: do not know/no opinion.

the respondents are optimistic that the procedures will be better, 21 per cent believe there will be no change, 8 per cent expect the procedures to be worse, and 29 per cent expressed no opinion.

In terms of the standards of regulation, 49.5 per cent of the respondents believe they will get better, 21.5 per cent see no change, 6.5 per cent assume they will be worse, and 22.5 per cent expressed no opinion. Regarding recognition of professional qualifications, 46 per cent are optimistic that it will be better, 15.5 per cent see no change, 8.5 per cent perceive it will get worse, and 30 per cent have no idea.

For investment process in ASEAN countries, 47.5 per cent of the overall sample are optimistic that the process will be better, 13.5 per cent suggest no change, 1 per cent think it will be worse, and 38 per cent expressed no opinion. About 63 per cent of the respondents believe that connectivity in terms of transport and communication services across the ASEAN region will be better, 12.5 per cent believe there will be no change, 1.5 per cent assume it will be worse, and 23 per cent expressed no opinion.

As indicated in Table 3.20, LEs are more optimistic on the impact of AEC key changes than SMEs. Overall, 59 per cent of LEs believe AEC key changes will be better relative to SMEs' average of 46 per cent. Besides, LEs understand AEC better than SMEs. For LEs, the average share of respondents that claimed do not know or expressed no opinion is 10 per cent while SMEs' response is 35 per cent.

4.3. Participation in Regional Integration

Regional integration can be promoted through trade, investment, joint business activities and so on. From our survey (see Table 3.21), we found that 45 per cent of the respondents, which are actively engaged in exporting or importing, established business relations with companies in the ASEAN region. On the contrary, less than 1 per cent of non-exporting/importing respondents have business relations with ASEAN partners. These findings complement the vision of ASEAN governments to form an integrated ASEAN economy.

TABLE 3.21
Cross Tabulation of Export-Import Activities and Business Relations

= 1 if exporting or importing	= 1 if have business relations in ASEAN		
	0	1	Total
0	119	1	120
	99.17%	0.83%	100.00%
1	44	36	80
	55.00%	45.00%	100.00%
Total	163	37	200
	81.50%	18.50%	100.00%

Foreign owned companies are more active in establishing business relations in the ASEAN region. From our survey, we found that 60 per cent of foreign owned and actively trading firms established business relations with partners around the region (see Table 3.22). On the contrary, non-foreign owned firms are less likely to establish business relations in the region, as the survey found that 58 per cent of actively trading respondents without foreign ownership do not have business relations in the region. This evidence supports the initiative to promote foreign direct investment in the development of regional economic integration.

TABLE 3.22
Cross Tabulation of Foreign Ownership and Business Relations for Actively Trading Firms

= 1 if have foreign ownership	=1 if have business relations in ASEAN		
	0	1	Total
0	38	27	65
	58.46%	41.54%	100.00%
1	6	9	15
	40.00%	60.00%	100.00%
Total	44	36	80
	55.00%	45.00%	100.00%

Whether the formation of an economic community would impact trading activities in the region is one of the important questions for ASEAN. Tariffs have been lowered in the region for many years and came to complete zero in 2016 with the establishment of AEC. However, in order to utilize this provision, firms must complete the administration process related to Free Trade Agreement (FTA). Our survey found that a larger percentage of firms did not use FTA forms (63 per cent) compared to firms that used the forms (37 per cent), even though they were all actively engaged in exporting (see Table 3.23). Meanwhile, the same percentage (50:50) of those that were not aware of AEC used/did not use FTA forms.

TABLE 3.23
Cross Tabulation of Usage of FTA Forms and Awareness of AEC for
Actively Exporting Firms

= 1 if aware of AEC	= 1 if use FTA forms		
	0	1	Total
0	2	2	4
	50.00%	50.00%	100.00%
1	38	22	60
	63.33%	36.67%	100.00%
Total	40	24	64
	62.50%	37.50%	100.00%

Our survey found that the reasons for not using FTA forms are very low trade volume, lack of knowledge on how to utilize FTA forms, difficulty in obtaining the certificates of origin, and unable to fulfill rules of origin (ROO) requirements. Our survey found that the most dominant reason is the lack of knowledge in using FTA forms (see Figure 3.12).

FIGURE 3.12
Reasons for Not Utilizing FTA Forms

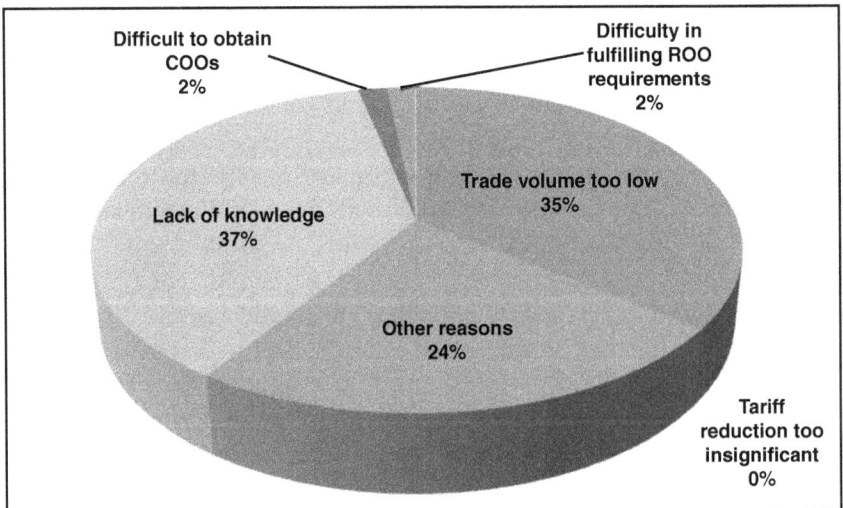

The government is always expected to support business conduct, including the implementation of AEC. However, evidence from our survey found that business-to-business relations in ASEAN is not really affected by government support (see Table 3.24). About 70 per cent of the surveyed firms that received government support for their operation, apparently, did not establish business relations in ASEAN. An even larger proportion happened for companies that did not receive government support. As we already know, business-to-business relations is more dependent on economical profits.

TABLE 3.24
Government Support and Business Relations in ASEAN

= 1 if receive government support for its operation	= 1 if have business relations in ASEAN		
	0	1	Total
0	121	21	142
	85.21%	14.79%	100.00%
1	42	16	60
	70.00%	26.67%	96.67%
Total	163	37	200
	81.50%	18.50%	100.00%

The perception of respondents on how FTAs will affect their businesses is summarized in Table 3.25. Overall, 29.5 per cent of the respondents indicate that FTAs will increase their domestic sales, 32 per cent imply no change, 14 per cent assume it will cause the domestic sales to decrease, and 24.5 per cent expressed no opinion. Regarding the impact of FTAs on export sales, 34.5 per cent of the respondents believe FTAs will increase their export sales, 22.5 per cent see no change, 3.5 per cent assume the export sales to decrease, and 39.5 per cent expressed no opinion. With regard to the cost of import, 13 per cent of respondents believe that it will increase, 23.5 per cent suggest no change, 17.5 per cent believe it will decrease, while 46 per cent have no idea. About 41.5 per cent of the respondents think that profits will increase, 23.5 per cent believe it will not change, 12 per cent assume it will decrease, and 23 per cent expressed no opinion.

TABLE 3.25
Perception of Respondents: How FTAs Will Affect Their Businesses

	Overall Sample (% of Firms)				SMEs (% of Firms)				LEs (% of Firms)			
	A	B	C	D	A	B	C	D	A	B	C	D
Domestic sales	29.5	32.0	14.0	24.5	27.8	31.9	14.1	28.2	46.0	32.4	13.5	8.1
Export sales	34.5	22.5	3.5	39.5	29.5	20.9	3.1	46.6	56.8	29.7	5.4	8.1
Import cost	13.0	23.5	17.5	46.0	10.4	20.3	15.3	54.0	24.3	37.8	27.0	10.8
Profits	41.5	23.5	12.0	23.0	36.8	23.3	13.5	26.4	62.2	24.3	5.4	8.1
Competition in local market	54.8	23.6	2.0	19.6	53.1	22.8	1.9	22.2	62.2	27.0	2.7	8.1
Competition in foreign market	40.0	15.5	1.0	43.5	36.8	13.5	1.2	48.5	54.1	24.3	8.1	13.5

Note: A: increase; B: no change; C: decrease; D: do not know/no opinion

Regarding the impact of FTAs on competition in the local market, 54.8 per cent of the respondents believe it will increase the competition, 23.6 per cent see no change, 2 per cent indicate a decline in competition, and 19.6 per cent expressed no opinion. Competition in foreign market is projected to increase by 40 per cent of the respondents, 15.5 per cent expect no change, 1 per cent foresee a decrease, and 43.5 per cent do not have any idea.

The study shows that SMEs' awareness of FTAs seemed lower than LEs'. It was evidenced by the response of the SMEs, especially on how FTAs will impact their export sales, import cost, and competition in foreign market. For these aspects, more than 45 per cent of SMEs expressed no opinion. On average, 37.7 per cent of SME respondents have no idea about the impact of FTAs. This percentage is much higher relative to LEs in which on average, 9.5 per cent expressed no opinion.

4.4. Assessing the Relationship between FTA Utilization and Exports/Imports: Probit Analysis

In order to analyse the relationship between FTA utilization and trade (exports and imports) in a more comprehensive perspective, we applied the probit model which was developed on the dependent variable of whether the firms conduct exports or imports, and on independent factors that could promote exporting or importing activities. We developed one particular probit model for export and one for import.

From our econometric analysis, we found that FTA utilization is significantly related to exporting activities. Use of FTA is positively related to the probability of firms in conducting export activities. Predictive margins showed 62.5 per cent of export probability is caused by FTA utilization. In other words, FTA utilization could really encourage firms to export their products. From the export model, we also found that having business relation with ASEAN counterparts and awareness of AEC have significant impacts on the probability of exporting.

TABLE 3.26
Description of Variables

Variables	Description
Dexport	Conduct exports, 1 = yes; 0 = otherwise
Dimport	Conduct imports, 1 = yes; 0 = otherwise
FTA	FTA utilization, 1 = if respondent utilizes FTA; 0 = otherwise
Dum_ict	Utilization of internet on business process, 1 = yes; 0 = otherwise
Dum_Assoc	Engagement in business association, 1 = yes; 0 = otherwise
Relation_asean	Having business relation with other firms in ASEAN, 1 = yes; 0 = otherwise
Gov_support	Received goverment support, 1 = yes; 0 = otherwise
AEC_aware	Awareness of AEC, 1 = yes; 0 = otherwise
lasset14	Log of fix asset in 2014
Foreign	Foreign Ownership, 1 = yes; 0 = otherwise
Age	Firms' operational year
export_pct	Share of export
Linnov	Log of innovation expenditure

FTA utilization is also significantly related to the probability of firms importing their products. In econometric analysis for import data, there is a significant positive relation between FTA utilization and import probability. However, the impact of FTAs in the import model is less than in the export model. Import probability increased by 50.3 per cent due to the existence of FTA utilization. Other than

TABLE 3.27
Probit Model for Export

Independent Variable	Dependent Variable: Conduct Exports (Dexport)
FTA utilization (FTA)	1.2708*** (0.3173)
Utilization of internet on business process (Dum_ict)	0.5174 (0.3579)
Engagement in business association (Dum_Assoc)	0.0011 (0.2351)
Having business relation with other firms in ASEAN (relation_asean)	1.5920*** (0.3060)
Received government support (gov_support)	0.3127 (0.2478)
Awareness of AEC (aec_aware)	0.9883*** (0.3658)
Constant	−2.3958*** (0.4652)
Number of observations	200
LR chi2(6)	89.26
Prob>chi2	0.0000
Pseudo R2	0.3560

Standard errors in parantheses; *** $p < 0.01$, ** $p < 0.05$, * $p < 0.1$

Predictive Margin			Number of obs.	=	200
Model VCE	:	OIM			
Expression	:	Pr(dexport), predict ()			
1._at	:	Fta	=	0	
2._at	:	Fta	=	1	

	Margin	Delta-method Std. Err	Z	P>|z|	[95% Conf. Interval]	
_at						
1	0.2659243	0.290278	9.16	0.000	0.2090309	0.3228178
2	0.6256644	0.836457	7.48	0.000	0.4617218	0.7896071

that, information technology and business relation with ASEAN firms are also significantly associated with higher import.

TABLE 3.28
Probit Model for Import

Independent Variable	Dependent Variable: Conduct Imports (Dimport)
FTA utilization (FTA)	1.0339*** (0.2764)
Utilization of internet on business process (Dum_ict)	0.9024** (0.3547)
Engagement in business association (Dum_Assoc)	−0.0371 (0.2411)
Having business relation with other firms in ASEAN (relation_asean)	0.8045*** (0.2758)
Received government support (gov_support)	−0.3514 (0.2529)
Awareness of AEC (aec_aware)	−0.4518 (0.2812)
Constant	−1.4234*** (0.3534)
Number of observations	200
LR chi2(6)	42.8
Prob>chi2	0.0000
Pseudo R2	0.1963

Standard errors in parantheses; *** $p < 0.01$, ** $p < 0.05$, * $p < 0.1$

Predictive Margin				Number of obs.	= 200
Model VCE	:	OIM			
Expression	:	Pr(dimport), predict ()			
1._at	:	Fta	=	0	
2._at	:	Fta	=	1	

	Margin	Delta-method Std. Err	Z	P>|z|	[95% Conf. Interval]	
_at						
1	0.1798946	0.029151	6.17	0.000	0.1227596	0.2370295
2	0.5031636	0.0882452	5.7	0.000	0.3302061	0.676121

Our econometric analysis also tried to examine factors that could encourage the usage of FTA forms. We applied the dummy dependent variable of FTA utilization and several independent variables on the probit method. The result shows that company size and export activities are significantly related to FTA forms usage. The larger the firms, the greater the chance they will utilize FTA forms. Similarly, the larger the proportion of exports from their production, the bigger the chance in utilizing FTA forms. Therefore, we could conclude that usage of FTAs would increase following the development of business entities resulting from regional integration.

TABLE 3.29
Probit Model for FTA

Independent variable	Dependent variable: FTA Utilization (FTA)
Awareness of AEC (aec_aware)	−0.5790 (0.4273)
Log of fix asset in 2014 (lasset14)	0.1599** (0.0635)
Foreign Ownership (Foreign)	−0.0018 (0.0050)
Firms' operational year (Age)	0.0095 (0.0075)
Share of exports (export_pct)	0.0159*** (0.0049)
Log of innovation expenditure (Linnov)	−0.0085 (0.0182)
Engagement in business association (Dum_Assoc)	0.3117 (0.3471)
Having business relation with other firms in ASEAN (relation_asean)	0.5805 (0.3595)
Received government support (gov_support)	0.3373 (0.3644)
Constant	−5.4249*** (1.4162)
Number of observations	200
LR chi2(6)	41.26
Prob>chi2	0.0000
Pseudo R2	0.3173

Standard errors in parantheses; *** $p < 0.01$, ** $p < 0.05$, * $p < 0.1$

4.5. Government Support

As summarized in Table 3.30, the respondents had been asked whether they ever received support for participation in events abroad, support for organizing meetings with potential partners, financial support, and assistance in business expansion abroad through their countries' bilateral FTAs. In terms of support for participation in events in foreign countries, 11 per cent of the respondents have received support from the central government, 15 per cent from the provincial government, and 10 per cent from the local government. As for support to organize meetings with potential partners, 5 per cent of the respondents claimed that they have received such supports from the central government, 5 per cent from the provincial government, and 3 per cent from the local government. Regarding financial support, 4 per cent of respondents have received help from the central government, 4 per cent from the provincial government, and 1 per cent from the local government. In terms of the government's assistance in business expansion abroad through bilateral FTAs, 1 per cent of the respondents have received help from the central government and 1 per cent from the provincial government.

The survey results have shown that government support has been mostly received by SMEs. Regarding support to participate in events in foreign countries, 11 per cent of SMEs have received assistance from the central government, 17 per cent from the provincial government, and 10 per cent from the local government. On the other hand, 11 per cent of LEs have received help from the central government, 5 per cent from the provincial government, and 5 per cent from the local government. In terms of support to organize meetings with potential partners, 6 per cent of SMEs received help from the central government, 6 per cent from the provincial government, and 4 per cent from the local government, whereas none of the LEs have received such assistance. Regarding financial support, 3 per cent of SMEs have received such support from the central government, 4 per cent from the provincial government, and 1 per cent from the local government. As for the LEs, 5 per cent of the total respondents have received financial support from the central government. For support to expand business through FTAs, 1 per cent of SMEs admitted that they ever received help from the central government, and 1 per cent from the provincial government, while LEs revealed that they have never received such support.

TABLE 3.30
Percentage of Respondents Who Received Government Support

Type of Support	Overall				SMEs				LEs		
	Central	Provinces	Local	Central	Provinces	Local	Central	Provinces	Local
Support for participation in events in countries abroad	11%	15%	10%	11%	17%	10%	11%	5%	5%
Support for organizing meetings with potential partners	5%	5%	3%	6%	6%	4%			
Provision of financial support	4%	4%	1%	3%	4%	1%	5%		
Assistance in business expansion abroad through bilateral FTAs	1%	1%		1%	1%				

5. Conclusions and Policy Recommendations

5.1. Conclusions

SMEs are important in Indonesia as well as in the integration process of ASEAN. When AEC was about to be launched, the Economic Research Institute for ASEAN and East Asia (ERIA) and the Institute of Southeast Asian Studies (ISEAS) jointly conducted studies across ten ASEAN countries, including Indonesia, to evaluate SMEs' participation in AEC in early 2015. The study aims at examining the extent and nature of the participation of Indonesia's SMEs in ASEAN economic integration based on a survey of 200 SMEs with more than ten employees/workers in the manufacturing sector.

The survey shows that most firms in Indonesia have a relatively superficial knowledge about the AEC as 79 per cent of the respondents are aware of AEC but only 18 per cent of them know about the ASEAN Blueprint for SMEs. A greater number of the large firms know about AEC than the small firms. The opinions of the respondents on the impact of AEC are mixed with the largest proportion suggesting positive impacts (increased domestic sales, increased exports, increased profits and better access to intermediate inputs). Firms are also aware of more intense competition with the AEC, both in the domestic and foreign markets. A large proportion of the firms also agreed that AEC affects their businesses through lower import duties, lower export tariffs, better custom procedures, better standard regulations and recognition of professional qualifications.

The survey also shows that firms which are actively engaged in exporting and importing, established business relations with companies in the region. On the contrary, fewer non-exporting/importing respondents have business relations with ASEAN partners. These findings complement the vision of ASEAN governments to form an integrated ASEAN economy.

The survey also shows that foreign owned companies are more active in establishing business relations in the region. On the contrary, non-foreign owned firms are less likely to establish business relations in the region. These evidences support the initiative to promote foreign direct investment in the development of regional economic integration.

The survey also found that a larger percentage of firms did not utilize FTA forms compared to firms that used the forms even though they were all actively engaged in exporting. Meanwhile, the same percentage (50:50) of those who were not aware of AEC used/did not use FTA forms. The many reasons cited for not using FTA forms are very low trade volume, lack of knowledge on how to utilize FTA forms, difficulty in obtaining certificates of origin, and unable to fulfill ROO requirements. Our survey found that the most dominant reason is the lack of knowledge in using FTA forms.

The econometric exercise shows a significant relationship between FTA utilization and exporting activities. FTA utilization is positively related to the probability of firms in conducting export activities. FTA utilization could enhance firms' ability to export their products. Similarly, business relations with ASEAN counterparts and awareness of AEC are significantly related to export probability. On imports, FTA utilization is a significant variable. However, the relationship of FTA utilization with imports is less than with exports. The econometric exercise also suggests that company size and export activities are significant variables for FTA forms usage. The larger the firms, the greater the chance they will utilize the FTA forms. Similarly, the larger the proportion of exports from their production, the bigger the change in utilizing FTA forms. Therefore, we could conclude that usage of FTAs would increase following the development of business entities resulting from regional integration.

5.2. Policy Recommendations

The survey reveals two important findings. First, FTA utilization has positive relations with both exports and imports, with exports having a bigger coefficient size. Second, larger firms know of and utilize AEC more than the smaller firms.

Given these findings, usage of FTAs would increase following the development of business entities. However, if the government plans to accelerate the process, it is recommended that the government does so by lowering the transaction cost in utilizing FTAs for smaller firms through better dissemination of information about FTAs, simplification of COO procedures, zero cost for COOs, and facilitating SMEs in obtaining COOs. More importantly, it is recommended that the government should assist smaller firms in establishing connections (supply chain) with larger exporting firms in the domestic market.

APPENDIX 3.1
MSMEs Across ASEAN

Country	Definition of MSME	SME Agency	MSME Key Sector
Indonesia	• Micro: assets (US$5,500); sales (US$33,002) • Small: assets (US$5,500–55,000); sales (US$33,002–275,014) • Medium: assets (US$1.1 million); sales (US$275,014–5,500,290)	Ministry of Cooperatives and SMEs (MOCSME)	1. Manufacturing 2. Trade 3. Primary Industry
Malaysia	**Manufacturing sector:** • Micro: sales (< US$91,645); workers (< 5 workers) • Small: sales (US$91,645–4.5 million); workers (5–74 workers) • Medium: sales (US$4.5–15.3 million); workers (75–200 workers) **Service and other sectors:** • Micro: sales (< US$91,645); workers (< 5 workers) • Small: sales (US$91,645–916,449); workers (5–29 workers) • Medium: sales (US$916,449–6.1 million); workers (30–75 workers)	1 National SME Development Council (NSDC) 2. Small and Medium Industries Development Corporation (SMIDEC)	1. Service 2. Manufacturing 3. Agriculture
Thailand	SMEs in Thailand are categorized into four main groups: manufacturing (including agricultural businesses), trade (wholesale), trade (retail), and service. The definition of Thai SMEs is based on two criteria, namely: the number of employees and fixed asset value.	Office of Small and Medium Enterprises Promotion (OSMEP)	1. Trade and maintenance 2. Service 3. Manufacturing

APPENDIX 3.1 (*continued*)

Country	Definition of MSME	SME Agency	MSME Key Sector
Singapore	Enterprises with annual sales turnover of not more than US$73.53 million or employment size of not more than 200 workers.	SPRING (Agency under the Ministry of Trade and Industry)	Almost all sectors (especially service)
Brunei Darussalam	No detailed definition	1. Ministry of Industry and Primary Resources 2. Brunei Economic Development Board (BEDB)	
Philippines	• Micro: assets (<= US$67,000) • Small: assets (US$67,000–333,000) • Medium: assets (US$333,000–2.22 million)	Bureau of Small and Medium Enterprises Development (BSMED)	1. Wholesale and retail trade 2. Repair of motor vehicles and motorcycle industries 3. Information and communications 4. Financial and insurance activities
Vietnam	Classified into three MSME criteria based on regional scale: • Agriculture, forestry and fishery • Industrial and construction • Trade and services	1. Central level: Agency for Enterprise Development 2. Provincial level: Department of Planning and Investment	Almost all sectors (trade, service, manufacturing, construction)

APPENDIX 3.1   (*continued*)

Country	Definition of MSME	SME Agency	MSME Key Sector
Cambodia	• Micro: workers (< 10 workers); assets (< US$50,000) • Small: workers (11–50 workers); assets (US$50,000–250,000) • Medium: workers (51–100 workers); assets (US$250,000–500,000)	The General Department of Industry (GDI), under the Ministry of Industry, Mines, and Energy	1. Service and Trade 2. Production sector, including agricultural processing, manufacturing, and mining
Lao PDR	• Small: workers (<= 19 workers); assets (<= US$30,271); turnover/year (<= US$48,433) • Medium: workers (> 19–99 workers); assets (<= US$145,300)	Department of SME Promotion, Ministry of Industry and Commerce	1. Trade 2. Service
Myanmar	Citeria by number of workers: • Micro: workers (< 10 workers) • Small: workers (10–50 workers) • Medium: workers (51–100 workers)	Industrial Development Committee	1. Agriculture, livestock and fisheries and forestry 2. Processing and manufacturing

Source: ASEAN, *Directory of Outstanding ASEAN SMEs 2015* (Jakarta: ASEAN Secretariat, 2015); conversion of local currency to USD using the exchange rate in 2010 (data from the World Bank).

NOTES

1. Email: tanas@presisi-indonesia.com; Carlos Mangunsong and Nur Afni Panjaitan from Presisi Indonesia provided research assistance.
2. For sales, one firm can have multiple outputs and sales to different types of buyers.

REFERENCES

Abonyi, George. "Best Policy Practices for Internationalization of SMEs' Trade and Investment for ASEAN and East Asia". In *Innovation, Technology Transfers, Finance, and Internationalization of SMEs' Trade and Investment: Policy Best Practices for ASEAN and East Asia*, edited by Sothea Oum, Patarapong Intarakumnerd, George Abonyi and Shigeo Kagami. ERIA Research Project Report FY2013, No. 14. Jakarta: Economic Research Institute for ASEAN and East Asia (ERIA), 2015, pp. 37–96.

Aldaba, Rafaelita M. *ASEAN Economic Community 2015 SME Development: Narrowing Development Gap Measure.* PIDS discussion paper series no. 2013-05. Makati City, Philippines: Philippine Institute for Development Studies (PIDS), 2013.

ASEAN. *Directory of Outstanding ASEAN SMEs 2015*. Jakarta: ASEAN Secretariat, 2015.

Asian Development Bank (ADB). *Asia SME Finance Monitor 2014*. Mandaluyong City, Philippines: ADB, 2014.

Aswicahyono, Haryo and Hal Hill. "Survey of Recent Developments". *Bulletin of Indonesian Economic Studies* 50, no. 3 (2014*a*): 319–46.

———. "Does Indonesia have Competitiveness Problems?" Unpublished paper, 2014*b*.

Burger, Nicholas, Charina Chazali, Arya Gaduh, Alexander D. Rothenberg, Indrasari Tjandraningsih, and Sarah Weilant. *Reforming Policies for Small and Medium Enterprises in Indonesia*. Jakarta, Indonesia: Rand Corporation in collaboration with Tim Nasional Percepatan Penanggulangan Kemiskinan, 2015.

ERIA SME Research Working Group. *ASEAN SME Policy Index 2014: Towards Competitive and Innovative ASEAN SMEs*. ERIA Research Project Report 2012, No. 8. Jakarta: Economic Research Institute for ASEAN and East Asia (ERIA), 2014.

Harvie, Charles. "SMEs and Production Networks – Framework". In *Integrating Small and Medium Enterprises (SMEs) into the More Integrated East Asia*, edited by Vo Tri Thanh, Dionisius Narjoko and Sothea Oum. ERIA Research Project Report 2009 No. 8. Jakarta: Economic Research Institute for ASEAN and East Asia (ERIA), 2010*a*, pp. 46–67.

————. "SMEs and Regional Production Networks". In *Integrating Small and Medium Enterprises (SMEs) into the More Integrated East Asia*, edited by Vo Tri Thanh, Dionisius Narjoko and Sothea Oum. ERIA Research Project Report 2009 No. 8. Jakarta: Economic Research Institute for ASEAN and East Asia (ERIA), 2010*b*, pp. 19–45.

Harvie, Charles, Dionisius Narjoko, and Sothea Oum. "Constraints to Growth and Firm Characteristics Determinants of SME Participation in Production Networks". In *Integrating Small and Medium Enterprises (SMEs) into the More Integrated East Asia*, edited by Vo Tri Thanh, Dionisius Narjoko and Sothea Oum. ERIA Research Project Report 2009 No. 8. Jakarta: Economic Research Institute for ASEAN and East Asia (ERIA), 2010*a*, pp. 68–133.

————. "Firm Characteristic Determinants of SME Participation in Production Networks". ERIA Discussion Paper 2010-11. Jakarta: Economic Research Institute for ASEAN and East Asia (ERIA), 2010*b*.

Hill, Hal. "Small and Medium Enterprises in Indonesia: Old Policy Challenges for a New Administration". *Asian Survey* 41, no. 2 (2001): 248–70.

Machmud, T.M. Zakir and Rizki N. Siregar. "Small and Medium Enterprises in Regional Production Networks: An Indonesian Case". In *Integrating Small and Medium Enterprises (SMEs) into the More Integrated East Asia*, edited by Vo Tri Thanh, Dionisius Narjoko and Sothea Oum. ERIA Research Project Report 2009 No. 8. Jakarta: Economic Research Institute for ASEAN and East Asia (ERIA), 2010, pp. 334–73.

Prassetya, Rully and Ponciano S. Intal. "AEC Blueprint Implementation Performance and Challenges: Standards and Conformance". ERIA Discussion Paper Series No. 2015-42. Jakarta: Economic Research Institute for ASEAN and East Asia (ERIA), 2015.

Presisi Indonesia. *Innovation Driven Businesses in Bandung*. Report for EU–Indonesia TCF, 2015.

Tambunan, Tulus and Alexander C. Chandra. "Utilisation Rate of Free Trade Agreement (FTAs) by Local Micro-, Small- and Medium-sized Enterprises: A Story of ASEAN". *Journal of International Business and Economics* 2, no. 2 (2014): 133–63.

Thanh, Vo Tri, Sothea Oum and Dionisius Narjoko. "Overview: Integrating Small and Medium Enterprises (SMEs) into a More Integrated East Asia". In *Integrating Small and Medium Enterprises (SMEs) into the More Integrated East Asia*, edited by Vo Tri Thanh, Dionisius Narjoko and Sothea Oum. ERIA Research Project Report 2009 No. 8. Jakarta: Economic Research Institute for ASEAN and East Asia (ERIA), 2010, pp. 1–18.

U.S. International Trade Commission (USITC). *Small and Medium-sized Enterprises: Characteristics and Performance*. Investigation No. 332-510. USITC Publication 4189. Washington, D.C.: USITC, 2010.

Wignaraja, Ganeshan. "Can SMEs Participate in Global Networks? Evidence from ASEAN Firms". In *Global Value Chains in a Changing World*, edited by Deborah K. Elms and Patrick Low. WTO Publications. Geneva: World Trade Organization, 2013a, pp. 279–312.

———. "Do SMEs Matter in Asian Production Networks?" In *The Future of The World Trading System: Asian Perspectives*, edited by Richard Baldwin, Masahiro Kawai and Ganeshan Wignaraja. London: Centre for Economic Policy Research, 2013b, pp. 45–54.

———. *Engaging Small and Medium Enterprises in Production Networks: Firm-Level Analysis of Five ASEAN Economies*. ADBI Working Paper Series No. 361. Tokyo: Asian Development Bank Institute (ADBI), 2012.

Wignaraja, Ganeshan and Yothin Jinjarak. *Why Do SMEs Not Borrow More from Banks? Evidence from the People's Republic of China and Southeast Asia*. ADBI Working Paper Series No. 509. Tokyo: Asian Development Bank Institute (ADBI), 2015.

World Economic Forum (WEF). *The Global Competitiveness Report 2015–2016*. Geneva: WEF, 2015.

Zhang, Yuhua and Akhmad Bayhaqi. *SMEs' Participation in Global Production Chains*. Singapore: APEC Policy Support Unit, 2013.

4

LAO SME PARTICIPATION IN REGIONAL ECONOMIC INTEGRATION

Phouphet Kyophilavong

1. Introduction

Laos has maintained relatively high economic growth rates for about two decades. However, the country's future long-term economic growth faces risks arising from the country's dependence on resource sectors such as mining and hydropower sectors. Empirical studies have showed that resource-rich countries tend to experience slower growth compared to resource-poor countries. Laos might face the "Dutch disease" or "resources curse" problem (Kyophilavong 2016; Kyophilavong and Toyoda 2008; Corden 1981; Corden 1984; and Corden and Neary 1982). Even though the Lao economy has been growing at about 7 per cent per year in recent years, several challenges remain. Lao firms have low productivity and lack competitiveness. Lao firms also face various obstacles such as high tax rate, access to finance, increasing costs of doing business, and regulatory changes (Kyophilavong 2008; GIZ 2014; World Bank 2013). To overcome these problems, the Lao government has established several enterprises development plans and strategies such as SMEs Development Strategy and Industrial Development

Plan. However, due to the lack of qualified human capital and funds, it appears that these plans and strategies have not achieved their targets.

Therefore, it is difficult for Lao enterprises to rival other enterprises in the region due to a lack of competitiveness. As such, in order to promote economic development in the long run, it is important to increase competitiveness of the enterprises. There are many ways to do this. One of the most important ways is to promote enterprise participation in production networks by improving access to external business resources and knowledge, technology, and finance sources. Getting SMEs to participate in production networks and regional economic integration could provide a short cut to enhancing firm competitiveness. However, participation in regional economic integration is affected by various factors, such as government policies, firm-specific advantages, and other barriers. According to our knowledge, there are very few studies on Lao SMEs' participation in regional economic integration.

This chapter aims to investigate the current situation of Lao SMEs with regards to their participation in the regional economy. There are three main specific objectives: (1) to investigate SMEs' awareness of economic integration (ASEAN Economic Community (AEC), ASEAN Free Trade Area (AFTA) and World Trade Organization (WTO)) and its impact; (2) to identify the determinants of the use of preferential tariff utilization; and (3) to assess the determinants of SMEs exporting. This study uses data from the enterprise survey conducted by GIZ, and secondary data from Vanhnalat et al. (2015).

This chapter is organized as follows. Section 2 provides an overview of the Lao economy. Section 3 discusses trade and investment. Section 4 discusses Lao SMEs' development policy and SMEs characteristics. Section 5 explains SMEs' perception of regional economic integration. Session 6 is about the determinants of the use of preferential tariff utilization. Session 7 examines the determinants of enterprises exporting. The last section provides the conclusion and policy recommendations.

2.   Overview of Lao Economy and Poverty

Since the introduction of the New Economic Mechanism (NEM) in 1986, Laos has been transitioning from a centrally planned economy to a more market-oriented economy. As a result, with the exception of the

TABLE 4.1
Macroeconomic Situation in Laos

Macroconomic Indicator	2011–13	2006–10	2001–5	1996–2000	1990–95
Population growth (%)	2.04	2.16	1.58	2.07	2.71
GDP growth (%)	7.98	7.98	6.24	6.17	6.28
GDP per capita (constant 2000 US$)	1,329	841	371	302	243
GDP per capita growth (%)	6.10	5.90	4.58	4.00	3.44
Money supply growth (%)	31.90	38.34	20.18	66.04	30.92
Inflation CPI (%)	5.92	4.98	10.31	57.00	15.27
Trade balance/GDP (%)	–0.30	–0.59	–10.43	–17.03	–13.02
External debt stock (% of GDP)	76.50	101.10	129.86	152.99	160.25
Budget deficit/GDP (%)–including grants	–2.85	–2.53	–4.13	–4.87	–7.95
Budget deficit/GDP (%)–excluding grants	–9.26	–6.05	–6.04	–8.88	–11.52
Exchange rate (kip per US$)	8,018	9,056	10,164	4,094	727

Sources: World Bank online database, World Development Indicators, Asian Development Bank (ADB).

Asian financial crisis in the 1990s, Laos has achieved high economic growth. Economic growth averaged about 8.02 per cent over 2006–13, which is higher than the previous periods of 1990–95 (6.28 per cent), 1996–2000 (6.17 per cent), and 2001–5 (6.24 per cent).[1]

Even though Laos has maintained high economic growth, low inflation, and a stable exchange rate, serious macroeconomic challenges remained. Firstly, Laos faces chronic twin deficits in government and trade balances. Secondly, there is a huge gap between savings and investment. The savings rate is low because the average income is low. Thirdly, Laos also faces a high external debt burden. Fourthly, because Laos' economy depends highly on its resource sectors,[2] this limits the growth of its other sectors, resulting in a negative long-term impact known as the "Dutch disease".

The national goal of Laos is to eradicate poverty by 2020. In order to achieve this, the Lao government has implemented the National Growth and Poverty Eradication Strategy (NGPES), which is an overall development and poverty alleviation framework (GoL 2004a). The World Bank and Department of Statistics (2009) shows that the incidence of poverty has fallen from 46 per cent in 1993 to 39 per cent in 1998, 33.5 per cent in 2003 and 28 per cent in 2008. Inequality has also changed since 1993. The Gini coefficient index increased from 30.5 in 1993 to 34.9 in 1998. But it declined to 32.6 in 2003 and increased to 35.4 in 2008.

As Laos faces various economic challenges and has high poverty rate, an investigation of the SMEs' participation in regional economic integration is important to promote long-term economic development and poverty reduction.

3. Trade and Investment

3.1. Trade Policy and Trade Characteristics

Since trade policies are the core of the overall development strategy, their formulation and implementation generally synchronize with the stages of economic development in Laos.

Prior to 1986, the Lao government had controlled foreign trade (Otani and Pham 1996, p. 11). A battery of interventions, including foreign exchange controls, protective tariffs, and import restrictions, were employed to save foreign exchange. Both exports and imports were monopolized by the state, except trade made by joint public and private companies or a few state enterprises.

However, the external trade system was liberalized in 1987 following major economic reforms in 1986, resulting in the elimination of most of these restrictions on trade in 1988.

Together with the continued domestic liberalization, Laos has been integrating into the regional and global economy. Laos joined ASEAN in 1997 for geopolitical and economic development reasons.

The potential trade-increasing effects of allowing international trade expansion in Laos provided a number of new opportunities and challenges. The opportunities included the access to a larger variety of intermediate products and capital equipment by many rural people, which enhanced the productivity of their own resources; and the stimulation of cross-border learning of production methods, product design, organization methods, and market conditions. Unfortunately, not all of the effects of increases in trade are positive. At present, Laos could gain limited benefits from AFTA as the country is characterized by small and medium-sized enterprises (SMEs), producing low value-added products. Therefore, integrating Lao SMEs into the regional production network is becoming a major challenge for reaping the full benefits from AFTA. Furthermore, since Laos' key export products have concentrated on mining and hydropower (MoIC 2011), policies aimed at increasing exports of these products could lead to the scarcity of water resources for rural people through increased use for mining activities and hydropower development. Finally, removing all tariff barriers could lead to more severe trade deficits which could result in a depletion of international monetary reserves, currency instability, and a slowdown of economic growth. The expansion of Laos' foreign trade has the potential to raise domestic production, but could also cause some forms of macroeconomic instability and environmental deterioration if more prudent macroeconomic policies are not designed and standards of governance are not raised simultaneously.

Trade trends indicate that Laos has been facing a chronic trade deficit since introducing NEM in 1986, although the situation has recently changed. Laos imports various goods from other countries, from light and heavy manufacturing goods to processed food, textiles and clothing. Imports from Thailand accounted for 60 per cent of all imported goods in 2008 (see Appendices 4.1 and 4.2). Laos' main export commodities in 2004 were textiles and clothing, light manufacturing, and products of mining. However, the export structure of the country has since changed. The heavy manufacturing held the highest share of exports in 2008, higher than textiles and clothing and mining (see Appendix 4.3). The main export destinations are Thailand, the European Union, East Asia and Vietnam (see Appendix 4.4). This shows that Lao trade is highly dependent on Asian countries, especially its neighbouring countries. As tariff rates for Laos and its trading partners are already low, Laos might not gain much from the effects of AFTA through tariff cuts.

3.2. Investment Policy and FDI Characteristics

Laos has introduced NEM which transformed its economy from a planned economy to a market-oriented economy since 1986. The privatization of state enterprises was a main objective. Laos introduced FDI Law 1988. This law was revised three times in 1994, 2004 and 2009.

The new features of the FDI Law are as follows: (1) combine the domestic investment law and foreign direct investment law to create a "level-playing field" for both domestic and foreign investors; (2) shorten procedures to open new businesses; (3) no terms of investment for promoted activities; (4) extend investment incentives: education and healthcare sectors are the top priorities; (5) foreigners can have access to local financial sources; (6) foreign-invested companies can own a piece of land for building their offices/residences (certain conditions to be applied); (7) foreigners can invest in the real estate sector; and (8) promote the development of Special Economic Zone (SEZ) and Industrial Park (Vongsay 2013).

Concerning the terms of investment, it included: (1) no terms of investment of general business activities (Article 20); (2) terms of the concession projects are up to 99 years (Article 28); and (3) access to credits — both foreign and domestic investors can have access to credits at commercial banks and financial institutions in Lao PDR and abroad (Article 53) (Vongsay 2013). The rights of land use for residential purpose is also included in the law. Investors are granted purchasing rights of land use for their residential purpose (Article 58), if the following conditions are satisfied: (1) import of registered capital (in cash) of at least US$500,000; (2) must be government-owned land and designated by the government; (3) obtain certificate on location of investment which is issued by the local authority; (4) provide land use rights of not than 800 m^2 to build facilities for residential or business purpose; (5) the government will allocate land to investors for duration consistent with the investment duration (Vongsay 2013). In addition, the foreign investment law in 2009 divided investment zones into four zones. Zone 1 includes mountainous areas that lack infrastructure. Foreign investors in this zone receive seven years of tax exemption, and pay a 10 per cent tax on profit after the tax exemption period ends. Zone 2 refers to areas with infrastructure. In this zone, foreign investors receive five years of tax exemption, and pay 7.5 per cent tax on profit after three years and 15 per cent after the tax exemption period (Vongsay 2013).

The first FDI law in 1988 allowed 100 per cent foreign ownership. However, the initial progress of economic reform has not provided much incentive to FDI inflows, as indicated by the total FDI inflow to Laos which has increased slowly from US$15 million in 1989 to US$120 million in 1992. As the first investment law lacked in implementation details and with the relatively high profit tax (which ranged between 20 and 50 per cent), FDI inflows fluctuated between US$74 million and US$540 million during 1992–96.

FDI inflows to Laos shrank sharply from US$120 million in 1997 to US$38 million in 2001. The Asian Financial Crisis during the period of 1997–99 was a significant factor that caused major FDI outflows, especially FDI from ASEAN countries. Nevertheless, the amount of capital inflows to Laos showed a tremendous increase of nearly fivefold, from US$1,200 million in 2002 to US$5,000 million in 2008. This was due to the revision of the FDI policy in 2004 which allowed foreign investors an extended and longer investment period between 50 and 75 years, compared to 15–20 years previously, and the profit tax reduced to 20 per cent across all sectors. In addition, a single investment window has been implemented in order to shorten document progress and reduce transaction costs. The flows of FDI show a fluctuation during the period of 2009–13 before falling to US$720 million in

2014 (see Appendix 4.5). The government suspended natural resource projects to evaluate the effectiveness of previous foreign investment approval. This might be a significant factor that caused FDI inflows to decline.

A major source of FDI inflows into Laos is Thailand. The total accumulated registered capital is US$5,600 million, which accounted for 23.7 per cent of total FDI. However, China is considered to be a dominant country that made the largest number of investment projects (45,156), which accounted for 18.9 per cent of the total investment. Vietnam is the third largest investor in terms of both registered capital (US$3,800 million) and number of projects (24,236). The major foreign investment sources are from neighbouring countries due to the proximity of geographical location and similar economic policy and political system. In addition, total FDI inflows from ten European countries are US$3,399.20 million, followed by South Korea and Japan which have experienced development in the electronics and automotive industries. The total accumulated FDI from South Korea and Japan are US$1,100 million and US$580 million, respectively (see Appendix 4.6).

The FDI inflows into Laos by sectors during the period 1988–2014 are summarized in Appendix 4.7. The FDI inflows into Laos are dominated by hydropower and mining sectors (based on number of investment projects). The total accumulated FDI inflows are 7,700 and 6,100 projects respectively, which accounted for 32.5 per cent and 25.8 per cent of total investment. Since the country is rich in natural resources, especially water resources, the Mekong River and its tributaries are estimated to hold a hydropower potential in excess of 20 times the current power production (Fraser 2010). In addition, investment laws have been revised in 2010 to provide a longer land accession up to 99 years for both mining and hydropower projects.

Furthermore, FDI inflows for agriculture, and industry and handicraft sectors were revealed to have the highest value in terms of registered capital. The total accumulated FDI are US$91,836 million and US$70,044 million respectively, which accounted for 38.4 per cent and 29.3 per cent of total register investment capital. Due to the fact that more than half of the Lao population have involved in agricultural production, the share of agriculture and industry sectors to GDP accounted for 25 per cent and 29 per cent respectively in 2014.

4.　SMEs Characteristics and Their Development Policy

4.1. Definition of SMEs

The Prime Minister's Office of Laos defines SMEs as enterprises that are legally registered and operating according to the prevailing laws of Laos. It classifies SMEs into the following categories: (1) small enterprises are those having an annual average number of employees not exceeding 19 people, or total assets not exceeding 250 million kip, or an annual turnover not exceeding 400 million kip; (2) medium-sized enterprises are those having an annual average number of employees not exceeding 99 people, or total assets not exceeding 1,200 million kip, or an annual turnover not exceeding 1 billion kip. In order to promote SME and private sector development in Laos, the government has promulgated Primary Office Decree No. 42/PM. The goals of this decree are as follows: (1) to improve the regulatory environment; (2) to enhance the competitiveness of establishments; (3) to expand domestic and international market access; (4) to improve access to finance; (5) to encourage the development of business organizations; and (6) to enhance entrepreneurial attitudes and characteristics within society. Furthermore, Prime Minister's Degree No. 42/PM established the SME Promotion and Development Office (SMEPDO). The main objective of SMEPDO is to promote the establishment and sustainable development of SMEs.

TABLE 4.2
Definition of SMEs

Type of Enterprises	Average Annual Number of Employees	Total Asset in kip	Annual Turnover in kip
Small Enterprise	<=19	<= 250 million	<= 400 million
Medium Enterprise	20–99	<= 1.2 billion	<= 1 billion

SMEs are classified into three categories by sector:
1. SMEs operating in the production of commercial goods,
2. SMEs operating in the trade sector, and
3. SMEs operating in the service sector.

Source: Department of SME Promotion (2015).

4.2. SMEs' Characteristics and Their Challenges

More than 99 per cent of enterprises in Laos are SMEs and about 95 per cent of them are small enterprises (see Table 4.3). In terms of industry, SMEs are dominant in wholesale and retails trade as well as car and motorbike repair which accounts for 62 per cent of all activities in these industries. The corresponding figures in other industries are manufacturing (12 per cent), accommodation and food service (11 per cent), and others (13 per cent) (see Table 4.4). Lao enterprises face various internal and external constraints. According to GIZ (2014), which conducted a survey covering more than 700 samples in five provinces in Laos, it was revealed that one of the most important external constraints for enterprises in Laos is high taxes and duties. The most important internal constraint facing enterprises is the lack of capital (see Table 4.5).

TABLE 4.3
SMEs' Contribution

	2006	2013
By unit of enterprises		
SMEs (%)	99.8	99.8
Small Enterprises (%)	100.0	95.2
Medium Enterprises (%)	0.9	4.6
By employment		
SMEs (%)	81.4	82.4
Small Enterprises (%)	69.2	62.0
Medium Enterprises (%)	12.2	20.4

Source: Department of SME Promotion (2015).

TABLE 4.4
SMEs by Activities

Activities	Number	Share
Trading on wholesale and retails and car and motorbike repair	78,407	62.80%
Manufacturing	15,573	12.50%
Accomodation and food service	14,549	11.70%
Others	16,344	13.00%
Total	124,873	100%

Source: Department of SME Promotion (2015).

TABLE 4.5
External and Internal Constraints of Enterprises

Rank		2007	2009	2011	2013
External constraints					
1		Too high taxes and duties	Too high taxes and duties	Too high taxes and duties	Competition with domestic competitors
2		Fuel prices	Competition with domestic competitors	Competition with domestic competitors	Electricity prices
3		Electricity prices	Re-registering with tax office	Electricity prices	Too high taxes and duties
Internal constraints					
1		Low productivity/efficiency	Lack of capital	Lack of capital	Lack of capital
2		Lack of market information	Lack of management	Lack of management	Lack of management
3		High labour costs	Lack of market information	Lack of market information	Low level of technology

Source: GIZ (2014).

4.3. SMEs' Development Policy

Policies promoting enterprise development have been in place since the New Market Mechanism was introduced in 1980. In order to promote the private sector, the government began to privatize state-owned enterprises (SOEs) and introduced modern commercial laws and regulations in the mid-1990s. Before the introduction of the New Market Mechanism, most large enterprises were SOEs.

The Government of Laos (GoL) has enhanced private sector development to promote growth (GoL 2004). In order to promote SME and private sector development in Laos, GoL has promulgated the Primary Office Decree No. 42/PM. The institutional framework of SMEs in Laos is based on the Seventh Five-Year National Socio-Economic Development Plan (2011–15) (GoL 2011*a*) and Small and Medium Enterprise (SME) Promotion Law (GoL 2011*b*). To support the law, the Lao government issued the Degree of Implementation on SME Law (2012), and the Decree on the Promotion and Development of Small and Medium Sized Enterprises (GoL 2004*c*). SMEPDO had transformed into the Department of SME (DSME) under the Ministry of Industry and Commerce (MIoC) in 2013. This transformation might have limited the roles and duties of institutions to coordinate with inter-government agencies and formulate and implement policies related to SMEs promotion and development in Laos.

Moreover, the Lao government has the SME Development Plan 2016–2020, which focuses on six main areas as follows: (1) promote productivity, technology and innovation; (2) enhance access to finance; (3) enhance access to business development services (BDS); (4) enhance SME accession to expanding domestic and international markets; (5) create and develop entrepreneurs; (6) create an enabling environment for the establishment and operation of SME businesses.

As SMEs face issues in terms of access to finance, the Lao government has set up the SME Promotion and Development Fund (SME Fund) to support SMEs. This involved transforming a state-owned commercial bank to a SME-oriented bank since 2008 (Lao Development Bank: LDB).

The SME Promotion and Development Fund (SME Fund) was established since 2010. The objectives of the fund are: (1) to support promotional projects and activities requested by business membership organizations and other government agencies involved in SME promotion; (2) to provide SMEs with access to finance via participating banks with minimum fee; (3) to provide credit guarantee to banks and financial institutions; and (4) to establish joint investments.

Moreover, the Lao government also established the Business Assistance Facility (BAF) to help SMEs access information and strengthen their capacity. BAF is a subcomponent of the diversification and a competitiveness component of Second Trade Development Facility Project (TDF-2). BAF has been established to assist Lao PDR's private sector manufacturers and enterprises expand by implementing business growth plans agreed in advance with BAF.

5. Perception of SMEs in Regional Economic Integration

5.1. Awareness of AEC/AFTA and its Impact

Laos began to integrate into the global economy by joining AFTA, and this was followed by its successful WTO accession in 2013. Economic integration leads to a reduction in trade barriers, which is expected to increase interlinkages and lead to higher Lao exports and imports.

Figure 4.1 shows the percentage of firms that indicated they are aware of such free trade agreements (FTAs) in each enterprise survey administered between 2007 and 2013. The percentages of enterprises that are aware of AFTA (27.7 per cent) or WTO (28.9 per cent) peaked in 2009 and have since decreased to a current rate of less than 20 per cent for both AFTA and WTO. There are various reasons for the low awareness of AFTA and WTO. First, this might be due to the fact that the most common types of enterprises surveyed are micro and small enterprises, which have limited access to information and markets. Second, it might be that government campaigns to promote awareness of AFTA and WTO have declined over the last several years.

Figure 4.2 shows the percentage of firms that indicated they are aware of AEC, AFTA and WTO agreements in 2013. Overall, a substantial percentage of entrepreneurs (37.45 per cent) are unaware of any of these three FTAs. However, there are marked differences in awareness based on enterprise size. Whereas the majority of micro enterprises (69.74 per cent) are not aware of AEC, AFTA, and WTO, most medium and large enterprises are familiar with at least one of the three.

FIGURE 4.1
Awareness of AFTA and WTO (ES2007, ES2009, ES2011, ES2013)

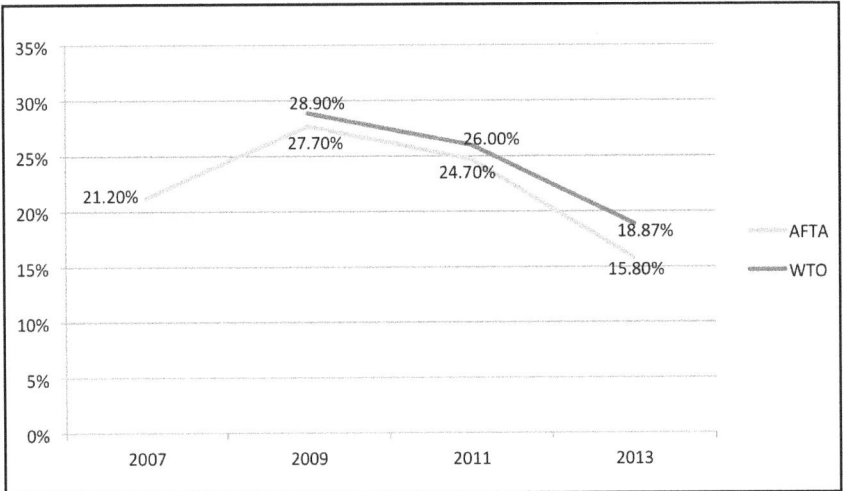

Source: Enterprise survey from GIZ in 2013.

FIGURE 4.2
Awareness of AEC, AFTA and WTO

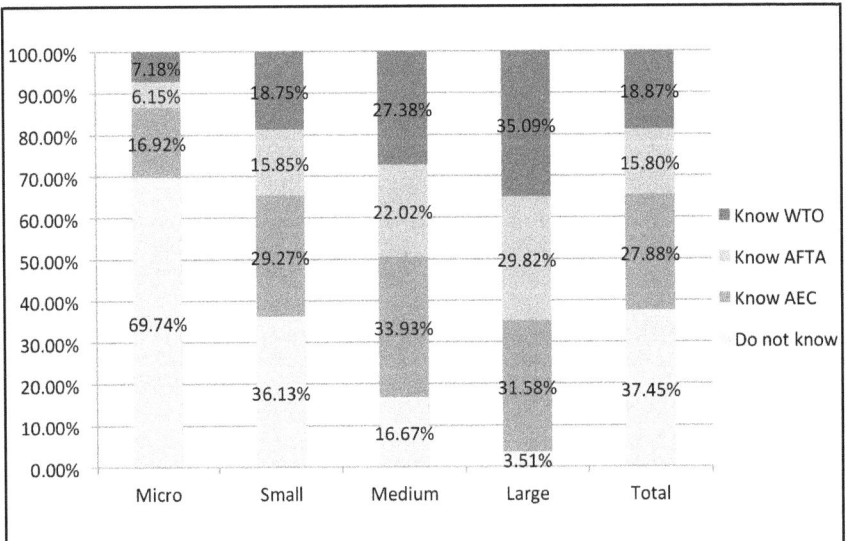

Source: Enterprise survey from GIZ in 2013.

In general, entrepreneurs are optimistic about the implementation of AEC, as shown in Figure 4.3, which indicates that more than half of the respondents believe it will have a positive effect on their businesses. Overall, more than 20 per cent of enterprises feel that AEC will provide new opportunities to import cheaper products and services and/or it will provide Lao exporters with better access to the markets of AEC members (see Appendix 4.8). These two benefits are particularly important for micro, small and medium enterprises. Large enterprises also believe that as a result of AEC implementation, both FDI inflows to Laos as well as competition from imported products and services will increase.

FIGURE 4.3
Perceptions of How AEC Will Affect Businesses

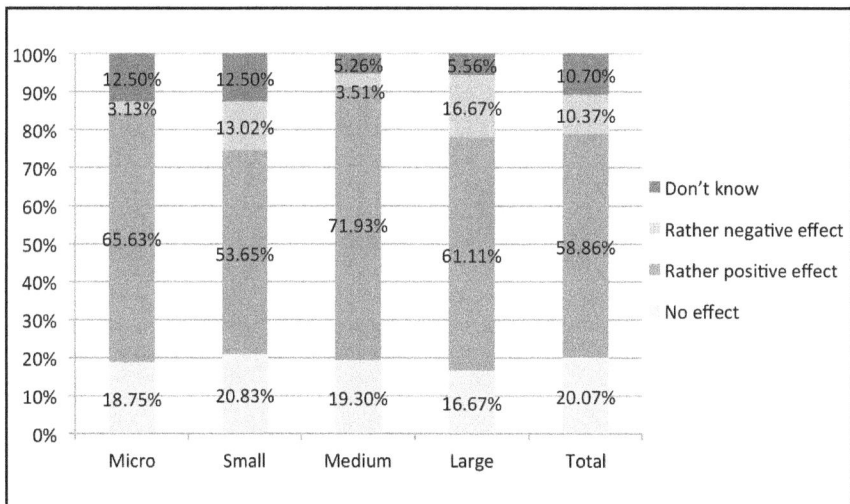

Source: Enterprise survey from GIZ in 2013.

More than 40 per cent of enterprises expect that AEC will provide new opportunities to export and import products from new markets. Large enterprises expect Laos to become a more attractive destination for foreign investors (27.03 per cent) and there will be more competition from imported products and services (21.62 per cent). On the other hand, micro, small and medium enterprises expect that AEC will generate a good opportunity to diversify their import products and services and provide access to new markets for export. These two components made up 52.94 per cent, 40.44 per cent and 48.57 per cent of micro, small and medium enterprises, respectively (see Appendix 4.8).

Despite the fact that most entrepreneurs expect AEC implementation to have a positive effect on their businesses, many firms do not have any plans to prepare for this implementation. Appendix 4.9 shows firms' preparation for AEC implementation in 2015. Overall, about 25.48 per cent of enterprises have done nothing to prepare for AEC implementation. In particular, 67.65 per cent of micro enterprises and 29.71 per cent of small enterprises have not done any preparation. This shows that there is low level of preparation for AEC, especially among micro and small enterprises.

AFTA took effect in 2008. As a consequence, most import tariffs were removed under the Common Effective Preferential Tariff (CEPT) Agreement. Figure 4.4 indicates that more than half of the entrepreneurs

FIGURE 4.4
Overall Effects of AFTA

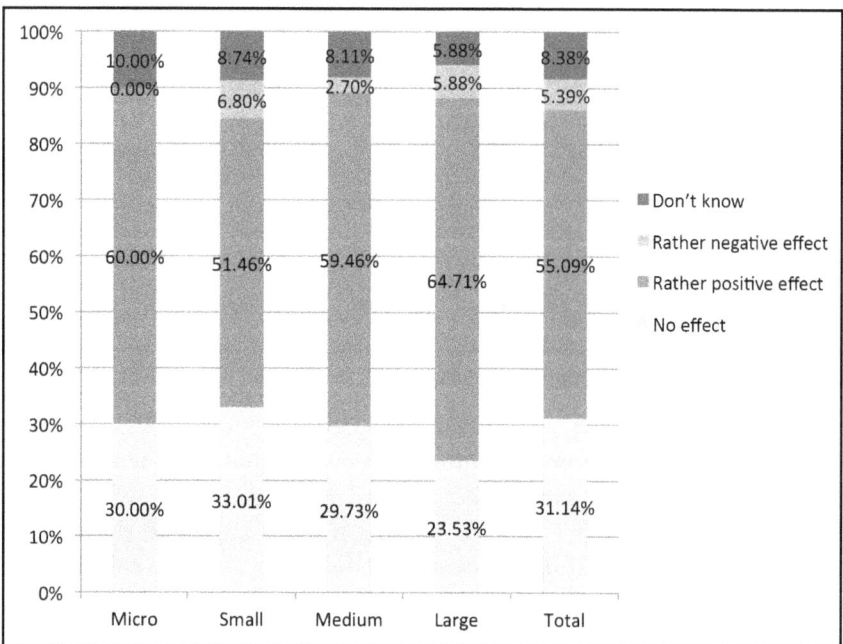

Source: Enterprise survey from GIZ in 2013.

are optimistic about AFTA implementation, believing that it will have a positive effect on their businesses. Appendix 4.10 further specifies the different ways in which enterprises expect AFTA to affect their businesses. Overall, just over 20 per cent of enterprises believe AFTA will increase FDI and make it easier to import products from other member countries as a consequence of the removal of all import tariffs. At the same time, almost 20 per cent believe there will be fiercer competition after the AFTA commitment is fully applied.

5.2. Awareness of WTO and its Impact

Laos' successful accession to the WTO in February 2013 signalled an important step towards more closely integrating the Lao economy into global markets. Although the WTO is quite a new phenomenon for most Lao entrepreneurs, more than half of the total respondents (52.50 per cent) believe that it will bring positive effects to their businesses (see Figure 4.5).

FIGURE 4.5
Overall Effects of WTO

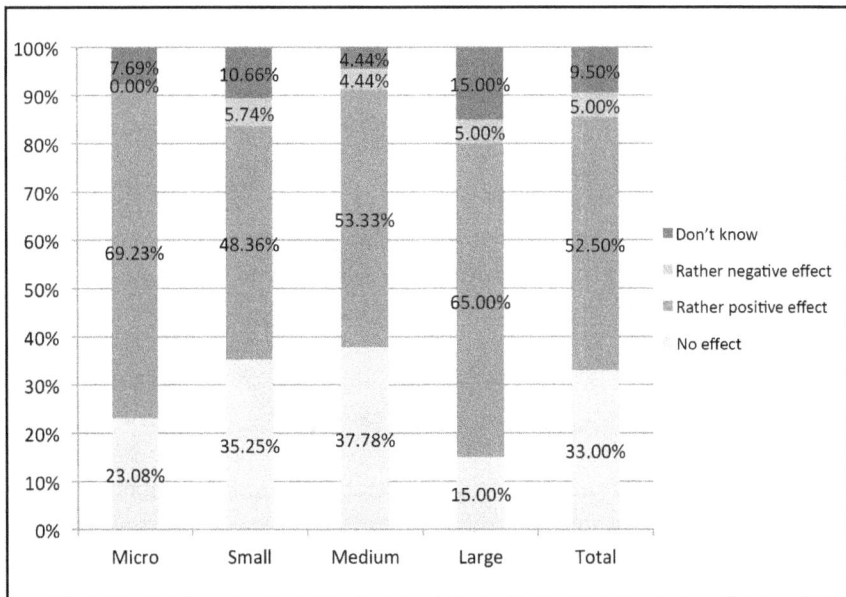

Source: Enterprise survey from GIZ in 2013.

Appendix 4.11 details the more specific impacts the WTO is expected to have. Overall, a number of enterprises believe the WTO will improve new market access for exporting goods and services (20.37 per cent), provide both new opportunities (17.04 per cent) and easier access (16.30 per cent) to import products and services, and attract more FDI (16.30 per cent). At the same time, almost 14.07 per cent of enterprises expect increased competition as a consequence of import tariffs reduction.

6.   Determinants of Use of Preferential Tariff Utilization

Regional economic integration has played a crucial role in improving market access and export performance of local enterprises in Laos. The objective of this section is to analyse preferential tariff utilization (PTU) after the signing of FTAs. The probit model is applied in order to calculate the determinants of firm-level use of FTA preferences. Based on the study of Katsuhide and Shujiro (2008), Demidova and Krishna (2008), and Wignaraja (2013), the probit model is formally defined as:

$$Pr\left(y = \frac{1}{x}\right) = \beta_0 + \beta_1 Edu + \beta_2 Age + \beta_3 Loc + \beta_4 WTO$$
$$+ \beta_5 Own + \beta_6 EXF + \beta_7 Cco + \beta_1 FTA\_T + \varepsilon$$

where the dependent variable in this model, y, is a binary variable, which can be used as a proxy for the probability of using FTAs at firm-level. If a firm decides to use an FTA, then y takes the value of 1; and if the firm decides not to use an FTA, then y is equal to 0. X is the matrix of explanatory variables related to firm and industry characteristics, β is the matrix of coefficients, and ε is the matrix of error terms.

The data used in this research were obtained from surveys conducted by Vanhnalat et al. (2015) in four provinces — Vientiane Capital, Savannakhet, Khammouane and Champassack. In order to understand the characteristics of firms using FTA preferences, a questionnaire survey was developed and randomly distributed to 250 exporting firms through face-to-face interviews with business owners. The data were collected from 237 questionnaire forms, which accounted for 94.80 per cent of the total observations. Champassack province represents the largest number, with 96 firms, about 40.5 per cent of the total sample size. Vientiane Capital ranks second, with 69 firms, accounting for 29.1 per cent. This is followed by Savannakhet province with 55 firms at 23.2 per cent and Khammouane province with 17 firms at 7.2 per cent of the total sample size.

The characteristics of firms could be explained as follows. In terms of gender, males tend to be the main owners of firms — they account for more than 60 per cent of all firms. On average, female firm owners account for approximately one-third of the total sample size. With regards to educational attainment, 78.4 per cent of the owners have attained a Bachelor's degree or a higher qualification. The firm owners in Vientiane Capital have the highest education level, with 34.4 per cent of them holding a Master's degree.

On average, firms have been established for 8.5 years. With regards to the average number of employees and registered capital in each province, with the exception of some large firms in Vientiane Capital, most firms are categorized as small and medium-sized firms defined as the number of employees at less than 100 people. The type of ownership is classified as 61.4 per cent domestic firms, 30.7 per cent foreign owned firms and 7.9 per cent joint venture firms (Vanhnalat et al. 2015). The average PTU is approximately 55 per cent. Regarding the exporting profile of the surveyed firms, most firms started to export from the year of establishment or within the first two years. Overall, the AFTA scheme is the most utilized at 31.1 per cent, followed by the Lao–Viet Free Trade Agreement (LVFTA) and the ASEAN–Japan Framework Agreement for Comprehensive Economic Partnership (AJFACEP), which are at the rate of 12.6 per cent each. The ASEAN–China Free Trade Agreement (ACFTA) and the ASEAN–South Korea Free Trade Agreement (ASKFTA) are also often utilized at 10.8 per cent and 7.2 per cent, respectively (Vanhnalat et al. 2015).

With regards to the firms' experience of receiving training for FTA utilization, the findings indicate that half or more of the firms did not receive any training. However many firms, especially in Savannakhet and Khammouane, did not have an opportunity to receive training. This calls for more efforts on public awareness from the government. For those who have received training, the study shows that they only received one or two types of training which were outlined in the questionnaire. The most pressing issue is that many firms have not yet received any training for the preparation of AEC. Training for the preparation of the AEC is essential to firms and relevant agencies. Based on the enterprise survey, 45 per cent of exporting firms did not apply preferential tariffs (PT) to their exports. The main reasons are that import tariffs of trading partners are relatively low (29.55 per cent) and they are not aware that their goods are eligible for the tariffs (25.84 per cent). The findings also illustrate that some firms do not have access to PT information, and government promotions of PTU is insufficient. Additional explanations include usage of FTA preferences not required by import partners (38.20 per cent) and difficulties in obtaining Certificates of Origin (COs) (33.71 per cent). The government has introduced a single process to simplify document procedure for exports. However, in practice, it depends on the characteristic of the products, especially for the export of natural resources because it takes longer to coordinate between several government organizations.

The results illustrate that firms with a higher exposure to international trade have a larger firm export performance and are foreign owned. Subsequently these firms have a higher cost of CO and are more inclined to utilize FTAs. This confirms a positive relationship between firm export performance and FTA utilization at approximately 90 per cent statistical significance. This is consistent with the findings of Hayakawa (2012) and Arudchelvan and Wignaraja (2015), who argued that firms with more exposure to international trade, had a higher probability of using FTAs.

Another significant determinant of FTA utilization is firm ownership. Estimated results show that domestic firms use FTAs less than foreign owned firms by 53.3 per cent at a statistical significance of 99 per cent. This depicts that foreign owned firms are aware of international markets and trade regulations including import tariffs, FTA preferences, and rules of origin (Takahashi and Urata 2008; Wignaraja et al. 2009).

Firms with high costs of COs tended to have greater FTA utilization. The results indicate that every one US dollar increase for CO rises the probability of firms using FTAs by 4.24 per cent at a statistical significance of 99 per cent. Although the cost of COs may present a barrier for exporters to use FTAs, it is considered to be a small significance compared

TABLE 4.6
Determinants of Preferential Tariff Utilization

Variable	Whole Sample		Vientiane Capital	
	Probit	Marginal Effects	Probit	Marginal Effects
Education	−0.051 (0.053)	−0.019 (0.020)	0.026 (0.063)	0.008 (0.020)
Firm's Age	0.012 (0.023)	0.004 (0.008)	−0.020 (0.026)	−0.006 (0.008)
Firm's Size	−0.0002 (0.0004)	−0.0001 (0.0001)	2.29e-05 (0.0003)	7.18e-06 (0.0001)
Located in the Capital	−0.306 (0.262)	−0.116 (0.100)	–	–
Awareness of WTO	0.367 (0.289)	0.139 (0.109)	0.740* (0.387)	0.232** (0.116)
Export Performance	0.0003* (0.0002)	0.0001* (7.99e-05)	0.018 (0.019)	0.005 (0.006)
Domestic Firm	−1.402*** (0.242)	−0.533*** (0.093)	−0.244 (0.448)	−0.076 (0.141)
Cost of CO	0.112*** (0.036)	0.042*** (0.014)	0.139*** (0.050)	0.043*** (0.016)
Training on FTAs	1.824*** (0.307)	0.693*** (0.111)	1.114*** (0.395)	0.350*** (0.118)
Constant	−0.064 (0.801)		−2.001* (1.122)	
Observations	237		69	
Pseudo R^2	0.318		0.257	

Notes: (1) Robust Standard errors in parentheses.
(2) *** $p < 0.01$, ** $p < 0.05$, and * $p < 0.1$
(3) Model 2 estimates for Vientiane Capital only.
(4) Absence of any strong correlation among independent variables has been confirmed by using a correlation matrix.
Source: Author's calculations based on survey data (2015).

to export values. Hence there is a positive relationship between CO cost and FTA utilization; the more exposure firms have to international trade, the more inclined they are to utilize FTAs.

Furthermore, the results demonstrate that having knowledge about FTAs has an immense impact on whether FTAs are utilized. There is a correlation between firm owners or managers who have been trained in FTAs and FTA utilization. The results from the sample size denote that owners and managers who have FTA knowledge are 69.3 per cent more likely to utilize FTAs than those who do not have the knowledge. However, other determinants such as the education level of firms owners or managers, the age and size of the firms, and awareness of economic integration do not show any statistical relationship with the firms' FTA utilization within Laos.

7. Determinant Factors of Enterprises' Exports

Export promotion is an important element of long-term development in Laos. The Lao economy is highly dependent on the resource sector (mining and hydropower sectors). On the other hand, natural resources sector has a negative impact on long-term development. The high dependence on natural resources tends to decrease the capacity of an enterprise to export due to declining competitiveness. According to empirical analysis in many countries, resource sector-dependent development will lead to an appreciation in the real exchange rate and a decline in non-resource sectors (agriculture and manufacturing), which is called "Dutch disease". In order to overcome this issue, a diversified economy is necessary, and improving the capacity of firms to export is an important strategy. There are a number of studies on the determinants of enterprises' exports in many countries (Biggs and Shah 2006; Koenig 2009; Lefebvre et al. 2003; Nazar and Saleem 2009; Rosenbusch et al. 2011; Özçelik and Taymaz 2004; Tomiura 2007; Pangarkar 2008; Watson 2007; Wilkinson and Brouthers 2006; and Yi et al. 2013). According to our knowledge, (until now) there has been no study conducted on the case of Laos. As a result, it is not clear what are the determinants of Lao firms' exports. The main objective of this section is to investigate the factors that affect a firm's exports by using the logit model. This empirical study provides important information for policymakers to formulate and implement policies related to the promotion of exports.

This model is particularly suited to the task at hand because it is designed to handle regressions involving dichotomous dependent variables. This consideration is singularly important since business owners were asked whether their firms export or not. Firms that export are coded one and those that do not are coded zero, making this the/a binary dependent variable. The logit model shows the probability of each factor affecting a firm's exports. The factors determining a firm's exports are demonstrated by the logit model as follows:

$$\text{Prob}(EX = 1) = Ln(P_i/1 - P_i) = \alpha + \beta(COE) + \lambda(TSO) + \phi(COB)$$
$$+ \eta(EBG) + \gamma(SEB) + \delta(TLE) + \pi(OFS) + e_i$$

EX denotes a firm's exports, with exporting firms coded as one and non-exporting firms coded zero. COE is a vector of characteristics of the entrepreneurs; TSO is a vector of training skills for owner-managers; COB is a vector of characteristics of the business; EBG is a vector of business growth; SEB is a vector of firm size; TLE is a vector of technologies level used by the enterprise; and OFS is a vector of other factors. α is the constant; β, λ, ϕ, η, γ, δ and π are corresponding vectors of coefficients, and e_i is a normally distributed random error term. The details of the variables used in the model are shown in Appendix 4.12.

To examine the determinants of exporting, we used the Enterprise Survey 2013 of Lao-German HRDME Programme from GIZ, which was conducted in October 2013 with 722 enterprises from five main provinces in Laos,[3] namely Vientiane Capital, Champasack, Savannakhet, Luangprabang and Luangnamtha.

We define each variable used in the model in Appendix 4.12. The logit model determines the probability of each factor affecting the enterprises' exports. The empirical results are shown in Table 4.7. Eleven factors were found to be statistically significant on enterprises exporting. The factors that have a positive effect on enterprises exporting include: the characteristics of the entrepreneurs, particularly the age of the owner-manager (AOB), which is statistically significant at 90 per cent confidence level. This result is consistent with the study of Kyophilavong (2008). This could be due to older entrepreneurs

TABLE 4.7
Factor Determinants of SMEs Exporting Using the Logit Model

Independent Variable	dy/dx	z
Characteristics of the Entrepreneur (COE)		
AOB Age of owner-manager	0.0027*	1.64
GOM Gender of owner-manager	0.0349	0.88
NOM Nationality of owner-manager	0.1126	1.32
EDU1 Eduction level of owner-management as completed upper secondary	0.0798	1.51
EDU2 Eduction level of owner-management as completed vocational/technical	0.0560	0.82
EDU3 Eduction level of owner-management as completed university and higher	−0.0131	−0.24
BRB Before starting current business the owner ran another business but it closed	0.1713	1.27
BTR Before starting current business the owner was trader	0.0597	0.78
BWF Before starting current business the owner worked for family business	0.0780	0.71
BEA Before starting current business the owner was employed by another business	0.0484	0.42
OIP Owner enterprise has investment plan for business	0.0298	0.79
OLR Owner-manager knows business laws and regulations relating to the business	0.0267	0.60
Training Skills for Owner-manager (TSO)		
OCS Owner-manager completed vocational and technical skills training	−0.0273	−0.57
OTS Owner-manager had management training when started business	−0.0012	−0.02
OMT Owner-manager had management training since started business	0.0056	0.11

OAD	Owner-manager received some advice for developing the business	-0.0124	-0.32
OSI	Owner-manager wants to learn some skills in order to improve the business	0.0012	0.03

Characteristics of the Business (COB)

AFI	Age of the firm at the time of incorporation	-0.0027	-0.97
EML	Enterprise as a member business organization of LNCCI	0.0087	0.10
EMC	Enterprise as a member business organization of Provincial CCI	-0.1384**	-2.41
EMA	Enterprise as a member business organization of Business Association	0.0501	0.68
EMG	Enterprise as a member business organization of Business Group	0.1484**	2.24
FEI	Enterprise as individual enterprise form	-0.2096*	-1.62
FES	Enterprise as sole limited company form	-0.0543	-0.53
FEL	Enterprise as limited company form	-0.1652**	-2.37
FEM	Enterprise as mixed company form	-0.1290	-0.89
EPC	Enterprise as public company form	-0.0998	-0.51
ESJ	Enterprise status as joint-venture	0.0498	0.42
EOF	Enterprise status as wholly owned foreign	0.0751	0.44

TABLE 4.7 *(continued)*

Independent Variable	dy/dx	z
Enterprise/Business Growth (EBG)		
OUI Output was increased (in 2013 compared to 2012)	−0.1792*	−1.91
TUI Turnover has increased (in 2013 compared to 2012)	0.1897	1.12
PRI Profit has increased (in 2013 compared to 2012)	0.0547	0.41
Size of Enterprise/Business (SEB)		
NOE1 Number of employees (5–19 persons)	0.0616	1.30
NOE2 Number of employees (20–99 persons)	−0.0271	−0.38
NOE3 Number of employees (more than 99 persons)	0.2813*	1.64
PFE Percentage of female employees	−0.0003	−0.42
ASS1 Company asset between 100–250 million kip	0.0360	0.63
ASS2 Company asset between 250–750 million kip	0.1211*	1.62
ASS3 Company asset between 750–1,200 million kip	−0.1483***	−2.67
ASS4 Company asset above 1,200 million kip	0.0266	0.38
Other Factors (OFS)		
TUR1 Company turnover between 200–400 million kip	0.1331**	2.20
TUR2 Company turnover between 401–700 million kip	0.0269	0.35
TUR3 Company turnover between 701–1,000 million kip	0.1234	1.14

TUR4	Company turnover of more than 1,000 million kip	0.0914	1.05
OEE	Owner-manager evaluates current economic situation compared to 2 years ago	0.0020	0.05
IBP	The inputs were imported for business production	0.1287***	2.76
EIC	Enterprise has used internet/email for business communications	-0.0091	-0.20
Number of obs.	=	722
LR chi2(47)	=	100.03
Prob > chi2	=	0
Pseudo R2	=	0.1147

Note: Estimate coefficient statistically significant at a (*) 90 per cent, (**) 95 per cent, and (***) 99 per cent confidence levels.

having more experiences running businesses and larger business networks, which could increase the probability of exporting to other countries. In terms of the characteristics of the business, the study found that being a member of a business group (EMG) contributed to expanding the market of a firm to foreign customers, which is similar to the results of Yi et al. (2013). It is statistically significant at 90 per cent confidence level. This can imply that if an enterprise is a member of EMG, it has a higher probability of exporting compared to other enterprises who are non-members. Focusing on the size of enterprise or business, which is defined as the number of employees and amount of assets, we found that enterprises with more than 99 employees (NOE3) and firms with assets valued between 250 and 750 million kip (ASS2) are more likely to export than other firms. This is statistically significant at 90 per cent confidence level. From this, it can be concluded that the size of firm is an important factor to determine exports; this result is consistent with the studies of Yi et al. (2013), Koenig (2009), Özçelik and Taymaz (2004), and Titman and Wessels (1988). In addition, other factors are also important for SMEs' exports. Having a turnover value between 200 and 400 million kip (TUR1) and importing some inputs for the business production process (IBP) are positively correlated with exports and are significant at the 90 per cent and 99 per cent confidence levels respectively. These factors have contributed to enterprises' exports, which are similar to the results of Biggs and Shah (2006) and Koenig (2009).

On the other hand, there are also some factors that have negative effects on enterprises' exports. The individual enterprise form (FEI) has a coefficient with an expected negative sign, and it is statistically significant at the 95 per cent confidence level. This indicates that there is a negative relationship between FEI and SMEs exporting. Some reasons for the negative effect are that these firms have low regional and international competitiveness because they lack some elementary inputs such as insufficient capital, lack of skills to run the businesses, limited products, unable to access large markets, limited business networks, etc. Enterprises which are members of the Provincial CCI (EMC) and in the form of limited companies (FEL) are negatively correlated with SMEs exporting and are significant at the 90 per cent and 95 per cent confidence levels respectively. Their coefficients are unexpected. Overall, we concluded that FEI, EMC, and FEL have a lower probability to export compared to others, due to a lack of access to finance, lack of skills to run the businesses, limited products, limited business networks, and low ability to compete. Both an increase in a firm's output (OUI) in 2013 compared to 2012 and a firm asset value of between 750 and 1,200 million kip (ASS3) are negative determinants of a firm's exports. They are significant at the 90 per cent and 99 per cent confidence levels respectively and their coefficients are unexpected. These results contrast with the results of some studies that demonstrated that business growth and firm size have positive effects on a firm's exports, such as the studies by Vos et al. (2007) and Titman and Wessels (1988). This study found the OUI and ASS3 have negative effects on enterprises' exports. This is perhaps because 84.63 per cent of the enterprises included in this survey are small enterprises, therefore their outputs are increased by small quantities for domestic customers and not enough are available for export.

However, these findings are consistent with the results of studies in other countries. The findings are important to policymakers for SME export promotion. It is very important to understand these factors because Laos has already joined WTO in 2013 and AEC in 2015. This regional and international trade liberalization will have significant impacts on SMEs' development in Laos because most of the SMEs lack in export competitiveness.

Promoting exports is one of the most important challenges facing enterprises in Laos. However, there is no clear understanding of the factors influencing firms' exports. This chapter aims to investigate these factors. There are a small portion of Lao firms that export goods and services. However, we found that they lack in competitiveness compared to firms from other countries.

As Laos has joined WTO in 2013 and AEC in 2015, promotion of exports is one of the most important policies of the Lao government. Empirical results show that owners-managers' experience, membership of a business organization or business group, number of employees, company assets, company turnover, and imported inputs are the major determinants of Lao firms' exports. In order to promote exports, there are two main policies to follow. First is to encourage firms to join business organizations or business groups. This will help firms access knowledge and information to export. Second is to promote growth in terms of employment, output, turnover and benefits. In order to do this, it is important to improve the business climate and provide firms with financial, technical, and management skills support.

8. Conclusion and Policy Recommendations

Regional economic integration is vital for linking Lao firms to regional and international production networks and to improve their productivity. The main objective of this chapter is to investigate the factors that influence Lao firms' participation in regional economic integration. There are three specific objectives as follows: (1) to investigate the awareness of economic integration (AEC, AFTA and WTO) and its impact; (2) to identify the determinants of use of PTU; and (3) to assess the determinants of SMEs' export. We used data from the enterprise survey conducted by GIZ, and secondary data from Vanhnalat et al. (2015), as well as the logit model for quantitative analysis.

The level of awareness of the AEC, AFTA and WTO agreements amongst Lao firms are relatively low. Only 18.89 per cent of firms are aware of the WTO agreement and 15.80 per cent are aware of AFTA. Lao firms are very optimistic about the impacts of economic integration, such as WTO accession and AEC. There are very few firms that used preferential tariffs for their exports. The average PTU is approximately 55 per cent. Awareness of WTO, export performance, firms of foreign ownership, and training on FTAs are significant determinants of the utilization of preferential tariffs.

Most of the Lao firms produce their goods for domestic use and only a few firms export. Less than 20 per cent of firms are exporters in our sample size. Variables such as the age of the owners/managers, membership in business organizations or business groups, number of employees, amount of assets and turnover, and firms that import materials are all positively correlated to the firms exporting.

In addition, we have some recommendations as follows. Even though Laos has signed several FTAs, their benefits to exporters appear to be relatively small. It is important for policymakers to provide FTA training to export-oriented firms and potential exporters, together with a wider promotion of FTA utilization to ensure their effectiveness.

APPENDIX 4.1
Imports by Commodity (%)

Commodity	2004	2008
Grains and crops	1.74	1.48
Livestock and meat products	0.25	0.26
Mining and extraction	2.70	1.28
Processed food	15.03	10.12
Textiles and clothing	10.19	6.44
Light manufacturing	18.44	26.77
Heavy manufacturing	46.58	49.13
Utilities and construction	0.53	2.46
Transport and communications	0.82	1.08
Other services	3.72	0.97
Total	100.00	100.00

Source: GTAP databases 7 and 8.

APPENDIX 4.2
Imports by Country of Origin (%)

Country of Origin	2004	2008
Australia, New Zealand	1.87	1.20
Cambodia	0.06	0.00
East Asia	11.91	17.64
European Union 25	13.54	6.50
Indonesia	0.20	0.24
Latin America	0.26	0.10
Malaysia	0.29	0.62
Middle East and North Africa	0.95	0.10
North America	2.66	1.49
Philippines	0.03	0.03
Rest of Southeast Asia	0.01	0.01
Singapore	5.10	0.44
South Asia	0.44	0.27
sub-Saharan Africa	1.43	0.22
Thailand	53.67	66.06
Vietnam	5.70	4.16
Rest of the world	1.85	0.91
Total	100.00	100.00

Source: GTAP databases 7 and 8.

APPENDIX 4.3
Exports by Commodity (%)

Commodity	2004	2008
Grains and crops	5.62	4.36
Livestock and meat products	0.90	0.46
Mining and extraction	9.00	10.07
Processed food	1.56	1.05
Textiles and clothing	27.26	12.74
Light manufacturing	21.20	9.73
Heavy manufacturing	4.91	42.87
Utilities and construction	1.11	2.72
Transport and communications	12.76	9.90
Other services	15.67	6.11
Total	100.00	100.00

Source: GTAP databases 7 and 8.

APPENDIX 4.4
Exports by Country (%)

Country	2004	2008
Australia, New Zealand	0.64	0.78
Cambodia	0.05	0.01
East Asia	7.11	15.75
European Union 25	46.29	24.65
Indonesia	0.14	0.38
Latin America	0.97	1.01
Malaysia	0.16	2.49
Middle East and North Africa	2.34	0.50
North America	11.16	7.67
Philippines	0.05	0.07
Rest of Southeast Asia	0.00	0.01
Singapore	0.53	0.50
South Asia	0.39	0.78
sub-Sahara Africa	0.55	0.93
Thailand	15.79	27.87
Vietnam	10.63	13.31
Rest of the world	3.20	4.06
Total	100.00	100.00

Source: GTAP databases 7 and 8.

APPENDIX 4.5
Registered Capital and Number of Projects

Year	Number of Projects		Registered Capital	
	Number	Growth (%)	(USD million)	Growth (%)
1988	6		2.4	
1989	168	2,700.0	15	525.0
1990	176	4.8	60	300.0
1991	372	111.4	52	−13.3
1992	834	124.2	120	130.8
1993	2,062	147.2	93	−22.5
1994	884	−57.1	360	287.1
1995	135	−84.7	74	−79.4
1996	347	157.0	540	629.7
1997	473	36.3	120	−77.8
1998	494	4.4	110	−8.3
1999	1,092	121.1	250	127.3
2000	377	−65.5	40	−84.0
2001	814	115.9	38	−5.0
2002	2,062	153.3	1,200	3,057.9
2003	3,080	49.4	130	−89.2
2004	5,347	73.6	200	53.8
2005	11,828	121.2	250	25.0
2006	19,953	68.7	2,400	860.0
2007	45,803	129.6	1,100	−54.2
2008	62,807	37.1	5,000	354.5
2009	31,552	−49.8	1,100	−78.0
2010	38,501	22.0	2,800	154.5
2011	3,482	−91.0	1,700	−39.3
2012	3,482	0.0	1,700	0.0
2013	2,373	−31.8	3,500	105.9
2014	353	−85.1	720	−79.4
Total	238,857		23,674.4	

Source: Ministry of Planning and Investment.

APPENDIX 4.6
FDI Sources Inflows to Laos

No.	Country	Number of Projects		Registered Capital	
		Number	Share (%)	USD million	Share (%)
1	Thailand	26,079	10.9	5,600	23.7
2	China	45,156	18.9	5,100	21.5
3	Vietnam	24,236	10.1	3,800	16.1
4	France	6,762	2.8	1,200	5.1
5	South Korea	10,961	4.6	1,100	4.6
6	Netherland	374	0.2	870	3.7
7	Norway	40	0.0	860	3.6
8	Japan	3,122	1.3	580	2.4
9	Malaysia	3,236	1.4	410	1.7
10	India	550	0.2	370	1.6
11	England	1,184	0.5	330	1.4
12	Hong Kong	1,385	0.6	210	0.9
13	Singapore	2,115	0.9	200	0.8
14	America	2,834	1.2	130	0.5
15	Taiwan	2,548	1.1	94	0.4
16	Canada	1,321	0.6	72	0.3
17	Italy	1,765	0.7	54	0.2
18	Russia	389	0.2	52	0.2
19	Maori	91	0.0	50	0.2
20	Switzerland	518	0.2	43	0.2
21	Australia	320	0.1	29	0.1
22	Cambodia	286	0.1	16	0.1
23	Turkey	12	0.0	15	0.1
24	Sweden	474	0.2	13	0.1
25	Germany	820	0.3	11	0.0
26	Belgium	216	0.1	3.2	0.0
27	New Zealand	234	0.1	2.5	0.0
28	Myanmar	592	0.2	1.8	0.0
29	Panama	53	0.0	1.8	0.0
30	Others	1,019	0.4	256.1	1.1
	Laos	100,165	41.9	2,200	9.3
	Total	238,857	100.0	23,674.4	100.0

Source: Ministry of Planning and Investment.

APPENDIX 4.7
FDI by Sector

Sector	Number of Projects		Registered Capital	
	Number	Share (%)	USD million	Share (%)
Electricity	7,700	32.5	600	0.3
Mining	6,100	25.8	11,741	4.9
Services	2,300	9.7	30,913	12.9
Agriculture	2,300	9.7	91,836	38.4
Hotel industries	1,000	4.2	17,776	7.4
Construction	570	2.4	1,523	0.6
Banking	220	0.9	79	0.0
Telecom	620	2.6	32	0.0
Industry, handicaft, others	1,958	8.3	70,044	29.3
Wood industries	390	1.6	4,580	1.9
Trade	320	1.4	5,956	2.5
Consulting	61	0.3	2,249	0.9
Education	31	0.1	633	0.3
Garment	89	0.4	868	0.4
Healthcare	15	0.1	27	0.0
Total	23,674	100.0	238,857	100.0

Source: Ministry of Planning and Investment.

APPENDIX 4.8
Expected Impacts of AEC

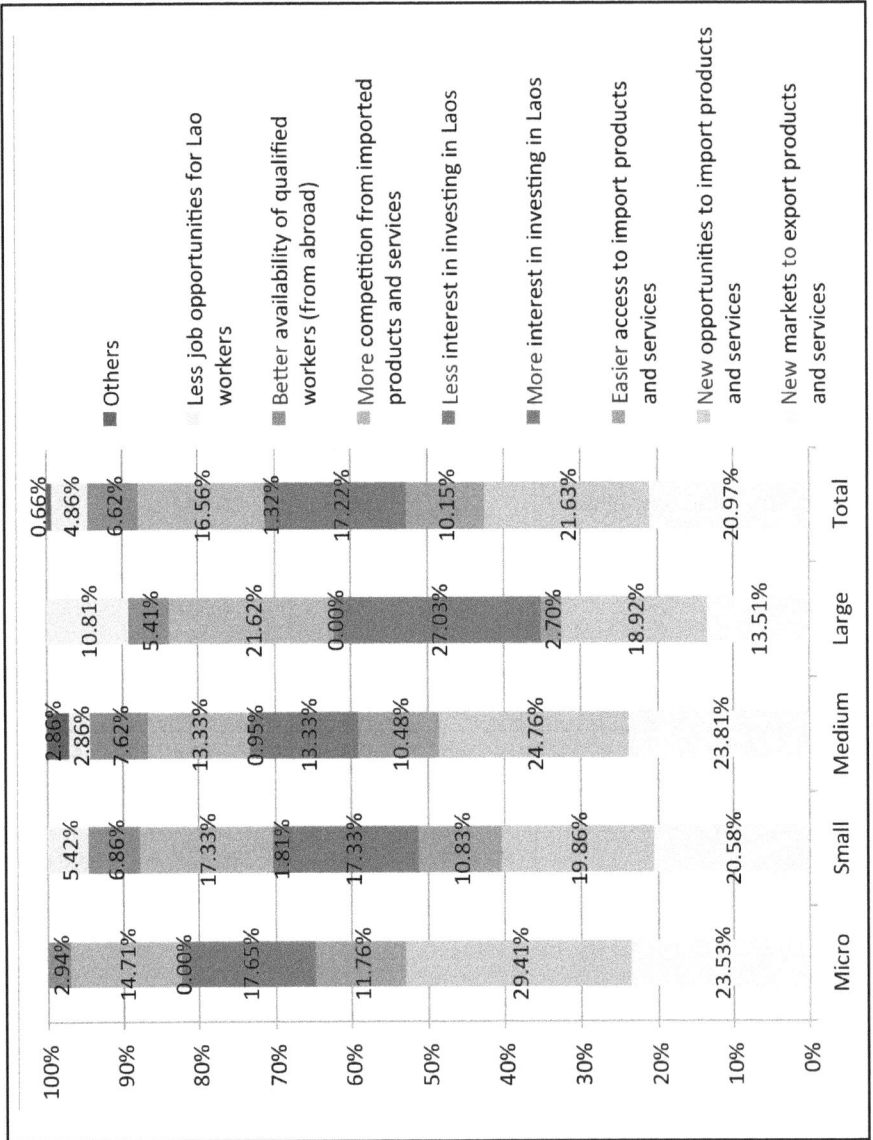

Legend:
- Others
- Less job opportunities for Lao workers
- Better availability of qualified workers (from abroad)
- More competition from imported products and services
- Less interest in investing in Laos
- More interest in investing in Laos
- Easier access to import products and services
- New opportunities to import products and services
- New markets to export products and services

Category	Micro	Small	Medium	Large	Total
Others	2.94%	5.42%	2.86%	10.81%	0.66%
Less job opportunities for Lao workers	14.71%	6.86%	2.86%	5.41%	4.86%
Better availability of qualified workers (from abroad)	0.00%	17.33%	7.62%	21.62%	6.62%
More competition from imported products and services	17.65%	1.81%	13.33%	0.00%	16.56%
Less interest in investing in Laos	11.76%	17.33%	0.95%	27.03%	1.32%
More interest in investing in Laos	29.41%	10.83%	13.33%	2.70%	17.22%
Easier access to import products and services	23.53%	19.86%	10.48%	18.92%	10.15%
New opportunities to import products and services		20.58%	24.76%	13.51%	21.63%
New markets to export products and services			23.81%		20.97%

Source: Enterprise survey from GIZ in 2013.

APPENDIX 4.9
Preparation for AEC Implementation in 2015

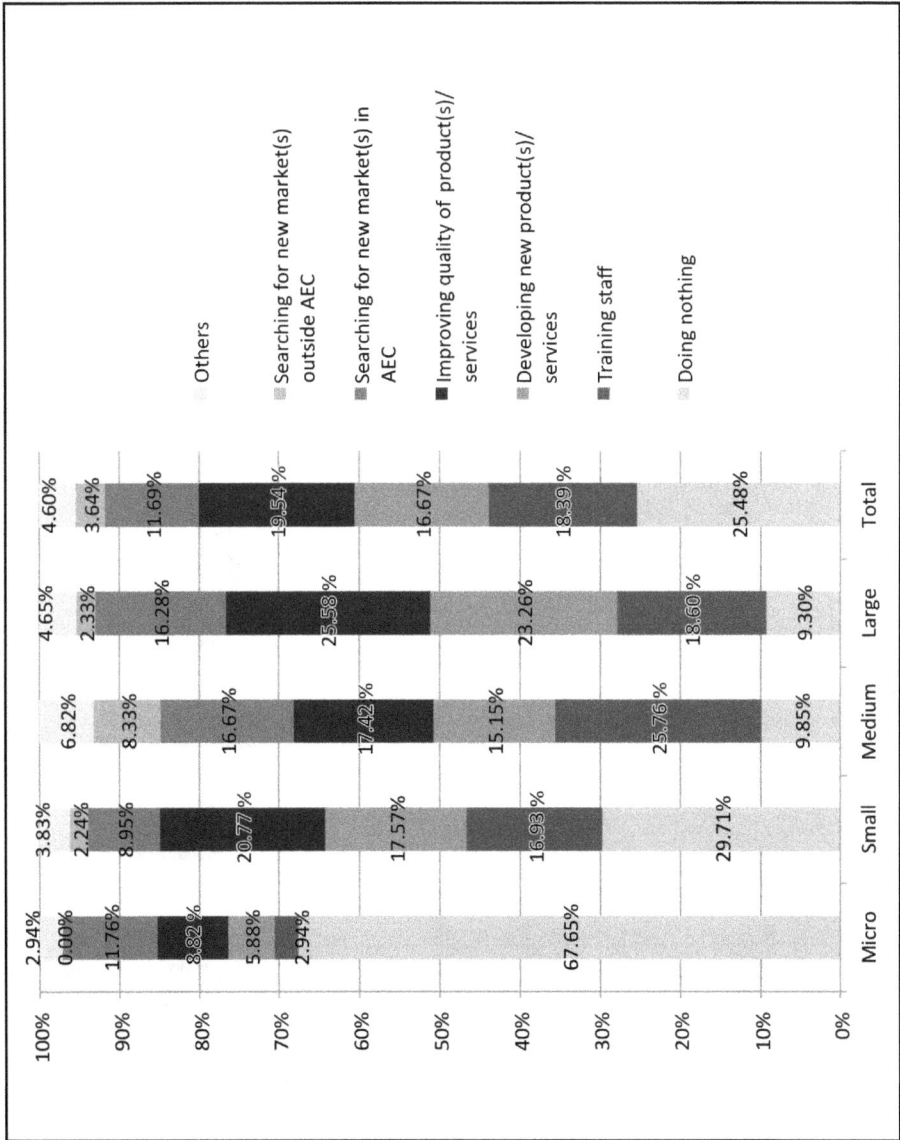

	Micro	Small	Medium	Large	Total
Others	2.94%	3.83%	6.82%	4.65%	4.60%
Searching for new market(s) outside AEC	0.00%	2.24%		2.33%	3.64%
Searching for new market(s) in AEC	11.76%	8.95%	8.33%	16.28%	11.69%
Improving quality of product(s)/services	8.82%	20.77%	16.67%	25.58%	19.54%
Developing new product(s)/services	5.88%	17.57%	17.42%	23.26%	16.67%
Training staff	2.94%	16.93%	15.15%	18.60%	18.39%
Doing nothing	67.65%	29.71%	25.76%	9.30%	25.48%
			9.85%		

Source: Enterprise survey from GIZ in 2013.

APPENDIX 4.10
Specific Impacts of AFTA

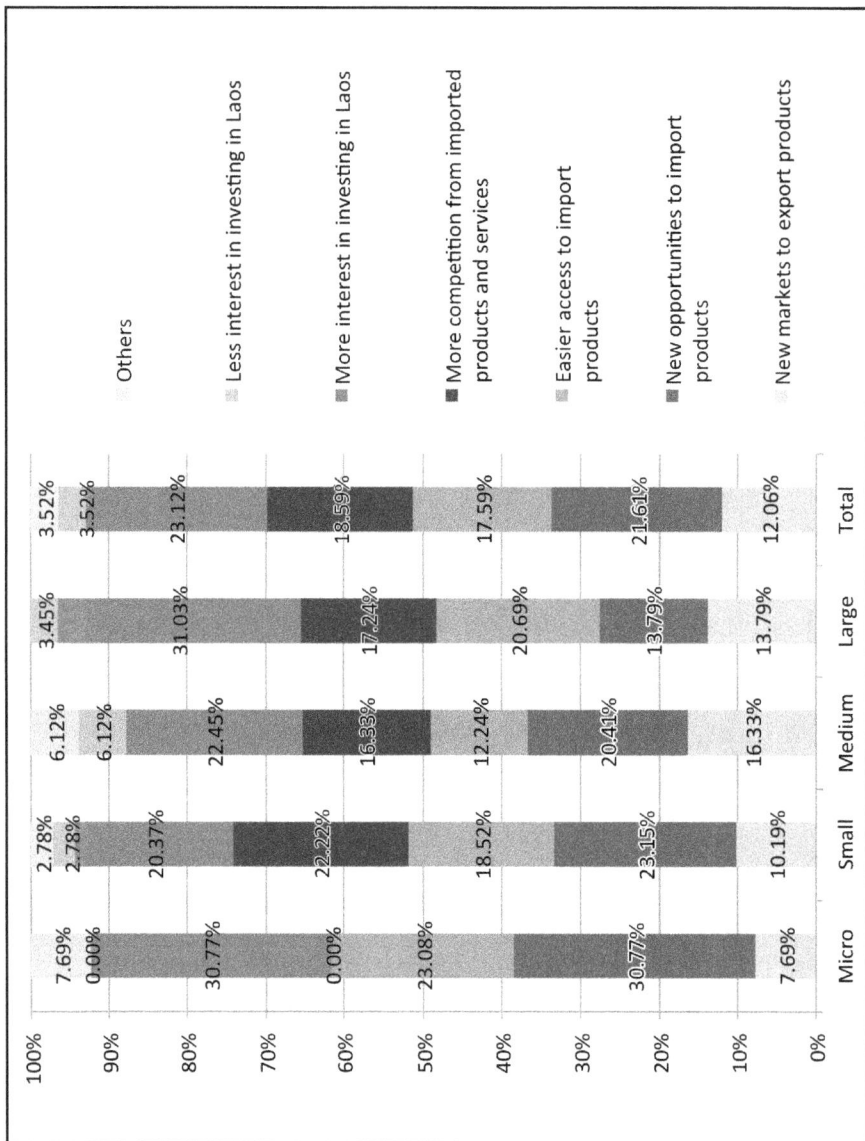

Legend:
- Others
- Less interest in investing in Laos
- More interest in investing in Laos
- More competition from imported products and services
- Easier access to import products
- New opportunities to import products
- New markets to export products

	Micro	Small	Medium	Large	Total
	7.69%	2.78%	6.12%	3.45%	3.52%
	0.00%	2.78%	6.12%		3.52%
	30.77%	20.37%	22.45%	31.03%	23.12%
	0.00%	22.22%	16.33%	17.24%	18.59%
	23.08%	18.52%	12.24%	20.69%	17.59%
	30.77%	23.15%	20.41%	13.79%	21.61%
	7.69%	10.19%	16.33%	13.79%	12.06%

Source: Enterprise survey from GIZ in 2013.

APPENDIX 4.11
Specific Impacts of WTO

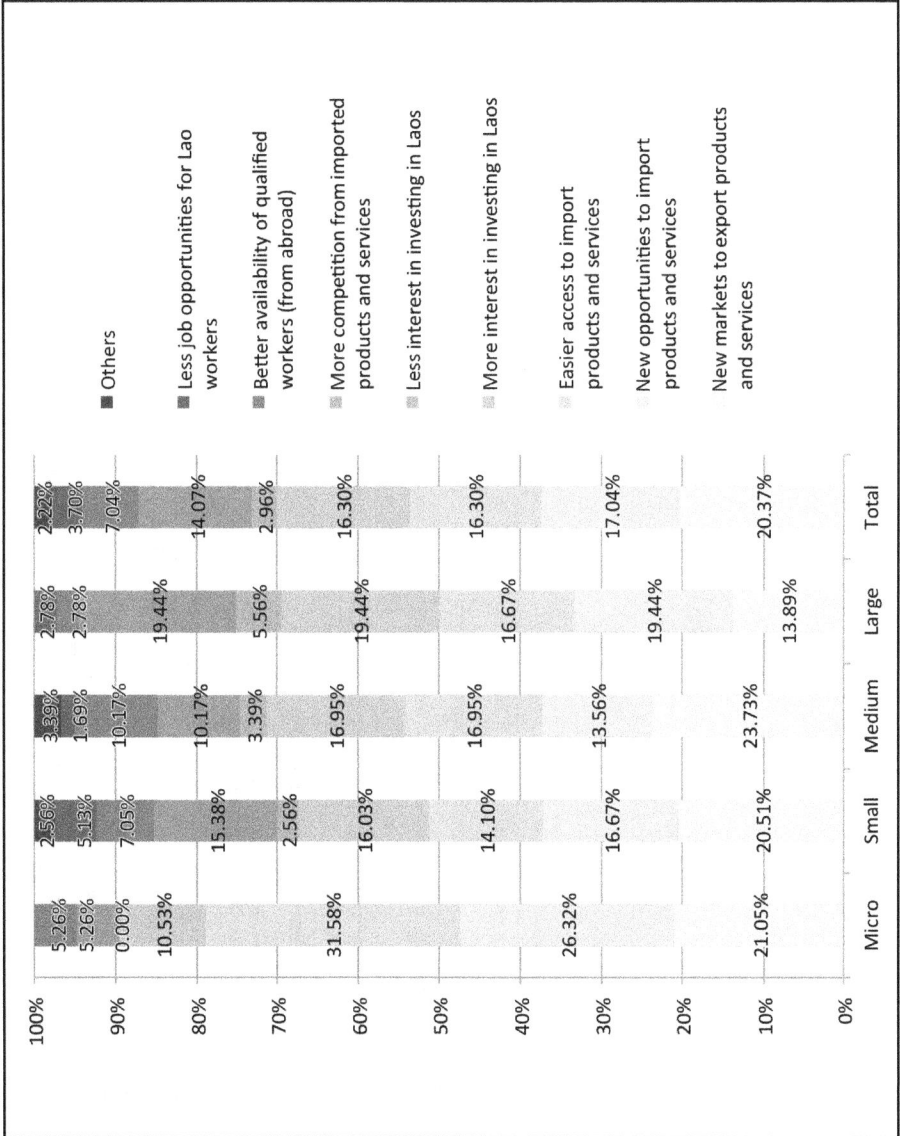

Legend:
- Others
- Less job opportunities for Lao workers
- Better availability of qualified workers (from abroad)
- More competition from imported products and services
- Less interest in investing in Laos
- More interest in investing in Laos
- Easier access to import products and services
- New opportunities to import products and services
- New markets to export products and services

	Micro	Small	Medium	Large	Total
Others	5.26%	2.56%	3.39%	2.78%	2.22%
Less job opportunities for Lao workers	5.26%	5.13%	1.69%	2.78%	3.70%
Better availability of qualified workers (from abroad)	0.00%	7.05%	10.17%	19.44%	7.04%
More competition from imported products and services	10.53%	15.38%	10.17%		14.07%
	31.58%	2.56%	3.39%	5.56%	2.96%
Less interest in investing in Laos		16.03%	16.95%	19.44%	16.30%
More interest in investing in Laos	26.32%	14.10%	16.95%	16.67%	16.30%
Easier access to import products and services		16.67%	13.56%		17.04%
New opportunities to import products and services	21.05%	20.51%	23.73%	19.44%	20.37%
New markets to export products and services				13.89%	

Source: Enterprise survey from GIZ in 2013.

APPENDIX 4.12

Variables and Their Definitions For Using on the Logit Model

Variables	Definition of Variables		Expected Sign
Dependent variable			
Exports	The products of SMEs are exports (provides to customers abroad)	1 = if exports; 0 = otherwise	
Independent variables			
Characteristics of the Enterpreneur (COE)			
AOB	Age of owner-manager	year	Positive
GOM	Gender of owner-manager	1 = female; 0 = otherwise	Negative
NOM	Nationality of owner-manager	1 = Lao; 0 = otherwise	Positive
EDU1	Educational level of owner-management as completed upper secondary	1 = yes; 0 = otherwise	Positive
EDU2	Educational level of owner-management as completed vocational/technical	1 = yes; 0 = otherwise	Positive
EDU3	Educational level of owner-management as completed university and higher	1 = yes; 0 = otherwise	Positive
BRB	Before starting current business the owner ran another business but it closed	1 = yes; 0 = otherwise	Negative
BTR	Before starting current business the owner was trader	1 = yes; 0 = otherwise	Positive
BWF	Before starting current business the owner worked for family business	1 = yes; 0 = otherwise	Positive
BEA	Before starting current business the owner was employed by another business	1 = yes; 0 = otherwise	Positive
OIP	Owner enterprise has investment plan for business	1 = yes; 0 = otherwise	Positive
OLR	Owner-manager knows business laws and regulations relating to the business	1 = yes; 0 = otherwise	Positive

Training Skills for Owner-manager (TSO)

Code	Description	Coding	Expected sign
OCS	Owner-manager completed vocational and technical skills training	1 = yes; 0 = otherwise	Positive
OTS	Owner-manager had management training when started business	1 = yes; 0 = otherwise	Positive
OMT	Owner-manager had management training since started business	1 = yes; 0 = otherwise	Positive
OAD	Owner-manager received some advice for developing the business	1 = yes; 0 = otherwise	Positive
OSI	Owner-manager wants to learn some skills in order to improve the business	1 = yes; 0 = otherwise	Positive

Characteristics of the Business (COB)

Code	Description	Coding	Expected sign
AFI	Age of the firm at the time of incorporation	year	Positive
EML	Enterprise as member business organization of LNCCI	1 = yes; 0 = otherwise	Positive
EMC	Enterprise as member business organization of Provincial CCI	1 = yes; 0 = otherwise	Positive
EMA	Enterprise as member business organization of Business Association	1 = yes; 0 = otherwise	Positive
EMG	Enterprise as member business organization of Business Group	1 = yes; 0 = otherwise	Positive
FEI	Enterprise as individual enterprise form	1 = yes; 0 = otherwise	Negative
FES	Enterprise as sole limited company form	1 = yes; 0 = otherwise	Positive
FEL	Enterprise as limited company form	1 = yes; 0 = otherwise	Positive
FEM	Enterprise as mixed company form	1 = yes; 0 = otherwise	Positive
EPC	Enterprise as public company form	1 = yes; 0 = otherwise	Negative
ESJ	Enterprise status as joint-venture	1 = yes; 0 = otherwise	Positive
EOF	Enterprise status as wholly owned foreign	1 = yes; 0 = otherwise	Positive

Enterprise/Business Growth (EBG)

Code	Description	Coding	Expected sign
OUI	Output was increased (in 2013 compared to 2012)	1 = yes; 0 = otherwise	Positive
TUI	Turnover has increased (in 2013 compared to 2012)	1 = yes; 0 = otherwise	Positive
PRI	Profit has increased (in 2013 compared to 2012)	1 = yes; 0 = otherwise	Positive

APPENDIX 4.12 *(continued)*

Variables	Definition of Variables		Expected Sign
Independent variables			
Size of Enterprise/Business (SEB)			
NOE1	Number of employees (5–19 persons)	1 = yes; 0 = otherwise	Negative
NOE2	Number of employees (20–99 persons)	1 = yes; 0 = otherwise	Positive
NOE3	Number of employees (more than 99 persons)	1 = yes; 0 = otherwise	Positive
PFE	Percentage of female employees	per cent (%)	Positive
ASS1	Company asset between 100–250 million kip	1 = yes; 0 = otherwise	Positive
ASS2	Company asset between 250–750 million kip	1 = yes; 0 = otherwise	Positive
ASS3	Company asset between 750–1,200 million kip	1 = yes; 0 = otherwise	Positive
ASS4	Company asset above 1,200 million kip	1 = yes; 0 = otherwise	Positive
Other factors (OFS)			
TUR1	Company turnover between 200–400 million kip	1 = yes; 0 = otherwise	Positive
TUR2	Company turnover between 401–700 million kip	1 = yes; 0 = otherwise	Positive
TUR3	Company turnover between 701–1,000 million kip	1 = yes; 0 = otherwise	Positive
TUR4	Company turnover of more than 1,000 million kip	1 = yes; 0 = otherwise	Positive
OEE	Owner-manager evaluates current economic situation compared to 2 years ago	1 = better; 0 = otherwise	Positive
IBP	The inputs were imported for business production	1 = yes; 0 = otherwise	Positive
EIC	Enterprise has used internet/email for business communications	1 = yes; 0 = otherwise	Positive

NOTES

1. The engine of growth during this period was FDI inflows into the mining and hydroelectricity sectors through production and exports. For a more detailed discussion of the impact of FDI on the mining and hydroelectricity sectors on the Lao economy, see Kyophilavong and Toyoda (2008).
2. According to the World Bank (2010), the resource sector contributed about 2.5 percentage points to the growth rate from 2005 to 2010. The resource sector accounted for about 70 per cent of all exports in 2010, a share that is expected to increase under expected ongoing development in the hydroelectricity and mining sectors. Revenue from the resource sector as a share of total revenue rose to 2.6 per cent of GDP in 2010, a share that is again expected to increase.
3. A total of 722 samples were collected from five main provinces — Vientiane Capital, Champasack, Savannakhet, Luangprabang and Luangnamtha covering 23.82 per cent, 22.16 per cent, 21.75 per cent, 21.61 per cent and 10.66 per cent respectively of the total sample collected.

REFERENCES

Biggs, Tyler and Manju Kedia Shah. "African SMES, Networks, and Manufacturing Performance". *Journal of Banking & Finance* 30 (2006): 3043–66.

Bird, Kelly and Hal Hill. "Tiny, Poor, Land-lock, But Growing: Lesson for Late Reforming Transition Economies from Lao". *Oxford Development Studies* 38, no. 2 (2010).

Corden, W. Max and J. Peter Neary. "Booming Sector and De-industrialization in a Small Open Economy". *Economic Journal* 92 (1982).

GIZ. *HRDME Enterprise Survey 2013 for Lao PDR*. Vientiane, July 2014.

Government of Laos (GoL). "The Seventh Five-Year National Socio-Economic Development Plan (2011–2015)". Vientiane, Lao PDR: Ministry of Planning and Investment, 2011*a*.

———. "Small and Medium Enterprises (SME) Promotion Law". Vientiane, Lao PDR: Lao National Assembly, 2011*b*.

———. "The National Growth and Poverty Eradication Strategy (NGPES)". Vientiane, Lao PDR: Committee of Planning and Investment, 2004*a*.

———. "National Growth and Poverty Eradication Strategy". Vientiane, Lao PDR: Government of Laos, 2004*b*.

———. "Decree on the Promotion and Development of Small and Medium Sized Enterprises". Vientiane Capital, Lao PDR: Prime Minister's Office, 2004*c*.

Hayakawa, Kazunobu. "Impacts of FTA Utilization on Firm Performance". IDE Discussion Paper No. 366 (2012).

Koenig, Pamina. "Agglomeration and the Export Decisions of French Firms". *Journal of Urban Economics* 66 (2009): 186–95.

Kyophilavong, Phouphet. "SME Development in Lao PDR". In *SMEs in Asia and Globalization*, edited by Hank ERIA Research Project Report 2007–5. Jakarta: The Economic Research Institute for ASEAN and East Asia (ERIA), 2008, pp. 191–215.

Kyophilavong, Phouphet and Toshihisa Toyoda. "Impacts of Foreign Capital Inflows on the Lao Economy". In *Empirical Research on Trade and Finance in East Asia*, edited by Toshihisa Toyda. Hiroshima: Hiroshima Shudo University, 2008.

Lefebvre, Elisabeth, Louis A. Lefebvre, and Stephane Talbot. "Determinants and Impacts of Environmental Performance in SMEs". *R&D Management* 33 (2003): 263–83.

Manchin, Miriam and Annette O. Pelkmans-Balaoing. "Rules of Origin and the Web of East Asian Free Trade Agreements". *World Bank Policy Research Working Paper No. 4273*. Washington, D.C.: World Bank, 2007.

Ministry of Industry and Commerce (MoIC). *Policy and Priority Task: 2013*. Lao: Enterprise Registration and Management Department, Ministry of Industry and Commerce, 2013.

⸻. "Statistics: Ministry of Industry and Commerce". MoIC website, 2011. Available at <http://www.moic.gov.la/statistic.asp> (accessed 20 March 2011).

National Statistics Centre (NSC) and United Nations Development Programme (UNDP). *International Trade and Human Development: Lao PDR 2006*. The Third Lao PDR National Human Development Report. Vientiane Capital, Lao PDR: NSC; UNDP, 2006.

Nazar, Muhammad Suhail and Hassan Mujtaba Nawaz Saleem. "Film-Level Determinants of Export Performance". *Internationl Business & Economics Research Journal* 8 (2009): 105–12.

Oh, Jeong-Soo and Phouphet Kyophilavong. "Does ASEAN–Korea FTA Reduce Poverty in Laos? The Roles of FDI and Trade Facilitation". *Journal of Social Development Sciences* 5, no. 2 (2014): 50–57.

Otani, Ichiro and Chi Do Pham. *The Lao People's Democratic Republic: Systemic Transformation and Adjustment*. Occasional Paper No. 137. Washington D.C.: International Monetary Fund, 1996.

Özçelik, Emre and Erol Taymaz. "Does Innovativeness Matter for International Competitiveness in Developing Countries? The Case of Turkish Manufacturing Industries". *Research Policy* 33 (2004): 409–24.

Pangarkar, Nitin. "Internationalization and Performance of Small- and Medium-sized Enterprises". *Journal of World Business* 43 (2008): 475–85.

Rosenbusch, Nina, Jan Brinckmann, and Andreas Bausch. "Is Innovation Always Beneficial? A Meta-analysis of the Relationship between

Innovation and Performance in SMEs". *Journal of Business Venturing* 26 (2011): 441–57.

Suvannaphakdy, Sithanonxay. "An Empirical Study of Trade and Foreign Direct Investment in Laos". Unpublished doctoral dissertation. Hiroshima: Hiroshima Shudo University, 2013.

Titman, Sheridan and Roberto Wessels. "The Determinants of Capital Structure Choice". *The Journal of Finance* 43 (1988): 1–19.

Tomiura, Eiichi. "Effects of R&D and Networking on the Export Decision of Japanese Firms". *Research Policy* 36 (2007): 758–67.

Ulloa, Alfie and Rodrigo Wagner-Brizzi. "Why Don't All Exporters Benefit from Free Trade Agreements? Estimating Utilization Costs". Mimeo, 2013.

Vongsay, Manothong. "Lao PDR FDI Policy". Investment Promotion Department, Ministry of Planning and Investment, 2013.

Vos, Ed, Andrew Jia-Yuh Yeh, Sara Carter, and Stephen Tagg. "The Happy Story of Small Business Financing". *Journal of Banking and Finance* 31 (2007): 2648–72.

Watson, John. "Modeling the Relationship between Networking and Firm Performance". *Journal of Business Venturing* 22 (2007): 852–74.

Wignaraja, Ganeshan. "Regional Trade Agreements and Enterprises in Southeast Asia". ADBI Working Paper Series No. 442. Tokyo: Asian Development Bank Institute, 2013.

Wilkinson, Timothy and Lance E. Brouthers. "Trade Promotion and SME Export Performance". *International Business Review* 15 (2006): 233–52.

World Bank. "Development with a Rapidly Expanding Natural Resources Sector: Challenges and Policy Options for PDR". Lao PDR Development Report 2010. World Bank, 2010.

World Bank and Department of Statistics, Laos. *Poverty in Lao PDR 1992/3–2007/8*. Washington D.C. and Vientiane, Laos: World Bank and Department of Statistics, 2009.

Yi, Jingtao, Wang Chengqi and Mario Kafouros. "The Effects of Innovative Capabilities on Exporting: Do Institutional Forces Matter?". *International Business Review* 22 (2013): 392–406.

5

GOVERNMENT POLICIES, REGIONAL TRADING AGREEMENTS AND ECONOMIC PERFORMANCE OF NATIONAL ELECTRONIC COMPONENTS SMALL AND MEDIUM-SIZED ENTERPRISES IN MALAYSIA

Rajah Rasiah and Govindamal Thangiah

1. Introduction

The importance of small and medium-sized enterprises (SMEs) in economic development is now widely acknowledged (Acs and Audretsch 1988).[1] However, despite the significant role they play, SMEs have historically been vulnerable to competition owing to their size disadvantage, especially in industries characterized by economies of scale. Although the evolution of science parks and university-industry research linkages have enabled SMEs to participate in intensive research and development activities, minimum scale efficiencies are still important in scale-based industries, such as automobile assembly, wafer fabrication, and integrated circuits and printed circuit board assemblies (Rasiah

2003). SMEs are also prone to market failures because of information asymmetries, especially when faced with weak institutions. There are also other impediments, such as limited access to finance, legal constraints, lack of skills and technological capabilities that limit the capacity of SMEs to compete with large firms. Despite these shortcomings, governments continue to promote SME development as they are not only competitive in scope-oriented activities, but also act as a conduit to stimulate entrepreneurship. The focus on SMEs has taken on a new dimension in Malaysia following the streamlining of trade and investment policies in the ASEAN Economic Community (AEC) that came into effect in 2015.

Hence, this chapter seeks to examine government policies to promote SMEs in Malaysia in general, and the influence of regional trading agreements (RTAs) on the export performance of national electronic components firms in particular. The in-depth analysis is confined to the electronics industry to obtain an informed industry-specific assessment of SMEs. National firms were preferred for this exercise because their participation in export markets is far less than foreign multinational companies (MNCs) that primarily engaged in export-oriented assemblies. Also, there is already considerable work on foreign electronics firms in Malaysia (Rasiah 1988, 1994, 1995, 1998, 2010; Narayanan and Lai 2000). Therefore, this chapter focuses for the first time on a large set of data on national firms. The rest of the chapter is organized as follows. Section 2 discusses the significance of SMEs in Malaysia's economy. Section 3 discusses government policies targeted at promoting SME development. Section 4 presents the methodology and data used in the chapter. Section 5 analyses the results. Section 6 finishes with the conclusions.

2. Significance of SMEs

Recognizing the important role SMEs play in economic development, the Malaysian government has introduced several programmes to support their development. SMEs have been targeted in Malaysia to perform a crucial role in generating employment opportunities, improving income distribution, increasing the growth of per capita income, and improving economic stability. Census data showed that there were 645,135 SMEs, which accounted for 97.3 per cent of business establishments in Malaysia in 2010 (DOS 2011).

Value added growth of SMEs recorded relatively strong rate of 6.0 per cent, which compared well against the 5.0 per cent growth recorded by the overall economy in 2014 (see Figure 5.1).

FIGURE 5.1
Average Annual Value Added Growth of SMEs and GDP in Malaysia, 2006–14 (%)

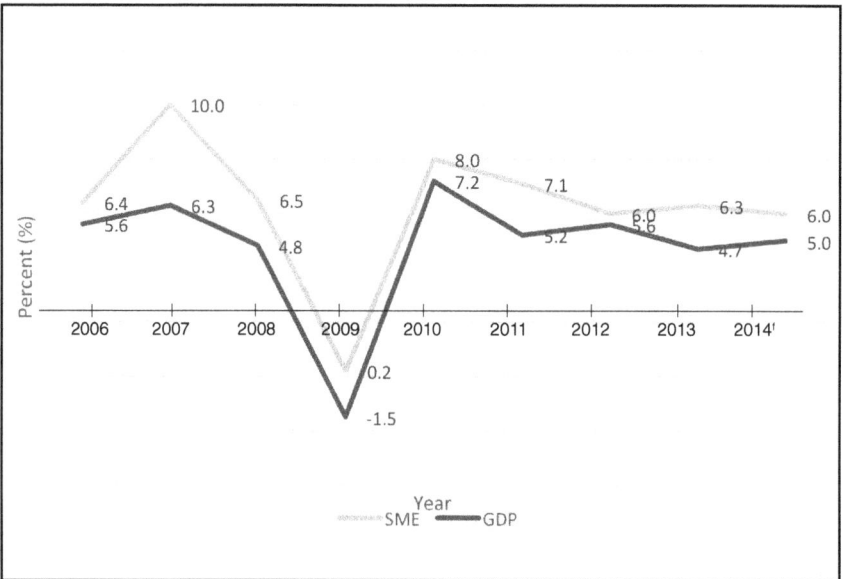

Note: f refers to forecast.
Source: SME Corp., *SME Annual Report 2011/12, 2012/13* and *2014/15*.

As a percentage of GDP contribution, SME value added increased from 29.4 per cent in 2005 to 33.1 per cent in 2013 (see Figure 5.2). However, SMEs' share in Malaysia's GDP has remained low compared to Japan, Taiwan and Hong Kong (OECD 2015).

Nevertheless, SMEs were the largest contributors to national employment in the period 2009–13, accounting for nearly 58 per cent of the total employment of 9.0 million in 2013. Employment by SMEs grew from 4.1 million in 2009 to 5.2 million in 2013 while that of large enterprises grew from 2.8 million in 2009 to 3.8 million in 2013 (see Table 5.1).

FIGURE 5.2
SMEs' Value-added Share of GDP in Malaysia, 2005–13 (%)

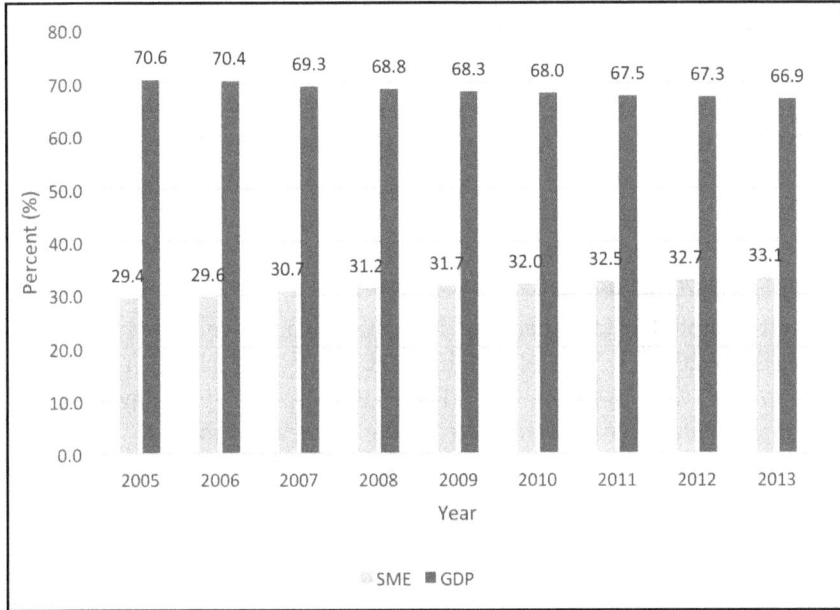

Source: SME Corp., *SME Annual Report 2011/12, 2012/13* and *2014/15*.

TABLE 5.1
Employment by SMEs and Large Enterprises in Malaysia, 2009–13 (millions)

	2009	2010	2011	2012	2013
SMEs	4.1	4.4	4.6	4.9	5.2
Large Enterprises	2.8	3.3	3.4	3.6	3.8
Total Employment	6.9	7.7	8.0	8.5	9.0

Source: SME Corp., *SME Annual Report 2011/12, 2012/13* and *2014/15*.

Thus, it is obvious that SMEs have not only played an important role, but have also become increasingly important in Malaysia's economy. Efforts to further synergize the role of SMEs in the Malaysian economy will not only offer them the opportunity to become as versatile and competitive as their counterparts in Taiwan, Italy and Japan, but also set the foundations for the harmonization of trade, investment and technology flows across the AEC. We will discuss SME development policies in the next session.

3. SME Development Policies

SME policies have faced significant changes over the years in Malaysia. While the legislative changes and coverage of services provided to SMEs have evolved considerably, we focus here on the aspects that are relevant to this chapter.

3.1. Institutional Support

The government established the National SME Development Council (NSDC) in 2004, which is the highest body that charts the policy direction of SMEs in the country. The SME Corporation Malaysia[2] (SME Corp. thereafter) was established as the dedicated body to formulate policies and coordinate the implementation of SME programmes in the country. SME Corp. also serves as the Secretariat to NSDC to ensure that the decisions of NSDC are effectively implemented.

In the manufacturing sector (including electronics), SMEs are classified as businesses with sales turnover not exceeding RM 25 million or full-time employees not exceeding 150. The government has allocated funds to support the development of SMEs (see Table 5.2).[3] A Master

TABLE 5.2
SME Development Programmes, 2014

Focus Area	Programmes	Financial Commitment (RM million)	SMEs Benefitted
Human Capital Development	61	162.8	127,594
Innovation & Technology Adoption	34	112.3	3,036
Access to Financing	45	4,254.6	325,183
Market Access	31	36.6	225,192
Infrastructure	12	110.8	258
Total	183	4,677.1	681,263

Source: SME Corp., *SME Annual Report 2011/12*.

Plan with goals, targets and action plans to enhance the contribution of SMEs to Malaysia's economic development was launched in 2012, which charts out the government's role till 2020. The higher growth achieved by SMEs over the overall economy has been attributed to the launch of a focused policy-driven approach by NSDC in 2004 and SME Corp's effective implementation of supportive policies.

The government's action plans on the development of SME support services in Malaysia have been entrusted to a number of ministries and agencies but SME Corp. coordinates these development programmes. Among the programmes under the governance of SME Corp. are the Business Accelerator Programme (BAP), Enrichment & Enhancement Programme (E²), 1-Innovation Certification for Enterprise Rating & Transformation (1-InnoCERT), SME Competitiveness Rating for Enhancement (SCORE), The National Mark of Malaysian Brand, Enterprise 50 Award Programme, Malaysia–Japan Automotive Industries Cooperation (MAJAICO A-1), Brand Innovation Centre, SME Expert Advisory Panel (SEAP), Skills Upgrading Programme, SME-University Internship Programme and Business Matching.[4] Meanwhile, the Technology Park Malaysia (TPM) and the Standards and Industrial Research Institute of Malaysia (SIRIM) have continued to provide start-up entrepreneurs with mentoring, training, networking, technical assistance and access to finance in their incubation centres. Under the Green Lane Policy, incentives such as finance, tax exemption and prioritized participation in government procurement programmes are offered to innovative SMEs that have been approved by SME Corp., the Malaysian Biotechnology Corporation (BioTech Corp.), the Multimedia Development Corporation (MDeC) and the Malaysian Technology Development Corporation (MTDC).

3.2. Connectivity and Coordination

To provide relevant information related to SMEs, SME Corp. has established the One Referral Centre (ORC) located in its headquarters in Kuala Lumpur. ORC is the focal point for SMEs to get business advice and information. As the Central Coordinating Agency, one of the functions of SME Corp. is to serve as a centre for advisory and information services so as to provide and disseminate relevant and updated information to the SMEs as well as to channel feedback from SMEs to related ministries and agencies. ORC is taking the lead in providing advisory and other support services, including business development services to SMEs. Among the facilities available in ORC are information kiosk, SME Toolkit Kiosk and resource centre.

E-commerce is widely used in business transactions and has been accepted as a new way of doing business in digital networks in Malaysia. The government recognizes that the promotion of e-commerce and enhancing its use will enable Malaysian SMEs to compete more effectively domestically and in the global market. All important and relevant information on SMEs can be accessed through the SME Info Portal,[5] which serves as the one-stop online SME node providing information on all programmes available for SMEs, such as access to finance, markets, infrastructure, technology and advisory services and information. SMEs can also obtain relevant information through the SME Corp. The conscious efforts of SME Corp to improve the registration process has enabled SMEs to obtain the registration certificate in one day while the registration process normally requires three administrative steps.

To encourage the establishment of new businesses, and particularly innovative SMEs, the government through the Malaysian Technology Development Corporation (MTDC), established the Business Start-up Fund (BSF) to fund new technology-based start-up companies. The Fund incorporates elements of loan and equity, offering companies flexible funding via convertible notes and/or preference shares. The objective of BSF is to support and encourage entrepreneurship and the creation of new strategic businesses that are important and potentially scalable, and to fund companies within eco-systems led by high technology firms.[6]

To provide a conducive business environment to enhance the competitiveness of firms, the Malaysia Productivity Corporation (MPC) had established a Regulatory Review Department in October 2010 to monitor, review and provide recommendations for smart regulations, and is targeting to substantially reduce the regulatory burden to businesses. Government agencies undertake consultations with relevant stakeholders as and when necessary during the planning stages of the drawing up of legislation and public policies. Many ministries have adopted an open policy and encourage feedback from both the private and public sectors with regard to problems faced on a daily basis.

3.3. Finance

The Central Bank of Malaysia is the central collateral registry office in the country. In addition, the legal framework of Malaysia allows firms to use movable assets as collaterals for loan applications, as well as uncollateralized loans. For instance, microfinance that is provided by the financial institutions requires no collateral in Malaysia. Microfinance is open to all sectors. Micro entrepreneurs involved in business for at least six months with a valid business license may apply for microfinance (financing up to RM 50,000). Minimal documentation is required to apply for such an application. What are required are proof of income, proof of business in operation, and utility bills.

The credit guarantee schemes offered by the Credit Guarantee Corporation Malaysia Berhad (CGC) are available to all viable SMEs nationwide. CGC was established in 1972 by the Central Bank of Malaysia with all the commercial banks as shareholders. CGC provides guarantee cover between 30 and 100 per cent of the loan amount, and the guarantee fee is between 0.5 and 5.75 per cent based on risk adjusted pricing. The interest rate depends on the scheme but not more than 50 per cent of the amount guaranteed by the financial institutions.

The Credit Bureau of Malaysia, which is owned and operated by the private sector, is another leading provider of comprehensive and credible credit information and ratings on SMEs in Malaysia. It is a joint venture between CGC and Dun and Bradstreet Malaysia — a global provider of credit information on businesses, and the Association of Banks in Malaysia to enhance SMEs' access to financing and to create a sound credit culture amongst the business community in the country. Endorsed by the Central Bank of Malaysia, the Bureau is essentially a platform for SMEs to build, maintain and enhance their credit ratings and ultimately facilitate wider and easier access to financing. The Bureau also assists SMEs by providing them with an avenue for recourse and ensures accurate and up-to-date information is reflected in their reports and ratings. The Bureau undertakes this role by generating independent credit ratings of SMEs from credit and corporate business information obtained from credible sources, such as the Central Bank of Malaysia and the Companies Commission of Malaysia.

The leasing activities in Malaysia are regulated by the Banking and Financial Institutions Act 1989 (BAFIA) that came into force on 1 October 1989. Leasing companies constitute a relatively small portion of the financial sector in Malaysia. The number of leasing companies registered increased to 227 companies in 2011. As at end-2011, the amount of SME outstanding balance for both factoring and leasing was only 0.7 per cent of the total amount (i.e. RM 128.1 billion) of SME financing outstanding (NSDC 2012).

The Securities Commission of Malaysia is the regulator for risk capital. The Venture Capital Tax Incentives Guidelines were released by the Securities Commission on 29 September 2009 to incorporate the new tax incentives for the venture capital industry. Under the Income Tax Order 2009, Venture Capital Corporations (VCCs) registered with the Securities Commission are eligible for tax exemptions for five years of assessment, subject to them investing at least 30 per cent of their invested funds in the form of seed capital, start-ups and/or early stage financing in approved investee companies (see Figure 5.3).

FIGURE 5.3
Sources of Venture Capital Funds

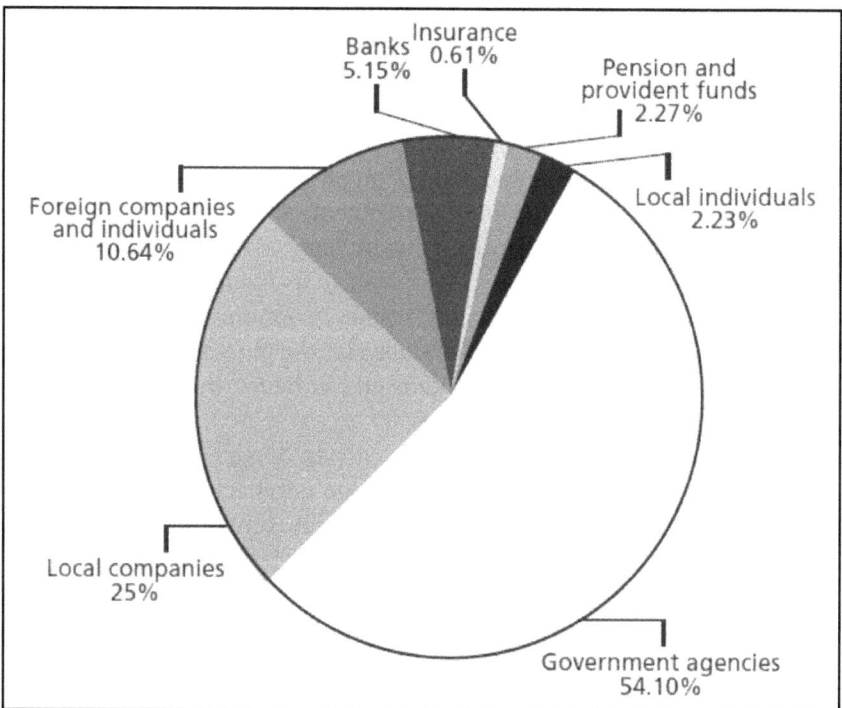

Source: Securities Commission Malaysia, SC Annual Report 2011 (Kuala Lumpur: Securities Commission Malaysia, 2012).

Bursa Malaysia restructured its business units in 2009 to unify the lower capitalized firms of the Second Board with the Main Market. The Access, Certainty, Efficiency (ACE) Market accepts SMEs from all sectors of the economy for listing, while Malaysian Exchange of Securities Dealing and Automated Quotation (MESDAQ) is restricted to the listing of high growth and technology-related firms. The listing requirements of ACE are less stringent than MESDAQ. Table 5.3 compares the listing requirements of MESDAQ and ACE. There is no minimum paid up or track record requirement for ACE.

Table 5.3
Incubators in Malaysia, 2010

Incubators	No.
NINA Members (Tech-based Incubators)	25
MARA (Indigenious/*Bumiputera*)	18
Banks	18
State Economy Development Corporations	17
MARDI (Agro-based)	10
Handicraft Incubators	9
Universities	4
MECD	2
Others	3
TOTAL	**106**

Source: National Incubator Network Association.

3.4. Technology

The government has officially supported technology development in SMEs since the introduction of the Industrial Master Plan in Malaysia in 1986. The government formed the Agensi Inovasi Malaysia (AIM) in 2011 to assist Malaysian SMEs to move up the value chain through innovation by taking advantage of novel methodologies, policies and outcomes (Malaysia 2013).[7] The SME Corp., through its InnoCERT programme, has since attempted to identify

and recognize the most innovative SMEs. These companies have been
further guided and coached to implement innovation systems, processes
and new business models.[8] Certified companies have been offered the
Green Lane Incentive that qualifies them to have fast access to funding
and market opportunities. To improve SMEs capabilities, a tool for
capacity building, known as SCORE, was also introduced. SCORE is
used to rate SMEs in terms of their capabilities in various aspects,
which enables SME Corp. to identify the strengths and weaknesses of
SMEs and recommend improvement measures. Indeed, the programme
allows SME Corp. to facilitate linkages between them and other
SMEs, and large firms (including MNCs) with those with export
capabilities to link with Malaysia External Trade Development
Corporation (MATRADE). Various efforts have been taken to promote
technological dissemination among SMEs and to stimulate technological
upgrading in SMEs. In addition, the SME Masterplan has identified
innovation and technology adoption as one of the most important
performance levers for SMEs with two high impact programmes
specifically designed to promote SMEs in this area namely, the
Technology Commercialisation Platform and Inclusive Innovation.

SME Corp. and various ministries and agencies, including AIM,
have taken measures to disseminate information on innovation
support services. However, the information that is available is mainly
targeted at creating awareness among SMEs on the importance of
innovation. Nevertheless, specific innovation advisory services for SMEs
are available through SME Corp. and MPC (via its productivity and
innovation enhancement programmes).[9] Training programmes have
been designed to improve performance excellence, process innovation,
customer excellence and management and performance development.
Indeed, the 1-InnoCert programme provides SMEs with innovation
support services whereas the SCORE programme provides support for
SMEs to assess their capabilities including its innovation capabilities.[10]
SME innovation support system is available through SME Info Portal
that has comprehensive information for various support systems.[11]
While much of these developments augurs well for SMEs in Malaysia,
the availability of experienced innovation advisors to review the
business cases and implement plans for the SMEs innovative projects
are still lacking. Several incubators programmes have been launched
and supported by the government to assist start-ups in the country
(see Table 5.3).

SME Corp. works closely with SIRIM to help SMEs in Malaysia attain product certification internationally. SIRIM is also the secretariat of the World Association of Industrial and Technological Organisations (WAITRO) and currently has 160 members in 80 countries. SIRIM, which is Malaysia's national standard development agency, is actively involved in international standards development with participation in over 80 ISO Technical Committees and Subcommittees. Consequently, a wide range of standards and products have been recognized and accredited in Malaysia.[12] SIRIM is well equipped with testing facilities and equipment to help SMEs.[13] Furthermore, efforts to develop Malaysian brands by the government, which began in March 2009, have helped SMEs build their branding efforts. A total of 59 SMEs have been certified with the National Mark of Malaysian Brand.[14]

The government strengthened the intellectual property (IP) environment in Malaysia through legislation and the opening of the patent system implementation agency (Chandran and Wong 2011). Malaysia has also joined the ASEAN IPR SME helpdesk to provide information about intellectual property rights (IPRs).[15] The Malaysian Intellectual Property Organisation (MyIPO) is actively involved in promoting IP awareness among SMEs in the country.[16] The MSC Malaysia Intellectual Property Grant Scheme was designed to provide subsidies up to 70 per cent of cost incurred for filing IPs. Indeed, SME Corp. manages reimbursable grants for the development and promotion of brands among SMEs. Malaysia Debt Venture Berhad will also finance SMEs wishing to develop IPRs. In addition, SMEs are allowed to assign IPRs as collateral and a total of RM 19 million has been allocated to create an IPR market platform and training for IP evaluators.[17]

Malaysia enjoyed broadband penetration of 60 per cent nationwide. The government has formulated the National Broadband initiatives with an objective to deploy high speed broadband rollout with a speed of more than 10 Mbps at strategic areas with high economic impact, especially in Johor, Klang Valley and Penang so that broadband facilities reached 60 per cent penetration nationwide in 2012 (Rasiah et al. 2014). Microsoft and SME Corp. have teamed up to provide cloud computing facilities for SMEs.[18]

MATRADE is the agency that is responsible for promoting Malaysian products in export markets, including those produced by SMEs. Two of MATRADE programmes assist SMEs to undertake activities to integrate into export markets — the Market Development Grant (MDG)[19] and

Brand Promotion Grant (BPG). For MDG, companies can obtain a 50 per cent reimbursable matching grant on approved costs of eligible activities. Meanwhile, for BPG, SMEs that are developing and promoting brands can apply for either a 100 per cent reimbursable grant subject to a maximum of RM 1 million per company per brand, or a combination of 100 per cent and 50 per cent reimbursable grants, subject to a maximum of RM 2 million per company per brand. Based on the Economic Census 2011, about 19 per cent of the total 645,136 SMEs have export experience. The preferential trading environment evolved by the ASEAN Free Trade Area (AFTA) and the formation of AEC in 2015 have already provided the fillip for integrating the operations of SMEs in regional markets.

The financial facilities for SMEs to export are available nation-wide from the Export-Import Bank of Malaysia Berhad (EXIM Bank), which was incorporated in 1995 as a government-owned development financial institution with a mandated role to provide credit facilities to finance and support exports and imports of goods, services and overseas projects with an emphasis on non-traditional markets as well as export credit insurance services, export financing insurance, overseas investments insurance and guarantee facilities.[20]

The Human Resources Development Fund (HRDF)[21] under the Ministry of Human Resources (MOHR) offers double deduction incentives to SMEs to stimulate formal training. Nevertheless, training providers are required to register with HRDF. The HRDF training programmes were found to have significant impacts on labour productivity (2.4 per cent), wages (1.5 per cent), total factor productivity (3.2 per cent), value added (3.6 per cent) and investment in machinery and equipment capital intensity (8 per cent).[22] Efforts have also been made to provide grants for training, especially for online distance learning and on-the-job training. The National Human Resources Centre was established in 2011[23] to provide training toolkits mainly on solutions for human resource practices for SMEs. This programme is useful as SMEs are generally reluctant to send their workers for training due to staffing problems. In 2011, RM 162.8 million was invested in 61 programmes that benefitted 127,594 SMEs. These programmes were implemented by MOHR through Pembangunan Sumber Manusia Berhad (PSMB). They are Retraining and Skills Upgrading programme (successfully trained 114,523 SME employees), Evaluation-on-Effectiveness of Training programme (a total of 157 trainers and human resource officers were trained), Master Trainer programme (successfully produced 50 training experts for SMEs in the various fields), SME Training Needs Analysis Consultancy Scheme, and SMEs Outreach Programme that is aimed at inculcating training culture among SMEs and establishing close linkages with private organizations and academic institutions.[24]

Entrepreneurial education in Malaysia takes place generally in formal settings through training institutes related to SME management. Nevertheless, workers get substantial learning from on-the-job training. Both government promotional programmes as well as conditions imposed by buyers and suppliers (including from export markets) have helped raise training in SMEs in Malaysia. Such initiatives have also reached the unemployed who are looking to enter the labour market.

It can be seen that the institutional environment in Malaysia has targeted SMEs for strong support in all the critical areas that support competitiveness. Electronic components firms are some of the major beneficiaries of these policies. Hence, we examine in this chapter the impact of RTAs on the export performance of SMEs in Malaysian national electronic components firms.

4. Data and Methodology

The survey was financed by the Economic Research Institute for ASEAN and East Asia (ERIA). Primary data was collected by two survey officers under the guidance of the authors. A stratified random sampling procedure based on firm size was adopted to gather data from the electronic components industry (MSIC code 21610–21639). Ownership was not used because the focus is on SMEs and none of the foreign firms had an employment size below 250. The data collection instrument used was supplied by ERIA. The analysis in this chapter is confined to 2014 as the information supplied by the firms on R&D expenditure and training cost were largely for only that year.

The survey questionnaire was sent to all 279 national electronic components firms in Malaysia with a sampling frame of 56 large firms (employment size exceeding 150) and 223 SMEs (employment size of 150 or less). The response rate was 92.9 per cent of large firms and 78.6 per cent of SMEs (see Table 5.4). We avoided using responses such as profits, a detailed breakdown of production costs and education qualifications of employees to ensure that the response rate does not

TABLE 5.4
Electronic Components Firms by Size, Malaysia, 2014

	Large	SME	Total
Questionnaires sent	56	223	279
Questionnaires received	52	174	226
Response rate (%)	92.9	78.6	81.0

Source: ERIA survey (2015).

fall below 70 per cent of the sample to meet the Cronbach-Alpha validity test statistics.

The sub-industries were classified by technological sophistication and product similarity as defined by industry experts from the pilot test conducted earlier. The largest group in the sample was component parts manufacturing where SMEs dominate (see Table 5.5). Indeed, 52.9 per cent of electronic components SMEs are engaged in component parts manufacturing followed by printed and flexible circuit board manufacturing (12.6 per cent) and smartcard manufacturing (12.1 per

TABLE 5.5
National Electronic Components Firms by Industry Breakdown,
Malaysia, 2014

	Large	SMEs	Total
Product testing	0 (0.0)	5 (2.9)	5
Component parts	11 (21.2)	92 (52.9)	103
Transistors, bipolar and integrated circuits	16 (30.8)	10 (5.7)	26
Smartcards	0 (0.0)	21 (12.1)	21
Displays, and flashers	2 (3.8)	6 (3.4)	8
Resistors, capacitors, connectors, cathode ray tubes and lead frames	10 (19.2)	18 (10.3)	28
Printed circuit and flexible circuit boards	13 (25.0)	22 (12.6)	35

Note: Figures in parentheses refer to percentages.
Source: ERIA Survey (2015).

cent). Only SMEs were engaged in smartcard production suggesting that this is an activity where scale is not important. Large firms are more evenly distributed but none are in product testing (stress and durability tests) and smartcard manufacturing. The largest numbers are found in transistor, bipolar and integrated circuit manufacturing (30.8 per cent), and printed and flexible circuit board production (25 per cent).

Data was analysed using the IBM Statistical Package for Social Sciences (SPSS), version 22.0. The univariate prevalence and descriptive statistics of variables used in the study are described in Table 5.6.

TABLE 5.6
Descriptive Statistics of Variables

Variables	Prevalence, n (%)	Mean ± SD	Minimum	Maximum
Type of Industry				
1 (1, 4 & 5)	34 (15.0)			
2	103 (45.6)			
3	26 (11.5)			
4 (6)	28 (12.4)			
5 (7)	35 (15.5)			
RTAs				
Yes	130 (57.5)			
No	96 (42.5)			
Firm Size				
Large	52 (23.1)			
SME	173 (76.9)			
IHRD	226	0.45 ± 0.348	0.0	1.20
FW	226	24.475 ± 24.86	0.0	86.4
Fema	222	49.108 ± 21.64	5.0	82.0
ET	226	12.677 ± 10.54	1.0	100.0
TEP	226	1.525 ± 0.76	0.1	3.0
XS	226	10.14 ± 22.91	0.0	100
XSa	226	12.5 ± 28.28	0.0	100
Firm age	226	14.5 ± 8.31	3.00	41.00

Note: SD – Standard Deviation.
Source: Authors' calculation.

The association and the significant differences of percentages between industries, RTAs (1 = yes, 0 = no) and firm size (1 = SME, 0 = large) were assessed using a bivariate analysis or a chi-square test. Using the one-way ANOVA test, the differences in mean scores of in-house R&D (IHRD) in sales, share of female workers in workforce (Fema), engineers and technicians in the workforce (ET), training expenditure in payroll (TEP), ASEANSALES, exports to ASEAN countries in Sales (XS) (%), and exports to Northeast Asia (China, South Korea and Taiwan) in Sales (XSa) (%) between industries will be examined. If the normality and homogeneity of variance assumptions of the test were not met, a non-parametric one-way ANOVA test, the Kruskal-Wallis analysis, will be performed to examine the differences in mean scores of IHRD, Fema, ET, TEP, ASEANSALES, XS and XSa among the industries. In doing so, if there are significant differences, a consequent Dunn-Bonferroni post-hoc analysis will be conducted to examine the pairwise comparisons among the industries. In addition, an independent t-test was used to compare the differences in IHRD, Fema, ET, TEP, Sales, ASEANSALES, XS and XSa between firms that reported to have used RTAs and those that have not used RTA, as well as between large firms and SMEs. This parametric test is done only when the assumptions on homogeneity of variances and normality are met. Alternatively, a non-parametric independent t-test, Mann-Whitney U t-test, was used when these assumptions are violated. All the analysis was statistically significant at 0.05 significance level. Since industries 1 and 5 have few observations with frequencies of 5 and 8 respectively, we integrated them with industry 4 resulting in a total of 34 observations.

4.1. Specification of Equations

We specify in this section two fundamental equations to test the relative importance of SMEs vis-à-vis large firms in exports and technology among national electronic components firms in Malaysia.

In the first equation we used in-house R&D (IHRD) in sales as the dependent variable with participation in RTAs, firm size (FS), share of foreign workers in the workforce (FW), share of engineers and technicians in the workforce (ET) and training expenditure in payroll

(TEP) as independent variables. The equations are as follows:

$$IHRD = \alpha + \beta_1 FS + \beta_2 RTA + \beta_3 A + \beta_4 FW + \beta_5 ET + \beta_6 TEP + \mu \qquad (1)$$

In the second equation we test the hypothesis that firms accessing RTAs are likely to export more to ASEAN members than otherwise. We also included FS, FW, ET and TEP among the independent variables.

$$XS = \alpha + \beta_1 FS + \beta_2 RTA + \beta_3 A + \beta_4 FW + \beta_5 ET + \beta_6 TEP + \mu \qquad (2)$$

We substituted exports to ASEAN with exports to Northeast Asia (China, Japan, South Korea, and Taiwan) in the third equation owing to the proliferation of China–ASEAN, South Korea–ASEAN and Japan–ASEAN free trade agreements. We also included FS, FW, ET and TEP among the independent variables.

$$XSA = \alpha + \beta_1 FS + \beta_2 RTA + \beta_3 A + \beta_4 FW + \beta_5 ET + \beta_6 TEP + \mu \qquad (3)$$

A generalized linear model (GLM) was used to examine the relationship between the dependent variables (IHRD, XS, and XSa) and FS, RTA, A, FW, ET and TEP owing to the non-normal distribution of the dependent variables. Since the outcome variables are continuous, a multiple linear regression is analysed. The standard errors of the respective regressions are computed using a sandwich estimator. Hence, the error terms are minimized and are considered statistically robust.

5.   Results and Analysis

We screened the data first to identify the variables that show relationship with the dependent variables of IHRD, XS and XSa. Hence, this first exercise focuses on descriptive analysis, both univariate and bivariate. In the second exercise we use the significant variables to carry out a multivariate analysis of influences on IHRD, XS and XSa. The multicollinearity issue was negated as the value of the variance inflation factor (VIF) did not exceed 5 or 10.

5.1. Descriptive Analysis

The sample is largely skewed towards industry 2 (45.6 per cent). Among the firms, 57.5 per cent have used RTAs, while 76.9 per cent were SMEs. The average ET, IHRD, FW, Fema, TEP, XS and XSa with standard deviation are 12.677 ± 10.54, 0.45 ± 0.348, 24.475 ± 24.86, 49.108 ± 21.64, 1.525 ± 0.76, 10.14 ± 22.91, and 12.5 ± 28.28 respectively (see Table 5.6).

Table 5.7 shows a significant bivariate relationship between the types of industry and RTAs at 1 per cent significance level. However, there was no association shown between industry and firm size, as well as between firm size and RTAs. Also, the bivariate association between the tertiles of XS and XSa and RTAs is significant at 1 per cent, though these variables are not associated with firm size. Since the normality test and homogeneity of variance were not met, a non-parametric one-way ANOVA test, the Kruskal-Wallis test, was used to assess the differences in mean scores of IHRD, FW, Fema, ET, TEP, Sales, ASEANSALES, XS and XSa among the industries. The analysis showed no significant differences among the industries in FW and Sales. However, there are significant differences among the industries in IHRD, Fema, ET, TEP, ASEANSALES, XS and XSa.

TABLE 5.7
Bivariate Association Between Industry, Firm Size and RTAs

Variables	Size, n (%)			
Industry	SMEs	Large	Total, n (%)	Chi-square
1	27 (79.4)	7 (20.6)	34 (100)	
2	84 (81.6)	19 (18.4)	103 (100)	
3	22 (84.6)	4 (15.4)	26 (100)	7.72
4	18 (66.7)	9 (33.3)	27 (100)	
5	22 (62.9)	13 (37.1)	35 (100)	
	Size, n (%)		Total, n (%)	
Tertiles of XS	SMEs	Large		
Q1	111 (76.0)	35 (24.0)	146 (100)	2.25[a]
Q2	2 (50.0)	2 (50.0)	4 (100)	
Q3	60 (80.0)	15 (20.0)	75 (100)	
	Size, n (%)		Total, n (%)	
Tertiles of XSa	SMEs	Large		
Q1	116 (76.8)	35 (23.2)	151 (100)	
Q2	22 (75.9)	7 (24.1)	29 (100)	0.038
Q3	35 (77.8)	10 (22.2)	45 (100)	

TABLE 5.7   (*continued*)

Industry	RTA, n (%) No	RTA, n (%) Yes	Total, n (%)	
1	31 (91.2)	3 (8.8)	34 (100)	
2	70 (68.0)	33 (32.0)	103 (100)	
3	6 (23.1)	20 (76.9)	26 (100)	44.52***
4	11 (39.3)	17 (60.7)	28 (100)	
5	12 (34.3)	23 (65.7)	35 (100)	
Firm Size	RTA, n (%) No	RTA, n (%) Yes	Total, n (%)	
SMEs	99 (57.2)	74 (42.8)	173 (100)	0.094
Large	31 (59.6)	21 (40.4)	52 (100)	
Tertiles of XS	RTA, n (%) No	RTA, n (%) Yes	Total, n (%)	
Q1	123 (83.7)	24 (16.3)	147 (100)	129.17[a] ***
Q2	1 (25.0)	3 (75.0)	4 (100)	
Q3	6 (8.0)	69 (92.0)	75 (100)	
Tertiles of XSa	RTA, n (%) No	RTA, n (%) Yes	Total, n (%)	
Q1	123 (80.9)	29 (19.1)	152 (100)	105.20***
Q2	5 (17.2)	24 (82.8)	29 (100)	
Q3	2 (4.4)	43 (95.6)	45 (100)	

Note: *** Significant at 1 per cent significance level, [a] Fisher's exact test was used to analyse the bivariate association since there were cells with expected counts of less than 5.
Source: Authors' calculation.

A Dunn-Bonferroni's post hoc test was performed (see Table 5.8). The following are the pairwise mean differences between industries for each continuous variable. The post hoc test revealed that IHRD is higher for industries 3 and 4 compared to industry 1, and is statistically significant. However, industry 4 has a higher mean IHRD compared to industries 5 and 2. Industries 2, 3, 4 and 5 have a significantly higher Fema compared to industry 1. Similarly, industries 4 and 5 have a higher Fema compared to industry 2. Also, industry 5 has a higher mean percentage of Fema compared to industry 3. The ET of industry 5 is higher than industries 1 and 2 and is statistically significant.

TABLE 5.8
Mean Values of Key Variables by Industry, National Electronic
Components Firms

Variables	Industry (Mean ± SD)					p-value[m]
	1	2	3	4	5	
IHRD	0.25 ± 0.322[ab]	0.424 ± 0.373[d]	0.65 ± 0.324[a]	0.67 ± 0.244[bcd]	0.42 ± 0.215[c]	0.000
Fema	26.47 ± 18.50[abcd]	43.88 ± 18.73[aef]	55.84 ± 18.92[bg]	59.87 ± 14.05[ce]	71.77 ± 6.71[dfg]	0.000
ET	9.74 ± 8.16[def]	8.73 ± 5.93[abc]	20.81 ± 19.34[be]	20.07 ± 11.58[cf]	15.20 ± 5.05[ad]	0.000
TEP	1.04 ± 0.802[abc]	1.36 ± 0.807[de]	1.68 ± 0.687[a]	1.95 ± 0.325[bd]	2.04 ± 0.174[ce]	0.000
ASEANSALES	1.47 ± 8.58[ab]	3.01 ± 11.45[cd]	17.98 ± 27.88[ac]	5.71 ± 20.08[e]	37.46 ± 32.65[bde]	0.000
XS	0.032 ± 0.13[abc]	0.13 ± 0.26[def]	0.47 ± 0.37[cf]	0.40 ± 0.44[ad]	0.38 ± 0.33[be]	0.000
XSa	0.032 ± 0.13[abc]	0.13 ± 0.27[def]	0.42 ± 0.38[cf]	0.35 ± 0.42[ad]	0.37 ± 0.34[be]	0.000

Notes: [a, b, c, d, e, f, g, h, i, j] The same superscripts across industries indicate the data were significantly different.
[m] The Kruskall–Wallis test analysed the significance across the different industries while Dunn-Bonferroni post-hoc testing was carried out for pairwise comparisons between industries. All p-values < 0.05 indicate significance.
Source: Authors' calculation.

In addition, industry 2 has a lower mean value of ET compared to industries 3, 4 and 5. Industry 1 also has a lower mean ET value compared to industry 4. Industries 3, 4 and 5 have a significantly higher mean TEP value compared to industry 1. Also, industry 2 has a significantly lower mean value of TEP than industries 4 and 5. Industry 5 has a significantly higher mean ASEANSALES compared to the rest of the industries. Industry 3 also has a higher mean ASEANSALES compared to industries 2 and 1. There is also a significant mean difference in XS and XSa of industries 3, 4 and 5 compared to industries 1 and 2.

Since the normality and homogeneity of variances assumption were not met, the Mann Whitney U t-test was used to identify the differences between the groups by firm size and RTA. Table 5.9 shows that there are no significant differences between SMEs and large firms for ET, IHRD, FW, Fema, TEP, ASEANSALES and Sales. However, there is

TABLE 5.9
Economic Characteristics of Electronic Components Firms by Firm Size and RTAs

Characteristics	Firm Size (n = 225)		p-value	RTA (n = 226)		p-value
	SME (Mean ± SD)	Large (Mean ± SD)		No, (Mean ± SD)	Yes, (Mean ± SD)	
IHRD	0.45 ± 0.35	0.44 ± 0.323	0.755	0.31 ± 0.31	0.65 ± 0.29402	0.000
FW	24.8 ± 25.29	22.7 ± 23.19	0.757	22.1 ± 25.52	27.6 ± 23.6821	0.000
Fema	48.3 ± 21.7694	51.3 ± 21.06	0.298	37.7± 20.0	64.4 ± 12.3205	0.000
ET	12.1 ± 8.8061	13.9 ± 14.10	0.314	8.4 ± 5.79	18.4 ± 12.6488	0.000
TEP	1.5 ± 0.7759	1.6 ± 0.71	0.656	1.2 ± 0.79	2.0 ± 0.3353	0.000
ASEANSALES	10 ± 23.061	12 ± 22.80	0.453	2 ± 9.43	21 ± 30.196	0.000
XS	0.24 ± 0.35	0.19 ± 0.30	0.477	0.024 ± 0.10	0.5 ± 0.35	0.000
XSa	0.22 ± 0.34	0.20 ± 0.32	0.841	0.028 ± 0.12	0.46 ± 0.36	0.000

Note: n – sample size, SD – Standard Deviation.
Source: Authors' calculation.

statistically significant difference between the dummy variable RTA and all other variables except for Sales. Hence, RTAs matter in ET, IHRD, FW, Fema, TEP, and ASEANSALES. Higher RTAs are associated with increases in ASEANSALES, ET, FW, IHRD, TEP, Fema, XS, and XSa.

Overall, FW, Fema, ET, TEP, and ASEANSALES show significant differences among firms that have used RTA instruments and those that did not use them. Hence, we use these variables in the multivariate analysis in the next section to examine the determinants of IHRD, XS and XSa.

5.2. Multivariate Analysis

Tables 5.10, 5.11, and 5.12 show the variables that are likely to have an influence on IHRD, XS, and XSa respectively. Table 5.10 focuses on IHRD, which is a proxy of firms' participation in the highest knowledge generating activity. RTA, TEP and firm age have an impact on IHRD. Firms that have used instruments of RTA significantly increase IHRD by 9.7 per cent compared to firms that did not. Also, a 1 per cent increase in TEP and firm age increases and decreases IHRD by 0.354 and 0.006, respectively.

TABLE 5.10
Fitted Estimates of Variables that have an Impact on IHRD

Characteristics	Coefficient ß,	S.E.	95% CI Lower Bound	95% CI Upper Bound	VIF
RTA					1.897
Yes	0.097**	0.0394	0.019	0.174	
No	(ref.)	(ref.)	(ref.)	(ref.)	
Firm Size					1.012
SMEs	0.035	0.0314	−0.026	0.097	
Large	(ref.)	(ref.)	(ref.)	(ref.)	
FW	0.000	0.0005	−0.001	0.001	1.051
ET	0.001	0.0018	−0.002	0.005	1.665
TEP	0.354***	0.0234	0.308	0.399	1.961
Firm age	−0.006**	0.0031	−0.012	0.000	2.648
Constant	−0.087	0.054	−0.193	0.018	

Note: ***,** Significant at 1 per cent and 5 per cent significance levels respectively; VIF – variance inflation factor, S.E. – standard error, CI – confidence interval, ref. – reference category.
Source: Authors' calculation.

Firms that used RTA instruments are significantly highly correlated at 1 per cent with XS compared to firms that did not, such that an increase of 1 per cent in RTA incidence will raise XS by 0.380 (see Table 5.11). XS also significantly increases by 0.3 per cent when FW rises by one unit, though it is only significant at 10 per cent

TABLE 5.11
Fitted Estimates of Variables that have an Impact on XS

| Characteristics | Coefficient, ß | S.E. | 95% CI | | VIF |
			Lower Bound	Upper Bound	
RTA					1.897
Yes	0.380***	0.1339	0.118	0.643	
No	(ref.)	(ref.)	(ref.)	(ref.)	
Firm Size					1.012
SMEs	0.183*	0.1108	−0.001	0.367	
Large	(ref.)	(ref.)	(ref.)	(ref.)	
FW	0.003*	0.0019	0.00	0.007	1.051
ET	−0.002	0.0064	−0.011	0.007	1.665
TEP	−0.211	0.1386	−0.505	0.084	1.961
Firm age	0.000	0.0076	−0.013	0.012	2.648
Constant	−0.604	0.3308	−1.253	0.044	

Note: ***, * Significant at 1 per cent and 10 per cent significance levels respectively; VIF – variance inflation factor, S.E. – standard error, CI – confidence interval, ref. – reference category.
Source: Authors' calculation.

significance level. SMEs compared to large firms significantly increase XS by 0.183, though this association is significant only at 10 per cent level. Interestingly, the intensity of exports to ASEAN countries rises when the share of foreign workers and SMEs are involved, though the association is only significant at the 10 per cent level.

Export intensity to East Asia (XSa) increases by 0.261 when the incidence of RTA instruments use rises by 1 per cent, though this association is significant only at 10 per cent level (see Table 5.12). In contrast, XSa falls by 0.232 for a 1 per cent increase in TEP incidence, though it is significant only at the 10 per cent level. Also, a 1 per cent rise in firm age will lead to a 0.06 per cent fall in XSa. FW and ET are not significant.

TABLE 5.12
Fitted Estimates of Variables that have an Impact on XSa

Characteristics	Coefficient, β	S.E.	95% CI Lower Bound	95% CI Upper Bound	VIF
Regional Trade Agreement					1.897
Yes	0.261*	0.1493	−0.032	0.553	
No	(ref.)	(ref.)	(ref.)	(ref.)	
Firm Size					1.012
Small and Medium Enterprise (SME)	0.105	0.1091	−0.109	0.319	
Large	(ref.)	(ref.)	(ref.)	(ref.)	
Foreign Worker (%)	0.002	0.0019	−0.002	0.006	1.051
ET	−0.004	0.0067	−0.017	0.010	1.665
TEP	−0.232*	0.1328	−0.492	0.028	1.961
Firm age	−0.003	0.0075	−0.018	0.012	2.648
Constant	−0.254	0.3393	−0.919	0.411	

Note: * Significant at 10 per cent significance level, VIF – variance inflation factor, S.E. – standard error, CI – confidence interval, ref. – reference category.
Source: Authors' calculation.

6. Conclusions

It can be seen that explicit development policies to support SMEs have evolved strongly in Malaysia to take advantage of the export opportunities opened up by RTAs. This is reflected in the rising share of SMEs' contribution to value added and employment in the country, including manufacturing. However, while SMEs' contribution to employment has exceeded that of large firms, their contribution to value added has remained small in the national economy. Nevertheless, strong government support to link SMEs with ICT networks, technical training and exports have reduced the disadvantages faced by these firms compared to large firms. The bivariate relationships show strong relationships between the variables of FW, ET, and TEP, and industry, firm size, RTA, IHRD, XS and XSa.

The incidence of participation in IHRD is higher among firms that have used RTA instruments compared to firms that have not and it is significant at the 5 per cent level. Also, the relationship between TEP and IHRD is statistically highly significant (1 per cent), demonstrating that firms that participate in IHRD undertake significant levels of training. Firm size is not significant suggesting that it did not matter in the capacity of firms to undertake R&D in-house.

The statistical results confirm an association between export intensities to both ASEAN and Northeast Asia and RTAs. This association is statistically highly significant with exports to ASEAN (1 per cent) and slightly significant with exports to Northeast Asia (10 per cent). The probability of SMEs exporting more than large firms to ASEAN is slightly significant (10 per cent) but is not significant with exports to East Asia.

Overall, the results show that SME electronic components firms in Malaysia have competed well with large firms to export. SMEs show a stronger participation in exports to ASEAN countries than large firms. The intensity of IHRD use did not show a bias towards large firms as firm size and IHRD did not show any relationship. The government's initiatives to support SMEs with ICT infrastructure and to promote trade may have been successful but a proper statistical analysis is necessary before this can be confirmed. Also, RTAs show significant importance as the relationship between firms using them and intensity of exports to ASEAN and Northeast Asia is positive and strong.

NOTES

1. While the evidence advanced by Acs and Audrestch (1988) is convincing, their claim that SMEs are more competitive than large firms lacks an understanding of economies of scale in particular industries (Scherer 1984).
2. The functions of SME Corp. include coordinating policies and programmes, providing business support, act as the centre for advisory and information services, data management and research, and as the Secretariat of the NSDC.
3. In collaboration with the World Bank, the Malaysian government undertook an impact assessment on 15 SME Development Programmes. The results indicate that every 1 per cent increase in programme assistance increases their performance by 1–5 per cent. In other words, the HRDF programmes have generated positive gains in SME performance. However, while the

impact of HRDF programmes on labour productivity was limited, they had no impact on wages.

4. See <http://www.scribd.com/doc/56613116/SME-Corp-Malaysia-Website>.
5. See <http://www.smeinfo.com.my/>.
6. See <http://www.nef.org.my/v_2010/financial-assistance/mtdc-business-start-up-fund-bsf/>.
7. See <http://innovation.my/pdf/AIM_NIS.pdf>.
8. See Rasiah, Rosli and Sanjivee (2011).
9. See <http://www.mpc.gov.my/home/index.php?kod1=k&kod2=events&item= 000096&sstr_lang=en&t=3>.
10. See <http://www.smecorp.gov.my/vn2/node/51 and http://www.smecorp. gov.my/vn2/node/48>.
11. See <http://www.smeinfo.com.my/index.php?option=com_content& view=article&id=1166&Itemid=825&lang=en>.
12. See <http://www.sirim.my/web/core>.
13. See <http://www.sirim-qas.com.my/>.
14. The National Mark of Malaysian Brand is available to SMEs in order to promote Malaysian brands that are recognized for quality and excellence. See <http://www.sirim-qas.com.my/index.php/en/our-services/national-mark-of-malaysian-brand>.
15. See <http://www.ukabc.org.uk/wp-content/uploads/2013/05/Malaysia-Factsheet.pdf>.
16. See <http://www.myipo.gov.my>.
17. See <http://www.mdv.com.my/v2/archives/news-post/budget-2013-venture-company-mdv-to-launch-intellectual-property-fund-for-smes>.
18. See <http://www.skmm.gov.my/Sectors/Broadband/National-Broadband-Initiative.aspx> and <http://www.smebroadband.com.my/broadband-packages/time-fibre-broadband-plan/>.
19. See <www.matrade.gov.my/en/component/joomdoc/doc_download/1147-new-mdg-guidelines-2012>.
20. See <http://www.exim.com.my/media-centre/annual-reports>.
21. See <www.hrdf.com.my>.
22. See *SME Masterplan 2012-2020*.
23. See <http://www.nhrc.com.my/home>.
24. See SME Corp., *SME Annual Report*, chapter 4.

REFERENCES

Acs, Zoltan J. and David B. Audretsch. "Innovation in Large and Small Firms: An Empirical Analysis". *American Economic Review* 78, no. 4 (1988): 678–90.

Chandran Govindaraju, V.G.R and Chan-Yuan Wong. "Patenting Activities by Developing Countries: The Case of Malaysia". *World Patent Information* 33, no. 1 (2011): 51–57.

Department of Statistics (DOS). "Data on Electric and Electronics Firms". Unpublished data. Putrajaya: Department of Statistics, Malaysia, 2011.

Malaysia. *National Science, Technology and Innovatioon Policy 2013–2020*. Putrajaya: Ministry of Science, Technology and Innovation, 2013.

———. *SME Master Plan*. Kuala Lumpur: SME Corp., 2012.

Narayanan, Suresh and Lai Yew Wah. "Technological Maturity and Development Without Research: The Challenge for Malaysian Manufacturing". *Development and Change* 32, no. 2 (2000): 435–57.

National SME Development Council (NSDC). "Economic Census 2012 – Profile of SMEs", 2012. Available at <http://www.smecorp.gov.my/index.php/en/policies/sme-statistics> (accessed 15 December 2015).

Organization for Economic Cooperation and Development (OECD). *New Approaches to SME and Entrepreneurship Financing: Broadening the Range of Instruments*. Paris: OECD, 2015.

Rasiah, Rajah. "Are Electronics Firms in Malaysia Catching Up". *Journal of the Asia Pacific Economy* (2010).

———. "Expansion and Slowdown in the Electronics Industry in Malaysia". *Journal of the Asia Pacific Economy* (2009).

———. "The Export Manufacturing Experience of Indonesia, Malaysia and Thailand: Lessons for Africa". Discussion paper no. 137. Geneva: United Nations Conference for Trade and Development, 1998.

———. *Foreign Capital and Industrialization in Malaysia*. Basingstoke: Macmillan, 1995.

———. "Flexible Production Systems and Local Machine Tool Subcontracting: Electronics Component Transnationals in Malaysia". *Cambridge Journal of Economics* 18, no. 3 (1994): 279–98.

———. "The Semiconductor Industry in Penang: Implications for the New International Division of Labour Theories". *Journal of Contemporary Asia* 18, no. 1 (1988): 24–46.

Rasiah, Rajah, Mohd Rosli Bin Mohamad, and Puvanesvaran Sanjivee. "Production Linkages, Technological Intensities and Economic Performance: Small and Medium Enterprises in the Manufacturing Sector in Malaysia". *Asian Journal of Technology Innovation* 19, no. 2 (2011): 279–96.

Rasiah, Rajah, V.G.R Chandran Govindaraju, Boon Kwee Ng and Saad Mohd Said. "SME Policy Index of Malaysia". Jakarta: Economic Research Institute for ASEAN and East Asia (ERIA), 2014.

Scherer, Frederic M. *Innovation and Growth: Schumpeterian Perspectives*. Cambridge: MIT Press, 1984.

Securities Commission Malaysia. *SC Annual Report 2011*. Kuala Lumpur: Securities Commission Malaysia, 2012.

SME Corp. *SME Masterplan 2012–2020*. Kuala Lumpur: SME Corp., 2012.

———. Annual Report, various issues. Kuala Lumpur: SME Corp., various years.

6

MYANMAR SMEs' PARTICIPATION IN ASEAN AND EAST ASIAN REGIONAL ECONOMIC INTEGRATION
With a Focus on Food and Apparel Manufacturing[1]

Thomas Bernhardt, S. Kanay De and Giles Dickenson-Jones

1. Myanmar's Historical and Macroeconomic Context

For decades, Myanmar's economic system has been characterized by central planning and economic isolation, the latter partly self-imposed and partly due to international sanctions that were put in place in response to military rule. Today, however, Myanmar is leaving this past behind and things are changing rapidly. The shift towards a market-oriented economic system actually started in 1988. Back then, a number of reforms were initialized, aiming at liberalizing the economic system, encouraging private sector development, and promoting external trade as well as foreign direct investment. These developments have gained momentum with changes in the political sphere where a transition towards democracy was initiated in the late 2000s with a constitutional referendum in 2008 and multi-party elections in 2010. The international community welcomed these reforms and gradually re-integrated Myanmar.

As a result, today there is widespread agreement that the country has great potential for rapid development in the future, in particular thanks to its vast natural resources, its abundance of (especially young) labour, and its geostrategic location (being a member state of the Association of Southeast Asian Nations (ASEAN) and bordering the two most important and dynamic emerging economies, i.e. China and India). In fact, since Myanmar's leadership adopted a market-oriented system in 1988, the number of private manufacturing firms has increased threefold.[2] At the same time, numerous challenges remain. Neither the economic nor the political transition can be expected to be easy and without hiccups. Myanmar is still one of the poorest country in the region. Its economy is dominated by agriculture, characterized by low levels of productivity, and hamstrung by underdeveloped infrastructural and financial systems. Moreover, despite the lifting of sanctions there is still a long way to go for the country in terms of integrating into regional and international economic systems.

Tables 6.1–6.3 report a number of different macroeconomic statistics that reflect both the positive developments that Myanmar has achieved but also the challenges that were encountered. Table 6.1, for example, shows that Myanmar has seen impressive economic growth. While more recent GDP growth rates did not quite match the two-digit growth rates recorded at the beginning of the millennium, they still remained at high levels and, in fact, accelerated again since 2010 (from about 5 per

TABLE 6.1
Key Macroeconomic Indicators for Myanmar

	2000	2005	2010	2011	2012	2013	2014
Real GDP growth (in %)	13.7	13.6	5.3	5.9	7.3	8.3	7.7
GDP per capita (in US$)	222	288	998	1,121	1,103	1,113	1,221
Total investment (% of GDP)	12.4	13.2	16.0	14.9	18.0	23.1	25.7
Inflation (in %)	−1.7	10.7	8.2	2.8	2.8	5.7	5.9

Source: IMF World Economic Outlook database, April 2015.

cent to around 8 per cent per year). This has also led to a tremendous increase in average income per capita, with GDP per capita quintupling from a mere US$222 in 2000 to US$1,221 in 2014. Simultaneously, investment has grown, raising its share in GDP from a low 12 per cent in the year 2000 to a promising 26 per cent in 2014. In some sense, this growing investment also reflects the increased confidence in the future of Myanmar's economy. In its latest Article IV Consultation report for Myanmar, the International Monetary Fund (IMF) estimated that Myanmar's economy has again grown by 6.7 per cent this fiscal year (FY 2017/18) and that it will grow at a similar rate next year, thanks to strong domestic demand and spurred by rapid expansion of credit to the private sector which in FY 2016/17 grew by 34 per cent. At the same time, however, this economic dynamism, together with expansionary macroeconomic policies (see below), has resulted in strong inflationary pressures. The annual inflation rate peaked at 10 per cent in FY 2015/16 before moderating to 6.8 per cent in FY 2016/17 and 5.1 per cent in FY 2017/18. However, the IMF projects it to increase again to around 6 per cent in the coming FYs (IMF 2018). Overall, medium- to long-term prospects remain "favourable", provided structural reforms, foreign direct investment and macroeconomic stability continued (IMF 2018). In fact, the World Bank (2015a) reckons that Myanmar is likely to be the world's fourth fastest growing economy until 2017.

Meanwhile, Table 6.2 displays how the government's role in the economy has developed in the last 15 years. In the year 2000, government revenue corresponded to a meagre 12 per cent of GDP. At the same

TABLE 6.2
Myanmar Government Revenues, Expenditures and Deficit (% of GDP)

Country	Subject Descriptor	Units	2000	2005	2010	2011	2012	2013	2014	2015	2016	2017
Myanmar	General government revenue	Per cent of GDP	12.0	10.5	9.1	9.8	19.0	20.1	22.0	18.7	18.8	18.0
Myanmar	General government total expenditure	Per cent of GDP	19.2	13.2	14.6	13.4	18.1	21.4	22.9	23.2	21.3	20.8
Myanmar	General government net lending/borrowing	Per cent of GDP	−7.1	−2.7	−5.5	−3.5	0.9	−1.3	−0.9	−4.4	−2.5	−2.7

Source: International Monetary Fund, World Economic Outlook database, October 2018.

time, government expenditure amounted to 19 per cent of GDP, leaving a large funding gap of over 7 per cent of GDP. On the positive side, Myanmar's government has since managed to significantly increase its tax collection, with its revenues in 2017 corresponding to almost a fifth (namely 18 per cent) of GDP. Moreover, this expansionary fiscal policy has also supported Myanmar's impressive economic growth record described above. However, on the negative side, in all the years since 2000, except 2012, Myanmar's government has not managed to match its expenditures with its revenues. That is, with the exception of 2012, there has not been a single year where Myanmar's government has managed to balance its budget so that it has been running a fiscal deficit ever since the turn of the millennium. The IMF reports that Myanmar's fiscal deficit for the FY 2016/17 was 2.5 per cent of GDP, a consolidation compared to the election year deficit of about 4.4 per cent of GDP in 2015/16, but it predicts that as a result of continuing expansionary fiscal policies, Myanmar will again increase its fiscal deficit to reach around 4 per cent of GDP in the next few years to come. As deficits continue to grow, the Central Bank of Myanmar (CBM) will be required to provide declining but still significant financing for this funding gap while credit growth will also accelerate, resulting in continuous inflationary pressures (IMF 2018).

Looking at Myanmar's international economic transactions reveals a mixed picture (see Table 6.3). On the one hand, exports have expanded very fast, in many years even at two-digit rates. On the other hand, imports have grown even faster, especially since 2006 which is the last year in which Myanmar recorded a current account surplus. That is, Myanmar's current account has been in deficit for a decade and, even

TABLE 6.3
International Transactions: Myanmar's Current Account

	2000	2005	2010	2011	2012	2013	2014
Annual growth of imports (in %)	−2.8	0.8	14.7	23.0	17.2	13.4	21.0
Annual growth of exports (in %)	17.8	15.3	10.3	9.6	5.0	12.3	13.1
Current account balance (in billion US$)	−0.6	0.8	−0.6	−1.1	−2.4	−2.9	−4.5
Current account balance (% of GDP)	−5.9	6.1	−1.2	−1.9	−4.3	−5.1	−7.2

Source: IMF World Economic Outlook database, April 2015.

worse, this deficit has been growing in the last couple of years, reaching 7.2 per cent of GDP in 2014. While this trend of a *growing* deficit is not expected to continue, the IMF forecasts a *persistent* current account deficit of more than 5 per cent of GDP for FYs 2017/18 and 2018/19, with foreign currency reserves falling to the equivalent of just 3 months of Myanmar imports (IMF 2018). As a result, the exchange rate has been under strong downward pressure, with CBM data[3] showing the Myanmar Kyat depreciating by more than 60 per cent vis-à-vis the US dollar over the last five years.

The previous paragraphs have provided a snapshot of the political and macroeconomic context in which Myanmar SMEs operate today. As has been highlighted, a lot of positive developments have taken place; at the same time, there are certain macroeconomic risks related to high inflation and the rapid depreciation of the kyat. Moreover, the recent elections had created some political uncertainty and worries about stability and the continuation of economic reforms. However, the unambiguous election results and the landslide victory by Aung San Suu Kyi's National League for Democracy (NLD) have helped to ease concerns and raised the hope of stability among both local and foreign business communities (Hammond 2015*a*, 2015*b*; Chan Mya Htwe 2015; Htin Lin Aung 2015; Kyaw Hsu Mon 2015). Finally, the launch of the ASEAN Economic Community (AEC) at the end of 2015 generated both opportunities and challenges for Myanmar's SMEs. On the one hand, they have easier access to inputs and markets in the ASEAN region. On the other hand, they face increased competition both in domestic and regional markets.

It is in this context that the present chapter undertakes an investigation into the extent of Myanmar SMEs' participation in ASEAN and East Asian regional economic relations as well as the challenges they face and the policy support they need for deeper integration. More specifically, the chapter attempts to address the following four questions: What is the state of Myanmar SMEs' participation in regional trade, production networks, and investment activities? What are the enabling factors and obstacles to SME participation in regional trade, production networks, and investment activities? How have regional and preferential trade agreements affected SMEs' activities and performance? What are the policy imperatives at national and regional levels to promote active participation of Myanmar SMEs in regional trade, production networks, and investment?

To find answers to these questions, the chapter, on the one hand, analyses existing, publicly available secondary data while, on the other hand, draws on a new dataset collected through a survey among Myanmar enterprises conducted for the purpose of this research project. Using these two different sources of information is crucial as each data source on its own suffers from certain shortcomings: for the existing secondary data, there is only little data currently available; as for the primary data collected through the enterprise survey, questionnaires returned by companies were often incomplete as they were unwilling to provide responses on certain topics. The latter can largely be explained by, first, a certain survey fatigue among companies (who have been surveyed a lot in recent years by both local and international institutions) and, second, the specific historical context in which the survey was carried out where many firms were concerned and felt uncertain because of ongoing negotiations on a new minimum wage on the one hand and the upcoming elections on the other hand (see Appendix 6.2 for more details).

Overall, it is important to recognize that, mostly due to the country's political conditions and its many years of isolation, existing research on Myanmar's economic system and performance is quite limited. Our study, therefore, has to be viewed primarily as a baseline research and its main contribution will be to complement other efforts to take stock of, and improve knowledge on, Myanmar's current economic setup, with a focus on SMEs. It is essential to do this contextualization and framing of our research right at the outset to make clear the important limitations that this implies.

The remainder of this chapter is structured as follows: section 2 takes a bird's eye view on the external relations of Myanmar's economy and, using available secondary data, analyses Myanmar's trade and investment relations with the world, ASEAN and the East Asian region while also providing a quick overview of Myanmar's trade agreements and preferential market access. In section 3, the chapter starts to shift from an economy-wide perspective towards a firm-level perspective; it introduces the concept of SMEs, briefly discusses their role in the economies of countries around the world, presents Myanmar's definition of SMEs, and gives a summary on the availability and sources of information on SMEs in Myanmar. Drawing on these different data sources and particularly our own survey, section 4 digs deeper and presents key characteristics of SMEs in Myanmar. Section 5 focuses on SMEs' participation in the international economy; after some general considerations, it analyses Myanmar SMEs' integration into global and regional trade, production networks and investment flows. Section 6 concludes and presents some policy implications emerging from the preceding analyses.

2. Myanmar's Trade and Investment Relations with the World, ASEAN and the East Asian Region

2.1. Myanmar's Trade Performance in the Recent Past

Due to its political regime, Myanmar's overall level of integration in the world economy has been very low for several decades. Besides trading with its neighbours and other countries in the East Asian region, Myanmar also had relevant trade linkages with Western countries such as the United States (which was the most important market for its apparel exports, for example), the United Kingdom, Germany and other European countries. However, with the imposition of economic sanctions by the United States starting in 1997 and many European countries following suit, Myanmar's external trade saw a re-orientation towards its own region (Kudo 2008 or Martin 2012, for example). Two of the main reasons for this re-orientation were, first, the fact that the countries in the region did not follow the United States in imposing sanctions and, second, that many of them (most notably China) were experiencing high levels of economic dynamism and growth. Since 2013, however, Myanmar is re-engaging with Western markets in Europe and the United States.

Figure 6.1 shows the developments of Myanmar's total exports and imports of goods and services from 1995 to 2013. It reveals that Myanmar's exports to the world have continuously grown from US$1.1 billion in 1995 to US$10.4 billion in 2013. The same trend could already be seen in Table 6.3 which shows that exports have expanded very fast, in many years even at two-digit rates. The impact of the sanctions can be seen in that there is a small disruption of this trend in 2003, when U.S. trade sanctions were tightened. Myanmar's imports of goods and services from the world, on the other hand, have seen quite a different development. They by far exceeded exports in 1995 but were on a slight downward trend between 1995 and 2004, after which they started to grow rapidly (from US$2.0 million in 2004 to US$10.4 million in 2013) to finally surpass exports in the year 2011. As noted above, according to other data sources this gap widened dramatically in 2014.

FIGURE 6.1
Myanmar's Exports and Imports in USD Million (left axis) and as Share of GDP (right axis), 1995–2013

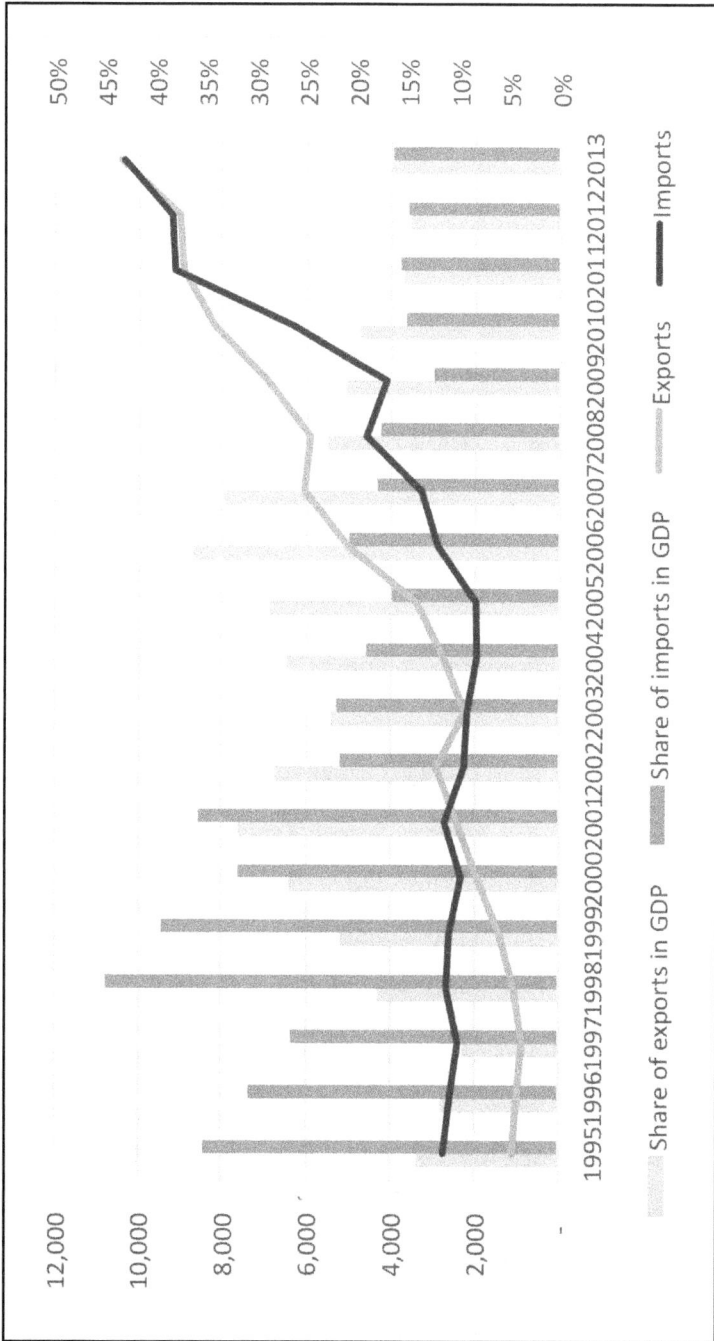

Source: United Nations Statistics Division (UNSD) National Accounts Main Aggregates Database.

In relations to total economic activity in Myanmar, both exports and imports corresponded to around 16.5 per cent of GDP in 2013 (see the right axis of Figure 6.1). This is quite low compared to other countries in the region. According to data from the World Bank's World Development Indicators (WDI) database, the share of exports in GDP ranges from 24 per cent in Indonesia and 28 per cent in the Philippines to 40 per cent in Laos, 68 per cent in Cambodia, 75 per cent in Thailand, 80 per cent in Malaysia, 86 per cent in Vietnam and a staggering 188 per cent in Singapore, the region's international trade hub. Similarly, imports amounted to 24 per cent of GDP in Indonesia, 31 per cent in the Philippines, 49 per cent in Laos, 68 per cent in Thailand, 76 per cent in Cambodia, 83 per cent in Vietnam, and up to 163 per cent in Singapore. Overall, this shows Myanmar's comparatively low degree of integration into the world trading system.

2.2. Myanmar's Trade with ASEAN

Myanmar joined ASEAN as a member state in July 1997. ASEAN is an important market for Myanmar's exports. As can be seen in Figure 6.2, over 40 per cent of Myanmar's exports are destined for other ASEAN countries. This is the second highest share among all ASEAN member states, only topped by Laos. Moreover, Myanmar sources about 40 per cent of all its imports from other ASEAN countries. Only Laos and Brunei get a higher share of their imports from within ASEAN. By contrast, Vietnam is at the bottom of the ranking, with merely 12 per cent of its exports going to other ASEAN countries and sourcing only 15 per cent of its imports from within ASEAN (see also Appendices 6.2 and 6.3).

Appendix 6.1 gives a detailed overview of ASEAN trade flows for each ASEAN member country as well as a number of East Asian countries. For Myanmar, exports to ASEAN grew from US$2,090 million in 2005 to US$4,633 million in 2013. In other words, Myanmar's exports to other ASEAN countries more than doubled during these eight years. While this is quite an impressive record, it is just the sixth-best export growth performance among the ten ASEAN countries as only Brunei's, Malaysia's, the Philippine's and Singapore's exports to ASEAN have grown more slowly during the same time period (see also Figure 6.3). In terms of export values, Myanmar ranks only

FIGURE 6.2
Share of ASEAN in Member States' Total Exports
and Imports, 2013

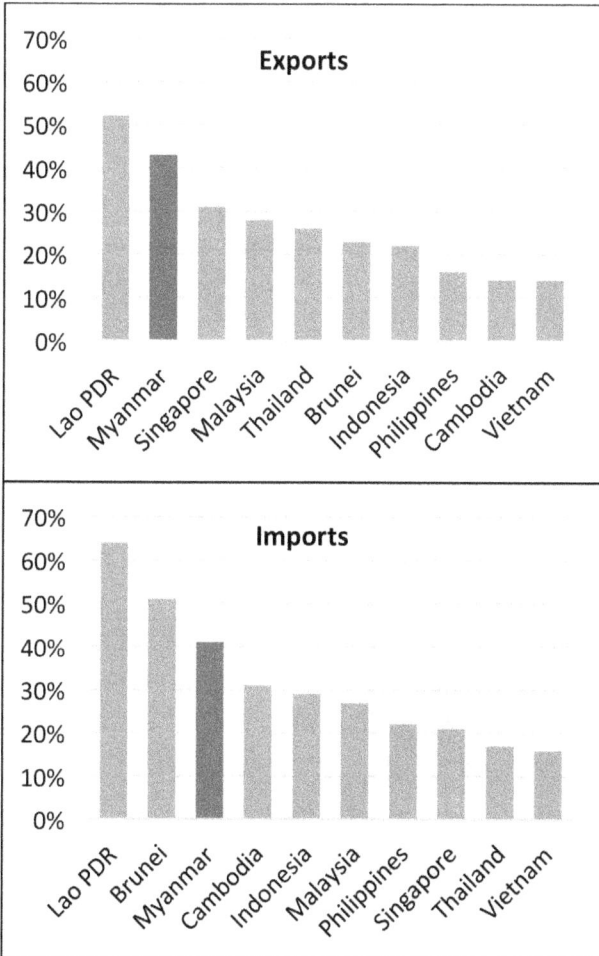

Source: ASEAN Merchandise Trade Statistics Database.

seventh among the ten ASEAN members. Its 2013 ASEAN exports worth US$4,633 million are higher than Brunei's, Cambodia's and Laos' but fall significantly short of Thailand's (US$59,287 million) or Vietnam's (US$18,584 million), for example.

Looking at the import side, Figure 6.3 reveals that among ASEAN members Myanmar has recorded the second-fastest growth of imports sourced from ASEAN after Laos. In fact, Myanmar's imports from ASEAN have increased from US$1,644 million in 2005 to US$7,559 million in 2013. This not only implies a growth rate of 360 per cent in these eight years but also that Myanmar's ASEAN trade balance turned from a surplus of US$446 million in 2005 to a deficit of US$2,269 million in 2013. This is a result of Myanmar's imports from ASEAN growing almost three times as fast as its exports to ASEAN (360 per cent vs. 122 per cent) between 2005 and 2013. Still, in value terms, its imports from ASEAN exceed only those from the smaller ASEAN members, i.e. Brunei, Cambodia and Laos, but fall considerably short of those of other members (e.g. Thailand's US$41,737 million or Vietnam's US$21,287 million in 2013).

FIGURE 6.3
Growth Rates of Exports to and Imports from ASEAN, 2005–13 (%)

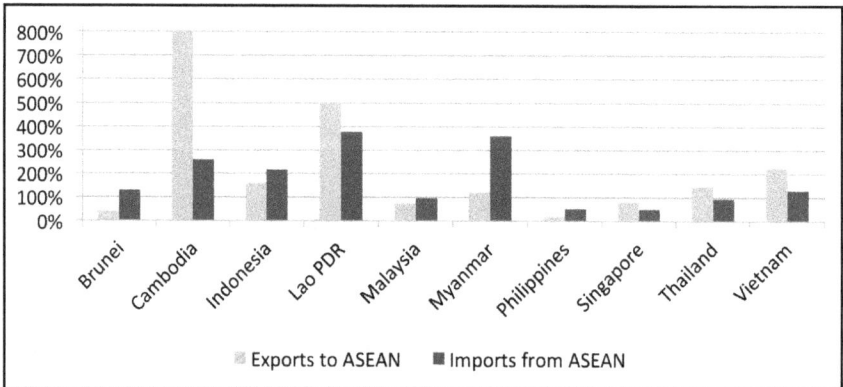

Source: UN Comtrade Database.

Since ASEAN member countries differ significantly in terms of population size, it makes sense to scale their exports and imports by population to get per capita export and import figures which are more suitable for cross-country comparisons. As can be seen in Figure 6.4, per capita ASEAN exports and imports are highest in Singapore and Brunei, partly reflecting their small population size. In Myanmar, imports per capita exceed exports per capita, reflecting

FIGURE 6.4
Per Capita Exports to and Imports from ASEAN, 2013 (USD)

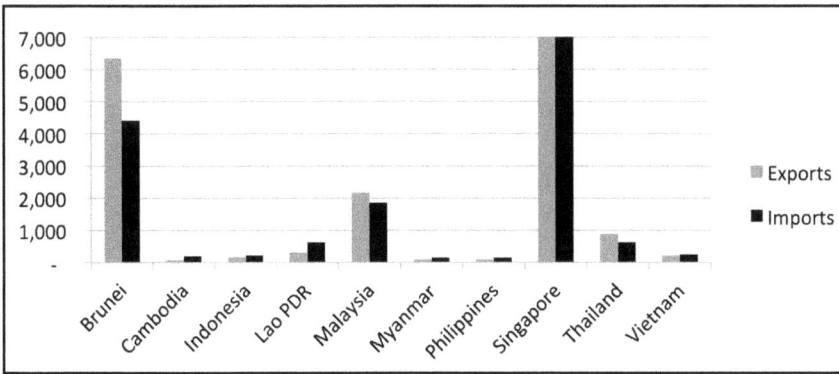

Note: For better legibility, the graph has been capped at US$7,000 line. As a result, the bars for Singapore were cut. Its ASEAN exports per capita actually stood at US$23,852 while its imports from ASEAN amounted to US$14,426 per capita.
Source: UN Comtrade and WDI databases.

the deficit in its trade with other ASEAN countries mentioned above. With Cambodia, Indonesia, Laos, the Philippines and Vietnam, these five other ASEAN members also have a deficit — which follows from the fact that some members' surpluses have to be matched by other members' deficits.

In any case, at US$87, Myanmar's ASEAN exports per capita are the second lowest after Cambodia's at US$85. However, they have more than doubled since 2005 when they stood at US$42, almost closing the gap to the Philippines whose ASEAN exports per capita in 2013 amounted to US$88. Yet, Myanmar's ASEAN exports per capita are still much lower than Laos', Vietnam's and Indonesia's and a far cry from the levels seen in Thailand and Malaysia (see Appendix 6.2 for more details).

On the import side, in 2013 Myanmar's purchased goods and services worth US$142 per capita from other ASEAN countries. This is actually the lowest value seen in the whole grouping, although only narrowly falling short of the US$144 observed for the Philippines and the US$187 seen in Cambodia. At the same time, Myanmar's ASEAN imports per capita have seen the fastest growth rate among all ASEAN countries, growing by 333 per cent since 2005 (when they stood at US$33) (see Appendix 6.3 for more details).

Overall, Myanmar is still a very small player even within ASEAN. As Figure 6.5 shows, the share of Myanmar in total intra-ASEAN exports (i.e. of total exports by ASEAN countries to other ASEAN member states) is a slim 1.4 per cent and, thus, only somewhat higher than Brunei's, Cambodia's and Laos'. This reflects that Myanmar is a newcomer to world trade but also to ASEAN trade, despite recent efforts of opening up and liberalization. All the evidence presented above suggests that there is quite some room for Myanmar to catch up and to intensify its trade relations with other ASEAN member states.

FIGURE 6.5
Share of Myanmar in Total Intra-ASEAN Exports, 2013

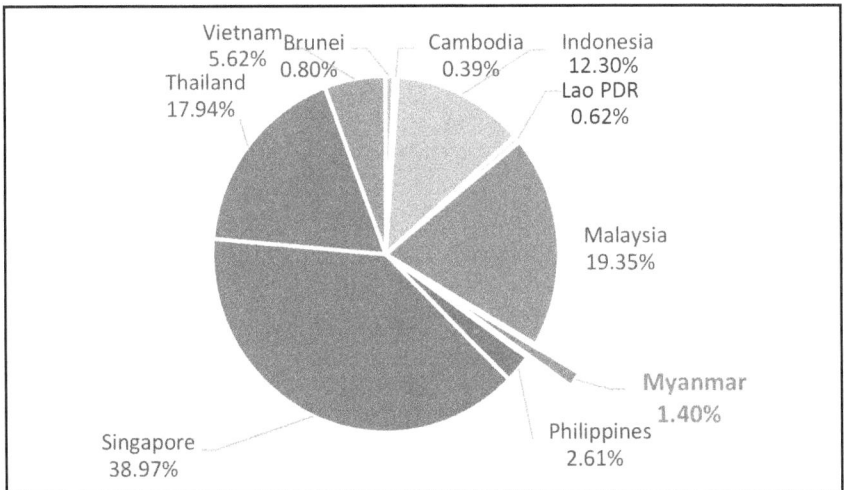

Source: UN Comtrade database.

2.3. Decomposing Myanmar's ASEAN and East Asian Trade

As can be seen in Table 6.4, Thailand is by far Myanmar's most important export market within ASEAN. In 2013, Myanmar exported goods and services worth US$4.033 billion to Thailand, corresponding to around 87 per cent of Myanmar's total ASEAN exports which stood at US$4.633 billion. Moreover, Myanmar's exports to Thailand more than doubled between 2005 and 2013. All other ASEAN countries are rather small export markets for Myanmar. Malaysia and Singapore each purchased Myanmar merchandise worth somewhat less than US$200 million in 2013 while Vietnam was the destination of Myanmar exports valued at US$124 million. However, while exports to Singapore and especially Malaysia have seen a rather uneven development, in the case of Vietnam there is a clear upward trend since 2005.

Looking at Myanmar's regional exports beyond ASEAN reveals that Japan, Korea and particularly China are important export markets in the East Asian region. In 2013, Myanmar's exports to China amounted to almost US$3 billion which makes it the second largest regional export market after Thailand. In the same year, Myanmar's exports to Japan and Korea were valued at US$759 million and US$488 million, respectively, which is more than Myanmar's exports to any ASEAN country except for Thailand. Moreover, Myanmar's shipments to these three regional markets have expanded rapidly during the last few years. Between 2010 and 2013, Myanmar's exports to China and Korea tripled while its exports to Japan doubled. By contrast, Hong Kong and Macao remain rather minor markets for Myanmar products (see Table 6.4).

TABLE 6.4
Myanmar's Bilateral Exports to ASEAN and East Asian Countries
(USD thousand)

	2005	2010	2011	2012	2013
Brunei	n.a.	n.a.	n.a.	184	857
Cambodia	422	52	132	114	263
Indonesia	14,155	31,847	71,279	63,533	73,151
Malaysia	133,585	229,229	233,749	183,412	198,161
Philippines	1,337	13,313	20,539	29,929	24,765
Singapore	107,866	82,941	85,905	79,035	179,231
Thailand	1,787,181	2,813,866	3,268,318	3,673,985	4,032,926
Vietnam	45,778	102,824	84,801	109,476	123,515
ASEAN-10 total	*2,090,323*	*3,274,070*	*3,764,723*	*4,139,667*	*4,632,869*
China	274,395	966,087	1,679,873	1,298,226	2,856,867
Hong Kong	48,315	41,086	47,463	47,042	40,994
Japan	203,572	385,935	590,014	672,031	759,296
Korea	56,257	159,892	298,681	351,164	487,769
Macao	33	1,920	2,706	2,585	2,241

Source: UN Comtrade database.

Table 6.5 shows that Myanmar's exports to ASEAN are dominated by raw materials and resource-based products. Actually, gas and crude

TABLE 6.5
Myanmar's Top-20 Export Products to ASEAN

Rank	HS Code	Product Group	Export Value in 2013 (mn. US$)	Share of Total Exports
1	2711	Petroleum gases and other gaseous hydrocarbons	3,674.73	79.4%
2	2709	Crude petroleum oils	152.81	3.3%
3	0713	Dried leguminous vegetables, shelled	137.24	3.0%
4	4403	Wood in the rough	130.17	2.8%
5	4001	Natural rubber, balata and similar natural gums	69.30	1.5%
6	2505	Natural sands of all kinds	35.32	0.8%
7	0306	Crustaceans	33.89	0.7%
8	1202	Groundnuts, not roasted or otherwise cooked	33.30	0.7%
9	7403	Refined copper and copper alloys, unwrought	32.54	0.7%
10	4407	Wood sawn or chipped lengthwise, sliced or peeled	31.77	0.7%
11	0102	Live bovine animals	31.76	0.7%
12	0302	Fish, fresh or chilled	23.90	0.5%
13	0303	Fish, frozen, excluding fish fillet	14.35	0.3%
14	1006	Rice	14.25	0.3%
15	2609	Tin ores and concentrates	13.41	0.3%
16	7307	Tube or pipe fittings	10.22	0.2%
17	4402	Wood charcoal	9.17	0.2%
18	0703	Onions, shallots, garlic, leeks and alliaceous vegetables	9.11	0.2%
19	2617	Other ores and concentrates	8.84	0.2%
20	9001	Optical fibres and optical fibre bundles	8.70	0.2%
		TOTAL	**4,628.98**	

Note: These figures are based on mirror data on product groups at the four-digit level of product disaggregation according to the Harmonized Commodity Description and Coding System, also known as the Harmonized System (HS); "nes" stands for "not elsewhere specified".
Source: UN Comtrade database.

oil account for over 80 per cent of all exports. Myanmar's top-20 export products also include agricultural and food products (dried vegetables, rice, onions, groundnuts, natural rubber), fishery products (fresh and frozen fish, crustaceans), forestry products (wood in the rough, sawn wood) as well as metals and minerals (natural sands, tin, ores, refined copper). Manufactured products are almost entirely absent from this top-20 list.

Similar to the export side, Thailand is also Myanmar's most important source of imports within ASEAN. However, Thailand is much less dominant as an origin of Myanmar imports than it is as a market for Myanmar exports. In 2013, Myanmar purchased goods and services worth US$3.8 billion from Thailand, corresponding to roughly half of Myanmar's total ASEAN imports which amounted to US$7.6 billion, while Singapore accounted for about 30 per cent of Myanmar's ASEAN imports. An additional 9.5 per cent and 7.4 per cent of Myanmar's ASEAN imports came from Malaysia and Indonesia, respectively (but these imports were valued at less than US$1 billion each). Since 2010, Myanmar's imports from these four countries almost doubled each. During the same time period, imports from Vietnam have grown the fastest (+364 per cent); still, Vietnam currently accounts only for about 3 per cent of Myanmar's ASEAN exports.

However, Myanmar's most important source of imports in the region is by far China. In 2013, Myanmar imported almost as much from China (US$7.3 billion) as it did from all the ASEAN countries together (US$7.6 billion). Moreover, Myanmar's imports from China have more than doubled since 2010. Yet, imports from Japan have expanded even faster during these three years, growing from US$262 million in 2010 to over US$1 billion in 2013, implying a quadrupling in the value of goods purchased from Japan. Meanwhile, imports from Korea have seen a more unsteady development. They grew between 2005 and 2012 when they peaked at US$1.3 billion before dropping to US$705 million in 2013, putting it more or less at par with Malaysia (see Table 6.6).

The composition of Myanmar's imports from ASEAN is quite different from the structure of its exports. First and foremost, it is much more diversified and much less concentrated in a few products. Table 6.7 reveals that petroleum oils again top the ranking of imports (accounting for 19 per cent of Myanmar's total ASEAN imports), but unlike on the export side (where crude oil dominates) in this case it is refined petroleum. The rest of the ranking mostly consists of manufactured products, including processed food and beverages, construction materials,

TABLE 6.6
Myanmar's Bilateral Imports from ASEAN and East Asian Countries (USD thousand)

	2005	2010	2011	2012	2013
Brunei	38	n.a.	n.a.	27	36
Cambodia	70,283	2	79	83	675
Indonesia	77,990	284,172	359,471	401,590	556,375
Malaysia	245,562	369,510	558,968	704,519	716,951
Philippines	9,087	11,233	14,129	19,132	22,682
Singapore	594,888	1,159,348	1,212,957	1,339,308	2,245,413
Thailand	704,851	2,072,955	2,845,830	3,127,141	3,786,941
Vietnam	11,978	49,521	82,458	117,813	229,747
ASEAN-10 total	*1,644,426*	*3,946,741*	*5,073,892*	*5,709,613*	*7,558,819*
China	934,847	3,475,524	4,821,497	5,673,756	7,338,689
Hong Kong	1,563	986	537	799	889
Japan	91,811	261,854	502,932	1,257,544	1,057,427
Korea	120,013	478,809	666,742	1,330,892	705,109
Macao	0	n.a.	n.a.	n.a.	n.a.

Source: UN Comtrade database.

TABLE 6.7
Myanmar's Top-20 Import Products from ASEAN

Rank	HS Code	Product Group	Import Value in 2013 (mn. US$)	Share of Total Imports
1	2710	Refined petroleum oils	1,450.88	19%
2	1511	Palm oil and its fractions	515.11	7%
3	9406	Prefabricated buildings	288.47	4%
4	2523	Portland cement, aluminous cement	209.43	3%
5	2202	Waters, including mineral waters	153.66	2%
6	2106	Food preparations nes	134.69	2%
7	8525	Transmission apparatus for radio or television	130.68	2%
8	1901	Malt extract; food preparations of flour, groats, meal, starch or malt extract	115.84	2%
9	7304	Tubes, pipes and hollow profiles	106.70	1%
10	3004	Medicaments	104.02	1%
11	8431	Machinery parts	102.29	1%
12	2203	Beer made from malt	93.52	1%
13	2101	Extracts, essences and concentrates of coffee or tea	92.38	1%
14	8703	Motor cars and other motor vehicles	90.57	1%
15	8471	Automatic data processing machines	80.25	1%
16	8502	Electric generating sets and rotary converters	73.93	1%
17	4011	New pneumatic tyres, of rubber	71.52	1%
18	8507	Electric accumulators	64.88	1%
19	2208	Undenatured ethyl alcohol	64.51	1%
20	8454	Converters, ladles, ingot moulds and casting machines used in metallurgy or in metal foundries	63.73	1%
		TOTAL	**7,474.13**	

Note: These figures are based on mirror data on product groups at the four-digit level of product disaggregation according to the Harmonized Commodity Description and Coding System, also known as the Harmonized System (HS); "nes" stands for "not elsewhere specified".
Source: UN Comtrade database.

machinery, vehicles, and medicaments. Interestingly, some of the products on this top-20 list are also produced in Myanmar itself, including palm oil, food preparations, beer, waters and also rubber tyres. This not only raises the question of why these products are sourced abroad and where local products fall short in terms of competitiveness vis-à-vis foreign products, but also points to possible import substitution opportunities.

2.4. Myanmar's Trade Agreements and Preferential Market Access

Myanmar has entered into a number of Free Trade Agreements (FTAs). As can be seen from Table 6.8, most of Myanmar's FTAs are through ASEAN. In addition to the ASEAN FTA, Myanmar is also a signatory of an ASEAN FTA with Australia and New Zealand as well as of ASEAN Comprehensive Economic Partnership or cooperation agreements with China, India, Japan and South Korea. All of these agreements were signed and have been in force since the second half of the 2000s. These agreements facilitate trade in goods and services as well as investment flows among signatories. In addition, Myanmar is part of trade negotiations launched between ASEAN and Hong Kong as well as through the Bay of Bengal Initiative for Multi-Sectoral Technical and Economic Cooperation (BIMSTEC). Finally, Myanmar signed a Trade and Investment Framework Agreement (TIFA) with the United States in 2013 which creates a platform for ongoing dialogue and cooperation on trade and investment issues between the two countries.

Apart from that, Myanmar also enjoys preferential access to the markets of a number of countries. As a Least Developed Country (LDC), it is a beneficiary of the Generalized System of Preferences (GSP) through which a number of countries offer lower tariffs for imports from eligible countries. For example, Myanmar benefits from the most favourable regime available under the EU's GSP, namely the "Everything But Arms" (EBA) scheme which gives LDCs duty-free access to the EU market for the export of all products, except arms and ammunition. The EU had temporarily withdrawn these GSP preferences from Myanmar in 1997 but they were reinstated in 2013. Similarly, Myanmar enjoys preferential tariff treatment under the GSP schemes of other advanced economies such as Australia, Japan, New Zealand, Iceland, Norway and Switzerland (with the latter three being European countries but not EU members). Canada and the United States are also operating GSP

TABLE 6.8
Myanmar's Free Trade Agreements

FTA Name	FTA Partner Country/ Countries	Status
ASEAN Free Trade Area (AFTA)	Brunei, Cambodia, Indonesia, Laos, Malaysia, Philippines, Singapore, Thailand, Vietnam	Signed and in effect since 1992
ASEAN–Australia and New Zealand Free Trade Agreement (AANZ)	ASEAN + Australia and New Zealand	Signed and in effect since 2010
ASEAN–India Comprehensive Economic Cooperation Agreement (incl. AIFTA)	ASEAN + India	Signed and in effect since 2010
ASEAN–Japan Comprehensive Economic Partnership (incl. AJFTA)	ASEAN + Japan	Signed and in effect since 2008
ASEAN–People's Republic of China Comprehensive Economic Cooperation Agreement (incl. ACFTA)	ASEAN + China	Signed and in effect since 2005
ASEAN–Korea Comprehensive Economic Cooperation Agreement (incl. AKFTA)	ASEAN + Republic of Korea	Signed and in effect since 2010
ASEAN–Hong Kong, China Free Trade Agreement	ASEAN + Hong Kong	Negotiations launched in 2014
Regional Comprehensive Economic Partnership	ASEAN + Australia, China, India, Japan, Korea, and New Zealand	Negotiations launched in 2009
Myanmar–US FTA	USA	Framework Agreement signed in 2013
Bay of Bengal Initiative for Multi-Sectoral Technical and Economic Cooperation (BIMSTEC) Free Trade Area	Bangladesh, Bhutan, India, Nepal, Sri Lanka, Thailand	Framework Agreement signed in 2004 and negotiations launched

Source: ADB (<http://aric.adb.org/fta-country>); UNESCAP (<http://artnet.unescap.org/APTIAD/agg_db.aspx>).

schemes but have not (yet) extended their benefits to Myanmar. More recently, a number of emerging economies have also introduced GSP schemes and Myanmar is a beneficiary of those offered by Belarus, Kazakhstan and Russia. Finally, as an LDC, Myanmar is also granted preferential treatment through the preferential market access schemes in favour of LDCs implemented by China, India and South Korea (UNCTAD 2013a, 2015).

2.5. ASEAN and East Asian Investment in Myanmar

Capital is typically a scarce factor of production in countries at the early stage of economic development as Myanmar's. As a consequence, such countries tend to be recipients rather than sources of international capital flows. That is, outward foreign direct investment (FDI) is a rare occurrence in such countries. In the following, we will therefore focus on inward FDI into Myanmar.

Since the re-opening of Myanmar's economy to international transactions in 2011, overall FDI inflows have grown rapidly. In the late 1990s and early 2000s, Myanmar attracted only few foreign investors and most of them were from East Asian countries such as China, Thailand and South Korea. Moreover, the bulk of foreign investments during that time were in natural resource extraction and export-oriented hydropower projects. However, since the new government came to power, Myanmar has not only seen a significant increase in the number of FDI projects but also a diversification in terms of sectors and the countries of origin of foreign investors. While six years ago, the Myanmar Investment Commission (MIC) approved only five FDI projects, in FY 2013/14 it approved 123 projects with an estimated value of over US$4.1 billion. Although there are still investments in natural resource and hydropower projects, most new FDI projects are in manufacturing (especially in the garment sector), hotels and tourism, telecommunications, and other non-extractive sectors.[4]

Recently, other ASEAN countries have become an important source of FDI inflows for Myanmar. This can be seen in Figure 6.6 which display how inward FDI is distributed between intra-ASEAN inflows (i.e. FDI coming in from another ASEAN member state) and extra-ASEAN inflows (which originate from non-ASEAN countries) in each of the ten ASEAN member countries. As Figure 6.6 shows, the share of ASEAN in total inward FDI was more than 70 per cent in Myanmar

FIGURE 6.6
Intra- and Extra-ASEAN FDI Inflows, 2014

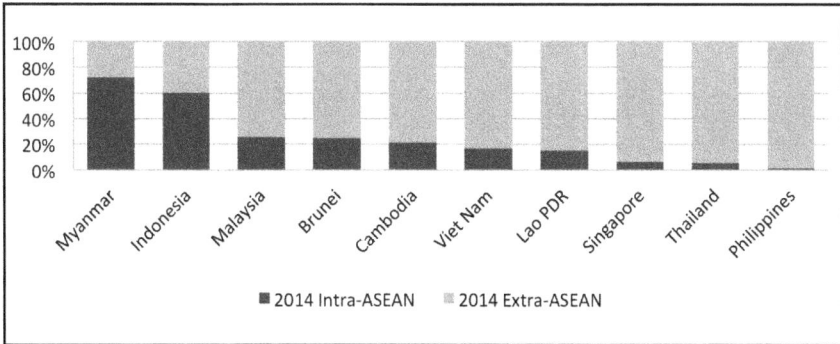

Legend: ■ 2014 Intra-ASEAN　■ 2014 Extra-ASEAN

Source: ASEAN Foreign Direct Investment Statistics Database.

in 2014, the highest figure reported among ASEAN member states. At the other extreme is the Philippines which get almost all their FDI from non-ASEAN countries (i.e. almost all their inward FDI is extra-ASEAN FDI).

Looking back in time reveals that today's situation in Myanmar is actually a reversal of the past. Table 6.9 indicates that in 2013 and particularly in 2012 extra-ASEAN FDI inflows exceeded intra-ASEAN FDI inflows. In fact, in 2012 Myanmar received only a slim US$151 million of FDI from within ASEAN but US$1,203 million of FDI from outside ASEAN. In 2013, intra-ASEAN FDI (US$1,187 million) and extra-ASEAN FDI (US$1,434 million) were already almost even.

As can be seen in Table 6.10, which gives details on bilateral FDI flows between Myanmar and ASEAN as well as East Asian countries, this reversal of trends was primarily driven by Singapore and Thailand. What is important to emphasize here is that the figures reported in Table 6.10 are only "approved" FDI amounts, i.e. Myanmar authorities (e.g. Directorate of Investment and Company Administration (DICA) or the Myanmar Investment Commission (MIC)) have approved investment projects that amount to these sums. This implies that these are *not* actual investment flows. In fact, actual investments might fall short of these amounts. However, what these figures show is a renewed interest among foreign, including ASEAN, investors to invest in Myanmar, in particular starting in 2009–10. In recent years, Singapore has by far

TABLE 6.9
Intra- and Extra-ASEAN FDI Inflows (USD million)

Country	2012			2013			2014		
	Intra-ASEAN	Extra-ASEAN	Total net inflow	Intra-ASEAN	Extra-ASEAN	Total net inflow	Intra-ASEAN	Extra-ASEAN	Total net inflow
Brunei	31.5	833.3	864.8	−58.0	783.5	725.5	141.2	427.0	568.2
Cambodia	523.0	1,034.1	1,557.1	298.8	976.1	1,274.9	372.5	1,354.0	1,726.5
Indonesia	7,587.9	11,550.0	19,137.9	8,721.1	9,722.7	18,443.8	13,458.8	8,817.5	22,276.3
Lao PDR	73.6	220.7	294.4	104.6	322.1	426.7	137.9	775.3	913.2
Malaysia	2,813.9	6,586.1	9,400.0	2,187.5	10,109.9	12,297.4	2,771.1	7,943.0	10,714.0
Myanmar	151.2	1,203.0	1,354.2	1,186.8	1,434.1	2,620.9	683.6	262.6	946.2
Philippines	145.2	2,651.8	2,797.0	−41.7	3,901.5	3,859.8	78.6	6,121.9	6,200.5
Singapore	8,302.0	52,678.3	60,980.3	3,665.0	52,473.3	56,138.3	4,532.7	67,565.6	72,098.3
Thailand	−342.0	11,041.2	10,699.2	1,256.8	11,743.0	12,999.8	653.9	10,884.0	11,537.9
Vietnam	1,262.5	7,105.5	8,368.0	2,078.6	6,821.4	8,900.0	1,547.1	7,653.0	9,200.1
Total	20,540	94,904	115,453	19,400	98,288	117,687	24,377	111,804	136,181

Methodological note: FDI figures are on a net basis and computed as follows: Net FDI = Equity + Net Inter-company Loans + Reinvested Earnings. The net basis concept implies that the followings should be deducted from the FDI gross flows: (1) reverse investment (made by a foreign affiliate in a host country to its parent company/direct investor; (2) loans given by a foreign affiliate to its parent company; and (3) repayments of intra-company loan (paid by a foreign affiliate to its parent company). As such, FDI net inflows can be negative.
Source: ASEAN Foreign Direct Investment Statistics Database.

TABLE 6.10
Approved FDI of ASEAN and East Asian Countries in Myanmar (USD million)

Country of Origin	Fiscal Year										
	2005–2006	2006–2007	2007–2008	2008–2009	2009–2010	2010–2011	2011–2012	2012–2013	2013–2014	2014–2015	April–June 2015
Brunei	0	0	0	0	0	0	0	1.0	2.3	43.9	5.1
Cambodia	0	0	0	0	0	0	0	0	0	0	0
Indonesia	0	0	0	0	0	0	0	0	0	0	13.2
Laos	0	0	0	0	0	0	0	0	0.9	0	0
Malaysia	0	0	0	0	237.6	76.8	51.9	4.3	616.1	6.7	3.6
Philippines	0	0	0	0	0	0	0	0	0	0.5	0
Singapore	0	81	38	0	39.2	226.2	0	418.2	2,300	4,297	1,430
Thailand	6,034	0	16.2	15	15.3	2,146	0	1.3	529.1	166	22
Vietnam	0	0	0	20	0	0	18.1	329.4	142	175.4	0
China	0.7	281.2	0	856	2.5	8,269	4,346	232	56.2	511.4	30.5
Hong Kong	0	0	0	0	6.0	5,798	0	84.8	107.1	625.6	50.2
Japan	0	0	1.4	3.8	0	7.1	4.3	54.1	55.7	85.7	106.2
Korea	0	37.0	12.0	0	0	2,676	25.6	37.9	81.2	299.6	13.5
Macao	0	0	0	0	0	0	0	0	0.9	0	0

Note: These figures report approved FDI amounts; however, approved FDI does not necessarily materialize so these figures do not describe actual foreign investments.
Source: DICA.

been the most important source of FDI for Myanmar, followed by other countries in the region including China, Thailand, Hong Kong, South Korea and Vietnam. At the moment at least, investors from non-Asian countries play a minor role in Myanmar.

Overall, however, Myanmar is a rather small recipient of intra-ASEAN FDI inflows. As can be seen in Figure 6.7, less than 3 per cent of all intra-ASEAN FDI flows went to Myanmar while Indonesia received over 55 per cent of them in 2014. Still, this share was higher than Cambodia's, Laos', Thailand's, Brunei's and the Philippines', and also higher than Myanmar's share in intra-ASEAN exports (see Figure 6.5).

FIGURE 6.7
Share of Myanmar in Intra-ASEAN FDI Inflows, 2014

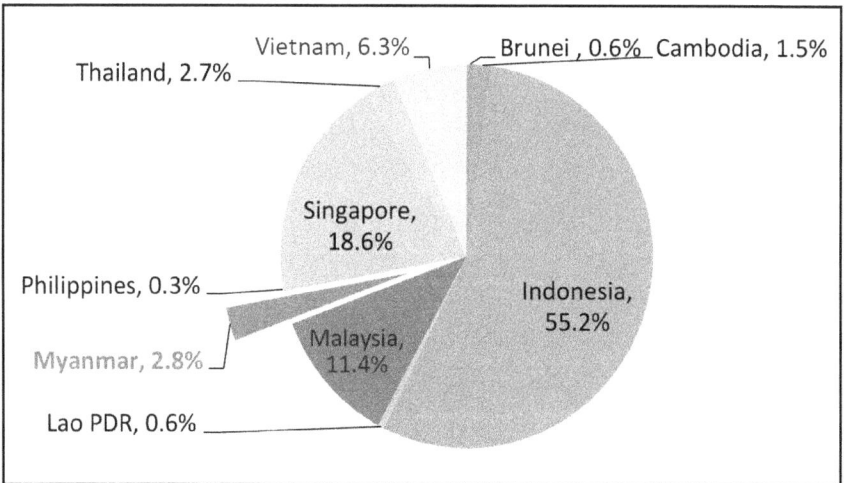

Source: ASEAN Foreign Direct Investment Statistics Database.

3.   SMEs in the World, in the Region and in Myanmar: Some Quick Facts

3.1. The role of SMEs in a country's economy

In almost any country in the world, the large majority of companies are SMEs. They are, therefore, widely recognized as significant drivers of economic output and employment creation, thereby generating income and contributing to poverty alleviation. In many contexts,

SMEs are also seen as important agents of innovation, introducing new products and novel production processes that help increase productivity and economic growth. In developing countries, this often takes the form of "frugal innovation", i.e. homegrown technological solutions that respond to needs of a specific low-income and cultural context. In view of this, governments around the world acknowledge that supporting the development of SMEs is an effective mechanism to promote socioeconomic development (Abe and Dutta 2014; Harvie 2010*a*, 2010*b*; UNESCAP 2012).

A study by the World Bank indicates that SMEs contribute over 60 per cent of GDP and more than 70 per cent of employment in low-income countries (Ayyagari et al. 2003). Meanwhile, the United Nations Economic and Social Commission for Asia and the Pacific (UNESCAP 2012) estimates that SMEs represent over 95 per cent of private enterprises and account for more than 50 per cent of employment in the Asia-Pacific region. However, the same publication also makes clear that there is quite a wide variation across countries in terms of SMEs' contribution to their national economies. For example, SMEs account for only 16 per cent of total exports in Singapore but for almost 70 per cent of exports in China. SMEs' role in exports is somewhere in between these two extremes in other countries such as Malaysia (where they contribute 19 per cent of exports), Indonesia (20 per cent), Vietnam (20 per cent), Thailand (31 per cent), and South Korea (39 per cent). Similarly, SMEs' shares in total employment range from 52 per cent in Singapore and 59 per cent in Malaysia to 69 per cent in Thailand, 75 per cent in China, 77 per cent in Vietnam, 88 per cent in South Korea and over 99 per cent in Indonesia. According to another study by the International Consulting Group, SMEs in fellow ASEAN member countries such as the Philippines, Vietnam and Indonesia contribute more than 30 per cent to their country's GDP.

Given the limited available data on the SME sector in Myanmar, it is difficult to precisely determine their contribution to the country's economic activities. In a presentation on "SME Development in Myanmar", Daw Wint Wah Lwin from the Yangon Institute of Economics estimated that Myanmar SMEs contribute 69 per cent of total output and 80 per cent of national export while employing 80 per cent of the local workforce. However, looking at other data sources suggests that these figures, especially the estimate on SMEs' contribution to exports, seemed too high (see Table 6.29 and Figure 6.12, for example). Anyway, it is estimated that there are only about 2.6 (registered) SMEs per 1,000 citizens in Myanmar — a figure that is well below the averages of 9 for the group of LDCs and 27 for developing countries (Smurra 2014).

3.2. Definition of SMEs in Myanmar and Elsewhere

Definitions of what constitutes an SME actually vary, often quite significantly, across countries. Some countries even stipulate different definitions for SMEs depending on the business sector concerned, i.e. the definition of an SME in agriculture differs from that of an SME in the manufacturing sector. In fact, countries do not always use the same criteria to define SMEs. Most SME definitions, however, use a company's number of employees as one criterion. While in some countries the size of the workforce is the sole criterion to distinguish small, medium-sized and large enterprises, others use additional criteria such as annual sales, value of assets or value of invested capital (UNESCAP 2012).

In Myanmar, the definition of what constitutes an SME was recently changed through the enactment of the 2015 SME Law. Before that, SMEs were defined according to the 1990 revised Industry Law on the basis of four criteria: power used (in horsepower), number of employees, capital investment, and value of annual production. The new definition reduced the number of criteria from four to three, dropping the criterion on power usage (see Table 6.11).

At the same time, however, a much more granular application of the employment criterion was introduced and thresholds between size categories were changed significantly. In the old definition, small firms were those with 10–50 workers, medium-sized firms were those with 51–100 workers, and large enterprises were those with over 100 employees. In the new definition, there is no lower boundary for the small enterprise category so that, effectively, it also includes micro enterprises (typically defined as firms with less than 10 employees). Moreover, the new definition now distinguishes between different economic sectors (manufacturing, services, others) and even between different business activities within these sectors (labour-intensive manufacturing vs. other manufacturing; wholesale vs. retail vs. other services business) — this is where the granular application of the employment criterion kicks in. Overall, Myanmar's new SME definition can, thus, be deemed quite complex.

TABLE 6.11
New SME Definition in Myanmar According to the 2015 SME Law

	Categories	No. of Employees	Capital (million Kyat)	Turn-over (million Kyat)
1	**Small**			
(a)	Manufacturing sector	Up to 50	Up to 500	
(b)	Labour-intensive manufacturing sector	Up to 300	Up to 500	
(c)	Wholesale business	Up to 30		Up to 100
(d)	Retail business	Up to 30		Up to 50
(e)	Servicing business	Up to 30		Up to 100
(f)	Other services business	Up to 30		Up to 50
2	**Medium**			
(a)	Manufacturing sector	51 to 300	500 to 1,000	
(b)	Labour-intensive manufacturing sector	301 to 600	500 to 1,000	
(c)	Wholesale business	31 to 60		100 to 300
(d)	Retail business	31 to 60		50 to 100
(e)	Servicing business	51 to 100		100 to 200
(f)	Other services business	31 to 60		50 to 100

Source: <www.smedevelopmentcenter.gov.mm/?q=en/def_sme>.

3.3. Availability of Information on SMEs in Myanmar: Registries and Surveys

In many other countries, data on businesses is regularly collected through business surveys by government authorities, such as Statistics Offices or Ministries of Industry. In Myanmar, such a regular and comprehensive exercise has not yet been established although plans exist to do so. Some data seems to exist within the Ministry of Industry (MoI) as well as within the Central Statistics Office (CSO). However, data collection does not seem to be undertaken based on a stringent methodology in line with international standards nor according to a given schedule and programme. As a result, no reliable data on business enterprises in general and SMEs more specifically exists in Myanmar. It is for this reason that different sources report different figures on the number of SMEs in the country.

According to the Central Department of Small and Medium Enterprises, for example, as of March 2015 there are 39,062 firms that have registered as small and medium industries (SMIs) under the Private Industrial Enterprise Law, accounting for 87.4 per cent of total registered industries (ADB 2015).[5] However, this data only covers manufacturers and cottage industries because the Central Department of Small and Medium Enterprises is only one of the public agencies/departments where firms can register. Other entities where companies can register include DICA, MIC, the Directorate of Industrial Supervision and Inspection (DISI), the Small Scale Industries Department (SSID) in the Ministry of Cooperatives, and the different city development committees such as the Yangon City Development Committee (YCDC). SME estimates coming from the Central Department of Small and Medium Enterprises are therefore typically incomplete and should be taken as a lower boundary estimate.

Meanwhile, the United Nations Development Programme (UNDP)'s "One Pager Business Census 2013–2014" for Myanmar looked at four different business registries, i.e. those from DICA, MIC, DISI and SSID, yielding a total number of 31,093 firms that are operating. Among these, the large majority, namely 80.6 per cent, had 10 or less employees, making them micro enterprises, while another 15.5 per cent can be considered small firms (with 11–49 workers), 2.9 per cent medium-sized firms (with 50–199 workers) and 1 per cent large firms (comprising 0.6 per cent of firms with 200–499 workers and 0.4 per cent of firms with 500 or more employees). At the same time, these large enterprises account for 41 per cent of total employment in UNDP's sample (UNDP 2014, pp. 10–11). There is, thus, quite a polarization in Myanmar's private sector into small and very large firms. In other words, these figures point to the existence of a "missing middle", i.e. the underrepresentation of medium-sized firms in Myanmar's enterprise population — a phenomenon that is not uncommon in developing countries.

However, other sources report higher numbers of SMEs. An article published in the *Myanmar Times*, for example, mentions that there are more than 80,000 SMEs registered (Htin Lynn Aung 2015). Meanwhile, according to an article published in *The New Light of Myanmar*, there are 126,968 registered companies of which 126,237 (or 99.4 per cent) are SMEs. The same source also states that, in addition, there are an estimated 620,000 informal (i.e. unregistered) firms operating in Myanmar, corresponding to 83 per cent of all businesses (*The New Light of Myanmar* 2013).

This discrepancies across sources point to an important task for the future, namely to establish a system for regularly collecting reliable data on SMEs in Myanmar. This will allow the government to take more informed decisions in their policy-making for SMEs and also to better monitor and evaluate the impact of their interventions.

In view of this gap in terms of reliable information, a number of donor agencies recently conducted a series of surveys in Myanmar. These include an SME survey by the German Institute for Development Evaluation (DEval 2015), a business survey conducted jointly by the Organization for Economic Cooperation and Development (OECD), the Union of Myanmar Federation of Chambers of Commerce and Industry (UMFCCI) and UNESCAP (Soans and Abe 2015), a "One Pager Business Census" by UNDP (2014) as well as the World Bank's Enterprise Survey, its Investment Climate Survey and its Doing Business Survey (World Bank 2014*a*, 2015*b*, 2015*c*). However, while these surveys have helped to improve the availability of information available on Myanmar's business sector, they differ in surveying methods, sample sizes, and topics covered. This means that the data produced by these surveys are not always fully comparable and this also explains why these surveys, in some cases, have produced divergent findings. UNDP's "One Pager Business Census" probably has been the most comprehensive exercise, and based on the most representative sample, covering over 31,000 firms drawn from different business registries. Meanwhile, the DEval survey focuses purely on SMEs, which are privately owned and operate in cities and in the manufacturing and services sectors. The OECD–UMFCCI–UNESCAP survey, on the other hand, did not only cover SMEs but also larger firms and also included agricultural and state-owned firms. While the DEval survey was carried out among a random sample of companies, the OECD–UMFCCI–UNESCAP survey sample was based on business registries from UMFCCI which implies a certain sample bias. In both cases, however, the survey samples were quite sizeable, covering over 2,200 firms. By comparison, the World Bank's Enterprise Survey was based on a rather small sample of 632 registered small, medium, and large firms. However, the latter clearly over-sampled medium and large firms and excluded agricultural firms from the sample.

In the following sections, we will discuss some characteristics and present some analyses on SMEs in Myanmar, drawing on information taken from these data sources and surveys and complementing it with information collected through a business survey conducted for the purpose of this study. Our survey was carried out from July to November 2015 among a sample of around 200 manufacturing firms operating in different industrial zones in Yangon Region and Mon State of Myanmar.

Our survey sample was drawn, through convenience sampling, from two sets of enterprise lists: first, lists provided by different industrial zone management committees and, second, a list of apparel producers provided by the Myanmar Garment Manufacturers Association (MGMA). Survey participants were then selected randomly from these two sets of enterprise lists. We acknowledge that this sample is not representative of the full firm population of Myanmar companies, for the following reasons:

–   The sampling frame was incomplete due to, first, the non-availability of a complete registry of businesses in Myanmar and, second, the choice of enterprise lists from industrial zone management committees and MGMA as representation of the underlying firm population.
–   The survey had a deliberate focus on the manufacturing sector, i.e. it does not cover firms operating in the agriculture or services sectors.
–   Within manufacturing, the survey focuses on two of the key industries in Myanmar, namely food processing and apparel manufacturing.
–   The survey had a regional focus on Yangon Region and Mon State while excluding other regions and states in Myanmar.

Despite these shortcomings, however, the data collected through our survey complements the existing stock of enterprise-level data for Myanmar and allows for some useful and interesting analyses. Above all, our survey had a specific focus on companies' participation in international economic activities and regional integration in ASEAN in particular. In addition, apart from asking respondents about the extent and nature of their participation in regional trade, production networks, and investment activities, our survey also collected information on Myanmar businesses' awareness of regional economic integration initiatives such as the AEC, their perceptions on the likely impacts of AEC, their knowledge and usage of FTAs, and their views on the effects of trade liberalization through FTAs. Such information is not available from existing datasets.

Table 6.12 gives an overview about how the sample for our survey looks like. It comprises a total of 198 firms (one of which did not provide employment information, therefore inhibiting us from classifying it as small, medium or large enterprise), 52 per cent of which operate in the apparel sector and 45 per cent in food manufacturing. While not being fully representative of Myanmar's business population our survey allows us, however, to focus on two of the most important manufacturing industries in Myanmar, i.e. apparel and food, and to do more in-depth analysis on them.

Following the Economic Research Institute for ASEAN and East Asia (ERIA)'s definition of SMEs (whereby small firms are those with 11–49 workers and medium-sized are those with 50–249 workers), our sample is composed of 27 per cent of small firms, 27 per cent of medium-sized firms and 45 per cent large firms. Almost all the firms in our sample operate in labour-intensive industries. Therefore, if we had

TABLE 6.12
Survey Sample Characteristics

Industry (ISIC CODE)	Firm Size				Share in Total
	Small	Medium	Large	Total	
	No.	No.	No.	No.	
10. Manufacture of food products	52	27	10	89	45%
14. Manufacture of wearing apparel	1	22	79	102	52%
16. Manufacture of wood and wood products	1	1	0	2	1%
17. Manufacture of paper and paper products	0	1	0	1	1%
32. Other manufacturing	0	3	0	3	2%
Total number	54	54	89	197	
Share in TOTAL	27%	27%	45%	100%	

applied the SME definition stipulated in Myanmar's SME Law, whereby small and medium-sized companies in labour-intensive manufacturing sectors are defined as those with less than 300 employees and between 301 and 600 employees, respectively (see Table 6.11), the composition of our sample would have looked differently: 60 per cent would have been classified as small firms, 14 per cent as medium-sized firms, and 26 per cent as large enterprises. To ensure comparability across the different country studies commissioned by ERIA, however, we decided to apply ERIA's definition of SMEs when analysing the data collected through our survey. More details on our survey are provided in Appendix 6.4.

4. Characteristics of SMEs: In General and in Myanmar

This section will first discuss some typical characteristics of SMEs around the globe, while recognizing their heterogeneity, and then zoom in on Myanmar's SMEs to give a portrayal of them along a variety of parameters, based on data from our survey as well as other data sources. The analyses undertaken here will also allow us to identify and understand both enabling factors and obstacles to Myanmar SMEs' participation in regional trade, production networks, and investment activities — a topic which will be analysed in more detail in the subsequent sections.

4.1. General Characteristics and Heterogeneity of SMEs

At the outset, it has to be emphasized that the category "SMEs" typically comprises a very heterogeneous group of enterprises. This has important implications for SME policy-making. The challenges of SMEs and their related need for policy support can vary quite significantly across the SME population of a country, according to different parameters.

First of all, the category SMEs includes firms of quite different sizes. Apart from small firms (usually those with less than 50 employees) and medium-sized firms (often defined as those firms with less than 250 workers, but sometimes also defined as those with less than 400 or even more employees[6]), the category often also includes micro firms (those with less than 10 workers). The operations, strategies and challenges of firms of different sizes typically differ quite a lot.

Second, SMEs operate in a wide range of sectors, including agriculture, manufacturing, construction and services, and a large variety of industries within these sectors. Examples of SMEs include a single artisan producing agricultural implements for the village market; a tea shop at the corner; an internet cafe; a medium-sized engineering company; a small software firm selling to overseas markets; or an automotive parts manufacturer selling to multinational car producers which, in turn, trade to both domestic and foreign markets. Obviously, the operational setups, opportunities, challenges and needs of, say, a small-scale farmer are quite different from those of a medium-sized manufacturing firm or those of a micro-sized firm shop in the retailing industry.

Third, SMEs are operating in different locations and in very different markets (urban, rural, subnational, national, regional and international). The challenges and needs of SMEs operating in rural areas are quite different from those of SMEs operating in urban areas. Within urban areas, one can further distinguish between firms that are set up within industrial zones and those outside such zones. Other locational factors include proximity to rivers or the sea, climate, and the likeliness of natural disasters. Finally, SMEs embody different levels of skills and capital, and show different levels of sophistication and growth orientation; and they may operate in the formal or in the informal economy.

However, there is also a lot that many SMEs have in common. Their operations are typically labour intensive and characterized by low investment requirements. There is often little separation between ownership and management and they tend to respond to market needs quickly with a flatter organizational structure and flexible operations that can readily adapt to a rapidly changing environment. Moreover, SMEs tend to have a niche market focus and comparatively high levels of customer-orientation (UNESCAP 2012).

This heterogeneity was clearly also identified in the data collected through our survey, even under the relatively small sample (see Tables 6.13 and 6.15). For instance, the number of employees of surveyed firms varies greatly across industry, with the surveyed food manufacturers tending to be relatively smaller when compared with apparel manufacturers, as measured by both the larger share of small-sized companies (see Table 6.12) and the lower average number of workers per firm (see Table 6.13).[7] Although it is unclear to what extent this is representative of both industries, it provides a grounded example of the different economic, policy and market contexts serviced by firms in either industry.

TABLE 6.13
Selected Firm Characteristics by Industry

Industry	Member of Business Association	Share of Family Business	Firms with Foreign Ownership	Average No. of Workers per Firm	Firms that Export
10. Manufacture of food products	70%	92%	3%	105	27%
14. Manufacture of wearing apparel	97%	60%	61%	657	84%
TOTAL (incl. Paper, Wood and Others)	84%	75%	32%	391	61%

Moreover, it appears that food manufacturers tend to be family businesses (92 per cent of the respondents). They are also more likely to serve just the domestic market, with only 27 per cent of survey firms indicating that they export. While this is likely due to food manufacturers catering to local tastes and preferences, it is also likely a result of Myanmar's domestic economy being predominantly agrarian, thereby providing a ready supply of inputs for manufacturing food.

On the other hand, apparel manufacturers surveyed tend to supply to foreign markets (84 per cent considered themselves exporters), and almost two thirds of them are reportedly partially or wholly foreign-owned. Although the factors driving these differences will not be explored in detail here, it is likely that both the higher export orientation and the larger size of apparel manufacturing firms are consequences of the predominance of the very labour-intensive Cut-Make-Pack (CMP) production model, which is the model of a large proportion of the firms sampled here (ILO 2015; MGMA 2015; MoC and ITC 2015a, and further below for more details). The higher membership of business associations evident in the apparel sector on the one hand reflects the fact that MGMA is quite a competent, proactive and strong business association. On the other hand, it can, to a large extent, also be explained by the requirement of apparel manufacturers to be an MGMA member if they want to obtain import permits, which is crucial given that local supply of essential input materials such as fabrics, yarn or accessories is very limited.[8]

4.2. Sectoral Distribution of SMEs in Myanmar

In terms of the sectoral distribution of SMEs, different data sources report quite different statistics. However, given that they make up the bulk of all companies in Myanmar, it can safely be assumed that SMEs dominate every sector of the economy. The most reliable statistics are available only for those SMIs that are registered with the Central Department of Small and Medium Enterprises which collects and reports data on SMIs. As mentioned above, there are almost 40,000 such SMIs in Myanmar, accounting for around 87 per cent of total domestic manufacturing firms. These SMIs include micro (or "cottage") enterprises of which 78 per cent operate in the manufacturing sector (cottage handicraft) and about 21 per cent in the service sector. Among those SMIs that are not involved in cottage industries, more than 60 per cent operate in the food processing sector. This includes rice mills, oil mills, powdering machines, sugar mills, bean and pulses processors, ice factories and confectionaries, which account for about 90 per cent of food processing SMIs. An additional 7.6 per cent of total SMIs operate as construction material producers. Meanwhile, mineral and petroleum producers make up a further 5.1 per cent and garment firms another 4.5 per cent of SMIs (ADB 2015).[9]

Quite a different picture on the sectoral distribution of SMEs emerges when looking at other data sources. The sample for the DEval SME survey included a majority of firms (54 per cent) engaged in manufacturing and 46 per cent of firms in the service sector. As mentioned, however, this survey did not cover the agricultural sector so these distribution figures are incomplete. According to the DEval data, within manufacturing most SMEs focus on the production of machinery and equipment, vehicles and metal products (12 per cent); food, beverages or tobacco/cheroots (12 per cent); and textile and/or shoes (10 per cent). Within the service sector, the main branches are restaurants and hotels (16 per cent) and retail (14 per cent).

In the following, a number of additional characteristics of SMEs in Myanmar will be presented. Apart from presenting results from our own survey, additional information is drawn from the DEval survey and the World Bank's Enterprise Survey because these two surveys provide data disaggregated by firm size. However, both for our survey and the World Bank's Enterprise Survey, it should be noted that they are based on relatively small samples of 198 firms and 630 firms, respectively, so that any interpretation and generalization of the figures presented in the following should be done with some caution. Moreover, it should also be noted that the definition of what constitute small, medium and large enterprises applied in the World Bank's Enterprise Survey (with small firms being those with 5–19 employees, medium-sized firms are those with 20–99 employees, and large firms are those with more than 100 employees) differs considerably from those applied in other surveys, including ours (where small firms have 11–49 workers, medium firms 50–249 workers, and large firms 250 or more workers).

4.3. Levels of Registration and Informality of Myanmar Firms

Overall registration rates of businesses are very low in Myanmar, implying that there is a substantial informal sector. As mentioned above, it is estimated that there are 620,000 informal (i.e. unregistered) firms operating in Myanmar, corresponding to 83 per cent of all businesses (*The New Light of Myanmar* 2013). Reasons for low registration levels are manifold, including an outdated and often cumbersome registration system involving different agencies, limited administrative coverage, business distrust against government entities and policies (e.g. regarding protection of poverty rights, usage of tax revenues, etc.) and also lack of knowledge of where to register and the intention to avoid taxes among firms (Bissinger and Maung Maung 2014, for example).

As a consequence, by far not all SMEs have registered with a government authority. However, existing survey data tend to underestimate the extent of informality as informal firms are heavily underrepresented in the samples. Within the DEval sample, around 21 per cent of firms are not registered. However, large variations were found when the sizes of these firms were investigated. Specifically, while the vast majority of medium-sized enterprises are registered, the same is true for only 74 per cent of micro businesses. Overall, the figures reported by the OECD–UMFCCI–UNESCAP Business Survey were quite similar; according to that survey, around 13 per cent of SMEs indicated that they had not registered yet. The World Bank's Enterprise Survey, by contrast, found somewhat lower levels of informality. According to that survey, around 14 per cent of small firms and only 7 per cent of medium-sized firms did not formally register when starting their operations. Moreover, in most cases, SMEs were found to operate only for about one year without formal registration (see Table 6.14).

TABLE 6.14
Informality Among Myanmar Firms

Subgroup	Percentage of Firms Formally Registered When They Started Operations	Number of Years Firm Operated Without Formal Registration	Percentage of Firms Competing Against Unregistered or Informal Firms
Small (5–19)	86.3	1.1	29.5
Medium (20–99)	93.0	0.6	36.1
Large (100+)	95.2	0.3	31.8

Source: World Bank Enterprise Survey Database.

4.4. Age, Ownership and Legal Status of Myanmar Companies

The average age of SMEs sampled by the World Bank's Enterprise Survey is around 12 years. Similarly, both the DEval and the OECD–UMFCCI–UNESCAP surveys found that a clear majority of firms have been operating for more than 10 years. This corroborates our survey results which show an average age of 11 years among the companies in our sample (see Table 6.14).

Only around 23 per cent of all SMEs covered by the DEval survey had started operations during the previous four years. This suggests that the average age of SMEs in Myanmar is quite high. On the one hand, this signals that survival rates of SMEs are pretty high, which, however, might just reflect low levels of competition. On the other hand, this might be interpreted as a sign that not many new firms have started operating, pointing to a lack of dynamism and potentially also to the fact that starting a business is quite cumbersome and difficult in Myanmar. Indeed, DEval (2015, p. 13) concludes that "[i]t thus seems that the transition and liberalisation process in Myanmar has not yet led to a significant increase in the number of private SMEs." UNDP (2014), however, comes to a somewhat different conclusion when looking at their sample of businesses. They found that in the year 2013, the share of new firms (defined as those having started operations in 2012 or 2013, i.e. those with a maximum age of one year) was 8.5 per cent — a percentage that is slightly higher than the average typically found in Asia (around 5 per cent). They deemed this "consistent also with the process of deregulation of the economy that allowed the creation of new businesses in such a large scale" (UNDP 2014, p. 24).

In our sample, the percentage of firms younger than five years, at around 38 per cent, is markedly higher than in the DEval sample. The explanation for this is that there is a clear tendency for firm creation rates to vary across industries. As can be seen in Table 6.15, the firms surveyed in the food manufacturing sector are almost twice the age of those in the apparel manufacturing sector. At the same time, the share of rather "new firms" (age less than five years) is more than three times higher in the apparel sector (57 per cent) than in the food processing sector (15 per cent). Although it is difficult to determine the extent to which the firms surveyed here are representative of the industry as a whole in Myanmar, these stark differences in age may suggest differing levels of competition and exposure to international markets as well as a number of recent domestic and international developments.

TABLE 6.15
Age Distribution of Survey Firms

Industry	Age Range				Average Age (in Years)
	<=5 Years	5<Age<20 Years	>20 Years	Total	
10. Manufacture of food products	15	58	16	89	15.2
14. Manufacture of wearing apparel	57	42	3	102	7.4
All survey firms	75	101	21	197	11.1

Specifically, Myanmar has become an increasingly attractive location for apparel manufacturing over the last five years, with relative increases in manufacturing wages in neighbouring countries such as China, factory accidents in Bangladesh, the easing of sanctions, and foreign investment reforms as important push and pull factors (Berg and Hedrich 2014). In addition to these reforms likely making Myanmar's apparel industry more competitive internationally, it also resulted in a relatively recent "boom" in SME establishment in the apparel sector. Indeed, the MGMA reports that it gained 65 new members, mostly foreign companies, in 2014 while in the first three quarters of 2015 already 55 new members joined MGMA (MGMA 2015).[10] By contrast, the more locally-oriented food manufacturing sector has not experienced such a boom of new business entries and incumbents seem to dominate the market.

According to both the World Bank's Enterprise Survey and our own survey, the legal status of almost all Myanmar SMEs is sole proprietorship. Apart from that, around 4 per cent of small companies and about 5 per cent of medium-sized enterprises operate with the legal status of partnership (see Figure 6.8) with state-owned SMEs representing a clear minority. The predominance of sole proprietorship and partnership as the most common ownership structures echo a tendency for SME ownership and management to be relatively fluid.

FIGURE 6.8
Legal Status of Myanmar Companies

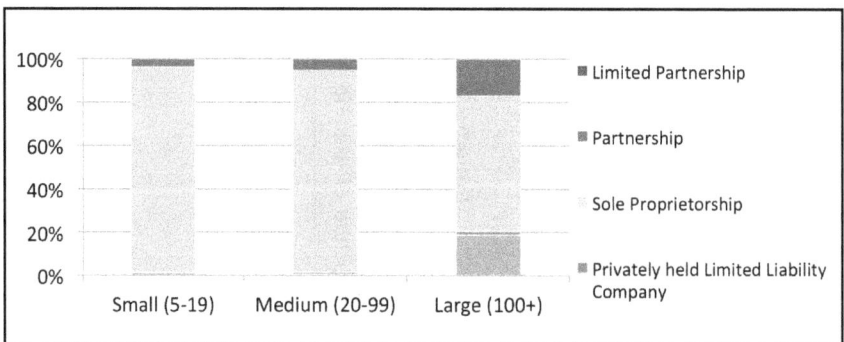

Source: World Bank Enterprises Survey Database.

Interestingly, the World Bank's Enterprise Survey also suggested that SMEs with foreign ownership are a clear minority. However, as can be seen from the results from our survey in Tables 6.16 and 6.17, this masks important variations across sectors and different firm sizes. For instance, among the firms we surveyed, 3 per cent of food manufacturers and 59 per cent of apparel manufacturers reported to have at least partial foreign ownership.[11] Furthermore, larger firms were more likely to have some form of foreign ownership while not a single small firm reported foreign ownership, as opposed to around 17 per cent of medium-sized firms and 62 per cent of large firms. This tendency for larger firms to report foreign ownership applies across industries, although seemingly to a lesser extent for food manufacturers, likely reflecting the comparatively higher attractiveness of apparel as a boom sector.

TABLE 6.16
Domestic vs. Foreign Ownership According to Firm Size

	Firm Size			Total (All Firms)
	Small	Medium	Large	
Domestically Owned	100%	83%	38%	68%
Foreign invested Firms	0%	17%	62%	32%

4.5. Innovation and Use of Technology

According to the World Bank's Enterprise Survey, the level of technology usage and technological sophistication is quite low among Myanmar SMEs (see Table 6.17). Only about 1.5 per cent of small firms and 0.5 per cent of medium-sized firms have an internationally recognized quality certification. Among medium-sized firms, only 2.8 per cent use technology licensed from foreign companies while licensing of foreign technology is almost non-existent among small Myanmar firms. Usage of modern communications technology is also not very common among small Myanmar firms covered by the World Bank's Enterprise Survey: only 7 per cent have their own website and just 20 per cent interact with clients or suppliers via email. Among medium-sized firms, these percentages are considerably higher (at 29 per cent and

TABLE 6.17
Share of Foreign-invested Firms by Firm Size and Industry

	Firm Size			Proportion of Sector that is Foreign-Invested
	Small	Medium	Large	
10. Manufacture of food products	0%	4%	20%	3%
14. Manufacture of wearing apparel	0%	32%	67%	59%

46 per cent, respectively) but still fall short of those for large enterprises. Finally, usage of external business services is not very widespread among SMEs in Myanmar. This is reflected in the fact that just 8.5 per cent of small firms and 42 per cent of medium-sized firms get their financial statements reviewed by external auditors.

Upon comparing results of the World Bank's Enterprise Survey with our own, similar trends emerge, with both surveys indicating a relatively small proportion of Myanmar SMEs employing Information and Communications Technologies (ICT), such as email or online sales (see Table 6.19). Interestingly, both surveys also suggest that email usage and having a website tended to be more likely for larger firms, likely reflecting the lower diffusion and higher costs of ICT in Myanmar in general, making it only a worthwhile investment for larger firms. It is also likely that the benefits of adopting such technologies would differ across sectors, with the relatively low use of technology, such as online purchasing, by domestic consumers making ICT adoption less worthwhile for firms supplying the domestic market, such as those in the food manufacturing sector (see Table 6.20).

However, outside of email usage and having a website, the uptake of ICT by Myanmar firms appears to be extremely low with less than 6 per cent of firms reporting the use of ICT for online sales, purchases and payment. Interestingly, this tendency does not appear to change across firms of different size, likely illustrating both the small benefits of adopting these technologies in Myanmar and different commercial contexts across sectors (see Table 6.19). Although this low level of adoption would tend to imply this as a key area of reform for Myanmar, it is important to note that this represents both a supply and demand side problem, with electronic payment systems only recently being adopted domestically and only in urban centres, where the minority of the population lives.

Table 6.18
Innovation and Use of Technology among Myanmar Firms

Company Size	Per Cent of Firms with an Internationally-recognized Quality Certification	Per Cent of Firms Using Technology Licensed from Foreign Companies	Per Cent of Firms Having Their Own Website	Per Cent of Firms Using Email to Interact with Clients/Suppliers	Per Cent of Firms with an Annual Financial Statement Reviewed by External Auditors
Small (5–19)	1.5	0.2	7.0	20.2	8.5
Medium (20–99)	0.5	2.8	29.0	46.2	42.1
Large (100+)	9.3	28.3	52.6	87.7	71.9

TABLE 6.19
Percentage of ICT Usage by Size

	Email Use	Website	Online Purchases	Online Sales	Online Marketing	Online Payment	ICT Use — Others
Small	24%	8%	2%	4%	2%	2%	4%
Medium	78%	20%	2%	4%	2%	6%	10%
Large	95%	30%	2%	2%	1%	5%	2%

TABLE 6.20
ICT Usage Score by Firm Size, Ownership and Industry

ICT Use Score	Small	Medium	Large	Domestic	Foreign-invested	Manufacture of Food Products	Manufacture of Wearing Apparel	Total
0	73%	20%	0%	37%	2%	49%	6%	24%
1	18%	55%	69%	41%	73%	27%	72%	52%
2	4%	16%	27%	15%	24%	16%	20%	18%
3	0%	6%	1%	3%	0%	4%	0%	2%
4	2%	2%	1%	2%	2%	1%	2%	2%
5	0%	2%	1%	2%	0%	2%	0%	1%
6	2%	0%	0%	1%	0%	1%	0%	1%

To explore this further, an "ICT usage score" was given to firms in the sample depending on how many ICT tools they reported using. This was done by providing each firm with a score of 1 for each technology used, with the lowest score possible being 0 and the highest being 7. For instance, a firm with a website and using email would receive a score of '2', whereas a firm using no form of ICT would receive a score of '0'. Results have been provided in Table 6.20. From this exercise a number of trends appear clear. For instance, as before there is a clear trend for larger firms to be more likely to use some form of ICT, as reflected in their higher scores. Almost half of all food manufacturers do not use any ICT (thus having a score of '0') while 43 per cent use one or two ICT services; in the apparel sector, the large majority (92 per cent) uses one or two different ICT services while only 6 per cent reported no ICT usage at all. As before, it can be assumed that much of this reflects the ownership structure and industry of firms with the apparel sector tending to use a larger number of ICT tools, likely both out of the need to communicate with overseas headquarters and/or international customers and reflecting the greater levels of competition they face.

Although the small uptake of ICT by SMEs in Myanmar is somewhat unsurprising given Myanmar's relatively recent efforts to engage in reforms in the telecommunications sector, it does illustrate the potential space SMEs may have to improve efficiency and access expanded markets through ICT. Despite this, when viewing firms by their efforts to innovate and technologically upgrade, a number of interesting tendencies emerge. First of all, as can be seen in Figure 6.9, between 2012 and 2014 only a very small percentage of survey firms have engaged in innovation and technology efforts. This corroborates the findings from the OECD–UMFCCI–UNESCAP survey where more than 60 per cent of all respondents reported having made zero investment in research and development (R&D) and innovation (Soans and Abe 2015, p. 34). Second, SMEs are more likely than large enterprises to report investing in innovation and technology efforts in all but the 'R&D outsourcing' category. Although the precise nature of this investment is not clear from the survey, it is likely that the 19 per cent of SMEs that reported acquisition of machinery, equipment or software are engaged in plant modernization such as the replacement of old machinery and technology with the

FIGURE 6.9
Innovation and Technology Efforts, Classified by Firm Size and Sector,
2012–14

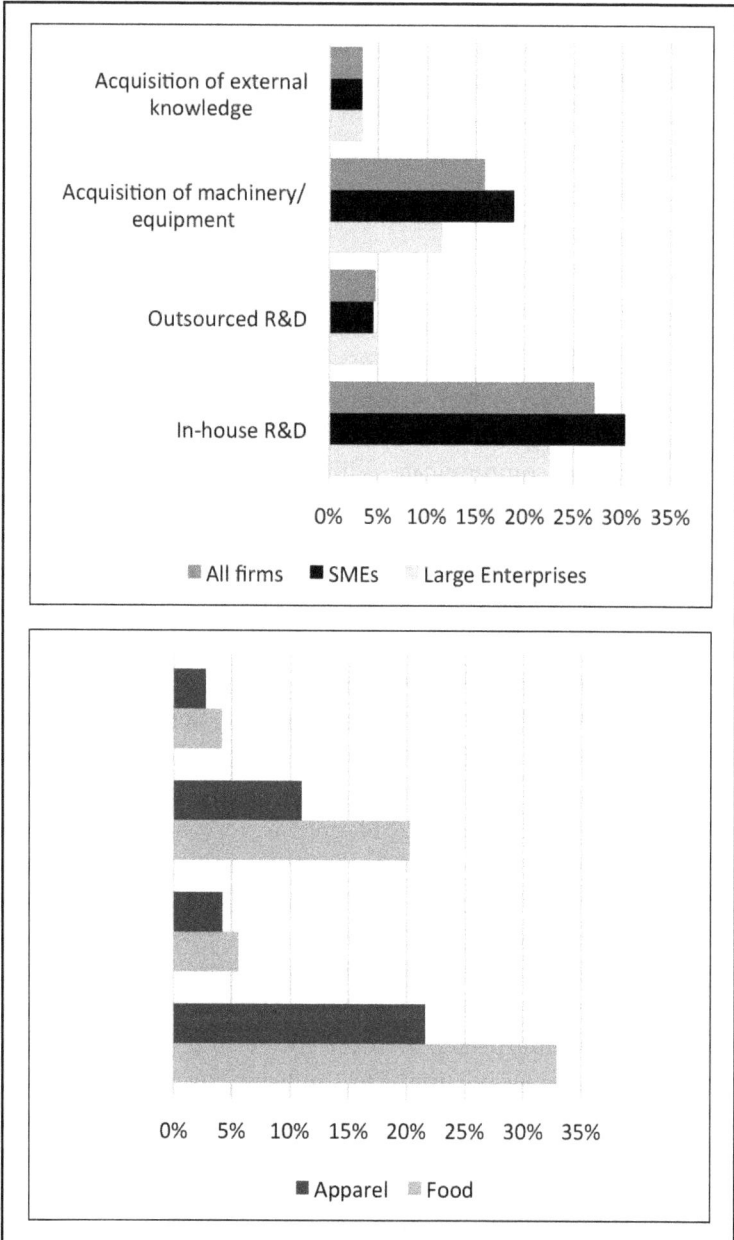

vision of producing new and/or better products. In contrast, only 11 per cent of large firms in the sample reported expenditures on the acquisition of machinery, equipment or software, possibly reflecting that these firms already have newer plants and use more modern technology and equipment. Comparing across sectors, we can see from Figure 6.9 that the food processing firms in our sample have engaged much more in innovation and technology efforts than apparel producers. As mentioned above, most Myanmar garment manufacturers are integrated into regional and global value chains where they operate under the CMP model, governed by foreign-lead firms and basically carrying out simple and labour-intensive assembly activities without much requirements in terms of innovativeness.

Interestingly, this tendency for SMEs to invest more heavily in innovation and technology efforts also seems to be reflected in a higher propensity to introduce new or significantly improved products and/or services, with large firms being the least likely to report having introduced a new product and/or service (see Table 6.21). Overall then around one-third of all firms surveyed introduced a new product and/or service between 2012 and 2014. Interestingly, the lowest percentage (22 per cent) can be found among large firms while 37 per cent of small and 39 per cent of medium-sized firms reported the introduction of a new product and/or service between

TABLE 6.21
Introduction of a New Product and/or Service by Firm Size and Ownership, 2012–14

	No	Yes
Small	63%	37%
Medium	61%	39%
Large	78%	22%
Domestic	63%	37%
Foreign-invested	82%	18%
Total	69%	31%

2012 and 2014. Another intriguing observation is that the share of firms introducing a new product and/or service is higher among fully domestically owned firms than among firms with foreign ownership (see Table 6.20). Comparing across sectors, we found that the percentage of food manufacturers in our sample that introduced new or significantly improved products and/or services between 2012 and 2014 is higher than that for apparel manufacturers (see Table 6.22). This observation echoes the finding that food manufacturers have invested more in R&D and other innovation efforts than apparel producers. It may equally be a reflection of rather rapid changes in the tastes and preferences of food consumers, to which food manufacturers have to respond with new offerings, as well as low requirements on innovativeness of apparel firms operating under the CMP model.

TABLE 6.22
Share of Firms Having Introduced a New Product or New Service, 2012–14

	Introduced a New Product		Introduced a New Service	
	No	Yes	No	Yes
10. Manufacture of food products	62%	38%	67%	33%
14. Manufacture of wearing apparel	87%	13%	90%	10%
Overall (all Industries)	75%	25%	78%	22%

4.6. Access to Finance

Access to finance is not a topic covered in our survey. The World Bank's Enterprise Survey, however, interestingly found that only less than a third of Myanmar SMEs identify access to finance as a major constraint to doing business. However, looking at a range of financial access indicators suggests that this is rather a consequence of SMEs' lack of awareness of and familiarity with modern financial services than of a well-functioning financial sector. For example, just 20 per cent of small enterprises and less than half of medium enterprises have a checking or savings account. Less than 8 per cent of SMEs use banks to finance working capital and less than 4 per cent use banks to finance investments. In fact, most SMEs finance their investments through internal funds (see Table 6.23). As a consequence, only about 3 per cent of small firms and 13 per cent of medium-sized firms currently have a bank loan or line of credit. One of the reasons

TABLE 6.23
Access to Finance for Myanmar Firms

Company Size	Per Cent of Firms with a Checking or Savings Account	Per Cent of Firms Using Banks to Finance Investments	Proportion of Investments Financed Internally (%)	Proportion of Investments Financed by Banks (%)	Per Cent of Firms Using Banks to Finance Working Capital	Proportion of Working Capital Financed by Banks (%)	Per Cent of Firms Identifying Access to Finance as a Major Constraint
Small (5–19)	19.4	1.4	90.4	0.8	2.0	1.0	18.3
Medium (20–99)	46.3	4.0	95.4	1.6	7.6	2.2	33.2
Large (100+)	92.7	8.8	85.2	5.5	26.8	6.2	8.8

Source: World Bank Enterprise Survey Database.

for this low percentage is the heavy collateral requirement. Typically, loans have to be almost 100 per cent collateralized (see Table 6.24).

TABLE 6.24
Access to Bank Loans for Myanmar Firms

Company Size	Per Cent of Firms with A Bank Loan/Line of Credit	Per Cent of Firms Not Needing a Loan	Proportion of Loans Requiring Collateral (%)	Per Cent of Firms Whose Recent Loan Application was Rejected
Small (5–19)	3.1	55.8	88.9	17.6
Medium (20–99)	13.2	55.7	100.0	7.7
Large (100+)	37.3	72.8	93.7	23.7

Source: World Bank Enterprise Survey Database.

The company perceptions captured by the OECD–UMFCCI–UNESCAP survey seem to be more in line with these hard facts. Among the top-10 major obstacles to business operations reported by companies surveyed by OECD, UMFCCI, and UNESCAP, four actually related to access to finance (Soans and Abe 2015, p. 24). In a similar vein, around 54 per cent of SMEs surveyed by DEval reported that they have additional, unmet funding needs (DEval 2015, p. 45). Accordingly, Myanmar ranks only 174th out of 189 economies on the ease of getting credit in the World Bank's *Doing Business 2016* Report (World Bank 2015c, p. 55).

4.7. Workforce

According to UNDP's "One Pager Business Census", the average number of workers per firm is 15 while the median is only 4, pointing to a very heterogeneous and polarized distribution (UNDP 2014, p. 12). From both the UNDP's "One Pager Business Census" and our own survey we know that there is quite some variations across sectors. As highlighted above, the average food manufacturer in our sample employs 105 workers while the average apparel company in our sample has 657 employees. These averages are higher than those that UNDP (2014, p. 12) found for both the food and the apparel sectors (namely 8 and

106, respectively) and also for other sectors (e.g. manufacture of wood products: 10; manufacture of textiles: 27; manufacture of electronics: 66; manufacture of electrical equipment: 51).

Only a tenth of small enterprises covered by the World Bank's Enterprise Survey offers formal training to its workforce. This percentage is a bit higher for medium-sized enterprises where about a quarter offers employees formal training (see Table 6.25). In most cases, training is provided informally through in-house on-the-job training. Interestingly, the share of unskilled workers among production workers is lower for SMEs than for large firms. Similarly, top managers of SMEs, on average, have more years of work experience in the firm's sector than top managers of large firms. This might reflect the fact that top managers of SMEs are often the owner and founder of the company who have been with the business since its establishment. Overall, according to the World Bank's Enterprise Survey data, SMEs expanded their workforce by about 4 per cent during the previous year. Only few of them (between 6 per cent of small firms and 9 per cent of medium firms) perceive labour regulations as a major constraint for doing business, while between 12 of small firms and 15 per cent of medium firms view an inadequately educated workforce as a major obstacle (see Table 6.24). In the OECD–UMFCCI–UNESCAP survey, this percentage is a bit higher, with around 20 per cent of survey participants identifying access to skilled labour as a severe obstacle for current business operations. These percentages may seem rather low, possibly reflecting that skill requirements are generally low in Myanmar. However, with its 20 per cent mentioning rate among survey respondents, availability of skilled labour is actually the second most frequently cited "very severe" constraint in the OECD–UMFCCI–UNESCAP survey (Soans and Abe 2015, p. 24). So, while filling low-skilled positions is easy in the context of an abundant supply of young and unskilled labour, finding adequate candidates for jobs that require higher skill sets seems tougher for firms. For example, nearly half of the SMEs interviewed by DEval (2015, pp. 35–36) regarded hiring skilled workers as quite or very difficult.

In addition to labour market bottlenecks at the workers' level, both findings from the OECD–UMFCCI–UNESCAP survey (Soans and Abe 2015, pp. 37–39) and anecdotal evidence from qualitative research suggest weaknesses at the managerial level as well. In a number of firms that we interviewed, there was just a general manager or a factory

TABLE 6.25
Workforce Characteristics of Myanmar Companies

Company Size	Per Cent of Firms Offering Formal Training	Proportion of Workers Offered Formal Training (%)	Years of Top Manager's Experience Working in the Firm's Sector	Proportion of Unskilled Workers (out of all production workers) (%)	Per Cent of Firms Identifying Labour Regulations as a Major Constraint	Per Cent of Firms Identifying an Inadequately Educated Workforce as a Major Constraint
Small (5–19)	10.3	62.5	12.0	20.5	5.6	11.6
Medium (20–99)	25.6	49.3	10.8	31.2	9.1	14.9
Large (100+)	31.4	38.9	9.5	59.2	1.9	11.3

Source: World Bank Enterprise Survey Database.

manager or a head of administration but there was no functional division into different branches of management. That is, these firms did not have separate finance, marketing, procurement, production, or in some cases even human resource managers. Instead, one general manager took care of the entire portfolio. Typically, the quality of management in such an arrangement without a division of labour between different branches of management and without formalized management practices is suboptimal (Bloom et al. 2010). In addition, information collected through qualitative interviews with a number of different stakeholders points to deficiencies in the capabilities of staff in managerial positions. Their knowledge is often outdated or they have only limited formal education in the area they now work in. In fact, 35 per cent of SMEs surveyed by DEval (2015, p. 36) said that finding good management staff was quite or very difficult. This difficulty in finding suitable candidates in the local labour market is one of the reasons why some firms hire foreign managers, as we will see below.

As noted earlier, the results from our own survey suggest that 92 per cent of food manufacturing and 60 per cent of apparel manufacturing firms are family-operated (see Table 6.12). Our survey then asked respondents from family-operated firms to indicate the highest educational achievements of their founder or owner. They seem to vary across sectors. In particular, the founders or owners of family-run apparel manufacturing firms tended more likely to be university educated when compared with food manufacturering firms. In general, quite a large share of respondents (around 90 per cent) indicated that the business founder or owner has secondary or even university education (see Table 6.26). Although strictly comparable questions

TABLE 6.26
Education Level of Founders/Owners of Family-run Businesses

	10. Manufacture of Food Products	14. Manufacture of Wearing Apparel
No Formal Education	3%	2%
Primary Education	9%	0%
Vocational/Diploma	0%	2%
Secondary	29%	18%
University	59%	78%

FIGURE 6.10
Percentage of Firms Reporting Expenditures on Worker Training

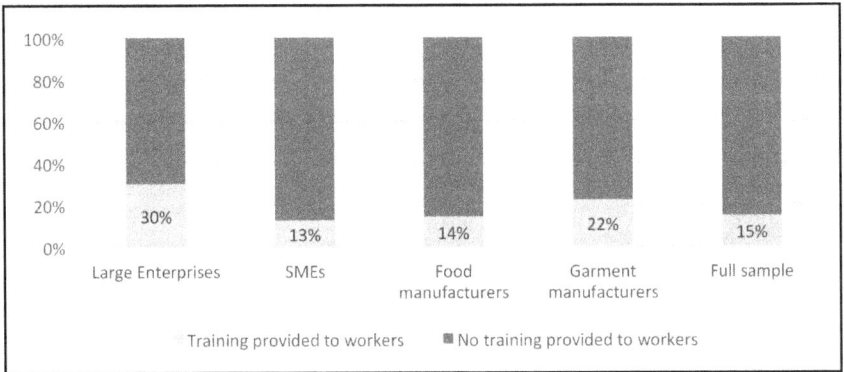

were not asked as part of the World Bank's Enterprise Survey, it is interesting to note that smaller firms tended to have such well-educated managers.

In terms of a firm's investment in training, our survey seems to confirm what was found by the World Bank's Enterprise Survey, with a relatively small proportion of responding firms (15 per cent) reporting expenditures on trainings for their workers (see Figure 6.10). The proportion of garment producers reporting training expenses was somewhat higher than that of food manufacturers (22 per cent vs. 14 per cent). Comparing across firm sizes, the large enterprises in our sample were found to be more than twice as likely than SMEs to invest in training expenditures (30 per cent vs. 13 per cent). Although it is not clear why such differences exist between SMEs and large firms, it is possible that this predominantly reflects larger organizations being more aware of the benefits of trainings and having more formalized structures and more financial potency for staff development. Furthermore, because this measure focuses on expenditure on trainings, it is likely that more informal training mechanisms, such as mentoring and on-the-job training, were not reported in our survey. At the same time, such more informal mechanisms of skills development and skills upgrading seem particularly important for SMEs. The DEval survey found that a large majority of SMEs (between 75 and 80 per cent) provide some sort of in-house training for their staff (DEval 2015, p. 32). Similarly, data from the OECD–UMFCCI–UNESCAP survey shows that when businesses experience a lack of skilled workers, they mainly organize in-house trainings (Soans and Abe 2015, pp. 38–39).

One of the factors that possibly shapes firms' spending behaviour on training for their workers is the extent to which they source skills domestically or from abroad. The hiring of foreign experts might be viewed as a substitute for organizing formal trainings for workers in that it is hoped that foreign experts will transfer knowledge and know-how to the local workforce. Although it is not possible to directly determine this from our survey, the extent of employment of foreign staff provides a useful indication of this. As can be seen in Table 6.27, most of the sample firms have not hired any foreign worker.

TABLE 6.27
Share of Firms Employing Foreign Staff in Different Occupations

	Number of Foreign Employees							
	1	2	3	4	5	6 to 10	11 and above	None
Managers and professionals	10.6%	6.1%	2.0%	1.0%	1.0%	2.5%	1.0%	75.8%
Engineers and technicians	7.1%	3.5%	1.5%	2.0%	2.0%	4.5%	2.5%	76.8%
Supervisory and clerical	2.0%	0.0%	0.0%	0.0%	0.5%	0.5%	1.5%	95.5%
Plant and machine operators and assemblers	0.5%	0.0%	0.0%	0.0%	0.0%	0.0%	0.0%	99.5%

The occupational group most commonly filled with foreign staff is managers and professionals. More specifically, 24 per cent of all firms reported having foreign managers and professionals, although of these, the majority employ only two or less. Similarly, 23 per cent of firms in our sample employed foreign engineers and technicians. In their case, employment numbers appear to be more equally distributed with 7.1 per cent of firms reporting to have just one foreign engineer or technician, another 7 per cent employing two to four foreign engineers and technicians, while another 7 per cent of firms having hired six or more foreign engineers and technicians. This higher frequency of larger numbers of foreign engineers and technicians is likely a reflection of them being necessary at a relatively constant rate as a firm grows. Finally, only 4.5 per cent of firms reported employing foreigners as supervisory and clerical workers, with this small number likely being a result of both the fact that it is possible to source these skills locally and due to the importance of language requirements for such roles.

Figure 6.11 shows the percentages of firms in our sample that employ either one, two to five, six to ten, or more than eleven foreign staff in different occupational groups, respectively, while comparing the usage of foreign staff across sectors and firm sizes. As can be seen in the upper panel of Figure 6.11, the share of large firms reporting employment of foreign staff by far exceeds the corresponding share of SMEs for all three occupational groups displayed. The difference is particularly striking for the employment of foreign managers and professionals, and the employment of foreign engineers and technicians. While almost half of the large enterprises in our sample reported having at least one foreign manager or professional in their workforce, the same is true for only 6 per cent of SMEs. Moreover, 19 per cent of large enterprises indicated that 2–5 foreign managers or professionals work for them, 4.5 per cent said that they have 6–10 foreign managers or professionals, and 2.2 per cent reported having more than 11 foreigners in these positions. At 2.8 per cent, 0.9 per cent and 0 per cent, respectively, the corresponding percentages for SMEs are significantly lower. In a similar vein, 43 per cent of large enterprises but only 7 per cent of SMEs in our survey reported having at least one foreign engineer or technician among their staff. Again, large firms are more likely to employ larger numbers of foreign engineers and technicians, with 15 per cent of them having 5 or more of them while the same is true for only 0.9 per cent of SMEs. Overall, thus, hiring foreign staff seems to be more difficult or less important for SMEs. One possible explanation might be SMEs' lower degree of integration into regional and global value chains; when firms become suppliers to international lead firms, the latter often send foreign managers and specialists to supplier firms in developing country locations in order to serve as liaison between headquarters and production facility, to improve operations and to smooth coordination and integration more generally.

FIGURE 6.11

Share of Firms Employing Foreign Staff in Different Occupations, Classified by Firm Size and Sector

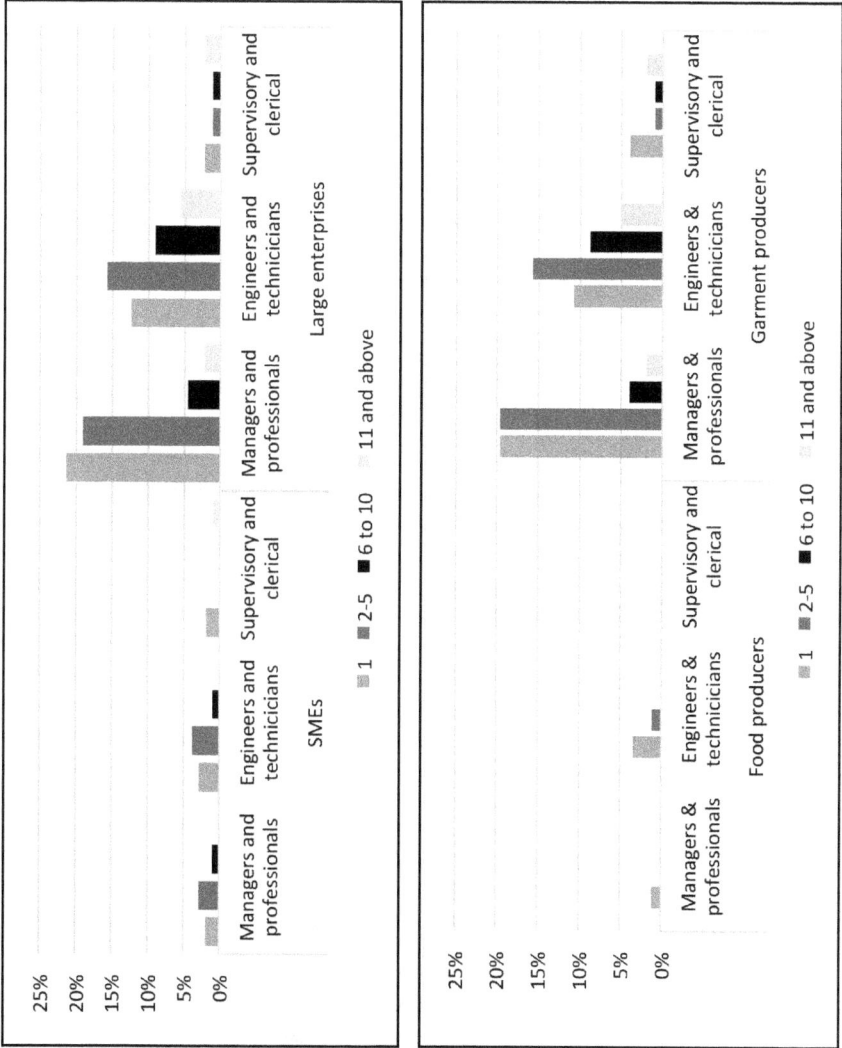

Comparing across sectors, the lower panel of Figure 6.11 reveals that the share of garment producers in our sample that employs foreign staff is much higher than that of food manufacturers. More precisely, only 4.5 per cent of food manufacturers have foreign engineers or technicians in their workforce and a mere 1.1 per cent have a foreign manager or professional. By contrast, 45.1 per cent of the garment producers in our sample employ at least one foreign manager or professional (and 5.9 per cent even more than five) while 40.2 per cent of them have at least one foreign engineer or technician in their workforce (and 13.7 per cent have more than five). To a certain extent, this reflects garment firms' higher degree of integration into cross-border value chains (see also Tables 6.28, 6.30 and 6.33).

TABLE 6.28
Countries of Origin of Foreign Investors in Myanmar by Sector and Firm Size

	Share of Respondents				
	Full Sample	SMEs	Large Enterprises	Food Producers	Garment Producers
Korea	9.80%	0.00%	21.60%	0.00%	19.40%
Japan	9.30%	2.90%	17.00%	2.20%	16.30%
China	6.20%	1.00%	12.50%	1.10%	11.20%
Hong Kong	6.20%	2.90%	10.20%	1.10%	11.20%
Taiwan	2.60%	0.00%	5.70%	0.00%	5.10%
EU countries	1.60%	1.00%	2.30%	1.10%	2.00%
Australia	1.00%	1.00%	1.10%	0.00%	2.00%
India	1.00%	1.00%	1.10%	0.00%	1.00%
Thailand	1.00%	0.00%	2.30%	0.00%	2.00%
Indonesia	0.50%	0.00%	1.10%	0.00%	1.00%
Norway	0.50%	0.00%	1.10%	0.00%	1.00%
Malaysia	0.50%	0.00%	1.10%	0.00%	1.00%
Singapore	0.50%	0.00%	1.10%	1.10%	0.00%
No foreign investment (locally-owned)	66.80%	92.30%	36.40%	96.60%	38.80%

Note: Multiple responses are possible per respondent.

In the previous section we have shed light on some key characteristics of SMEs in Myanmar in general, and those operating in the food and apparel manufacturing sectors more specifically. This section looks at Myanmar SMEs' interactions with companies in foreign countries, with a specific focus on countries in ASEAN and East Asia. In doing so, it undertakes an investigation into the extent of Myanmar SMEs' integration into regional and global economic relations, addressing the following questions: What is the state of Myanmar SMEs' participation in regional trade, production networks, and investment activities? How have regional and preferential trade agreements affected SMEs' activities and performance?

5.1. SMEs, FDI, GVCs and Trade: Some Conceptual Foundations

In today's world economy, the production of an increasing number of goods and services is fragmented internationally and carried out in regional or international production networks whereby individual production step takes place in different locations around the world. That is, countries often no longer specialize in producing certain products in their entirety but rather specialize in a set of tasks that makes up a given stage of production of an individual product. As a result, international trade increasingly takes place within regional and global value chains that are governed by lead firms and multinational corporations. While implying new challenges, these developments have also created new opportunities for SMEs in developing countries to integrate into international trade flows by linking to and supplying to such regional and global value chains (Bamber et al. 2014; Gereffi 1994; Harvie 2010b; Harvie and Charoenrat 2015; Kaplinsky 2005; Lim and Kimura 2010; UNCTAD 2010; Wignaraja 2013.

In many cases, the spreading of such cross-border value chains involves FDI flows whereby lead firms from advanced economies (including large retailers, brand marketers and brand manufacturers) set up production facilities or enter joint ventures with local producers in developing countries (UNCTAD 2013b; World Bank 2014b). SMEs in developing countries can benefit from FDI inflows and the integration into regional and global value chains in various ways. First, the spreading of regional and global value chains opens up opportunities for SMEs not only to engage in direct exporting but also in indirect exporting, i.e. acting as subcontractors and second-tier suppliers to companies that export. Second, many foreign companies that subcontract certain productive tasks to SMEs in developing countries provide (at least initial) trainings to these suppliers to familiarize them with better production processes and help them to improve quality and productivity. Third, in some cases doing business with foreign companies involves the transfer of technology and know-how. In such cases, local producers are given more modern machinery or at least support in making the right choices for new investments. Moreover, they may benefit from the transfer of know-how not only on production processes but also in terms of non-production activities such as managerial practices, R&D sourcing, marketing, logistics or distribution. Fourth, foreign buyers are often quite demanding when it comes to volume, quality and consistency of supplies. They typically require their suppliers to have a minimum level of capacity to comply with technical, quality and other standards (both public and private standards). Being confronted with such stringent requirements can provide a stimulus to SMEs to improve production processes and the quality of their products and to become more productive and competitive (Bamber et al. 2014; UNCTAD 2010; UNIDO 2015; World Bank 2014b).

However, participating in international markets also comes with a lot of challenges. The most important one is probably the intensified competition with suppliers from other countries both in foreign and domestic markets. More productive foreign competitors are able to offer various products more cheaply and with better quality. Moreover, many SMEs in developing countries struggle to meet the consistency requirements of foreign buyers, both in terms of the quantities demanded and the compliance with their stringent technical and quality standards. Entering foreign markets also involves the need to obtain information about them and knowledge on distribution channels. Obtaining such information and developing such knowledge implies costs which many SMEs cannot easily afford. Participating in international trade is quite a risky undertaking, given that buyers locate in different countries with different political and legal systems as well as using different currencies. This is why most firms engaging in cross-border transactions seek to cover themselves against these commercial and political risks inherent in international trade. However, SMEs often lack the resources for such hedging (Harvie 2010a; Harvie and Charoenrat 2015; Puusaag et al. 2015; UNESCAP 2012). For SMEs in a country like Myanmar that only recently re-opened to the international economy, these challenges might be too much to overcome, not least due to a lack of experience.

5.2. FDI in Myanmar

As discussed, recent years have seen an increasing international fragmentation of production, the spreading of global value chains (GVCs) and the increasing integration of developing countries in such GVCs with lead firms deciding where to locate production tasks and functions according to comparative and cost advantages of the host country. FDI is a key driver behind these developments, supporting the setting up, expansion and upgrading of production facilities in developing countries. These trends are also observable in Myanmar which has seen a rapid increase in FDI inflows ever since it opened its economy in 2011. As mentioned above, around the turn of the millennium, Myanmar attracted few foreign investors, mostly from East Asia, who almost exclusively invested in natural resource extraction and export-oriented hydropower projects. By contrast, in recent years, Myanmar has not only seen a significant increase in the number of FDI projects but also a diversification in terms of sectors and investor countries of origin. While there are still investments in natural resource and power projects, a lot of new FDI projects are in manufacturing, tourism, telecommunications, and other non-extractive sectors with an increasing interest also from Western investors (ASEAN and UNCTAD 2014).[12]

As we have seen in Table 6.10, Singapore, Thailand, Vietnam and Malaysia have been the most prominent ASEAN foreign investors in Myanmar while China, Hong Kong and South Korea have been important sources of FDI from the East Asia region. By contrast, investors from non-Asian countries, for now at least, still play a rather subdued role in Myanmar. This is also revealed in Table 6.28 which shows the ranking of the countries of origin of foreign investors who have invested in the manufacturing firms in our survey sample. As can be seen there, 9.3 per cent of respondents reported that they have foreign investment from Japan; this includes both fully foreign-owned firms as well as joint ventures with Japanese assets-holding. This is interesting as, according to Table 6.10, Myanmar has not received much FDI from Japan in the recent past. The fact that Japan ranks number 1 as FDI source among our survey companies, thus, largely reflects older Japanese investment from the early and mid-2000s, particularly in the garment sector (Kudo 2013). Another 9 per cent of our survey firms reported having foreign investment from Korea while about 6 per cent each indicated that they had investment from China and Hong Kong. By comparison, countries from the EU are the most important non-Asian source of FDI for the Myanmar enterprises in our survey sample — but their overall significance is limited as only 1.6 per cent of companies surveyed reported investment from the EU, followed by 1 per cent who reported investment from Australia and 0.5 per cent who reported investment from Norway.

Table 6.28 also shows that the share of large enterprises in our sample that are foreign-invested is much higher than that of foreign-invested SMEs. While 92.3 per cent of the SMEs in our sample are entirely locally owned (i.e. have no foreign asset holders), the same is true for only 36.4 per cent of large enterprises. Among the SMEs, 2.9 per cent each reported to have at least some Japanese and Hong Kong investment, while 1 per cent reported foreign investment from China, India, Australia and the EU. By contrast, 21.6 per cent of large enterprises have foreign investment from Korea, 17 per cent from Japan, 12.5 per cent from China and 10.2 per cent from Hong Kong. There are also some that reported foreign investment from Taiwan, EU, Thailand and other Southeast Asian countries. Table 6.28 also allows comparisons between the food and the garment sectors. In the former, the share of fully domestically owned enterprises (96.6 percent) is much higher than in the latter (38.8 per cent), reflecting that garment firms tend to be both larger and more integrated into cross-border value chains than food manufacturers. Most prominent among foreign investors in Myanmar garment producers are those from Korea, Japan, China, and Hong Kong; between 10 and 20 per cent of garment firms in our sample reported foreign investment from these countries. While Japanese, Chinese and Hong Kong investors are also the most important sources of foreign capital in the food manufacturing sector, the percentage of food producers with investment from these countries is much smaller (between 2.2 per cent and 1.1 per cent). The Myanmar food processing sector, thus, is still largely in Myanmar hands.

5.3. Participation of Myanmar companies in global trade

Exports to foreign countries almost play no role for most of Myanmar SMEs. Compared to other ASEAN countries, Myanmar's SMEs appear to be less likely to export their produce (see Table 6.29 and Figure 6.12).

Myanmar SMEs' Participation in Regional Economic Integration

TABLE 6.29
SME Participation in International Trade for Selected ASEAN Countries

Economy and Survey Year	Firm Size (no. of employees)	Per Cent of Firms Exporting Directly or Indirectly (at least 1% of sales)	Per Cent of Firms Exporting Directly (at least 1% of sales)	Proportion of Total Sales that are Exported Directly (%)	Proportion of Total Sales that are Exported Indirectly (%)	Per Cent of Firms Using Material Inputs and/ or Supplies of Foreign Origin	Proportion of Total Inputs that are of Foreign Origin (%)
Cambodia 2013	Medium (20–99)	5.3	4.4	3.0	0.5	n.a.	0.0
	Small (5–19)	1.8	1.0	0.7	0.4	n.a.	0.0
Indonesia 2009	Medium (20–99)	14.2	8.3	3.8	4.3	12.5	6.0
	Small (5–19)	1.6	0.9	0.3	0.5	2.5	1.1
Lao PDR 2012	Medium (20–99)	33.0	22.6	18.4	8.2	53.3	33.5
	Small (5–19)	19.4	9.9	6.4	6.9	25.4	11.3
Malaysia 2007	Medium (20–99)	54.5	51.6	23.3	3.4	43.5	25.4
	Small (5–19)	30.0	25.1	13.5	3.1	30.3	16.8
Myanmar 2014	Medium (20–99	4.2	3.0	2.5	0.3	26.8	14.3
	Small (5–19))	0.8	0.6	0.6	0.2	12.6	8.5
Philippines 2009	Medium (20-99)	16.5	11.3	7.3	3.6	57.3	40.3
	Small (5–19)	5.0	2.0	0.5	2.2	20.9	12.2
Thailand 2006	Medium (20–99)	58.3	27.7	12.8	1.3	100.0	n.a.
	Small (5–19)	40.7	16.7	7.3	0.7	100.0	n.a.
Vietnam 2009	Medium (20–99)	23.2	12.0	7.0	6.2	58.7	39.4
	Small (5–19)	5.1	4.6	4.4	0.3	42.5	15.2

Note: Figures reported are averages; sample sizes and survey years differ across countries.
Source: World Bank Enterprise Survey Database.

233

FIGURE 6.12
Percentage of SMEs Exporting Directly or Indirectly (at least 1% of sales)

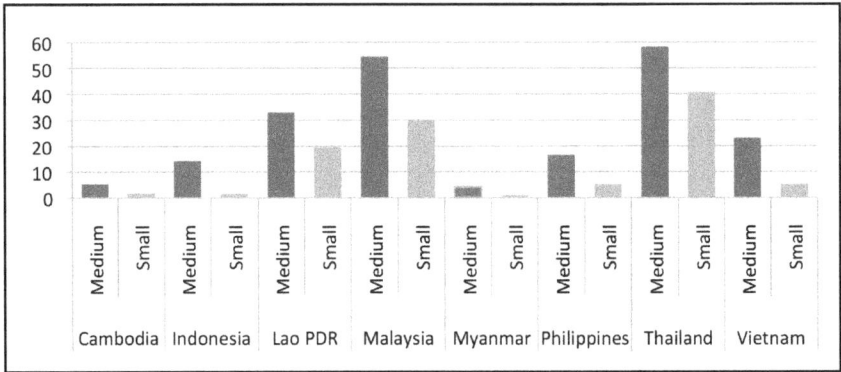

Note: Small enterprises are defined as having 5–19 employees while medium enterprises are defined as having 20–99 employees; figures reported are averages; sample sizes and survey years differ across countries.
Source: World Bank Enterprise Survey Database.

According to the World Bank's Enterprise Survey, only 4.2 per cent of medium-sized companies and 0.8 per cent of small enterprises export directly or indirectly at least 1 per cent of sales. Similarly, among the SMEs surveyed by DEval, only around 4 per cent stated that they export at all. These percentages are considerably lower than those for fellow ASEAN member states, which is at least partly a reflection of the long period that Myanmar had been closed off internationally.

Overall, the DEval survey found that "the main marketing channel for micro and small enterprises are their own shop(s) and wholesalers in the same region [see Figure 6.13]. In general, micro enterprises tend to trade within their local areas, whereas small and medium enterprises also market their goods and services through traders from other regions" (DEval 2015, p. 20) while "[e]xports to foreign countries are largely irrelevant" (DEval 2015, p. 21).

However, there are some variations across sectors. In fact, in our survey 7 per cent of small firms, 56 per cent of medium-sized firms, and 91 per cent of large firms indicated that they export at least some of their output (see Table 6.33). With that, the share of exporting firms in our sample is significantly higher than those in the World Bank's Enterprise Survey and the DEval survey. The explanation for this significant difference lies in the fact that firms from export-oriented

FIGURE 6.13
Main Marketing Channels (%)

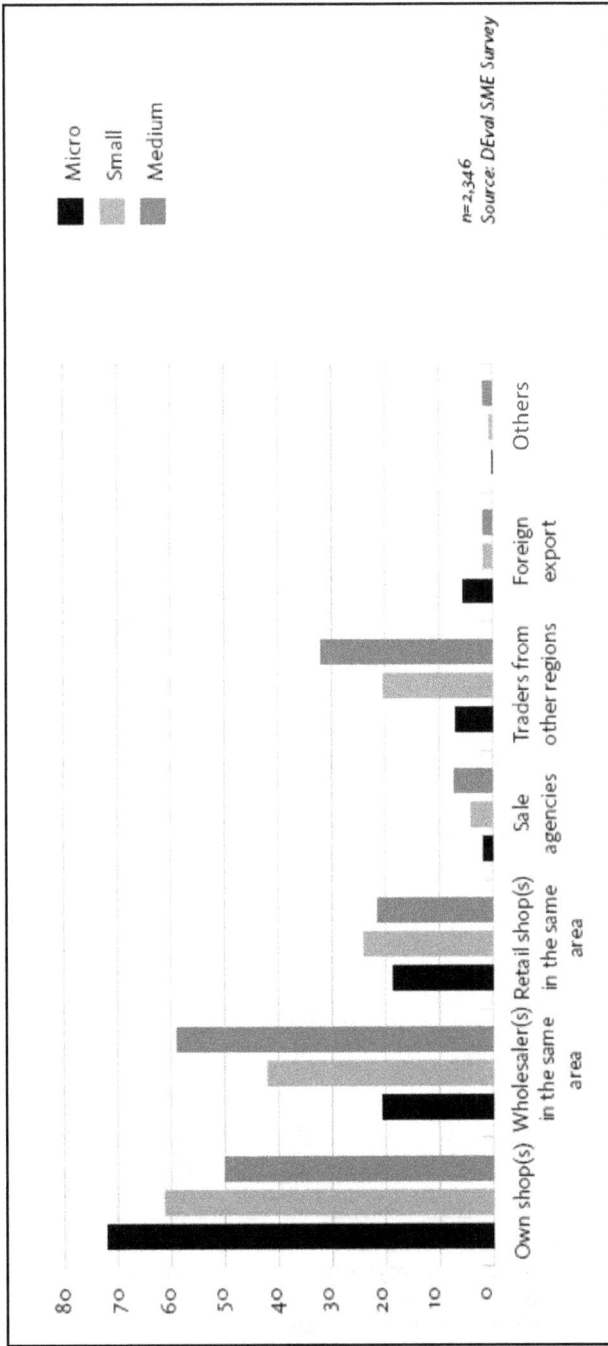

Note: DEval (2015, p. 20).

sectors dominate our survey sample. In fact, more than half of the firms in our sample operate in the apparel sector (which is heavily export-oriented in Myanmar; see MGMA 2015 and also Table 6.33 which shows that 84 per cent of all apparel companies surveyed are exporters) while another 45 per cent of survey firms are food manufacturers (of which 27 per cent export; again see Table 6.33).

Looking at the import side, Myanmar's SMEs appear to source less of their material inputs and supplies from abroad, compared to other ASEAN countries, which points to their lower degree of integration into international production networks. More precisely, according to the World Bank's Enterprise Survey, the proportion of total inputs that Myanmar SMEs source from foreign suppliers (14.3 per cent in the case of medium-sized firms and 8.5 per cent in the case of small firms) is smaller than in other ASEAN countries (see Table 6.29). The World Bank's Enterprise Survey also found that 27 per cent of medium-sized firms and 13 per cent of small enterprises in Myanmar use material inputs and/or supplies of foreign origin. These percentages are significantly lower than those seen in Laos, Malaysia, the Philippines or

FIGURE 6.14
Percentage of SMEs Using Material Inputs and/or Supplies of Foreign Origin

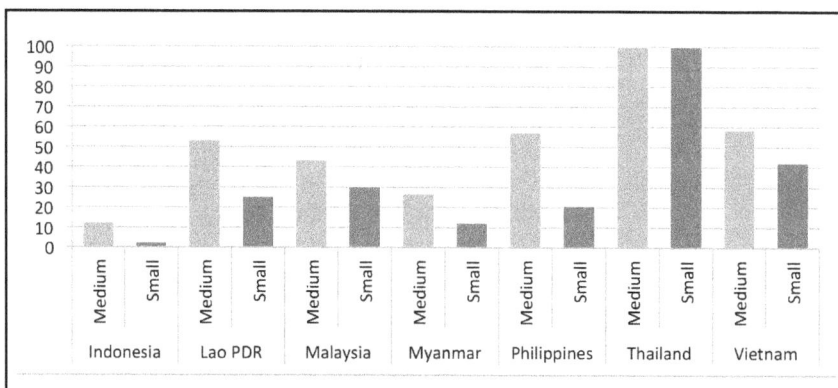

Note: Small enterprises are defined as having 5–19 employees while medium enterprises are defined as having 20–99 employees; figures reported are averages; sample sizes and survey years differ across countries.
Source: World Bank Enterprise Survey Database.

Vietnam, for example, where between 40 and 60 per cent of medium-sized firms and between 20 and 40 per cent of small enterprises source inputs or supplies from abroad (see Figure 6.14).

Again, however, there are differences across sectors. According to our survey, 88 per cent of Myanmar food manufacturers source all their inputs domestically with just 2 per cent sourcing all their inputs from abroad and 10 per cent sourcing at least some of their inputs from foreign suppliers. By contrast, foreign inputs are much more important for the Myanmar apparel sector. A staggering 45 per cent of the apparel firms in our sample indicated that they get all their inputs from abroad and another 50 per cent source at least some inputs from foreign suppliers while just 5 per cent of respondents said that they source all their inputs locally (see Table 6.30). This can be explained by the peculiar integration of Myanmar's garment sector into regional and global value chains: at present, the large majority of Myanmar apparel factories operate under the CMP model which is a form of contract work where foreign buyers take care of all the sourcing. That is, the buyer ships all necessary inputs to the Myanmar garment factory which then just carries out the labour-intensive CMP activities, assembling garment components that are purchased and supplied by the buyers themselves. In other words, the Myanmar apparel industry currently has little backward integration as the local textile and the packaging industries are underdeveloped and are not

TABLE 6.30
Source of Inputs by Industry and Firm Size

	INDUSTRY		SIZE			
	10. Food	14. Apparel	Small	Medium	Large	Full sample
All inputs sourced locally	88%	5%	74%	36%	5%	55%
All inputs sourced abroad	2%	45%	9%	36%	36%	18%
At least some inputs sourced abroad	10%	50%	17%	27%	59%	27%
Total	100%	100%	100%	100%	100%	100%

able to supply inputs in the quantity and/or quality needed by the export-oriented garment producers (ILO 2015; MoC and ITC 2015*a*; MGMA 2015).

These cross-sectoral differences and sectoral specificities also explain why the findings from our survey deviate somewhat from those of the World Bank's Enterprise Survey. According to our survey, 26 per cent of small companies and 64 per cent of medium-sized enterprises source some or even all their inputs from abroad (see Table 6.30). These percentages are higher than those found by the World Bank's Enterprise Survey — with these differences being driven by the fact that apparel factories, which have to import a lot of their inputs, make up over 50 per cent of our sample. However, the SMEs in our sample are still less likely than the large enterprises to import supplies from abroad — with 95 per cent of the latter reporting that they source some or even all their inputs from foreign suppliers.

5.4. Integration of Myanmar's SMEs into Regional Trade and Production Networks

In the previous sub-section, we looked at the extent to which Myanmar SMEs interact with global markets, in terms of both exporting products and importing inputs. This sub-section addresses the question of what the current state is in terms of Myanmar SMEs' participation in regional trade, production networks, and investment activities. When we say *regional*, we mean, on the one hand, ASEAN and, on the other hand, the East Asia region.

Tables 6.31 and 6.32 give an overview of the extent and type of business relations that survey firms have with companies in other ASEAN member states. They show that Myanmar is hardly integrated into ASEAN business networks. As can be seen in Table 6.31, only 13 per cent of responding firm reported having any business relationship with companies in other ASEAN countries. The share is largest among medium-sized firms (16.7 per cent), followed by large enterprises (16.1 per cent) while only a minority of small firms (5.7 per cent) engage in businesses with companies in other ASEAN countries. Table 6.31 also shows that firms with foreign ownership are slightly more likely to have ASEAN business relations than fully domestically owned firms (15.6 vs. 11.9 per cent).

TABLE 6.31
Share of Firms with ASEAN Business Relations by Firm Size and Foreign Ownership

	ASEAN Business Relations?	
	No	Yes
Small	94.3%	5.7%
Medium	83.3%	16.7%
Large	83.9%	16.1%
Domestically Owned (%)	86.6%	11.9%
Foreign-invested (%)	82.8%	15.6%
Total (%)	85.4%	13.1%

TABLE 6.32
Business Relationships with ASEAN Countries

	Percentage of Respondents Importing from	Percentage of Respondents Exporting to	Percentage of Respondents with Investment in/from
Thailand	4.6%	2.6%	NA
Malaysia	3.1%	3.1%	1.0%
Singapore	1.0%	2.1%	NA
Vietnam	0.5%	1.5%	NA
Cambodia	0.5%	NA	0.5%
Indonesia	0.5%	NA	NA
ASEAN Total	8.2%	7.2%	1.5%
Non-ASEAN	2.1%	1.5%	0.5%

Table 6.32 provides more details on the type of business relations and the countries of origin of the business partners. As can be seen from the table, three of the nine other ASEAN member states do not show up as business relationship partners for Myanmar, namely: Brunei, Laos, and the Philippines. That is, none of our survey companies reported any business relationship with companies in these three countries. By contrast, Thailand, Malaysia and Singapore seem to be

the most important business partner countries within ASEAN. Thailand is the source of imports for 4.6 per cent of the respondents and the destination for exports for 2.6 per cent of the respondents. As for Malaysia, it is the source of imports for 3.1 per cent of the respondents, the destination for exports for another 3.1 per cent of respondents, and the country where 1 per cent reported having investment relations. By contrast, business interactions of survey firms with companies in Cambodia, Indonesia and Vietnam are almost negligible at the moment.

In relative terms, the most important type of ASEAN business relationship is import: 8.2 per cent of survey firms reported that they import from one other ASEAN member state. Meanwhile, 7.2 per cent of respondents said they export to at least one other ASEAN country while only 1.5 per cent reported any investment relationship with ASEAN businesses. Overall, thus, there is still very little business engagement of Myanmar firms with counterparts in other ASEAN countries.

Please note that, when asked to identify the countries of origin of their ASEAN business partners, some respondents actually mentioned non-ASEAN countries such as China, Japan, Hong Kong or Taiwan. The percentage of respondents mentioning non-ASEAN countries is given in the last row of Table 6.32. The fact that some respondents mistake China, Japan, Hong Kong or Taiwan for ASEAN member states reinforces the notion that awareness of and knowledge about ASEAN is still quite limited among Myanmar enterprises.

Looking in more detail at the composition of firms exporting to ASEAN, we see that while only 4 per cent of small firms reported exports to ASEAN, the corresponding shares are 9 per cent for medium-sized and 7 per cent for large enterprises (see Table 6.33). Overall, East Asia seems to be a more important export destination than ASEAN: while merely 7 per cent of responding firms reported exports to ASEAN, 41 per cent reported exports to East Asia. For medium-sized and large firms, in particular, East Asia appears to be an important market: 35 per cent of medium-sized and 67 per cent of large survey firms export to East Asia — while the corresponding percentages for ASEAN exports are much smaller at 9 per cent and 7 per cent, respectively. Small companies are the only group where the share of exporters to ASEAN (4 per cent) is higher than that to East Asia (3 per cent).

TABLE 6.33
Exporting Firms by Industry, Firm Size and Export Markets

Size	Share of Exporting Firms (All)	Share of Firms Exporting to ASEAN	Share of Firms Exporting to East Asia
Small	7%	4%	3%
Medium	56%	9%	35%
Large	91%	7%	67%
Industry			
10. Manufacture of food products	27%	11%	15%
14. Manufacture of wearing apparel	84%	3%	59%
Total	61%	7%	41%

Again there are important differences across sectors. While ASEAN is a more important export market for Myanmar food manufactures (of which 11 per cent export to other ASEAN countries) than for Myanmar apparel producers (of which only 3 per cent reported exports to ASEAN), the reverse is true for East Asia. Almost 60 per cent of Myanmar apparel firms export to East Asia but just 15 per cent of food producers do so (see Table 6.33). This reflects the fact that in view of U.S. and EU sanctions starting in 2003, Myanmar apparel producers began to target the East Asian countries of Japan and Korea as substitute export markets and these two countries are still the most important destinations for Myanmar apparel exports today (Kudo 2008; MoC and ITC 2015a).

Indeed, as can be seen in the right panel of Table 6.34, 46 per cent of all apparel firms in our sample reported exports to Japan (making it the single most important export destination among the survey firms) while another 25 per cent export to Korea (giving it a ranking of fourth). However, as can also be seen in the table, the lifting of sanctions in recent years (and especially the EU's reinstatement of Myanmar into its GSP) led to both the United States and the EU gaining ground again as export markets for Myanmar garment products. In fact, 33 per cent of apparel producers in our sample named the United States as an export destination and 32 per cent of respondents said

TABLE 6.34
Myanmar's Major Export Destinations by Industry

Export Market	Food		Apparel	
	Percentage of Respondents	Rank	Percentage of Respondents	Rank
Japan	10.0%	(1)	46.1%	(1)
EU countries	5.0%	(2)	31.6%	(3)
China	5.0%	(2)	6.6%	(5)
Thailand	5.0%	(2)	2.6%	(8)
Malaysia	5.0%	(2)	2.6%	(8)
Singapore	5.0%	(2)	1.3%	(11)
Australia	3.3%	(7)	3.9%	(6)
Hong Kong	3.3%	(7)	1.3%	(11)
United Arab Emirates	3.3%	(7)	NA	NA
Vietnam	3.3%	(7)	NA	NA
United States	1.7%	(11)	32.9%	(2)
Korea	1.7%	(11)	25.0%	(4)
Taiwan	1.7%	(11)	2.6%	(8)
Kuwait	1.7%	(11)	NA	NA
Asian countries	1.7%	(11)	NA	NA
Saudi Arabia	1.7%	(11)	NA	NA
Qatar	1.7%	(11)	NA	NA

they ship products to the EU countries. The United States and the EU, thus, rank second and third in terms of frequency of being mentioned as export markets by the survey participants.[13]

Apart from these top four export destinations (Japan, the United States, the EU countries, Korea), other export markets were mentioned only by a small minority of survey respondents. Most of these other apparel export markets are in the region, however: China was mentioned by 6.6 per cent of Myanmar apparel producers (rank fifth), Australia by 3.9 per cent, and Malaysia, Taiwan and Thailand by 2.6 per cent each.

The picture is quite different for the food manufacturing sector. While Japan also ranks as the most frequently mentioned export market, it was mentioned by only 10 per cent of the respondents (compared to 46 per cent in the apparel sector). Similarly, the three other markets that dominated the ranking in the apparel sector are much less important as export markets for Myanmar food manufacturers: only 1.7 per cent of the respondents reported exporting to the United States, 5 per cent to the EU, and 1.7 per cent to Korea. Other countries seem equally important as buyers of Myanmar food products. This includes countries that play no or just a minor role as export markets for Myanmar apparel, both within the region (Malaysia, Singapore, Thailand and Vietnam as ASEAN members as well as China, Hong Kong and Taiwan in East Asia) and outside the region, particularly in the Middle East. Unlike in the apparel sector, the United Arab Emirates, Kuwait, Qatar and Saudi Arabia are mentioned as importers of Myanmar food products.

Overall, thus, a comparison of the food and the apparel sectors based on the figures presented in Table 6.34 suggests three conclusions: first, a smaller share of Myanmar food producers actually export; second, export markets for Myanmar food products seem to be more diversified (or, conversely, Myanmar apparel exports are more concentrated in a few, in fact, four dominant markets); and, third, more generally, Myanmar food exporters target other foreign markets than Myanmar apparel producers.

Meanwhile, Table 6.35 compares the export orientation of Myanmar SMEs against that of large firms. It shows the percentage of respondents which reported exporting to different foreign markets, ranking these export markets according to their frequency of mention. Comparing the figures for SMEs with those for large firms, first of all, reveals that the latter are much higher, reflecting the fact that large firms in Myanmar have a much higher export propensity than SMEs. Looking at the rankings of export markets of SMEs vs. large enterprises shows that large firms are able to export to high-income markets (such as Japan, the EU and the United States), where customers are typically more demanding with regard to the quality, sophistication and consistency of supply, whereas most SMEs are unable to do so. Among large firms, 35 per cent said they export to the EU and 32 per cent to the United States, whereas only 5.6 per cent of SMEs reported exporting to these two markets. Japan ranks first as the most frequently mentioned

TABLE 6.35
Myanmar's Major Export Destinations by Firm Size

Export Market	All Firms		SMEs		Large Firms	
	Percentage of Respondents	Rank	Percentage of Respondents	Rank	Percentage of Respondents	Rank
Japan	29.7%	(1)	12.5%	(1)	47.0%	(1)
EU countries	19.6%	(2)	5.6%	(2)	34.8%	(2)
US	18.8%	(3)	5.6%	(2)	31.8%	(3)
Korea	14.5%	(4)	2.8%	(6)	24.2%	(4)
China	6.5%	(5)	5.6%	(2)	9.1%	(5)
Thailand	3.6%	(6)	2.8%	(6)	4.5%	(6)
Malaysia	3.6%	(6)	4.2%	(5)	3.0%	(9)
Australia	3.6%	(6)	2.8%	(6)	4.5%	(6)
Singapore	2.9%	(9)	2.8%	(6)	3.0%	(9)
Hong Kong	2.2%	(10)	1.4%	(11)	3.0%	(9)
Taiwan	2.2%	(10)	NA	NA	4.5%	(6)
Russia	2.2%	(10)	1.4%	(11)	3.0%	(9)

export market among both SMEs and large enterprises — while 47 per cent of large firms in our survey indicated exporting to Japan, only 12.5 per cent of SMEs did so.

By contrast, regional markets with less demanding customers seem comparatively more important for SME exporters. For example, China was mentioned as often as the EU and the United States as export market for Myanmar SMEs participating in our survey (whereas among large firms it was mentioned three times less than the EU and the United States). In a similar vein, Malaysia ranks as the fifth most frequently mentioned export market for SMEs — while it ranks only ninth among large firms.

So far, we have only looked at the export side of Myanmar SMEs' integration into regional trade and production networks. In the following paragraphs, we shed some light on their backward integration, i.e. import relationships with ASEAN and East Asian countries. We have already seen in Table 6.30 that 74 per cent of small Myanmar firms indicated that they source all their inputs locally while only 17 per cent source at least some inputs from abroad and 9 per cent import all their inputs. Among medium-sized firms, the situation is the opposite with just 36 per cent getting all their inputs domestically and 64 per cent sourcing at least some inputs from foreign suppliers.

Table 6.36 provides some details on the countries of origin of these foreign inputs as well as on the differences between the food industry and the apparel industry. As can be seen from the table, in general, non-Asian countries play a negligible role as foreign suppliers of inputs. That is, if Myanmar companies source inputs from abroad, they mostly do so from ASEAN and East Asian countries. Overall, China is the most important foreign source of inputs with 24 per cent of the respondents importing supplies from there, followed by Thailand and Japan (10 per cent of respondents each). For Myanmar food manufacturers, however, Malaysia is the most important source of foreign inputs; 5 per cent of surveyed food firms indicated they obtain at least some of their supplies there. China and Thailand rank as the second most frequently mentioned countries of origin of imported inputs in the food sector (with 3 per cent of respondents each, indicating that they source inputs from there).

By contrast, for the apparel sector it can be observed, first, that a much larger share of respondents source at least some inputs from abroad and, second, that China and Japan are the most important

TABLE 6.36
Sources of Foreign Inputs by Sector and Country of Origin

Import Source	Full Sample Percentage of Respondents	Food Percentage of Respondents	Apparel Percentage of Respondents
China	24%	3%	57%
Thailand	10%	3%	16%
Japan	10%	0%	30%
Malaysia	9%	5%	11%
Korea	6%	2%	16%
EU countries	5%	0%	11%
Indonesia	4%	0%	11%
Taiwan	4%	0%	11%
Vietnam	3%	0%	8%
Hong Kong	2%	0%	5%
Singapore	2%	2%	3%
United States	2%	2%	3%

countries of origin of these foreign supplies, followed by Thailand and Korea. More precisely, more than half of the respondents source inputs from China, almost a third from Japan, and 16 per cent each from Thailand and Korea. Given this high incidence of regional sourcing and the great importance of East Asian markets for exports that was documented above, it can be said that apparel production is the most pronounced case of a Myanmar industry being integrated into regional production sharing and regional value chains.

In summary, Myanmar SMEs appear to have a relatively low level of export orientation. At the same time, in some sectors, most notably garments, Myanmar companies depend to a large extent on foreign inputs. More generally, owing to the progressive opening of the country's economy, Myanmar SMEs increasingly come under pressure in their domestic markets (both for intermediate and final goods) from cheaper imports and foreign competition. The common preferential tariff scheme applied in the ASEAN community, for example, has led to an influx of often higher quality and cheaper products from other ASEAN countries, threatening the future of many SMEs in Myanmar as they push the prices of products in the local market down to levels that local SMEs cannot achieve. In markets for products such as canned and snack foods, plastic products and toys, for example, local producers must compete with products from Thailand. Similarly, household products, appliances and consumer electronic products are facing price competition from cheaper products, especially from China (Abe and Dutta 2014). This competitive pressure from foreign firms is expected to intensify with the launch of AEC at the end of 2015. Yet, local companies, and SMEs in particular, do not seem to be fully aware of this. This will be discussed in the next sub-section.

5.5. Awareness and Perceptions of AEC, Trade Agreements and Implications of Regional Integration

Most of Myanmar SMEs do not (yet) seem to be prepared to keep up with the global transformation of business strategies and practices. That is, they are unable to take advantage of the benefits and opportunities provided by global and especially regional integration. This is partly due to their lack of awareness about business opportunities in foreign markets, for example those arising from trade preferences. Accordingly, the OECD–UMFCCI–UNESCAP survey found that firms still have more localized concerns and do not view issues such as foreign competition and international sanctions as particularly severe obstacles to their businesses (Soans and Abe 2015).

In a similar vein, our survey found that a significant share of Myanmar SMEs are actually not aware of the AEC, let alone its implications and the possible opportunities (e.g. in terms of access to ASEAN markets) that it offers. Figure 6.15 shows that only around 25 per cent of the SMEs responding to our survey each indicated being aware of the AEC and of the ASEAN Blueprint for SME Development. Interestingly, however, this is still a higher level of awareness than among the large enterprises in our survey. This is quite a striking finding which requires further investigation. Similarly, when asked about how the AEC has affected or will affect their businesses in different areas, half or more of the respondents said that they "don't know" or have "no opinion". That is, only half or less of the survey participants expressed an opinion on the impacts they expect the AEC to have on their businesses[14] — their responses are displayed in Figure 6.16. As can be seen from the figure, optimism trumps pessimism when it

FIGURE 6.15

FIGURE 6.15
Awareness of AEC and ASEAN Blueprint for SME Development by Industry and Firm Size

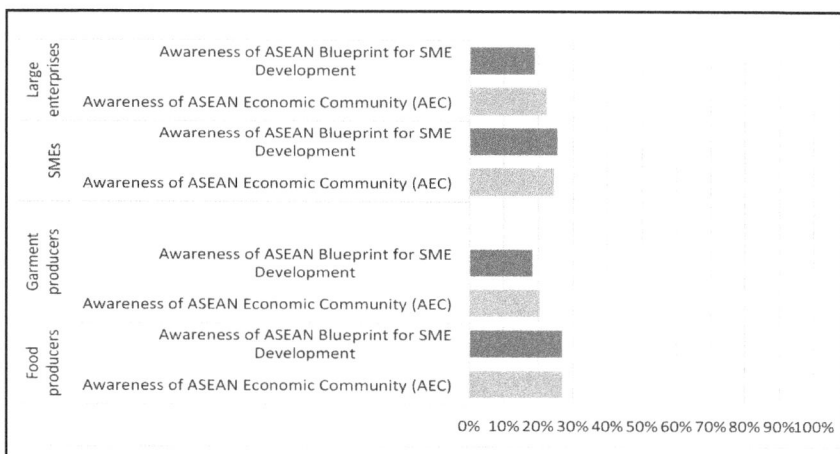

comes to profits, access to intermediate inputs and particularly exports (where the share of respondents expecting an increase is larger than that expecting a decrease). In general, large enterprises appear to be more optimistic with regard to these variables (and especially exports) than SMEs. Moreover, large enterprises also tend to be more optimistic with respect to domestic sales while among SMEs the share of skeptics (who are afraid domestic sales will decrease) is as large as the share of optimists (who expect domestic sales to increase).

Figure 6.16 shows that, in general, there are also concerns related to import cost, competition in the local market and especially competition in foreign markets where more respondents expect an increase rather than a decrease in competition. Interestingly, there are quite some differences between SMEs and large firms in their expectations for these variables. Large enterprises seem particularly worried about losing out to competition in foreign markets, which 52 per cent of them (but only 25 per cent of SMEs) expect competition to increase and none expects it to decrease. Similarly, large enterprises tend to be more pessimistic about import cost — which a third of them, but only a fifth of SMEs, expect import cost to rise. By contrast, SMEs are more concerned about competition in the local market; 32 per cent of them expect competition to intensify while only 24 per cent of large firms

FIGURE 6.16

Firms' Responses to the Question: "How Has AEC Affected or Will Affect Your Business?"

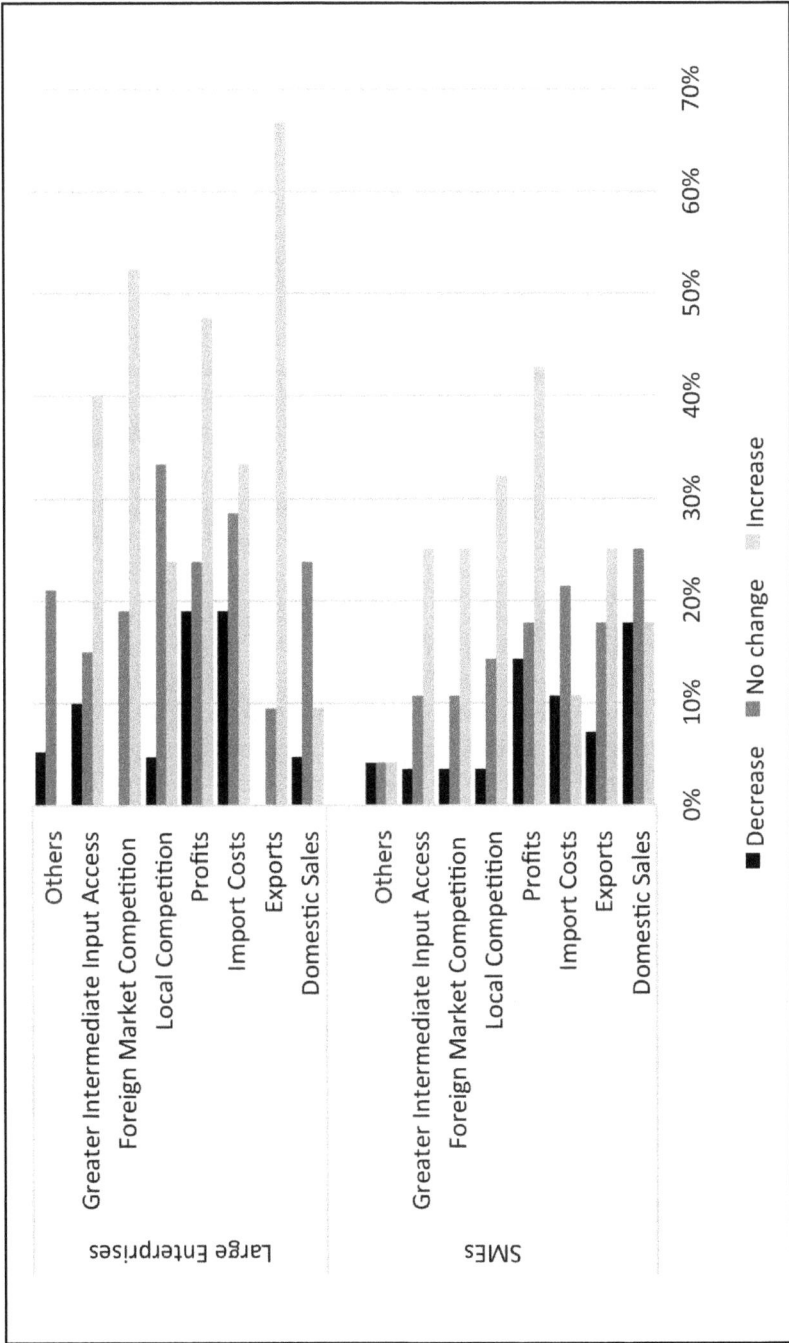

do so. These findings seem to reflect a general orientation of SMEs towards the domestic market and a higher degree of integration into international trade flows of large firms. Overall, these responses also point to survey participants' concerns that the AEC will expose them to more competition while the export and foreign market opportunities that it offers will be hard to capture.

Figure 6.17 sheds some light on the underlying mechanisms that respondents think will drive these expected changes. Overall, responses do not differ too much between SMEs and large firms. As can be seen from the figure, around 40 per cent of responding SMEs and more than half of the surveyed large enterprises expect connectivity in terms of transport and communication services to improve, thanks to the AEC. Overall, slightly more than a quarter of respondents expect both export and import tariffs and duties to decrease as a result of the AEC; however, SMEs are more optimistic in this regard than large enterprises. All these should facilitate market access to other countries within ASEAN for any ASEAN firm, thereby potentially leading to fiercer competition in the market of the individual ASEAN countries.

Figure 6.17 also reveals that around 40 per cent of the respondents (with slightly higher proportions among SMEs than large enterprises) expect customs procedure, standards regulation, and the investment process in ASEAN countries to "increase". However, it is not entirely clear what exactly they imply with their responses. There might have been different interpretations and understandings of the underlying questions. When stating that they expect an "increase in customs procedures" due to the AEC, respondents likely meant an "improvement" in customs procedures — although some might actually have expressed their expectation that customs procedures will become more numerous and cumbersome. When indicating that they anticipate an "increase in standards regulation", respondents may have had more and/or stricter regulations in mind (given that such quality and safety standards are more stringent in the more advanced ASEAN economies such as Singapore, Malaysia or Thailand than they currently are in Myanmar) — although some might as well have meant an "increase in harmonization" of standards regulation across ASEAN (given related initiatives at the ASEAN level) (MoC and ITC 2015b; UNIDO 2015). Meanwhile, when declaring that they expect an "increase" in the "investment process in ASEAN countries" due to the AEC, respondents likely meant that investment procedures within

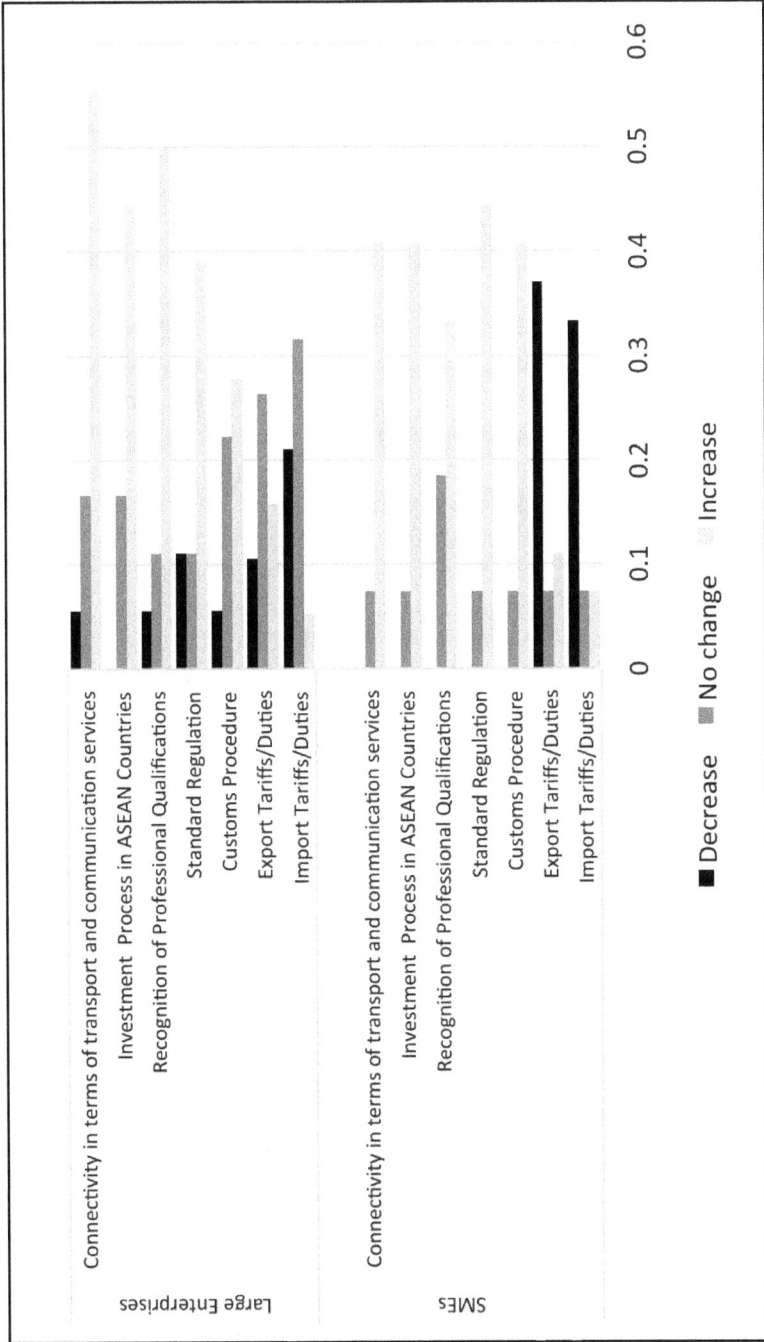

FIGURE 6.17

Firms' Responses to the Question: "What are Key Changes due to AEC that Affect Your Business?"

ASEAN will be simplified for ASEAN investors or that intra-ASEAN investment flows will grow — and probably not that the investment process will become more lengthy and cumbersome.

In a final note on Figure 6.17, it should be highlighted that 40 per cent or more of the respondents answered that they "don't know" or that they have "no opinion" on key changes related to the AEC that will affect their businesses.[15] This, again, reinforces the notion that awareness and understanding of the AEC are rather low among the respondents, regardless of firm size.

In separate questions, survey participants were also asked to provide additional comments, first, on how they think ASEAN economic integration will affect their firms and, second, on how increased competition from firms based in other countries in the region will affect their businesses. These comments can help better understand their concerns described above and implied by their responses in Figure 6.16. In these comments, some firms indicated that they are afraid of lacking the technological capabilities needed for withstanding the increase in competition particularly in foreign markets, while others fear that the size of their firms will become too small in the context of such market expansion. Moreover, quite a number of respondents stated that to become or stay competitive in more integrated regional markets, it will become more important to pay attention to product quality and quality control while there will also be an increased need for product and process innovation as well as for the ability to deliver at shorter lead times. All these likely require new investments for which some respondents fear they lack the capital.

The additional comments that respondents provided in the questionnaire also help us to better appreciate the concerns that they have with regard to the changes they expect for the situation in the domestic market. Here, one big concern is the influx of imports from more competitive foreign producers. Many respondents expect an increase in competition for market share while some are afraid that this could trigger a price war that hurts their businesses. Another concern that some respondents voiced relates to the labour market where they are afraid to lose out to foreign-invested firms coming to Myanmar, resulting in an increase in competition for labour and a shortage of skilled labour. Skilled workers will rather take jobs at foreign-invested firms as they are better paid, making it difficult for local firms to find sufficiently skilled labour. A few respondents are also concerned that increasing regional integration will stimulate labour emigration, further aggravating the shortage of skilled labour. One possible root cause of this concern can be seen in Figure 6.17: 47 per cent of the respondents expect the recognition of professional qualifications to increase due to the AEC, theoretically making it easier for qualified Myanmar labour to find (often better-paid) jobs in other ASEAN countries. Finally, a number of survey participants anticipate an increase in competition for raw materials, possibly leading to higher prices.

There are, however, also comments that suggest that some respond- ing firms are more optimistic about the effects of ASEAN economic integration. An admittedly rather small subgroup of respondents indicated that they hope for better access to foreign markets, more opportunities for export expansion, an improvement in the business environment (including better rules and regulations), as well as better transportation and lower logistics/transaction costs. Some companies expect the AEC to bring improved access to technology and packaging supplies, foreign investment inflows and an increased potential for joint ventures. There is also some disagreement among the more optimistic firms with the predictions of the more pessimistic respondents: for example, the former expect access to raw materials and intermediate goods to actually become easier and cheaper thanks to the ASEAN economic integration. A few respondents even see bright spots for the labour market, predicting more and better job opportunities as well as an increase in the capacity of labour due to intensified competition resulting from the ASEAN economic integration.

So far, our analysis has focused more narrowly on economic integration within ASEAN and related perceptions and expectations among participants in our survey. Taking a somewhat wider perspective, we will now discuss companies' behaviour and views with regard to Myanmar's trade agreements and trade opportunities more generally. Similar to our findings on ASEAN economic integration, both survey data and anecdotal evidence point to firms having very low levels of awareness and understanding of Myanmar's duty-free and quota-free access to the markets of various high-income countries, particularly through the GSP (Tin Mg Oo 2014). There is also little knowledge of the various FTAs which Myanmar has signed, which give Myanmar producers preferential access to the markets of other signatories. Figure 6.18 shows that only 14 per cent of large enterprises and merely 3 per cent of SMEs participating in our survey have ever made use of an FTA. Figure 6.19 specifies the usage rates of different FTAs and trade preference schemes by the Myanmar enterprises that

FIGURE 6.18
Usage of FTAs and Reasons for Not Using Any FTA

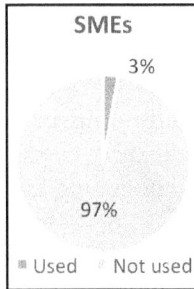

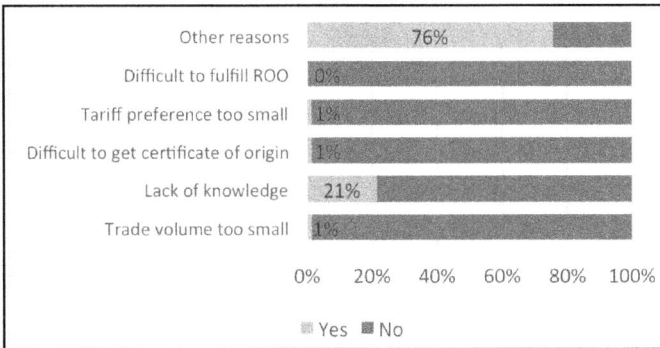

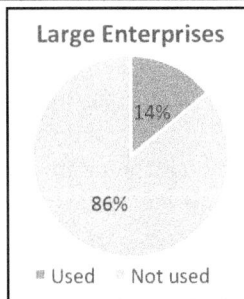

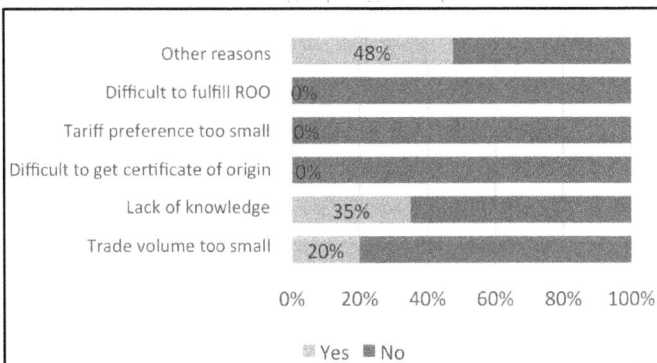

FIGURE 6.19
Reported Usage of Different FTAs and Trade Preference Schemes

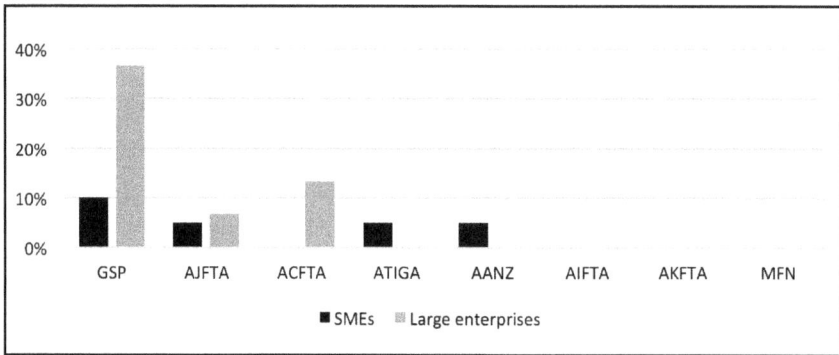

responded to our survey. As can be seen from the table, most FTAs have hardly been used; only the GSP and the ASEAN–China Free Trade Area (ACFTA) have been used by more than 20 per cent of all respondents. There are, however, quite some differences between firms of different sizes and between different FTAs. While 37 per cent of large enterprises have used GSP and 7 per cent have used ASEAN–Japan Free Trade Area (AJFTA), the same is true for only 10 per cent and 5 per cent of SMEs, respectively. ACFTA was used by 13 per cent of the large firm respondents but not by a single SME. By contrast, 5 per cent of SMEs but no large enterprise reported having used ATIGA. This is also true for AANZ.

A lack of knowledge is the main reason for survey firms not using FTAs and trade preference schemes, followed by too small trade volume (see Figure 6.18). Interestingly, the share of respondents indicating these two reasons for non-usage of FTAs is larger among large enterprises than SMEs (35 per cent and 20 per cent vs. 21 per cent and 1 per cent). Under "other reasons", quite a number of survey firms mentioned that they feel that the FTAs are not relevant for their businesses or that they do not relate to their areas of business. One responding firm also indicated that it lacks the capacity to make use of FTA preferences and that it is "still far from using the FTA-related forms" (which need to be submitted to the Customs Department to enjoy FTA benefits). By contrast, difficulties to fulfill Rules of Origin (ROO) requirements or to obtain certificates of origin are not mentioned as important reasons for not using FTAs (see Figure 6.18 again).

When asked about how FTAs have affected or will affect their businesses in various aspects, around 60 per cent of the respondents are not able (or willing) to provide a concrete answer, saying that they "don't know" or have "no opinion". In other words, only two fifths of respondents expressed an opinion on the impacts that FTAs have on their businesses. Figure 6.20 provides details on their responses, revealing some differences across firm sizes. In general, SMEs seem more optimistic about FTAs' effects on domestic sales (which 11 per cent perceive to have increased) than large enterprises (among whom only 3 per cent reported an increase). By contrast, almost half of the large survey firms but only around 10 per cent of SMEs indicated that FTAs have increased or will increase their export sales. Similarly, the share of large enterprises saying that profits have increased or will increase is more than twice as high as that of SMEs (23 per cent vs. 11 per cent). These figures are somewhat lower than for comparable questions on the AEC where more than a quarter of SMEs and more than half of large firms expect an increase in exports and profits, respectively (see Figure 6.16). By and large, respondents, thus, seem to be a bit more optimistic about reaping benefits from regional integration within ASEAN than from FTAs with countries outside ASEAN.

Meanwhile, SMEs seem equally concerned about FTAs leading to increases in competition in domestic and foreign markets whereas large enterprises appear to be more concerned about increases in competition in foreign markets than about increases in competition in local markets, possibly reflecting their higher degree of export orientation. Overall, looking at the full survey sample, 15 per cent and 23 per cent of respondents said that FTAs have increased or will increase competition in local markets and competition in foreign markets, respectively. Again, these percentages are somewhat lower than for comparable questions on the AEC where 35 per cent and 41 per cent of respondents indicated that they anticipate an increase in local competition and foreign market competition, respectively. In a similar vein, only 4 per cent of respondents stated that FTAs have reduced or will reduce their domestic sales while a three times larger share of respondents (i.e. 12 per cent) expect the same to happen as a result of the AEC. This implies that respondents are more concerned about regional competitors within ASEAN than about competitors from non-ASEAN countries with which Myanmar has signed FTAs.

FIGURE 6.20
Perceived Impact of FTAs on Businesses

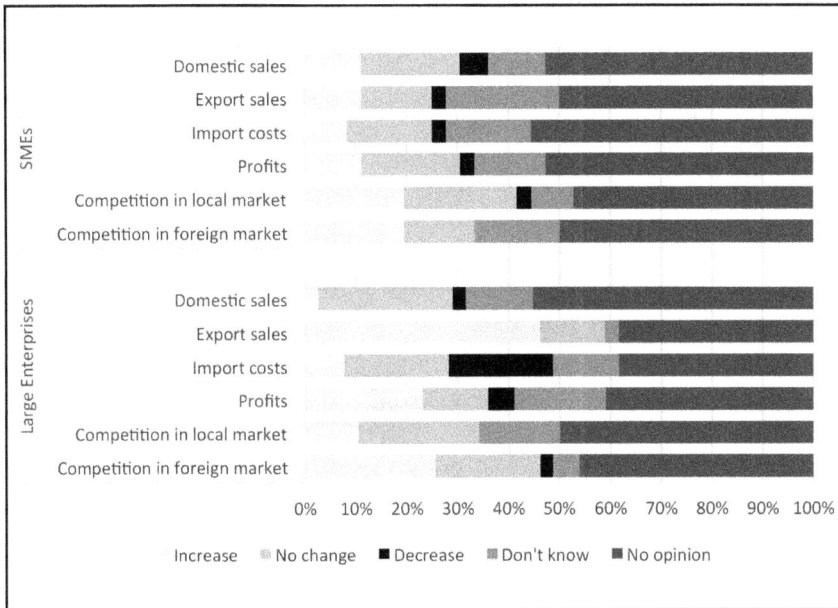

A final, open-ended question in our survey invited respondents to provide comments on what they view as the three most important reasons that impede their firms' participation as suppliers to other firms locally or internationally. These comments provide interesting insights on what firms see as the key constraints to being successful. The most common response pointed to the scarcity or lack of raw materials; this mostly came from apparel companies which currently have to import (almost) all their inputs since there is no local supply chain which many view as jeopardizing their competitiveness. The scarcity of skilled labour and access to finance are the second and third most frequently mentioned impediments to firms' integration as suppliers into value chains. Both were already discussed to some extent above.

Another area that many respondents identified as a key impediment relates to deficiencies in the business environment (government procedures, getting permits, consistency of laws and government policies), the lack of government support, and political instability. Technology limitations, including the quality of machinery, and low investment rates were also mentioned by a fair share of respondents. Finally, survey participants also cited exchange rate fluctuations, infrastructure (e.g. transportation), and concerns about the quality of their products and their ability to comply with international standards and certification requirements as important reasons that impede their firms' participation as suppliers to other local or international firms. This list of constraints to local, regional or international integration as suppliers to other firms can be taken to point to some areas where policy support could be helpful. This is the topic to which the next, final section will be dedicated.

6. Concluding Remarks and Policy Implications

The opening of Myanmar's economy in general and the intensification of regional economic integration more specifically bring both opportunities and challenges to Myanmar's SMEs. However, the results from our survey suggest that most of them do not seem to be well prepared for or even aware of the changes that such intensification of economic linkages with other countries in the region and the world will imply.

Myanmar's economic policy mix will be an important factor in shaping the prosperity of Myanmar's SMEs in general and their survival and success in the context of increasing regional integration, most notably through the AEC, more specifically. Obviously, some Myanmar SMEs will be more exposed to international and regional economic forces than others, depending, inter alia, on the sector they operate in. Accordingly, the need for policy support will vary across sectors and companies.

At present, Myanmar's SMEs seem to receive relatively little support from the government. Figure 6.21 presents different areas of possible government support for companies' internationalization and shows the percentage of our survey firms receiving such assistance during 2012 to 2014, distinguishing between support from the central government and state/local government. The overall picture is clear: only a minority of firms said that they have received any government assistance.

Two general observations can be made from Figure 6.21: first, by and large, state/local government was identified as being more active

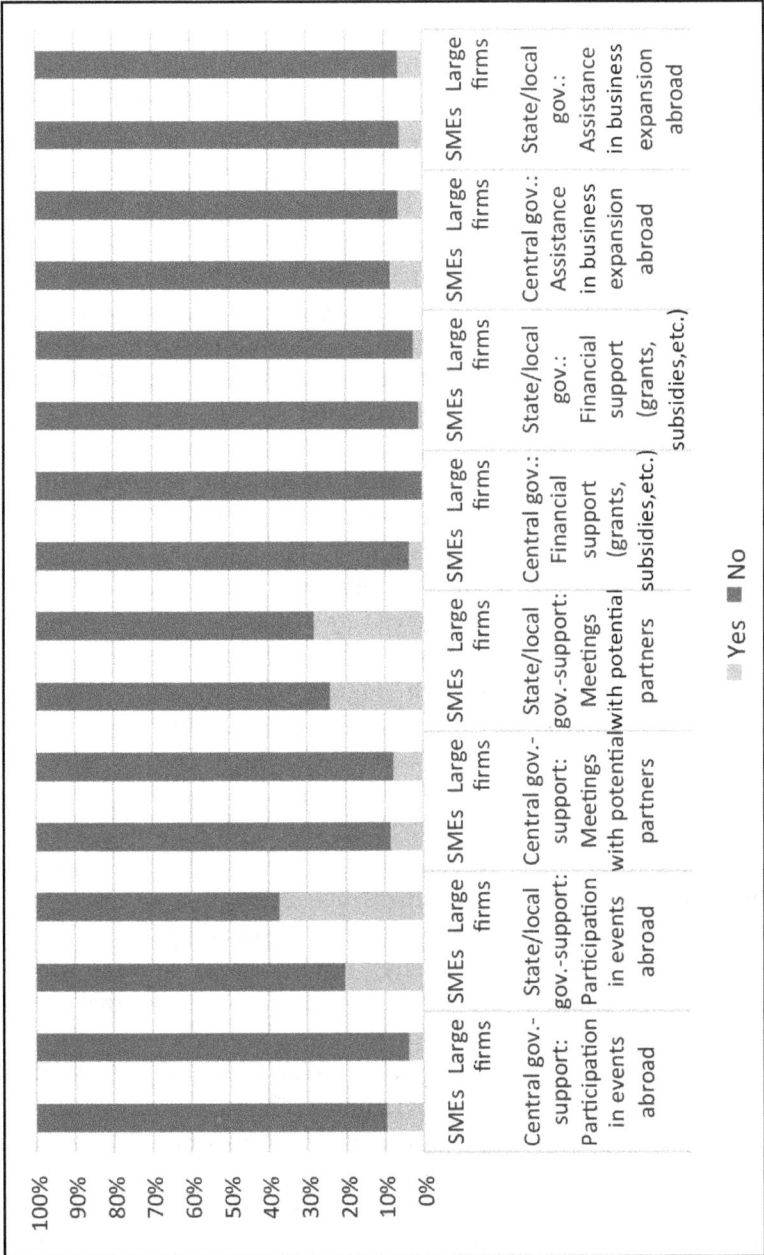

FIGURE 6.21
Extent and Nature of Government Support by Firm Size, 2012–14

in supporting firms' internationalization efforts. In most of the four policy areas shown in Figure 6.21, the share of respondents reporting support from the state/local government is higher than that from the central government. The area where the government seems most active is the provision of support for companies' participation in events abroad (e.g. fairs and exhibitions). Around 37 per cent of large enterprises and 20 per cent of SMEs indicated having received such support from the state/local government while 4 per cent of large firms and 10 per cent of SMEs have obtained such support from the central government. By contrast, almost no company indicated to have benefitted from the provision of financial support (e.g. grants, subsidies, loans). In between these two extremes, the government has extended some assistance to companies in terms of providing support for meetings with potential partners (about a quarter of firms received such support from the state/local government and 8 per cent of firms from the central government) and in terms of providing assistance in business expansion abroad through bilateral FTAs and AEC (benefitting about 6 per cent of the respondents).

Second, and even more interestingly, the share of large firms reporting that they have received government support is higher than that of SMEs acknowledging government assistance for almost every policy area covered in Figure 6.21. In other words, during 2012 to 2014 Myanmar SMEs were less likely to receive government support than large firms, which is a striking finding. This seems to be particularly true for assistance from the local/state government. The only exceptions are central government support for companies' participation in events abroad (of which 10 per cent of responding SMEs but just 4 per cent of large firms benefitted) and central government financial support (which 4 per cent of responding SMEs but no large firm enjoyed). Overall, thus, large firms seem to be more successful in securing government support. One reason for this is that larger firms are more knowledgeable about existing government support schemes. They tend to have a higher capacity to search for and process information about public policies and programmes. They are also more likely than SMEs to have the time and resources to go through the application processes for such government support and to submit application materials of higher quality. A second reason may be that large firms tend to have better connections to policymakers and more ability and clout to lobby for government support.

Myanmar is in the middle of a profound and forceful political and economic transition. Despite comprehensive and ambitious reform efforts, operating a business in Myanmar is still not simple and exposure to foreign competitors will further grow in parallel with the increasing opening and regional and global economic integration of Myanmar's economy. The list of challenges for Myanmar companies is long. Accordingly, there is an almost infinite number of items that can be suggested for a policy reform agenda, ranging from infrastructure, tax legislation, business environment and investment climate to financial sector development or trade, technology and industrial policies. Recently, a number of different experts and stakeholders have published work that discusses wide-ranging policy imperatives for SME support in Myanmar (Abe and Dutta 2014; ADB 2014, 2015; OECD 2013; Puusaag et al. 2015; or Soans and Abe 2015, for example). Here, instead of attempting to cover the whole universe of possible policy suggestions, we will focus on those that result from our analysis of the data collected by both our survey and others on enterprises in Myanmar. In the following paragraphs, we will, thus, present some policy conclusions that emerge from our analyses, highlighting a few rather broad policy areas where government measures appear to be most needed or most promising.

1. Efforts should be made to encourage firm registration and formalization

A large number of firms are currently not registered and operating in the informal sector in Myanmar. We have seen that the number of SMEs per 1,000 citizens in Myanmar (namely 2.6) is far below the averages for LDCs (namely 9) and developing countries (at 27). While this possibly also reflects generally lower levels of private sector activity, one explanation for this small number also lies in the low rate of registration by SMEs in Myanmar. Although, on the one hand, this is unsurprising given registration and licensing have historically been cumbersome and expensive (Tin Mg Oo 2014; *Eleven Myanmar* 2015), it does provide an indication of weaknesses in the current regulatory regime; clearly, for many firms the cost of registration outweighs its benefits. Policies designed to encourage firm registration, therefore, require that these benefits and costs be examined, both at the point of firm registration and for operating within the formal system. The data collected through firm registration should be fed into a central business registry which would thereby provide a useful pool of information on Myanmar's business population.

Increasing the proportion of SMEs that are formally registered would, hence, not only allow policymakers to better understand the characteristics and needs of Myanmar's SME population but also provide a potential means of encouraging SMEs' engagement in wider institutional and economic reforms by allowing registered firms greater participation in policy-making around economic reforms. In addition, if structured properly, such measures to increase registration levels could both help government distribute the tax burden more equitably across a larger population, while also allowing better targeting of government support measures for SMEs, which hence would see the benefits of being registered. More generally, businesses need to feel that they benefitted from formalizing and registering, e.g. better financial support, access to information and training programmes, infrastructure improvements, getting a voice in policy decision-making, or assistance in business match-making and in participation in trade fairs and other events. Overall, this would provide a first step to rebuilding the social contract between government, businesses and the wider community.

While it is suggested that further research be conducted in the area, there exist a number of entry points that might assist in increasing business registration rates such as reducing registration fees and streamlining the registration process. One of the most cited impediments to being a supplier to other local or foreign firms provided by the respondents to our survey relates to the business environment and government regulations. This also echoes the World Bank's Doing Business survey which ranks Myanmar at 160th out of 189 economies in terms of the costs of starting a business. Specifically, the World Bank survey estimates that starting a business costs the equivalent of 97.1 per cent of Myanmar's average per capita income, requiring 11 separate registration processes and taking 13 days on average to process (World Bank 2015c). In addition to this likely discouraging registration procedure, many of these fees, such as stamp duty, are charged at a flat rate, implying that they are regressive and likely to increase the barriers to the establishment of small firms, thereby discouraging competition in domestic markets.

Given this, one means of improving firm registration could be to ensure business registration fees are not used as a means of generating revenue, while also streamlining the complexity and number of processes required for a business to register and obtain licenses. Although attempts have already been made to do this, our survey suggests that this is likely still an issue. One idea would be to establish one-stop services for business registration and licensing procedures and making them easily accessible throughout the country. However, perhaps of equal importance is the need to ensure that efforts to reduce registration costs are coupled with wider reforms to make sure the formalized systems that businesses are subject to upon registering (e.g. payment of taxes, renewal of licenses, application for government support measures, etc.) are not excessively burdensome so that businesses benefit from registering and remaining in the formal sector.

Such reform measures could and should actually have the wider objective of not only encouraging the registration of existing (informal) firms but also promoting the establishment of new firms. That is, a simplification of registration and licensing procedures could be linked to a programme to promote new business start-ups, i.e. to stimulate new entrants in addition to just encouraging registration of existing firms. This could be complemented by measures to promote and trainings to develop entrepreneurship in the country. The existence of an entrepreneurial spirit is, to a certain extent, reflected in vibrant informal sector activities, which could be taken as a latent advantage yet to be fully exploited.

2. Improve data availability and collection to allow for better evidence-based policy-making

When using data from different sources, at various occasions we encountered conflicting information on one and the same issue. These discrepancies across data sources point to an important shortage in the supply of reliable data. At the same time, effective evidence-based policy-making requires the availability of reliable information and datasets. In view of this, establishing a system of regular and systematic data collection on businesses in Myanmar would be helpful. The collected data should then be harmonized and stored in a centralized database. The first step in this exercise would be to carry out a business census among, if possible, the entire population of Myanmar enterprises. This would result in an official count and record that would allow Myanmar's business population to be mapped. The availability of a central business registry, the establishment of which was suggested above, would obviously facilitate this undertaking. The more complete this central business registry is, the more comprehensive and reliable the resulting census dataset will be; and also from this perspective it is important to achieve high business registration rates. After the initial census, it will be necessary to conduct regular business surveys in order to keep the stock of information updated. For the implementation of such data collection efforts, the government could seek support from international organizations such as the World Bank, UNDP or UNIDO. The availability of such data would allow the government to take more informed decisions in its policy-making for SMEs and also to better monitor and evaluate the impact of its policy interventions.

3. Increase awareness of and knowledge about ASEAN and FTAs

The results from our survey clearly point out that there is very little awareness and knowledge among Myanmar SMEs about ASEAN integration, the AEC and FTAs in general. On the one hand, this means that a lot of SMEs are not aware of possible business opportunities related either to attracting foreign investors (e.g. for joint ventures) or the availability of preferential access to foreign markets. Part of the issue is that many firms have only very limited knowledge of how to make use of these trade preferences (i.e. what they need to do, which documents they need to prepare, etc.). On the other hand, this also means that they are unaware of the challenges they might face, e.g. increased foreign competition as a result of the opening of Myanmar's markets through the AEC and FTAs. Lacking this awareness, they might be slow and reluctant to take the necessary measures to prepare themselves for the new circumstances.

Against this backdrop, the government could take measures to help SMEs increase their awareness of and knowledge about AEC and the FTAs that Myanmar has signed. It could consider launching a public campaign on ASEAN integration and the AEC, including seminars, forums, workshops and other events for SMEs. This could involve the dissemination of reference materials. In fact, the Central Department of

SME Development under the Ministry of Industry has already translated key documents and handbooks, including one on the AEC, one on law and competition policies for businesses in the ASEAN region, and an SME Guidebook towards the AEC; these would be more useful and effective if they are more widely disseminated. The government could also help organize industry and trade fairs with a specific focus on business opportunities within ASEAN. These events could also be used not only to disseminate the reference materials mentioned above but also to share market intelligence about the characteristics and dynamics of ASEAN markets, helping SMEs to identify potential markets to access and to better understand opportunities and challenges. Currently, most workshops and seminars for the business community are held in cities such as Yangon, Mandalay and Naypyitaw, making participation costly for SMEs located in other townships. Therefore, spreading such workshops and seminars more widely across Myanmar would help increase participation rates.

To raise awareness and to disseminate information, the government can work with industry associations (such as UMFCCI, MGMA, etc.) and also piggyback on existing initiatives such as the "Business Forum", a platform for public–private dialogue between the business community and the government initiated by previous President Thein Sein, and the "Saturday Talks" organized by the Department of SME Development. The latter in particular would, however, need some upscaling since so far it has been organized irregularly.

Facilitating access to information is a very valuable support that the government can provide to SMEs. This is because, in general, SMEs often do not have the resources or capacities to regularly and consistently search for information, screen different sources of information, access information and process the information obtained. This is particularly grave in the case of Myanmar, where the ICT infrastructure is still pretty underdeveloped and ICT usage is low, thus making information collection even more time-consuming and cumbersome. Moreover, after years of economic isolation, limited exposure to international competition and markets trends, and generally low private business dynamics, a lot of Myanmar entrepreneurs lack the attitude and habit of seeking up-to-date information. At the same time, getting accurate and timely information on market opportunities, possibilities to partner with foreign investors, financial assistance, government support offerings or technology updates are becoming more and more important in an increasingly open economy setting characterized by a more competitive environment. By helping Myanmar SMEs to obtain such information, the government can help them to better prepare for the challenges and be more aware of the opportunities that regional economic integration processes such as the AEC will bring with them.

4. Human resource development

On the one hand, the results from our survey suggest that the typical education level attained by owners and founders of family-run businesses is high, with more than half in the food manufacturing sector and more than three quarters in the apparel manufacturing sector having graduated from university. Although the survey does not allow for this to be directly compared with the average education level of workers, based on the tendency for firms to import labour for higher-level positions and the lack of skilled labour being commonly cited as a business constraint in our survey, it appears probable that there exists a wide gap in educational attainment across firms, with local workers being used for unskilled labour.

More specifically, many firms are already indicating that they have a hard time finding skilled labour. What is more, a considerable share of respondents in our survey expect the shortage of skilled labour to become even more severe under the AEC since an increasing number of foreign companies are anticipated to enter Myanmar and to compete with local businesses for skilled workers. In addition, we have seen that quite a number of firms in our survey have hired foreign managers; one of the reasons for this is that they have difficulties finding suitable candidates in the local labour market.

Although this is not totally unexpected in a country with dynamic economic growth and in transition from isolation to liberalization, the apparent skill gap between local labourers, foreign workers and owners, combined with the tendency for firms not to spend money on formal trainings, presents a risk that enterprises may soon face a ceiling in terms of how much they can improve productivity. The skill gap also presents a risk that local labour continues to be used for low value-added and poorly compensated activities. Furthermore, if the incentives are not created to encourage the transfer of skills and technology with foreign investment and foreign skilled labour, the local economy will likely lose an opportunity to encourage the creation of more economically productive and profitable domestic industries.

Although it is difficult to extrapolate the results of our survey across all SMEs in Myanmar, the evidence collected suggests that the limited supply of skilled labour is a clear impediment to corporate competitiveness. Given this, it is suggested that government efforts should be focused on increasing the domestic supply of skilled labour. These efforts should not only cover technical skills needed by workers but also skills needed for white-collar, clerical and managerial jobs. On the one hand, from a longer-term perspective, this implies the need to upgrade the quality and increase the funding of the education system at all levels. This ideally also involves the establishment of new Technical and Vocational Education and Training (TVET) institutes with a focus on the skill needs of priority sectors for the country. On the other hand, in the short- to medium-term, government policy should take aim at expanding the supply of government-provided trainings as well as supporting and strengthening existing private training institutes (such as the one owned by MGMA which offers technical trainings to garment workers, for example).

At the same time, in order to ensure that companies increase their demand for skill development programmes and trainings, the government should consider introducing measures that incentivize firms to send workers or staff to trainings or even to incur expenditures for formal, external staff training. This could come in the form of grants, subsidies or tax breaks, for example.

Finally, although further analysis would need to be undertaken to ensure this is properly designed and targeted, it is possible that programmes which encourage the internal mentoring and training of staff as well as programmes which expand access to formal training programmes domestically and overseas would assist to expand the local availability of skilled labour. Ultimately, more skilled labour would help firms to become more productive and produce goods and services of higher quality.

5. Technology and investment

Both our survey and others revealed that the level of technological sophistication is pretty low among Myanmar SMEs with usage of modern or foreign technology being quite limited. Moreover, the percentage of SMEs that put efforts and investments in innovation and in acquiring technology is small. At the same time, quite a number of participants in our survey recognize this as an issue. As mentioned above, a considerable share of survey respondents mentioned technological limitations, quality of machinery and low investment as important factors that impede their participation as suppliers to other local or foreign firms. Some fear that they do not have the technological capabilities needed to withstand the increase in competitive pressures that they expect to result from AEC and regional integration in general. They therefore feel an increased need both for more capital investment and for process and product innovation.

The government could play an important role in supporting such efforts. However, it has to be said that, up to now, technology development and innovation are areas that have largely been overlooked by Myanmar policymakers. Combined with low levels of education and difficulty in accessing capital, this lack of government support has resulted in very reduced levels of innovative activities. The inception of the AEC should be taken as a trigger to change this. Indeed, in a positive development, technology adoption has been identified as a priority future policy area by the Department of SME Development, although a coherent and consistent strategy and action plan for related policies and programmes is still missing. This should be changed in an effort that receives sufficient budgetary funding and that involves all relevant ministries, e.g. the Ministry of Industry and the Ministry of Science and Technology.

Policy measures to consider include the strengthening of linkages between SMEs and innovation and technology agents (such as universities, R&D centres and laboratories) and the establishment of pilot science and technology parks (possibly within existing industrial zones or within the Special Economic Zones (SEZs) currently under development). Moreover, the existing network of both technological and, in particular, business incubators could be expanded and accessibility increased for private SMEs (since at present incubators mainly supply their services to state-owned enterprises).

Regarding investments in technology and productive capacity more at large, from the firms' perspective, part of the problem is the difficulty in accessing finance in Myanmar, particularly loans with longer maturities which are essential for investments in equipment and machinery. While this topic was not covered in our survey, other surveys highlight this as a key constraint for Myanmar companies and SMEs in particular (Soans and Abe 2015; World Bank 2014*a*). Generally, the government tries to facilitate access to finance for SMEs through a subsidized loan scheme administered by the Small and Medium Industrial Development Bank (SMIDB), a semi-governmental bank operating under the guidance of the Ministry of Industry, and through a credit guarantee scheme for SMEs that has been set up as a department under the Myanmar Insurance Company. However, the pick-up rates have been very low so far, mostly due to very strict credit conditions (related to collateral requirements and repayment periods). To increase borrowing by SMEs, policy measures should aim at making credit available at more attractive conditions, raise awareness of existing government support schemes, and have programmes to increase financial literacy among SMEs and also banks. To facilitate financing of enterprise activities aimed at technology development and innovation more specifically, the government could envisage setting up direct support schemes such as grants (including matching grants), subsidies or other incentives.

Access to finance for investments could also be an important element to address the "missing middle" issue in Myanmar, i.e. the polarization of the private sector into small and very large firms. As mentioned above, the large majority of firms in Myanmar are very small (with less than 10 employees) while large companies account for a significant share of employment. One way to help broaden and strengthen the medium-size segment of Myanmar's enterprise population is to support small companies to develop. To do this, companies need to make investment which requires the availability of capital. By facilitating access to finance and fostering capacity-building (including technical, organizational, technological and managerial capacities), the government could play an important role in supporting the expansion of small firms so that they develop into more stable and competent medium-sized firms.

Apart from that, FDI can be important both as a channel for technology transfer and for bringing additional capital into the country. Myanmar's SMEs could possibly benefit from FDI by either becoming suppliers to foreign-invested companies or, if they are more mature, by entering into joint ventures with foreign companies. They may also benefit from spillover effects, i.e. positive externalities resulting from backward linkages from foreign firms to the local supplier base, knowledge diffusion through labour turnover as well as "competition effects" and "demonstration effects" (World Bank 2014b). However, for these linkages and spillover effects to materialize, a smartly designed and effective regulatory framework for FDI needs to be in place to provide security to foreign investors and also to incentivize them to establish such linkages. The levels of FDI that Myanmar currently receives per capita, both from ASEAN and other countries of origin, are still quite low by regional and international standards. The fact that the national elections in November 2015 went smoothly and brought a change in government signals that the transition to democracy is more solid than some skeptics have feared, which should help alleviate reluctance and hesitation among foreign investors. However, an important task for the new government was to pass new legislations relevant for investment. In fact, the Myanmar Investment Commission had started drafting a new Myanmar Investment Law which combines the existing Foreign Investment Law and the Myanmar Citizens Investment Law in 2014 but its enactment was delayed several times. Amongst other things, the new law includes stipulations on the approval and treatment of foreign investment as well as on investment incentives. It was originally envisaged that parliament passes the new Myanmar Investment Law as well as a revision of the Myanmar Companies Act, which dates from 1914 and is utterly outdated, in the course of 2015 but incorporating suggestions submitted from a wide range of stakeholders meant that the process was delayed. In fact, the new Myanmar Investment Law was enacted in October 2016 whereas the Myanmar Companies Law took effect in August 2018 only. While the processing of amendments should have been quicker, the enactment of the new law by parliament was important to provide investors, both local and foreign, with the clarity and predictability they need to make investments with confidence.

Finally, given the underdevelopment of Myanmar's own capital goods industry, importing capital goods and technology could be another potential avenue for technological upgrading and productivity enhancements. The government could consider to facilitate the import of such capital goods, at least for priority sectors, e.g. through trade policy measures (such as reduced import tariffs or duty drawback schemes), support for companies' participation in technology fairs and exhibitions (where they can learn about the newest technologies and the different models of acquiring them, e.g. through licensing or leasing), and/or the lifting of restrictions on payment arrangements for international transactions.[15] However, the possible adverse effects on Myanmar's trade balance, which is already in deficit, need to be kept in mind. Not only for this reason, in the longer run, it is desirable that Myanmar strengthens its own capital goods industry.

6. Encourage ICT usage of SMEs

This point is somewhat related to the previous point but offers insights into some intricacies related to ICT usage that merit a separate focus. The results from our survey and others have shown that Myanmar SMEs currently use ICT to a limited extent only. This is hardly surprising in a country that has opened up again only a few years ago and where liberalization of and investment in modern telecommunications have started only recently. Rigid regulations, a monopolized tele-communications sector, and lack of economic opportunities for decades have left Myanmar SMEs behind their regional peers when it comes to ICT proficiency and usage. However, in the wave of several political and economic reforms, the telecommunications sector has received more attention, attracted foreign investment and, thereby, become more modern and competitive which, in and of itself, increases the potential for new economic opportunities. However, the density, quality and penetration of ICT infrastructure and services in Myanmar still lag far behind that of more advanced countries in the region such as Malaysia, Thailand or Vietnam. Further government efforts, through either direct investments, public–private partnerships or tendering, would be necessary in the future to expand the underlying infrastructure, to enhance connectivity, and to improve the reliability, quality, speed and diffusion of ICT service provision.

Apart from these infrastructural shortcomings, another main reason for the very low usage of ICT, both among SMEs and enterprises more generally, is that there is a generation gap among Myanmar entrepreneurs. Older entrepreneurs and SME owners who have started their busi-nesses under the old regime often do not have the habit of seeking ICT solutions for their businesses. Many of them are therefore still relying on traditional ways of communicating, networking, trading, organizing production, and managing. At the same time, there is a large younger generation of potential or would-be entrepreneurs and employees with great interest in and appetite for ICT applications. These differences should be taken into account by the government when it designs policies and programmes to encourage ICT usage among Myanmar SMEs.

One way to encourage ICT usage could be through subsidization or provision of other incentives. The government could, for example, grant certain tax breaks if registration or license applications are done online, or if annual reports including balance sheets are submitted online. Financial support could be provided to SMEs that want to introduce business management software or set up web-based portals for online sales and online payment. SMEs that introduce such online services could also be given free entry to participate in local and national product exhibitions to present their solutions. Another option to consider is to offer mobile ICT training for SMEs across the country, targeting especially older entrepreneurs and the rural areas, to enhance SMEs' awareness of the advantages of applying ICT in their businesses and increase their knowledge on how to use ICT. Policy initiatives like these would encourage the usage of ICT among Myanmar SMEs by increasing their understanding of the likely benefits (such as reduction of information search costs, transaction costs, and communication costs, particularly over the long run) and by letting them be aware of the opportunities that ICT usage could bring to their businesses, for example in terms of improving efficiency.

7. Simplify the SME definition

A final suggestion may be to simplify the definition of what constitutes an SME, at least the definition to be applied when designing policy support measures targeted at SMEs. Admittedly, the new SME Law has been enacted only recently, namely in 2015, thus changing it again for such a minor issue would not make much sense. However, the SME definition stipulated there is quite complex and not much in line with definitions in other ASEAN countries or elsewhere.

This situation may contribute to complicating or even hindering the proper implementation of policies targeting SMEs, both at national and regional levels. A simpler SME definition will make it easier for government agencies to determine whether or not applicants for certain government support programmes and measures are eligible in the first place, or whether or not certain exemptions from rules and regulations apply to a given company. Similarly, it will help other stakeholders involved in SME support programmes, such as banks extending loans to SMEs under the SME credit guarantee insurance scheme offered by the Myanmar Insurance Company or training providers offering subsidized training programmes to SMEs, to distinguish those companies that qualify from those that do not. Overall, a simpler SME definition could, thus, contribute to guiding and designing more targeted SME development policies and other promotion measures.

Future research

Our analyses also pointed to areas where further research would be beneficial. For one, the survey which forms a focus of the analyses undertaken here is restricted to a relatively small sample of firms from Yangon Region and Mon State which predominately operate in the food processing and apparel manufacturing sectors. Additionally, due to the unavailability of adequate business registration data the sample frames used for selecting firms to be surveyed were based on non-representative sources, such as business association membership lists and lists obtained from industrial zone management committees. This, when coupled with the survey being conducted during sensitive political and economic times dominated by uncertainty related to upcoming national elections and minimum wage negotiations, also limited the willingness of some firms to participate and their likeliness to answer honestly.

Given these difficulties and the clear importance of SMEs to the Myanmar economy, future research addressing similar research questions and using a similar survey instrument could be useful while building on this work. This future research agenda could be envisaged to include (but is not limited to) the development and application of a more representative sample frame of randomly selected firms; and the implementation of a more detailed survey over a bigger sample of firms, covering a larger number of sectors and regions within Myanmar, so as to allow more detailed and also more representative analyses and sector-specific insights. Conducting such a new survey under more stable political circumstances should also help to achieve a higher response rate. A bigger survey sample and a higher response rate would, moreover, allow for more meaningful econometric analysis, for example on the determinants of Myanmar SMEs' participation in regional trade and production networks or on the factors that act as barriers or enablers of such regional integration.

Another interesting task for future investigations would be to do research on the extent and nature of Myanmar's bilateral economic relationships with its ASEAN peers. Such research could examine in more depth the obstacles that inhibit further deepening of bilateral economic ties with individual ASEAN member states, as well as identify opportunities for the further strengthening of bilateral economic linkages. Finally, additional research could also look more specifically at policy conclusions for the regional level which would serve as useful inputs into policy debates at fora such as the ASEAN Secretariat or AEC negotiation roundtables.

APPENDIX 6.1
Exports to and Imports from ASEAN and East Asian Countries, 2005–13

Exporter	Export value (mn. US$)			Growth rate (2005–13)	Import value (mn. US$)			Growth rate (2005–13)
	2005	2010	2013		2005	2010	2013	
Brunei	1,892	n.a.	2,651	40%	803	n.a.	1,843	130%
Cambodia	143	703	1,293	805%	792	1,684	2,832	258%
Indonesia	15,825	33,348	40,630	157%	17,040	38,912	53,851	216%
Lao PDR	339	1,048	2,049	504%	887	2,381	4,237	378%
Malaysia	36,849	50,498	63,926	73%	28,168	44,580	54,828	95%
Myanmar	2,090	3,274	4,633	122%	1,644	3,947	7,559	360%
Philippines	7,150	11,545	8,615	20%	9,325	16,434	14,171	52%
Singapore	71,929	106,634	128,781	79%	52,119	74,650	77,890	49%
Thailand	23,969	44,333	59,287	147%	21,624	30,328	41,737	93%
Vietnam	5,744	10,365	18,584	224%	9,326	16,408	21,287	128%
China	55,367	138,160	244,040	341%	74,994	154,678	199,559	166%
Hong Kong	1,567	1,938	2,159	38%	38,446	63,392	69,779	81%
Japan	75,575	112,859	110,970	47%	72,587	101,021	117,791	62%
Korea, Rep.	27,432	53,195	81,989	199%	26,064	44,099	53,339	105%
Macao	29	23	12	−58%	333	327	494	48%

APPENDIX 6.2
Exports to ASEAN and East Asian Countries, 2005–13 (per capita and as % of total)

Exporter	Exports to ASEAN per capita (US$)			Share of ASEAN in total exports (US$)		
	2005	2010	2013	2005	2010	2013
Brunei	5,144	n.a.	6,345	25%	n.a.	23%
Cambodia	11	49	85	5%	13%	14%
Indonesia	70	139	163	18%	21%	22%
Lao PDR	59	164	303	56%	51%	52%
Malaysia	1,426	1,786	2,151	26%	25%	28%
Myanmar	42	63	87	55%	49%	43%
Philippines	83	124	88	17%	22%	16%
Singapore	16,862	21,005	23,852	31%	30%	31%
Thailand	366	668	885	22%	23%	26%
Vietnam	70	119	207	18%	14%	14%
China	42	103	180	7%	9%	11%
Hong Kong, China	230	276	300	8%	13%	11%
Japan	591	881	871	13%	15%	16%
Korea, Rep.	570	1,077	1,633	10%	11%	15%
Macao	63	44	n.a.	2%	8%	5%

Note: Figures for Laos and Myanmar are mirror data; for Brunei, data for 2005 is actually from 2006.
Source: UN Comtrade database and WDI databank.

APPENDIX 6.3
Imports from ASEAN and East Asian Countries, 2005–13 (per capita and as % of total)

Importer	Imports from ASEAN per capita (US$)			Share of ASEAN in total imports (US$)		
	2005	2010	2013	2005	2010	2013
Brunei	2,182	n.a.	4,412	48%	n.a.	51%
Cambodia	59	117	187	31%	34%	31%
Indonesia	76	162	216	30%	29%	29%
Lao PDR	153	372	626	79%	74%	64%
Malaysia	1,090	1,577	1,845	25%	27%	27%
Myanmar	33	76	142	52%	44%	41%
Philippines	109	176	144	19%	28%	22%
Singapore	12,218	14,704	14,426	26%	24%	21%
Thailand	330	457	623	19%	17%	17%
Vietnam	113	189	237	25%	19%	16%
China	58	116	147	12%	12%	11%
Hong Kong	5,643	9,025	9,708	13%	14%	11%
Japan	568	789	925	14%	15%	14%
Korea, Rep.	541	893	1,062	10%	10%	10%
Macao	711	611	872	9%	6%	4%

Note: Figures for Laos and Myanmar are mirror data; for Brunei, data for 2005 is actually from 2006 while the 2013 data for Macao is actually from 2014.
Source: UN Comtrade database and WDI databank.

Appendix 6.4
Survey Methodology

For the purpose of this study, a survey was conducted among a sample of Myanmar firms in order to compile a new enterprise-level dataset with a focus on regional economic integration issues. The questionnaire used in this survey was provided by ERIA. It consisted of different types of questions, including dichotomous questions, multiple-choice questions, constant sum questions, rank order scaling questions, demographic questions and closed-ended questions.

Survey sampling:

The survey sample was determined through convenience sampling, selecting companies from two sets of enterprise lists: first, lists provided by different industrial zone management committees and, second, a list of apparel producers provided by the MGMA. Survey participants were then selected randomly from these two sets of enterprise lists. Part of the convenience sampling was to restrict survey locations to Yangon Region and Mon State in Myanmar, and to focus on certain industries, primarily the manufacturing of food products and wearing apparel, while also surveying a few firms from the wood products, paper, and other manufacturing sectors. As discussed above, we acknowledge that this sample is not representative of the full business population of Myanmar companies. In total, 205 companies were contacted and asked to participate in the survey. Seven of them refused to do so, leaving a sample size of 198 enterprises.

Pre-testing and survey implementation:

Before its actual implementation, a pre-testing of the survey was undertaken in June 2015. Ten garment firms operating in Yangon Region were randomly selected and visited by MDRI-CESD's research team leader, a research associate, and a research assistant who then conducted face-to-face interviews, using the questionnaire that had been provided by ERIA. This pre-testing revealed that, on average, it took about two hours to complete the survey and that many respondents were not able to provide answers to questions that required numeric information such as asset values, sales values, export ratios, production costs, number of employees and their wages. In view of this, it was decided to divide the questionnaire into two parts in order to elicit and collect as much information as possible from survey firms. This meant that the first part of the questionnaire was to be covered by face-to-face interviews during firm visits while the second part was to be left with respondents for a week to give them time to check back their accounting records, contact different departments, or contact the owner (in cases where lower-level ranks served as respondents) in order to gather the information needed to answer the survey questions.

The actual survey was then carried out from July to November 2015 among a sample of firms operating in different industrial zones in Yangon Region and Mon State. Based on the lists received from the industrial zone management committees and MGMA, participating firms were randomly selected and then contacted for appointments. Implementation support was provided by the different industrial zone management committees who helped the survey team to contact firms and to arrange survey appointments and questionnaire collection times. Further support was provided by the Ministry of Labour, Employment and Social Security (MOLES) through issuing request letters to firms, arranging survey appointments, and sending officers from labour departments to serve as enumerators for data collection. In general, the survey team who visited firms to conduct face-to-face interviews consisted of the research team leader, research associates, research assistants and enumerators from MOLES.

Company owners and high-level management staff were targeted as respondents. In practice, however, sometimes mid-level administration officers were delegated to respond to the survey team's questions during factory visits. In various cases, this proved to be an issue as the overall knowledge about the firm and the ability to respond to certain questions often vary according to the positional rank of the respondent. Overall, respondents included business owners, directors, managing directors, factory heads, HR managers, general managers, admin officers, and accounting officers.

As mentioned, Part I of the questionnaire was covered through on-the-ground interviews which typically took about an hour but sometimes longer if extensive explanations of survey questions were necessary. Part II of the questionnaire was left at the companies with the request to return it within a week; if that did not happen, the survey team followed up about once a week. A total of 198 firms responded to Part I of the questionnaire. However, by the end of November 2015, only 108 firms returned (at least partially) completed Part II of the questionnaire.

Difficulties:

The survey team had to face certain difficulties. It often proved hard to make an appointment with firm owners or higher-level management such as directors, managing directors, general managers, especially for large and medium-sized firms. In some cases, the interest from respondents and their willingness to avail more than 30 minutes were limited, resulting in a low degree of reflection about survey questions.

Leaving Part II of the questionnaire with the firm proved to create problems of its own as respondents who were not owners, directors, managing directors or general managers often did not fully understand some of the questions and had to ask higher-level management to respond, but the latter then often did not take the time, not least due to a lack of knowledge about the survey context. In some cases, lower-ranking respondents also had to ask permission from higher management to provide certain types of information in response to survey questions, but this permission was not always granted.

As such, questionnaires returned by companies were often incomplete as they were unwilling to provide responses on certain topics. This can largely be explained by, first, a certain survey fatigue among companies (which have been surveyed a lot in recent years by both local and international institutions) and, second, the specific historical context in which the survey was carried out where many firms were concerned and felt uncertain because of ongoing negotiations on a new minimum wage on the one hand and the upcoming national elections on the other hand.

Usage of complementary sources of information:

To deal with the issue of incomplete questionnaires, the data collected through the survey, especially that on garment factories, was complemented with some additional data from the following sources:

(1) balance sheets submitted to the survey team by participating firms;
(2) the MGMA company directory, primarily to get information on the number of full-time employment in apparel firms, whether or not they are exporting, whether or not they had foreign ownership, and whether or not they had a website;
(3) company websites, where applicable;
(4) social security cards and registration numbers, to calculate employee numbers;
(5) qualitative interviews by MDRI-CESD researchers at the margins of factory visits; and
(6) notes from enumerators; some firms, while not responding to the questions in the questionnaire, provided narrative answers (e.g. on the total number of workers) which enumerators could write down on separate sheets of paper.

Data caveats:

Survey data collected on the value of fixed assets such as land and building have to be interpreted with caution. These should just be taken as approximate values since most firms provided the expected value based on market prices — but land and building prices are currently inflated in Myanmar (and especially in Yangon) due to a bubble.

Similarly, it cannot be guaranteed that respondents provided accurate figures on sales values and production costs as they do not want to admit making profits, not even in a survey like ours. Several respondents even openly told the survey team that they do not want to provide true values in order not to disclose their avoidance of profit taxes.

NOTES

1. Acknowledgements: The authors would like to thank Dr Zaw Oo for his overall guidance on this research and Aung Phyo Kyaw, Aung Thet Paing, Mi Win Thida, Phoo Pwint Phyu, Tun Min Sandar, Thandaar Soe and Thant Zin Tun for their invaluable support in implementing the enterprise survey and in processing the data collected. The authors are also grateful to the project coordinators and to participants at the workshops of ERIA/ISEAS – Yusof Ishak Institute in Singapore and Bali for their helpful comments on earlier drafts of this chapter. All remaining errors are the authors.

2. See <https://ntsblog.wordpress.com/2013/06/14/sme-development-and-management-in-myanmar/>.

3. See <https://forex.cbm.gov.mm/index.php/fxrate>.

4. See the "Data and Statistics" section of the Directorate of Investment and Company Administration's (DICA) website, available at <https://www.dica.gov.mm/>.

5. See also <www.smedevelopmentcenter.gov.mm/>.

6. As we have seen above, in Myanmar's new SME Law, SMEs include even companies with up to 600 employees if they operate in labour-intensive sectors. See <www.smedevelopmentcenter.gov.mm/?q=en/def_sme>.

7. It is interesting to note, however, that for both industries the average number of employees per firm that we found in our sample is significantly higher than that by UNDP (2014, p. 18), which reported that an average food processing firm employs 8 workers and an average apparel manufacturer has 106 workers. There, thus, seems to be a certain bias towards larger firms in our sample.

8. When apparel companies want to obtain an import license, they need to apply to MGMA for their endorsement. After MGMA has assessed the application, and the endorsement is granted, the apparel companies can then apply to the Ministry of Commerce (MoC) for the import license. MoC issues the license based on MGMA's endorsement and their internal checking. MGMA conducts the checking on behalf of the MoC as the garment industry requires expertise knowledge, which MoC deemed MGMA to be the appropriate entity to conduct the check on their behalf.

8. See also <www.smedevelopmentcenter.gov.mm/>.

10. See also <www.myanmargarments.org/about/about-mgma/>.

11. Note that our category of "foreign-invested firms" or "firms with foreign ownership" include both firms that are fully foreign-owned and firms that have at least some foreign ownership.

12. See also the Directorate of Investment and Company Administration's (DICA) website, available at <https://www.dica.gov.mm/>.

13. Note that these percentages only refer to the share of survey respondents mentioning a given country as an export market. They do not reveal anything about trade volume or value. That is, while the share of respondents mentioning the United States and the EU as export markets is higher than that identifying Korea as an export destination, this does not necessarily imply that the total export volume or value to the United States and the EU is higher than that to Korea. Given that business relationships are still in their infancy, shipment sizes to the United States and the EU might still be smaller than to Korea.

14. This is also why the percentages displayed in Figure 6.16 for the different categories do not add up to 100 per cent. The balance actually corresponds to the share of respondents that chose "don't know" or "no opinion" as answer.

15. This is the reason why the percentages shown in Figure 6.17 do not add up to 100 per cent in each of the different categories. The balance corresponds to the share of respondents that chose "don't know" or "no opinion" as answer.

16. In some industries it is standard practice that purchases of large capital goods (e.g. farm machinery) require the importer to make a down payment prior to shipment. Myanmar law restricts citizens from making down payment on imported goods prior to receipt without a substantial burden of documentation, severely reducing enterprises' access to certain capital goods (MoC and ITC 2015c).

REFERENCES

Abe, Masato and Madhurjya Kumar Dutta. "A New Policy Framework for Myanmar's SME Development". *ARTNeT Working Paper Series No. 142*. Bangkok: UNESCAP, February 2014.

ASEAN and UNCTAD. *ASEAN Investment Report 2013–2014: FDI Development and Regional Value Chains*. Jakarta: ASEAN Secretariat, 2014.

Asian Development Bank (ADB). *Asia SME Finance Monitor 2014*. Manila: ADB, 2015.

———. *Myanmar: Unlocking the Potential. Country Diagnostic Study*. Manila: ADB, 2014.

Ayyagari, Meghana, Thorsten Beck, and Asli Demirgüç-Kunt. "Small and Medium Enterprises Across the Globe". *World Bank Policy Research Working Paper No. 3127*. Washington D.C.: World Bank, 2003.

Bamber, Penny, Karina Fernandez-Stark, Gary Gereffi, and Andrew Guinn. "Connecting Local Producers in Developing Countries to Regional and Global Value Chains: Update". *OECD Trade Policy Papers No. 160*. Paris: OECD Publishing, 2014.

Berg, Achim and Saskia Hedrich. "What's Next in Apparel Sourcing". In *Perspectives on Retail and Consumer Goods Number 3*, edited by McKinsey & Company. McKinsey & Company, Summer 2014.

Bissinger, Jared and Linn Maung Maung. "Subnational Governments and Business in Myanmar". *Subnational Governance in Myanmar Discussion Paper No. 2*. MDRI-CESD and The Asia Foundation, February 2014.

Bloom, Nicholas A., Aprajit Mahajan, David McKenzie, and John Roberts. "Why Do Firms in Developing Countries Have Low Productivity?" *American Economic Review* 100, no. 2 (2010): 619–23.

Chan Mya Htwe. "Hope of Stability for Local Business as NLD Takes Lead". *Myanmar Times*, 12 November 2015. Available at <www.mmtimes.com/index.php/business/17572-hope-of-stability-for-local-business-as-nld-takes-lead.html> (accessed 16 November 2015).

Eleven Myanmar. "SME Registration Fee to Remain at Ks 1 Million", 9 July 2015. Available at <www.elevenmyanmar.com/business/sme-registration-fee-remain-ks-1-million> (accessed 12 November 2015).

Gereffi, Gary. "The Organization of Buyer-driven Global Commodity Chains: How US Retailers Shape Overseas Production Networks". In *Commodity Chains and Global Capitalism*, edited by Gary iguel. Westport, CT: Greenwood Press, 1994, pp. 95–122.

German Institute for Development Evaluation (DEval). *Small and Medium Enterprise Survey Myanmar 2015*. Bonn: DEval, 2015.

Hammond, Clare. "Investors Relieved, Optimistic After Provisional Results". *Myanmar Times*, 10 November 2015a. Available at <www.mmtimes.com/index.php/business/17523-investors-relieved-optimistic-after-provisional-results.html> (accessed 16 November 2015).

———. "Moody's Views NLD Landslide as Credit Positive". *Myanmar Times*, 18 November 2015b. Available at <www.mmtimes.com/index.php/business/17668-moody-s-views-nld-landslide-as-credit-positive.html> (accessed 20 November 2015).

Harvie, Charles. "East Asian Production Networks: The Role and Contribution of SMEs". *International Journal of Business and Development Studies* 2, no. 1 (2010a): 27–62.

———. "SMEs and Regional Production Networks". In *Integrating Small and Medium Enterprises (SMEs) into the More Integrate East Asia*, edited by ri hanhDionisius othea. ERIA Research Project Report 2009-8. Jakarta: Economic Research Institute for ASEAN and East Asia (ERIA), 2010b, pp. 19–45.

Harvie, Charles and Teerawat Charoenrat. "SMEs and the Rise of Global Value Chains". In *Integrating SMEs into Global Value Chains: Challenges and Policy Actions in Asia*. Manila: Asian Development Bank Institute (ADBI) and Asian Development Bank (ADB), 2015, pp. 1–26.

Htin Lin Aung. "Foreign Investment Down 5.1%". *Myanmar Times*, 26 November 2015. Available at <www.mmtimes.com/index.php/business/17819-foreign-investment-down-5-1.html> (accessed 27 November 2015).

Htin Lynn Aung. "No Taker of Credit Guarantee Insurance in Last Year". *Myanmar Times*, 4 August 2015. Available at <www.mmtimes.com/index.php/business/15816-no-takers-for-credit-guarantee-insurance-in-last-year.html> (accessed 27 November 2015).

International Labour Organization (ILO). *Myanmar Garment Sub-Sector Value Chain Analysis*. Geneva: ILO, 2015.

International Monetary Fund (IMF). "Myanmar – Staff Report for the 2017 Article IV Consultation". IMF Country Report No. 18/90. Washington D.C.: IMF, 9 February 2018.

Kaplinsky, Raphael. *Globalization, Poverty and Inequality: Between a Rock and a Hard Place*. Malden, M.A.: Polity Press, 2005.

Kudo, Toshihiro. "Myanmar's Apparel Industry in the New International Environment: Prospects and Challenges". *IDE Discussion Paper No. 430*. Chiba: Institute of Developing Economies-Japan External Trade Organization (IDE-JETRO), 2013.

———. "The Impact of U.S. Sanctions on the Myanmar Garment Industry". *Asian Survey* 48, no. 6 (2008): 997–1017.

Kyaw Hsu Mon. "Business Leaders see Brighter Future in NLD Win". *The Irrawaddy*, 13 November 2015. Available at <www.irrawaddy.org/election/news/business-leaders-see-brighter-future-in-nld-win> (accessed 16 November 2015).

Lim, Hank and Fukunari Kimura. "The Internationalization of Small and Medium Enterprises in Regional and Global Value Chains". *ADBI Working Paper Series No. 231*. Tokyo: Asian Development Bank Institute (ADBI), 2010.

Martin, Michael F. "U.S. Sanctions on Burma". Congressional Research Service (CRS) Report for Congress, 19 October 2012. Available at <https://www.fas.org/sgp/crs/row/R41336.pdf> (accessed 24 September 2015).

Myanmar Garment Manufacturers Association (MGMA). *Myanmar's Garment Sector: Opportunities & Challenges in 2015*. Yangon: MGMA, 2015.

Myanmar Ministry of Commerce (MoC) and the International Trade Centre (ITC). *National Export Strategy 2015–2019. Sector Strategy: Textiles and Garments*. Nay Pyi Taw: Ministry of Commerce of the Republic of the Union of Myanmar, 2015*a*.

———. *National Export Strategy 2015–2019. Cross-Sector Strategy: Quality Management*. Nay Pyi Taw: Ministry of Commerce of the Republic of the Union of Myanmar, 2015*b*.

————. *National Export Strategy 2015–2019. Cross-Sector Strategy: Access to Finance*. Nay Pyi Taw: Ministry of Commerce of the Republic of the Union of Myanmar, 2015c.

The New Light of Myanmar. "SMEs Lie at the Core of National Economic Growth in Developing Countries and Some Developed Countries: President U Thein Sein", 12 January 2013.

Organisation for Economic Co-operation and Development (OECD). *Multi-dimensional Review of Myanmar: Volume 1. Initial Assessment*. OECD Development Pathways series. Paris: OECD Publishing, 18 July 2013.

Puusaag, Kamile, David Abonyi, and Masato Abe. "Business and Development in Myanmar: A Policy Handbook for Private Sector Development". *Studies in Trade and Investment No. 82*. Bangkok: United Nations Economic and Social Commission for Asia and the Pacific (UNESCAP), 2015.

Smurra, A. "SMEs Development: Issues and Actions". *IGC Policy Note*. Yangon: International Growth Centre, 29 October 2014.

Soans, Aaron and Masato Abe. *Myanmar Business Survey: Data Analysis and Policy Implications*. Bangkok: UNESCAP and Mekong Institute, 2015.

Tin Mg Oo. "SME Registration Processing Time Slashed to One Day". *Myanmar Business Today*, 11 December 2014. Available at <www.mmbiztoday.com/articles/sme-registration-processing-time-slashed-one-day> (accessed 15 November 2015).

United Nations Conference on Trade and Development (UNCTAD). *Generalized System of Preferences: List of Beneficiaries*. Geneva: UNCTAD, 2015.

————. "GSP Newsletter No. 12". Geneva: UNCTAD, April 2013a.

————. *World Investment Report 2013. Global Value Chains: Investment and Trade for Development*. Geneva: UNCTAD, 2013b.

————. *Integrating Developing Countries' SMEs into Global Value Chains*. Geneva: UNCTAD, 2010.

United Nations Development Programme (UNDP). *Myanmar One Pager Business Census 2013–2014. First General Report*. Yangon: UNDP Myanmar, 2014.

United Nations Economic and Social Commission for Asia and the Pacific (UNESCAP). *Policy Guidebook for SME Development in Asia and the Pacific*. Bangkok: UNESCAP, 2012.

United Nations Industrial Development Organization (UNIDO). *Meeting Standards, Winning Markets: Trade Standards Compliance 2015*. Vienna: UNIDO, 2015.

Wignaraja, Ganeshan. "Can SMEs Participate in Global Production Networks? Evidence from ASEAN Firms". In *Global Value Chains in a Changing World*, edited by Deborah Elms atrick. Geneva: World Trade Organization, 2013.

World Bank. *Global Economic Prospects: The Global Economy in Transition*. Washington D.C.: World Bank, June 2015a.

————. *Myanmar Investment Climate Assessment: Sustaining Reforms in a Time of Transition*. Washington D.C. and Yangon: World Bank, 2015*b*.

————. *Doing Business 2016: Measuring Regulatory Quality and Efficiency. Economy Profile 2016: Myanmar*. Washington D.C.: World Bank, 2015*c*.

————. *Myanmar Enterprise Survey 2014: Early Findings*. Yangon: World Bank, 2014*a*.

————. *Making Foreign Direct Investment Work for Sub-Saharan Africa: Local Spillovers and Competitiveness in Global Value Chains*. Washington D.C.: World Bank, 2014*b*.

Zaw Htike. "Firms Slow to Use GSP Benefits". *Myanmar Times*, 28 July 2014. Available at <https://www.mmtimes.com/business/11172-firms-slow-to-use-gsp-benefits.html> (accessed 27 November 2015).

7

PHILIPPINE SME PARTICIPATION IN ASEAN AND EAST ASIAN REGIONAL ECONOMIC INTEGRATION

Rafaelita M. Aldaba

1. Introduction

Small and medium-sized enterprises (SMEs) are expected to benefit from the opportunities arising from increasing globalization and regional economic integration through greater participation in global value chains (GVCs) and global and regional production networks.[1] The ASEAN Economic Community was established not only to create a single market but also to serve as a regional production base that will attract more foreign direct investment (FDI). Regional production networks are at the heart of intraregional trade and investment and are the key drivers of economic growth in ASEAN and East Asia. This phenomenon is characterized by the exports of parts, components, capital equipment and other industrial inputs to be assembled into finished goods for export.

MNCs have established these production networks with domestic firms, particularly SMEs, serving as potential suppliers of outsourced parts or services that have increasingly grown in sectors such as automotive, machineries, electronics, and garments. Participation in regional and global production networks provides SMEs with access not only to export markets but also to newer technologies. To increase their overall competitiveness in international markets, lead multinational firms provide their local affiliates and local suppliers with more rapid technological upgrading and greater attention to quality control, cost control, and human resource development.

However, participation in these production networks is not easy and there are many challenges that SMEs need to overcome in order to participate in GVCs and production networks. SMEs must be financially strong to carry out the necessary upfront investment, have the ability to comply with stringent standards and other international business practices, and are able to constantly upgrade and innovate in order to maintain their competitiveness. Given their small size and age, government support for SMEs is crucial to facilitate their productive participation in GVCs.

It is important to note that SMEs participating in production networks are different from non-participants and are often characterized by substantially higher growth and higher productivity (Aldaba et al. 2010). Given the large number of barriers that SMEs must face, making small and medium manufacturers internationally competitive is a major challenge that would require government support particularly by addressing financing, market information, business linkages, technology development, training and counselling and advice.

Access to finance has been identified as one of the most binding constraints affecting SME growth and development in the Philippines. Aldaba (2011) illustrated the continued dependence of SMEs on internal sources of financing such as personal savings of owners, retained earnings, and loans from friends and relatives not only during the start-up phase but also for current operations.

Studies analysing the participation of Philippine enterprises in free trade agreements (FTAs) have shown low utilization rates. Aldaba et al. (2015) indicated a utilization rate of 31 per cent for the 108 establishments surveyed while Kawai and Wignaraja (2011) indicated that only 20 per cent of 155 firms surveyed used FTAs. For SMEs, the lack of information was cited as the biggest impediment to using FTAs along with small trade volume and to some extent, complicated certificate of origin (COO) requirements.

In view of the increasing regional economic integration in ASEAN and East Asia, the present study aims to take a more in-depth look at the extent and nature of SME participation in ASEAN economic integration. It also aims to identify the enabling factors and obstacles to SME participation in regional trade, production networks and investment activities. A survey of 205 establishments was conducted to examine the state of SME participation in the regional economic integration in ASEAN and East Asia.

This chapter is divided into five parts. After the introduction, part two reviews the current state and performance of Philippine SMEs along with government policies and programmes to promote SME competitiveness and integrate them with GVCs. Part three describes the regional and preferential trade agreements that the Philippines has signed while part four presents the survey results and the analysis of findings. The last part crafts policy recommendations to promote active participation of SMEs in regional trade, production networks, and investment.

2. Economic Growth, Government Policies, and SME Performance

2.1. Growth and Overall Economic Performance

Philippine economic growth performance has been quite remarkable, averaging at 6.4 per cent from 2010 to 2014 (see Figure 7.1). The manufacturing industry has been leading the country's growth with an average of 8.2 per cent while services posted an average growth of 6.7 per cent. Agriculture, hunting, forestry, and fishing lagged behind as its average growth registered only 1.7 per cent during the same period. In terms of contribution to GDP, the share of manufacturing went up from 22.8 per cent in 2013 to 23.2 per cent in 2014 (see Table 7.1). Its growth accelerated from an average of 4.1 per cent during 2008–12 to 10.3 per cent in 2013 and 8.1 per cent in 2014.

Food manufacturing continued to dominate the manufacturing industry with a share of 35.6 per cent in 2014 (see Table 7.1). This is followed by the radio, television and communication equipment and apparatus sector with a share of 16.6 per cent and chemical and chemical products with a share of 11.4 per cent. Furniture and fixtures contributed 5.8 per cent to total manufacturing value added while beverages registered a contribution of 4.4 per cent.

FIGURE 7.1
Quarterly Industry Growth, 2009–14

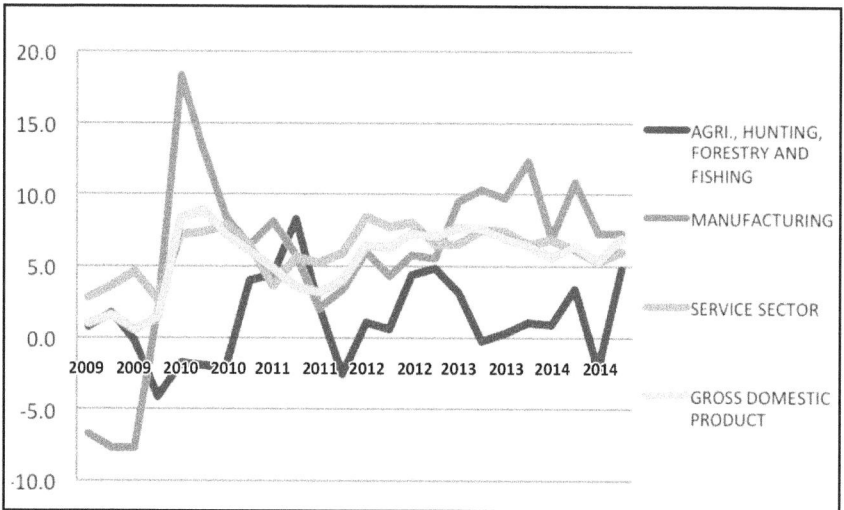

In terms of growth, furniture and fixtures has witnessed steady growth from an average of 34.8 per cent during 2008–12 to 44.5 per cent in 2013. In 2014, it registered a growth rate of 24.8 per cent. Chemical and chemical products also sustained its growth, averaging from 7.8 per cent during the 2008–12 period to 93.5 per cent in 2013 and 3.3 per cent in 2014. Food manufacturing, rubber and plastic, fabricated metal, and machinery and equipment excluding electrical posted increases in their growth rates between 2013 and 2014. A recovery seemed to be apparent in office, accounting and computing machinery as its growth rate went up to 13.4 per cent in 2014. Electrical machinery and apparatus grew by 2.2 per cent in 2014 after a decline in 2013. Radio, television and communication equipment and apparatus grew by 10 per cent in 2013 but slowed down in 2014. On the average, transport equipment grew by 11.5 per cent from 2008 to 2012. However, its growth decelerated in 2013 but quickly increased to 7.1 per cent in 2014.

To sustain a high growth level, the government is currently focusing on a new industrial policy aiming at revitalizing the manufacturing industry. The goal is to develop a globally competitive manufacturing industry supported by strong forward and backward linkages and

TABLE 7.1
Manufacturing Structure and Growth Performance

Manufacturing Subsectors	Share			Growth		
	2008–12	2013	2014	2008–12	2013	2014
Food manufactures	38.4	36.1	35.6	4.4	4.4	6.8
Beverage industries	4.2	3.8	4.4	5.2	–2.8	25.1
Tobacco manufactures	0.6	0.3	0.2	–16.7	–7.0	–5.1
Textile manufactures	2.5	1.7	1.8	–3.5	–12.2	15.0
Wearing apparel	2.5	2.2	1.9	4.0	–15.7	–4.6
Footwear & leather & leather products	0.5	0.5	0.4	–4.3	11.5	2.6
Wood, bamboo, cane & rattan articles	1.1	0.9	0.8	–2.7	–7.0	0.6
Paper & paper products	1.0	0.8	0.8	5.5	–6.5	6.4
Publishing & printing	0.7	0.5	0.9	–1.0	–3.3	88.7
Petroleum & other fuel products	4.2	2.8	3.0	–4.2	–11.3	14.3
Chemical & chemical products	6.4	12.0	11.4	7.8	93.5	3.3
Rubber & plastic products	1.6	1.5	1.5	8.3	3.1	5.7
Non-metallic mineral products	2.5	2.7	2.4	8.8	8.9	–2.8
Basic metal industries	2.0	2.0	1.9	–6.2	49.4	1.2
Fabricated metal products	1.1	0.9	1.2	1.2	0.7	46.2
Machinery & equipment ex electrical	1.5	1.4	1.6	3.1	5.7	22.3
Office, accounting & computing machinery	1.4	1.4	1.4	5.1	0.0	13.4
Electrical machinery & apparatus	2.3	2.2	2.1	10.7	–6.6	2.2
Radio, television and communication equipment & apparatus	17.8	17.0	16.6	3.6	10.0	5.3
Transport equipment	2.2	1.7	1.7	11.5	–19.3	7.1
Furniture and fixtures	2.3	5.0	5.8	34.8	44.5	24.8
Miscellaneous manufactures	3.2	2.6	2.4	7.8	–10.5	–0.7
Manufacturing	22.2	22.8	23.2	4.1	10.3	8.1

Source: Philippine Statistics Authority.

deepen the participation of manufacturing firms, especially SMEs, in GVCs in automotive, electronics, machinery, garments, and food industries. The government will address the most binding obstacles to the entry and growth of domestic firms and implement measures to create the right policy framework to encourage the development of the private sector along the lines of the country's comparative advantage. These will entail programmes and policies to address the high cost of power, high cost of domestic shipping and logistics, inadequate infrastructure, and complex government rules and regulations affecting business operations. The strategies include human resource development and skills training programmes, SME development, innovation, investment promotion (especially FDI that would bring in new technologies), and improvement in the business environment.

2.2. Policies and Programmes for SME Development

In the Philippines, SMEs are defined based on employment size and total assets. The former which is more frequently used defines the different size categories as follows: small enterprises have ten to 99 employees; medium enterprises have 100 to 199 employees while large enterprises have 200 or more employees. In terms of assets, small enterprises are those with three to 15 million total assets; medium enterprises have total assets of between 15 and 100 million pesos; while large enterprises have assets of 100 million pesos and above. Enterprises with less than ten workers or with total assets amounting to three million pesos or less are classified as micro enterprises.

There are currently three major legislations affecting the development of micro, small, and medium enterprises (MSMEs):

- Republic Act 6977 Magna Carta for Small Enterprises (1991): creation of the Micro, Small and Medium Enterprise Development (MSMED) Council as the primary agency responsible for the promotion, growth and development of MSMEs; creation of the Small Business Guarantee and Finance Corporation to implement comprehensive policies and programmes to assist MSMEs; mandatory allocation of credit resources to MSMEs of at least 8 per cent for micro and small enterprises and at least 2 per cent for medium enterprises of banks' total loan portfolio.

- Republic Act 9178 Barangay Micro Business Enterprises Act (2002): granting of incentives to micro enterprises such as income tax exemption, exemption from the Minimum Wage Law, and other benefits.
- Republic Act 10644 Go Negosyo Act (2015): establishment of Negosyo Centers in all provinces, cities, and municipalities to serve as one-stop shops for MSME needs such as business registration assistance, business advisory services, and business information and advocacy.

The Department of Trade and Industry (DTI) is the primary coordinator for the development of Philippine SMEs including micro enterprises. The DTI Bureau of Small and Medium Enterprises Development (BSMED) is mandated to develop and promote MSMEs by advocating policies, programmes and projects addressing the needs of MSMEs in accessing markets, developing human resources, and upgrading technology. The BSMED also acts as a secretariat to the MSMED Council and is tasked to monitor the implementation of the above laws as well as to review policies and strategies for MSME development. BSMED also coordinates, monitors, and evaluates the implementation of the activities under the MSME Development Plan. Its major programmes for MSME development cover the following:

- Negosyo Centers: these are one-stop shops that provide information, advisory, and consulting services in productivity improvement, technology upgrading, market information, product and market development, trade promotion, financing, and entrepreneurial development.
- SME Roving Academy: a learning programme to promote entrepreneurship and raise MSME competitiveness through continuous capacity building activities in partnership with local government units, academe, trade and industry associations, chambers of commerce, financial institutions, and government and non-government organizations.
- Shared Services Facilities: in cooperation with the Department of Science and Technology (DOST), academe, local government units and private organizations, this entails setting up common service facilities or production centres to provide MSMEs with better technology and more modern equipment.

DTI has other line bureaus and support offices to assist MSMEs and MSME exporters. The Center for International Trade Expositions and Missions (CITEM) is the export marketing arm of the DTI and provides global trade platforms for MSMEs primarily in home and fashion lifestyle and food industries. The Design Center of the Philippines (DCP) provides product design services to MSMEs to improve the quality and competitiveness of their products. The Philippine Trade Training Center (PTTC) designs and develops training curricula and conducts training programmes for MSMEs on entrepreneurship development, business capability building, and quality and productivity. The Bureau of Export Trade Promotion (BETP) provides frontline assistance, information, and specialized consultancy services to MSME exporters.

DOST is the main agency responsible for providing technology support to MSMEs. Like the DTI, it also has various offices and line agencies to support MSMEs' technology needs. The Advanced Science and Technology Institute (ASTI) implements research and development (R&D) programmes in information and communications technology, microelectronics, and technology transfer programmes through technology diffusion/commercialization and collaborative R&D. The Industrial Technology Development Institute (ITDI) conducts applied research in industrial manufacturing, mineral processing, energy and environment using local raw materials and provides analytical and testing services, food engineering services, calibration and metrology, process engineering, and packaging R&D. The Metals Industry Research and Development Center (MIRDC) provides trainings for engineers and technicians in the metals and engineering industry, quality control and testing of metal products, and R&D. The Philippine Council for Agriculture, Aquatic and Natural Resources Research and Development (PCAARRD) provides strategic R&D programme covering ten industry clusters: export fruit crops, vegetables, legumes and root crops, coffee and abaca, coconut and oil palm, ornamentals, rice and white corn, sugarcane, swine poultry yellow corn, pasture ruminants and forestry. The Philippine Council for Industry, Energy and Emerging Technology Research and Development (PCIEERD) provides R&D, technology transfer and information dissemination services in the following sectors: electronic and semiconductor, mining and minerals, metals and engineering, food processing as well as in energy (bio-fuels, renewable, energy efficiency) and emerging technologies (materials science/nanotechnology, genomics, biotechnology, among others).

3. Current State and Performance of SMEs

Table 7.2 shows that as of 2013, the Philippines has 941,174 enterprises, 99.6 per cent of which are MSMEs. A great bulk or 46.4 per cent of the total enterprises consist of MSMEs in the wholesale and retail trade and repair of motor vehicles and motorcycles. A far second or 13.6 per cent of the total comprise of MSMEs engaged in accommodation and food service activities. MSMEs in the manufacturing industry account for 12.5 per cent of the total.

TABLE 7.2
Number of Establishments by Industry and Employment Size, 2013

Sector	Number			% Share	
	MSMEs	LEs	Total	MSMEs	LEs
Agriculture, Forestry & Fishing	8,329	188	8,517	0.9	4.9
Mining & Quarrying	962	50	1,012	0.1	1.3
Manufacturing	117,524	1,048	118,572	12.5	27.2
Electricity, Gas, Steam & Air Conditioning Supply	940	101	1,041	0.1	2.6
Water Supply; Sewage Waste Management, Remediation Activities	1,271	19	1,290	0.1	0.5
Construction	3,242	240	3,482	0.3	6.2
Wholesale and Retail Trade; Repair of Motor Vehicles, Motorcycles	434,847	388	435,235	46.4	10.1
Transportation & Storage	4,877	135	5,012	0.5	3.5
Accommodation & Food Service Activities	127,128	78	127,206	13.6	2.0
Information & Communications	39,455	115	39,570	4.2	3.0
Financial & Insurance Activities	33,159	178	33,337	3.5	4.6
Real Estate Activities	9,602	48	9,650	1.0	1.2
Professional Scientific & Technical Activities	18,495	80	18,575	2.0	2.1
Administrative & Support Service Activities	16,172	755	16,927	1.7	19.6
Education	17,728	222	17,950	1.9	5.8
Human Health & Social Work Activities	27,988	153	28,141	3.0	4.0
Arts Entertainment & Recreation	15,045	41	15,086	1.6	1.1
Other Service Activities	60,563	8	60,571	6.5	0.2
Total	937,327	3,847	941,174	100	100

Source: Philippine Statistics Authority.

In terms of employment contribution, Table 7.3 shows that MSMEs posted a share of 63.7 per cent of the total. The wholesale and retail trade and repair of motor vehicles and motorcycles generated the largest contribution of 35.8 per cent. This is followed by the manufacturing industry with a share of 16.5 per cent while accommodation and food service activities registered a share of 14 per cent.

TABLE 7.3
Total Employment by Industry and Size, 2013

Sector	Number			% Share	
	MSMEs	LEs	Total	MSMEs	LEs
Agriculture, Forestry & Fishing	105,275	122,331	227,606	2.2	4.5
Mining & Quarrying	14,311	45,182	59,493	0.3	1.7
Manufacturing	785,908	759,612	1,545,520	16.5	27.9
Electricity, Gas, Steam & Air Conditioning Supply	27,219	43,673	70,892	0.6	1.6
Water Supply; Sewage Waste Management, Remediation Activities	25,956	12,544	38,500	0.5	0.5
Construction	78,944	162,317	241,261	1.7	6.0
Wholesale and Retail Trade; Repair of Motor Vehicles, Motorcycles	1,707,217	152,184	1,859,401	35.8	5.6
Transportation & Storage	81,925	81,701	163,626	1.7	3.0
Accommodation & Food Service Activities	674,273	33,625	707,898	14.1	1.2
Information & Communications	129,628	92,523	222,151	2.7	3.4
Financial & Insurance Activities	165,482	179,381	344,863	3.5	6.6
Real Estate Activities	67,096	19,978	87,074	1.4	0.7
Professional Scientific & Technical Activities	106,687	54,605	161,292	2.2	2.0
Administrative & Support Service Activities	146,779	769,981	916,760	3.1	28.3
Education	275,065	98,574	373,639	5.8	3.6
Human Health & Social Work Activities	122,446	72,554	195,000	2.6	2.7
Arts Entertainment & Recreation	62,462	15,087	77,549	1.3	0.6
Other Service Activities	193,772	3,314	197,086	4.1	0.1
Total	4,770,445	2,719,166	7,489,611	100	100

Source: Philippine Statistics Authority.

Within the manufacturing industry, micro enterprises accounted for 88 per cent of total establishments while small enterprises recorded a share of 11 per cent in 2013 (see Table 7.4). Medium and large enterprises registered a share of 0.8 per cent and 0.9 per cent, respectively. In terms of employment share, large firms contributed the highest with a share of 49 per cent of the total. Small and medium enterprises contributed 22 per cent and 9 per cent respectively while micro enterprises posted a share of 21 per cent. Medium enterprises constitute a small share not only of the SME sector but also the overall manufacturing industry.

TABLE 7.4
Total Number of Manufacturing Enterprises and Employees

Number of Enterprises

Year	Micro	%	Small	%	Medium	%	Large	%	Total
1995	86,900	89	8,928	9	1,027	1	982	1	97,837
2000	108,998	87	14,121	11	1,110	0.9	1,238	1	125,467
2003	107,398	89	11,910	10	853	0.7	1,024	0.8	121,184
2006	105,083	90	10,274	9	1,004	0.9	985	0.8	117,346
2010	100,779	90	9,334	8	809	0.7	924	0.8	111,846
2011	100,837	89	10,029	9	899	0.8	1,024	0.9	112,789
2012	103,037	87	13,473	11	1,091	0.9	1,121	0.9	118,722
2013	103,845	88	12,718	11	961	0.8	1,048	0.9	118,572

Number of Employees

Year	Micro	%	Small	%	Medium	%	Large	%	Total
1995	271,699	22	227,949	18	137,384	11	615,874	49	1,252,906
2000	354,025	22	354,328	22	150,734	9	730,127	46	1,589,214
2003	360,576	25	285,027	19	118,896	8	698,173	48	1,462,672
2006	259,664	19	252,931	18	132,332	10	727,984	53	1,372,911
2010	258,117	20	240,340	19	112,388	9	680,459	53	1,291,304
2011	253,945	18	270,123	20	124,524	9	724,775	53	1,373,367
2012	316,036	20	353,715	22	148,997	9	766,102	48	1,584,850
2013	318,899	21	334,621	22	132,388	9	759,612	49	1,545,520

Source: Philippine Statistics Authority and National Statistics Office.

While some notable improvements in terms of the number of enterprises and employment contribution were registered, the overall economic performance of SMEs in the last decade has been subdued. Special tabulations from the Philippine Statistics Authority show that in terms of contribution to total value added, SMEs in the formal sector of the economy accounted for only 31 per cent in 2012. Within the manufacturing industry, SMEs' contribution to total manufacturing value added declined from 21 per cent in 2006 to 17 per cent in 2012. Employment contribution also dropped from 34 per cent in 2006 to only 29 per cent in 2012. On the whole, SMEs have not substantially generated sufficient value added and employment to increase competition, improve industrial structure and increase the country's overall manufacturing growth. The weak performance of SMEs has been largely attributed to a large number of barriers, particularly access to finance, technology, and skills as well as the presence of information gaps and difficulties with product quality and marketing. Despite the substantial trade and investment liberalization in the country along with increasing regional integration, penetrating the export market has not been easy for SMEs. Making small and medium manufacturers internationally competitive and integrating them into GVCs are major challenges that the Philippines faces especially in the light of increasing globalization and greater economic integration through the ASEAN Economic Community and other FTAs that the Philippines has signed.

4. Philippine Commitments in Regional and Preferential Trade Agreements

The Philippines has continued to maintain an open trade policy and currently, after substantial unilateral liberalization since the 1980s, average tariffs are low. Tariffs have been reduced from an average nominal rate of 34.6 per cent in 1981 to only 7.02 per cent in 2010. Since 2004, no major unilateral tariff changes have been made; mostly the tariff reductions carried out were those covered by the ASEAN Free Trade Area–Common Effective Preferential Tariff (AFTA–CEPT) scheme.

Compared to some of its ASEAN neighbours, the Philippines seems to be more cautious in its FTA policy. Currently, the country has a total of seven concluded FTAs consisting of Philippines–Japan

FTA, ASEAN–Korea FTA, ASEAN–China FTA, ASEAN Trade in Goods Agreement (ATIGA), ASEAN–Australia and New Zealand FTA, ASEAN–India FTA and ASEAN–Japan FTA. As Table 7.5 shows, the simple average tariff under the ASEAN/ATIGA is already almost zero and covers all product lines. Average tariffs are also very low under the ASEAN–China FTA at 0.35 per cent and ASEAN–Korea FTA at 0.44 per cent with 92 per cent and 90 per cent of product lines enjoying zero tariffs, respectively. Average tariff is slightly lower under the ASEAN–Japan FTA than the bilateral agreement with Japan. In terms of zero duty coverage, ASEAN–Japan FTA is slightly higher than Philippines–Japan FTA. Under the ASEAN–India FTA, the average tariff is 4.9 per cent and only 4.3 per cent of all goods enjoy zero duty.

The government continues to engage in further discussions on possible bilateral partnerships such as with the European Union, European Free Trade Area States, and Taiwan along with regional cooperation such as the Regional Comprehensive Economic Partnership (RCEP) and Trans Pacific Partnership (TPP). The government sees FTAs not only as tools for market access but also as opportunities to attract investments, services, trade facilitation, institution building and technology upgrading.

Previous studies indicated low FTA utilization by firms in the Philippines. For instance, in a survey of Japanese-affiliated companies operating in ASEAN, Hiratsuka et al. (2009) found that the utilization rate by exporting firms was only 15 per cent during 2006–7 and it even declined to 11.8 per cent in 2008. In a survey of 155 firms from the transport, electronics and food sectors, Wignaraja et al. (2010) reported that 20 per cent of these firms used FTAs. The major reasons for the low FTA utilization cited by these studies are the lack of information on FTAs along with difficulties in complying with Rules of Origin (ROO)[2] requirements and high administration costs.

In a more recent survey covering 108 firms, Aldaba et al. (2015) found that only 30.6 per cent are FTA users, mostly from the automotive, electronics, apparel and leather sectors. For SMEs, the most common reason for non-FTA use is the lack of information. Large enterprises, most of which are located in eco zones, are less inclined to use FTAs because they are already enjoying duty and tax free importation of raw materials, supplies, capital equipment, and spare parts. Other reasons cited are small trade volume and complicated COO requirements.

TABLE 7.5
Tariff Profile by FTA

FTA Agreement	Enactment/Date of Implementation	2010		2011		End Dates
		Average Tariff	Percentage of Duty Free Tariff Lines to All Goods	Average Tariff	Percentage of Duty Free Tariff Lines to All Goods	
ASEAN/ATIGA	2006 (EO 489)	0.00	Approx 100.00	0.00	Approx 100.00	2015
ASEAN–China	2005 (EO 485)	0.35	92.24	0.35	92.24	2018
ASEAN–Korea	2007/2008 (EO 638)	0.44	89.69	0.44	89.69	2016
ASEAN–Japan	2009/2010 (EO 852)	2.33	63.22	1.55	71.45	2018
ASEAN–Australia/New Zealand	2009/2010 (EO 851)	3.38	59.52	3.08	60.76	2020
ASEAN–India	2011 (EO 25)			4.90	4.28	2022
Philippines–Japan	2008 (EO 767)	2.68	64.63	2.38	65.57	2018

Source: Department of Trade and Industry.

5. Survey on SME Participation in ASEAN Economic Integration: Major Findings

5.1. Overall Profile and Business Information

The survey aims to examine the extent and nature of SME participation in the ASEAN economic integration. The sample consisted of 205 manufacturing establishments located in the National Capital Region (NCR) and the Cavite, Laguna, Batangas, Rizal and Quezon (CALABARZON) area. These two regions were selected due to the relatively large size of their manufacturing industries and their importance in terms of economic contribution. In 2013, NCR and CALABARZON combined represented 34 per cent of the total number of establishments in the Philippine manufacturing industry and contributed 56 per cent to total manufacturing employment. In 2014, the two regions accounted for 59 per cent of total manufacturing value added and 54 per cent of the gross domestic product (Philippine Statistics Authority and National Statistics Office).

The survey covered a wide range of manufacturing subsectors composed of food and beverage; textile, wearing apparel, leather; wood, paper; chemical and chemical products; rubber and plastic; basic metals; electronics, motor vehicle, furniture, and others as described in Figure 7.2. Since there is no published list of enterprises, names and addresses of manufacturing companies gathered from different offices and bureaus of the Department of Trade and Industry were assembled. Using a systematic sampling design, samples were drawn from this list of manufacturing companies.

Table 7.6 summarizes the overall profile and business information of the sample firms. In terms of employment size (small enterprises: 10–99 workers; medium enterprises: 100–199 workers; and large enterprises: 200 and above), 40 per cent of the establishments are small enterprises, 19 per cent are medium enterprises, and 38 per cent are large enterprises. The average establishment age is 22 years. The bulk of the sample firms or 88 per cent are legally organized as stock corporations, 9 per cent are single proprietorships while 3 per cent are partnerships. In terms of ownership structure, 36 per cent of the establishments are 100 per cent locally owned, 32 per cent are fully foreign-owned while 32 per cent have mixed ownership. Only 38 per cent are considered as family business.

Among SMEs, 87 per cent are stock corporations with only 11 per cent single proprietorships. Forty-nine per cent are locally owned while

FIGURE 7.2
Distribution by Manufacturing Sector

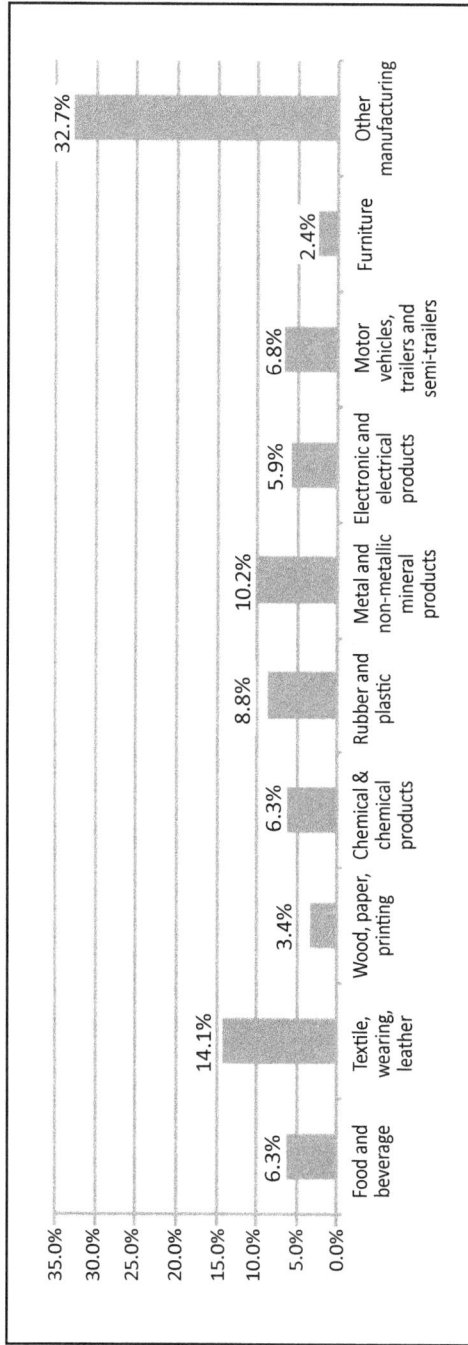

TABLE 7.6
Profile of the Sample Firms

	Full Sample		SMEs		LEs	
Employment Size	**Number**	**Share**	**Number**	**Share**	**Number**	**Share**
Small	80	40.49%	80	66.67%		
Medium	40	19.02%	40	33.33%		
Large	75	37.56%			75	
No reply	10	2.93%				
Total	205	100.00%	120	100%	75	100%
Legal Organization	**Number**	**Share**	**Number**	**Share**	**Number**	**Share**
Single Proprietorship	18	8.78%	13	10.83%	4	5.33%
Partnership	6	2.93%	0	0.00%	3	4.00%
Government Corporation	0	0.00%	3	2.50%	0	0.00%
Stock Corporation	181	88.29%	104	86.67%	68	90.67%
Total	205	100.00%	120	100%	75	100%
Ownership Structure	**Number**	**Share**	**Number**	**Share**	**Number**	**Share**
Local	73	35.61%	59	49.17%	11	14.67%
Partially Local (Majority)	22	10.73%	13	10.83%	7	9.33%
Partially Local (Half)	0	0.00%	0	0.00%	0	0.00%
Partially Local (Minority)	44	21.46%	22	18.33%	20	26.67%
Foreign	66	32.20%	26	21.67%	37	49.33%
Total	205	100.00%	120	100%	75	100%
Family Business	**Number**	**Share**	**Number**	**Share**	**Number**	**Share**
Yes	77	37.56%	62	51.67%	14	18.67%
No	125	60.98%	57	47.50%	59	78.67%
No response	3	1.46%	1	0.83%	2	2.67%
Total	205	100.00%	120	100%	75	100%
Managed by Founder/ Family Member	**Number**	**Share**	**Number**	**Share**	**Number**	**Share**
Yes	72	93.51%	57	91.94%	14	100%
No	5	6.49%	5	8.06%	0	0.00%
Total	77	100.00%	62	100%	14	100%

TABLE 7.6 (*continued*)

Highest Academic Qualification of Founder/Family Member	Full Sample		SMEs		LEs	
	Number	Share	Number	Share	Number	Share
Primary	1	1.39%	1	1.75%	0	0.00%
Secondary/High School	2	2.78%	2	3.51%	0	0.00%
Vocational/Diploma	2	2.78%	1	1.75%	1	7.14%
University	67	93.06%	53	92.98%	13	92.86%
Total	72	100.00%	57	100%	14	100%
Total Fixed Assets	**2013**	**2014**	**2013**	**2014**	**2013**	**2014**
Mean	PHP 441M	PHP 1,005M	PHP 108M	PHP 115M	PHP 851M	PHP 2,385M
Parent Company	**Number**	**Share**	**Number**	**Share**	**Number**	**Share**
Yes	124	60.49%	61	50.83%	57	76.00%
No	81	39.51%	59	49.17%	18	24.00%
Total	205	100.00%	120	100%	75	100%
Size of Parent Company	**Number**	**Share**	**Number**	**Share**	**Number**	**Share**
11–49 full-time workers	24	19.35%	15	24.59%	7	12.28%
50–249 full-time workers	35	28.23%	25	40.98%	9	15.79%
More than 250 full-time workers	54	43.55%	17	27.87%	34	59.65%
Unknown (no response)	11	8.87%	4	6.56%	7	12.28%
Total	124	100.00%	61	100%	75	100%
Ownership of Parent Company	**Number**	**Share**	**Number**	**Share**	**Number**	**Share**
Local	29	23.39%	20	32.79%	7	12.28%
Foreign	91	73.39%	38	62.30%	49	85.36%
Both	1	0.81%	1	1.64%	0	0.00%
No response	3	2.42%	2	3.28%	1	1.75%
Total	124	100.00%	61	100%	57	100%
Membership	**Number**	**Share**	**Number**	**Share**	**Number**	**Share**
Yes	110	53.66%	65	54.17%	41	54.67%
No	88	42.93%	52	43.33%	31	41.33%
No response	7	3.41%	3	2.50%	3	4.00%
Total	205	100.00%	120	100%	75	100%

22 per cent are foreign-owned. Fifty-two per cent are family-owned enterprises. Meanwhile, the bulk of large enterprises (91 per cent) are also organized as stock corporations. Forty-nine per cent are foreign-owned and 15 per cent are domestically-owned. Only 19 per cent are family-owned enterprises.

Among the family-owned establishments, 94 per cent are managed by the founder/family member. In terms of the academic qualification of the founder/family member who manages the business, 93 per cent have university degrees. For SMEs, 92 per cent of family-owned enterprises are managed by the founder/family member with 93 per cent of them possessing a university degree.

The average total fixed assets of the firms in the sample were 441 million pesos in 2013 and 1,005 million pesos in 2014. Sixty per cent of the respondents have parent companies, 44 per cent of which have more than 250 full-time workers. Seventy-three per cent of the parent companies are foreign-owned and only 23 per cent are locally owned. In terms of industry networks, 54 per cent are members of industry associations.

SMEs have mean fixed assets amounting to 115 million pesos in 2014 while for large enterprises, mean fixed assets amounted to almost 2.4 billion pesos during the same year. Among SMEs, 51 per cent have parent companies of which 41 per cent have between 50 and 249 workers. The parent companies are mostly foreign-owned (62 per cent). For large enterprises, 76 per cent have parent companies, most of which have more than 250 workers (60 per cent) and are largely foreign-owned (85 per cent).

6. Firm Characteristics: Sales, Production Costs, Employment, and Innovation

For the whole sample, mean sales increased by 14 per cent between 2013 (2.44 billion pesos) and 2014 (2.79 billion pesos). On the average, the firms export 40 per cent of their production. Mean sales for SMEs rose by 5 per cent from 375 million pesos in 2013 to 395 million pesos in 2014. Large enterprises' mean sales increased by 17 per cent from 5.792 billion pesos in 2013 to 6.79 billion pesos in 2014. In terms of market orientation, SMEs export 33 per cent of their production while large enterprises sell 54 per cent of their products abroad.

Table 7.7 presents the sales distribution by customer type (parent, sister, subsidiary, other companies, direct customers, or state-owned

TABLE 7.7
Sales Activities

| | Total Sample | | | | Small and Medium Enterprises | | | | Large Enterprises | | | |
| | Intermediate | | Final | | Intermediate | | Final | | Intermediate | | Final | |
	No.	%	No.	%	No.	%	No.	%	No.	%	No.	%
a. Parent Company												
Yes	34	17	36	18	17	14	20	17	15	20	15	19
No	170	83	168	82	102	85	99	83	60	80	60	80
NR	1	0	1	0	1	1	1	1	0	0	0	0
Total	205	100	205	100	120	100	120	100	75	100	75	100
b. Sister Company												
Yes	23	11	22	11	10	8	12	10	13	17	8	11
No	181	88	181	88	109	91	106	88	62	83	67	89
NR	1	0	2	1	1	1	2	2	0	0	0	0
Total	205	100	205	100	120	100	120	100	75	100	75	100
c. Subsidiary Company												
Yes	13	6	11	5	5	4	5	4	8	11	6	8
No	191	93	192	94	114	95	114	95	67	89	68	91
NR	1	0	2	1	1	1	1	1	0	0	1	1
Total	205	100	205	100	120	100	120	100	75	100	75	100

d. Other Companies

	63	31	88	43	36	30	56	47	26	35	39	39
Yes	63	31	88	43	36	30	56	47	26	35	39	39
No	140	68	116	57	83	69	63	53	48	64	46	61
NR	2	1	1	0	1	1	1	1	1	1	0	0
Total	205	100	205	100	120	100	120	100	75	100	75	100

e. State-owned Enterprise

Yes	3	1	16	8	1	1	10	8	2	3	5	7
No	200	98	187	91	118	98	108	90	72	96	70	93
NR	2	1	2	1	1	1	2	2	1	1	0	0
Total	205	100	205	100	120	100	120	100	75	100	75	100

f. Directly to Consumers

Yes	61	30	41	34	16	21
No	142	69	78	65	58	77
NR	2	1	1	1	1	1
Total	205	100	120	100	75	100

Note: NR: no reply.

enterprises); product type (intermediate or final) as well as by size (SMEs or large enterprises). For the total sample, 31 per cent of the firms sell intermediate products to other companies, 17 per cent supply these to their parent companies, 11 per cent to their sister companies, and 6 per cent to subsidiary companies. Meanwhile, 43 per cent of the firms sell final products to other companies, 30 per cent sell these directly to consumers, 18 per cent to parent companies, 11 per cent to sister companies, 5 per cent to subsidiary companies, and 8 per cent to government-owned enterprises.

Thirty per cent of SMEs sell their intermediate products to other companies, 14 per cent to parent company, 8 per cent to sister companies, and 4 per cent to subsidiary companies. For final products, 47 per cent of SMEs sell these to other companies, 34 per cent directly to customers, 17 per cent to parent companies, and 10 per cent to sister companies. For large enterprises, the same pattern is observed with 35 per cent selling their intermediate products to other companies, 20 per cent to parent companies, and 17 per cent to sister companies. For final products, 39 per cent of large enterprises sell these to other companies, 21 per cent directly to customers, 19 per cent to parent companies, and 11 per cent to sister companies.

Table 7.8 presents the production activities, cost breakdown and sources of inputs. Sixty-two per cent of the respondent firms carry out their processes completely in-house while 33 per cent have combined in-house and outsourced activities. On the average, the percentage of inputs outsourced abroad and outsourced domestically are even at 50 per cent. Three per cent of the firms completely outsource their production activities, with 72 per cent outsourced abroad while the remaining 28 per cent outsourced locally.

Among SMEs, 67 per cent have completely in-house production while 3 per cent completely outsource their production. Thirty per cent have both in-house and outsourced production with 64 per cent outsourced abroad and 36 per cent outsourced domestically. Among large enterprises, 56 per cent of firms carry out their production completely in-house. Meanwhile, 4 per cent completely outsource their production, with 67 per cent outsourced abroad and 33 per cent outsourced domestically. Thirty-six per cent of large firms have both in-house and outsourced production with 36 per cent outsourced abroad and 64 per cent outsourced domestically.

TABLE 7.8
Production Activities

Production Activities	Overall Sample		SMEs		LEs	
	2013	2014	2013	2014	2013	2014
Production	**Number**	**Per Cent**	**Number**	**Per Cent**	**Number**	**Per Cent**
Completely in-house	127	62%	80	67%	42	56%
Completely outsourced	6	3%	3	3%	3	4%
Foreign outsourced	72%		80%		67%	
Domestic outsourced	28%		20%		33%	
Both in-house & outsourced	68	33%	36	30%	27	36%
Foreign outsourced	50%		64%		36%	
Domestic outsourced	50%		36%		64%	
No response	4	2%	1	1%	3	4%
Production Cost	PHP 1,847 M	PHP 2,016 M	PHP 249 M	PHP 287 M	PHP 4,504 M	PHP 4,828 M
% Breakdown	**2013**	**2014**	**2013**	**2014**	**2013**	**2014**
Raw materials	58%	57%	60%	60%	55%	52%
Intermediate inputs	6%	7%	6%	6%	7%	8%
Utilities (water, gas, and electricity)	7%	7%	7%	7%	6%	7%
Interest payments	2%	1%	2%	1%	1%	1%
Salaries and wages	19%	19%	18%	18%	20%	21%
Overhead	9%	9%	8%	7%	12%	12%
Sources of Inputs (2014)	**Number**	**Per Cent**	**Number**	**Per Cent**	**Number**	**Per Cent**
Local	34	17%	26	22%	6	8%
Partially Local (Majority)	33	16%	17	14%	12	16%
Local (Half)	1	0%	1	1%	0	0%
Local (Minority)	69	34%	38	32%	30	40%
Partially Local	5	2%	3	3%	2	3%
Foreign	44	21%	26	22%	16	21%
No response	19	9%	9	8%	9	12%
Local Source Mean (% of Total Inputs)	41%		43%		35%	
Foreign Source Mean (% Total Inputs)	59%		57%		65%	

Average production costs went up by 9.1 per cent from 1.85 billion pesos in 2013 to 2.02 billion pesos in 2014. A large proportion of total production costs is accounted for by raw materials with a share of 57 per cent in 2014. This is followed by salaries and wages whose share remained at 19 per cent in 2014. In terms of input sources, 64 per cent of the firms source their intermediate inputs from other companies while 27 per cent source these from their parent companies. For final inputs, 34 per cent buy these from other companies, 13 per cent from their parent companies and 10 per cent from their sister companies. In terms of major sources of inputs, 41 per cent of total inputs are sourced locally while 59 per cent are sourced abroad.

Among SMEs, production costs increased by 15 per cent from 249 million pesos in 2013 to 287 million pesos in 2014. Raw materials comprised 60 per cent of total production costs in 2014, followed by salaries and wages which accounted for 18 per cent of the total. In 2013, salaries and wages represented the same percentage. For large enterprises, production costs went up by 7 per cent from 4.5 billion pesos in 2013 to 4.8 billion pesos in 2014. Raw materials costs which comprise the bulk of production costs accounted for 55 per cent in 2013 but this declined to 52 per cent in 2014. Salaries and wages followed with a share of about 21 per cent in 2014. Other manufacturing overhead is next with a share of 12 per cent of the total costs in 2014. On the average, SMEs source 43 per cent of their inputs locally while large enterprises source only 35 per cent locally.

Table 7.9 shows that in terms of employment, the respondent firms reported an average employment of 448 workers in 2013 and 452 workers in 2014. Foreign workers' share was around 7 per cent in 2013 and 6 per cent in 2014. Female employees represented a share of 37 per cent in 2013 and 38 per cent in 2014. Plant and machine operators and assemblers comprised the bulk of the total salaries accounting for 43 per cent of the total. Managers and professionals followed with a share of 19 per cent along with supervisory and clerical workers with a share of 17 per cent while service and sales workers accounted for a share of 9 per cent. A large proportion of the workforce or 47 per cent of the total obtained secondary/high school level of education; 30 per cent have university degrees while 21 per cent have attended vocational/diploma courses. Training expenditures amounted to 0.83 million pesos in 2014 and 0.93 million pesos in 2013. Thirty-nine per cent of the respondents hire foreign workers.

TABLE 7.9
Employment Profile

Employment, Salaries, Qualification	Overall Sample		SMEs		LEs	
	2013	2014	2013	2014	2013	2014
Employment Profile						
Full-time workers	448	452	77	77	1,045	1,052
Part-time workers	65	59	22	25	138	117
Foreign employees mean	7%	6%	5%	5%	9%	8%
Female employees mean	37%	38%	33%	33%	43%	45%
Workforce and Salaries	Per Cent of Total Salaries	Number of Workers	Per Cent of Total Salaries	Number of Workers	Per Cent of Total Salaries	Number of Workers
Managers and professionals	19%	13.82	22%	6.54	11%	25.31
Engineers and technicians	7%	29.21	7%	5.04	7%	67.76
Supervisory and clerical	17%	44.25	17%	15.63	18%	94.64
Plant and machine operators, and assemblers	43%	342.55	39%	50.65	52%	839.93
Service and sales workers	9%	15.27	11%	9.36	4%	25.19
Academic Qualification of Workers	Per Cent of Total Workers		Per Cent of Total Workers		Per Cent of Total Workers	
No formal education	0%		0%		0%	
Primary	1%		1%		0%	
Secondary/High School	47%		45%		52%	
Vocation/Diploma	21%		20%		23%	
University Degree	30%		33%		24%	
Training Expenditures	PHP 933 K	PHP 829 K	PHP 133 K	PHP 138 K	PHP 2,018 K	PHP 1,839 K
Hiring of Foreign Workers	Number	Share	Number	Share	Number	Share
Yes	80	39%	35	29%	41	55%
No	123	60%	84	70%	34	44%
No response	2	1%	1	1%	0	1%

TABLE 7.10
Innovation Activities

Innovation Activities	Overall Sample		SMEs		LEs	
	Number	Value	Number	Value	Number	Value
Innovation Expenditure						
In-house R&D activities		PHP 22.2 M		PHP 36 M		PHP 2 M
Outsourcing of R&D activities	18	PHP 206 K	12	PHP 25 K	4	PHP 510 K
Acquisition of machinery, equipment and software		PHP 33.6 M		PHP 16 M		PHP 64.9 M
Acquisition of external knowledge	20	PHP 27 K	13	PHP 24 K	6	PHP 2 K
Innovation expenditure (% of total costs)	15%		25%		2%	
Introduction of Innovation (2012–14)	Number	Per Cent	Number	Per Cent	Number	Per Cent
Yes	85	41%	45	38%	33	44%
No	109	53%	71	59%	35	47%
No response	11	5%	4	3%	5	9%
New and Improved Services	Number	Per Cent	Number	Per Cent	Number	Per Cent
Yes	52	25%	25	21%	21	29%
No	136	66%	87	73%	46	61%
Percentage of New and Improved Products in Sales	Mean		Mean		Mean	
New to the market	11%		9%		11%	
Process Innovation Introduced (2012–14)					Number	Per Cent
Methods of Manufacturing						
Yes	92	45%	48	40%	36	48%
No	105	51%	67	56%	37	49%
No response	8	4%	5	4%	2	3%
Logistics						
Yes	73	36%	39	33%	28	37%
No	124	60%	76	63%	45	60%
No response	8	4%	5	4%	2	3%
Supporting Processing Activities						
Yes	82	40%	42	35%	32	43%
No	116	57%	74	62%	41	55%
No response	7	3%	4	3%	1	3%

On the average, SMEs had only 77 full-time workers in 2014 while large enterprises had 1,052 full-time workers. Female employees employed by SMEs accounted for 33 per cent of total employment and 45 per cent for large enterprises. On the average, SMEs have 25 part-time workers while for large enterprises, the average is 117. SMEs employed foreign workers which accounted for 5 per cent of the total; for large enterprises, foreign workers represented 8 per cent of the total.

Among SMEs, 29 per cent hire foreign workers while among large enterprises, a higher proportion is obtained at 55 per cent. The bulk of SME workforce is composed largely of plant and machine operators and assemblers with an average of 51 workers and in terms of salaries, they represented 39 per cent of the total. The same holds for large enterprises with an average of 840 plant and machine operators and assemblers whose salaries accounted for 52 per cent of the total. On the average, 45 per cent of the SME workforce and 52 per cent of large enterprises have secondary/high school education. SMEs spent an average of 0.138 million pesos on training in 2014 while large enterprises spent 1.84 million pesos on the average.

Table 7.10 shows innovation expenditure from 2012 to 2014. Only 9 per cent of the firms outsource their R&D activities, spending an average of 0.21 million pesos. Mean expenditures for in-house R&D and for the acquisition of machinery, equipment and software amounted to 22 million pesos and 33.6 million pesos, respectively. Ten per cent of the firms invest in acquiring external knowledge with an average expenditure of 0.03 million pesos.

In terms of product innovation, 41 per cent of the firms introduced new and improved goods while 25 per cent introduced new and improved services. Eleven per cent of the products that have been introduced are new to the market and 10 per cent are new to the establishment. In terms of process innovation, 45 per cent of the firms introduced new or improved methods of manufacturing during 2012–14. Thirty-six per cent introduced new or improved logistics while 40 per cent introduced new or improved supporting activities.

Among SMEs, 10 per cent of the firms engage in outsourcing R&D activities, spending 0.025 million pesos on the average. SME expenditure for in-house R&D and for the acquisition of machinery, equipment and software amounted to 36 million pesos and 16 million pesos, respectively.

The same proportion of SMEs spent an average of 0.024 million pesos for the acquisition of new knowledge. Among large enterprises, only 5 per cent outsource their R&D activities, spending an average of 0.510 million pesos. Large enterprises' average expenditure for in-house R&D activities and for the acquisition of machinery, equipment and software amounted to 2 million pesos and 64.9 million pesos, respectively. In terms of R&D outsourcing and acquisition of machinery, equipment and software, large enterprises' expenditures are higher than that of SMEs. However, for in-house R&D and acquisition of external knowledge, average SME spending is relatively higher.

Thirty-eight per cent of SMEs and 44 per cent of large enterprises introduced new and improved products. In terms of services, 21 per cent of SMEs and 29 per cent of large enterprises introduced new and improved services. On the average, new and improved products represented 9 per cent of SME sales while for large enterprises, these accounted for a slightly higher proportion at 11 per cent.

For process innovation, 40 per cent of SMEs introduced new or improved methods of manufacturing; for large enterprises, the share is much higher at 48 per cent. For new and improved logistics, 33 per cent of SMEs and 37 per cent of large enterprises introduced this. Similarly, both SMEs (35 per cent) and large enterprises (43 per cent) introduced new or improved supporting services.

In terms of internet services, Table 7.11 shows that 96 per cent of the respondent firms use email and 49 per cent have company websites. There is only a slight difference between SMEs and large enterprises as 95 per cent of SMEs use email while for large enterprises, the proportion is slightly higher at 97 per cent. The same proportion of SMEs and large enterprises (48 per cent) have company websites.

On the whole, only 9 per cent of the respondent firms have online sales, 18 per cent use online purchases and procurement, 13 per cent use online marketing, and 35 per cent use online payment services. For online sales and online purchases/procurement, the proportion of SMEs is slightly higher than large enterprises. Ten per cent of SMEs have online sales and 19 per cent use online purchases while only 7 per cent and 15 per cent of large enterprises do so, respectively. For online marketing, the proportion of SMEs is the same as large enterprises at roughly 12 per cent, but for online payment, the proportion of large enterprises is higher (43 per cent) than that of SMEs (30 per cent).

TABLE 7.11
Use of Internet-related Services

Internet Services	Overall Sample		SMEs		LEs	
a. Email	Number	Share	Number	Share	Number	Share
Yes	197	96%	114	95%	73	97%
No	5	2%	3	3%	2	3%
No response	3	1%	3	3%	0	0%
b. Company website	Number	Share	Number	Share	Number	Share
Yes	101	49%	58	48%	36	48%
No	101	49%	59	49%	39	52%
No response	3	1%	3	3%	0	0%
c. Online sale	Number	Share	Number	Share	Number	Share
Yes	19	9%	12	10%	5	7%
No	183	89%	105	88%	70	93%
No response	3	1%	3	3%	0	0%
d. Online purchase/procurement	Number	Share	Number	Share	Number	Share
Yes	36	18%	23	19%	11	15%
No	166	81%	94	78%	64	85%
No response	3	1%	3	3%	0	0%
e. Online marketing	Number	Share	Number	Share	Number	Share
Yes	26	13%	14	12%	9	12%
No	176	86%	103	86%	66	88%
No response	3	1%	3	3%	0	0%
f. Online payment	Number	Share	Number	Share	Number	Share
Yes	71	35%	36	30%	32	43%
No	130	63%	80	67%	43	57%
No response	4	2%	4	3%	0	0%

7. AEC and FTA Utilization

1) AEC Awareness

As seen in Table 7.12, on the overall, majority of the respondents (52 per cent) have business relations with other firms in ASEAN, primarily through imports (85 per cent) and exports (56 per cent). Furthermore, 7 per cent of the firms indicated that they have services relations with other firms in ASEAN while 3 per cent have investment relations. Among SMEs, 46 per cent have business relations with other firms in ASEAN while among large enterprises, the proportion is much higher at 61 per cent.

TABLE 7.12
ASEAN Economic Community 2015

AEC Awareness	Overall Sample		SMEs		LEs	
Business Relations with Other Firms in ASEAN	Number	Share	Number	Share	Number	Share
Yes	106	52%	55	46%	46	61%
No	95	46%	61	51%	29	39%
No data	4	2%	4	3%	0	0%
Business Relations According to Activity	Number	Share	Number	Share	Number	Share
Import	90	85%	44	80%	42	91%
Export	59	56%	28	51%	28	61%
Investment	3	3%	0	0%	1	2%
Services	7	7%	2	4%	4	9%
Awareness of AEC Policy Blueprint/Strategic Action Plan for SME Development 2004–14	Number	Share	Number	Share	Number	Share
Yes	74	36%	33	28%	36	48%
No	127	62%	86	72%	37	49%
No response	4	2%	1	1%	2	3%
Awareness of ASEAN Economic Community	Number	Share	Number	Share	Number	Share
Yes	109	53%	58	48%	45	60%
No	91	44%	61	51%	28	37%
No response	5	2%	1	1%	2	3%

The AEC Blueprint has focused on SME development through the ASEAN Policy Blueprint for SME Development (APBSD) 2004–2014. The Blueprint promotes the idea that ASEAN SMEs should be part of the regional and global supply chains. The Strategic Action Plan for ASEAN SME Development (SAPASD) 2010–2015 has been formulated to engage businesses on issues of access to finance, technology, and human resource development among others to enhance SME competitiveness.

On the overall, only 36 per cent of the respondent firms indicated that they are aware of AEC Policy Blueprint/Strategic Action Plan for SME Development. For SMEs, a smaller proportion of 28 per cent expressed awareness while for large enterprises, almost half of the firms are aware of the plan. For the ASEAN Economic Community, 53 per cent of the total respondent firms expressed awareness; 48 per cent of SMEs and 60 per cent of large enterprises expressed awareness.

2) How AEC Affected Businesses

Table 7.13 summarizes the overall firm responses on how AEC has affected their businesses. In terms of the impact on domestic sales, 21 per cent indicated no change, 16 per cent expressed an increase in sales, while 10 per cent pointed out a drop in sales. A large proportion of the respondents of about 53 per cent had no opinion, no response or no knowledge. Export sales are expected to increase by 21 per cent of the respondents. However, 59 per cent had no opinion, no response, or no knowledge while 17 per cent indicated no change. Import costs are expected to decline by 20 per cent of the respondents, although 17 per cent indicated no change while 12 per cent expressed an increase in costs and 52 per cent had no opinion, no response, or no knowledge. In terms of the impact on their profits, 18 per cent indicated an increase in profits, 15 per cent expressed no change, 11 per cent expressed a decrease in profit, and again a large proportion of the respondents (57 per cent) had no reply, no opinion, or no knowledge. Competition in the domestic market is expected to increase by 27 per cent of the respondents, 13 per cent expressed no change, but a huge proportion of the respondents (58 per cent) had no opinion, no response or no knowledge. Competition in the foreign market is also expected to increase by 23 per cent of the respondents, 13 per cent indicated no change and 61 per cent had no opinion, no response or no knowledge. Access to intermediate outputs is perceived to rise by 23 per cent of

TABLE 7.13
Perceptions on the Impact of AEC on Businesses (%)

AEC Impact	Overall Sample				SMEs				LEs			
	A	B	C	D	A	B	C	D	A	B	C	D
a) How AEC affected business												
Domestic sales	16	21	10	53	8	22	13	57	29	20	4	47
Export sales	21	17	3	59	13	20	2	66	36	12	5	47
Import cost	12	17	20	52	11	21	11	58	15	11	32	43
Profits	18	15	11	57	13	16	12	60	27	15	8	51
Competition in local market	27	13	3	58	24	13	2	62	31	15	4	51
Competition in foreign market	23	13	2	61	17	14	1	68	35	12	3	51
Greater access to intermediate outputs	23	14	2	60	18	18	2	63	32	11	3	55
Average	20	16	7	57	15	18	6	62	29	14	8	49
b) AEC key changes affecting business												
Import tariffs/duties	9	21	23	47	8	25	17	51	12	15	32	41
Export tariffs/duties	8	23	14	56	7	22	11	61	11	23	19	48
Customs procedure	15	21	9	55	9	20	8	63	27	21	9	43
Standards regulation	16	23	5	56	13	20	3	64	23	27	8	43
Recognition of professional qualifications	14	24	1	61	13	20	1	66	16	27	3	55
Investment process in ASEAN countries	15	17	4	64	12	17	3	69	19	16	7	59
Connectivity in terms of transport and communication services	22	20	2	55	21	18	3	58	27	21	3	49
Average	14	21	8	56	12	20	6	62	19	21	11	48

Note: A = increase; B = no change; C = decrease; D = do not know/no opinion/no reply.

the respondents, 14 per cent expressed no change, and 60 per cent had no opinion, no response or no knowledge.

For SMEs, 22 per cent indicated that there would be no change in their domestic sales, 13 per cent indicated a decrease in sales and only 8 per cent indicated an increase. For the impact on export sales, 20 per cent indicated no change, 13 per cent expected an increase in sales while 2 per cent indicated a decline. Only 11 per cent indicated a decrease in import cost, 21 per cent indicated no change, and 11 per cent indicated an increase. Sixteen per cent indicated no change in profits, 13 per cent indicated an increase while 12 per cent indicated a decline. Twenty-four per cent expected increased competition in the domestic market while 13 per cent indicated no change. Seventeen per cent expected competition in the foreign market to increase while 14 per cent indicated no change. Eighteen per cent perceived greater access to intermediate outputs, although the same proportion indicated no change. A large proportion of the SME respondents had no reply, no opinion or no knowledge about the impact of AEC on their business activities.

Among the large enterprises, 29 per cent indicated an increase in domestic sales while 20 per cent expressed that there would be no change. For exports, 36 per cent indicated an increase while 12 per cent indicated no change. Import costs are expected to decline by 32 per cent of large enterprises, 15 per cent indicated an increase in cost while 11 per cent indicated no change. Profits are expected to increase by 27 per cent of the large enterprises while 15 per cent indicated no change. Thirty-one per cent expected competition in the local market to increase while 35 per cent indicated an increase in competition in foreign market. Thirty-two per cent expressed greater access to intermediate outputs.

3) Key Changes in AEC Affecting Businesses

Table 7.13 also shows the key changes (due to AEC) that might have affected businesses. On the overall, 23 per cent of the firms indicated a decrease in AEC import tariffs/duties while 21 per cent indicated no change. Nine per cent of the firms perceived import tariffs to increase. A large proportion (47 per cent) of the respondents either did not know, had no opinion or no reply.

For AEC export tariffs/duties, 23 per cent indicated no change, 14 per cent indicated a decrease in export tariffs and 8 per cent expressed an increase. Again, majority of the firms (56 per cent) either did not know, had no opinion, or no reply. In terms of AEC customs procedure, 21 per cent expressed no change, 9 per cent indicated a decrease in customs procedure while 15 per cent perceived an increase. A large proportion (55 per cent) did not know, had no opinion, or no reply.

For AEC standards of regulation, 23 per cent of the firms indicated no change, 5 per cent perceived a decrease in harmonization of product standards and conformance regulations across the ASEAN region and 16 per cent expected an increase. Still, a large proportion of the firms either did not know, had no opinion, or no reply. In terms of recognition of professional qualifications, 24 per cent of the respondents had no perceived changes and 14 per cent indicated an increase in movement of professional workers. However, 61 per cent of the respondents did not know, had no opinion, or no reply. For investment process in ASEAN countries, 15 per cent of the respondents indicated an increase in investment facilitation, 17 per cent expressed no change and 64 per cent either did not know, had no opinion, or no reply. In terms of transport and communication services, 22 per cent expressed an increase in their businesses due to improved connectivity in these services, 20 per cent indicated no change while 55 per cent either did not know, had no opinion, or no reply.

For SMEs, 25 per cent of the respondents indicated that there would be no change in their businesses arising from AEC tariffs, 17 per cent expressed a decline in tariffs and 8 per cent indicated an increase. In terms of export tariffs, 22 per cent expressed that there would be no change, 11 per cent indicated a decline and only 7 per cent indicated an increase. Majority of the responses did not know, had no opinion or no reply.

For customs procedure, 20 per cent of the SME respondents indicated no change, 9 per cent expressed an increase, and 8 per cent indicated a decline. For standards regulation, 20 per cent of the respondents expressed that there would be no change; the same holds for recognition of professional qualifications. For investment process in ASEAN and connectivity in terms of transport and communication services, 17 per cent and 18 per cent, respectively, indicated no change. Twenty-one per cent of the respondents indicated an increase in their businesses due to improved connectivity while 12 per cent expressed an increase due to investment process in ASEAN. Thirteen per cent indicated an increase, both for standards regulation and recognition of professional qualifications. The proportion of respondents who did not know, had no opinion or no reply remained high ranging from 51 per cent to 69 per cent.

For large enterprises, 12 per cent of the respondents indicated an increase in ASEAN import tariffs, 11 per cent in export duties, 27 per cent in customs procedure, 23 per cent in standards regulation, 16 per cent in recognition of professional qualification, 19 per cent in investment process in ASEAN, and 27 per cent due to connectivity. For export tariffs, 23 per cent indicated no change along with standards regulation (27 per cent) and recognition of professional qualifications (27 per cent). Thirty-two per cent of the respondents indicated a decrease in import tariffs. Compared with SMEs, the proportion of those who did not know, had no opinion or no reply are much lower ranging from 41 per cent to 59 per cent.

4) FTA Utilization

In terms of FTA utilization, Table 7.14 shows that 41 per cent of the 205 respondents use FTAs. By size structure, 57 per cent of the FTA users are SMEs while 39 per cent are large enterprises.[3] Fifty-eight per cent of the FTA users use more than one FTA while the remaining 42 per cent use only one FTA. Among the single FTA users, 71 per cent are SMEs while 23 per cent are large enterprises. Among the multiple FTA users, 47 per cent are SMEs while 51 per cent are large firms.

Based on FTA use, Figure 7.3 shows that ATIGA has the most number of users accounting for 28 per cent, ACFTA (ASEAN–China FTA) follows with a share of 18 per cent, AJFTA (ASEAN–Japan FTA) is next with a share of 14 per cent, and AKFTA (ASEAN–Korea FTA) with a share of 11 per cent. Generalized System of Preferences (GSP)[4] users accounted for 11 per cent.

In terms of FTA use in the two groups of enterprises, there is not much difference between SMEs and large enterprises. Among SMEs and large enterprises, the proportions of firms using FTAs are 40 per cent and 44 per cent, respectively. The percentage of single FTA users among SMEs is higher (52 per cent) than that among large firms

TABLE 7.14
FTAs

	Overall Sample		SMEs		LEs	
Use of FTAs	**Number**	**Share**	**Number**	**Share**	**Number**	**Share**
FTA users	84	41%	48	40%	33	44%
Non-users	107	52%	63	53%	37	49%
No reply	14	7%	9	8%	5	7%
No. of FTAs Used	**Number**	**Share**	**Number**	**Share**	**Number**	**Share**
Single FTA	35	42%	25	52%	8	24%
More than one FTA used	49	58%	23	48%	25	76%
Reasons for Not Using FTA	**Number**	**Share**	**Number**	**Share**	**Number**	**Share**
Small trade volume	20	19%	14	22%	3	8%
Lack of knowledge/do not know how to use	51	48%	31	49%	17	46%
Difficult to get certificate of origin	13	12%	5	8%	6	16%
Small tariff preference by FTA	9	8%	6	10%	3	8%
Difficult to fulfill the requirements of Rules of Origin	16	15%	9	14%	6	16%
Others	19	18%	11	17%	8	22%

FIGURE 7.3
FTA Use

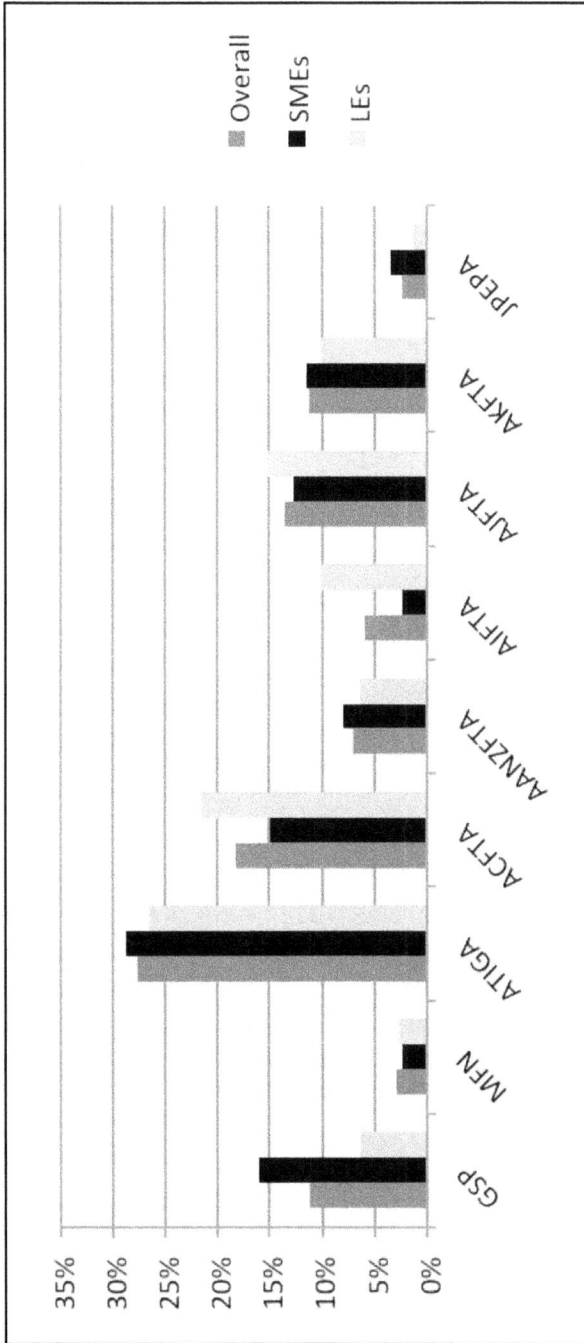

(24 per cent). Large enterprises tend to be multiple users of FTAs with 76 per cent of the firms using more than one FTA. Among SMEs, only 48 per cent are multiple FTA users.

The major reasons cited for non-use of FTAs are lack of knowledge on how to use FTAs (48 per cent); small trade volume (19 per cent); difficulties in complying with ROO requirements (15 per cent); and difficulties in getting COOs (12 per cent). Other reasons for non-use of FTAs are as follows: for companies that are registered under the Philippine Economic Zone Authority, they are already enjoying duty and tax free importation of raw materials, and some companies have the United States and Mexico as their major markets, while others have established customers in other markets. Moreover, some firms mentioned that they do not use FTAs because they are focusing mainly on the domestic market. Others indicated that they are operating as subcontractors, some as toll manufacturers, while others have brokers who handle directly the processing of their trade documents. There are also firms who mentioned that it is their mother companies that make decisions on these matters.

For both SMEs and large enterprises, the most important reason for not using FTAs is the lack of information. For SMEs, the other major constraints cited are small trade volume and difficulties in complying with ROO requirements. Large enterprises also cited difficulties in complying with ROO requirements and obtaining COOs.

5) Impact of FTAs on Businesses

As seen in Table 7.15, in terms of the impact of FTAs on domestic sales, 25 per cent of the total respondents indicated no change, 16 per cent expressed an increase in domestic sales, while 10 per cent indicated a decline in this aspect. As pointed out earlier, a large proportion of the respondents expressed no opinion, had no reply, or no knowledge. For export sales, 21 per cent indicated an increase, 19 per cent expected no change, 4 per cent a decrease, and 55 per cent had no opinion, no reply, or no knowledge. Import costs are expected to decline by 28 per cent of the respondents, 19 per cent stated no change, 9 per cent expected an increase, and 44 per cent had no opinion, no reply, or no knowledge. Profits are expected to increase by 23 per cent of the respondents, 16 per cent expected no change, 11 per cent expressed a decrease, and 50 per cent had no opinion, no reply, or no knowledge.

TABLE 7.15
Perceptions on the Impact of FTAs on Businesses

How FTAs Affect Businesses	Overall Sample				SMEs				LEs			
	A	B	C	D	A	B	C	D	A	B	C	D
Domestic sales	16	25	10	49	12	26	13	50	24	23	4	49
Export sales	21	19	4	55	15	19	6	60	31	19	3	48
Import cost	9	19	28	44	8	22	25	46	13	17	28	41
Profits	23	16	11	50	18	19	13	51	32	11	9	48
Competition in local market	26	20	1	52	22	22	2	55	31	20	0	49
Competition in foreign market	28	15	1	56	23	18	1	59	36	12	0	52
Average	21	19	9	51	16	21	10	53	28	17	7	48

Note: A = increase; B = no change; C = decrease; D = do not know/no opinion/no reply.

Competition in the domestic market is expected to intensify by 26 per cent, 20 per cent indicated no change, and 52 per cent had no opinion, no reply, or no knowledge. For competition in the foreign market, 28 per cent expected this to increase, 15 per cent expressed no change, and 56 per cent had no opinion, no reply, or no knowledge.

For SMEs, 26 per cent of the respondents indicated no change in domestic sales, 13 per cent expressed a decline while 12 per cent indicated an increase. In terms of the impact of FTAs on export sales, 19 per cent of the SME respondents indicated no change, 15 per cent expected an increase, while 6 per cent indicated a decline. For import costs, 25 per cent of the respondents indicated a decline; however, 22 per cent expressed no change while 8 per cent indicated an increase. For the impact on profits, 19 per cent indicated no change while 18 per cent expressed an increase with 13 per cent expecting a decline. Competition in the local market is expected to increase by 22 per cent of SMEs, 22 per cent indicated no change, while 2 per cent indicated a decline. For the foreign market, competition is expected to increase by 23 per cent and no change by 18 per cent of the respondents. For the bulk of the SMEs, the respondents had no opinion, no response or no knowledge about the impact of FTAs on their business activities.

The proportion of firms that perceived positive impact of FTAs on their businesses is much higher for large enterprises than for SMEs. Twenty-four per cent of large enterprises expected an increase in their domestic sales, 31 per cent expressed an increase in export sales and 28 per cent indicated a decline in their import cost. Profits are expected to increase by 32 per cent of the firms. Thirty-one per cent indicated that competition in the local market will increase while 36 per cent expected more intense competition in the foreign market arising from FTA implementation. Still a high proportion of large enterprises had no opinion, no response or no knowledge on the impact of FTAs on their business activities; although the share is relatively smaller than that among SMEs.

8. Major Characteristics of FTA Users

Table 7.16 contains a summary of the characteristics of FTA users. In terms of basic firm characteristics, FTA users are older (mean age is

TABLE 7.16(a)
Characteristics of FTA Users

	Overall Sample		FTA Users		FTA Non-users	
Age of Firms	22		24		20	
Firm Size	Number	Share	Number	Share	Number	Share
Small	80	39.02%	29	34.52%	44	41.12%
Medium	40	19.51%	19	22.62%	19	17.76%
Large	75	36.59%	33	39.29%	37	34.58%
Unknown	10	4.88%	3	3.57%	7	6.54%
Ownership Structure	Number	Share	Number	Share	Number	Share
Local	73	36%	24	28.57%	45	42.06%
Partial (Majority)	22	11%	9	10.71%	10	9.35%
Partial (Half)	0	0%	0	0.00%	0	0.00%
Partial (Minority)	44	21%	21	25.00%	20	18.69%
Foreign	66	32%	30	35.71%	32	29.91%
Family Business	Number	Share	Number	Share	Number	Share
Yes	77	38%	25	29.76%	47	43.93%
No	125	61%	59	70.24%	59	55.14%
	2013	2014	2013	2014	2013	2014
Fixed Assets	PHP 441 M	PHP 1,005 M	PHP 420 M	PHP 424 M	PHP 469 M	PHP 1,502 M
Parent Company	Number	Share	Number	Share	Number	Share
Yes	124	60%	63	75.00%	52	48.60%
No	81	40%	21	25.00%	55	51.40%
Size of Parent	Number	Share	Number	Share	Number	Share
11–49 full-time workers	24	19%	15	23.81%	8	15.38%
50–249 full-time workers	35	28%	16	25.40%	19	36.54%
More than 250 full-time workers	54	44%	28	44.44%	19	36.54%
Membership	Number	Share	Number	Share	Number	Share
Yes	110	54%	54	64.29%	45	42.06%
No	88	43%	27	32.14%	59	55.14%
	2013	2014	2013	2014	2013	2014
Total Sales	PHP 2.44 B	PHP 2.79 B	PHP 2.81 B	PHP 3.3 B	PHP 2.41 B	PHP 2.67 B

TABLE 7.16(b)
Characteristics of FTA Users

Product Sold	Number	Share	Number	Share	Number	Share
Intermediate only	55	27%	24	29%	25	23%
Final only	108	53%	40	48%	63	59%
Mixed	38	19%	19	23%	17	16%
% Exported	40%		39%		40%	
Production	**Number**	**Share**	**Number**	**Share**	**Number**	**Share**
Completely in-house	127	62%	45	53.57%	76	71.03%
Completely outsourced	6	3%	5	5.95%	1	0.93%
Foreign outsourced mean	72%		90%		0%	
Domestic outsourced mean	28%		10%		100%	
Both in-house and outsourced	68	33%	31	36.90%	29	27.10%
Foreign outsourced mean	50%		60%		39%	
Domestic outsourced mean	50%		40%		61%	
Input Sources	**Number**	**Share**	**Number**	**Share**	**Number**	**Share**
Local	34	17%	4	4.76%	29	27.10%
Partially local (Majority)	33	16%	9	10.71%	23	21.50%
Local (Half)	1	0%	0	0.00%	1	0.93%
Local (Minority)	69	34%	39	46.63%	26	24.30%
Partially local	5	2%	2	2.38%	3	2.80%
Foreign	44	21%	24	28.57%	17	15.89%
No response	19	9%	6	7.14%	8	7.48%
Local source (% of total inputs)	41%		25.35%		55.30%	
Foreign source (% total inputs)	59%		74.65%		44.70%	
Employment	**2013**	**2014**	**2013**	**2014**	**2013**	**2014**
Full-time workers	448	452	364	381	524	517
No. of part-time workers	65	59	70	64	63	57
Foreign employees	7%	6%	9.10%	7.80%	3.20%	3.40%
Female employees	37%	38%	31.40%	32.00%	42.30%	43.80%
Labour productivity	PHP 1,832 K	PHP 1,949 K	PHP 2,391 K	PHP 2,539 K	PHP 1,470 K	PHP 1,610 K
Workforce and Salaries	**% of Total Salaries**	**Number of Workers**	**% of Total Salaries**	**Number of Workers**	**% of Total Salaries**	**Number of Workers**
Managers and professionals	19%	13.82	18.36%	14.98	18.09%	13.47
Engineers and technicians	7%	29.21	7.54%	24.25	7.11%	34.15
Supervisory and clerical	17%	44.25	18.20%	54.29	17.67%	38.22
Plant & machine operators, assemblers	43%	342.55	44.10%	277.96	43.33%	390.9
Service & sales workers	9%	15.27	5.90%	19.91	11.00%	9.87

TABLE 7.16(b)   *(continued)*

Academic Qualification	% of Total Workers		% of Total Workers		% of Total Workers	
Primary	1%		2.00%		1.00%	
Secondary/High School	47%		43.00%		51.00%	
Vocation/Diploma	21%		20.00%		21.00%	
University Degree	30%		34.00%		26.00%	
Training Expenditures	**2013**	**2014**	**2013**	**2014**	**2013**	**2014**
	PHP 933 K	PHP 829 K	PHP 1,011 K	PHP 813 K	PHP 940 K	PHP 893 K
Hiring of Foreign Workers	**Number**	**Share**	**Number**	**Share**	**Number**	**Share**
Yes	80	39%	36	42.86%	38	35.51%
No	123	60%	47	55.95%	69	64.49%
Innovation Expenditure	**Yes**	**Mean**	**Yes**	**Mean**	**Yes**	**Mean**
In-house R&D activities		PHP 22.23 M		PHP 49.95 M		PHP 3.43 M
Outsourcing of R&D activities	18	PHP 206 K	12	PHP 485 K	6	PHP 18 K
Acquisition of machinery, equipment and software		PHP 33.56 M		PHP 48.96 M		PHP 25.88 M
Acquisition of external knowledge	20	PHP 27 K	14	PHP 64 K	4	PHP 0
Innovation expenditure (% of total costs)	15%		34%		3%	
Innovation						
a. New & Improved Goods	**Number**	**Share**	**Number**	**Share**	**Number**	**Share**
Yes	85	41%	44	52.38%	38	35.51%
No	109	53%	36	42.86%	67	62.62%
b. New & Improved Services	**Number**	**Share**	**Number**	**Share**	**Number**	**Share**
Yes	52	25%	21	25.00%	29	27.10%
No	136	66%	54	64.29%	76	71.03%
% of New & Improved Products	**Mean**		**Mean**		**Mean**	
New to the market	11%		13.00%		12.00%	
New to firm	10%		12.00%		9.00%	
Process Innovation						
a. Manufacturing Methods	**Number**	**Share**	**Number**	**Share**	**Number**	**Share**
Yes	92	45%	44	52.38%	45	42.06%
No	105	51%	38	45.24%	57	53.27%
b. Logistics	**Number**	**Share**	**Number**	**Share**	**Number**	**Share**
Yes	73	36%	36	42.86%	35	32.71%
No	124	60%	46	54.76%	67	62.62%

TABLE 7.16(b) (continued)

c. Supporting Activities	Number	Share	Number	Share	Number	Share
Yes	82	40%	40	47.62%	40	37.38%
No	116	57%	43	51.19%	62	57.94%
Internet						
a. Email	Number	Share	Number	Share	Number	Share
Yes	197	96%	83	98.81%	100	93.46%
No	5	2%	1	1.19%	4	3.74%
b. Company Website	Number	Share	Number	Share	Number	Share
Yes	101	49%	49	58.33%	45	42.06%
No	101	49%	35	41.67%	59	55.14%
Business Relations	Number	Share	Number	Share	Number	Share
Yes	106	52%	59	70.24%	40	37.38%
No	95	46%	22	26.19%	66	61.68%
Activity	Number	Share	Number	Share	Number	Share
Import	90	85%	52	88.14%	32	80.00%
Export	59	56%	38	64.41%	16	40.00%
Investment	3	3%	2	3.39%	1	2.50%
Services	7	7%	3	5.08%	4	10.00%
Action Plan for SME	Number	Share	Number	Share	Number	Share
Yes	74	36%	40	47.62%	30	28.04%
No	127	62%	44	52.38%	75	70.09%
AEC Awareness	Number	Share	Number	Share	Number	Share
Yes	109	53%	58	69.05%	43	40.19%
No	91	44%	25	29.76%	62	57.94%
Government Support	Number	Share	Number	Share	Number	Share
Yes	44	21%	24	29%	18	17%
No	123	60%	43	51%	77	72%
Risk Preference	Number	Share	Number	Share	Number	Share
Risk taker	16	8%	7	8%	7	7%
Risk averse	85	41%	33	39%	50	47%

24 years). Compared to non-users, the percentage share of foreign-owned firms, non-family business firms, firms that have parent companies, and firms belonging to industry associations are higher among FTA users. Their average sales are also higher than that of non-users. Their sales consist mostly of final products (same with non-users). In terms of export orientation, their export ratio is slightly lower than non-users (39 per cent vs. 40 per cent) which could be due to non-user exporters operating under the Philippine Economic Zone Authority as well as those that export primarily to the United States and Mexico where the Philippines does not have FTAs. The bulk of their inputs is foreign-sourced (75 per cent vs. 45 per cent for non-users). Their average number of full-time workers is lower than non-users, but they have a higher average number of part-time workers. FTA users have a higher proportion of workers with a university degree (34 per cent vs. 26 per cent for non-users). In terms of proportion of foreign employees, the ratio is also higher for FTA users.

In terms of training expenditures, FTA users spent more than non-users in 2013. However, in 2014, non-users had slightly higher expenditures. In terms of innovation expenditure, FTA users are spending significantly much more than non-users for in-house R&D activities, acquisition of machinery, equipment and software, and acquisition of external knowledge. Innovation expenditure as a share of total costs is around 34 per cent for FTA users and only 3 per cent for non-users. More FTA users are also introducing new and improved products; new or improved methods of manufacturing; new or improved logistics; and new and improved supporting services. The proportion of firms with email and company websites is also higher for FTA users. Most FTA users have business relations with firms in ASEAN (70 per cent vs. 37 per cent for non-users). In terms of awareness of the AEC as well as the Policy Blueprint for SME Development, the proportion of FTA users that are aware is also much higher than non-users. The proportion of FTA users receiving government support (29 per cent) is higher than the proportion of non-FTA users receiving the same (17 per cent). There is roughly the same proportion of risk takers for both FTA and non-FTA users but in terms of risk averse firms, the proportion for non-FTA users is higher than FTA users.

9. Analysis of the Respondents' Perceptions on the Possible Impacts of FTAs

To further understand how the respondent firms perceive the impact of AEC and other FTAs, Tables 7.17 to 7.24 provide more detailed tabulations that link together the perceptions of the responses to questions on the implications of the AEC and FTAs with the respondents' characteristics. It is evident from the preceding sections that the respondents may be divided into four groups:

- Optimistic firms consist of respondents who perceive that the AEC and other FTAs had or would have a positive impact on their business operations.
- Pessimistic firms consist of respondents who perceive that the AEC and other FTAs had or would have a negative impact on their business operations.
- Neutral or indifferent firms are respondents who perceive that the AEC and other FTAs had or would have no impact on their business operations.
- Unaware or uninformed firms are those that have no response, no opinion, or do not know what the impact of the AEC or other FTAs had or would have on their business operations.

Table 7.17 links firm responses to questions on the impact of AEC to AEC awareness. In terms of the impact of the AEC on domestic sales, 53 per cent of the respondents expressed a lack of knowledge on its likely effect on their domestic business operations. The bulk of these uninformed respondents (70 per cent) are not aware of what the AEC is. Of the total respondents, 21 per cent are neutral or indifferent with respect to the impact of the AEC. The bulk of this group (74 per cent) are aware of the AEC. Sixteen per cent of the total respondents expressed optimism on the impact of the AEC on their domestic sales. The group is dominated by firms who are aware of the AEC (85 per cent). A small group of firms (10 per cent) are not optimistic and indicated that the AEC would lead to a reduction in their domestic sales. The bulk of this group is dominated by firms that are also aware of the AEC (90 per cent).

In terms of the impact of the AEC on export sales, import costs, profits, domestic competition, foreign competition and access to intermediate inputs, the same pattern is observed. Respondent firms belonging to the optimistic, pessimistic, and neutral groups are dominated by firms who are aware of the AEC while the biggest group consisting of unaware or uninformed respondent firms is dominated by firms who are not aware of the AEC.

TABLE 7.17
Awareness and Perceptions on the Impact of AEC

AEC Impact	Increase	Decrease	No Change	Don't Know/ No Opinion/ No Reply
Domestic Sales				
Aware of AEC (%)	85	90	74	30
Not aware of AEC (%)	15	10	26	70
Total number	33	20	42	105
Export Sales				
Aware of AEC (%)	89	57	76	35
Not aware of AEC (%)	11	43	24	65
Total number	44	7	33	116
Import Cost				
Aware of AEC (%)	71	85	79	70
Not aware of AEC (%)	29	15	21	30
Total number	24	40	34	102
Profits				
Aware of AEC (%)	89	73	72	35
Not aware of AEC (%)	11	27	28	65
Total number	37	22	29	112
Domestic Competition				
Aware of AEC (%)	80	83	77	35
Not aware of AEC (%)	20	17	23	65
Total number	55	6	26	113
Foreign Competition				
Aware of AEC (%)	85	75	73	38
Not aware of AEC (%)	15	25	27	62
Total number	48	4	26	122
Intermediate Inputs				
Aware of AEC (%)	83	50	82	37
Not aware of AEC (%)	17	50	18	63
Total number	48	4	28	120

In terms of the perceived impact of AEC on export sales, 21 per cent of the total respondents expressed an increase, of which 89 per cent are aware of the AEC. In terms of the impact on import cost, 20 per cent of the total respondents expected a decline, of which 85 per cent are aware of AEC. Similarly, 23 per cent of the total respondents expected an increase in access to intermediate goods, of which 83 per cent are aware of the AEC. Twenty-seven per cent expected domestic competition to increase, of which 80 per cent are aware of the AEC. Twenty-three per cent expected foreign competition to intensify as a result of the AEC and of which 85 per cent are aware of the AEC.

Though aware of the AEC, more cautious respondent firms expected a decline in their domestic and export sales. They also perceived their import costs to increase and domestic and foreign competition to reduce. Their access to intermediate inputs along with their profits are also expected to fall due to the AEC. There are also respondent firms that are aware of the AEC but perceive no change in their business operations arising from the AEC.

It is important to note that though firms expressed awareness of the AEC, their perceptions on its impact on their business operations differ widely with some expressing optimism while others are more cautious. There are also some that remained indifferent or neutral while others have no opinion on how the AEC could potentially affect their activities.

Table 7.18 links firm responses to questions on the impact of the AEC to firm size as measured by the number of workers. The bulk of the responses fall under the uninformed group which is largely dominated by SMEs. For instance, on the impact of AEC on domestic sales, the group represented 53 per cent of the total respondent firms, of which 66 per cent are SMEs. The neutral or indifferent group accounted for 21 per cent of the total and of which 62 per cent are SMEs who perceived that the AEC would have no impact on their domestic sales. The optimistic group represented 16 per cent of the total and is composed mainly of large enterprises, of which 69 per cent are large firms who perceived that AEC would lead to increases in their domestic sales.

The same general trend is evident in the perceptions of firms on the likely impact of the AEC on their business operations. Large enterprises expected their export sales to increase (65 per cent), import costs to fall (66 per cent), profits to increase (58 per cent), along with increases in both domestic (45 per cent) and foreign competition (57 per cent). Large enterprises also perceived their access to intermediate inputs to increase due to the AEC (53 per cent).

TABLE 7.18
Firm Size and Perceptions on the Impact of AEC

AEC Impact	Increase	Decrease	No Change	Don't Know/ No Opinion/ No Reply
Domestic Sales				
SME (%)	31	84	62	66
LE (%)	69	16	38	34
Total Number	32	19	42	106
Export Sales				
SME (%)	35	29	73	70
LE (%)	65	71	27	30
Total Number	43	7	33	116
Import Cost				
SME (%)	54	34	73	69
LE (%)	46	66	27	31
Total Number	24	38	34	103
Profits				
SME (%)	42	67	63	66
LE (%)	58	33	37	34
Total Number	36	21	30	112
Domestic Competition				
SME (%)	55	40	58	66
LE (%)	45	60	42	34
Total Number	53	5	26	115
Foreign Competition				
SME (%)	43	25	65	69
LE (%)	57	75	35	31
Total Number	47	4	26	122
Intermediate Inputs				
SME (%)	47	50	72	65
LE (%)	53	50	28	35
Total Number	45	4	29	117

There are also large enterprises that perceived negative effects from the AEC. Seventy-one per cent expected their export sales to fall, 46 per cent perceived their import costs to increase, while 50 per cent expected their access to intermediate inputs to drop. Furthermore, 33 per cent of large firms perceived their profits to shrink due to the AEC. Respondents that are indifferent on the implications of AEC on their operations consisted mostly of SMEs. They expected no change in their export sales (73 per cent), import costs (73 per cent), profits (63 per cent), domestic and foreign competition (58 per cent and 65 per cent respectively), and access to intermediate inputs (72 per cent).

Table 7.19 links perceptions on the impact of AEC to the export activities of the firm respondents. In general, the four groups are largely dominated by firm exporters indicating that there are different perceptions on the implications of the AEC even among exporters. Table 7.20 links perceptions on the impact of AEC to FTA use. The biggest group consisting of unaware or uninformed firms is made up largely of non-FTA users. The group of firms that is indifferent to the impact of the AEC consists mainly of FTA users. Similarly, the group of optimistic firms is dominated by FTA users. The bulk of the more cautious firms show a mix of both FTA and non-FTA users. The responses on the decline of domestic sales (67 per cent) and decrease in import costs (71 per cent) are dominated by FTA users while the responses on the decline in export sales (86 per cent), profits (55 per cent), domestic competition (67 per cent), and access to intermediate inputs (100 per cent) are dominated by non-FTA users.

Table 7.21 tries to relate the perceptions on the impact of AEC to the firms' risk preference. All the groups are dominated by risk averse firms. Table 7.22 links the perceptions on the impact of AEC to the hiring of foreign workers. As the results show, the unaware group is dominated by firms without foreign workers.

Table 7.23 links perceptions on the impact of AEC to introduction of new products, a measure of firm innovativeness. The group of optimistic firms is dominated by firms that introduced new products while the unaware or uninformed group is composed largely of firms that did not introduce new products. Firms that have introduced new products perceived increases in domestic sales (70 per cent), increases in export sales (60 per cent), reduction in import costs (61 per cent), increases in profits (61 per cent), increases in domestic and foreign competition (63 per cent and 62 per cent respectively), and increases in access to intermediate inputs (68 per cent).

TABLE 7.19
Export Activity and Perceptions on the Impact of AEC

AEC Impact	Increase	Decrease	No Change	Don't Know/ No Opinion/ No Reply
Domestic Sales				
Exporter (%)	64	50	71	67
Non-exporter (%)	36	50	29	33
Total Number	28	18	38	102
Export Sales				
Exporter (%)	93	86	71	52
Non-exporter (%)	7	14	29	48
Total Number	41	7	31	107
Import Cost				
Exporter (%)	71	67	78	60
Non-exporter (%)	29	33	22	40
Total Number	21	36	32	97
Profits				
Exporter (%)	67	60	84	62
Non-exporter (%)	33	40	16	38
Total Number	33	20	25	108
Domestic Competition				
Exporter (%)	57	80	75	66
Non-exporter (%)	43	20	25	34
Total Number	47	5	24	110
Foreign Competition				
Exporter (%)	90	100	70	59
Non-exporter (%)	10	0	30	41
Total Number	45	4	23	114
Intermediate Inputs				
Exporter (%)	86	50	72	64
Non-exporter (%)	14	50	28	36
Total Number	44	4	25	113

Table 7.20
FTA Use and Perceptions on the Impact of AEC

AEC Impact	Increase	Decrease	No Change	Don't Know/ No Opinion/ No Reply
Domestic Sales				
FTA User (%)	63	67	51	32
Non-FTA user (%)	37	33	49	68
Total Number	32	18	37	104
Export Sales				
FTA User (%)	69	14	61	32
Non-FTA user (%)	31	86	39	68
Total Number	42	7	28	114
Import Cost				
FTA User (%)	57	71	55	27
Non-FTA user (%)	43	29	45	73
Total Number	23	38	31	99
Profits				
FTA User (%)	67	45	54	34
Non-FTA user (%)	33	55	46	66
Total Number	36	20	26	109
Domestic Competition				
FTA User (%)	62	33	61	32
Non-FTA user (%)	38	67	39	68
Total Number	53	6	23	109
Foreign Competition				
FTA User (%)	68	50	39	35
Non-FTA user (%)	32	50	61	65
Total Number	47	4	23	117
Intermediate Inputs				
FTA User (%)	60	0	68	34
Non-FTA user (%)	40	100	32	66
Total Number	47	4	25	115

TABLE 7.21
Risk Preference and Perceptions on the Impact of AEC

AEC Impact	Increase	Decrease	No Change	Don't Know/ No Opinion/ No Reply
Domestic Sales				
Risk Taker (%)	14	18	21	18
Risk Averse (%)	86	82	79	82
Total Number	14	11	24	52
Export Sales				
Risk Taker (%)	11	0	27	14
Risk Averse (%)	89	100	73	86
Total Number	18	4	22	57
Import Cost				
Risk Taker (%)	10	16	24	15
Risk Averse (%)	90	84	76	85
Total Number	10	19	17	55
Profits				
Risk Taker (%)	18	18	6	18
Risk Averse (%)	82	82	94	82
Total Number	17	11	18	55
Domestic Competition				
Risk Taker (%)	17	0	14	17
Risk Averse (%)	83	100	86	83
Total Number	24	4	14	59
Foreign Competition				
Risk Taker (%)	18	0	19	15
Risk Averse (%)	82	100	81	85
Total Number	22	1	16	62
Intermediate Inputs				
Risk Taker (%)	17	0	19	16
Risk Averse (%)	83	100	81	84
Total Number	23	4	16	58

TABLE 7.22
Hiring of Foreign Workers and Perceptions on the Impact of AEC

AEC Impact	Increase	Decrease	No Change	Don't Know/ No Opinion/ No Reply
Domestic Sales				
With Foreign Workers (%)	42	45	43	36
Without Foreign Workers (%)	58	55	57	64
Total Number	33	20	42	108
Export Sales				
With Foreign Workers (%)	57	43	52	29
Without Foreign Workers (%)	43	57	48	71
Total Number	44	7	33	119
Import Cost				
With Foreign Workers (%)	50	45	52	31
Without Foreign Workers (%)	50	55	48	69
Total Number	24	40	33	106
Profits				
With Foreign Workers (%)	51	41	55	31
Without Foreign Workers (%)	49	59	45	69
Total Number	37	22	29	115
Domestic Competition				
With Foreign Workers (%)	44	50	44	36
Without Foreign Workers (%)	56	50	56	64
Total Number	55	6	25	117
Foreign Competition				
With Foreign Workers (%)	46	100	42	34
Without Foreign Workers (%)	54	0	58	66
Total Number	48	4	26	125
Intermediate Inputs				
With Foreign Workers (%)	44	25	50	36
Without Foreign Workers (%)	56	75	50	64
Total Number	48	4	28	123

TABLE 7.23
Introduction of New Products and Perceptions on the Impact of AEC

AEC Impact	Increase	Decrease	No Change	Don't Know/ No Opinion/ No Reply
Domestic Sales				
Introduced New Products (%)	70	47	54	32
No New Products (%)	30	53	46	68
Total Number	30	19	37	108
Export Sales				
Introduced New Products (%)	60	50	52	36
No New Products (%)	40	50	48	64
Total Number	40	6	31	117
Import Cost				
Introduced New Products (%)	64	61	42	34
No New Products (%)	36	39	58	66
Total Number	22	36	33	103
Profits				
Introduced New Products (%)	61	43	50	38
No New Products (%)	39	57	50	62
Total Number	33	21	26	114
Domestic Competition				
Introduced New Products (%)	63	50	52	33
No New Products (%)	37	50	48	67
Total Number	51	6	23	114
Foreign Competition				
Introduced New Products (%)	62	0	50	38
No New Products (%)	38	100	50	62
Total Number	42	4	24	124
Intermediate Inputs				
Introduced New Products (%)	68	50	46	34
No New Products (%)	32	50	54	66
Total Number	44	4	26	120

TABLE 7.24
Selected Firm Characteristics and Perceptions on the Impact of AEC

AEC Impact	Increase	Decrease	No Change	Don't Know/ No Opinion/ No Reply
Domestic Sales				
Age	20	28	24	19
Labour Productivity	6,298,646	8,196,138	5,005,662	3,359,440
In-house R&D Spending	1,359,107	203,000,000	4,275,048	2,110,249
Machinery, Equipment and Software Expenditure	39,300,000	18,100,000	117,000,000	2,398,003
Export Sales				
Age	22	18	23	20
Labour Productivity	5,941,545	5,938,827	5,551,808	3,797,449
In-house R&D Spending	1,143,203	2,339,026	1,054,932	37,100,000
Machinery, Equipment and Software Expenditure	61,300,000	144,286	102,000,000	5,941,725
Import Cost				
Age	21	25	21	19
Labour Productivity	3,301,596	9,402,309	6,028,701	2,709,896
In-house R&D Spending	4,255,230	3,797,561	119,000,000	1,948,606
Machinery, Equipment and Software Expenditure	20,400,000	74,800,000	89,500,000	3,442,281

Profits

Age	19	20	23	25
Labour Productivity	3,685,149	2,988,876	6,626,613	7,964,057
In-house R&D Spending	3,439,113	404,609	184,000,000	1,769,576
Machinery, Equipment and Software Expenditure	6,383,400	101,000,000	20,500,000	71,700,000

Domestic Competition

Age	19	22	25	24
Labour Productivity	2,701,497	4,514,611	5,457,267	8,802,773
In-house R&D Spending	1,749,915	7,071,609	5,762,197	74,500,000
Machinery, Equipment and Software Expenditure	18,300,000	74,400,000	1,667	50,800,000

Foreign Competition

Age	19	22	35	23
Labour Productivity	3,769,179	5,120,826	3,416,426	6,733,933
In-house R&D Spending	34,200,000	1,647,089	0	3,428,150
Machinery, Equipment and Software Expenditure	6,434,927	112,000,000	0	64,900,000

Intermediate Inputs

Age	20	19	10	25
Labour Productivity	2,872,647	5,820,982	5,264,317	8,032,376
In-house R&D spending	34,900,000	290,198	3,643,295	4,234,765
Machinery, Equipment and Software Expenditure	27,000,000	55,900,000	2,500	39,900,000

Table 7.24 compares the mean age, labour productivity, in-house R&D spending, and machinery, equipment, and software expenditures of the different groups. The optimistic group is the oldest in terms of age and has the highest level of labour productivity while the unaware group is the youngest and has the lowest level of productivity. It is important to note that all groups are investing quite substantially in R&D and innovation.

10. Regression Analysis: Determinants of FTA Use

DTI conducted a similar survey that examines firms' FTA awareness and their perceptions on its possible impact on their business operations. The DTI preliminary survey results generated 734 respondent firms from the manufacturing industry. These are combined with the current survey's 205 respondent firms. Table 7.25 summarizes the major characteristics of the sample consisting of a total of 939 enterprises which are made up largely of SMEs (59 per cent small firms and 16 per cent medium enterprises). The average age of the firms is 21 years.

TABLE 7.25
Characteristics of the Firm Respondents

Characteristics	Total	SMEs	LEs
Number of Firms	939[1]	704	224
Sales	PHP 1.26 B	PHP 309 M	PHP 4.24 B
Export Share	25%	20%	41%
Full-time Workers	269	60	926
Fixed Assets (mean 2014)	PHP 501.8 M	PHP 167 M	PHP 1.5 B
Labour Productivity (mean)	PHP 1.3 M	PHP 971 K	PHP 2.2 M
FTA Users (number)	207[2]	116	88

Notes: [1] Eleven firms did not provide employment data.
[2] Two firms did not provide employment data.

A probit model is estimated to examine the determinants of FTA participation. The following regression framework is employed:

$\Pr(FTA\ Participation_i = 1)$
$= F(FirmSize_i,\ Prody_i,\ Foreign_i,\ Age_i,\ Export_i,\ Innovation_i,\ Association_i)$

equation 1

TABLE 7.26
Definition of Variables

Variable	Definition	Observations	Mean
Firm Size	Dummy variable = 1 if a firm is a large enterprise (200 or more workers), 0 if a firm is small or medium (less than 200 workers)	Yes = 224 No = 704	
Age	Firm age	929	21
Labour Productivity (in pesos)	Value added per worker = [Sales less raw material cost]/ number of workers	875	1,282,735
Capital Intensity (in pesos)	Fixed assets/number of workers	891	2,204,970
Exporter	Dummy variable = 1 if firm is an exporter, 0 otherwise	Yes = 323	
		No = 551	
Innovation	Dummy variable = 1 if firm has introduced a new good, 0 otherwise	Yes = 280	
		No = 640	
Member of Industry Association	Dummy variable = 1 if firm is a member of an industry association, 0 otherwise	Yes = 267	
		No = 667	
Foreign Ownership	Dummy variable = 1 if firm has foreign equity, 0 otherwise	Yes = 345	
With Foreign Equity		No = 594	
With Government Support	Dummy variable = 1 if firm has received government support, 0 otherwise	Yes = 146	
		No = 793	
AEC Awareness	Dummy variable = 1 if firm is aware of the AEC, 0 otherwise	Yes = 411	
		No = 523	
FTA User	Dummy variable = 1 if firm uses FTA, 0 otherwise	Yes = 207	
		No = 718	

where i indexes firms and the dependent variable is set to one if the firm has used any FTA. The explanatory variables are firm characteristics covering the following: firm size measured by the number of workers (*Firm Size*), labour productivity (*Prody*), foreign ownership (*Foreign*), capital intensity (*KL*), export activity (*Export*), introduction of a new good as an indicator of a firm's innovation activity (*Innovation*), and membership in industry association (*Association*). Table 7.25 provides a description of the explanatory variables.

Based on equation 1, the probit results explaining the probability of FTA use by a given firm are presented in Table 7.27. Model I is the basic specification that looks at firm characteristics such as size, age, labour productivity, foreign ownership, export activity, innovation, and membership in industry association. Model II introduces an additional variable, AEC awareness; while Models III and IV add government support and capital intensity, respectively.

For all specifications, the coefficients on firm size, age, foreign ownership, exporter, innovation, membership in industry association, and awareness of the AEC are all positive and significant. The results indicate that firms that are larger, older, with foreign partners, are exporters, innovative in terms of introducing new products, are members of industry associations and knowledgeable about the AEC have a higher probability of using FTAs. The results imply that a marginal change in age from the average of 21 years is associated with a 1.4 per cent increase in FTA use. As a firm ages, it is able to gradually adapt to a changing and competitive market environment, establishes itself over time, and is more likely to use FTAs. Firm level innovations and technology activities are also positively correlated with FTA use. Firms that introduce new products have a 34 per cent higher probability of FTA use (under Model 1). Industry associations serve as networks for information and knowledge sharing and as the results show, membership in industry associations is associated with a 63 per cent increase in FTA use. Awareness of AEC also has a positive influence; firms that are aware of AEC have a 55 per cent higher probability of using FTAs. Exporting firms have a 57 per cent higher probability of using FTAs. Given their knowledge of international markets and trade rules and regulations, exporters would most likely use FTAs.

Larger firms have a higher probability of using FTAs given their access to resources like skills, finance, and information and are in a better position to use FTAs than relatively smaller firms. Small firm size

TABLE 7.27
Regression Results

	Model I	Model II	Model III	Model IV
	dy/dx	dy/dx	dy/dx	dy/dx
Size	0.335404*** (0.129599)	0.2547619** (0.1277337)	0.2534164** (0.1275004)	0.2452525* (0.1277066)
Age	0.0140125*** (0.0038339)	0.0144412*** (0.0037512)	0.0147724*** (0.0037965)	0.0148831*** (0.0037708)
Prody	2.13e-09 (2.01e-09)	2.79e-09 (2.00e-09)	2.68e-09 (1.96e-09)	4.55e-09 (6.88e-09)
Foreign	0.3094332** (0.1238472	0.3119623** (0.1243052)	0.3187206*** (0.1242592)	0.3155207*** (0.1241414)
Exporter	0.5676457*** −0.1250125)	0.5957399*** (0.1250095)	0.5956917*** (0.1252257)	0.5958617*** (0.1255237)
Innovation	0.3429228*** (0.1121779)	0.3038641*** (0.1153437)	0.2913557** (0.1149989)	0.2857702*** (0.1151519)
Association	0.6348786*** (0.1158784)	0.5495445*** (0.1189469)	0.543287*** (0.1190274)	0.5356668*** (0.1191338)
AEC aware		0.5508128*** (0.1127748)	0.5380652*** (0.113106)	0.5376706*** (0.1131508)
Government support			0.1999338	0.1957138
			−0.1485729	−0.148057
KL				−6.29e-09 (1.77e-08)
Constant	−1.919432*** (0.1314788)	−2.16736*** (0.1426665)	−2.199012*** (0.1458123)	−2.183423*** (0.1457843)
Log Likelihood	−343.73924	−331.91464	−330.9773	−329.75915
Pseudo R2	0.1984	0.226	0.2282	0.2246
Number of Obs	809	809	809	800

Notes: The reported coefficients are marginal effects representing the change in the marginal probability of firm exit at the mean of the regressors. (#) dy/dx is for discrete change of dummy variable from 0 to 1. Robust standard errors in parentheses. *** significant at 1 per cent level, ** significant at 5 per cent level, and * significant at 10 per cent level.

reduces the likelihood of using FTAs. Foreign ownership is positive and significant indicating that firms with foreign equity participation have a higher probability of using FTAs. Multinational companies have established global or regional production bases along with extensive marketing networks and are likely to use FTAs. In the case of labour productivity, though its coefficient is positive, it is not statistically significant for all specifications. This might be due to the low level of labour productivity which on the average amounted to only 1.3 million pesos for the overall sample with SMEs' average labour productivity representing only about 44 per cent of the average productivity level of large enterprises (see Table 7.25). According to the World Bank (2005), the value added per worker of SMEs relative to all firms is approximately 46 per cent in the Philippines as compared to 64 per cent in Indonesia, 65 per cent in Malaysia and 84 per cent in Thailand. All these imply the need to improve productivity and strengthen competitiveness of firms, especially SMEs. The coefficient on government support is positive but not statistically significant while capital intensity is negative and insignificant.

In terms of government support and assistance, the survey results indicated that only a small proportion of the respondent firms are reached by existing government programmes. Only 9 per cent of the firms received national support for participating in events in countries abroad; 6 per cent for organizing meetings with potential partners; 4 per cent for financial support; and 4 per cent for assistance in business expansion abroad. The numbers for companies that are able to receive similar local and provincial support are also miniscule. It is probably due to the limited number of firms receiving government assistance that the coefficient on government support, though it has the correct sign, turned out to be insignificant. This implies a thorough review and assessment of the breadth and depth of government programmes aimed at providing support for SMEs especially financing, supplier development and business linkages, networking, market information, and technology and innovation.

11. Conclusions and Policy Recommendations

In the Philippines, SMEs formed the backbone of the economy accounting for 99.6 per cent of the total number of enterprises and employing a substantial share (65 per cent) of the domestic workforce. In order to benefit from rising globalization and increasing economic integration through AEC and other FTAs, it is important to focus on making small and medium manufacturers internationally competitive and integrating them into GVCs.

The results of the survey have shown that out of 205 firms, 41 per cent are FTA users, of which 48 (or 40 per cent) are SMEs while 33 (44 per cent) are large enterprises. Relative to non-users, FTA users are characterized by the following: older; foreign-owned; have parent companies; members of industry associations; higher average sales consisting mostly of final products; lower export ratio than non-users; inputs are foreign-sourced; lower average number of full-time workers but have a higher average number of part-time workers.

FTA users have a higher proportion of workers with a university degree and employ a higher share of foreign employees. They have higher training expenditures, higher innovation expenditures, have more business relations with firms in ASEAN and higher level of awareness of the AEC, as well as the Policy Blueprint for SME Development.

The respondent firms may be divided into four groups depending on their perceptions on how the AEC and other FTAs affect their business operations:

- Optimistic firms consist of respondents who perceive that the AEC and other FTAs would have a positive impact on their business operations.
- Pessimistic firms consist of respondents who perceive that the AEC and other FTAs would have a negative impact on their business operations.
- Neutral or indifferent firms are respondents who perceive that the AEC and other FTAs would have no impact on their business operations.
- Unaware or uninformed firms are those that have no response, no opinion, or do not know what the impact of the AEC or other FTAs would have on their business operations.

For the overall perceived impact of AEC on SMEs covering domestic sales, export sales, import cost, profits, competition in the domestic and foreign markets, and access to intermediate inputs, 62 per cent of the SMEs on the average have no knowledge, no opinion or no response. On the average, 18 per cent of the SMEs expected no change in their businesses while 15 per cent indicated an increase. In contrast, large enterprises have a lower average proportion of firms that have no knowledge, no opinion or no response (49 per cent). The average proportion of firms that expected an increase is also higher at 29 per cent while those that expected no change in their businesses represented a lower average of 14 per cent.

Large enterprises expressed a more positive outlook on the impact of the AEC on their businesses. Twenty-nine per cent of large enterprises indicated an increase in their domestic sales; 36 per cent expressed an increase in export sales; 32 per cent indicated a decline in import cost; 27 per cent expected an increase in profits; 31 per cent indicated an increase in domestic competition; 35 per cent expressed an increase in foreign competition; and 32 per cent expected an increase in access to intermediate inputs.

Regarding current or possible key changes due to the AEC (covering import tariffs, export duties, customs procedures, standards of regulation, recognition of professional qualifications, investment process, and connectivity in terms of transport and communication services), the great bulk of SME respondents (62 per cent) have no opinion, no response or no knowledge. Some SMEs indicated that there have been no change in import tariffs (25 per cent), export tariffs (22 per cent), customs procedures (20 per cent), standards of regulation (20 per cent), recognition of professional qualifications (20 per cent), investment process (17 per cent), and connectivity (18 per cent).

For large enterprises, there is a relatively lower proportion (48 per cent) of firms that have no opinion, no response or no knowledge. Those who perceived no change accounted for an average of 21 per cent while those who expected an increase accounted for 19 per cent. No changes were indicated in export tariffs by 23 per cent of the respondents, 27 per cent in standards of regulation, and 27 per cent in recognition of professional qualifications. For 32 per cent of the respondents, decreases in import tariff affected their businesses while increases in customs procedures (27 per cent), investment process (19 per cent) and connectivity (27 per cent) affecting large businesses were indicated.

On the perceived effects of FTAs on SMEs, almost the same general results are obtained with the bulk of the respondents (53 per cent) indicating that they have no opinion, no response or no knowledge. Twenty-one per cent of the SME respondents indicated that there are no changes and only 16 per cent expected an increase in their businesses. For large enterprises, the results show a much lower but still substantial proportion of firms (48 per cent) that have no knowledge, no opinion or no response. Relative to SMEs, there is a higher proportion of firms (28 per cent) that expected an increase in their businesses and a lower proportion that perceived no change (17 per cent) due to AEC.

Relating firm perceptions on the impact of AEC with AEC awareness indicated that though firms expressed awareness of the AEC, their perceptions on its impact on their business operations widely differ ranging from optimism, cautiousness, indifference, to no opinion. Respondent firms belonging to the optimistic, pessimistic, and neutral groups are dominated by firms that are aware of the AEC while the biggest group consisting of unaware or uninformed respondent firms is dominated by firms who are not aware of the AEC.

Linking firm responses on the impact of the AEC to firm size (measured by the number of workers) showed that the bulk of the responses fall under the uninformed group which is largely dominated by SMEs. Looking at perceptions on the impact of AEC and FTA use, the biggest group which consists of unaware or uninformed firms is made up largely of non-FTA users. With respect to the hiring of foreign workers, the results indicated that the unaware group is dominated by firms without foreign workers. Regarding perceptions on the impact of AEC and introduction of new and improved products (a measure of firm level innovation), the group of optimistic firms is dominated by firms that introduced new products while the unaware or uninformed group is composed largely of firms that did not introduce new products. In terms of selected firm characteristics, the optimistic group is the oldest in terms of age and has the highest level of labour productivity while the unaware group is the youngest and has the lowest level of productivity.

Combining the survey results with a larger data set based on a similar survey by DTI, a regression analysis was carried out to examine the determinants of FTA use. The results showed that the coefficients on firm size, age, exporting, foreign ownership, engaging in innovation, membership in industry association, and awareness of the AEC are all positive and significant. Firms that are larger, older, have foreign partners, are exporters, innovative in terms of introducing new products, members of industry associations and have knowledge about the AEC have a higher probability of using FTAs. Larger firms have a higher probability of using FTAs because given their access to resources like skills, finance, and information, they are in a better position to use FTAs than relatively smaller firms.

In terms of government support and assistance, the survey results indicated that only a small proportion of the respondent firms are reached by existing government programmes. It is due to this very limited number of firms receiving government assistance that the coefficient on government support though positive is not statistically significant. This implies a thorough review and assessment of the breadth and depth of government programmes aimed at providing support for SMEs especially financing, supplier development and business linkages, networking, market information, and technology and innovation is needed.

The above findings are consistent with the major reason cited by firms for not using FTAs, i.e., lack of knowledge/do not know how to use. Though most firms are aware of the AEC (53 per cent of the respondents indicate that they are aware), the results tend to imply the prevailing limited knowledge about the more specific impact of AEC on their businesses. This reaffirms the need for more substantial awareness programmes, especially on how to use FTAs and how firms can take advantage of the opportunities arising from the increased market access provided by the AEC integration and other FTAs. It would also be useful to create a central database on how to do businesses in other ASEAN countries with information on market opportunities and domestic rules and regulations. The government can make intensive use of ICT (creating more interactive websites) in order to increase the efficiency, scope and reach of its promotional and technical training programmes (Aldaba et al. 2015).

At the same time, organizing and conducting more trade and investment missions and industry exchange visits in the ASEAN region would be very useful in deepening the awareness of firms, exploring business opportunities and engaging in more direct interactions through linkages and networks with other firms in the region. Government support in these activities would be crucial, especially for SMEs.

Other reasons why firms do not use FTAs include difficulties in complying with ROO requirements as well as in getting COOs. To address these issues, the government can enhance FTA utilization by easing ROO compliance and administration by pursuing reforms toward electronic COO and self-certification, and linkages to the National Single Window. These reforms are expected to facilitate the entry, especially of MSMEs, in using FTAs. Unlike large companies that have departments directly managing these trade processes, SMEs do not have the same capacity. Equally important are efforts at the regional level to harmonize ROOs to deepen FTA utilization across ASEAN member countries and other FTAs, particularly the RCEP.

Finally, programmes that help improve the productivity and competitiveness of SMEs would have to be intensified and effectively implemented. This is crucial in order to lodge in or deepen participation in global and regional production networks especially in automotive, electronics, machinery, garments, and processed food industries. It is important to attract FDI in these sectors especially those that would bring in new technology. Policies and programmes should focus on developing the parts and components sector by addressing fundamental constraints to SME growth and development such as access to finance, access to technology and skilled workers, supply chain gaps, network linkages strengthening, high cost of transport and logistics, and providing R&D support and incubation facilities for start-up companies along with incentives to encourage universities and researchers to interact more with industries, especially SMEs.

NOTES

1. In regional/global production networks, multinational corporations (MNCs) fragment their production process generally by separating the capital-intensive segments from the labour-intensive ones with the latter being transferred to developing countries.
2. Rules of Origin (ROOs) refer to the set of criteria used to determine where goods are manufactured. Firms must prepare the required documents and secure a Certificate of Origin (COO) to prove that a good is produced in a particular country and qualify for preferential tariffs. ROOs vary with each FTA and hence there are different COO forms for different FTAs.
3. Three enterprises did not report their employment levels and hence could not be classified.
4. Under GSP schemes of preference-giving countries, selected products originating in developing countries are granted reduced or zero tariff rates over the most favoured nation (MFN) rates.

REFERENCES

Aldaba, Rafaelita M. "SMEs Access to Finance: Philippines". In *Small and Medium Enterprises (SMEs) Access to Finance in Selected East Asian Economies*, edited by Charles Harvie, Sothea Oum, and Dionisius Narjoko. ERIA Research Project Report 2010–14. Jakarta: Economic Research Institute for ASEAN and East Asia (ERIA), 2011, pp. 291–350.

Aldaba, Rafaelita M., Erlinda M. Medalla, Fatima del *Prado* Prado and Donald Yasay. "Integrating SMEs into the East Asian Region: The Philippines". In *Integrating Small and Medium Enterprises (SMEs) into the More Integrated East Asia*, edited by Vo Tri Thanh, Dionisius Narjoko and Sothea Oum. ERIA Research Project Report 2009–8. Jakarta: Economic Research Institute for ASEAN and East Asia (ERIA), 2010, pp. 374–428.

Aldaba, Rafaelita M., Erlinda M. *Medalla*, Josef T. *Yap*, Mureen Ane D. *Rosellon*, Fatima del *Prado*, Melalyn C. *Mantaring* and Veredigna M. *Ledda*. "Survey Report on the Use of Free Trade Agreements in the Philippines". In *The Use of FTAs in ASEAN: Survey-based Analysis*, edited by Lili Yan Ing and Shujiro Urata. ERIA Research Project Report 2013–5. Jakarta: Economic Research Institute for ASEAN and East Asia (ERIA), 2015, pp. 185–214.

Hiratsuka, Daisuke, Kazunobu Hayakawa, Kohei Shiino, and Seiya Sukegawa. "Maximizing Benefits from FTAs in ASEAN". In *Deepening East Asian Economic Integration*, edited by Jenny Corbett and So Umezaki. ERIA Research Project Report 2008–1. Jakarta: Economic Research Institute for ASEAN and East Asia (ERIA), 2009, pp. 407–545.

Kawai, Masahiro and Ganeshan Wignaraja, eds. *Asia's Free Trade Agreements: How is Business Responding?* Cheltenham: Edward Elgar, 2011.

Wignaraja, Ganeshan, Dorothea Lazaro, and Genevieve DeGuzman. "FTAs and Philippine Business: Evidence from Transport, Food, and Electronics Firms". *ADBI Working Paper Series No. 185*. Tokyo: Asian Development Bank Institute, 2010.

World Bank. "Fostering Linkages between Multinational and Domestic Firms in the Philippines". Paper presented during the "Policies to Strengthen Productivity in the Philippines Conference", AIM Policy Center, Makati City, 27 June 2005.

8

THAILAND'S SME PARTICIPATION IN ASEAN AND EAST ASIAN REGIONAL ECONOMIC INTEGRATION

Teerawat Charoenrat and Charles Harvie

1. Introduction

Thailand's small and medium-sized enterprises (SMEs) have played a pivotal role in the country's economic and social development (OSMEP 2014). They constituted 99 per cent of all enterprises in the country and contributed 73 per cent of total employment during the period 2007 to 2012. During this period, they contributed 33 per cent of total exports on average and approximately 38.8 per cent of total GDP at current prices on average (OSMEP 2013). Of the total SMEs over the period 2007 to 2012, almost one-third were in the manufacturing sector. Manufacturing SMEs employed around 27.1 per cent of the private sector workforce on average over the period 2007 to 2012 and their contribution to total SME GDP was 28.7 per cent over the same period.[1]

The contribution of SMEs, especially manufacturing SMEs, is indicated in Table 8.1. While the contribution of SMEs to total business

Teerawat Charoenrat and Charles Harvie

TABLE 8.1
Contribution of Manufacturing SMEs to the Thai Economy, 2007–12

Enterprises	2007	2008	2009	2010	2011	2012
Business numbers						
SMEs (% of total firms)	99.6	99.7	99.8	99.6	99.8	99.5
Manufacturing SMEs (% of SME firms)	28.2	19.2	18.9	18.7	17.8	17.7
Manufacturing SMEs (% of total firms)	28.2	19.2	18.9	18.6	17.8	17.4
SME employment						
SMEs (% of total employment)	76.0	76.2	78.2	77.9	83.9	80.4
Manufacturing SMEs (% of SME employment)	38.9	38.8	34.2	33.2	29.6	32.7
Manufacturing SMEs (% of total employment)	29.6	29.6	26.8	25.9	24.8	26.3
GDP of SMEs						
SMEs (% of total GDP)	38.2	38.1	37.8	37.1	36.6	37.5
Manufacturing SMEs (% of SME GDP)	30.7	30.8	30.4	32.3	31.2	30.9
Manufacturing SMEs (% of total GDP)	11.7	11.8	11.5	12	11.4	11.4
SME exports						
Total exports (% of total GDP)	61.9	64.5	57.4	60.5	63.6	62.3
SME exports (% of total exports)	30.1	28.9	30.1	27.3	29.4	28.8
SME exports (% of SME GDP)	48.8	48.9	45.8	44.5	51.1	48.5
SME exports (% of total GDP)	18.7	18.6	17.3	16.5	18.7	18.0

Source: OSMEP (2007–12).

numbers remained stable, accounting for approximately 99.5 per cent of total enterprises over the period 2007–12, the contribution of manufacturing SMEs to total SMEs and the contribution of manufacturing SMEs to total enterprises declined from around 28.2 per cent and 28.2 per cent in 2007 respectively to around 17.7 per cent and 17.4 per cent in 2012, respectively.The contribution of SMEs to employment has gained a high level of importance due to their employment of more than 78.8 per cent of total workers over the period 2007–12. In terms of the contribution of manufacturing SMEs to the economy, around one-third of total workers employed by SMEs are in manufacturing SMEs which was equivalent to 26 per cent of total employment in 2012 (OSMEP 2007–13).

From Table 8.1 it can also be observed that SMEs accounted for around 37.5 per cent of GDP, at current prices, over the period 2007–12. These figures imply that large enterprises accounted for only 0.5 per cent of business establishments in the country over the period 2007–12, but contributed around 62.5 per cent of GDP over the same period. Punyasavatsut (2008, p. 294) pointed out that the contribution of SMEs to GDP remained restricted due to numerous common limitations on their operations, such as a lack of management capabilities, limited access to market information and promotional support from government agencies, a shortage of financial support or working capital, inadequate access to skilled labour, and uncertainties in government support programmes. Similarly, Charoenrat et al. (2013) revealed that SMEs face severe barriers to their future growth and development, which include access to finance, poor exporting capacity, limited marketing, information technology, innovation and management skills, and excessive government bureaucracy and regulations. SMEs, however, still play significant roles and functions in assisting large enterprises, particularly in the context of regional production networks as they help link all important units of industry together, and fill gaps in industrial clusters which might not be completed by large enterprises alone (Regnier 2000). They also supply goods, services, information and knowledge for large enterprises, and play a pivotal role in the production process of export goods (Tapaneeyangkul 2001).

The contribution of exports to growth and development continues to remain important to the Thai economy, constituting around

57–64 per cent of total GDP over the period 2007–12. In terms of contribution to total exports, however, Thai SMEs have become less important compared with that of large enterprises over the period 2007–12. This contribution was equivalent to 18 per cent of GDP by 2012 even though they accounted for 99.5 per cent of all business establishments in the country.[2] Consequently, this implies that large enterprises play a leading role in the country's international trade even though they contributed only 0.5 per cent of total enterprises. OSMEP (2011) also pointed out that Thailand's exports rely greatly on large enterprises, and, therefore, both the public and private sectors should pay attention to promoting greater international trade participation by SMEs. Punyasavatsut (2007) also acknowledged that Thai manufacturing SMEs are not ready to face the rigours of "international competition" in competitive global markets arising from the country's increased opening and economic integration, and concurrent intense competition from lower labour cost countries. More importantly, Thai business segments, particularly Thai SMEs, are now under the "Nut-Cracker Effect" which implies that Thailand is now trapped between countries with lower price competitiveness, such as China, Vietnam and Indonesia and countries with higher value-added production and services, such as Japan, South Korea and Taiwan. Finally, OECD (2011) also recommended that internationalization should be promoted for Thai SMEs, especially Thai small enterprises.

Hence, Thai SMEs in general have made, and continue to make, a significant contribution to the country's social and economic development (Regnier 2000; Brimble et al. 2002; Mephokee 2003; Pholphirul and Biatasevi 2012). This contribution is multi-dimensional in nature in terms of business numbers, employment, GDP and exports. This section conducts a brief overview of this contribution with a focus on the period 2007 to 2012. The hiatus of manufacturing SMEs in particular occurred in 1997 before the full effects of the Asian Financial Crisis began to have an impact. They have not regained such a level of importance, although they still remain important in terms of their contribution to the number of SME enterprises, employment, GDP and exports. They will remain important in the future but the extent of this will likely depend upon enhancing their competitiveness.

The major aims of this study are: (1) to identify the role, significance and contribution of Thai SMEs; (2) to examine the factors that can affect the export participation of Thai manufacturing SMEs; (3) to identify key issues facing Thai manufacturing SMEs; and (4) to identify plans and policies to improve the performance of Thailand's manufacturing SMEs. Data compiled for the 2015 ERIA–ISEAS SME survey of Thailand will be utilized for the empirical analysis conducted in this chapter.

2. An Overview of Thai SMEs

2.1. Definition of Thailand's SMEs

The two most common means of defining an SME are: the number of employees and the amount of fixed assets. The Ministry of Industry (MOI) regulation of 11 September 2002 adopted employment or fixed assets, excluding land, as the criteria in defining SMEs. The criteria changes, however, according to sector. Hence, Thai SMEs are classified into four business sectors[3] (see Table 8.2) (Brimble et al. 2002; OSMEP 2002, 2003).

TABLE 8.2
Summary: Definitions of Thai SMEs by Sector

Sectors	Number of Employees (Workers)	Fixed Assets (THB, Million)
1. Manufacturing		
1.1 Small Enterprises	≤ 50	≤ 50
1.2 Medium Enterprises	51–200	51–200
2. Wholesale		
2.1 Small Enterprises	≤ 25	≤ 50
2.2 Medium Enterprises	26–50	51–100
3. Retail		
3.1 Small Enterprises	≤ 15	≤ 30
3.2 Medium Enterprises	16–30	31–60
4. Service		
4.1 Small Enterprises	≤ 50	≤ 50
4.2 Medium Enterprises	51–200	51–200

Source: OSMEP (2003).

Manufacturing Sector

An enterprise in the manufacturing sector employing less than 50 workers or has fixed assets, excluding land, not exceeding THB 50 million is considered a small enterprise. An enterprise employing between 51 and 200 workers or has fixed assets, excluding land, worth between THB 50 million and THB 200 million is defined as a medium-sized enterprise.

Wholesale Sector

A small enterprise in the wholesale sector is defined as having less than 25 workers or has fixed assets, excluding land, not exceeding THB 50 million. An enterprise employing 26–50 workers or has fixed assets, excluding land, worth between THB 50 million and THB 100 million, is defined as a medium-sized enterprise.

Retail Sector

An enterprise in the retail sector employing less than 15 workers or has fixed assets, excluding land, not exceeding THB 30 million is defined as a small enterprise. A medium-sized enterprise is defined as employing 16–30 workers or has fixed assets, excluding land, worth between THB 30 million and THB 60 million.

Service Sector

A small enterprise in the service sector is defined as employing less than 50 workers or having fixed assets, excluding land, not exceeding THB 50 million in value. An enterprise employing between 51 and 200 workers or has fixed assets, excluding land, worth between THB 50 million and THB 200 million is defined as a medium-sized enterprise.

2.2. SME Business Numbers: Aggregate, Sector and Region

Aggregate

Table 8.3 shows that the number of SMEs generally increased during the period 2007–13. The number even increased across all categories of firm size during the period of the Global Financial Crisis (GFC)

TABLE 8.3
Number and Percentage of SMEs and Enterprises by Size, 2007–12

Enterprises	2007	2008	2009	2010	2011	2012
SMEs	2,199,595	2,239,280	2,274,525	2,359,312	2,827,633	2,896,106
Small Enterprises	2,189,966	2,229,353	2,264,734	2,347,531	2,815,560	2,884,041
Medium Enterprises	9,629	9,927	9,791	11,781	12,073	12,065
Large Enterprises	4,323	4,444	4,292	4,324	4,586	4,653
Other Enterprises	5,989	5,994	8,240	6,915	4,158	N/A
Total	**2,209,907**	**2,249,718**	**2,287,057**	**2,377,466**	**2,836,377**	**2,900,759**
Percentage of All Enterprises (%)						
Small Enterprises	99.1	99.09	99.02	98.74	99.27	99.42
Medium Enterprises	0.44	0.44	0.43	0.5	0.43	0.42
Large Enterprises	0.2	0.2	0.19	0.18	0.16	0.16
Other Enterprises	0.27	0.27	0.36	0.29	0.15	N/A
Total	**100**	**100**	**100**	**100**	**100**	**100**

Source: OSMEP (2007–12).

(2007–8) and subsequent global economic downturn (2008–9). The number of SMEs remained remarkably buoyant during this period suggesting that they had become more financially resilient to regional and global crises and certainly in comparison to the financial crisis in 1997–98. The number of SMEs increased rapidly from 2007 to 2012, driven by the growth in the number of small enterprises, mainly on the back of a government promotion policy during this period (see for example OSMEP 2013).

Sector

Table 8.4 shows the decline in the number of SMEs in the manufacturing sector after 2010. In 2007 the Office of the Board of Investment of Thailand promoted 675 projects involving SMEs, the total value of which amounted to US$3,960 million (OSMEP 2007). Of these projects, 573 involved manufacturing SMEs in such areas as raw steel, machines, car spare parts, mining, ceramics, electronic and electronic appliances, paper and plastic products, services and utilities (Sahakijpicharn 2007). As a consequence of these projects and increased export growth by manufacturing sectors such as computers, automotive and auto parts, home appliances and electronics, there was a dramatic increase in the number of manufacturing SMEs until 2010.

A study by the ADB (2013) argued that Thai manufacturing SMEs were not ready to face the rigours of international competition arising from the country's increased opening to foreign trade/investment and economic integration, more intense competition from lower labour cost countries in the region and poorer efficiency and competitiveness.

On the other hand, SMEs in the service sector steadily increased in number from 2007–12. The service sector became the second most SME-dense sector, with the retail sector a close third. SMEs in the retail sector experienced a decline in numbers due to increased competition from the establishment of giant discount stores in Thailand such as Tesco Lotus, Carrefour, and Big C (OSMEP 2013). This situation changed in 2008 with the newly established trade and repairs sector,[4] which quickly became the most SME-dense sector followed by services and manufacturing SMEs from 2007–12.

TABLE 8.4
Number and Percentage of SMEs by Sector, 2007–12

Sectors	2007	2008	2009	2010	2011	2012
Manufacturing	674,129	684,815	698,651	680,270	564,706	547,052
Wholesale	180,926	188,830	N/A	N/A	N/A	N/A
Retail	558,496	563,366	N/A	N/A	N/A	N/A
Service	561,797	577,663	636,626	709,841	946,812	975,552
Trade and Repairs	N/A	N/A	918,028	953,248	1,311,714	1,371,488
Other Enterprises	224,247	224,606	21,220	15,953	4,401	2,014
Total	**2,199,595**	**2,239,280**	**2,274,525**	**2,359,312**	**2,827,633**	**2,896,106**
Percentage of SMEs (%)						
Manufacturing	30.65	30.58	30.72	28.83	19.97	18.89
Wholesale	8.23	8.43	N/A	N/A	N/A	N/A
Retail	25.39	25.16	N/A	N/A	N/A	N/A
Service	25.54	25.8	27.99	30.09	33.48	33.68
Trade and Repairs	N/A	N/A	40.36	40.4	46.39	47.36
Other Enterprises	10.19	10.03	0.93	0.68	0.16	0.07
Total	**100**	**100**	**100**	**100**	**100**	**100**

Source: OSMEP (2007–12).

SME Contribution to Employment – Total by Sector

Table 8.5 presents the total employment and employment by enterprise size from 2007 to 2012. It is clear that SMEs are a pivotal source of jobs in the economy. They contributed more than 73 per cent, on average, to overall employment over the period 2007–12, mostly in small enterprises (around two-thirds of total employment). Over the period 2007–12, total employment in medium enterprises increased slightly while that of large enterprises decreased. Employment in small enterprises noticeably increased, even during the period of the GFC and its economic aftermath. This fluctuating number and percentage contribution of SMEs to overall employment is likely to have been contributed to by an improvement in statistical collection methods during this period (OSMEP 2013).

Table 8.6 shows SME employment classified by sector during 2006 to 2012. The manufacturing, service and retail sectors[5] dominated SME employment. By 2009, SMEs in the manufacturing, service, and trade and repairs sectors each contributed approximately one-third to total SME employment. According to OSMEP (2012), manufacturing and services SMEs are more labour-intensive than those in the retail and wholesale sectors. They have an average employed number of 4 workers for small enterprises and between 200 and 109 workers for medium-sized enterprises in the manufacturing and service sectors, respectively.

From Table 8.6 it can be seen that the share of manufacturing employment in total SME employment increased rapidly from 24.85 per cent in 2006 to 36.48 per cent in 2007 and remained fairly stable until 2010. As with the contribution to business numbers the hiatus of manufacturing SMEs to employment occurred just before the onset of the GFC. Subsequently, this contribution has declined, although it remained important at around 38–39 per cent of total SME employment or 30 per cent of total economy employment over the period 2006–12. On the other hand, the share of the service and trade and repairs sectors steadily increased during this same period. The declining share of manufacturing SMEs could be a reflection of their poor efficiency and lack of competitiveness which is the focus of this study.

TABLE 8.5
Number and Percentage of SME Employment and Enterprises by Size, 2007–12

Enterprises	2007	2008	2009	2010	2011	2012
SMEs	8,863,607	8,896,164	8,863,334	8,900,567	9,125,916	9,701,354
Small Enterprises	7,454,493	7,482,561	7,524,936	7,550,269	7,715,458	8,262,128
Medium Enterprises	1,409,114	1,413,603	1,338,398	1,350,298	1,410,458	1,439,226
Large Enterprises	2,887,261	2,894,932	2,687,938	2,810,767	2,891,756	2,704,243
Total	**12,000,000**	**12,000,000**	**11,551,272**	**11,711,334**	**12,000,000**	**12,405,597**
Percentage of SMEs (%)						
SMEs	75.43	75.45	76.73	76	76.23	78.2
Small Enterprises	63.44	63.46	65.14	64.5	64.2	66.6
Medium Enterprises	11.99	11.99	11.59	11.52	11.73	11.6
Large Enterprises	24.57	24.55	23.27	24	24.07	21.8

Source: OSMEP (2007–12).

TABLE 8.6
SME Employment by Number and Percentage, Classified by Sector, 2006–12

Sectors	2006[1]	2007	2008	2009	2010	2011	2012
Manufacturing	1,383,343	3,233,484	3,420,120	3,452,699	3,501,167	3,541,587	3,320,409
Wholesale	355,630	935,702	846,162	N/A	N/A	N/A	N/A
Retail	1,200,070	1,395,029	1,365,054	N/A	N/A	N/A	N/A
Service	1,803,012	2,567,485	2,378,657	2,687,284	2,819,684	3,066,933	3,467,763
Trade and Repairs[2]	N/A	N/A	N/A	2,376,968	2,431,432	2,501,941	2,912,678
Unspecified[3]	824,810	731,907	886,171	346,383	148,284	15,455	N/A
Total	**5,566,865**	**8,863,607**	**8,896,164**	**8,863,334**	**8,900,567**	**9,125,916**	**9,700,850**
Percentage of SMEs (%)							
Manufacturing	24.85	36.48	38.44	38.95	39.33	38.8	34.23
Wholesale	6.39	10.56	9.51	N/A	N/A	N/A	N/A
Retail	21.56	15.74	15.34	N/A	N/A	N/A	N/A
Service	32.39	28.97	26.74	30.31	31.68	33.6	35.75
Trade and Repairs[2]	N/A	N/A	N/A	26.81	27.31	27.42	30.02
Unspecified[3]	14.82	8.26	9.96	3.9	1.67	0.18	N/A
Total	**100**	**100**	**100**	**100**	**100**	**100**	**100**

Notes: [1] In 2006, the trade and repairs sector included the wholesale and retail sectors (OSMEP 2006).
[2] The trade and repairs sector was introduced as a new classification in 2006 and included the wholesale and retail sectors.
[3] OSMEP did not identify unspecified enterprises by sector.

Source: OSMEP (2007–12).

Contribution of SMEs to Thailand's GDP

Table 8.7 shows the structure of Thailand's GDP for the period 2007 to 2012. The SME contribution to GDP, at current prices, was 38.8 per cent over the period 2007–12, with small enterprises accounting for 23.7 per cent of this figure and medium enterprises accounting for the remaining 15.1 per cent. The SME share of GDP steadily declined after 2010, mainly due to a decline in the share from small enterprises. By 2012 SMEs contributed around 37.8 per cent to overall GDP, with small enterprises contributing 25.4 per cent of total GDP and medium enterprises contributing 12.4 per cent.

Table 8.7 also shows that the average annual real growth rate of SME output over the period 2007–12 was approximately 3.9 per cent. Comparing the average growth rate between 2007 and 2012 classified by size of enterprise (small and medium), the average annual real GDP growth rate of small enterprises was 3.6 per cent while that of medium enterprises was 4.5 per cent. The average annual real growth rate of large enterprises was 4.5 per cent.

Table 8.8 presents the GDP of SMEs classified by economic activity during the period 2007 to 2012. The trade and maintenance sector contributed the most to SME GDP with an annual average value of 32 per cent of total SME output during the period 2007 to 2012, followed by private services (31.2 per cent) and manufacturing (28 per cent). By 2012 private services contributed the highest SME GDP, accounting for 32 per cent of total SME GDP, followed by manufacturing (30.4 per cent) and trade and maintenance (29.9 per cent). The average annual real output growth of all SMEs at constant prices was around 4.1 per cent during 2007 to 2012, compared to 7 per cent for trade and maintenance SMEs, 6.9 per cent for manufacturing SMEs and 5.8 per cent for private service SMEs.

SMEs and Export Activity, 2007–12

The Thai authorities do not compile statistics on the exports of SMEs by sector of activity. Table 8.9, however, shows the value and percentage of exports classified by size of enterprise during the period 2007 to 2012. Large enterprises contributed, on average, 67 per cent of total exports over the period 2007 to 2012, while the SME average contribution was 33 per cent of total exports due to high demand

TABLE 8.7
GDP Classified by Size of Enterprise, 2007–12

Items	2007	2008	2009	2010	2011	2012
GDP at Current Price (Thai million baht)						
Agriculture	654,810	706,285	836,077	967,091	1,054,175	1,052,564
Non-agriculture	5,848,677	6,397,943	6,980,397	7,501,542	8,050,783	7,998,151
Large enterprises	2,954,382	3,260,301	3,589,655	3,881,340	4,214,807	4,154,278
SMEs	2,598,657	2,816,641	3,041,895	3,236,634	3,446,589	3,417,861
Small enterprises	1,761,455	1,901,333	2,043,460	2,170,069	2,295,711	2,300,196
Medium enterprises	837,202	915,307	998,435	1,066,564	1,150,877	1,117,665
Other enterprises	295,638	321,001	348,846	383,567	389,387	425,384
Total GDP	**6,503,487**	**7,104,228**	**7,816,474**	**8,468,633**	**9,104,959**	**9,050,715**
GDP at Current Price (%)						
Agriculture	10.1	9.9	10.7	11.4	11.6	11.6
Non-agriculture	89.9	90.1	89.3	88.6	88.4	88.4
Large enterprises	45.4	45.9	45.9	45.8	46.3	45.9
SMEs	40	39.6	38.9	38.2	37.9	37.8
Small enterprises	27.1	26.8	26.1	25.6	25.2	25.4
Medium enterprises	12.9	12.9	12.8	12.6	12.6	12.3
Other enterprises	4.5	4.5	4.5	4.5	4.3	4.7
Total GDP	**100**	**100**	**100**	**100**	**100**	**100**

Real GDP Growth Rate at Constant Price (%)

Agriculture	-2.4	-1.9	3.8	2.6	5	5.5
Non-agriculture	7.4	5.2	5.2	5.4	2.4	2.1
Large enterprises	7.4	5.6	5.4	6	2.9	3.1
SMEs	7.6	4.9	5.5	4.9	1.9	1.8
Small enterprises	6.9	4.7	5.4	4.7	1.7	1.7
Medium enterprises	9.1	5.2	5.5	5.3	2.3	2.5
Other enterprises	3.2	3.9	0	2.2	-1.1	N/A
GDP	**6.3**	**4.6**	**5.2**	**4.9**	**2.5**	**1.9**

Source: OSMEP (2007–12).

TABLE 8.8
GDP of SMEs in Aggregate, Classified by Economic Activity, 2007–12

Items	2007	2008	2009	2010	2011	2012
GDP of SMEs by Economic Activity at Current Price (Thai million baht)						
SMEs	2,598,657	2,816,641	3,041,895	3,236,634	3,446,589	3,417,861
Mining	31,636	40,159	46,545	49,902	57,073	54,686
Manufacturing	755,130	830,247	921,924	992,617	1,101,480	1,039,030
Construction	164,043	184,051	197,448	205,471	212,283	201,654
Trade and Maintenance	783,347	841,407	889,518	937,861	981,979	1,021,940
Private Services	857,892	913,893	975,561	1,043,155	1,085,581	1,093,715
Electric, Gas and Water Supply	6,610	6,882	7,900	7,628	8,190	10,254
Share of GDP SMEs by Economic Activity at Current Price (%)						
SMEs	40	39.6	38.9	38.2	37.9	37.76
Mining	1.2	1.4	1.5	1.5	1.7	1.6
Manufacturing	29.1	29.5	30.3	30.7	32	30.4
Construction	6.3	6.5	6.5	6.3	6.2	5.9
Trade and Maintenance	30.1	29.9	29.2	29	28.5	29.9
Private Services	33	32.4	32.2	32.2	31.5	32
Electric, Gas and Water Supply	0.3	0.2	0.3	0.2	0.2	0.3

GDP Growth Rate of SMEs at Constant Price (%)

SMEs	7.6	4.9	5.5	4.9	1.9	2.0
Mining	9.5	9	4.2	3.5	2.3	1.8
Manufacturing	10.1	5.2	5.9	6.2	3.9	4.0
Construction	5.5	5.7	4.3	1.6	1.2	1.8
Trade and Maintenance	4.5	4.4	3.9	5.5	2.5	1.9
Private Services	8.3	4.7	6.5	3.7	2.0	2.2
Electric, Gas and Water Supply	1.7	5.3	4.8	5	4.3	4.5

Source: OSMEP (2007–12).

TABLE 8.9
Value and Percentage of Exports, Classified by Size of Enterprise, 2007–12

Items	2007	2008	2009	2010	2011	2012
Exports (Thai million baht)						
Large Enterprises	1,816,000	2,611,085	3,060,290	3,448,181	3,634,414	4,042,799
SMEs	1,516,971	1,235,139	1,291,858	1,456,083	1,575,971	1,691,145
Total	3,332,971	3,846,224	4,352,148	4,904,264	5,210,385	5,733,944
Percentage of Exports						
Large Enterprises	64.85	67.89	70.32	70.30	69.75	70.50
SMEs	35.15	32.11	29.68	29.70	30.24	29.50
Total	100	100	100	100	100	100

Source: OSMEP (2007–12).

for manufactured products from Japan, the United States and ASEAN, particularly for plastic products, electronic products, computer parts, vehicle and automotive parts (OSMEP 2012). This was due to the flow on benefits from Thailand's closer economic integration with other economies in ASEAN as a result of its involvement in ASEAN–China FTA, ASEAN–India FTA, ASEAN–South Korea FTA, ASEAN–Australia–New Zealand FTA, Thailand–Australia FTA, Thailand–Peru FTA and Thailand–South Korea FTA, which all came into effect after 2002 (Chirathivat 2007; Sally 2007).[6] By 2012, the share of total exports by SMEs was 29.50 per cent (see Table 8.9) with the largest export market for Thai SMEs being ASEAN, which accounted for 22 per cent of total SME exports by value. The European Union (EU) was the second largest export market, representing 14.5 per cent of overall SME export value. The third ranked was the Japanese market which amounted to 9.7 per cent of the total export value of SMEs.

The trend in SME exports indicated only a gradual increase during the period 2007–12. Possible reasons for this are that Thai SMEs face specific barriers to exporting, they produce poor quality products and they experience inefficiencies and lack competitiveness compared to large enterprises. This could be due to non-tariff barriers to trade (e.g. logistics, labelling, warehousing etc.) which are typical problems faced by SMEs in other countries. Thai SMEs face intense competition from rapidly developing regional economies such as China, India, Vietnam and Indonesia which have much lower labour costs. Thai SMEs are lagging in terms of upgrading their knowledge and skills, technology, innovation and value-added activities (Amornkitvikai et al. 2010; OECD 2011). Consequently, this study is of particular importance as it will shed light on key issues facing Thai manufacturing SMEs.

Focusing on Thailand's trade, exports substantially increased after the 1997 Asian financial crisis due to the baht's depreciation, the easing of a reduction in the demand for labour, and reversal of persistent real wage growth experienced before the crisis (Lombaerde 2008). The trade deficit disappeared after 1997, averaging surpluses of 353,910 million baht and 304,479 million baht during 1998–2000 and 2007–9, respectively, as shown in Table 8.11. The country's trade balance, however, moved into deficit at 82,754 million baht on average during the period 2004–6 as a consequence of decelerating export growth along with faster import growth in 2005 (Bank of Thailand 2005).

TABLE 8.10
Value and Percentage of SME Exports, Classified by Country, 2007–12

Countries	2007	2008	2009	2010	2011	2012
SME Exports (Thai million baht)						
ASEAN	315,442	269,944	302,959	363,706	361,032	349,624
EU	44,498	186,648	201,368	222,422	228,434	230,434
USA	205,028	220,585	221,130	188,927	181,435	147,001
Japan	281,986	151,576	159,231	160,766	181,798	154,311
China	89,363	102,736	138,921	120,688	113,976	133,652
Hong Kong	90,573	64,801	66,612	98,672	124,565	143,982
Middle East	N/A	72,367	88,509	97,359	103,464	N/A
Australia	17,668	29,143	47,978	48,842	68,222	77,712
South Asia	N/A	35,761	39,824	45,550	48,432	N/A
Switzerland	N/A	12,234	15,368	26,631	46,230	90,584
Republic of Korea	13,755	23,235	23,516	26,120	39,916	N/A
Taiwan	N/A	26,803	26,419	29,609	30,779	N/A
South Africa	N/A	10,621	11,492	12,665	15,674	N/A
Canada	N/A	14,727	15,697	15,722	15,521	N/A
Unspecified Countries	458,658	70,676	97,058	118,294	131,669	261,900
Total	**1,516,971**	**1,291,858**	**1,456,083**	**1,575,971**	**1,691,145**	**1,589,200**

Percentage of Total SME Exports (%)

ASEAN	22.00	21.35	23.08	20.81	20.90	20.79
EU	14.50	13.51	14.11	13.83	14.45	2.93
USA	9.25	10.73	11.99	15.19	17.08	13.52
Japan	9.71	10.75	10.20	10.94	11.73	18.59
China	8.41	6.74	7.66	9.54	7.95	5.89
Hong Kong	9.06	7.37	6.26	4.57	5.02	5.97
Middle East	N/A	6.12	6.18	6.08	5.60	N/A
Australia	4.89	4.03	3.10	3.30	2.26	1.16
South Asia	N/A	2.86	2.89	2.73	2.77	N/A
Switzerland	5.70	2.73	1.69	1.06	0.95	N/A
Republic of Korea	N/A	2.36	1.66	1.62	1.80	0.91
Taiwan	N/A	1.82	1.88	1.81	2.07	N/A
South Africa	N/A	0.93	0.80	0.79	0.82	N/A
Canada	N/A	0.92	1.00	1.08	1.14	N/A
Unspecified Countries	16.48	7.79	7.51	6.67	5.47	30.24
Total	**100**	**100**	**100**	**100**	**100**	**100**

Source: OSMEP (2007–13).

The trade deficit was also observed at 179,497 million baht on average during the period 2010–13 as a consequence of declining foreign demand resulting from weak global economic conditions and limitations on production due to a major flood in 2011 (Bank of Thailand 2012). During the period 2010–13, Thailand mainly exported to ASEAN, followed by the NAFTA nations, EU and Japan. Thailand also mostly imported goods from Japan during the same period, followed by ASEAN, EU and the NAFTA nations (see Table 8.11).

Beginning in May 2004, the EU comprised twenty-five countries, adding Cyprus, Czech Republic, Estonia, Hungary, Latvia, Lithuania, Malta, Slovakia, Poland and Slovenia. In January 2007, the EU comprised twenty-seven countries, adding Bulgaria and Romania. Since July 2013, the EU has comprised twenty-eight countries, adding Croatia. Prior to 1999, ASEAN did not include Cambodia.

TABLE 8.11
Thailand's Merchandise Trade Value by Country and Trade Group, 1995–2013 (million baht)

Items	1995–97	1998–2000	2001–3	2004–6	2007–9	2010–13
Exports						
Japan	248,130	343,200	446,270	589,440	607,494	689,538
NAFTA	305,723	564,019	631,606	745,408	708,414	782,217
EU 1/	256,213	416,166	481,888	623,307	713,561	694,208
ASEAN 2/	333,867	452,738	608,292	952,512	1,184,992	1,722,196
Rest of the World	397,775	636,320	876,703	1,505,918	2,234,901	2,996,296
Total exports	**1,541,707**	**2,412,443**	**3,044,758**	**4,416,584**	**5,449,362**	**6,900,330**
Imports						
Japan	516,299	500,178	669,500	977,916	988,158	1,364,852
NAFTA	253,809	279,979	316,091	363,864	368,036	467,295
EU 1/	284,783	239,180	328,872	416,188	436,240	625,824
ASEAN 2/	242,383	328,056	478,426	805,236	908,448	1,223,736
Rest of the World	542,959	711,140	1,095,765	1,936,133	2,444,002	3,805,865
Total imports	**1,840,233**	**2,058,533**	**2,888,654**	**4,499,338**	**5,144,884**	**7,079,826**

Source: Customs Department (compiled by the Bank of Thailand 2013).

With respect to SME exports, the major export markets for Thai SMEs in 2011 were China, Hong Kong, Japan, the United States, Switzerland, Malaysia, Indonesia, Vietnam, Australia and Singapore, accounting for 11.6 per cent, 11.42 per cent, 10.71 per cent, 7.71 per cent, 5.07 per cent, 4.83 per cent, 4.44 per cent, 3.04 per cent, 2.79 per cent and 2.74 per cent of total SME export value, respectively (OSMEP 2008). Comparing the export value between SMEs and large enterprises in 2011, SME export value was about 29.94 per cent of the total value of exports. This is much lower compared to that of large enterprises even though the number of exporting SMEs is much larger than large exporting enterprises.

Punyasavatsut (2007) acknowledged that Thai manufacturing SMEs are not ready to face the rigours of international competition in competitive global markets arising from the country's increased opening and economic integration, as well as more intense competition from lower labour costs in other countries. According to OSMEP (2012), Thai business segments have fallen under the "Nut-Cracker Effect", implying that Thailand is trapped between countries with greater price competitiveness, such as China, Vietnam and Indonesia, and countries with more skilled labour and higher productivity that can differentiate their output by concentrating on higher value-added products and services, such as Japan, South Korea and Taiwan. More importantly, OECD (2011) suggested that internationalization is one of the important SME policies that can overcome the problem of the "missing middle" for Thai SMEs due to the lack of growth-oriented small enterprises and the relative under-representation of medium-sized enterprises, leading to a distinctly smaller proportion of the SME population involved in export markets than is the case in OECD countries and other non-OECD Asian countries (OECD 2011).

3. Key Issues Facing Thai SMEs

While SMEs represent a major component of the Thai economy in terms of employment, business establishments and GDP, they face a number of severe problems that act as barriers to their further growth and development. These include a lack of management and/or administration skills, limited marketing skills, lack of technology and related skills, inadequate skilled labour, limited access to information and promotion from Thai government agencies, and difficulty in gaining access to government funding and finance from lending institutions (Sarapaivanich 2003; Punyasavatsut 2007). In addition, SME failures can arise from a lack of experience, insufficient capital invested by the owner, an over-reliance on external funds and poor record-keeping (Brooks et al. 1990). According to Gregory, Harvie and Lee (2002), SMEs have to build their capacity through strengthening and improving their cooperation and integration with both domestic and overseas enterprises, participate in production networks and become embedded in knowledge sharing, with the aim of maintaining competitiveness worldwide and enhancing their knowledge and technology. We will discuss a number of these barriers in more detail.

3.1. Finance

There is considerable evidence to support the contention that SMEs face many barriers in accessing finance, mainly related to their limited resources, opaqueness in business operation and perceived risk by lenders (Oum et al. 2011, p. 42). Harvie (2011, p. 18) also emphasizes that access to finance is the most critical factor influencing the competitive readiness of SMEs. This in turn determines their ability to fully exploit and participate in the global market, take advantage of business opportunities stemming from regional economic integration, and participate in regional production networks (Tranh et al. 2009; Oum et al. 2011).

In the context of Thailand, a large number of SMEs face difficulties in accessing formal sources of funding due to limitations related to their characteristics such as small size, lack of fixed assets, lack of systematic accounting and lack of a business plan (OSMEP 2007a, 2009; OSMRJ 2008). A lack of access to capital causes them to encounter high financial costs and high failure rates (OSMEP 2003; Sarapaivanich 2003). They have also been unable to obtain capital through the Thai stock market and raise funds from banks and financial institutions (OSMEP 2003; Theingi 2004). This lack of interaction with financial markets and institutions has caused several problems for SMEs such as a lack of efficiency, usage of outdated technology, poor innovation, inadequate funds for investment and a lack of integration into domestic and international value-adding production networks (Brimble et al. 2002; OECD 2005; OSMRJ 2008).

3.2. Marketing

The role of marketing is one of the most important factors that can influence SMEs' success and prosperity (Simpson and Taylor 2002; Rose et al. 2006). Thai SMEs primarily remain in the domestic market because of intense competition in worldwide markets, their involvement in primarily low-skill and low value-adding activities, as well as due to the existence of tariff and non-tariff barriers in overseas markets. These factors add disproportionately to their costs. Most SMEs are not well-prepared for both domestic and international markets. The major reason for this is that they lack knowledge and know-how on how to increase the value-added content of their products, distribution channels, and market penetration. As a result, the marketing efforts of SMEs are frequently not fully competitive in both domestic and international markets. In the domestic market, Thai SMEs face intense competition from large enterprises and from imported products, such as from the modern trade discount and convenience stores (OSMEP 2007b; Punyasavatsut 2010; OECD 2011).

Exports

Thai SMEs have internal barriers that impede their export performance, such as a lack of managerial export experience and weak planning systems. SMEs lack export knowledge and have poor networking that leads to difficulties in finding new international markets (Chirasirimongkol and Chutimaskul 2005). They utilize less formal market research on international market opportunities. Thai SMEs encounter greater challenges in international markets than large-sized enterprises because they have to compete with several big companies and they lack access to market information (OSMEP 2004; Theingi 2004). The changing marketing environment has increased competition in both domestic and international markets, requiring Thai SMEs to improve their performance in order for them to survive in the global marketplace (OSMEP 2003). With regards to product quality and technological advances, Thai SMEs are unable to compete with SMEs in other countries such as Italy, Japan, Taiwan because they are heavily involved in labour-intensive, low-skill and low value-adding activities using outdated technology (OSMEP 2007a, 2007b; Tambunan 2008).

3.3. Information Technology

Thai SMEs also lack the ability to access and utilize information technology (IT) and to adopt e-commerce. Most SMEs still have a traditional style of business operation. The majority of SME entrepreneurs and employees have low education levels and skills, and lack the understanding of how to utilize IT effectively in their businesses (Lertwongsatien and Wongpinunwatana 2003). Hence, application of IT to SMEs is difficult and beyond their capacity to utilize efficiently, despite Thai government agencies having provided technological support to assist SMEs, such as the Software Park project in 1997. As a consequence, only a small number of SMEs received any benefit from this project, because Thai government agencies provided insufficient information about the IT project. Many are not aware of the benefits from IT services provided by government agencies (OSMEP 2009; Tippakoon 2009). In contrast, large enterprises have continued to develop and enhance their utilization of IT. They have applied IT to their administration and production process, for instance, the management of their supply chains, commodity inventories and e-commerce systems. The benefit of IT to large enterprises is to simplify their process of work, save production costs, and expand customer reach.

3.4. Innovation

Innovation[7] is related to creative thinking, improvement and innovative usage of technology to increase the economic value of products and services (Cooke 2001). Innovation is also important in the knowledge or so-called "new economy". According to Intarakamnerd et al. (2002), the innovation system in Thailand is not well-organized in many areas, such as in the macro-environment, innovation infrastructure, R&D and technology capabilities. Innovation is not explicitly emphasized in the Thai National Economic and Social Plan. Thus, SMEs in Thailand pay insufficient attention to innovation. This is a consequence of the low education level of employees in the SME sector that contributes to a lack of creativity. In addition, the educational system itself contributes to the problem, because in Thailand emphasis is placed on rote learning or memorizing and not on creative thinking. Baker and Rudd (2001) emphasize that creative thinking is the process of creating something new or having a new idea.

Varatorn (2005) points out that brainstorming is a form of creative thinking. Teaching students to think creatively must therefore be the priority of schools today (Baker and Rudd 2001). The absence of appropriate innovation among Thai SME entrepreneurs is a critical issue that leads to low product quality and production and it needs to be addressed by the Thai government (Brimble et al. 2002; OSMEP 2003). In terms of technology and quality control, SMEs are producing goods below export-quality standards, such as ISO, making them difficult to participate in the supply chains of multinational companies and international markets more generally (Brimble et al. 2002). Although the Thai government established an innovation development fund in 2000 to support entrepreneurs and employees, to date this fund has not been successful in terms of patents, product designs, trademarks, certification marks and local Thai wisdom (culture, art and knowledge in the community) (OSMEP 2003).

3.5. Human Resource Development

Human resources are a vital issue for SME development, particularly in the knowledge- and skills-intensive "new economy" today. The government of Thailand has supported the educational system by allocating a large amount of funds through successive budgets. However, the average education level of Thai workers is low and almost 70 per cent of the workforce in SMEs has only primary education or lower. The labour force in SMEs consists of largely unskilled labour. These workers have limitations and difficulties in learning and training, and knowledge acquisition and application. That part of the labour force which is more highly educated, such as at the secondary school or diploma levels, has a greater ability to learn and understand compared to workers who only have a primary education (OSMEP 2001, 2007b). Entrepreneurship skills is another issue facing Thai SMEs. The traditional style of running a business may be productive for the domestic market, but not for the international market (Mephokee 2003). Furthermore, most Thai SMEs are family businesses and informal, which limit their business and market expansion. They have limited capabilities in raising and managing finance, conducting market research, business administration, and analysing domestic and international markets (Theingi 2004).

3.6. Government Regulation

Another reason for the weakness of SMEs relates to the Thai government. The government has, until quite recently, not paid much attention to SMEs. Government agencies are not well-prepared to play an effective role in assisting SMEs (Mephokee 2003; Sahakijpicharn 2007; OSMEP 2007*a*). For example, the government should play the major role in providing necessary information for the SME sector. It should also encourage networking among SMEs for their mutual benefit and launch necessary measures to protect SMEs from unfair competition and international trade barriers (OSMEP 2003). Corruption in Thai government agencies and in corporate governance is the main reason for the lack of effective support. SMEs face various problems from the Thai government such as a lack of transparency of government agencies, an inadequate legal and regulatory framework, inconsistent SME promotion plans and confusion in the structure of government agencies and their support (Sahakijpicharn 2007; OSMEP 2007*b*).

4.   SME Policy Context

The SME policy environment in Thailand is determined within the context of SME promotion plans. To date, there have been three promotion plans since the Asian Financial Crisis, but only the first two of these are discussed here. The First SME Promotion Plan (2002–6)[8] aimed to enhance the efficiency and capacity of SMEs by means of creating a business environment in which they could prosper; improve firm efficiency and competitiveness; and promote grassroots businesses to facilitate income distribution and prosperity in regional economies. The specific objectives of the plan, as well as the outcomes and perceived problems by the government, are summarized in Table 8.12. The plan incorporated seven strategies: (1) managerial and technological upgrading; (2) human resource development; (3) expanding markets; (4) strengthening financial capabilities; (5) improving the business environment; (6) cultivating microenterprises and grassroots community businesses; and (7) establishing comprehensive linkages between enterprises (SMEs and large enterprises). To achieve the objective of the plan, the Thaksin government focused on investment promotion, financial assistance to SMEs, and the provision of technical and management consultancy services.

TABLE 8.12
Results of the First SME Promotion Plan, 2002–6

Targets of the Plan	Results	Problems and Limitations from the Government's Point of View
1. GDP share of SMEs to reach 50 per cent in 2011	• 38.9 per cent per year on average	• The GDP of SMEs in the manufacturing and service sectors increased gradually, while the trade sector decreased.
2. Increasing employment by SMEs at an average of 180,000 people annually	• Employment increased by about 354,533 workers per year during 2007–11.	• SMEs are labour-intensive enterprises. • Inadequate skilled labour • Job opportunities and working environment are insufficient for SMEs.
3. Boosting the value of SME exports by 6 per cent per year	• 9 per cent per year	• Most SME exports are in primary and labour intensive products. • Lack of product differentiation • Weak marketing infrastructure
4. Increasing new entrepreneurs by 50,000 per year	• 44,551 entrepreneurs per year	• New SMEs required government support due to market failures and policy biases.
5. Enhancing and promoting target groups of SMEs, such as enterprises with existing high potential and good record. Increasing groups[1] of SMEs by 10 per cent per year to reach 6,300 groups in 2011.	• 1,602 groups per year	• SMEs needed to focus on knowledge and quality. • SMEs required a strong integration of business networking.

Note: [1] SMEs that have a 3–5 star One Tambon One Product (OTOP) rating.
Source: OSMEP (2013).

During this period, Thailand's SME policy was more interventionist in nature and also involved the targeting of certain sectors (e.g. food processing, the fashion industries, automotive parts, electrical and electronics components) (Punyasavatsut 2008).

The Second SME Promotion Plan (2007–11) aimed to enable SMEs to grow with continuity, strength, and sustainability in terms of knowledge and skills. Consistent with the first plan, the second plan aimed to achieve three economic targets: (1) to raise the share of SMEs in GDP to 42 per cent; (2) to achieve higher SME export shares than total export growth; (3) to increase the total factor productivity of SMEs by an average of 3 per cent annually, including a minimum of 5 per cent labour productivity growth per annum. The second plan targeted sectors such as auto and electronic parts, software, logistics, healthcare, education, tourism-related industry, health foods, and rubber products. Measures specifically targeting manufacturing SMEs included: (1) improving product quality; (2) establishing business incubator centres in regional and local areas; (3) establishing trade fairs; (4) setting up exhibition centres for SME products throughout the country; (5) improving logistics or distribution channels; and (6) establishing industrial clustering and networks.

5. Literature Review

This section provides a review of the literature in relation to the factors that can influence the export decisions of firms, such as firm age, firm size, foreign ownership, R&D, financial support, and government assistance.

A number of studies have investigated both linear and non-linear relationships between firm size and export performance (Jongwanich and Kohpaiboon 2008; Dueñas-Caparas 2006; Althukorala et al. 1995). Jongwanich and Kohpaiboon (2008) utilized the 1997 Thai Industrial Census to examine the determinants of a firm's export decision in the Thai manufacturing sector. They found that firm size has a positive and significant impact on a firm's export decision, indicating that there are typically significant sunk costs related to entering export markets, hence larger firms are more likely to obtain advantages than smaller firms. However, a non-linear relationship between firm size and its export decision is not found in their study.

Dueñas-Caparas (2006) investigated the determinants of export performance in Philippine manufacturing firms. They found both positive linear and negative non-linear relationships between a firm's size and its export performance in the country's clothing sector, but insignificant results were found in the food processing and electronics sectors. Athukorala et al. (1995) used the Sri Lankan Survey of manufacturing firms in 1981 and found that firm size was significantly and positively correlated with the export decisions of 111 Sri Lankan manufacturing firms. They suggested that firm size could be an important factor for export participation where scale or size economies exist. Reaching an adequate size may be crucial for achieving success in export markets, since exporting is a costly and risky activity. Smaller firms, therefore, may be at a disadvantage in gathering market information, introducing overseas sales-promotion campaigns, withstanding exchange rate and other risks, and adapting their products to foreign markets.

However, a number of empirical studies have found that firm size can have a negative association with a firm's export decision (Biggs 2002; Wiboonchutikula 2002; Alvarez and Crespi 2003; Yang and Chen 2009; Le 2010). The benefits of being a small firm are as follows: (1) flexibility to adjust and diversify activities to become more efficient; (2) small firms add dynamism to business activities which can improve economic performance; (3) small firms are likely to have a cost advantage relative to medium- and large-sized firms (Biggs 2002; Biesebroeck 2005; Yang and Chen 2009; Le 2010).

Firm age, indicating a learning-by-doing experience, can be one of the factors that significantly affect export decisions, since old firms can compete with foreign companies due to their cumulative experience, business networks and reputation. Aggrey et al. (2010), however, pointed out that young firms are more proactive, flexible and aggressive than old firms. As a result, they are willing to adopt modern technology, whereas old firms are stuck with outdated physical capital. Focusing on empirical studies, Jongwanich and Kohpaiboon (2008) found that firm age has a significant and positive linear effect on export decisions among Thai manufacturing enterprises, implying that older firms tend to have more operating experience and higher efficiency through their learning-by-doing experience than younger firms. A negative and significant non-linear effect, however, was found among Thai manufacturing enterprises, indicating that after a certain threshold, a firm's experience does not exert a positive effect on its export performance. In other words, a negative relationship between a firm's age and its export activity may be observed, since firms firstly supply the local market, and diversification into exports does not occur until an expansion of their domestic markets has been exhausted (Jongwanich and Kohpaiboon 2008). However, Dueñas-Caparas (2006) found both positive linear and negative non-linear associations between a firm's age and its export performance in the Philippine clothing and electronics sectors, but an insignificant result was found in the food processing sector.

A number of empirical studies have found a significant and positive relationship between foreign ownership and firm export decisions (Greenaway et al. 2007; Jongwanich and Kohpaiboon 2008; Aggrey et al. 2010). For example, Greenaway et al. (2007) found that foreign ownership had a significant and positive effect on firm export participation for 9,292 UK manufacturing enterprises between 1993 and 2003. For Thailand, Jongwanich and Kohpaiboon (2008) used the 1997 Thai manufacturing census and found that foreign ownership has a significant and positive impact on firm export participation among Thai manufacturing enterprises. This positive result implies that an increase in foreign participation encourages firms to participate in export markets since foreign partners bring new foreign markets and distribution, new products, managerial know-how and advanced production technology (Jongwanich and Kohpaiboon 2008). Jongwanich and Kohpaiboon (2008, p. 21) also pointed out that foreign-owned firms can cover sunk costs and enter foreign markets more easily than domestically-owned firms.

With respect to R&D, Dueñas-Caparas (2006) found that R&D has a significant and positive effect on a firm's export decision in the Philippine electronics industry, but a significant and negative relationship was found in the country's clothing industry. Roper and Love (2002) also found small plants' export propensity is positively affected by informally and formally organized R&D activities, but only more formally organized R&D is useful for large plants.

Finally, government assistance can influence a firm's exporting decision. Such aid can be in the form of financial support (e.g., credit assistance, income tax exemption or reduction, and exemption from import duties on essential raw materials) and non-financial support (e.g., managerial and technical assistance, and training support). The coefficient estimates of the government support variable are positive. Wu and Cheng (1999) studied the determinants of export performance in China's township-village enterprises (TVEs), and found that government financial support contributes positively toward the international competitiveness of TVE export performance.

6. Review of the 2015 ERIA–ISEAS SME Survey and Data Obtained for Thailand

The main objective of the 2015 ERIA–ISEAS SME Survey for Thailand was to collect basic information on the distribution of establishments engaged in the manufacturing industry classified by ISIC: Revision 4, 2-digit code. It also collected information on the operation of manufacturing establishments by type of establishment, their cost of production, sales revenue and administrative expenses. The survey can be used for national account compilation and constructing economic performance indicators. The 2015 ERIA–ISEAS SME Survey consisted of nine parts: (1) general information on the establishments; (2) sales and exports; (3) production and inputs of the establishments; (4) employment and human resources of the establishments; (5) technology and innovation of the establishments; (6) knowledge and awareness of the ASEAN Economic Community (AEC); (7) utilization of free trade agreements; (8) government support; and (9) attitudes toward risk. The total number of Thai manufacturing enterprises participating in this survey was 301, of which 205 were SMEs.

Table 8.13 presents the number and percentage of total interviewed manufacturing firms in 2015 by various categories. With regard to the size of enterprises, the largest number of interviewed manufacturing enterprises were medium enterprises, amounting to 116 firms or 38.54 per cent of the total sample, followed by large enterprises and then small enterprises. In terms of submanufacturing sectors of interviewed enterprises, the manufacture of rubber and plastic products had the highest number of interviewed enterprises, amounting to 104 firms or 34.55 per cent of the total sample, followed by the manufacture of food products (31.56 per cent of the total sample), manufacture of machinery and equipment n.e.c (10.96 per cent of the total sample), manufacture of furniture (9.63 per cent of the total sample), manufacture of leather and related products (6.98 per cent of the total sample), manufacture

TABLE 8.13
**Number and Percentage of Interviewed Firms, Classified by Size,
Sub-manufacturing Sector and Type of Ownerships**

Items	Number of Observations	Percentage (%)
Size of Enterprises		
Small enterprises	89	29.57
Medium enterprises	116	38.54
Large enterprises	96	31.89
Total	**301**	**100**
Sub-manufacturing Sectors		
Manufacture of food products	95	31.56
Manufacture of textiles	10	3.32
Manufacture of leather and related products	21	6.98
Manufacture of rubber and plastic products	104	34.55
Manufacture of fabricated metal products, except machinery and equipment	9	2.99
Manufacture of machinery and equipment n.e.c.	33	10.96
Manufacture of furniture	29	9.63
Total	**301**	**100**
Type of Ownerships		
Sole Proprietor	6	1.99
Partnership	37	12.29
Private Limited Company	234	77.74
Public Limited Company	24	7.97
Total	**301**	**100**

Source: ERIA–ISEAS survey for Thailand (2015).

of textiles (3.32 per cent of the total sample), and manufacture of fabricated metal products, except machinery and equipment (2.99 per cent of the total sample). Focusing on the type of ownership of the interviewed enterprises, the number of private limited companies was 234 or 77.74 per cent of the total sample, representing the largest number of interviewed enterprises, followed by partnerships (12.29 per cent of the total sample), public limited companies (7.97 per cent of the total sample), and sole proprietorships (1.99 per cent of the total sample).

TABLE 8.14
Number and Percentage of Manufacturing Firms,
Classified by Firm Size and Sector

Manufacturing Sector	Size of Enterprises			
	Small	Medium	Large	Total
10. Manufacture of food products	31	22	42	95
13. Manufacture of textiles	2	4	4	10
15. Manufacture of leather and related products	14	2	5	21
22. Manufacture of rubber and plastic products	23	46	35	104
25. Manufacture of fabricated metal products	1	7	1	9
28. Manufacture of machinery and equipment	13	14	6	33
31. Manufacture of furniture	6	19	4	29
Total	**90**	**114**	**97**	**301**
Percentage of Manufacturing Sector				
10. Manufacture of food products	34.44%	19.29%	43.29%	31.56%
13. Manufacture of textiles	2.22%	3.50%	4.12%	3.32%
15. Manufacture of leather and related products	15.55%	1.75%	5.15%	6.97%
22. Manufacture of rubber and plastic products	25.55%	40.35%	36.08%	34.55%
25. Manufacture of fabricated metal products	1.11%	6.14%	1.03%	2.99%
28. Manufacture of machinery and equipment	14.44%	12.28%	6.18%	10.96%
31. Manufacture of furniture	6.66%	16.66%	4.12%	9.63%
Total	**100%**	**100%**	**100%**	**100%**

Source: ERIA–ISEAS survey for Thailand (2015).

Table 8.14 shows the number and percentage of manufacturing firms classified by sector and size in the 2015 survey. The largest number of firms were in the manufacture of rubber and plastic products sector, which consisted of 104 firms or 34.55 per cent of all enterprises in the survey. The total number of small firms in the manufacture of rubber and plastic products sector is 23, representing 25.55 per cent of all small firms in the survey, while medium and large firms contributed 46 and 35 enterprises in this same sector, respectively, equivalent to 40.35 per cent and 36.08 per cent, respectively, of all medium and large firms in the entire survey. The manufacture of food products sector is the second highest, with 95 enterprises or 31.56 per cent of all enterprises in the survey. The total numbers of small and medium firms in the manufacture of food products sector were 31 and 22, respectively, accounting for 34.44 per cent and 19.29 per cent, respectively of the total sample, while large firms accounted for 42 firms, representing 43.29 per cent of the total sample. The manufacture of machinery and equipment sector was third, with 33 firms or 10.96 per cent of the sample, followed by the manufacture of furniture sector, manufacture of leather and related products sector, manufacture of textiles sector, and manufacture of fabricated metal products sector.

Table 8.15 presents the number and percentage by firm ownership type classified by size and sector in 2015. Regarding the size of enterprises, it can be seen that almost all firms are operated as private limited companies, followed by partnerships, public limited companies, and sole proprietorships. Medium firms are mainly organized as private limited companies, representing 97 firms or 41.50 per cent of all private limited companies, while large and small enterprises have 74 and 63 firms, respectively, accounting for 31.60 per cent and 26.90 per cent of private limited companies, respectively. With respect to sub-manufacturing sectors, the largest number of firms is in the manufacture of rubber and plastic products sector and they are mainly organized as private limited companies, representing 84 firms or 35.90 per cent of all private limited companies, followed by the manufacture of food products sector, manufacture of furniture sector, manufacture of machinery and equipment sector, manufacture of leather and related products sector, manufacture of textiles sector, and manufacture of fabricated metal products sector.

Table 8.16 presents the number and percentage of type of family business and ownership of the parent company classified by size and sector. For the type of family business, most of the firms in terms of both enterprise size and sub-manufacturing sector of operation are not family businesses, representing 204 firms in total, while the rest of the firms are family businesses (97 firms). The majority of the firms are not family-run, accounting for 215 firms, while only 86 firms are family run. Focusing on ownership of the parent

TABLE 8.15
Number and Percentage of Ownership Type, Classified by Firm Size and Sector

Size of Enterprises	Ownership Type				
	Sole Proprietor	Partnership	Private Limited	Public Limited	Total
Small Enterprises	5	20	63	2	90
Medium Enterprises	1	12	97	4	114
Large Enterprises	0	5	74	18	97
Total	**6**	**37**	**234**	**24**	**301**
Percentage of Enterprises					
Small Enterprises	83.30%	54.10%	26.90%	8.30%	29.90%
Medium Enterprises	16.70%	32.40%	41.50%	16.70%	37.87%
Large Enterprises	0.00%	13.50%	31.60%	75.00%	32.22%
Total	**100.00%**	**100.00%**	**100.00%**	**100.00%**	**100%**
Manufacturing Sector					
10. Manufacture of food products	1	13	71	10	95
13. Manufacture of textiles	0	1	7	2	10
15. Manufacture of leather and related products	3	4	14	10	104
22. Manufacture of rubber and plastic products	2	8	84	10	104
25. Manufacture of fabricated metal products	0	3	6	0	9
28. Manufacture of machinery and equipment	0	7	25	1	33
31. Manufacture of furniture	0	1	27	1	29
Total	**6**	**37**	**234**	**24**	**301**

TABLE 8.15 *(continued)*

Size of Enterprises	Ownership Type					
	Sole Proprietor	Partnership	Private Limited	Public Limited	Total	
Percentage of Manufacturing Sector						
10. Manufacture of food products	16.70%	35.10%	30.30%	41.70%	31.60%	
13. Manufacture of textiles	0.00%	2.70%	3.00%	8.30%	3.30%	
15. Manufacture of leather and related products	50.00%	10.80%	6.00%	0.00%	7.00%	
22. Manufacture of rubber and plastic products	33.30%	21.60%	35.90%	41.70%	34.60%	
25. Manufacture of fabricated metal products	0.00%	8.10%	2.60%	0.00%	3.00%	
28. Manufacture of machinery and equipment	0.00%	18.90%	10.70%	4.20%	11.00%	
31. Manufacture of furniture	0.00%	2.70%	11.50%	4.20%	9.60%	
Total	**100.00%**	**100.00%**	**100.00%**	**100.00%**	**100.00%**	

Source: ERIA–ISEAS survey for Thailand (2015).

TABLE 8.16
Number and Percentage of Type of Family Business and Ownership of the Parent Company, Classified by Firm Size and Sector

Size of Enterprises	Type of Family Business				Ownership of the Parent Company	
	Not Family Business	Family Business	Not Run by Family	Run by Family	Local	Foreign
Small Enterprises	44	46	51	39	86	4
Medium Enterprises	78	36	82	32	113	1
Large Enterprises	82	15	82	15	92	5
Total	**204**	**97**	**215**	**86**	**291**	**10**
Percentage of Enterprises						
Small Enterprises	21.60%	47.40%	24.29%	43.33%	29.60%	40.00%
Medium Enterprises	38.20%	37.10%	39.05%	35.56%	38.80%	10.00%
Large Enterprises	40.20%	15.50%	36.67%	21.11%	31.60%	50.00%
Total	**100.00%**	**100.00%**	**100.00%**	**100.00%**	**100.00%**	**100.00%**
Manufacturing Sector						
10. Manufacture of food products	60	35	50	45	88	7
13. Manufacture of textiles	9	1	10	0	10	0
15. Manufacture of leather	8	13	10	11	21	0
22. Manufacture of rubber and plastic products	81	23	92	12	104	0
25. Manufacture of fabricated metal products	0	9	0	9	9	0
28. Manufacture of machinery and equipment	23	10	22	11	30	3
31. Manufacture of furniture	23	6	26	3	29	0
Total	**204**	**97**	**210**	**91**	**291**	**10**

TABLE 8.16 (continued)

Size of Enterprises	Type of Family Business				Ownership of the Parent Company	
	Not Family Business	Family Business	Not Run by Family	Run by Family	Local	Foreign
Percentage of Manufacturing Sector						
10. Manufacture of food products	29.40%	36.10%	23.80%	49.00%	30.20%	70.00%
13. Manufacture of textiles	4.40%	1.00%	4.80%	0.00%	3.40%	0.00%
15. Manufacture of leather and related products	3.90%	13.40%	4.80%	12.20%	7.20%	0.00%
22. Manufacture of rubber and plastic products	39.70%	23.70%	43.80%	13.30%	35.70%	0.00%
25. Manufacture of fabricated metal products	0.00%	9.30%	0.00%	10.00%	3.10%	0.00%
28. Manufacture of machinery and equipment	11.30%	10.30%	10.50%	12.20%	10.30%	30.00%
31. Manufacture of furniture	11.30%	6.20%	12.30%	3.30%	10.00%	0.00%
Total	100.00%	100.00%	100.00%	100.00%	100.00%	100.00%

Source: ERIA–ISEAS survey for Thailand (2015).

company, almost all firms are locally owned, representing 291 firms, whereas only 10 firms are foreign-owned.

Table 8.17 shows the qualifications of the founding members or their family relatives now operating the family businesses in the firm survey sample, classified by firm size and sector. It can be seen that the majority of founding members, or family relatives now operating these firms, have no formal education, representing 178 firms in the sample, while 117 firms have founders or relatives with a university degree, followed by vocational and diploma qualifications (4 firms), and secondary/high school qualifications (2 firms). From the sample, small enterprises have the highest number of founders or family relatives now running the businesses with a university degree, representing 51 firms or 43.6 per cent of all enterprises in that category, while medium and large enterprises have 42 firms and 24 firms, respectively, accounting for 35.90 per cent and 20.50 per cent, respectively of sample firms in that category.

For sub-manufacturing sectors, the manufacture of rubber and plastic products sector had the highest number of founding or family relatives running the businesses having no formal education, representing 80 firms or 45.2 per cent of all enterprises in that category. The second highest number of founding or family members running the businesses having no formal education is in the manufacture of food products sector, accounting for 41 firms or 23.2 per cent of all enterprises in that category, followed by the manufacture of furniture sector, manufacture of machinery and equipment sector, manufacture of textiles sector, and manufacture of leather and related products sector. Focusing on having a university degree, the manufacture of food products sector has the highest number of founding or family relatives running the businesses with a university degree, representing 49 firms or 41.9 per cent of all enterprises in this category. The manufacture of rubber and plastic products sector has the second highest number of founding or family relatives running the businesses having a university degree, accounting for 24 firms or 19.7 per cent of all enterprises in this category, followed by the manufacture of machinery and equipment sector, manufacture of leather and related products sector, manufacture of fabricated metal products sector, manufacture of furniture, and manufacture of textiles sector.

Table 8.18 presents the number and percentage of exporting and non-exporting enterprises classified by size and sector. In the sample of firms,

TABLE 8.17

Highest Academic Qualification of the Founder or Family Relative Running the Firms in the Sample, Classified by Firm Size and Sector

Size of Enterprises	Qualification of Family Member				
	No Formal Education	Secondary / High School	Vocational / Diploma	University	Total
Small Enterprises	37	0	3	51	91
Medium Enterprises	70	1	1	42	114
Large Enterprises	71	1	0	24	96
Total	**178**	**2**	**4**	**117**	**301**
Percentage of Enterprises					
Small Enterprises	21.00%	0.00%	75.00%	43.60%	30.00%
Medium Enterprises	39.00%	50.00%	25.00%	35.90%	38.00%
Large Enterprises	40.00%	50.00%	0.00%	20.50%	32.00%
Total	**100.00%**	**100.00%**	**100.00%**	**100.00%**	**100.00%**
Manufacturing Sector					
10. Manufacture of food products	41	1	3	49	94
13. Manufacture of textiles	9	0	0	1	10
15. Manufacture of leather and related products	8	0	0	13	21
22. Manufacture of rubber and plastic products	80	0	1	24	105
25. Manufacture of fabricated metal products	0	0	0	8	9

28. Manufacture of machinery and equipment	18	1	0	15	33
31. Manufacture of furniture	22	0	0	7	29
Total	**178**	**2**	**4**	**117**	**301**
Percentage of Manufacturing Sector					
10. Manufacture of food products	23.20%	50.00%	75.00%	41.90%	31.30%
13. Manufacture of textiles	5.10%	0.00%	0.00%	0.90%	3.30%
15. Manufacture of leather and related products	4.50%	0.00%	0.00%	11.10%	7.00%
22. Manufacture of rubber and plastic products	45.20%	0.00%	25.00%	19.70%	34.70%
25. Manufacture of fabricated metal products,	0.00%	0.00%	0.00%	7.70%	3.00%
28. Manufacture of machinery and equipment	9.60%	50.00%	0.00%	12.80%	11.00%
31. Manufacture of furniture	12.40%	0.00%	0.00%	6.00%	9.70%
Total	**100.00%**	**100.00%**	**100.00%**	**100.00%**	**100.00%**

Source: ERIA–ISEAS survey for Thailand (2015).

TABLE 8.18
**Number and Percentage of Exporting and Non-Exporting Enterprises,
Classified by Firm Size and Sector**

Size of Enterprises	Non-exporting	Exporting	Total
Small Enterprises	54	38	92
Medium Enterprises	54	59	113
Large Enterprises	51	45	96
Total	**159**	**142**	**301**
Percentage of Enterprises			
Small Enterprises	34.0%	26.8%	30.6%
Medium Enterprises	34.0%	41.5%	37.5%
Large Enterprises	32.0%	31.7%	31.9%
Total	**100.0%**	**100.0%**	**100.0%**
Manufacturing Sector			
10. Manufacture of food products	37	58	95
13. Manufacture of textiles	5	5	10
15. Manufacture of leather and related products	12	9	21
22. Manufacture of rubber and plastic products	71	33	104
25. Manufacture of fabricated metal products	0	9	9
28. Manufacture of machinery and equipment	18	15	33
31. Manufacture of furniture	16	13	29
Total	**159**	**142**	**301**
Percentage of Manufacturing Sector			
10. Manufacture of food products	23.3%	40.8%	31.6%
13. Manufacture of textiles	3.10%	3.50%	3.30%
15. Manufacture of leather and related products	7.50%	6.30%	7.00%
22. Manufacture of rubber and plastic products	44.70%	23.20%	34.50%
25. Manufacture of fabricated metal products	0.00%	6.30%	3.00%
28. Manufacture of machinery and equipment	11.30%	10.60%	11.00%
31. Manufacture of furniture	10.10%	9.30%	9.60%
Total	**100.0%**	**100.0%**	**100.0%**

Source: ERIA–ISEAS survey for Thailand (2015).

exporting firms accounted for 142 enterprises while non-exporting firms accounted for 159 enterprises.[9] With regards to exporting firms, medium enterprises made up the largest number, representing 59 enterprises or 41.5 per cent of all exporting firms in the sample, while large and small enterprises had 45 and 38 enterprises, accounting for 31.7 per cent and 26.8 per cent, respectively, of all exporting firms. For non-exporting firms, small and medium enterprises had the highest number, 108 in total or 68 per cent of overall non-exporting firms, whereas large enterprises have 51 firms or 32 per cent of overall non-exporting firms.

Focusing on the sub-manufacturing sector, the largest number of exporting firms is in the manufacture of food products sector, representing 58 firms or 40.8 per cent of all exporting firms. The second largest number of exporting firms is in the manufacture of rubber and plastic products sector, accounting for 33 firms or 23.2 per cent of all exporting firms, followed by the manufacture of machinery and equipment sector, manufacture of furniture sector, manufacture of fabricated metal products sector, manufacture of leather and related products sector, and manufacture of textiles sector. For non-exporting firms, the manufacture of rubber and plastic products sector had the highest number, accounting for 71 firms or 44.7 per cent of all non-exporting firms. The manufacture of food products sector had the second highest number of non-exporting firms, representing 37 firms or 23.3 per cent of all non-exporting firms, followed by the manufacture of machinery and equipment sector, manufacture of furniture sector, manufacture of leather and related products sector, and manufacture of textiles sector.

Table 8.19 presents the number and percentage of firms in the sample where production is carried out internally, through outsourcing, or using both of these, classified by firm size and sector. It can be seen that most of the sampled firms carried out production completely in-house, representing 250 out of 301 firms, whereas only 51 firms did not carry out their production completely in-house. With respect to completely outsourcing, most firms did not completely carry out their production through outsourcing, accounting for 279 out of 301 enterprises, while there are only 22 firms that carried out their production completely through outsourcing. Most firms in the sample carried out production either completely in-house or completely through outsourcing, representing 272 of the sampled firms, and only 29 sampled firms carried out their production using both in-house and outsourced production.

TABLE 8.19

Number and Percentage of Firms in the Sample Conducting Production Only In-house, Through Outsourcing or Using Both of These, Classified by Firm Size and Sector

Size of Enterprises	Completely In-house		Completely Outsourced		Both In-house and Outsourced	
	No	Yes	No	Yes	No	Yes
Small Enterprises	21	69	83	7	76	14
Medium Enterprises	21	93	106	8	101	13
Large Enterprises	9	88	90	7	95	2
Total	51	250	279	22	272	29
Percentage of Enterprises						
Small Enterprises	41.2%	27.6%	29.70%	31.80%	27.9%	48.3%
Medium Enterprises	41.2%	37.2%	38.00%	36.40%	37.1%	44.8%
Large Enterprises	17.6%	35.2%	32.30%	31.80%	34.9%	6.9%
Total	100.0%	100.0%	100.0%	100.0%	100.0%	100.0%
Manufacturing Sector						
10. Manufacture of food products	19	76	89	6	82	11
13. Manufacture of textiles	1	9	9	1	10	0
15. Manufacture of leather and related products	10	11	15	6	17	4
22. Manufacture of rubber and plastic products	4	100	99	5	105	1
25. Manufacture of fabricated metal products	9	0	8	1	1	8
28. Manufacture of machinery and equipment	8	25	30	3	28	5
31. Manufacture of furniture	0	29	29	0	29	0
Total	51	250	279	22	272	29

Percentage of Manufacturing Sector

Sector						
10. Manufacture of food products	37.3%	30.4%	31.9%	27.3%	30.1%	37.9%
13. Manufacture of textiles	2.0%	3.6%	3.2%	4.5%	3.7%	0%
15. Manufacture of leather and related products	19.6%	4.4%	5.4%	27.3%	6.3%	13.8%
22. Manufacture of rubber and plastic products	7.8%	40.0%	35.5%	22.7%	38.6%	3.4%
25. Manufacture of fabricated metal products	17.6%	0%	2.9%	4.5%	.4%	27.6%
28. Manufacture of machinery and equipment	15.7%	10.0%	10.8%	13.6%	10.3%	17.2%
31. Manufacture of furniture	0%	11.6%	10.4%	0%	10.7%	0%
Total	**100.0%**	**100.0%**	**100.0%**	**100.0%**	**100.0%**	**100.0%**

Source: ERIA–ISEAS survey for Thailand (2015).

For sub-manufacturing sectors, the manufacture of rubber and plastic products sector has the highest number of sampled firms that carried out production completely in-house, representing 100 firms or 40 per cent of all enterprises in this category. The second highest number of sampled firms carrying out production completely in-house is in the manufacture of food products sector, accounting for 76 firms or 30.4 per cent of all enterprises in this category, followed by the manufacture of furniture sector, manufacture of machinery and equipment sector, manufacture of leather and related products sector, and manufacture of textiles sector. With regards to completely outsourced production, the highest numbers of firms in the sample that completely outsourced production are the manufacture of food products sector and the manufacture of leather and related products sector, followed by the manufacture of rubber and plastic products sector. But the number of firms in each of these sectors was small. Focusing on both in-house and outsourced production, the manufacture of food products has the highest number of firms engaged in production that involved both in-house and outsourcing, representing 11 firms or 37.9 per cent of firms in this category, followed by the manufacture of fabricated metal products sector, manufacture of machinery and equipment sector, manufacture of leather and related products sector, and manufacture of rubber and plastic products sector. It is apparent that the simultaneous use of both in-house and outsourcing activities in production is utilized by only a small number of firms in the sample.

Table 8.20 presents the number and percentage of firms that spent on worker training and hired foreign workers, classified by size and sector. The majority of firms did not spend on worker training, representing 186 firms out of all sample enterprises, whereas 115 firms spent on worker training. In terms of hiring foreign workers, most firms did not hire foreign workers, accounting for 240 firms, while only 61 firms hired foreign workers. More large enterprises employed foreign workers, 35 firms overall, while 16 medium and 10 small enterprises employed foreign workers, respectively.

Focusing on sub-manufacturing sectors, the manufacture of rubber and plastic products sector had the highest number of firms that did not spend on worker training, representing 74 firms or 39.8 per cent of all enterprises in this category, followed by the manufacture of food products sector, manufacture of machinery and equipment sector, manufacture of furniture sector, manufacture of leather and related products sector, and manufacture of textiles sector. With regard to

TABLE 8.20
Number and Percentage of Firms that Spent on Worker Training and
Hired Foreign Workers, Classified by Firm Size and Sector

Size of Enterprises	Spend on Worker Training?		Hire Any Foreign Workers?	
	No	Yes	No	Yes
Small Enterprises	60	30	80	10
Medium Enterprises	66	48	98	16
Large Enterprises	60	37	62	35
Total	**186**	**115**	**240**	**61**
Percentage of Enterprises				
Small Enterprises	32.3%	26.1%	33.3%	16.4%
Medium Enterprises	35.5%	41.7%	40.8%	26.2%
Large Enterprises	32.3%	32.2%	25.8%	57.4%
Total	**100.0%**	**100.0%**	**100.0%**	**100.0%**
Manufacturing Sector				
10. Manufacture of food products	50	45	74	21
13. Manufacture of textiles	7	3	8	2
15. Manufacture of leather and related products	11	10	18	3
22. Manufacture of rubber and plastic products	74	30	80	24
25. Manufacture of fabricated metal products	0	9	8	1
28. Manufacture of machinery and equipment	22	11	27	6
31. Manufacture of furniture	22	7	25	4
Total	186	115	240	61
Percentage of Manufacturing Sector				
10. Manufacture of food products	26.9%	39.1%	30.8%	34.4%
13. Manufacture of textiles	3.8%	2.6%	3.3%	3.3%
15. Manufacture of leather and related products	5.9%	8.7%	7.5%	4.9%
22. Manufacture of rubber and plastic products	39.8%	26.1%	33.3%	39.3%
25. Manufacture of fabricated metal products	0%	7.8%	3.3%	1.6%
28. Manufacture of machinery and equipment	11.8%	9.6%	11.3%	9.8%
31. Manufacture of furniture	11.8%	6.1%	10.4%	6.6%
Total	**100.0%**	**100.0%**	**100.0%**	**100.0%**

Source: ERIA–ISEAS survey for Thailand (2015).

hiring foreign workers, the manufacture of rubber and plastic products sector had the largest number of firms that did not hire foreign workers, accounting for 80 firms or 33.33 per cent of all enterprises in this category. Despite this, the manufacture of rubber and plastic products sector had the highest number of firms employing foreign workers in the sample, 24 firms in total, while the manufacture of food products sector had 21 firms that hired foreign workers.

Table 8.21 shows the number and percentage of firms in the sample that spent on in-house R&D and outsourcing R&D activities, classified by firm size and sector. Most firms did not spend on in-house R&D activities, accounting for 229 firms, while only 72 firms engaged in in-house R&D spending. With regard to expenditure on outsourcing R&D activities, only 17 firms spent on this while 284 of the sample firms did not.

Focusing on sub-manufacturing sectors, the sector with the highest number of firms that did not spend on in-house R&D activities is the manufacture of rubber and plastic products sector, with 103 firms or 45 per cent of all enterprises in this category. The second highest sector not spending on in-house R&D activities is the manufacture of food products sector, accounting for 56 firms or 24.5 per cent of all enterprises in this category, followed by the manufacture of furniture sector, manufacture of machinery and equipment sector, manufacture of leather and related products sector, and manufacture of textiles sector. However, the manufacture of food products sector has 39 firms which spent on in-house R&D activities, followed by the manufacture of leather and related products sector (11 firms). For expenditure on outsourced R&D activities, the sector with the highest number of firms not spending on this is the manufacture of rubber and plastic products sector, followed by the manufacture of food products sector. However, only three sub-manufacturing sectors (the manufacture of machinery and equipment sector, manufacture of rubber and plastic products sector, and manufacture of food products sector) spent on outsourced R&D activities.

Table 8.22 presents the number and percentage of firms in the sample that have acquired machinery, equipment, software and external knowledge, classified by firm size and sector. It is important to note that most firms in the sample did not provide expenditure for the acquisition of machinery, equipment, and software, representing 242 firms, whereas only 59 firms had done so. Regarding expenditure on

TABLE 8.21
Number and Percentage of Firms in the Sample that Spent on In-house R&D and Outsourcing R&D Activities, Classified by Firm Size and Sector

Size of Enterprises	In-house R&D		Outsourced R&D	
	No	Yes	No	Yes
Small Enterprises	63	27	89	1
Medium Enterprises	83	31	100	14
Large Enterprises	83	14	95	2
Total	229	72	284	17
Percentage of Enterprises				
Small Enterprises	27.5%	37.5%	31.3%	5.9%
Medium Enterprises	36.2%	43.1%	35.2%	82.4%
Large Enterprises	36.2%	19.4%	33.5%	11.8%
Total	100.0%	100.0%	100.0%	100.0%
Manufacturing Sector				
10. Manufacture of food products	56	39	93	2
13. Manufacture of textiles	9	1	10	0
15. Manufacture of leather and related products	10	11	21	0
22. Manufacture of rubber and plastic products	103	1	98	6
25. Manufacture of fabricated metal products	0	9	9	0
28. Manufacture of machinery and equipment	24	9	24	9
31. Manufacture of furniture	27	2	29	0
Total	229	72	284	17
Percentage of Manufacturing Sector				
10. Manufacture of food products	24.50%	54.10%	32.7%	11.8%
13. Manufacture of textiles	3.80%	1.40%	3.5%	0%
15. Manufacture of leather and related products	4.40%	15.30%	7.4%	0%
22. Manufacture of rubber and plastic products	45.00%	1.40%	34.5%	35.3%
25. Manufacture of fabricated metal products	0.00%	12.50%	3.2%	0%
28. Manufacture of machinery and equipment	10.50%	12.50%	8.5%	52.9%
31. Manufacture of furniture	11.80%	2.80%	10.2%	0%
Total	100.0%	100.0%	100.0%	100.0%

Source: ERIA–ISEAS survey for Thailand (2015).

TABLE 8.22
Number and Percentage of Firms in the Sample that had Acquired Machinery, Equipment, Software and External Knowledge, Classified by Firm Size and Sector

	Acquisition of Machinery, Equipment, and Software		Acquisition of External Knowledge	
	No	Yes	No	Yes
Size of Enterprises				
Small Enterprises	80	17	80	10
Medium Enterprises	64	26	75	39
Large Enterprises	98	16	66	31
Total	**242**	**59**	**221**	**80**
Percentage of Enterprises				
Small Enterprises	26.4%	44.1%	36.2%	12.5%
Medium Enterprises	40.5%	27.1%	33.9%	48.8%
Large Enterprises	33.1%	28.8%	29.9%	38.8%
Total	**100.0%**	**100.0%**	**100.0%**	**100.0%**
Manufacturing Sector				
10. Manufacture of food products	56	39	63	32
13. Manufacture of textiles	10	0	7	3
15. Manufacture of leather and related products	10	11	18	3
22. Manufacture of rubber and plastic products	97	7	85	19
25. Manufacture of fabricated metal products	7	2	0	9
28. Manufacture of machinery and equipment	33	0	22	11
31. Manufacture of furniture	29	0	26	3
Total	**242**	**59**	**221**	**80**

Percentage of Manufacturing Sector

10. Manufacture of food products	23.1%	66.1%	28.5%	40.0%
13. Manufacture of textiles	4.1%	0%	3.2%	3.8%
15. Manufacture of leather and related products	4.1%	18.6%	8.1%	3.8%
22. Manufacture of rubber and plastic products	40.1%	11.9%	38.5%	23.8%
25. Manufacture of fabricated metal products	2.9%	3.4%	0%	11.3%
28. Manufacture of machinery and equipment	13.6%	0%	10.0%	13.8%
31. Manufacture of furniture	12.0%	0%	11.8%	3.8%
Total	**100.0%**	**100.0%**	**100.0%**	**100.0%**

Source: ERIA–ISEAS survey for Thailand (2015).

the acquisition of external knowledge, the majority of firms had not acquired external knowledge, accounting for 221 firms, while only 80 firms had done so.

Focusing on sub-manufacturing sectors, the sector with the highest number of firms in the sample that spent on the acquisition of machinery, equipment, and software is the manufacture of food products sector, followed by the manufacture of leather and related products sector, manufacture of rubber and plastic products sector, and manufacture of fabricated metal products sector. However, most of the firms in these manufacturing sectors did not spend on the acquisition of machinery, equipment, software and external knowledge.

Table 8.23 shows the number and percentage of firms in the sample introducing new or significantly improved goods and services classified by firm size and sector. It can be observed that most firms in the sample had introduced new or significantly improved goods and services, whereas a minority of firms had not done so. For sub-manufacturing sectors, the manufacture of rubber and plastic products sector and manufacture of food products sector had the highest number of firms that introduced new or significantly improved goods and services, followed by the manufacture of furniture sector, manufacture of machinery and equipment sector, manufacture of leather and related products sector, and manufacture of textiles sector.

Table 8.24 shows the number and percentage of firms in the sample that have introduced innovation and technology classified by firm size and sector. It can be seen that most firms in the sample had introduced innovation and new technology in manufacturing, logistics, delivery or distribution methods and supporting activities for processes, whereas a minority of firms had not done so. For sub-manufacturing sectors, the manufacture of rubber and plastic products sector and manufacture of food products sector had the highest number of firms in the sample that introduced innovation and new technology, followed by the manufacture of furniture sector, manufacture of machinery and equipment sector, manufacture of leather and related products sector, and manufacture of textiles sector.

Table 8.25 shows the number and percentage of sample firms using internet-related services classified by firm size and sector. Regarding the use of email, most of the sample firms used email in their businesses, representing 244 firms of all enterprises, while only 57 firms did not do

TABLE 8.23
Number and Percentage of Firms in the Sample
that Introduced New or Significantly Improved Goods and Services,
Classified by Firm Size and Sector

Size of Enterprises	New or Significantly Improved Goods		New or Significantly Improved Services	
	No	Yes	No	Yes
Small Enterprises	26	64	24	66
Medium Enterprises	31	83	31	83
Large Enterprises	12	85	11	85
Total	**69**	**232**	**66**	**234**
Percentage of Enterprises				
Small Enterprises	37.7%	27.6%	36.4%	28.2%
Medium Enterprises	44.9%	35.8%	47.0%	35.5%
Large Enterprises	17.4%	36.6%	16.7%	36.3%
Total	**100.0%**	**100.0%**	**100.0%**	**100.0%**
Manufacturing Sector				
10. Manufacture of food products	13	82	11	83
13. Manufacture of textiles	2	8	2	8
15. Manufacture of leather and related products	6	15	6	15
22. Manufacture of rubber and plastic products	18	86	17	87
25. Manufacture of fabricated metal products	9	0	9	0
28. Manufacture of machinery and equipment	16	17	15	18
31. Manufacture of furniture	5	24	6	23
Total	**69**	**232**	**66**	**234**
Percentage of Manufacturing Sector				
10. Manufacture of food products	18.8%	35.3%	16.7%	35.5%
13. Manufacture of textiles	2.9%	3.4%	3.0%	3.4%
15. Manufacture of leather and related products	8.7%	6.5%	9.1%	6.4%
22. Manufacture of rubber and plastic products	26.1%	37.1%	25.8%	37.2%
25. Manufacture of fabricated metal products	13.0%	0%	13.6%	0%
28. Manufacture of machinery and equipment	23.2%	7.3%	22.7%	7.7%
31. Manufacture of furniture	7.2%	10.3%	9.1%	9.8%
Total	**100.0%**	**100.0%**	**100.0%**	**100.0%**

Source: ERIA–ISEAS survey for Thailand (2015).

TABLE 8.24
Number and Percentage of Firms in the Sample that Introduced Innovation and Technology, Classified by Firm Size and Sector

Size of Enterprises	Methods of Manufacturing		Logistics, Delivery or Distribution Methods		Supporting Activities for Processes	
	No	Yes	No	Yes	No	Yes
Small Enterprises	25	65	24	66	25	65
Medium Enterprises	13	101	16	98	12	102
Large Enterprises	11	86	11	86	12	85
Total	**49**	**252**	**51**	**250**	**49**	**252**
Percentage of Enterprises						
Small Enterprises	51.0%	25.8%	47.1%	26.4%	51.0%	25.8%
Medium Enterprises	26.5%	40.1%	31.4%	39.2%	24.5%	40.5%
Large Enterprises	22.4%	34.1%	21.6%	34.4%	24.5%	33.7%
Total	**100.0%**	**100.0%**	**100.0%**	**100.0%**	**100.0%**	**100.0%**
Manufacturing Sector						
10. Manufacture of food products	15	80	12	83	15	80
13. Manufacture of textiles	1	9	1	9	1	9
15. Manufacture of leather and related products	7	14	5	16	5	16
22. Manufacture of rubber and plastic products	15	89	20	84	16	88
25. Manufacture of fabricated metal products	1	8	1	8	1	8
28. Manufacture of machinery and equipment	8	25	7	26	8	25
31. Manufacture of furniture	2	27	5	24	3	26
Total	**49**	**252**	**51**	**250**	**49**	**252**

Percentage of Manufacturing Sector

10. Manufacture of food products	30.6%	31.7%	23.5%	33.2%	30.6%	31.7%
13. Manufacture of textiles	2.0%	3.6%	2.0%	3.6%	2.0%	3.6%
15. Manufacture of leather and related products	14.3%	5.6%	9.8%	6.4%	10.2%	6.3%
22. Manufacture of rubber and plastic products	30.6%	35.3%	39.2%	33.6%	32.7%	34.9%
25. Manufacture of fabricated metal products	2.0%	3.2%	2.0%	3.2%	2.0%	3.2%
28. Manufacture of machinery and equipment	16.3%	9.9%	13.7%	10.4%	16.3%	9.9%
31. Manufacture of furniture	4.1%	10.7%	9.8%	9.6%	6.1%	10.3%
Total	**100.0%**	**100.0%**	**100.0%**	**100.0%**	**100.0%**	**100.0%**

Source: ERIA–ISEAS survey for Thailand (2015).

TABLE 8.25
Number and Percentage of Sample Firms Using Internet-related Services,
Classified by Firm Size and Sector

Size of Enterprises	Email		Company Website		Online Sales		Online Purchase		Online Marketing		Online Payment	
	No	Yes	No	Yes	No	Yes	No	Yes	No	Yes	No	Yes
Small Enterprises	20	70	51	39	85	5	86	4	86	4	58	32
Medium Enterprises	18	96	45	69	91	23	93	21	100	14	74	40
Large Enterprises	19	78	41	56	88	9	89	8	87	10	66	31
Total	**57**	**244**	**137**	**164**	**264**	**37**	**268**	**33**	**273**	**28**	**198**	**103**
Percentage of Enterprises												
Small Enterprises	35.1%	28.7%	37.2%	23.8%	32.2%	13.5%	32.1%	12.1%	31.5%	14.3%	29.3%	31.1%
Medium Enterprises	31.6%	39.3%	32.8%	42.1%	34.5%	62.2%	34.7%	63.6%	36.6%	50.0%	37.4%	38.8%
Large Enterprises	33.3%	32.0%	29.9%	34.1%	33.3%	24.3%	33.2%	24.2%	31.9%	35.7%	33.3%	30.1%
Total	**100**	**100**	**100**	**100**	**100**	**100**	**100**	**100**	**100**	**100**	**100**	**100**
Manufacturing Sector												
10. Manufacture of food products	17	78	32	63	85	10	83	12	82	13	47	48
13. Manufacture of textiles	5	5	5	5	9	1	10	0	9	1	9	1
15. Manufacture of leather and related products	7	14	16	5	20	1	18	3	21	0	14	7
22. Manufacture of rubber and plastic products	16	88	53	51	99	5	103	1	104	0	87	17
25. Manufacture of fabricated metal products	0	9	0	9	0	9	1	8	6	3	0	9
28. Manufacture of machinery and equipment	6	27	16	17	23	10	24	9	23	10	20	13
31. Manufacture of furniture	6	23	15	14	28	1	29	0	28	1	21	8
Total	**57**	**244**	**137**	**164**	**264**	**37**	**268**	**33**	**273**	**28**	**198**	**103**

Percentage of Manufacturing Sector

10. Manufacture of food products	29.8%	32.0%	23.4%	38.4%	32.2%	27.0%	31.0%	36.4%	30.0%	46.4%	23.7%	46.6%
13. Manufacture of textiles	8.8%	2.0%	3.6%	3.0%	3.4%	2.7%	3.7%	0%	3.3%	3.6%	4.5%	1.0%
15. Manufacture of leather and related products	12.3%	5.7%	11.7%	3.0%	7.6%	2.7%	6.7%	9.1%	7.7%	0%	7.1%	6.8%
22. Manufacture of rubber and plastic products	28.1%	36.1%	38.7%	31.1%	37.5%	13.5%	38.4%	3.0%	38.1%	0%	43.9%	16.5%
25. Manufacture of fabricated metal products	0%	3.7%	0%	5.5%	0%	24.3%	0.4%	24.2%	2.2%	10.7%	0%	8.7%
28. Manufacture of machinery and equipment	10.5%	11.1%	11.7%	10.4%	8.7%	27.0%	9.0%	27.3%	8.4%	35.7%	10.1%	12.6%
31. Manufacture of furniture	10.5%	9.4%	10.9%	8.5%	10.6%	2.7%	10.8%	0%	10.3%	3.6%	10.6%	7.8%
Total	100	100	100	100	100	100	100	100	100	100	100	100

Source: ERIA–ISEAS survey for Thailand (2015).

so. The majority of the firms had a company website, representing
164 firms out of all survey enterprises, while 137 firms did not have
a website. For online sales, online purchases and online marketing, it
can be observed that most of the sample firms did not utilize these in
their businesses, while a minority of firms did so. Focusing on the sub-
manufacturing sectors, the manufacture of rubber and plastic products
sector and manufacture of food products sector had the highest number
of sample firms that used email and had a company website. Most of
the sample firms in the various manufacturing sectors did not utilize
online sales, online purchases, online marketing, and online payment
in their businesses.

Table 8.26 shows the number and percentage of sample firms having
business relations with firms in other ASEAN countries, awareness of
the ASEAN SME Policy Blueprint/Strategic Action Plan and awareness
of the AEC classified by size and sector. It can be observed that most
of the sample firms did not have business relations with firms in other
ASEAN countries, accounting for 207 firms out of all survey enterprises,
whereas only 94 firms had such business relations. However, most firms
were aware of the ASEAN SME Policy Blueprint/Strategic Action Plan,
representing 207 firms out of overall enterprises, while 94 firms were
not aware. Regarding awareness of the AEC, the majority of firms
were aware of it, representing 196 firms out of all enterprises, while
105 firms were not aware.

Focusing on the various sub-manufacturing sectors, the manufacture
of food products sector has the largest number of firms that have
business relations with firms in other ASEAN countries, accounting for
43 firms or 45.7 per cent of all enterprises in this category, followed
by the manufacture of rubber and plastic products sector, manufacture
of machinery and equipment sector, manufacture of fabricated metal
products sector, and manufacture of furniture sector. For awareness
of the ASEAN SME Policy Blueprint/Strategic Action Plan, the
manufacture of food products sector has the largest number of firm
awareness, representing 74 firms or 35.7 per cent of all enterprises
in this category, followed by the manufacture of rubber and plastic
products sector, manufacture of machinery and equipment sector,
manufacture of furniture sector, manufacture of leather and related
products sector, and manufacture of fabricated metal products sector.
Regarding the awareness of the AEC, the manufacture of food products

TABLE 8.26
Number and Percentage of Firms Having Business Relations with Firms in Other ASEAN Countries, Awareness of the ASEAN SME Policy Blueprint/Strategic Action Plan and Awareness of the AEC, Classified by Firm Size and Sector

Size of Enterprises	Business Relations with Firms in Other ASEAN Countries		Awareness of ASEAN SME Policy Blueprint/ Strategic Action Plan		Awareness of AEC	
	No	Yes	No	Yes	No	Yes
Small Enterprises	67	23	28	62	30	60
Medium Enterprises	72	42	38	76	49	65
Large Enterprises	68	29	28	69	26	71
Total	207	94	94	207	105	196
Percentage of Enterprises						
Small Enterprises	32.4%	24.5%	29.8%	30.0%	28.6%	30.6%
Medium Enterprises	34.8%	44.7%	40.4%	36.7%	46.7%	33.2%
Large Enterprises	32.9%	30.9%	29.8%	33.3%	24.8%	36.2%
Total	100.0%	100.0%	100.0%	100.0%	100.0%	100.0%
Manufacturing Sector						
10. Manufacture of food products	52	43	21	74	22	73
13. Manufacture of textiles	7	3	4	6	4	6
15. Manufacture of leather and related products	17	4	8	13	8	13
22. Manufacture of rubber and plastic products	89	15	42	62	41	63
25. Manufacture of fabricated metal products	0	9	0	9	5	4
28. Manufacture of machinery and equipment	19	14	6	27	12	21
31. Manufacture of furniture	23	6	13	16	13	16
Total	207	94	94	207	105	196

TABLE 8.26 (*continued*)

Size of Enterprises	Business Relations with Firms in Other ASEAN Countries		Awareness of ASEAN SME Policy Blueprint/ Strategic Action Plan		Awareness of AEC	
	No	Yes	No	Yes	No	Yes
10. Manufacture of food products	25.1%	45.7%	22.3%	35.7%	21.0%	37.2%
13. Manufacture of textiles	3.4%	3.2%	4.3%	2.9%	3.8%	3.1%
15. Manufacture of leather and related products	8.2%	4.3%	8.5%	6.3%	7.6%	6.6%
22. Manufacture of rubber and plastic products	43.0%	16.0%	44.7%	30.0%	39.0%	32.1%
25. Manufacture of fabricated metal products	0%	9.6%	0%	4.3%	4.8%	2.0%
28. Manufacture of machinery and equipment	9.2%	14.9%	6.4%	13.0%	11.4%	10.7%
31. Manufacture of furniture	11.1%	6.4%	13.8%	7.7%	12.4%	8.2%
Total	**100.0%**	**100.0%**	**100.0%**	**100.0%**	**100.0%**	**100.0%**

Source: ERIA–ISEAS survey for Thailand (2015).

sector has the largest number of firms aware of AEC, accounting for 73 firms or 37.2 per cent of all enterprises in this category, followed by the manufacture of rubber and plastic products sector, manufacture of machinery and equipment sector, manufacture of furniture sector, and manufacture of leather and related products sector. Furthermore, Figure 8.1 presents a clustered column of the percentage of sample firms having business relations with firms in other ASEAN countries, awareness of the ASEAN Policy Blueprint/Strategic Action Plan, and awareness of the AEC.

Figures 8.2 and 8.3 show how the AEC has affected or will affect the businesses of sample firms classified by firm size and sector. It can be observed that the highest number of sample firms expected to be affected by the AEC using various measures are mainly in the manufacture of food products sector, followed by the manufacture of rubber and plastic products sector, manufacture of machinery and equipment sector, and manufacture of furniture sector.

FIGURE 8.1

Business Relations with Firms in Other ASEAN Countries, Awareness of the ASEAN SME Policy Blueprint/ Strategic Action Plan, and Awareness of the AEC

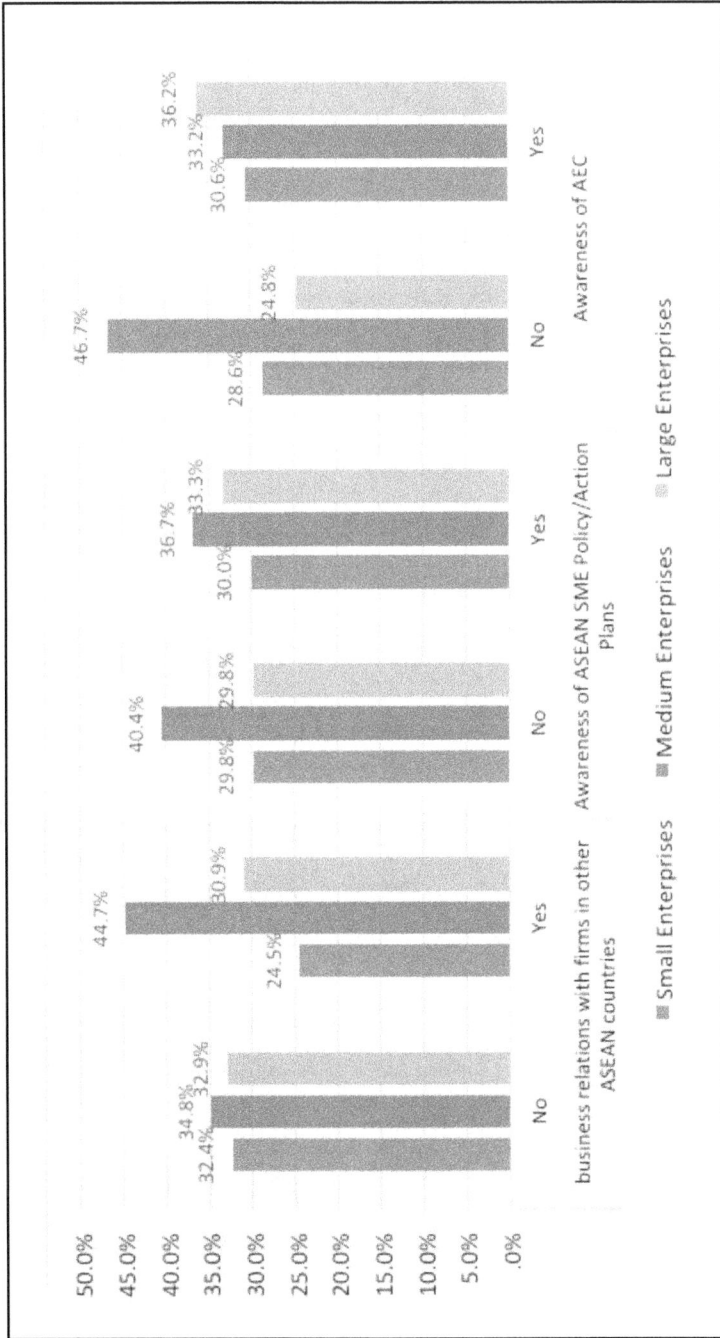

Source: ERIA–ISEAS survey for Thailand (2015).

FIGURE 8.2

How Has the AEC Affected or Will Affect the Businesses of Sample Firms, Classified by Firm Size

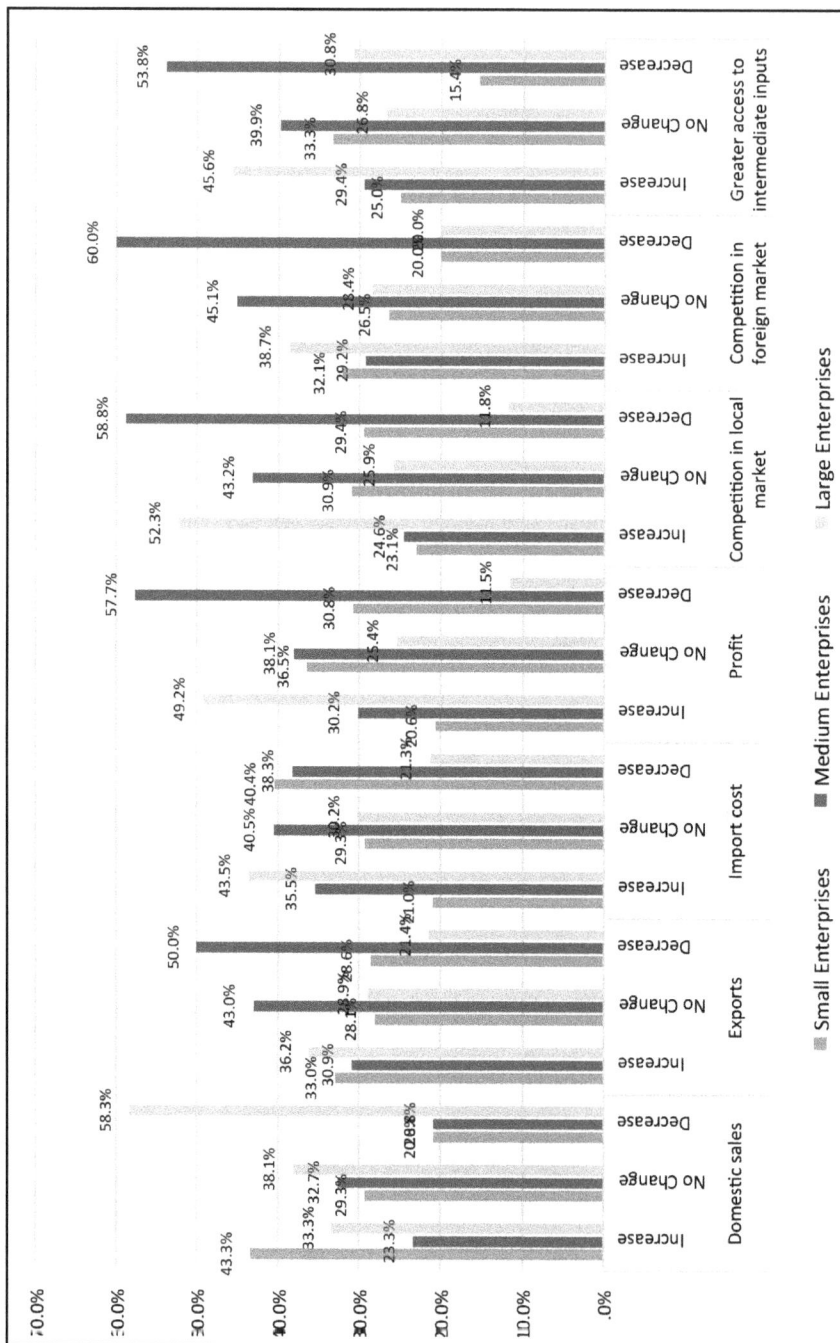

Source: ERIA–ISEAS survey for Thailand (2015).

FIGURE 8.3

How Has the AEC Affected or Will Affect the Businesses of Sample Firms, Classified by Sector

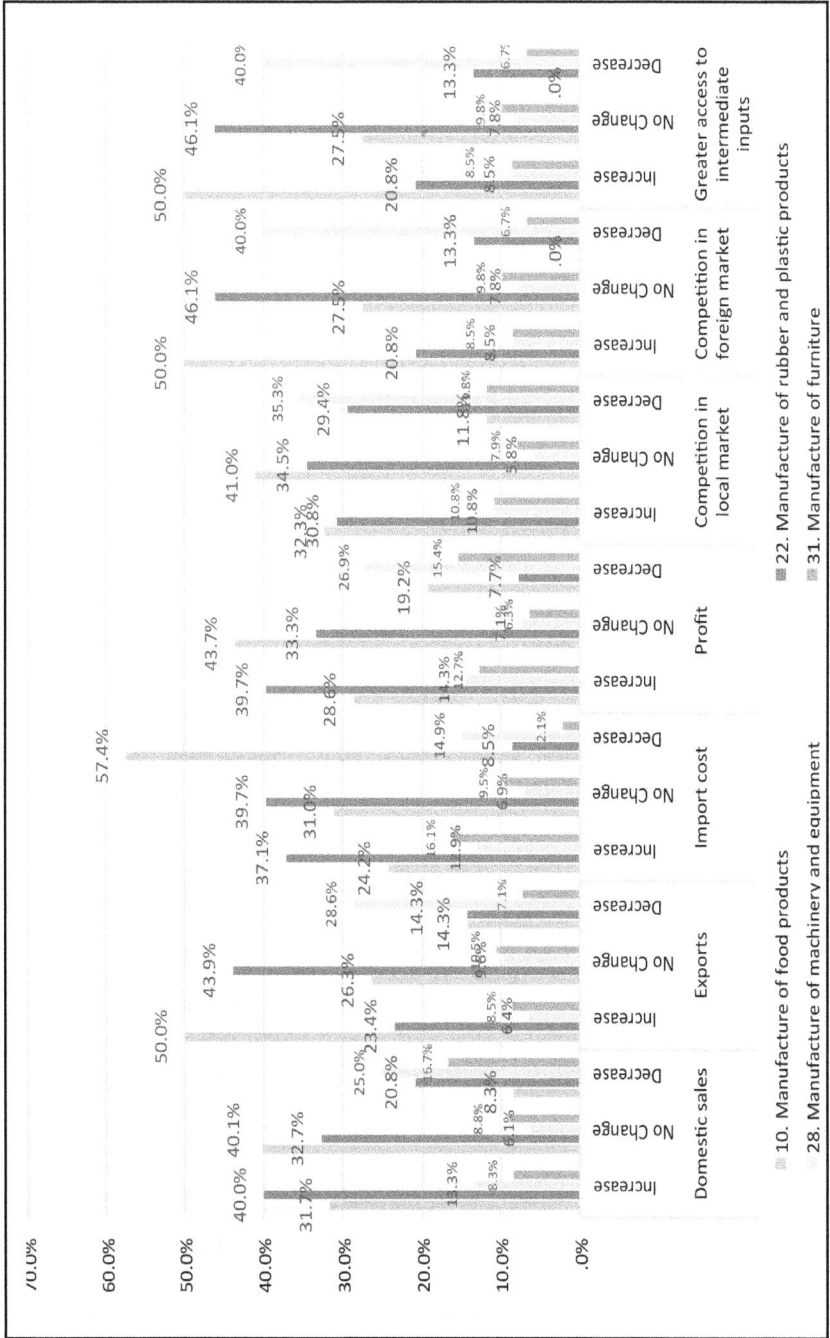

Legend:
- 10. Manufacture of food products
- 22. Manufacture of rubber and plastic products
- 28. Manufacture of machinery and equipment
- 31. Manufacture of furniture

Source: ERIA–ISEAS survey for Thailand (2015).

7. Empirical Model

In this section we present empirical results, identifying the most important variables impacting the export participation of our sample firms. A binary variable for export participation is used as the dependent variable. Therefore, the limited dependent variable models, such as the probit and logit models, are utilized to conduct this study, which can be illustrated as follows (Wooldridge 2006):

$$G(z) = \phi(z) = \int_{-\infty}^{z} \emptyset(v)dv \qquad \text{Probit Model}$$

$$G(z) = \frac{exp(z)}{1 + exp(z)} = \Lambda(z) \qquad \text{Logit Model}$$

Where:

$\phi(z)$ is the standard normal density as given by $(2\pi)^{-1/2}exp(-z^2/2)$

For probit and logit models, the relationship between dependent and independent variables is assumed to be an increasing function. For the binary response model, Wooldridge (2006, pp. 256, 582) also mentioned that the probit and logit models can overcome certain drawbacks of the linear probability model (LPM), since the LPM model violates the homoskedasticity assumption that is important for justifying the t and F statistics. The assumption of linear parameters between the dependent and independent variables is also generally required for the LPM model under the ordinary least squares (OLS) estimation. The probit model is also more popularly compared with the logit model, as economists are likely to favour the probit model's normality assumption (Wooldridge 2006, p. 385). In addition, the probit model's method of maximum likelihood estimation automatically accounts for the heteroskedasticity problem. However, these two estimation models are utilized to check the sensitivity of this study's results (Jongwanich and Kohpaiboon 2008). Applying the limited dependent variable model, the equation for the export decisions of all firms is identified as follows:

Equation 1:

$Z_{ij} = \beta_0 + \beta_1 FIRM\_AGE_{ij} + \beta_2 FIRM\_SIZE_{ij} + \beta_3 FOREIGN\_OWNERSHIP_{ij} + \beta_4 FAMILY\_BUSINESS_{ij} + \beta_5 IN-HOUSE\_R\&D_{ij} + \beta_6 OUTSOURCE\_R\&D_{ij} + \beta_7 FINANCIAL\_SUPPORT_{ij} + \beta_8 FTA_{ij} + \beta_9 ASSIST\_EXPANSION_{ij} + \beta_{10} AWARE\ AEC_{ij} + \beta_{11} AWARE\ ASEAN_{ij} + \beta_{12} BUSINESS\ ASSOCIATIONS_{ij} + u_{ij}$

Where

Z_{ij} = Dummy for export participation
Z_{ij} = 1 if firm i in industry j exports to foreign markets,
  = 0, otherwise;
FIRM AGE_{ij} = Age of firm i at time t, represented by the number of
      operating years;
FIRM $SIZE_{ij}$ = Size of firm i in industry j, represented by the
      number of workers;
FOREIGN $OWNERSHIP_{ij}$ = Dummy for foreign ownership
FOREIGN $OWNERSHIP_{ij}$ = 1 if firm i in industry j has foreign
          ownership,
        = 0 if firm i in industry j does not have
          foreign ownership;
FAMILY $BUSINESS_{ij}$ = Dummy for a family business
FAMILY $BUSINESS_{ij}$ = 1 if firm i in industry j is a family business,
        = 0 if firm i in industry j is not a family business;
IN–HOUSE $R\&D_{ij}$ = Dummy for in-house R&D activities
IN–HOUSE $R\&D_{ij}$ = 1 if firm i in industry j spends on in-house
      R&D activities,
    = 0 if firm i in industry j does not spend on
      in-house R&D activities;
OUTSOURCE $R\&D_{ij}$ = Dummy for outsourcing R&D
OUTSOURCE $R\&D_{ij}$ = 1 if firm i in industry j spends on outsourced
      R&D activities,
    = 0 if firm i in industry j does not spend on
      outsourced R&D activities;
FINANCIAL $SUPPORT_{ij}$ = Dummy for financial support
FINANCIAL $SUPPORT_{ij}$ = 1 if firm i in industry j obtains financial
        support,
      = 0 if firm i in industry j does not obtain
        financial support;
FTA_{ij} = Dummy for FTA
FTA_{ij} = 1 if firm i in industry j is involved[10] in an FTA,
    = 0 if firm i in industry j is not involved in an FTA;
ASSIST $EXPANSION_{ij}$ = Dummy for expansion assistance
ASSIST $EXPANSION_{ij}$ = 1 if firm i in industry j obtains assistance in
          business expansion abroad,
        = 0 if firm i in industry j does not obtain
          assistance in business expansion abroad,

AWARE AEC$_{ij}$ = Dummy for awareness of the ASEAN Economic
            Community (AEC)
AWARE AEC$_{ij}$ = 1 if firm i in industry j is aware of the AEC,
AWARE AEC$_{ij}$ = 0 if firm i in industry j is not aware of the AEC;
AWARE ASEAN$_{ij}$ = Dummy for awareness of the ASEAN SME
            Policy Blueprint/Strategic Action Plan
AWARE ASEAN$_{ij}$ = 1 if firm i in industry j is aware of the ASEAN
            SME Policy Blueprint,
            = 0 if firm i in industry j is not aware of the
            ASEAN SME Policy Blueprint;
BUSINESS ASSOCIATIONS$_{ij}$ = Dummy for business associations
BUSINESS ASSOCIATIONS$_{ij}$ = 1 if firm i in industry j belongs to a
            business association;
            = 0 if firm i in industry j does not belong
            to a business association.

8. Preliminary Results

Table 8.27 presents the results of maximum likelihood estimates of
probit and logit models for aggregate manufacturing based on our
sample of 301 firms in 2015, as specified by equation 1, where export
participation is the dependent variable. The table shows that only four
specific factors — in-house R&D, FTA, awareness of AEC, and business
association membership — are found to be statistically significantly
associated with the export participation of Thai manufacturing firms
in aggregate.

For in-house R&D, the coefficient estimates indicate a positive and
significant association with a firm's export participation for both the
probit and logit models in aggregate in 2015, indicating that R&D can
help improve the quality of a firm's products to compete in international
markets. With R&D, firms can produce goods of export-quality standards,
such as ISO, making it easier for them to participate in the supply
chains of multinational companies and international markets more
generally (see Table 8.27).

With regard to FTAs, as measured by the use of any forms of FTA,
the estimated coefficients indicate a positive and significant association
with export participation for both the probit and logit models in
aggregate. This result may imply that Thai manufacturing firms can
benefit from any form of FTAs, such as Form A (GSP), Form B (MFN)
and Form D (ATIGA).[11] For awareness of the AEC, it is found to be
positively and significantly associated with a firm's export participation

TABLE 8.27
Maximum Likelihood Estimates for Parameters of Probit and Logit Models for Aggregate Manufacturing Firms

Models	Aggregate Manufacturing Firms			
	Probit		Logit	
	Coefficients	Standard Errors	Coefficients	Standard Errors
Dependent Variable:				
Exports				
Obs Dep = 0	158		158	
Obs Dep = 1	142		142	
Total Observations	300		300	
Independent Variables:				
C	−2.750718*	0.578465	−5.395443*	1.387805
FIRM_AGE	0.003607	0.007552	0.007171	0.012883
FIRM_SIZE	−0.000051	0.000157	−0.000098	0.000278
FOREIGN_OWNERSHIP	0.323984	0.256076	0.447195	0.440409
FAMILY_BUSINESS	−0.006014	0.261171	−0.216694	0.46738
INHOUSE_R&D	2.538859*	0.745187	4.966479*	1.607925
OUTSOURCE_R&D	0.182182	0.442333	0.095798	0.752355
FINANCIAL_SUPPORT	−0.135557	0.273154	−0.029129	0.514985
FTA	1.664031*	0.516033	3.504951*	1.276917
ASSIST_EXPANSION	0.360287	0.405384	0.439634	0.689691
AWARE_AEC	3.113412*	0.574314	6.144167*	1.432129
AWARE_ASEAN	−0.111115	0.276927	−0.27922	0.492764
BUSINESS_ASSOCIATIONS	−0.788466*	0.246637	−1.503419*	0.434329
R^2/ Mc-Fadden R^2	0.533022		0.540655	
F-statistic /LR − statistic	221.2226		224.3906	
Prob (F/LR - statistic)	0.000000		0.000000	

Note: Huber/White robust standard errors (S.E.) are shown in the table for logit and probit models; * and ** indicate that the coefficients are statistically significant at the 5 per cent and 10 per cent levels, respectively.

Source: Authors' calculations.

for both the probit and logit models in aggregate, indicating that Thai firms may benefit from Thailand being a member of the AEC. Finally, the business association membership coefficient estimates are found to have a negative and significant effect on export decisions for both the probit and logit models in aggregate. This is an unexpected negative sign for Thai firms.

Table 8.28 shows the results of maximum likelihood estimates of the parameters of the probit and logit models for large manufacturing firms. The results from the probit and logit models show that there is only one specific factor, FTA, that is found to be statistically significantly associated with a large firm's export decision. The estimated coefficients for FTAs have a positive and significant effect on export decisions for both probit and logit models in aggregate, indicating that

TABLE 8.28
Maximum Likelihood Estimates for Parameters of Probit and Logit Models for Large Manufacturing Firms

| Models | Large Manufacturing Firms | | | |
| | Probit | | Logit | |
	Coefficients	Standard Errors	Coefficients	Standard Errors
Dependent Variable:				
Export				
Obs Dep = 0	51		51	
Obs Dep = 1	45		45	
Total Observations	96		96	
Independent Variables:				
C	−0.133544	0.494942	−0.116115	0.874096
FIRM_AGE	−0.010586	0.011070	−0.016369	0.019258
FIRM_SIZE	0.000191	0.000162	0.000295	0.000259
FOREIGN_OWNERSHIP	0.038962	0.339857	0.043792	0.600788
FAMILY_BUSINESS	0.14573	0.398914	0.187611	0.66932
INHOUSE_R&D	0.195342	0.813967	0.466340	1.586363
OUTSOURCE_R&D				
FINANCIAL_SUPPORT	0.189629	0.369637	0.345827	0.637864
FTA	1.239379**	0.551522	2.178653**	1.065373
ASSIST_EXPANSION	0.368319	0.545929	0.693145	0.939746
AWARE_AEC				
AWARE_ASEAN	−0.615597	0.377214	−1.172674	0.779445
BUSINESS_ASSOCIATIONS	−0.21128	0.321668	−0.502006	0.591507
R²/ Mc-Fadden R²	0.236426		0.241709	
F-statistic /LR − statistic	31.37587		32.07702	
Prob (F/LR − statistic)	0.000508		0.000389	

Note: Huber/White robust standard errors (S.E.) are shown in the table for probit and logit models; * and ** indicate that the coefficients are statistically significant at the 5 per cent and 10 per cent levels, respectively.

Source: Authors' calculations.

Thai manufacturing firms may benefit from any form of FTA, such as Form A (GSP), Form B (MFN) and Form D (ATIGA).

Table 8.29 presents the results of maximum likelihood estimates of the parameters from the probit and logit models for small manufacturing firms.[12] For foreign ownership, the estimated coefficients have a positive and significant effect on export participation for only the probit model for small firms, whereas the result for the

TABLE 8.29
Maximum Likelihood Estimates for Parameters of Probit and Logit Models for Small Manufacturing Firms

| Models | Small Manufacturing Firms | | | |
| | Probit | | Logit | |
	Coefficients	Standard Errors	Coefficients	Standard Errors
Dependent Variable:				
Export				
Obs Dep = 0	54		54	
Obs Dep = 1	38		38	
Total Observations	92		92	
Independent Variables:				
C	−2.41250*	0.601436	−4.195819*	1.030086
FIRM_AGE	0.001184	0.018069	0.000387	0.033596
FOREIGN_OWNERSHIP	1.745464**	0.771116	3.215921	1.818778
FAMILY_BUSINESS	−0.032781	0.479134	−0.045563	0.925657
INHOUSE_R&D				
OUTSOURCE_R&D				
FINANCIAL_SUPPORT	−1.239100	0.804763	−2.277885	1.691517
FTA	2.115818*	0.607967	3.699106*	1.165826
ASSIST_EXPANSION	2.228580*	0.851683	3.904561*	1.811201
AWARE_AEC	2.076015*	0.446307	3.674968*	0.855389
AWARE_ASEAN	−1.115936*	0.455531	−1.991216*	0.942825
BUSINESS_ASSOCIATIONS	−0.149978	0.450064	−0.242017	0.880457
R^2/ Mc-Fadden R^2	0.553382		0.549392	
F-statistic /LR − statistic	69.03007		68.5324	
Prob (F/LR − statistic)	0.00000		0.00000	

Note: Huber/White robust standard errors (S.E.) are shown in the table for probit and logit models; * and ** indicate that the coefficients are statistically significant at the 5 per cent and 10 per cent levels, respectively.

Source: Authors' calculations.

logit model is not statistically significant. This positive result implies that a rise in foreign ownership encourages firms to participate in export markets, since foreign partners bring new foreign markets and distribution, new products, managerial know-how and advanced production technology (Jongwanich and Kohpaiboon 2008). This result is also consistent with other empirical studies (Greenaway et al. 2007; Jongwanich and Kohpaiboon 2008; Aggrey et al. 2010).

With respect to FTA, coefficient estimates have a positive and significant effect on export participation for both the probit and logit models for small firms, indicating that small manufacturing firms may benefit from country membership of FTAs. For assistance in expansion, as measured by government assistance in the form of non-financial aid, the estimated coefficients have a positive and significant effect on a firm's export participation for both the probit and logit models.

For awareness of AEC, coefficient estimates are found to be positively and significantly associated with export participation for both the probit and logit models for small firms, implying that small firms may benefit from the AEC. However, the estimated coefficients for awareness of ASEAN are found to have a negative and significant effect on export participation for both the probit and logit models for small firms. This is an unexpected negative sign for Thai firms.

9.   Policy implications

Table 8.30 summarizes the main results from this study. For all the firms in the sample, the statistically significant factors associated with export participation are found to be — in-house R&D expenditure, participation in FTA, awareness of the AEC and the closer economic integration underlying this, and a relevant business association membership — using either the probit or logit model. Surprisingly, no statistically significant results for medium-sized firms are found using the probit and logit models. For the case of small firms in the sample, the following factors are found to be statistically significantly associated with export participation — foreign ownership (probit model only), participation in FTA, expansion assistance, awareness of the AEC and the ASEAN SME Policy Blueprint.

TABLE 8.30
A Summary of the Main Findings from This Study:
Statistically Significant Factors Impacting the
Export Participation of the Sample of Thai Firms

Aggregate of Firms	Large Firms	Small Firms
In-house R&D expenditure*	Participation in FTA*	Foreign ownership**
Participation in FTA*		Participation in FTA*
Awareness of AEC*		Awareness of AEC*
Business association membership*		Expansion assistance*
		Awareness of ASEAN SME Policy Blueprint/ Strategic Action Plan*

Notes: 1. * indicates statistical significance using both the probit and logit models.
2. ** indicates statistical significance using the probit model only.
3. For medium sized firms, the results from the probit and logit models produced insignificant results.
4. Total sample size is 301 firms.
Source: The authors.

These findings provide useful guidelines for SME policymakers in Thailand to enable small businesses to take advantage of closer regional integration through membership of ASEAN and the AEC. For example, measures to attract foreign ownership to locally-based small businesses carry numerous advantages such as technology transfer, managerial practices, attainment of product international standards, access to international markets and increased likelihood of participation in regional production networks (Harvie et al. 2015), access to finance from both domestic and foreign sources and spillover benefits to local firms. In this context, the provision of requisite skilled workers, good infrastructure, suppliers, a conducive and stable business and political environment would all be high priority policy dimensions. This is also linked to economic openness to domestic and international markets through participation in regional FTAs such as the ASEAN Free Trade Agreement as well as other higher forms of economic integration like AEC and the ASEAN SME Policy Blueprint/Strategic Action Plan. Suitable assistance policies in this framework, tailored to meet the needs of exporting SMEs, would further facilitate such firms in taking advantage of export market opportunities.

In a related study, Charoenrat and Harvie (2014)[13] used industrial census data and a stochastic frontier analysis to measure the technical efficiency of Thai SMEs as an indicator of their competitiveness and export readiness. They identified a number of important policy implications which are of relevance in the context of this study, as they complement the results presented here. Their key policy findings are as follows. First, there is a need to upgrade the skills of the existing workforce which will require improved provision of education and training aimed at providing appropriate skills for the labour force to meet contemporary business needs. Second, more investments in capital stock and an upgrading of technology are required. In this context, encouraging foreign investment and ownership is ideal and is consistent with the above discussion. A skilled workforce, improved capital stock and technology could be the catalysts to encourage more knowledge, skills intensive, innovative and higher value-added activities by Thai SMEs. This could enable an upgrading in the quality and production of differentiated products by local small firms enabling them to be more competitive in both the domestic and international markets, and, hence, encourage greater export participation. This improvement in product quality and in value-added activities will provide the Thai economy with the opportunity to move out of its middle income trap where it is currently situated.

As a third policy recommendation, Charoenrat and Harvie (2014) argued that more attention needs to be given to tackle ongoing regional and urban–rural inequity in the technical efficiency performance of SMEs, which is found to be sizeable and significant. This will require more investments in local physical infrastructure, improve local logistics and distribution channels, encourage and support local SME networks and value chains, promote local SME products through trade fairs and the establishment of exhibition centres for SME products domestically and internationally, encourage technology upgrading, establish business incubator centres in regional and local areas, establish and build upon existing local and regional industrial clusters, encourage the adoption of e-commerce through improved access to information and communications technology, improve local business support services, enhance the skills and capabilities of the local workforce and entrepreneurs through the provision of relevant local education and training facilities, encourage business start-ups in sectors of competitive advantage and establish special economic zones. All of these are aimed at addressing a regional disparity in the performance of SMEs with the objective of encouraging SMEs from all regions to participate in the market opportunities arising from closer regional integration.

As a fourth policy priority, Charoenrat and Harvie (2014) advocated the encouragement of all forms of entrepreneurial activity and SME ownership. Public and public limited type of ownership is given particular emphasis but this would only occur if SMEs can gain greater access to stock markets, which is currently prohibitively expensive, in particular, for small firms. Reducing the costs of this type of ownership should be addressed. The authors argued that this type of ownership has the potential to unlock greater access to finance and other resources for medium-sized SMEs in particular, facilitating their access to capital, technology and skilled labour, and enabling them to achieve faster growth, benefit from economies of scale and scope, improve their technical efficiency and competitiveness that will facilitate greater exporting activities. Reducing start-up costs and providing adequate funding for new firm start-ups and entrepreneurs are important. Establishing venture capital markets is important for start-ups in knowledge intensive and IT sectors as is the establishment of financial institutions designed to meet the financial needs of SMEs.

Fifth, and as confirmed from the sample of 301 firms used in this report, foreign ownership offers considerable potential to improve the competitiveness and exporting performance of local SMEs as it can promote technological upgrading, managerial skills and knowledge, promote good corporate governance and enable access to foreign markets. A sixth policy measure should address and highlight export market opportunities for existing products while at the same time encourage the export of higher value-added and more differentiated products. Finally, existing policy measures need to be reviewed and weaknesses addressed to achieve more broad-based and inclusive benefits to a broader range of domestic SMEs.

10. Summary

In summary, this chapter has presented a plethora of potential factors impacting the competitiveness and export participation of Thai SMEs. There are common threads in the evidence presented. Foreign ownership and investment in local enterprises is a potent force to rapidly upgrade firm competitiveness, technology and engagement in exporting.

The capital stock and technology of domestic Thai SMEs need to be improved. There is considerable regional inequality in the performance (technical efficiency) and export participation of Thai SMEs. This gap needs to be closed, otherwise certain regions in Thailand will not benefit from the effects of FTAs and regional economic integration in general, and inclusive growth and development, a key objective of the AEC, will not be achievable. There are market opportunities arising from ASEAN integration and for SMEs, in particular, from the AEC with its aim of encouraging cross border production and regional production networks. It is clear from this study that Thai small businesses are aware of these developments, and by implication the opportunities arising, and the challenges they face are to ensure that they are in a good position to take advantage of these opportunities. This can be achieved from appropriate business support measures, including access to finance, technology, skilled labour, market information and networking.

NOTES

1. The official definition of manufacturing SMEs in Thailand is based on the number of employees or the value of fixed assets. An enterprise employing up to 50 workers, or having fixed assets, excluding land, not exceeding THB 50 million (approximately US$1.65 million) in the manufacturing sector is considered a small enterprise. An enterprise employing between 51 and 200 workers or fixed assets, excluding land, between THB 51 million and THB 200 million (approximately US$1.68–6.6 million) is defined as a medium-sized enterprise in the manufacturing sector (OSMEP 2003).
2. Statistics on the exports of SMEs by sector of activity are not available as the Thai authorities do not compile these.
3. Micro enterprises are not defined separately from small enterprises.
4. Incorporating both the retail and wholesale sectors.
5. The retail sector was included in the trade and repairs sector from 2006.
6. Thailand has been very active in establishing bilateral FTAs and regional trade agreements in the Asia-Pacific region. Establishing bilateral FTAs has become a major priority of trade policy in Thailand (Chirathivat 2007; Sally 2007).
7. Innovation usually involves product, process and organizational innovations. SMEs usually focus on product innovation as this is less resource-intensive

and more in line with introducing new products or improving existing market products to meet rapidly changing market demand.

8. The First SME Promotion Plan is particularly pertinent in the context of the empirical analysis conducted in this chapter.

9. Exporting firms are those that export their products to foreign markets while non-exporting firms do not. Due to poor responses from the questionnaire on the share of production that is exported, a dummy variable approach is used in the empirical analysis. Here, an exporting firm is given a dummy variable value of 1 while a non-exporting firm is given a dummy variable of 0.

10. Defined to mean firm usage of any FTA in the conduct of their businesses.

11. Form A (GSP) is the Generalised System of Preferences (GSP), Form B (MFN) is the Most Favoured Nation treatment (MFN); Form D (ATIGA) is the ASEAN Trade in Goods Agreement (ATIGA).

12. For medium-sized firms, the results from the probit and logit models produced insignificant results as it perfectly predicts binary response failure.

13. See also Charoenrat et al. (2013) and Charoenrat and Harvie (2013).

REFERENCES

Aggrey, Niringiye, Luvanda Eliab, and Shitundu Joseph. "Determinants of Export Participation in East African Manufacturing Firms". *Current Research Journal of Economic Theory* 2, no. 2 (2010): 55–61.

Amornkitvikai, Yot, Charles Harvie, and Teerawat Charoenrat. "Measuring Technical Efficiency: The Case of Thai Manufacturing and Exporting Small and Medium Size Enterprises (SMEs)". The 7th SMEs in a Global Economy Conference: Challenges and Prospects, Kuching, Sarawak, Malaysia, 15–17 October 2010.

Baker, Matt and Rick Rudd. "Relationships between Critical and Creative Thinking". *Journal of Southern Agricultural Education Research* 51, no. 1 (2001): 173–88.

Brimble, Peter, David Oldfield, and Manusavee Monsakul. "Policies for SME Recovery in Thailand". In *The Role of SMEs in National Economies in East Asia*, edited by Charles Harvie and Boon-Chye Lee. Cheltenham: Edward Elgar Publishing, 2002.

Brooks, Albie, Suzanne Collings, and Peter Gonzales. *Accounting for Small Business: A Single Entry Approach*. Collingwood, Vic: VCTA Publishing, 1990.

Charoenrat, Teerawat and Charles Harvie. "The Efficiency of SMEs in Thai Manufacturing: A Stochastic Frontier Analysis". *Economic Modelling* 43 (December 2014): 372–93.

———. "Technical Efficiency of Thai Manufacturing SMEs: A Stochastic Frontier Analysis". *The Australasian Accounting, Business and Finance Journal* 7, no. 1 (2013): 100–21.

Charoenrat, Teerawat, Charles Harvie, and Yot Amornkitvikai. "Thai Manufacturing Small and Medium Sized Enterprise Technical Efficiency: Evidence from Firm-level Industrial Census Data". *Journal of Asian Economics* 27 (2013): 42–56.

Chirasirimongkol, Siriporn and Wichian Chutimaskul. "Information Technology for Thai Leather SME Development". The Fourth International Conference on eBusiness, Bangkok, 19–20 November 2005.

Chirathivat, Suthiphand. "Thailand's Strategy toward FTAs in the New Context of East Asian Economic Integration". *Chulalongkorn Journal of Economics* 19, no. 2 (2007): 185–214.

Cooke, Philip. "Regional Innovation Systems, Clusters, and the Knowledge Economy". *Industrial and Corporate Change* 10 (2001): 945–74.

Greenaway, David, Alessandra Guariglia, and Richard Kneller. "Financial Factors and Exporting Decisions". *Journal of International Economics* 73 (2007): 377–95.

Gregory, Gary, Charles Harvie, and Hyun-Hoon Lee. "Korean SMEs in the 21st Century: Strategies, Constraints and Performance in a Global Economy". *Economic Papers* 21, no. 3 (2002): 64–79.

Harvie, Charles. "Framework Chapter: SME Access to Finance in Selected East Asian Economies". In *Small and Medium Enterprises (SMEs) Access to Finance in Selected East Asian Economies*, edited by Charles Harvie, Sothea Oum and Dionisius Narjoko. Jakarta: Economic Research Institute for ASEAN and East Asia (ERIA), 2011.

Harvie, Charles, Dionisius Narjoko, and Sothea Oum. *Economic Integration in East Asia: Production Networks and Small and Medium Enterprises*. Singapore: Routledge, 2015.

———, eds. *Small and Medium Enterprises (SMEs) Access to Finance in Selected East Asian Economies*. Jakarta: Economic Research Institute for ASEAN and East Asia (ERIA), 2011.

Intarakamnerd, Patarapong, Pun-arj Chairatana, and Tipawan Tangchitpiboon. "National Innovation System in Less Successful Developing Countries: The Case of Thailand". *Research Policy* 31 (2002): 1445–57.

Jongwanich, Juthathip and Archanun Kohpaiboon. *Export Performance, Foreign Ownership, and Trade Policy Regime: Evidence from Thai Manufacturing*. ADB Economics Working Paper Series No. 140. Metro Manila, Philippines: Asian Development Bank, 2008.

Lertwongsatien, Chalermsak and Nitaya Wongpinunwatana. "E-commerce Adoption in Thailand: An Empirical Study of Small and Medium Enterprises (SMEs)". *Journal of Global Information Technology Management* 6, no. 3 (2003): 67–83.

Lombaerde, Philippe A.A. De. "The Paradoxes of Thailand's Pre-crisis Export Performance". *Global Economic Review* 37, no. 2 (2008): 249–64.

Mephokee, Chanin. *The Thai SMEs Development Policies: Country Report*. Bangkok: Thammasat University, 2003.

Office of Small and Medium Enterprises Promotion (OSMEP). *The White Paper on Small and Medium Enterprises of Thailand in 2012 and Trends 2013*. Bangkok: OSMEP, 2012.

————. *The White Paper on Small and Medium Enterprises of Thailand in 2011 and Trends 2012*. Bangkok: OSMEP, 2011.

————. *The White Paper on Small and Medium Enterprises of Thailand in 2010 and Trends 2011*. Bangkok: OSMEP, 2010.

————. *The White Paper on Small and Medium Enterprises of Thailand in 2009 and Trends 2010*. Bangkok: OSMEP, 2009.

————. *The White Paper on Small and Medium Enterprises of Thailand in 2008 and Trends 2009*. Bangkok: OSMEP, 2008.

————. *The White Paper on Small and Medium Enterprises of Thailand in 2007 and Trends 2008*. Bangkok: OSMEP, 2007.

————. *The 2nd SME Promotion Plan (2007–2011)*. Bangkok: OSMEP, 2007.

————. *The White Paper on Small and Medium Enterprises of Thailand in 2006 and Trends 2007*. Bangkok: OSMEP, 2006.

————. *The White Paper on Small and Medium Enterprises of Thailand in 2005 and Trends 2006*. Bangkok: OSMEP, 2005.

————. *The White Paper on Small and Medium Enterprises of Thailand in 2004 and Trends 2005*. Bangkok: OSMEP, 2004.

————. *The White Paper on Small and Medium Enterprises of Thailand in 2003 and Trends 2004*. Bangkok: OSMEP, 2003.

————. *The White Paper on Small and Medium Enterprises of Thailand in 2002 and Trends 2003*. Bangkok: OSMEP, 2002.

————. *Executive Summary of White Paper on SMEs in 2001*. Bangkok: OSMEP, 2001.

Organisation for Economic Co-operation and Development (OECD). *OECD Studies on SMEs and Entrepreneurship Thailand: Key Issues and Policies*. Paris: OECD, 2011.

————. *SME and Entrepreneurship Outlook*. Paris: OECD, 2005.

Organisation for Small & Medium Enterprises and Regional Innovation Japan (OSMRJ). *Small & Medium Enterprise Development Policies in Thailand*. Tokyo: OSMRJ, 2008.

Pholphirul, Piriya and Veera Biatasevi. "Challenges and Obstacles of Small and Medium Enterprises under a Creative Economy: The Case of Thailand". *International Business Management* 6, no. 3 (2012): 356–68.

Punyasavatsut, Chaiyuth. "Integrating SMEs into East Asia Production Networks: Thailand". In *Integrating Small and Medium Enterprises (SMEs) into the More Integrated East Asia*, edited by Vo Tri Thanh, Dionisius Narjoko and Sothea Oum. Jakarta: Economic Research Institute for ASEAN and East Asia (ERIA), 2010.

————. "SMEs in the Thai Manufacturing Industry: Linking with MNEs". In *SME in Asia and Globalization*, edited by Hank Lim. ERIA Research Project

Report 2007–5. Jakarta: Economic Research Institute for ASEAN and East Asia (ERIA), March 2008, pp. 287–321. Available at <http://www.eria. org/SMEs%20in%20The%20Thai%20Manufacturing%20Industry_Linking%20 with%20MNEs.pdf> (accessed 15 May 2009).

Regnier, Philippe. *Small and Medium Enterprises in Distress: Thailand, the East Asian Crisis and Beyond*. Burlington: Ashgate Publishing, 2000.

Rose, Raduan C., Naresh Kumar, and Lim L. Yen. "Entrepreneurs Success Factors and Escalation of Small and Medium-sized Enterprises in Malaysia". *Journal of Social Sciences* 2, no. 3 (2006): 74–80.

Sahakijpicharn, Krittakorn. "*Guanxi* Network and Business Performance of Sino-Thai SMEs". PhD thesis, School of Economics, Faculty of Commerce, University of Wollongong, 2007.

Sally, Razeen. "Thai Trade Policy: From Non-discriminatory Liberalisation to FTAs". *The World Economy* 30, no. 10 (2007): 1594–1620.

Sarapaivanich, Naruanard. "The Use of Financial Information in Financial Decisions of SMEs in Thailand". A paper for the Small Enterprise Association of Australia and New Zealand 16th Annual Conference, Ballarat, Australia, 28 September–1 October 2003.

Simpson, Mike and Nick Taylor. "The Role and Relevance of Marketing in SMEs: Towards a New Model". *Journal of Small Business and Enterprise Development* 9, no. 4 (2002): 370–82.

Tambunan, Tulus. "Development of SMEs in ASEAN with Reference to Indonesia and Thailand". *Chulalongkorn Journal of Economics* 20, no. 1 (2008): 53–58.

Tapaneeyangkul, Prasert. *Government Policies in Assisting SMEs for Sustainable Development*. Bangkok: The Office of Small and Medium Enterprise Promotion, 2001.

Theingi. "The Influence of Marketing Control and a Resource-Based View on Export Performance of SMEs in Thailand". PhD thesis, University of Western Australia, 2004.

Tippakoon, Phakpoom. "The Role of the Buyer in the Upgrading of Rural Enterprises in Thailand: Lessons from 13 Silk-Weaving Enterprises in Pak Thong Chai District, Nakhon Rachasima Province". *Forum of International Development Studies* 38 (March 2009): 157–79.

Tranh, Vo Tri, Dionisius Narjoko, and Sothea Oum. *Integrating Small and Medium Enterprises (SMEs) into the More Integrated East Asia*. ERIA Research Project Report 2009, No. 8. Jakarta: Economic Research Institute for ASEAN and East Asia (ERIA), March 2010.

Varatorn, Supannee. "Literacy through Child Activities: Community Children's Libraries and the Story – Book Projects". World Library and Information Congress: 71th IFLA General Conference and Council "Libraries – A Voyage of Discovery", Oslo, Norway, 14–18 August 2005.

9

VIETNAM SMEs' PARTICIPATION IN REGIONAL ECONOMIC INTEGRATION
Survey Results of Three Manufacturing Sectors

*Nguyen Dinh Chuc, Nguyen Ngoc Anh and
Nguyen Thi Kim Thai*

1. Introduction

During the course of development, small and medium-sized enterprises
(SMEs) are seen as the cornerstone of a national economy and
significant contributors to the prosperity of a country. SMEs play an
important role in a wide spectrum of industries in a country. The
number of SMEs dominates that of large and very large enterprises.
They contribute significantly to a country's economic growth and
employment creation of most countries. Most governments view the
SME sector as a key engine of the economy and a source of employment
creation (Harvie 2010).

The role of SMEs, however, was not recognized until the mid-1970s. Before that concentration and centralization of economic activities were seen as the main evidence of a firm's competitiveness and large firms received much attention. SMEs' contributions to economic activity only began to be a priority after the Bolton Report in the UK (1971) and the Wiltshire Report in Australia (1971) on the role of SMEs in the economies of the UK and Australia, respectively were published (Al-Qirim 2004).

In Europe, two-thirds of all new jobs are created by SMEs and more than 99 per cent of all enterprises are SMEs. In the United States, more than 99 per cent of all independent enterprises employ fewer than 500 employees, which is the definition of an SME in the United States. These SMEs employ 52 per cent of all U.S. workers (Devos et al. 2014).

In Australia, SMEs is a substantial sector, making up 95 per cent of all enterprises (Chau and Turner 2004). These enterprises contribute A\$530 billion to the economy in 2010–11, more than half of private sector economic activities, and employed over 7 million people, generating more than two thirds of private sector employment (Deloitte 2013).

In East Asia, SMEs account for about 98 per cent of all enterprises, equivalent to between 20 and 30 million businesses. In the three largest economies of East Asia — Japan, China and Korea — SMEs account for 70 per cent of enterprises in the region (China: 8 million; Japan: 5 million; and Korea: 2.6 million). The intensity ratio of SMEs is only 20 people per SME in developed countries. The regional developing countries have a ratio of about 100 people per SME, making an average of 85 people for every SME in the region. The SMEs sector creates about 60 per cent of the private sector employment and about 30 per cent of the total workforce, but contributes about 70 per cent of net employment growth of the region. Most SMEs in the region are micro enterprises with more than 80 per cent of them with less than 5 employees (Harvie and Lee 2005).

In Vietnam, SMEs accounted for 98 per cent of total enterprises in 2012, increased from 94.6 per cent in 2000. The SMEs sector created jobs for more than 5.4 million workers, 4.6 times higher than the number of jobs created by SMEs in 2000. More importantly, SMEs in Vietnam are cost effective in generating off-farm employment for the economy.[1]

Given the importance of SMEs in the economy and deeper integration into the world economy, the capacity of internationalization of SMEs in particular and competitiveness of domestic enterprise sector in general are important for the development of the country. Internationalization of SMEs is seen as a form of development of these enterprises and the domestic economic environment. The internationalization of SMEs, however, is affected by numerous factors, ranging from the size of home market, government policies, firm-specific advantages, and trade barriers (Nordstrom 1991).

With the increasing regional economic integration and the implementation of ASEAN Economic Community (AEC), this study looks into details the current situation of Vietnamese SMEs with regard to the participation into the regional economy. The study aims to identify enabling factors and obstacles to this process of Vietnamese SMEs in three sectors: (i) wooden products manufacturing; (ii) textile and garment; and (iii) food processing. A survey of 208 enterprises in these three sectors was conducted to establish a better understanding of the participation of Vietnamese enterprises in the regional economy.

With the exception of the introduction, this chapter is divided into four parts. The first part examines the current economic environment for the development of SMEs in Vietnam and discusses the Vietnamese SMEs' performance. The second part examines the current situation of the three survey sectors of the economy. The third part discusses results of the survey. The last part concludes the analyses and presents policy recommendations for strengthening integration of Vietnamese SMEs into the regional economy.

2. SMEs in Vietnam and Government Policies

SMEs' Definition

The SME definition varies from country to country in accordance to the development of the economy, characteristics of the sector and government policy. Most dominantly, the definition depends on enterprise sector situation in the countries and usually reflects the relative correlation between capital and labour in these countries. In the United States, an SME is defined as "one which is independently owned and operated and which is not dominant in its field of operation",[2] which is based on the position of the organization within the overall marketplace. Also, the definition of an SME differs according to sector in the United States, e.g. in the manufacturing sector, an SME has 500 employees or fewer, while in the services industry, an SME is defined in terms of annual receipts (US$6 million or less) (MacGregor and Vrazalic 2007).

In Australia, the Australian Bureau of Statistics (ABS) defines a small business as an enterprise employing up to 99 people, a medium one as having between 100 and 199 individuals, and a business with more than 200 employees is considered a large enterprise. In the UK, the UK Companies Act of 1989 declared an SME to be an enterprise having fewer than 50 employees and not a subsidiary of any other company (MacGregor and Vrazalic 2007).

The World Bank has its own definitions. A "micro" enterprise has less than 10 employees with total assets of less than US$10,000 and total annual sales of less than US$100,000. An enterprise is considered "small" if it employs fewer than 50 employees and has total assets or total annual sales of less than US$3 million. The medium enterprise is one with less than 300 employees and total assets or total annual sales of less than US$15 million.

In Vietnam, SMEs are officially defined by the government for the first time in Decree 90/2001/ND-CP as enterprises with registered capital of under VND 10 billion (about US$500,000) and fewer than 300 employees. These standards are generally maintained in the new definition on SMEs in Decree 56/2009/ND-CP, in which both labour and capital are used as criteria for defining SMEs. This follows international practice. In terms of labour, the practice is followed strictly, however, in terms of capital, the threshold is much lower (see Table 9.1). It reflects the fact that labour is abundant and the economy needs more capital.

TABLE 9.1
Vietnam's Definition of SMEs

Sector	Micro Enterprises	Small Enterprises		Medium Enterprises	
	Labour	Total Capital (billion VND)	Labour	Total Capital (billion VND)	Labour
Agriculture, forestry, aquaculture	<=10	<=20	10–200	20–100	200–300
Industry and construction	<=10	<=20	10–200	20–100	200–300
Trade and services	<=10	<=10	10–50	10–50	50–100

Source: Decree 56/2009/ND-CP.

SMEs in Vietnam

SMEs dominate the number of enterprises in Vietnam. According to the fourth establishment census[3] conducted by the General Statistics Office in 2012, there are about 4.9 million economic establishments in Vietnam. They create 18.9 million jobs for the economy. Among the economic establishments, 4.6 million are unregistered and operate as household businesses. It is estimated that 99.9 per cent of the total 4.9 million of economic establishments in the country are micro, small and medium businesses.

In terms of registered enterprises, SMEs accounted for 94.6 per cent of the total 41,964 enterprises in 2000 (see Figure 9.1 and Table 9.2), when the new Enterprise Law was enacted. Since then the establishment of new enterprises has been raising rapidly. The total number of enterprises has increased 7.7 times from 2000 to 2012. During this period, the number of large enterprises has increased 2.2 times and the

FIGURE 9.1
Share of SMEs in Total Number of Enterprises

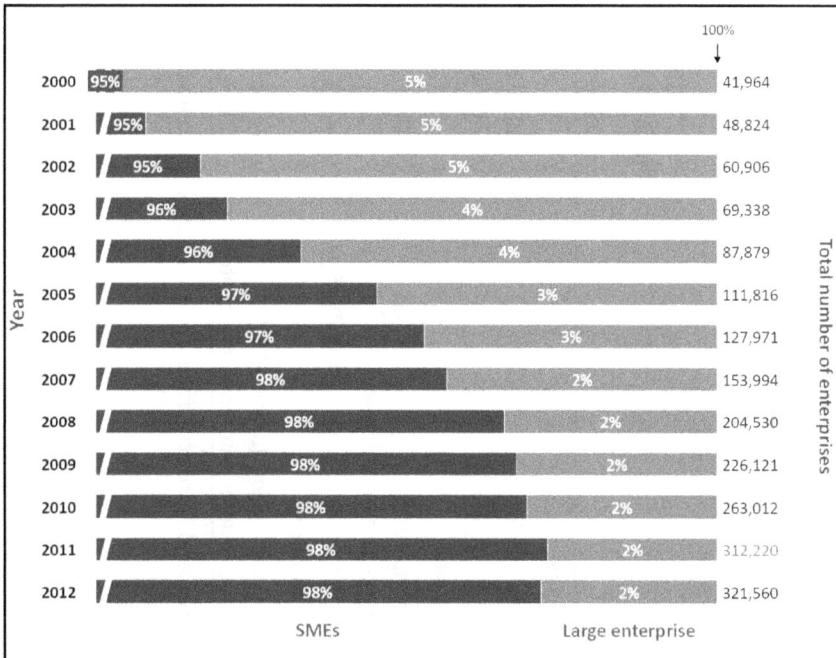

Year	SMEs	Large enterprise	Total number of enterprises
2000	95%	5%	41,964
2001	95%	5%	48,824
2002	95%	5%	60,906
2003	96%	4%	69,338
2004	96%	4%	87,879
2005	97%	3%	111,816
2006	97%	3%	127,971
2007	98%	2%	153,994
2008	98%	2%	204,530
2009	98%	2%	226,121
2010	98%	2%	263,012
2011	98%	2%	312,220
2012	98%	2%	321,560

Source: General Statistics Office, *Annual Enterprises Census 2001–2013*.

TABLE 9.2
SMEs in Vietnam, 2000–12

	2000	2005	2009	2010	2011	2012
Enterprises						
Number of SMEs	39,678	108,389	222,023	258,505	307,438	316,431
Percentage of all enterprises	94.6%	96.9%	98.2%	98.3%	98.5%	98.4%
Employment						
Employment (person)	1,168,611	2,373,046	4,263,976	4,824,587	5,423,237	5,616,141
Percentage of all employees	35%	40%	50%	50%	53%	49%
Persons engaged per enterprise (person)	29.5	21.9	19.2	18.7	17.6	17.7
Tax contribution						
Total tax contribution (billion VND)	18,582	53,504	138,566	219,291	189,889	241,996
Percentage of total enterprise tax contribution	30.7%	34.7%	43.2%	42.7%	45.0%	38.8%

Source: General Statistics Office, *Annual Enterprises Census, 2001–2013*.

number of SMEs has increased by nearly 8 times. It is clear that most of the newly established enterprises are SMEs. In 2011, they accounted for 98.5 per cent of total enterprises in Vietnam (see Figure 9.1).

The Vietnamese SMEs have similar characteristics with SMEs in other countries. An SME in Vietnam employs an average of 18 persons, which is very close to the average of 20 in Europe. The average size of SMEs in Vietnam has been reducing over the years, from 29.5 labours per enterprise in 2000 to 21.9 labours per enterprise in 2005 and only 17.7 labours per enterprise in 2012. Together SMEs in Vietnam have surpassed large enterprises in terms of jobs creation. Among registered enterprises, the share of employment created by SMEs has increased from 35 per cent of total employment in 2000 to 51 per cent in 2012 (see Figure 9.2).

FIGURE 9.2
Total Employment of Enterprises: SMEs vs. Large Enterprises

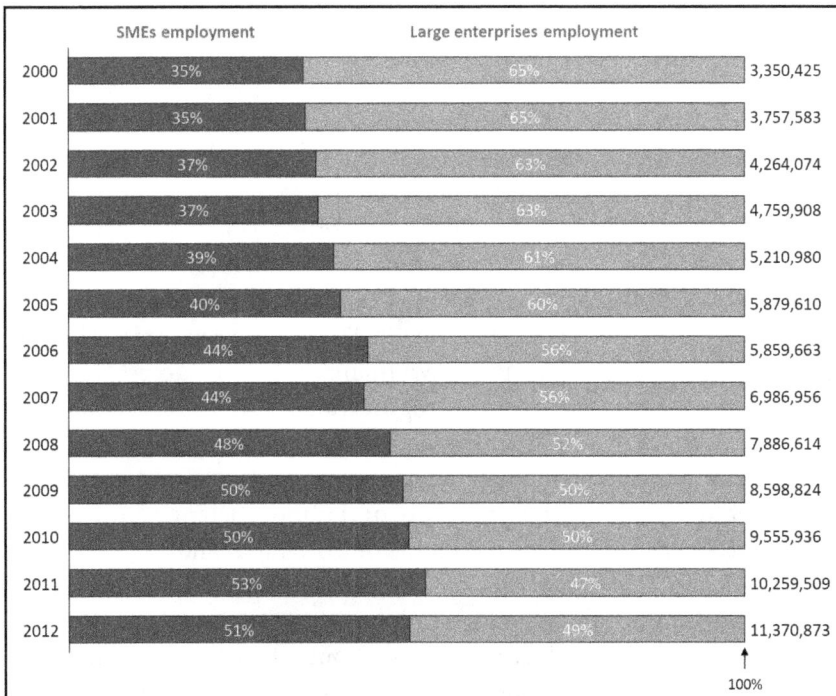

Year	SMEs employment	Large enterprises employment	Total
2000	35%	65%	3,350,425
2001	35%	65%	3,757,583
2002	37%	63%	4,264,074
2003	37%	63%	4,759,908
2004	39%	61%	5,210,980
2005	40%	60%	5,879,610
2006	44%	56%	5,859,663
2007	44%	56%	6,986,956
2008	48%	52%	7,886,614
2009	50%	50%	8,598,824
2010	50%	50%	9,555,936
2011	53%	47%	10,259,509
2012	51%	49%	11,370,873

100%

Source: General Statistics Office, *Annual Enterprises Census 2001–2013*.

SMEs in Vietnam consist primarily of non-state enterprises. Non-state SMEs accounted for 97 per cent of total Vietnamese SMEs in 2011. The ratio of SMEs in non-state enterprises has increased from 98.6 per cent in 2000 to 99.2 per cent in 2011. The ratio of SMEs in state-owned enterprises (SOEs) has reduced very slightly from 72.7 per cent in 2000 to 72.2 per cent in 2011. There was a small increase in the ratio of SMEs among foreign-invested enterprises (FIEs), which were 81.4 per cent in 2000 and 83.3 per cent in 2011 (see Table 9.3).

TABLE 9.3
SMEs by Ownership (%)

	2000	2005	2011
State-owned enterprises	72.7	64.9	72.2
Non-state enterprises	98.6	98.8	99.2
Foreign-invested enterprises (FIEs)	81.4	78.9	83.3

In terms of number of enterprises and jobs created, the performance of SMEs has been improving in the past years. Total revenue created by SMEs has increased from 47 per cent in 2000 to 55 per cent in 2011 before reducing to 50 per cent in 2012 (see Figure 9.3). Their share of contribution to stage budget has also increased from 31 per cent in 2000 to 39 per cent in 2012 (see Figure 9.4).

Despite making strong impression on the growth of the number of enterprises as well as the number of jobs created, there are still many difficulties faced by SMEs. Harvie (2007) summarizes impediments to the development of SMEs in Vietnam, including access to land, access to finance, troublesome regulations, access to technology, access to market, access to information, access to skilled human resources, access to information etc. According to the surveys conducted in 2002 and 2005 by the Institute of Labour Science and Social Affairs (ILSSA) in the Ministry of Labour, Invalids and Social Affairs (MOLISA) and University of Copenhagen (Denmark), most important constrains to growth as perceived by entrepreneurs include the shortage of capital and credit, harsh competition in the markets, products not satisfying needs of buyers and lack of access to production sites.

FIGURE 9.3
Share of SMEs in Total Revenue

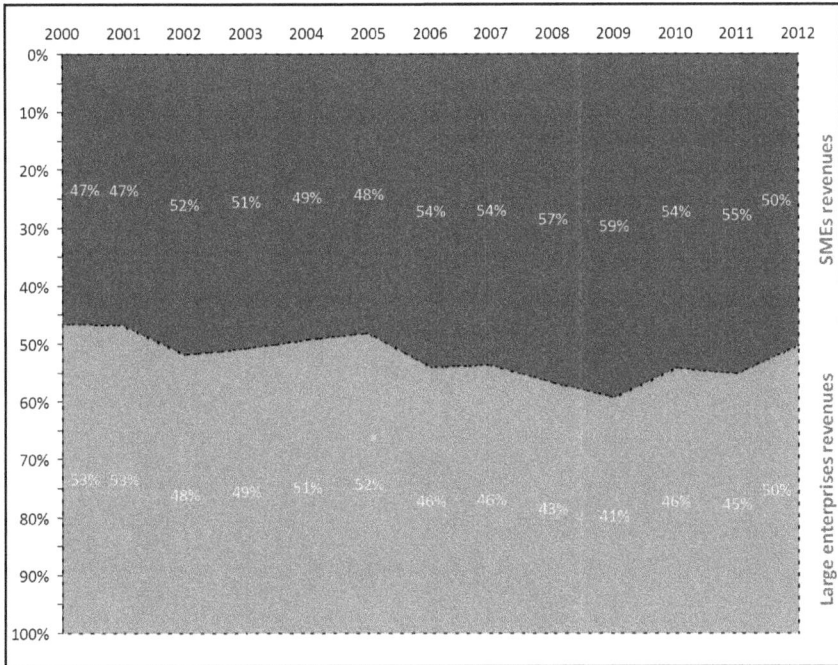

Source: General Statistics Office, *Annual Enterprises Census 2001–2013*.

Over the past decades, Vietnam has consistently implemented its economic liberalization policy. This results in a more open economy with many bilateral and multilateral trade agreements that have been concluded and implemented. In addition, the existence of FIEs creates huge pressure on domestic enterprises in terms of both mobilizing skilled labour force and competition in domestic market. Over the long term, with the fierce competition in the market and the "creative destruction" process, this will certainly result in a competitive SMEs sector in Vietnam. However, at the moment, SMEs are facing huge difficulties in development.

The development strategy for SMEs drafted by the Ministry of Planning and Investment (MPI) in 2012 pointed out that SMEs have low competitiveness partly due to their outdated technology and equipment. Estimation by MPI shows that the majority of Vietnamese

FIGURE 9.4
State Budget Contribution: SMEs vs. Large Enterprises

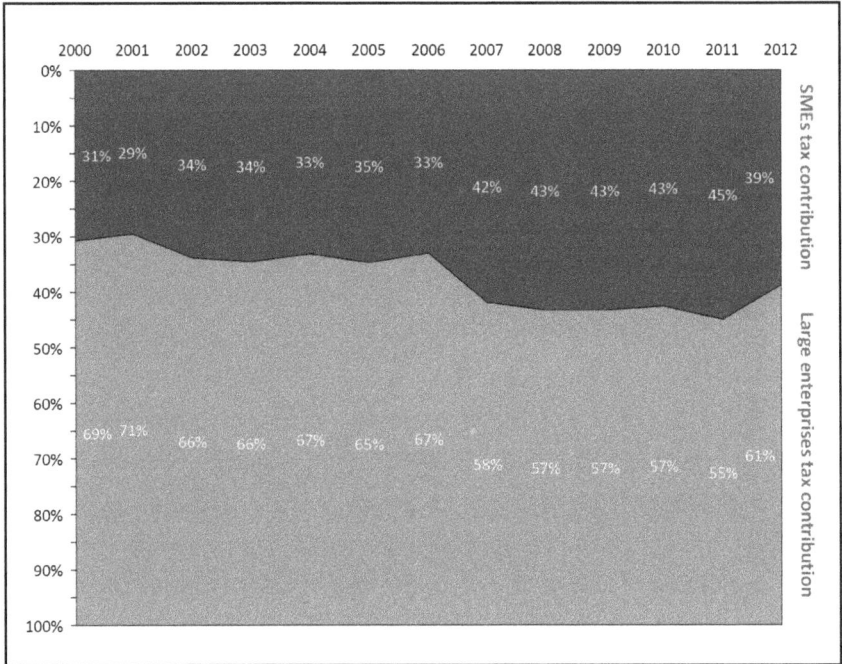

Source: General Statistics Office, *Annual Enterprises Census 2001–2013*.

enterprises are using technology of three or four generations behind the world's average.

Government Policies to Develop SMEs

Support for SMEs' development is given attention by the Vietnamese government. The support is given in various aspects, including establishment of enterprises, legal support, capital access, human resource development, market penetration, and technology development. The legal environment for the establishment and operation of SMEs in particular and firms in general has been improved significantly with the revised enterprise law and other related legal documents. Particularly, there are several reforms regarding the establishment and operation of enterprises specified in the Enterprise Law 2014. The law separates the establishment of an enterprise from the establishment of an investment project. In which, at the point in time for the establishment of an enterprise, business registration and licence for conditional business sectors are not taken care by the investors. The established enterprises are also proactive in conducting their businesses without concern on business registration as required by the previous enterprise law. In other words, the new enterprise law abandons the requirement for declaration of business sectors by enterprises.

The regulation on stamp of enterprises is also eased to allow enterprises to decide on the form, content, and number of stamps used. Enterprise documents are not required to be stamped, except those requested by their counterparts or by laws. The law redefines SOEs as those with 100 per cent state capital. Other enterprises with state capital of less than 100 per cent will be treated as normal shareholding or limited liability companies. The law also includes new regulations on social enterprises which are differentiated from other enterprises by their use of earned profits. Another reform is that an enterprise can assign their legal representative at their will, instead of a representative specified by law as previously did. These reforms by the revised enterprise law are expected to bring more motivation for the establishment and operation of enterprises in general and SMEs in particular in Vietnam.

In addition, the government has designed a programme to support human resource development for SMEs. The programme is managed by the Agency of Enterprise Development in the Ministry of Planning and Investment to provide start-up enterprises with knowledge and to strengthen governance capacity of entrepreneurs and managers of SMEs. The government supports up to 50 per cent of the total expenditure of training courses. Trainees who live in certain areas will be supported with 100 per cent of accommodation and living costs during the training course (AED 2014).

Internationalization and market penetration of SMEs also receive support from the Ministry of Industry and Trade via the national trade promotion programme. This programme provides various supports to SMEs, including provision of information, consultancy and short-term training courses, and funds for organizing and participating in international trade fairs and conferences. The government covers up to 100 per cent of total expenditure for such activities.

Financial access has been provided to SMEs under various programmes, including financing programmes for supporting industries, credit guarantee funds, SMEs development funds, and development credits and export credits of the Vietnam Development Bank (VDB). In addition, production of SMEs is also supported from the cleaner industrial manufacturing fund, industrial production supporting programme, technology market development programme, and national programme for technology innovation to 2020.[4]

In general, the government of Vietnam has realized the importance of SMEs in the economy and has paid attention to design various support programmes for SMEs. These support programmes provide SMEs with legal supports, management and governance knowledge and skills, financial access, trade promotion, market penetration, and technology upgrading. The results, however, are limited. The following analysis aims to get a better understanding of Vietnam SMEs' participation in regional economic integration and the enabling factors and obstacles to SMEs based on the survey conducted on the textile and garment, food and beverage, and wood processing industries.

3. Current Situation of the Surveyed Industries

In this research, three manufacturing sectors have been chosen for investigating the participation of Vietnamese SMEs in regional production networks. They are textile and garment, food and beverage, and wood processing industries. These are among the most active industries of Vietnam over the past few years. The following sections describe the three sectors in the economy of Vietnam and government policies towards their development.

Textile and Garment Industry

In recent years, the textile and garment industry has become one of the major exporting sectors of Vietnam. Joining the World Trade Organization (WTO) and signing free trade agreements (FTAs) have brought positive impacts on this sector. After becoming a member of WTO, the export turnover of this sector has increased from US$5.9 billion in 2006 to US$15.8 billion in 2011. In 2011, the textile and garment industry had occupied the leading position on export with a turnover of US$14.4 billion, increasing about 9.1 per cent

(US$1.2 billion) compared to 2010.[5] In 2012, the textile and garment sector had reclaimed the first place with an export value of US$13.2 billion, increasing 17.9 per cent compared with 2011.[6] In 2013, this sector had been ranked in second place after telephone, mobile phone, and components industry, with a turnover of US$17.9 billion, increasing 24.4 per cent in comparison with 2012.[7]

Vietnam's textiles and garments have been exported to over 180 countries and territories all over the world, including large and important markets such as the United States, Japan, Korea, Germany, Spain and United Kingdom. Table 9.4 shows the statistics for the top three largest markets — the United States, Japan and Korea.

TABLE 9.4
Export Turnover and Three Major Markets of Vietnam's Textile and Garment Industry, 2011–13

Export Value and Markets	2011		2012		2013	
	Export Value (billion USD)	Growth Rate (%)	Export Value (billion USD)	Growth Rate (%)	Export Value (billion USD)	Growth Rate (%)
Total Export Value	**13.2**	**17.9**	**14.4**	**9.1**	**17.9**	**24.4**
Main markets						
United States	6.8	10.9	7.44	8.9	8.8	17.8
Japan	1.7	52.7	1.96	17.2	2.4	21.5
Korea	0.807	98.4	1	25.4	1.6	56.3

Source: General Statistics Office, Vietnam's export and import of commodities in 2011, 2012, 2013.

It is expected that with the Comprehensive and Progressive Agreement for Trans-Pacific Partnership (CPTPP), FTAs with Korea, the European Union, and the Eurasian Customs Union, the opportunities for the development of Vietnam's textile and garment industry will expand. According to Vietnam Textile and Apparel Association, in 2015,[8] exports to the U.S., EU and Japanese markets are estimated to grow at 13 per cent, 17 per cent and 9 per cent, respectively. In other words, with the current growth momentum, Vietnam could be in the top ten leading countries in garment and textile by export turnover.

Vietnam's textile and garment industry has used the advantage of abundant and cheap labour to facilitate the development of the sector (Dinh 2013). With deep regional and global economic integration, it is expected that Vietnam's textile and garment enterprises will expand their market to developing countries, in addition to the current markets in developed countries. The industry can compete internationally and satisfy the demand of domestic and international markets, especially in the United States, European Union and Japan and orients toward potential markets in China, New Zealand, India and Russia.

The major obstacles facing the sector are intrinsic barriers including the quality of labour and input costs which outweigh the advantage of low-cost labour in Vietnam (Dinh 2013). Besides, Vietnam textile and garment industry has to face other restrictions and obstacles. One such barrier is the low starting point of the industry, which mainly follows CMT (Cutting–Making–Trimming) production modality that brings less value than FOB (Freight on Board) or ODM[9] (Original Design Manufacturer) production modalities. Furthermore, there are a number of obstacles to improving the competitiveness of the sector during the process of integration into the global economy. The main hindrances are that supporting industries have not been developed yet, primary materials have to be imported, the outsourcing ratio is high and competiveness is weaker than other countries in the region. The second barrier is the legal framework with unfinished and low-quality legal documents governing the operation of the industry. The third obstacle is that SMEs in Vietnam have no capacities to defend themselves in anti-dumping lawsuits, resulting in loses in trade disputes when many larger markets have utilized the barriers of technology, sanitary, safety, environment, social responsibility and anti-subsidy to protect domestic producers.

The textile and garment industry has always been a key sector of Vietnam's economy. With the rapid growth and strong development, this sector plays an important role not only in economic growth but also in maintaining trade balance. The government of Vietnam has planned for the industry to be ranked in the top second or third place among the world's textile exporters by 2017–20. Simultaneously, it is expected that Vietnam will have 5–7 per cent leading brands integrating into the global market by 2020.[10] Besides, textile enterprises also confirmed that Vietnam textile industry is a strong competitor in the international market.[11]

Besides implementing common policies, the textile and garment sector also focuses on a number of particular policies to facilitate sector development. In fact, textile and garment enterprises are paying attention on human resource policies. Given the current condition, policies towards the development of the labour force and training high quality workforce to fulfil market demand are preferable.[12] Furthermore, it is necessary to have better policies for female workers, who are a major workforce in this sector, and to establish gender equality in this industry.[13]

On the other hand, the capital invested in technology has been strengthened and modern equipment and machinery have been installed. However, as analysed above, the textile industry should concentrate on investment projects in order to complete the supply chain (fiber–fabric–dye–clothing manufacture); thus this sector can diversify supply sources, increase localization rates and shift to ODM production modality. If Vietnam's textile and garment industry succeeds in this orientation, it can enhance competitiveness as well as close the gap with the textile and garment industry in China.

The extensive integration into regional and global markets leads to Vietnam's textile and garment enterprises attempting to fulfill huge quantities and strict requirements on quality and origin of products.[14] Besides, it is important to affiliate with enterprises in this sector to boost export and enhance competitiveness.[15]

Food and Beverage Manufacturing

Food and beverage industry plays an important role and contributes significantly to improving the competitiveness of the economy in integrating into regional and global markets.[16] The industry includes alcohol-beer-beverages; milk and milk products; vegetable oil; processed food; starch and processed starch; and food industry. At present, the food and beverage industry contributes 15 per cent of GDP and this contribution is still increasing. The revenue of processed food industry outperformed that of the beverage industry.

According to the Ministry of Industry and Trade, food consumption is expected to grow by 5.1 per cent per year. Consumption per capita is about VND 5.8 million per year (equivalent to US$386 per year). In terms of profit, the statistics on the top 1,000 corporate taxpayers in 2013 illustrates that food and beverage industry has the second highest ROE (Return on Equity) and ROA (Return on Total Assets), behind the telecommunications sector. In the list of taxpayers, the food and beverage industry is also ranked in the top five, behind banking-finance-insurance, telecommunications, minerals and petroleum, and construction and real estate sectors.[17]

FIGURE 9.5
Revenue of the Food and Beverage Industry (billion VND)

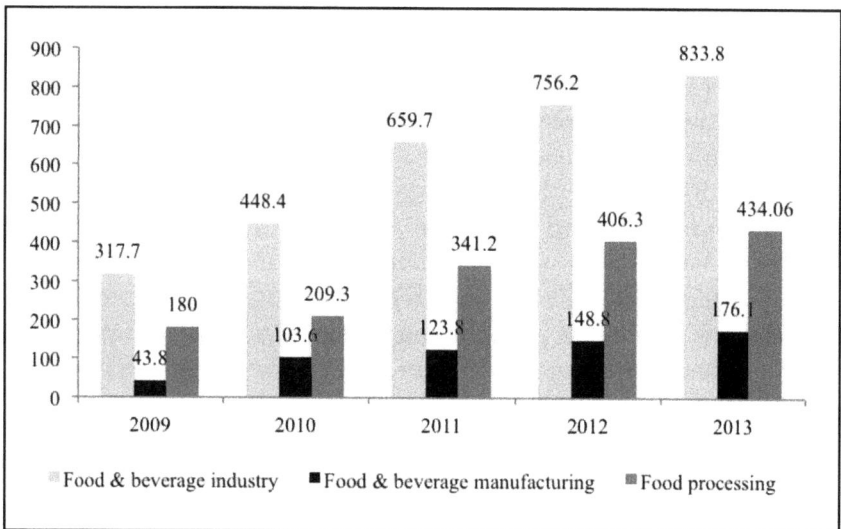

Source: Vietnam Economic Growth Report 2015.

With a population of nearly 90 million people and a high GDP growth rate, Vietnam has huge potential to develop the domestic market as the demand for fresh and processed food is becoming higher and more diversified. Along with that, the government is focusing on developing the agricultural sector, which provides businesses with an opportunity to develop their supply chain and linking networks with food service providers.

Vietnam's food and beverage industry has achieved certain results, such as better manufacturing facilities and equipment; using modern technology; making more diversified and high-quality products; greater contribution to the state's budget; and meeting customers' demand better. However, to develop the industry further, the state and enterprises ought to implement better micro and macro policies.

Human resources remains a major barrier, alongside the lack of modern facilities and advanced technology. Therefore, the government and its related ministries should revise and issue new policies to improve management capacity as well as workmanship to operate modern machinery and build advanced facilities. If high-quality manpower for this industry is met, there are chances that the industry can compete in quality and hence goods can be sold at higher prices.[18]

Today, businesses tend to accelerate the process of equitization and are restructuring to improve production efficiency, as well as adjusting to suit market conditions and increasing state management over food safety and hygiene. This is to raise product quality, marking and packaging, comply with requirements and regulations as well as adjust to suit consumers' habit to facilitate penetration into domestic and international markets. There is also the need to review, convert, and supplement the standards of quality, food safety and hygiene in Vietnam to match with international standards. If these measures are well conducted, the competitiveness of the industry can be improved even further.

Wood Processing Industry

The wood processing industry is one of the economic sectors with impressive growth rates, of which processed products are within the group of highest export turnover in many consecutive recent years. The wood processing and wood products industry is receiving the government's attention in terms of policies, mechanisms to support production, and trade development (Trang and Thuy 2014).

Wood producing and processing entities can be divided into three main groups. These three groups are: (1) wood and non-timber forest products processing enterprises; (2) wood processing facilities in wood villages; and (3) households producing and selling wood furniture.

Official statistics are only available for the first group (enterprises). The second group is only statistically counted at the wood village level (there are currently 349 wood villages nationwide). The third group is totally not statistically counted.

The number of official wood processing enterprises increased tremendously in recent times. Most wood processing enterprises are small scale (MARD 2013). In terms of the size of the workforce, 46 per cent of woods processing enterprises are micro enterprises, 49 per cent are small enterprises, 1.7 per cent are medium enterprises and 2.5 per cent are large enterprises. In terms of investment, the rate for micro and small scale enterprises is 93 per cent, medium scale enterprises is 5.5 per cent and only 1.2 per cent of the enterprises are large scale. In terms of the source of capital, 5 per cent are SOEs, the remaining 95 per cent are from the private sector. Enterprises with foreign direct investment make up 16 per cent.

As an export-oriented industry, the export capacity of the wood processing industry is a good indicator of its competitiveness. Among 3,400 enterprises in the wood industry,[19] about 600–700 enterprises (i.e. about 20 per cent of all enterprises) export directly to some Asian, EU and U.S. markets, while the rest either serve as the direct exporter, or focus on the domestic market.

FIGURE 9.6
Vietnam's Wood Product Exporting Markets, 2009 and 2013

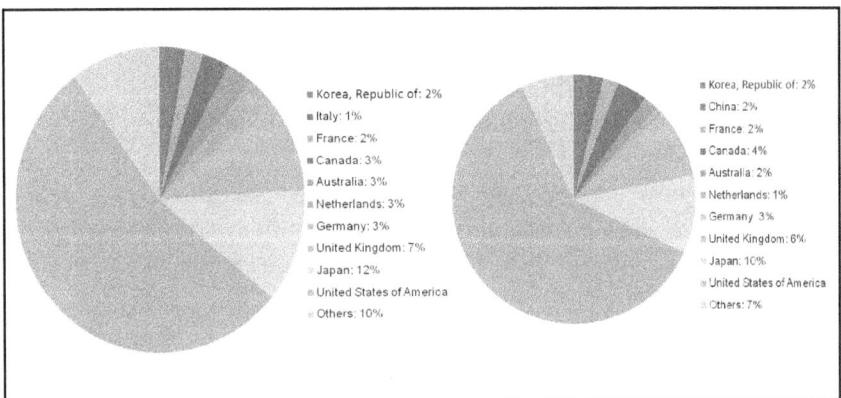

Source: trademap.org.

Currently, Vietnam's wood export ranks sixth in the ten key export sectors. At the global level, despite the differences between figures from different sources, Vietnam is among the world's largest exporters, ranked second in Asia and first in Southeast Asia. In particular, according to data from the Centre for Industrial Studies (CSIL), Vietnam is the world's sixth largest wood exporter, of which export accounts for above 80 per cent of the total value produced by Vietnam's wood processing industry. Data from the International Trade Centre (ITC) trademap of 2013 even shows that Vietnam is the world's fourth largest wood exporter (Trang and Thuy 2014).

Similar to other light industries, such as textile and garment industry and food and beverage industry mentioned above, the wood industry in Vietnam generally takes advantage of its abundant and cheap labour, and with virtue of its industrious workforce and a desire to upgrade, all of which are great advantages for the industry's development (Dinh et al. 2013). Alongside other advantages such as having a diversified and open market, and possessing better value than producers of other countries thanks to Vietnam's membership in the WTO and participation in multiple FTAs, these help to develop the export market of this industry.

Nevertheless, the small scale of both employees and investments in wood processing firms can significantly affect the sector's competitiveness and production stability. In addition, the small capital of the enterprises may also cause difficulties in responding to changes/enhancements about the requirements/technical conditions in the export markets. Thus, Vietnam's wood processing sector faces many challenges. One such challenge is the outsourcing of the processing of furniture exports, with the designs provided by clients, and the owners not dynamic in products as well as markets. A second problem is low added value. Nearly all exporters are currently selling their products under the FOB production modality, which has low profits and cannot reach out to the supply chains overseas. The third problem is low labour productivity. These are three major problems that the wood processing industry in Vietnam needs to pay special attention to overcome.

Until now, the timer industry operates mainly in households, and in small and medium enterprises. Most of the workers are from rural areas, have difficulties in apprenticeship and are slow in adapting to the working style of modern environments (Trang and Thuy 2014). Thus, it is necessary to link with stakeholders to improve the skills of the workers and to incorporate the use of the latest and most effective techniques in production.

Therefore, in order to take advantage of the opportunities and continue to increase export turnover, enterprises should proactively make adjustments to standardize the production process, and design and produce products branded in Vietnam. There is a need to identify segments of the supply chain to focus on reorganizing the production process and to create products suited for the market. Besides, it is necessary to step up marketing and promotion of the products, as well as building up the distribution system.

4. Survey on SMEs' Participation in Regional Economic Integration

Sample Characteristics

The survey was conducted with enterprises in three manufacturing sectors with an aim to examine their participation in regional economic integration. They include 78 wooden products-making firms, 82 textile and garment firms, and 48 food and beverage firms (see Figure 9.7). The sample consists of 208 enterprises operating in five provinces in the north and the south of Vietnam — Hanoi, Bac Ninh, Ho Chi Minh city, Binh Duong, Dong Nai — which are hubs to the sampled

FIGURE 9.7
The Survey Sample

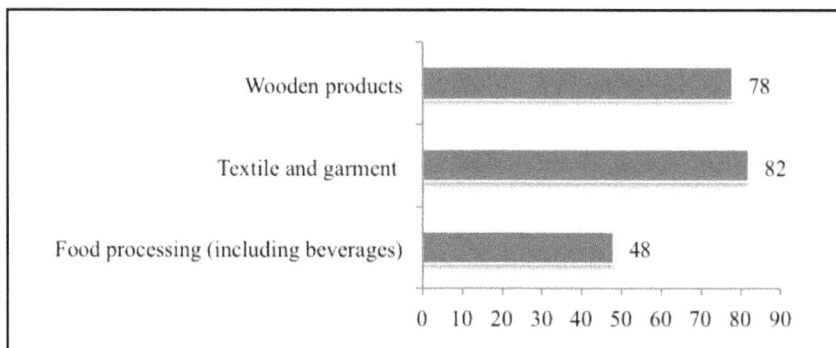

Source: Survey data.

industries. The sample is chosen randomly based on the population of enterprises in the three sectors of the five provinces and cities provided by the General Statistics Office census survey. The SMEs surveyed in the research have been established since 2000. SMEs accounted for 90 per cent of total enterprises in the research sample.

Of the total of 208 enterprises, only 2.4 per cent are SOEs; the other 97.6 per cent are not. In terms of enterprise type, 0.5 per cent are partnership enterprises, 10.6 per cent are private companies, 57.7 per cent are limited liability companies, 27.9 per cent are joint stock companies, and 3.4 per cent are cooperatives (see Table 9.5). Limited liability companies accounted for the largest share across all enterprise size, from 54 per cent of small enterprises to 75 per cent of large ones. Table 9.5 shows that all large enterprises are in the textile and garment industry, a labour-intensive sector, and 75 per cent of them have total local domestic ownership with 75 per cent in the form of limited liability companies.

One of the outstanding features of the enterprises in the sample is the closeness of the business management and ownership. This is different from other countries where joint stock companies are the main type of establishment. The number of limited liability companies accounted for 57.7 per cent of the sample, while joint stock companies are the second largest, accounting for 27.9 per cent. More importantly, enterprises in the sample are dominantly owned by family members. Table 9.5 shows that while the number of private enterprises which are mainly family type of businesses accounted for 10.6 per cent of the sample, the number of enterprises which are managed by families is 55 per cent of the total enterprises in the sample. This may imply that cooperation among different investors is limited in Vietnamese enterprises.

Among the family-owned enterprises, 94 per cent are currently managed by the founder of the enterprises. With regard to academic qualification of the managers of these enterprises, 43.5 per cent have university degrees. The second largest group in terms of academic qualification is managers with secondary or high school education at 32.4 per cent.

Among the sampled enterprises, only 6 per cent have parent companies, of which 41 per cent are medium enterprises. In terms of membership of industry and business associations, 19 per cent of the

TABLE 9.5
Basic Information of the Sample

Main Industry of Company	Micro		Small		Medium		Large		Full Sample	
	Number	Share	Number	Share	Number	Share	Number	Share	Number	Share
Food processing (including beverages)	4	20%	29	25.7%	15	21.1%	0	0%	48	23.1%
Textile and garment	7	35%	34	30.1%	37	52.1%	4	100%	82	39.4%
Wooden products	9	45%	50	44.2%	19	26.8%	0	0%	78	37.5%
Total	20	100%	113	100%	71	100%	4	100%	208	100%
Company Type	**Number**	**Share**	**Number**	**Share**	**Number**	**Share**	**Number**	**Share**	**Number**	**Share**
1. Partnership	0	0.0%	1	0.9%	0	0%	0	0.0%	1	0.5%
2. Private enterprise	2	10.0%	14	12.4%	6	8%	0	0.0%	22	10.6%
3. Limited liability	13	65.0%	61	54.0%	43	61%	3	75.0%	120	57.7%
4. Joint stock company	4	20.0%	34	30.1%	19	27%	1	25.0%	58	27.9%
5. Cooperative	1	5.0%	3	2.7%	3	4%	0	0.0%	7	3.4%
Total	20	100%	113	100%	71	100%	4	100%	208	100%
Local Domestic Ownership (%)	**Number**	**Share**	**Number**	**Share**	**Number**	**Share**	**Number**	**Share**	**Number**	**Share**
0	0	0%	6	5.3%	5	7.0%	1	25.0%	12	5.8%
50	0	0%	1	0.9%	0	0.0%	0	0.0%	1	0.5%
100	20	100%	106	93.8%	66	93.0%	3	75.0%	195	93.8%
Total	20	100%	113	100%	71	100%	4	100%	208	100%
Family Business	**Number**	**Share**	**Number**	**Share**	**Number**	**Share**	**Number**	**Share**	**Number**	**Share**
No	8	40%	44	39%	39	55%	2	50%	93	45%
Yes	12	60%	69	61%	32	45%	2	50%	115	55%
Total	20	100%	113	100%	71	100%	4	100%	208	100%

Managed by Founder	Number	Share	Number	Share	Number	Share	Number	Share	Number	Share
No	0	0%	5	7%	2	6%	0	0%	7	6%
Yes	12	100%	64	93%	30	94%	2	100%	108	94%
Total	12	100%	69	100%	32	100%	2	100%	115	100%
Highest Academic Qualification of Founder	**Number**	**Share**	**Number**	**Share**	**Number**	**Share**	**Number**	**Share**	**Number**	**Share**
No formal education	0	0.0%	1	1.6%	3	10.0%	0	0.0%	4	3.7%
Primary	1	8.3%	3	4.7%	0	0.0%	0	0.0%	4	3.7%
Secondary/High School	3	25.0%	22	34.4%	8	26.7%	2	100%	35	32.4%
Vocational/Diploma	3	25.0%	12	18.8%	3	10.0%	0	0.0%	18	16.7%
University degree	5	41.7%	26	40.6%	16	53.3%	0	0.0%	47	43.5%
Total	12	100%	64	100%	30	100%	2	100%	108	100%
Parent Company	**Number**	**Share**	**Number**	**Share**	**Number**	**Share**	**Number**	**Share**	**Number**	**Share**
No	19	95%	109	96%	66	93%	2	50%	196	94%
Yes	1	5%	4	4%	5	7%	2	50%	12	6%
Total	20	100%	113	100%	71	100%	4	100%	208	100%
Association Membership	**Number**	**Share**	**Number**	**Share**	**Number**	**Share**	**Number**	**Share**	**Number**	**Share**
No	18	90%	96	85%	52	73%	3	75%	169	81%
Yes	2	10%	17	15%	19	27%	1	25%	39	19%
Total	20	100%	113	100%	71	100%	4	100%	208	100%

Source: Survey data.

enterprises in the sample reported that they have such memberships, 42 per cent of which are small and medium enterprises.

Sales, Production Cost, Employment and Innovation

Table 9.6 presents the sales activities of surveyed enterprises to their parent company, sister company, subsidiary company, other companies, SOEs, and directly to customers. Their outputs are divided into intermediate and final. In general, sales to parent company, sister company and subsidiary company are insignificant. Only 0.5 per cent, 0.5 per cent and 1 per cent of enterprises sell their intermediate outputs and 1.9 per cent, 1 per cent and 0.5 per cent sell their final products respectively to their parent company, sister company and subsidiary company. The largest customers of enterprises are other companies. Most interestingly, all large enterprises are involved in selling their final products to other companies. The fact that all large enterprises are in the textile and garment industry and all of them sell their final products to other companies means that all large enterprises outsourced the production of their final products to other companies. The remaining 33.3 per cent of large enterprises sell their intermediate outputs to other companies.

In total, 34.6 per cent of enterprises sell their intermediate products and 67.3 per cent of enterprises sell their final products to other companies. For SMEs, in terms of immediate outputs, 25 per cent of micro enterprises, 35.4 per cent of small enterprises and 36.1 per cent of medium enterprises sell their immediate outputs to other companies. Regarding final products, the share of total sales to other companies is large. Sixty-five per cent of micro enterprises, 68.1 per cent of small enterprises and 65.6 per cent of medium enterprises sell their final products to other companies.

The second most important customer is final consumers. In the survey, 57.7 per cent of enterprises reported that they sell their final products directly to consumers. Majority of small enterprises sell their final products directly to consumers (60.2 per cent), while 55 per cent of micro enterprises, 55.6 per cent of medium enterprises and 33.3 per cent of large enterprises sell final products to these customers.

SOEs are important customers of enterprises in the survey. About 9.6 per cent of enterprises sell their intermediate outputs to SOEs, while 23.6 per cent sell their final products to these customers. For SMEs, SOEs are important buyers of final products with 35 per cent of micro

TABLE 9.6
Sales Activities

	Micro				Small				Medium				Large				Total			
	Intermediate		Final		Intermediate		Final		Intermediate		Final		Intermediate		Final		Intermediate		Final	
	No	%	No	%	No	%	No	%	No	%	No	%	No	%	No	%	No	%	No	%
1. To Parent Company																				
Yes	0	0	0	0	0	0	1	0.9	0	0	2	2.8	1	33.3	1	33.1	1	0.5	1	1.9
No	0	0	0	0	1	0.9	0	0	2	2.8	0	0	0	0	0	0	3	1.4	0	0
N.A.	20	100	20	100	112	99.1	112	99.1	70	97.2	70	97.2	2	66.7	2	66.7	204	98.1	204	98.1
Total	20	100	20	100	113	100	113	100	72	100	72	100	3	100	3	100	208	100	208	100
2. To Sister Company																				
Yes	0	0	0	0	0	0	2	1.8	1	1.4	0	0	0	0	0	0	1	0.5	2	1
No	0	0	0	0	2	1.8	0	0	0	0	1	1.4	0	0	0	0	2	1	1	0.5
N.A.	20	100	20	100	111	98.2	111	98.2	71	98.6	71	98.6	3	100	3	100	205	98.6	205	98.6
Total	20	100	20	100	113	100	113	100	72	100	72	100	3	100	3	100	208	100	208	100
3. To Subsidiary Company																				
Yes	0	0	0	0	2	1.8	1	0.9	0	0	0	0	0	0	0	0	2	1	1	0.5
No	0	0	0	0	0	0	1	0.9	0	0	0	0	0	0	0	0	0	0	1	0.5
N.A.	20	100	20	100	111	98.2	111	98.2	72	100	72	100	3	100	3	100	206	99	206	99
Total	20	100	20	100	113	100	113	100	72	100	72	100	3	100	3	100	208	100	208	100
4. To Other Companies																				
Yes	5	25	13	65	40	35.4	77	68.1	26	36.1	47	65.6	1	33.3	3	100	72	34.6	140	67.3
No	12	60	4	20	58	51.3	21	18.6	36	50	15	20.8	2	66.7	0	0	108	51.9	40	19.2
N.A.	3	15	3	15	15	13.3	15	13.3	10	13.9	10	13.9	0	0	0	0	28	13.5	28	13.5
Total	20	100	20	100	113	100	113	100	72	100	72	100	3	100	3	100	208	100	208	100

TABLE 9.6 (continued)

	Micro				Small				Medium				Large				Total			
	Intermediate		Final		Intermediate		Final		Intermediate		Final		Intermediate		Final		Intermediate		Final	
	No	%	No	%	No	%	No	%	No	%	No	%	No	%	No	%	No	%	No	%
5. To SOEs																				
Yes	1	5	7	35	13	11.5	26	23	6	8.3	16	22.2	0	0	0	0	20	9.6	49	23.6
No	7	35	1	5	21	18.6	8	7.1	15	20.8	5	6.9	0	0	0	0	43	20.7	14	6.7
N.A.	12	60	12	60	79	69.9	79	69.9	51	70.8	51	70.8	3	100	3	100	145	69.7	145	69.7
Total	20	100	20	100	113	113	113	100	72	100	72	100	3	100	3	100	208	100	208	100
5. Directly to Customers																				
Yes			11	55			68	60.2			40	55.6			1	33.3			120	57.7
No			0	0			0	0			1	1.4			0	0			1	0.5
N.A.			9	45			45	39.8			31	43.1			2	66.7			87	41.8
Total			20	100			113	100			72	100			3	100			208	100

Source: Survey data; Note: N.A. – not answered.

enterprises, 23 per cent of small enterprises and 22.2 per cent of medium enterprises sell their final outputs to SOEs. The share of SMEs selling their intermediate outputs to SOEs is much smaller. Large enterprises do not sell their products, either intermediate or final, to SOEs.

Table 9.7 shows that most of the enterprises carry out their production in-house. About 75.7 per cent of enterprises complete their outputs totally in-house, 2.4 per cent completely outsource their production activities and 21.8 per cent use both in-house and outsourced production. Regarding large enterprises, 100 per cent of them use in-house production. Among SMEs, 75.3 per cent have completely in-house production and only 2.5 per cent completely outsource their production. The share of SMEs using both in-house and outsourced production is 22.2 per cent.

In terms of production costs, raw materials accounted for the largest share of the total production costs at 40.62 per cent in 2013 and 41.14 per cent in 2014. While SMEs have very similar share of raw materials in production costs, large enterprises spend less on raw materials. Large enterprises spent 31.25 per cent of the total production costs on raw materials in both 2013 and 2014. These figures are lower than those of SMEs.

The second largest item in production costs of the surveyed enterprises is salaries and wages. In 2013, salaries and wages accounted for 22.61 per cent of total production costs; for 2014 the figure is 22.7 per cent. Among types of enterprises, salaries and wages of micro enterprises are the lowest, accounting for 16 per cent and 16.1 per cent of total production costs for 2013 and 2014 respectively. Compared with other types of enterprises, large enterprises pay more for salaries and wages. They accounted for 27.5 per cent in both 2013 and 2014.

Intermediate inputs are the third largest item in production costs of responded enterprises. They contributed 17.53 per cent in 2013 and 17.04 per cent in 2014 of the total costs of all enterprises. Large and micro enterprises pay higher share for intermediate input compared to small and medium firms. For large enterprises, it is intermediate inputs and not salaries and wages that are the second largest item in production costs.

In terms of sources for inputs in 2014, the survey results show that most of the enterprises use local inputs. The share of enterprises that use 75 to 100 per cent local inputs is 77.3 per cent. But the share of enterprises that use local inputs of less than 25 per cent is also

TABLE 9.7
Production Activities

	Micro		Small		Medium		Large		Total	
	No.	%	No.	%	No.	%	No.	%	No.	%
1. Production Process										
Completely in-house	13	72.2	87	77	53	73.6	3	100	156	75.7
Completely outsourced	2	11.1	2	1.8	1	1.4	0	0	5	2.4
Both in-house and outsourced	3	16.7	24	21.2	18	25	0	0	45	21.8
Total	18	100	113	100	72	100	3	100	206	100
2. Production Costs (%)	*2013*	*2014*	*2013*	*2014*	*2013*	*2014*	*2013*	*2014*	*2013*	*2014*
2.1. Raw materials	40.9	42.4	41.17	41.96	40.19	39.99	31.25	31.25	40.62	41.14
2.1. Intermediate inputs	24.6	25.75	16.66	15.95	16.34	15.56	26.25	28.75	17.53	17.04
2.3. Utilities costs	10.9	10.1	12.85	13.33	15.73	15.91	8.93	10.16	13.55	13.80
2.4. Interest payments	3.9	3.45	3.58	3.48	4.11	4.19	3.83	0.08	3.79	3.65
2.5. Salaries and wages	16	16.1	23.69	23.34	22.52	23.32	27.5	27.5	22.61	22.70
2.6. Others	2.1	2.2	2.05	1.94	1.10	1.02	2.25	2.25	1.74	1.67
3. Sources of Inputs (2014)	*No.*	*%*	*No.*	*%*	*No.*	*%*	*No.*	*%*	*No.*	*%*
3.1. Local										
Local inputs less than 25%	1	5	10	9.1	9	13.8	2	66.7	22	11.1
Local inputs from 25–50%	1	5	4	3.6	5	7.7	0	0	10	5.1
Local inputs from 50–75%	0	0	6	5.5	6	9.2	1	33.3	13	6.6
Local inputs from 75–100%	18	90	90	81.8	45	69.2	0	0	153	77.3
Total	20	100	110	100	65	100	3	100	208	100
3.2. Foreign	*No.*	*%*	*No.*	*%*	*No.*	*%*	*No.*	*%*	*No.*	*%*
Yes	3	15	33	29.2	43	40.3	3	100	68	32.7
No	17	85	80	70.8	29	59.7	0	0	140	67.3
Total	20	100	113	100	72	100	3	100	208	100

Source: Survey data.

significant at 11.1 per cent in 2014. Micro and small enterprises seemed to depend on local inputs for their production. The number of micro and small enterprises that use 75 to 100 per cent local inputs are 90 per cent and 81.8 per cent respectively. Large enterprises, however, are different. The share of large enterprises that use less than 25 per cent of local inputs accounted for 66.7 per cent.

The number of enterprises that use foreign inputs for their production is significant. The survey statistics shows that 32.7 per cent of enterprises use imported inputs. Hundred per cent of large enterprises use imported inputs, while 40.3 per cent of medium enterprises use imported inputs. Only 15 per cent of micro enterprises use foreign inputs for their production.

In terms of employment, responded enterprises employ on average 52.92 full-time and 17.92 part-time labours in 2013 and 56.4 full-time and 19.74 part-time labour in 2014 (see Table 9.8). There is a trend of expansion in terms of firm size during 2013 and 2014 from the employment aspect. Female workers accounted for more than 50 per cent of the total employees in surveyed enterprises. Large enterprises use more female workers than male workers. The shares of female workers in large enterprises are 68.3 per cent in 2013 and 71.6 per cent in 2014. Foreign workers accounted for a tiny share of the total number of workers. In 2013, foreign workers accounted for 5.6 per cent of total labour and this reduced to 0.4 per cent in 2014.

The largest share of employment comes from plant and machine operators, and assemblers. They accounted for 61 per cent of total employees, but earned only 46 per cent of total salaries and wages on average. Service and sales employees accounted for the second largest share in total employment at 14 per cent. Supervisory and clerical employees accounted for the third largest share and managers and professionals accounted for the fourth largest share of total employment.

The survey shows that the better paid employees are engineers and technicians, who accounted for 4 per cent of employment but 9 per cent of salaries and wages. Next are service and sales employees who made up 14 per cent of total employees but earned 22 per cent of salaries and wages of an average firm. The third better paid group is managers and professionals, who earned 13 per cent of the total salaries and wages while made up only 8 per cent of total employment. Supervisory and clerical employees are relative well earned since their

TABLE 9.8
Human Resources

	Micro		Small		Medium		Large		Total	
	2013	2014	2013	2014	2013	2014	2013	2014	2013	2014
Workforce										
Full-time workers (No.)	11.25	9	25.21	25.96	95.92	103.49	324	388	52.92	56.4
Part-time workers (No.)	11.1	10.5	15.95	16.28	23.57	28.5	0	0	17.92	19.74
Female workers (share in total)	50.80%	50.30%	46.40%	47.05%	54.90%	56.20%	68.30%	71.6	50.10%	50.80%
Foreign workers (share in total)	–	0	8.06%	0.68%	3.60%	0.28%	0.37%	0.11%	5.60%	0.40%
Workforce and Salaries (2014) *(average per firm)*	*No. of workers*	*Total wage (VND mill.)*	*No. of workers*	*Total wage (VND mill.)*	*No. of workers*	*Total wage (VND mill.)*	*No. of workers*	*Total wage (VND mill.)*	*No. of workers*	*Total wage (VND mill.)*
Managers and professionals	1.8	181.65	2.68	308.67	5.7	902.38	2.33	348	3.6	506.22
Engineers and technicians	0.47	198	1.18	196.48	3.51	545.88	1.67	378	1.9	356.9
Supervisory and clerical staff	1.37	151.5	2.91	217.04	10.21	775.34	10.33	622.67	5.4	436.07
Plant and machine operators, and assemblers	4.21	354	12.29	933.75	48.83	2827.31	252.33	17870	27.1	1861.5
Service and sales workers	1.47	217.67	3	382.69	12.23	1480.44	20	2880	6.3	882.8
Worker Qualification (%)		%		%		%		%		%
No formal education		0		0.3		0		0		0
Primary		5.2		3.7		5.6		6.8		4.5
Secondary/High School		58.6		62.9		60.1		82.3		61.8
Vocational/Diploma		21.8		19.6		21.7		7.3		20.9
University degree		14.2		13.3		12.3		3.4		12.9
Foreign Workers	*No.*	%	*No.*	%	*No.*	%	*No.*	%	*No.*	%
Yes	0	0	8	7.1	7	9.7	1	33.3	16	7.7
No	20	100	105	92.9	65	90.3	2	66.7	192	92.3
N.A.	0	0	0	0	0	0	0	0	0	0
Total	20	100	113	100	72	100	3	100	208	100

Source: Survey data; Note: N.A. – not answered.

12 per cent of employment accounted for 11 per cent of salaries and wages. The group of employees that earned the least is plant and machine operators, and assemblers.

In terms of education, employees of surveyed enterprises have good qualifications. About 33.8 per cent of them have vocational/ diploma or university and higher degrees. Workers who attended secondary and high schools accounted for 61.8 per cent of total employment. The survey also shows that hiring foreign workers is not popular in these three manufacturing sectors. Only 7.7 per cent of enterprises hire foreign workers and not a single micro enterprise has this practice.

Table 9.9 shows innovation expenditure, innovation activities and turnover from new products and services of enterprises in the survey. In terms of innovation expenditure, the mean expenditure for in-house R&D of an average enterprise is 10 per cent of total expenditure for innovation during the period 2012–14. Outsourcing R&D activities has an insignificant share of less than 1 per cent of total innovation expenditure of an average enterprise. Micro and medium firms do not spend on outsourcing R&D activities. Acquisition of machinery, equipment and software is the largest share of expenditure for innovation, at 88.3 per cent. Acquisition of external knowledge requires only 1 per cent of total expenditure for innovation.

Among the responded enterprises, medium enterprises spend the most on acquisition of machinery, equipment and software. An average medium enterprise spends about VND 7.53 billion on machinery, equipment and software while it spends only VND 0.78 billion on in-house R&D activities. They do not spend on outsourcing R&D activities and spend very little on acquisition of external knowledge. Large enterprises, in contrast, spend largely on in-house R&D activities, with an average of VND 2.67 billion while they spent VND 1 billion on machinery, equipment and software during 2012–14.

In terms of innovation activities, the most popular activity is producing new or significantly improved goods. About 51.4 per cent of enterprises stated that they have such activities. Only 7.7 per cent of enterprises said that they produced new or significantly improved services during 2012–14. In 2014, the turnover from products that are new to market of an average enterprise is quite high: 45.8 per cent. The turnover from products that are new to firm is also high, at 44.9 per cent.

TABLE 9.9
Innovation Activities

	Micro		Small		Medium		Large		Total	
Innovation Expenditure	Mean (VND million)	%	Mean (VND million)	%	Mean (VND million)	%	Mean (VND million)	%	Mean (VND million)	%
In-house R&D activities	10		78.5		783.61		2,666.67		353.32	
Outsourcing of R&D activities	0		4.48		0		316.67		7	
Acquisition of machinery, equipment, software	738.25		612		7,534.86		1,006.33		3,026.57	
Acquisition of external knowledge	8.75		8.55		92.36		0		37.46	
Innovation Activities	No.	%	No.	%	No.	%	No.	%	No.	%
New or significantly improved goods										
Yes	12	60	54	47.8	39	54.2	2	66.7	107	51.4
No	8	40	59	52.2	33	45.8	1	33.3	101	48.6
Total	20	100	113	100	72	100	3	100	208	100
New or significantly improved services										
Yes	2	10	3	2.7	11	15.3	0	0	16	7.7
No	18	90	110	97.3	61	84.7	3	100	192	92.3
Total	20	100	113	100	72	100	3	100	208	100
Turnover in 2014 from Products that are		Mean (%)		Mean (%)		Mean (%)		Mean (%)		Mean (%)
New to market		41.4		47.7		45.2		35		45.8
New to firm		35.2		50.2		41.3		50		44.9

Source: Survey data.

Regional Trade Participation

The survey results show that 85 per cent of enterprises in all three manufacturing sectors do not participate in international trade. This share is distributed fairly equal among the three sectors of which the shares of food and beverage enterprises, textile and garment enterprises, and wooden product enterprises are 85.4 per cent, 85.4 per cent and 83.3 per cent respectively (see Table 9.10).

TABLE 9.10
International Trade Participation

		Food & Beverage Enterprises	Textile and Garment Enterprises	Wooden Product Enterprises	Total
International Trade Activities					
Not participating in international trade	No.	41	70	65	176
	%	85.4	85.4	83.3	84.6
Participating in international trade	No.	7	12	13	32
	%	14.6	14.6	16.7	15.4
Total	No.	48	82	78	208
	%	100	100	100	100
Importing from ASEAN Countries					
Not importing	No.	47	76	72	195
	%	97.9	92.7	92.3	93.75
Importing	No.	1	6	6	13
	%	2.1	7.3	7.7	6.25
Total	No.	48	82	78	208
	%	100	100	100	
Exporting to ASEAN Countries					
Not exporting	No.	43	75	73	191
	%	89.6	91.5	93.6	91.8
Exporting	No.	5	7	4	16
	%	10.4	8.5	5.1	7.69
Total	No.	48	82	78	208
	%	100	100	100	

Source: Survey data.

In terms of import and export to ASEAN countries, in total only 6.25 per cent of enterprises import from ASEAN countries and 7.69 per cent export to ASEAN economies. With regards to importing from

ASEAN countries, 2.1 per cent of food and beverage enterprises, 7.3 per cent of textile and garment enterprises and 7.7 per cent of wooden product enterprises import from these countries. In terms of exporting to ASEAN countries, 10.4 per cent of food and beverage enterprises, 8.5 per cent of textile and garment enterprises, and 5.1 per cent of wooden product enterprises export to these countries.

Awareness of AEC and Its Impacts

About 15.4 per cent of total enterprises have business relations with enterprises in other ASEAN countries (see Table 9.11). This means that the majority of 84.6 per cent of enterprises do not have such business relations. The participation of surveyed enterprises in regional trade is therefore limited. In terms of awareness of AEC, 58 per cent of total enterprises are aware, while 42 per cent stated they are not. However, in terms of ASEAN policies and strategies for SMEs, only 25 per cent of the total enterprises are aware, while 75 per cent are not. Hence, there is a lack of awareness of ASEAN policies and strategies for SMEs in Vietnam.

TABLE 9.11
Awareness of the ASEAN Economic Community and Its Policies

AEC Awareness	Full Sample		Micro		Small		Medium		Large	
	No.	%	No.	%	No.	%	No.	%	No.	%
Business Relations with Firms in ASEAN										
Yes	32	15.4	1	5	14	12.4	16	22.2	1	33.3
No	176	84.6	19	95.0	99	87.6	56	77.8	2	66.7
N.A.	208		20		113		72		3	
Awareness of AEC Policy Blueprint/Strategic Action Plan for SME Development 2004–2014										
Yes	155	25.1	18	90	81	72.3	54	75	2	66.7
No	52	74.9	2	10	31	27.7	18	25	1	33.3
Total	207	100	20		112		72		3	
Awareness of ASEAN Economic Community										
Yes	120	58	8	40	66	58.4	44	62	2	66.7
No	87	42	12	60	47	41.6	27	38	1	33.3
Total	207	100	20		113		71		3	

Source: Survey data.

In terms of the perception of the influences of the AEC, the surveyed enterprises said that there is an increase in domestic revenue, export sales, profits, market competitiveness and access to intermediate outputs. Particularly, 45.2 per cent of the enterprises stated that their domestic revenue increased, 66.7 per cent said their export sales went up, 73.8 per cent answered that their profits rosed, 69 per cent stated that their competitiveness in domestic market increased, and 61.9 per cent confirmed that their competitiveness in the international market increased. Meanwhile, another benefit of the AEC is lowering import expenses. About 59.5 per cent of total enterprises stated that AEC reduced their import costs (see Tables 9.12 and 9.13). The AEC, therefore, has much influence on the businesses of the surveyed enterprises.

The perceptions of the impact of AEC on businesses are different in different sectors. About 47.4 per cent of textile and garment firms and 50 per cent of wooden products manufacturing firms said that domestic sales will increase with AEC. However, only 28.6 per cent of food and beverage firms believed that there will be such an increase. In terms of export sales, majority of firms in all three sectors believed that there will be an increase. About 71.4 per cent of food and beverages enterprises, 78.9 per cent of textile and garment enterprises, and 50 per cent of wooden products manufacturing firms said that there will be an increase in export sales.

Majority of the firms believed that there will be increases in competition, both at home and abroad. At the same time, there will be greater access to intermediate outputs for firms across all three sectors. For import cost, majority of the firms, except large firms, believed that AEC will bring about a decrease (see Tables 9.12 and 9.13).

From the perspective of enterprise size with regards to the impacts of AEC, Table 9.13 shows that the majority of small and medium firms believe in an increase in domestic sales with AEC. However, 75 per cent of micro firms believe that there will be no change and 33.3 per cent of medium firms believe in a decrease in domestic sales. In terms of export sales, 50 per cent of micro firms believe in an increase but the same share of firms also believes in no change in export sales. In contrast, majority of small and medium firms believe in an increase in export sales.

TABLE 9.12
Influence of the ASEAN Economic Community, by Sector (%)

AEC Impact	Full Sample (%)				Foods & Beverages (%)				Textile & Garment (%)				Wooden Products (%)			
	A	B	C	D	A	B	C	D	A	B	C	D	A	B	C	D
a) How AEC Affected Business																
Domestic sales	45.2	33.3	16.7	4.8	28.6	42.8	28.6	0	47.4	36.8	10.5	5.3	50.0	25.0	18.8	6.2
Export sales	66.7	21.4	2.4	9.5	71.4	14.3	0	14.3	78.9	15.8	0	5.3	50	31.2	6.2	12.4
Import cost	9.5	11.9	59.5	19	14.3	0	57.1	28.6	5.3	21.1	68.4	5.3	12.5	6.2	50	31.2
Profits	73.8	11.9	11.9	2.4	57.1	14.2	28.6	0	89.5	5.3	5.3	0	62.5	18.8	12.5	6.2
Competition in local market	69.0	21.4	7.1	2.4	71.4	14.3	14.3	0	63.2	31.6	5.3	0	75	12.5	6.2	6.2
Competition in foreign market	61.9	16.7	7.1	14.3	42.9	14.3	14.3	28.6	73.7	15.8	5.3	5.3	56.2	18.8	6.2	18.7
Greater access to intermediate outputs	69.0	21.4	0	9.6	57.1	14.3	0	28.6	73.7	26.3	0	0	68.8	18.8	0	12.5
b) AEC Key Changes Affecting Business																
Import tariffs/duties	9.5	26.2	45.2	19	0	28.6	71.4	0	15.8	31.6	31.6	21.1	6.2	18.8	50	25
Export tariffs/duties	9.5	21.4	42.9	26.2	0	42.9	14.2	42.9	15.8	21.1	42.1	21.1	6.2	12.5	56.2	25
Customs procedure	66.7	16.7	0	16.7	71.4	28.6	0	0	63.2	15.8	0	21	68.8	12.5	0	18.8
Standards of regulation	42.9	35.7	4.8	16.7	28.6	42.9	14.3	14.3	36.8	42.1	0	21	56.2	25	6.2	12.5
Recognition of professional qualifications	45.2	28.6	7.1	19	42.9	28.6	14.3	14.3	42.1	31.6	5.3	21	50	25	6.3	18.7
Investment process in ASEAN countries	42.9	16.7	0	40.5	42.9	28.6	0	31.6	63.2	5.3	0	31.6	18.8	25	0	56.3
Connectivity in terms of transport and communication services	76.2	4.8	0	19	100	0	0	0	68.4	5.3	0	26.3	75	6.2	0	18.7

Note: A = increase; B = no change; C = decrease; D = do not know/no opinion/no reply.
Source: Survey data.

TABLE 9.13
Influence of the ASEAN Economic Community, by Size (%)

AEC Impact	Full Sample (%)				Micro (%)				Small (%)				Medium (%)				Large (%)			
	A	B	C	D	A	B	C	D	A	B	C	D	A	B	C	D	A	B	C	D
a) How AEC Affected Business																				
Domestic sales	45.2	33.3	16.7	4.8	25	75	0	0	54.5	27.3	9.1	9.1	40	26.7	33.3	0	0	100	0	0
Export sales	66.7	21.4	2.4	9.5	50	50	0	0	59.1	22.7	4.5	13.6	80	13.3	0	6.7	100	0	0	0
Import cost	9.5	11.9	59.5	19	0	25	50	25	9.1	9.1	63.6	18.1	13.3	13.3	53.3	20	0	0	0	100
Profits	73.8	11.9	11.9	2.4	75	25	0	0	72.7	9.1	13.6	4.5	73.3	13.3	13.3	0	100	0	0	0
Competition in local market	69	21.4	7.1	2.4	100	0	0	0	81.8	9.1	4.5	4.5	46.7	40	13.3	0	0	100	0	0
Competition in foreign market	61.9	16.7	7.1	14.3	75	0	25	0	68.2	13.6	0	18.1	46.7	26.7	13.3	13.4	100	0	0	0
Greater access to intermediate outputs	69	21.4	0	9.6	75	25	0	0	59.1	27.3	0	13.6	80	13.3	0	6.7	100	0	0	0
b) AEC Key Changes Affecting Business																				
Import tariffs/duties	9.5	26.2	45.2	19	25	75	0	0	4.5	18.2	50	27.2	6.7	26.7	53.3	13.3	100	0	0	0
Export tariffs/duties	9.5	21.4	42.9	26.2	25	25	25	25	50	13.6	40.9	36.4	6.7	33.3	46.7	13.4	0	100	0	0
Customs procedure	66.7	16.7	0	16.7	75	25	0	0	63.6	13.6	0	22.7	73.3	13.3	0	13.4	100	0	0	0
Standards of regulation	42.9	35.7	4.8	16.7	50	50	0	0	40.9	31.8	0	27.2	40	40	13.3	6.7	100	0	0	0
Recognition of professional qualifications	45.2	28.6	7.1	19	50	50	0	0	45.5	18.2	9.1	27.2	40	40	6.7	13.3	100	0	0	0
Investment process in ASEAN countries	42.9	16.7	0	40.5	75	0	0	25	45.5	13.6	0	40.9	33.3	26.7	0	40	0	0	0	100
Connectivity in terms of transport and communication services	76.2	4.8	0	19	100	0	0	0	77.3	4.5	0	18.1	73.3	6.7	0	20	0	0	0	100

Note: A = increase; B = no change; C = decrease; D = do not know/no opinion/no reply.
Source: Survey data.

Key Changes in AEC Affecting Businesses

Tables 9.12 and 9.13 also show the possible changes caused by AEC that will influence the businesses of firms in the three sectors. In general, 45.2 per cent and 42.9 per cent of the surveyed firms indicate a decrease in import duties and a decrease in export duties, respectively as the key changes affecting their businesses. On the other hand, 66.7 per cent of firms believe in an increase in custom procedures, 42.9 per cent an increase of standards of regulation, 45.2 per cent an increase of recognition of professional qualifications, 42.9 per cent an increase of investment process, and 76.2 per cent an increase in connectivity in transportation and communication services as a result of the AEC.

For import duties, 75 per cent of micro firms believe in no change, while 50 per cent of small firms and 53.3 per cent of medium firms believe in a decrease. With regard to export duties, micro firms do not exhibit a trend, while 40.9 per cent of small firms and 46.7 per cent of medium firms believe in a decrease in export duties as a key impact on their businesses. On other changes, majority of SME firms believe in an increase in custom procedures, increase in standards of regulation, increase in recognition of professional qualifications, increase in investment process, and increase in connectivity in transportation and communication services as the key impacts affecting their businesses (see Table 9.13).

Utilization of FTAs and Their Influences

Table 9.14 shows that the surveyed firms are not well aware of FTAs. Less than half of the surveyed firms (42.3 per cent) are aware of FTAs. It is surprising that only 25 per cent of large firms are aware of FTAs. The type of enterprises that is most aware of FTAs is the medium enterprises with 50.7 per cent of them being aware of the FTAs between Vietnam and other countries.

The use of FTAs is very limited. Among 88 enterprises which are aware of FTAs, only 14 of them, or 15.9 per cent, are FTA users. All large enterprises that are aware of FTAs use such trade agreements. The next highest user of FTAs, surprisingly, is micro enterprises with 28.6 per cent of them which are aware of FTAs are FTA users. Among the FTA users, 42.9 per cent use only a single FTA while 57.1 per cent use more than one FTA.

TABLE 9.14
Awareness of FTAs

	Full Sample		Micro		Small		Medium		Large	
	No.	%	No.	%	No.	%	No.	%	No.	%
Awareness of FTAs										
Yes	88	42.3	7	35	44	38.9	36	50.7	1	25
No	120	57.6	13	65	69	61.1	35	49.3	3	75
Total	*208*	*100*	*20*	*100*	*113*	*100*	*71*	*100*	*4*	*100*
Use of FTAs										
FTA Users	14	15.9	2	28.6	5	11.4	6	16.7	1	100
Non-users	74	84.1	5	71.4	39	88.6	30	83.3	0	0
Total	*88*	*100*	*7*	*100*	*44*	*100*	*36*	*100*	*1*	*100*
Number of FTAs Used										
Single FTA	6	42.9	1	50	1	20	4	66.7	0	0
More than one FTA used	8	57.1	1	50	4	80	2	33.3	1	100
Total	*14*	*100*	*2*	*100*	*5*	*100*	*6*	*100*	*1*	*100*
Reasons for Not Using FTA										
Small trade volume with other countries	23	25	1	16.7	14	25.5	8	25.8	0	0
Lack of knowledge/do not know how to use	25	27.2	2	33.3	18	32.7	5	16.1	0	0
Difficult to get certificate of origin	5	5.4	0	0	4	7.3	1	3.2	0	0
Small tariff preference by FTA	3	3.3	0	0	2	3.6	1	3.2	0	0
Difficult to fulfil the requirements of Rules of Origin	3	3.3	0	0	2	3.6	1	3.2	0	0
Others	33	35.9	3	50	15	27.3	15	48.4	0	0
Total	*92*	*100*	*6*	*100*	*55*	*100*	*31*	*100*	*0*	*0*

Source: Survey data.

Among the FTA non-users who are aware of the trade agreements, three reasons that are most often cited for not using FTAs are (i) small trade volume with other countries, (ii) lack of knowledge, and (iii) other reasons. These same three reasons are also observed across the different firm sizes.

TABLE 9.15
Impact of FTAs on the Enterprises (%)

FTAs Impact	Full Sample (%)				Micro (%)				Small (%)				Medium (%)				Large (%)			
	A	B	C	D	A	B	C	D	A	B	C	D	A	B	C	D	A	B	C	D
Domestic sales	26.4	27.8	16.7	29.1	20	40	0	40	29.7	21.6	16.2	32.4	20.7	34.5	20.7	24.1	100	0	0	0
Export sales	29.2	30.6	2.8	37.5	20	40	0	40	27	21.6	5.4	45.9	31	41.4	0	27.5	100	0	0	0
Import cost	13.9	30.6	15.3	40.3	20	40	0	40	18.9	24.3	8.1	48.6	6.9	34.5	27.6	31	0	100	0	0
Profits	36.1	26.4	11.1	26.4	20	60	0	20	35.1	18.9	13.5	32.4	41.4	27.6	10.3	20.6	0	100	0	0
Competition in local market	40.3	25	2.8	31.9	20	40	20	20	45.9	16.2	0	37.8	37.9	34.5	3.4	24.1	0	0	0	100
Competition in foreign market	30.6	25	5.6	38.9	40	20	20	20	27	18.9	5.4	48.6	34.5	34.5	3.4	40.2	0	0	0	100

Note: A = increase; B = no change; C = decrease; D = do not know/no opinion/no reply.
Source: Survey data.

Regarding the impacts of FTAs on enterprises, Table 9.15 shows that about 27.8 per cent of enterprises said that domestic sales remain unchanged, 30.6 per cent stated that export revenue stays the same, and 30.6 per cent reported that import expenses are unchanged. However, the surveyed enterprises believed that there are significant changes in competition in the domestic market, with 40.3 per cent of them stating that competitiveness in domestic market has increased as a result of the FTAs. Also, the enterprises believed that competition in foreign markets will increase, although a large portion of the surveyed firms stated that they do not know or have no reply to this question.

The State Participation Promotion Policies at Regional and National Levels

It can be seen from Table 9.16 that there is little support from the central, city and local authorities for participating in overseas events (e.g. fairs, exhibitions) as well as in meeting with potential partners. A large number of enterprises also indicated "non applicable" in

TABLE 9.16
Government Support

Forms of Support from Government		Governmental level		
		Central (%)	Province/ City (%)	Local (%)
Support for participation in overseas events (e.g. fairs, exhibitions)	Support	3.8	3.4	5.8
	No support	2.9	3.4	1
	Not applicable	93.3	93.3	93.3
Support in meeting with potential partners	Support	1.9	1.9	3.8
	No support	2.4	2.4	0.5
	Not applicable	95.7	95.7	95.7
Financial support	Support	0.5	2.4	0
	No support	2.4	0.5	2.9
	Not applicable	97.1	97. 1	97.1
Support in expanding business overseas through international agreements	Support	0	1	0
	No support	1	0	1
	Not applicable	99	99	99

Source: Survey data.

receiving support for financial assistance and in business expansion. Thus, the support from the government remains to be seen.

The surveyed enterprises also raised issues on the impact of ASEAN economic integration on their businesses, competition between businesses in the region, and difficulties and obstacles when participating in providing intermediate goods for domestic and international enterprises.

The advantages enjoyed by businesses that have been participating in regional trade, production and investment include:

- In the process of regional economic integration, cheap labour and raw materials become available, and there are opportunities to work with capable affiliates and foreign companies.
- The market for local firms expanded as a result of ASEAN economic integration.
- Labour quality rose to meet the requirements of businesses.
- The expansion of production, business and investment, and regional market created new jobs.

However, there are certain difficulties. These include:

- With the pressure of commodity and market, businesses have to compete fiercely with others in order to survive. Therefore, business risk is high, and the risk of bankruptcy is even much higher.
- Competition for qualified workers is also one of the difficulties facing businesses.
- Poor quality products reduce the competitiveness of businesses in the market. Meanwhile, the domestic market is crowded out by foreign goods of good quality and design from China, Thailand etc.
- Constraints on access to capital for production and investment and tight production spaces.
- Some procedures and provisions on loans, production, and investment are cumbersome and complex.

5. Regression Analysis on Vietnam SMEs' Participation in the Production Networks

There are various theories explaining the participation of SMEs in production networks (Wignaraja 2012). One such explanation can be found in a new trade theory initiated by Melitz (2003). Melitz's seminal paper focuses on the heterogeneity of firms in international trade. Firms' decisions to export or not are influenced by two factors: firm productivity and sunk costs. Only highly efficient firms are able to export, invest in international market, and therefore participate in production networks, because they can overcome high entry costs, whereas less productive firms cannot and so have to concentrate on the domestic market.

The other explanation can be found in the fragmentation theory proposed by Jones and Kierzkowski (1990), which is applied popularly in rationalizing the formation of production networks. The theory emphasizes on the location of the production process, which is separated into several stages and located in different countries. There are three conditions affecting the feasibility of fragmentation. Firstly, firms can take advantage of dissimilarity in location, thereby saving production cost in fragmented production blocks. Secondly, service link costs that connect remotely located production blocks (e.g. costs of transportation, telecommunication, etc.) must be low. Finally, network set-up cost is low. A reduction in costs of these elements will improve the fragmentation of production networks. In the case of East Asian production/distribution networks, Kimura and Ando (2005) further develop fragmentation theory to cover the fragmentation by distance and fragmentation by firm disintegration (two-dimensional fragmentation).

According to Kimura and Ando (2005), fragmentation by distance raises the issues of higher transportation, telecommunication, distribution and coordination costs while possibly reducing production costs. Fragmentation by firm disintegration likely involves information costs as well as institution-related costs, but it might result in reduction of production costs due to more efficient supportive industries, availability of business partners, etc. In accordance with fragmentation theory, SMEs must overcome barriers related to types of fragmentation in order to participate in production networks.

To analyse the determinants of SME participation in the production networks of ASEAN countries, Harvie, Narjoko and Oum (2010) built a framework with external and internal factors on the basis of the empirical application of fragmentation theory. The statistical model used by Harvie, Narjoko and Oum (2010) is in the following form:

$$PN_i = \gamma_0 + \Gamma'^{X_i} + \varepsilon_i$$

Where the equation is on the participation in the production networks, i presents firm i and X_i is a vector of explainatory variables taking the SMEs' characteristics. The statistical model is a logistic one, that is used to overcome the fact that PNi is a (0, 1) variable reflecting the probability to participate in the production networks by SMEs.

Based on the results of the survey on the three manufacturing sectors, this study analyses further the determinants of the SMEs' participation in the regional production networks following the Harvie, Narjoko and Oum (2010) approach. The analysis is applied to the dependent variable of participation in production networks. With regards to the current database, the participating enterprises are mainly defined as those that export some of their products or import inputs for their production. Independent variables include firm size, age of firms, foreign ownership, labour productivity, skill intensity, industry variables and dummy variables regarding innovation activities, association membership and risk preference of firm managers.

In this analysis, age of firms is the number of years since the establishment of firms. Firm size is provided by the number of employees in the firms, foreign ownership stands for the control of foreign investors in the enterprises and measured by the share of foreign ownership. Labour productivity is measured by revenue per employee, while skill intensity is the share of employees with higher education in the total labour of firms.

Tables 9.17 and 9.18 show the differences in variables between enterprises of the three manufacturing sectors participating in production networks and those not in the networks. Table 9.17 indicates that SMEs that participate in production networks are significantly different from SMEs that do not participate in production networks in terms of size, foreign ownership, labour productivity and skill intensity. However, the two groups of SMEs do not differ in terms of operating years and training expenditure.

Two surprising facts include productivity and foreign ownership. These are puzzling since it is expected that foreign invested firms are more likely to join production networks, taking advantage of their relationship with the outside world. Also, productivity is usually assumed to be the most important characteristic that separate production network-participating firms from non-participating firms. Theories on production network participation emphasize the barriers to participate in production networks by SMEs and argue that productivity is one factor that helps SMEs to overcome these barriers.

TABLE 9.17
Average Value of SME Characteristics

	SMEs in Production Network	SMEs Not in Production Network	Statistically Different
Age (years)	8.3	9.1	No
Size (employees)	72.1	44.2	Yes***
Foreign ownership (%)	9.9	1.0	Yes***
Labour productivity (revenue/employee)	944.8	491.6	Yes**
Skill intensity (%)	38.9	27.7	Yes***
Training expense	33.4	23.2	No

Notes: * $p < 0.10$; ** $p < 0.05$; *** $p < 0.010$

TABLE 9.18
Comparison Between Participating and Non-participating Enterprises

	SMEs in Production Network	SMEs Not in Production Network	Statistically Different
Having new/improved products/services	56.6	45.4	No
Having new/improved methods	59.4	48.5	No
Having new/improved logistics/delivery	33.0	27.8	No
Having new/improved supporting activities	38.7	35.1	No
Belonging to industry/business associations	24.5	11.3	Yes**
Having risk preference	36.8	38.1	No

Notes: * $p < 0.10$; ** $p < 0.05$; *** $p < 0.010$

Statistical tests on other dummy variables show that the two groups of SMEs in consideration are not different in several variables standing for innovations of SMEs. Also these two groups do not differ from each other in the risk preference of managers. However, the two groups are different in business association membership. The test shows that SMEs that participate in production networks tend to belong to business associations more often than those that do not participate in production networks (see Table 9.18).

Table 9.19 presents the estimation results of the logistic regression for the sample of all SMEs with less than 300 employees. This table reports eight specifications with specifications (1) and (2) as the baseline. They include all variables except dummy variables for innovations, business association membership and risk preference. Specification (2) is different from specification (1) with the dummy variables for the sectors of enterprises.

Among the main characteristics of enterprises, age has a negative impact on the probability of production network participation. With the exception of specification (3), age of enterprises has significantly and negatively influenced production network participation. This fact implicates that younger enterprises tend to be more active in participating in production networks. The regression results suggest that firm size is an important factor in determining the participation of enterprises in production networks.

The results also imply that foreign ownership and productivity are two other important determinants of participation of enterprises in production networks. The foreign ownership coefficients as estimated significantly determine the participation of SMEs in production networks. This fact is in accordance with the hypothesis on the advantages of enterprises that have connections with foreign markets in their ownership. The magnitude of foreign ownership effects as estimated is large in all specifications. The estimated marginal effects for these coefficients ranged from 0.56 to 0.67 percentage points. They are as large as the marginal effects of firm size on the participation of SMEs in production networks. However, their statistical significance is not as high as those of firm size, fluctuating between 5 per cent and 10 per cent significant levels.

The estimated coefficients of labour productivity are statistically significant and positive across the eight specifications. They are mostly significant at the 10 per cent level. The magnitude of the marginal effects of labour productivity is, however, very small, ranging from 0.0095 to 0.011 percentage points. These results imply that labour productivity is still a determinant of the participation of SMEs in production networks but with very limited impact.

The other two characteristics of SMEs in the three manufacturing sectors that are not statistically significant determinants of production

TABLE 9.19
Determinants of SMEs to Participate in Production Networks

	(1)	(2)	(3)	(4)	(5)	(6)	(7)	(8)
			Dependent Variable: Participation in Production Networks					
Age	−0.0435*	−0.0441*	−0.0388	−0.0406*	−0.0436*	−0.0460*	−0.0527*	−0.0443*
	(−1.74)	(−1.72)	(−1.63)	(−1.65)	(−1.71)	(−1.73)	(−1.88)	(−1.72)
Firm size	0.0229***	0.0225***	0.0228**	0.0206**	0.0223**	0.0237***	0.0215**	0.0227***
	(2.68)	(2.61)	(2.54)	(2.31)	(2.56)	(2.68)	(2.46)	(2.62)
Firm size squared	−0.0000379	−0.0000369	−0.0000374	−0.0000313	−0.0000364	−0.0000386	−0.0000339	−0.0000377
	(−1.24)	(−1.20)	(−1.13)	(−0.99)	(−1.17)	(−1.23)	(−1.10)	(−1.22)
Foreign ownership	0.0231**	0.0231**	0.0273**	0.0235*	0.0230**	0.0229**	0.0247**	0.0227**
	(2.02)	(2.03)	(2.26)	(1.90)	(2.03)	(2.01)	(2.14)	(1.98)
Labour productivity	0.000393*	0.000392*	0.000475**	0.000394*	0.000393*	0.000398*	0.000407*	0.000385*
	(1.83)	(1.74)	(2.14)	(1.82)	(1.76)	(1.72)	(1.88)	(1.69)
Skill intensity	0.00921*	0.00898	0.00518	0.00985*	0.00903	0.00922*	0.00797	0.00936
	(1.65)	(1.61)	(0.89)	(1.72)	(1.62)	(1.67)	(1.38)	(1.61)
Training expense	0.000525	0.000527	−0.000127	0.000121	0.000505	0.000760	0.000334	0.000562
	(0.27)	(0.26)	(−0.06)	(0.06)	(0.25)	(0.38)	(0.17)	(0.28)
Food processing		0.206	0.0930	0.209	0.200	0.213	0.154	0.210
		(0.47)	(0.21)	(0.48)	(0.46)	(0.48)	(0.35)	(0.48)
Textile and garments		0.213	0.256	0.246	0.214	0.210	0.266	0.209
		(0.58)	(0.69)	(0.66)	(0.58)	(0.58)	(0.72)	(0.57)
Dummy var. for having new/improved goods/services			0.707**					
			(2.11)					
Dummy var. for having new/improved methods				0.463				
				(1.37)				

TABLE 9.19 (continued)

				Dependent Variable: Participation in Production Networks				
	(1)	(2)	(3)	(4)	(5)	(6)	(7)	(8)
Dummy var. for having new/ improved logistics					0.0469 (0.13)			
Dummy var. for having new/ improved supporting activities						−0.298 (−0.85)		
Dummy var. for belonging to business assoc.							0.877** (2.00)	
Dummy var. for risk preference								−0.0757 (−0.21)
Constant	−1.277*** (−2.84)	−1.371*** (−2.86)	−1.715*** (−3.35)	−1.612*** (−3.25)	−1.381*** (−2.83)	−1.318*** (−2.73)	−1.383*** (−2.82)	−1.353*** (−2.79)
Observations	196	196	196	196	196	196	196	196

Notes: t statistics in parentheses; * $p < 0.10$; ** $p < 0.05$; *** $p < 0.010$

network participation are skill intensity and training expenses. The estimated coefficients are positive for both variables, but not stable for skill intensity and not significant for training expenses.

Among the behavioural activities of SMEs in terms of innovation, the regression analysis shows that creating new products/services and membership of industry and business associations are statistically significant and have positive impacts on the participation of SMEs in production networks. The general finding from the regression analysis is that connections in the form of foreign investment or membership of industry and business associations are important determinants of production network participation of SMEs. The analysis also shows that domestic connection, i.e. membership of industry and business associations, has far more significant impacts on the decision to participate in production networks by SMEs. The estimated marginal effect of industry and business association membership is 20 percentage points, compared to 0.6 percentage points of marginal effect of foreign ownership variable. In the same manner, magnitude of product innovation of SMEs is far larger than other variables, reaching 17 percentage points of marginal effect.

6. Conclusions and Policy Recommendations

Similar to the structure of the economy, the results of the survey show that the surveyed firms are mostly micro, small and medium-sized enterprises. In terms of establishment, the most common type is limited liability companies. These companies are mainly run as family businesses, of which 94 per cent are managed by the founders.

This fact can also partly explain the limited participation in the regional production networks by Vietnamese SMEs. Vietnam SMEs' participation in regional production is limited with only 15.4 per cent of enterprises having business relations with firms in other ASEAN countries. The awareness of Vietnam's enterprises on ASEAN SMEs Development Plan is relative high (66.7 per cent), but can be improved.

In terms of the perception of the influences of the AEC, the surveyed enterprises believe in an increase in domestic revenue, export sales, profits, market competitiveness and access to intermediate outputs. Particularly, 45.2 per cent of the enterprises stated that their domestic revenue increased, 66.7 per cent said that their export sales went up,

73.8 per cent answered that their profits rosed, 69 per cent stated that their competitiveness in the domestic market increased, and 61.9 per cent confirmed that their competitiveness in international market increased. Meanwhile, another benefit of the AEC is lowering import expenses. About 59.5 per cent of total enterprises stated that AEC reduced their import costs. The AEC, therefore, has many influences as perceived by the surveyed Vietnamese enterprises in the three sectors.

In contrast with AEC, awareness of FTAs among Vietnamese SMEs is limited. Less than half of the surveyed firms (42.3 per cent) are aware of FTAs. It is surprising that only 25 per cent of large firms are aware of FTAs. The type of enterprises that is most aware of FTAs is the medium enterprises with 50.7 per cent of them being aware of the FTAs between Vietnam and other countries. The use of FTAs is also very limited. Among the 88 enterprises which are aware of FTAs, only 14 of them, or 15.9 per cent, are FTA users.

Among the FTAs non-users who are aware of the trade agreements, three reasons that are most often cited for not using FTAs are: (i) small trade volume with other countries, (ii) lack of knowledge, and (iii) other reasons.

Our regression analysis also shows that among the important determinants of production network participation, foreign ownership and productivity are two other important determinants of participation of enterprises in production networks. Among the behavioural activities of SMEs in terms of innovation, the regression analysis shows that creating new products/services and membership of industry and business associations are statistically significant and have positive impacts on the participation of SMEs in production networks. The general finding from the regression analysis is that connections in the form of foreign investment or membership of industry and business associations are important determinants of production network participation of SMEs. The analysis also shows that domestic connection, i.e. membership of industry and business associations, has far more significant impacts on the decision to participate in production networks by SMEs.

The analysis implies some policy recommendations to enhance the participation of Vietnamese SMEs in regional production networks.

Participating in production networks and development of SMEs is a two-way relationship. Policies to develop SMEs will certainly help to improve SME participation in regional production networks. Also, policies to promote labour productivity have the same implications. Policies to continue the international integration are proven to help SMEs involve in production networks by promoting foreign ownership.

From the enterprise perspective, new or significantly improved products or services and industry/business association membership will help to promote SME participation in production networks. Therefore, government policies to promote product innovation as well as expansion of industry and business associations are believed to be helpful. Also information on ASEAN SMEs' policies, AEC and other business related issues should be promoted to enterprises to raise their awareness. These will help to significantly improve the participation of Vietnam SMEs in regional production networks.

NOTES

1. An estimation by the World Bank shows that each job created by Vietnamese SMEs requires an investment of about US$800. Meanwhile, a state-owned enterprise (SOE) requires US$18,000 to create a new job.
2. Section 3 of the Small Business Act of 1953.
3. This census surveyed all business establishments (administrative and non-profit) in the country.
4. A comprehensive description of these support programmes can be found in the report by AED (2014).
5. General Statistics Office, Vietnam's export and import of commodities in 2011.
6. General Statistics Office, Vietnam's export and import of commodities in 2012.
7. General Statistics Office, Vietnam's export and import of commodities in 2013.
8. CTCK Rồng Việt, "Dệt may 2015 dự báo tiếp tục tăng trưởng tốt" [Textile and Apparel 2015 Forecast Continued Good Growth], 4 April 2015, available at <http://tinnhanhchungkhoan.vn/thuong-truong/det-may-2015-du-bao-tiep-tuc-tang-truong-tot-115828.html>.

9. Vũ Phong, "Dệt may cần ODM" [Textile Needs ODM], 8 July 2014, available at <http://nld.com.vn/kinh-te/det-may-can-odm-20140708180853189.htm>.

10. Thu Hiền, "Dệt may Việt Nam hưởng tới vị trí thứ 3 thế giới về xuất khẩu năm 2015" [Vietnam's Textile and Garment Industry is Aiming for the Third Position of Top Exporters in World Exports in 2015], available at <http://www.agtex.com.vn/zone/det-may-viet-nam-huong-toi-vi-tri-thu-3-the-gioi-ve-xuat-khau-nam-2015/258/424>.

11. Nguyễn Tấn Dũng, "Ngành Dệt may: Cả thế giới chọn Việt Nam là đối tưởng cạnh tranh" [Textile and Clothing: The Whole World Chooses Vietnam as a Competitive Destination], 16 January 2015, available at <http://nguyentandung.org/nganh-det-may-ca-the-gioi-chon-viet-nam-la-doi-tuong-canh-tranh.html>.

12. <http://tapchicongthuong.vn/>.

13. "Dữ liệu mới nhất về ngành dệt may ghi nhận cả tiến bộ và thách thức về bình đẳng giới" [The Latest Data on the Textile Industry Notes Both Progress and Challenges in Gender Inequality], 7 March 2015, available at <http://www.ilo.org/hanoi/Informationresources/Publicinformation/Pressreleases/WCMS_349654/lang--vi/index.htm>.

14. CTCK Rồng Việt, "Dệt may 2015 dự báo tiếp tục tăng trưởng tốt" [Textile and Apparel 2015 Forecast Continued Good Growth], op. cit.

15. Lien Hoa, "Liên kết các doanh nghiệp dệt may Việt Nam để tăng lợi thế cạnh tranh" [Link Vietnam's Garment Enterprises to Increase Competitive Advantage], 24 March 2015, available at <http://www.phongphucorp.com/news/lien-ket-cac-doanh-nghiep-det-may-viet-nam-de-tang-loi-the-canh-tranh-vi.html>.

16. Vietnam Economic Growth Report 2015, available at <http://vef.vn/2015-04-16-bao-cao-tang-truong-viet-nam-nam-2015>.

17. Luu Yen, "Công nghe thuc pham: Đón đau su phat trien", *huongnghiep24h*, available at <http://huongnghiep24h.com/tu-van-nghe-nghiep/cong-nghe-thuc-pham-don-dau-su-phat-trien.html>.

18. Hai Phan, "Ngành thuc pham - đo uong: Toa sáng tu canh tranh" [Food Industry: Shining from the Competition], *Vietnamnet.vn*, 3 January 2014, available at <http://vietnamnet.vn/vn/kinh-te/156350/nganqh-thuc-pham--do-uong--toa--sa-ng-tu-canh-tranh.html>.

19. "Mapping the Stakeholders for FLEGT VPA in Vietnam", Forest Trend 11/2011.

REFERENCES

Agency of Enterprise Development (AED). *Guidance on SMEs Support Programs (Vietnamese)*. 2014.

Al-Qirim, Nabeel. *Electronic Commerce in Small to Medium-Sized Enterprises: Frameworks, Issues and Implications.* U.S. and UK: Idea Group Publishing, 2004.

Chau, Stephen B. and Paul Turner. "An SME Experience of E-Commerce: Some Considerations for Policy Formulation in Australia". In *e-Business, e-Government and Small and Medium-Size Enterprises: Opportunities and Challenges,* by Brian J. Corbitt and Nabeel Al-Qirim. U.S. and UK: Idea Group Publishing, 2004.

Deloitte. *Connected Small Businesses: How Australian Small Businesses are Growing in the Digital Economy.* 2013. Available at <https://www2.deloitte.com/content/dam/Deloitte/au/Documents/Economics/deloitte-au-economics-connected-small-businesses-google-100413.pdf>.

Devos, Jan, Hendrik van Landeghem, and Dirk Deschoolmeester, eds. *Information Systems for Small and Medium-Sized: State of Art of IS Research in SMEs.* Berlin: Springer, 2014.

Dinh, Hinh T., *Light Manufacturing in Vietnam: Creating Jobs and Prosperity in a Middle-Income Economy.* Washington, D.C.: World Bank, 2013.

Dinh, Hinh T., Deepak Mishra, Le Duy Binh, Duc Minh Pham, and Pham Thi Thu Hang. *Light Manufacturing in Vietnam: Creating Jobs and Prosperity in a Middle-Income Economy.* Washington, D.C.: World Bank, 2013.

Forest Trend. "Mapping the Stakeholders for FLEGT VPA in Vietnam". Report, 2011.

Jones, Robert W. and Henryk Kierzkowski. "The Role of Services in Production and International Trade: A Theoretical Framework". In *The Political Economy of International Trade: Essays in Honour of Robert E. Baldwin,* edited by Ronald W. Jones and Anne O. Krueger. Oxford, UK: Basil Blackwell, 1990, pp. 31–48.

Harvie, Charles. "SMEs and Regional Production Networks". In *Integrating Small and Medium Enterprises (SMEs) into the More Integrated East Asia,* edited by Vo Tri Thanh, Dionisius Narjoko, and Sothea Oum. Jakarta: Economic Research Institute for ASEAN and East Asia (ERIA), 2010, pp. 19–45.

Harvie, Charles and Boon-Chye Lee. *Sustaining Growth and Performance in East Asia: The Role of Small and Medium Sized Enterprises.* Cheltenham, UK: Edward Elgar, 2005.

Harvie, Charles, Dionisius Narjoko, and Sothea Oum. "Firm Characteristic Determinants of SME Participation in Production Networks". ERIA Discussion Paper Series, ERIA-DP-2010-11. October 2010.

Kimura, Fukunari and Mitsuyo Ando. "Two-dimensional Fragmentation in East Asia: Conceptual Framework and Empirics". *International Review of Economics and Finance* 14, no. 3 (2005): 317–48.

MacGregor, Robert and Lejla Vrazalic. *E-Commerce in Regional Small to Medium Enterprises.* New York: IGI Publishing, 2007.

Melitz, Marc J. "The Impact of Trade on Intra-Industry Reallocations and Aggregate Industry Productivity". *Econometrica* 17, no. 6 (2003): 1695–1725.

Ministry of Agriculture and Rural Development (MARD). "Development Planning of the Wood Processing Industry". Report, 2013.

Nordstrom, Kjell A. "The Internationalization Process of the Film: Searching for New Pattern and Explanations". DBA dissertation, Stockholm School of Economics, Stockholm, 1991.

Tambunan, Tulus. *SMEs in Asian Developing Countries*. UK: Palgrave Macmillan, 2009.

Trang, N.T.T.T. and P.M. Thuy. *Supporting Business Association to Implement the Development Strategy of Wood Processing Industry (Vietnamese)*. 2014.

Wignaraja, Ganeshan. "Engaging Small and Medium Enterprises in Production Networks: Firm- level Analysis of Five ASEAN Economies". ADBI Working Paper 361. Tokyo: Asian Development Bank Institute, June 2012.

PART 2

Multinational Enterprise Studies

10

USE OF PREFERENCE AT EXPORT PLATFORM
Evidence from Export to China by Japanese Affiliates in ASEAN[1]

Kazunobu Hayakawa and Toshiyuki Matsuura

1. Introduction

Recently, multinational enterprises (MNEs) actively use regional trade agreements (RTAs) all over the world. In particular, there is a growing number of MNEs of which the overseas affiliates trade with third countries (i.e., neither home country nor host country) under RTA preferential schemes. For example, the White Paper on International Economy and Trade 2014 by the Japanese government introduces several case studies on Japanese affiliates in Southeast Asia using preferential schemes when trading with China, India, or Korea. Their use in trading with China or Korea is especially important since Japan has not yet concluded any RTA schemes with China and Korea. Namely, through trading via their overseas affiliates, MNEs enjoy preferential trade with countries with which their home country does not have preferential access.

In the academic literature, such export to third countries by MNEs is called the export platform foreign direct investment (FDI). This branch of research is motivated by the growing importance of platform-FDI activities. For instance, export sales accounted for over 40 per cent of total sales by foreign affiliates of Japanese MNEs in 2009, and export sales to third markets represented over 30 per cent of the export sales.[2] Despite its empirical importance, there have been only a few studies on export platform FDI. Ekholm et al. (2007) is one of the pioneering studies and considers various types of export platform FDI according to the destination market of the overseas plant.[3] The above-mentioned feature indicates that overseas affiliates by such export platform FDI enjoy preferential trade in their export.

In this study, we empirically identify significant firm characteristics in the use of preferences in export platform FDI. Specifically, we investigate the correlation of preference use with the share of "originating inputs", intensity of exports to the third country, and experience of preference use in exporting to other third countries. For example, if the export intensity is highly and positively correlated with preference use, the absolute magnitude of preferential exports will play a significant role in that use. We can also decompose "originating inputs" into labour inputs, originating material inputs, and other originating inputs. As a result, in order to directly find the bottleneck in preference use in export platform FDI, we just examine the correlation of preference use with firm performance indicators rather than its determinants, such as more fundamental firm characteristics including firm productivity.

We investigate the use of ASEAN–China Free Trade Agreement (ACFTA) when Japanese affiliates in ASEAN export to China. To do that, we employ a unique dataset for 2012 and 2013 collected by the Japan External Trade Organization (JETRO) in its "Survey of Japanese-Affiliated Firms in ASEAN, India, and Oceania" (hereafter, called the "JETRO survey"). This survey targets Japanese affiliates operating in Asia and includes some basic firm characteristics such as number of employees. In recent years, it includes information on affiliates' FTA usage in export or import activities in addition to detailed composition of inputs. Roughly, the survey for each year includes around one thousand manufacturing affiliates in ASEAN. The response rate of around 50 per cent seems to be sufficiently high despite the fact that this survey is not mandatory. This data will be suitable for our analysis.

There are mainly two reasons for our focus on export to China. One is to avoid the firms' complicated decisions on tariff schemes. ASEAN countries have multilateral RTAs with China, Korea, Japan, Australia, New Zealand, and India. In addition to these RTAs, most of the ASEAN countries also have bilateral RTAs with Japan, Australia, New Zealand, and India. When multiple FTA schemes are available, firms can choose the tariff scheme from among most favoured nation (MFN) rates, bilateral RTA rates, and multilateral RTA rates rather than simply choose between MFN rates and RTA rates. Since our aim is not to examine such complicated decisions on tariff schemes, we focus on the imports from China, which has a single RTA scheme with each of the ASEAN countries.

The other reason is that rules of origin (ROOs) in almost all products in ACFTA are regional value content (RVC) rules. According to Hayakawa and Laksanapanyakul (2017), in China in 2011, around 10 per cent of harmonized system (HS) six-digit codes followed duty free (i.e., zero MFN rates) or were excluded from liberalization. RVC is set in approximately 80 per cent of these codes. Almost all of the rest follow co-equal rule with the combination of RVC with change-in-tariff classification or technical requirement. In ACFTA, the cut-off of RVC is set to 40 per cent. Therefore, in almost all our sample for empirical analysis, information on the share of originating inputs becomes a good indicator on whether or not to comply with ROOs in ACFTA. In other words, we do not need to check the transformation from imported inputs to exported products in terms of HS classification.

After clarifying significant firm characteristics in the use of preferences in export platform FDI, we further investigate the differences in such characteristics according to the size of parent firms. Following the definition provided in Japan's Small and Medium-sized Enterprise (SME) Basic Law, we define large firms as those with 300 or more employees and whose paid-up capital or investment fund is over 30 million yen. Otherwise, firms are categorized into SMEs. For example, if input structures play a significant role in the use of preference and are further systematically different between large-sized firms and SMEs, such a difference results in the difference in preference use between these two kinds of firms. In other words, this analysis will contribute to clarifying why the use of preference from platform countries is different between overseas affiliates by large firms and SMEs.

Our chapter contributes to at least two literatures. One is that, as mentioned above, it is related to the studies on export platform FDI. Those studies have investigated significant firm characteristics or country characteristics when export platform FDI becomes the dominant strategy in MNEs. In the case of Japanese FDI in East Asia, most studies such as Hayakawa and Matsuura (2011; 2015) shed light on vertical or horizontal FDIs. However, Baldwin and Okubo (2014) showed that it is difficult to classify each Japanese affiliate into one specific type of FDI since their sales and procurement patterns are so complicated.[4] Nevertheless, defining affiliates exporting to the third country as export platform FDI, we examine preference use in export platform FDI for East Asia by Japanese multinationals. The analysis on the actual utilization of preference in export platform FDI will be important because such FDI seeks "platform" with better access (e.g., preference schemes) to the third country than home country.

The other is the literature that examines the role of firm characteristics or country characteristics in preferential use. Most of the previous studies on RTA utilization have employed the product-level trade data according to tariff schemes (Bureau et al. 2007; Cadot et al. 2006; Francois et al. 2006; Manchin 2006; Hakobyan 2015). In particular, these studies find that the utilization rates of preferential schemes are higher in products with larger preference margin, larger trade volume, and less restrictive ROOs. More recently, some studies start to employ firm-level data to examine firms' preference utilization (Takahashi and Urata 2010; Hayakawa 2015a, 2015b; Cherkashin et al. 2015). These studies have investigated the role of firm sizes in preference use, the effects of preference use on firm performance, and those of reduction of fixed cost for preference use. Compared with these studies, our chapter investigates the role of input structures at a more detailed level.

The rest of this chapter is organized as follows. The next section specifies our empirical methodology. Section 3 introduces our data sources in addition to a brief overview of ACFTA use. The estimation results are reported in Section 4. Lastly, Section 5 concludes this chapter.

2. Empirical Specification

This section specifies our empirical framework to examine the use of ACFTA in exporting to China by Japanese affiliates in ASEAN countries. Following Hayakawa (2015a), the empirical model of firms' choice on exporting and utilizing FTA schemes is specified as follows. Our selection equation describes firms' decision on whether to export or not:

$$y^*_{EX} \equiv \max\{\pi_{MFN}, \pi_{FTA}\} = \mathbf{z}\gamma + u_{EX}, \qquad y_{EX} = \begin{cases} 1 & \text{if } y^*_{EX} > 0 \\ 0 & \text{if } y^*_{EX} \leq 0 \end{cases}.$$

A vector of $\mathbf{z}$ includes various elements that affect gross profits from exporting. A vector of γ indicates coefficients to be estimated. u_{EX} is an error term. Namely, this equation indicates that firms choose to export if the gross profits from exporting under either MFN or FTA scheme become positive.

Then, the outcome equation describes firms' decision on whether using MFN schemes or FTA schemes:

$$y^*_{FTA} \equiv \pi_{FTA} - \pi_{MFN} = \mathbf{x}\beta + u_{FTA}, \qquad y_{FTA} = \begin{cases} 1 & \text{if } y^*_{FTA} > 0,\, y^*_{EX} > 0 \\ 0 & \text{if } y^*_{FTA} \leq 0,\, y^*_{EX} > 0 \end{cases}.$$

A vector of $\mathbf{x}$ shares elements with that of $\mathbf{z}$. However, it does not include fixed costs for exporting because those costs are eliminated by taking a difference between gross profits from exporting under two schemes.[5] A vector of β indicates coefficients to be estimated. u_{FTA} is an error term. This equation indicates that firms choose to export under FTA scheme if the gross profits from exporting under FTA scheme are greater than those under MFN scheme. The errors in these two equations are assumed to be as follows:

$$u_{EX} \sim N(0, 1), \qquad u_{FTA} \sim N(0, 1), \qquad \text{corr}(u_{EX}, u_{FTA}) = \rho.$$

As is evident from the fact that y_{FTA} can be defined if y_{EX} is unity, this model is the probit model with sample selection (Heckman probit), of which framework is provided in Van de Ven and Van Praag (1981).

The benefits and costs for the use of FTA schemes are as follows. The users of preferences can export their products with cheaper tariff rates than MFN rates. Therefore, not only the larger gap between MFN rates and FTA rates (called the "tariff margin") but also the larger volume of export result in the larger amount of tariff payment savings. On the other hand, the use of FTAs requires firms to incur some amount of additional cost. In order to meet ROO requirements, FTA users may need to change their procurement sources from the optimal pattern of procurement. Also, administrative costs for applying for the use of FTA might not be negligible. In particular, users need to collect several kinds of documents including a list of inputs, production flow chart, production instructions, invoices for each input, contract documents, and so on. These kinds of administrative procedures become a significant burden for potential FTA users getting engaged in exporting.

Based on these benefits and costs, we specify a vector of x as follows. First, in order to shed light on the magnitude of tariff saving, we introduce the share of exports to China in total sales, under controlling for the size of affiliates in terms of the number of employees, which is expected to control for total exports. The higher share of exports to China is expected to lead to larger benefits from the use of ACFTA. Second, the role of ROO compliance is examined by introducing the share of originating inputs in total production costs. Those in the context of ACFTA include labour inputs, material inputs from host countries, imports from other ACFTA member countries (i.e., other ASEAN countries and China), and miscellaneous expenses. Third, to highlight the role of the administrative costs, we introduce an indicator variable which takes the value one if an affiliate uses any FTA schemes in exporting to other third countries (i.e., countries other than China and Japan) and zero otherwise. The users of any other FTA schemes will already have knowledge of the bureaucratic requirements, and the system and organizational divisions to certify ROOs. Therefore, for such affiliates, the administrative costs for ACFTA use will be much lower.

Obviously, these elements in a vector of x are endogenous variables in a sense that these are simultaneously determined when firms make decision on the use of FTA schemes. Therefore, we need to interpret our estimates carefully. Also, we introduce industry fixed effects, export country fixed effects, and year fixed effects. The industry fixed effects may control for the differences in tariff margin to some extent. The differences in fees for certificates of origin (COOs), in addition to those in macroeconomic conditions across export countries such as wages, will be controlled by the export country fixed effects. The year fixed effects will control for the over-time changes of macroeconomic conditions in China such as demand sizes.

Finally, we need to specify "excluded variables". Namely, it is necessary to include in the selection equation the variables related to firms' decision on exporting but not their decision on FTA usage. From a theoretical point of view, as mentioned above, any proxy variable for fixed costs for exporting plays a good role of excluded variables. Therefore, we introduce export costs per container in export country. In addition, we also include an indicator variable which takes the value one if an affiliate gets engaged in exporting to any other third countries and zero otherwise. Since some components of fixed costs for exporting should be common across export destination countries, experience in exporting to other countries will lower the fixed costs for exporting. As a result, a vector of z includes elements in x in addition to these two variables.

3. Data Issues

This section introduces our data sources. As mentioned in the introductory section, we mainly use the JETRO survey for 2012 and 2013. The definition of Japanese affiliates is the usual one for FDIs, namely more than or equal to 10 per cent capital shares.[6] In 2012, for example, the response rate was 48 per cent. Specifically, 2,004 responses came from Japanese affiliates in the manufacturing industry. Of these, 711 came from Northeast Asia (China, Hong Kong, Macao, Korea, and Taiwan), 1,019 were from ASEAN countries (Thailand, Cambodia, Malaysia, Singapore, Indonesia, Lao PDR, the Philippines, Vietnam, and Myanmar), 191 came from South Asia (India, Bangladesh, Pakistan, and Sri Lanka), and 83 came from Oceania (Australia and New Zealand).

This survey includes nearly half of all Japanese affiliates in ASEAN covered by the "Basic Survey of Japanese Business Structure and Activities" conducted by the Ministry of Economy, Trade and Industry (hereafter, METI survey), which is the survey based on Statistics Act. Nevertheless, the mean values of some indicators such as employment or export share are similar between the JETRO survey and the METI survey. For example, the mean of employees in ASEAN is 741 in the

JETRO survey and 627 in the METI survey. That of export share is around 50 per cent in both surveys. As a result, our sample can be considered as representative to some extent. Using the JETRO survey, we obtain all affiliate-level variables.[7] The data on export costs are from the database of Doing Business by the World Bank.

Before reporting the estimation results, we take a brief overview of Japanese affiliates in ASEAN. The left panel in Table 10.1 reports the average of affiliate-level sales share in total sales according to destinations in addition to parent sizes, in 2013. As mentioned above, "large" is defined as the parent firm with 300 or more employees and whose paid-up capital or investment fund is over 30 million yen. The rest are categorized into SMEs. The highest share of sales can be found in local sales, i.e., sales in host countries. It accounts for around 50 per cent. The second largest sales destination is Japan, i.e., home country, followed by sales for other ASEAN countries and for China. Although some sales destinations show significantly different shares between SMEs and large parents, the differences are quantitatively negligible. The large difference can be found only in the case of Japan, which is 6 per cent point higher in the case of SME.

TABLE 10.1
Affiliate-level Share of Sales and Procurement According to Parent's Size: Average in Japanese Affiliates in ASEAN, 2013

	Sales Destination				Input Source			
	SME	Large	t-value		SME	Large	t-value	
Host	51%	48%	2.64	***	44%	41%	0.79	
Japan	28%	22%	−2.54	**	32%	31%	−3.64	***
ASEAN	10%	13%	−1.48		7.6%	12%	0.29	
China	2.6%	3.4%	−3.00	***	8.1%	7.8%	−1.41	
USA	2.0%	3.8%	−4.59	***	0.5%	0.9%	−0.33	
EU	1.4%	3.3%	1.21		1.0%	1.1%	1.38	
Others	5.3%	6.4%	−1.30		6.8%	6.7%	0.04	

Notes: 1. "Large" is defined as the parent firm with 300 or more employees and whose paid-up capital or investment fund is over 30 million yen. The rest are categorized into SMEs.
2. *** and ** respectively represent significance at the 1 per cent and 5 per cent statistical levels for the null hypothesis that shares are the same between the cases of SMEs and large parents.
3. The total number of affiliates in this computation is 982.

The right panel shows the average of affiliate-level material input share in total material inputs according to input sources in addition to parent sizes, in 2013. As in the case of sales, the first and second highest shares can be found in local inputs and imports from Japan, respectively. The import shares from both other ASEAN countries and China also show approximately 10 per cent. The share difference between SMEs and large parents is more negligible in the case of inputs than that of sales. It is statistically significant only in the case of imports from Japan but is just one per cent point difference. In sum, regardless of parent's size, Japanese affiliates in ASEAN have been well involved in global value chains in terms of diverging sales destinations and input sources. However, there are no significant differences between Japanese affiliates owned by SMEs and large parents, particularly in terms of input structure.

Next, we take a closer look at the share of originating inputs (i.e., the share of labour inputs, material inputs from host countries, imports from other ACFTA member countries, and miscellaneous expenses) in each affiliate in 2013, which is shown in Table 10.2. Its average is 78 per cent in affiliates owned by SMEs and 75 per cent in those owned by large parents. Both shares are much higher than the usual cut-off in RVC rules (e.g., 40 per cent). The average is a little larger in affiliates owned by SMEs. Decomposing originating inputs into originating materials (i.e., material inputs from host countries and imports from

TABLE 10.2
Affiliate-level Shares of Originating Inputs According to Parent's Size: Average in Japanese Affiliates in ASEAN, 2013

	SME	Large	t-value	
Share of originating inputs	78%	75%	2.05	**
Share of originating materials	34%	40%	−3.89	***
Share of labour inputs	21%	13%	9.82	***
Share of other inputs	23%	22%	0.80	

Notes: 1. "Large" is defined as the parent firm with 300 or more employees and whose paid-up capital or investment fund is over 30 million yen. The rest are categorized into SMEs.
2. *** and ** respectively represent significance at the 1 per cent and 5 per cent statistical levels for the null hypothesis that shares are the same between the cases of SMEs and large parents.
3. The total number of affiliates in this computation is 1,033.

other ACFTA member countries), labour inputs in host countries, and other inputs (miscellaneous expenses in host countries), we can see that such a higher share in affiliates owned by SMEs is sourced from a higher share of labour inputs. The difference in the labour input share is significant at 8 per cent point. On the other hand, affiliates owned by large parents have the higher share of originating materials. In sum, in terms of ROO compliance, both affiliates owned by SMEs and large parents seemed to have no difficulty in this area.

Then, we restrict our attention to ACFTA used by Japanese affiliates in ASEAN. Table 10.3 reports the number and share of Japanese affiliates according to status on export to China, status on ACFTA use, and parent's size. From this table, we can see that the share of export affiliates is around 10 per cent point lower in SMEs than in large parents. Also among exporters, the share of ACFTA users is lower in SMEs. These observations are found in export platform FDI but are similar to the findings in the previous studies such as Takahashi and Urata (2010), which examine the use of FTA schemes by Japanese firms in Japan. Namely, although we found above that input structure and the difficulty in ROO compliance are not so different between affiliates owned by SMEs and large parents, those by large parents are more likely to use preference schemes in exporting than those by SMEs.

TABLE 10.3
Export and ACFTA Use by Japanese Affiliates, 2013

			SMEs	Large
Export				
NO		Number	385	313
		Share in All (%)	77	65
YES		Number	113	168
		Share in All (%)	23	35
	ACFTA Use			
	NO	Number	90	119
		Share in All Exporters (%)	80	71
	YES	Number	23	49
		Share in All Exporters (%)	20	29
All		Number	498	481

Note: "Large" is defined as the parent firm with 300 or more employees and whose paid-up capital or investment fund is over 30 million yen. The rest are categorized into SMEs.

Lastly, we introduce affiliates' responses to the question on problems encountered when they export under FTA schemes. The number and share of each response in 2011 according to parent's size are shown in Table 10.4. The number of responding affiliates is 815, and multiple answers are allowed. The table shows that the shares of problems raised by the two kinds of affiliates are not so different. They consistently point out the time and effort needed for obtaining COOs as a major problem. Interestingly, it is not a serious issue whether an affiliate can technically comply with ROOs. This fact is consistent with the above high share of originating inputs. Therefore, the major issue in FTA utilization would be on how to obtain COOs rather than whether or not to comply with ROOs. In addition, "no problem" also records a high share.

TABLE 10.4
Problems Encountered when Japanese Affiliates in ASEAN Export under FTA Schemes

	SME		Large		Total	
	Number	Share (%)	Number	Share (%)	Number	Share (%)
Long time needed for obtaining COOs	101	21	146	22	247	21
Cumbersome works needed for obtaining COOs	69	14	89	13	158	14
Cumbersome ROOs across FTAs	50	10	80	12	130	11
Shortage of staffs	40	8	51	8	91	8
Unable to comply with ROOs	29	6	53	8	82	7
Expensive COO fee	25	5	35	5	60	5
No existence of FTAs	14	3	32	5	46	4
Others	22	5	24	4	46	4
Incooperative suppliers	17	4	22	3	39	3
Bad quota system	8	2	10	1	18	2
No problem	102	21	132	20	234	20
Total	375	100	542	100	917	100

Notes: 1. Multiple answers are allowed.
2. The number of responding affiliates is 815.
Source: Survey of Japanese-Affiliated Firms in ASEAN, India, and Oceania in 2011.

4. Empirical Results

This section reports our estimation results. The basic statistics for our empirical analysis are provided in Table 10.5. Our baseline results are shown in Table 10.6. In column (I), we estimate only the FTA equation by probit estimation technique for the purpose of comparison. The coefficient for the share of originating inputs is estimated to be insignificant, indicating that their share is not significantly associated with affiliates' ACFTA use. One possible reason is that there is no positively-linear relation between compliance of RVC and the share of originating inputs once it becomes greater than its cut-off (e.g., 40 per cent). Another reason is that, as shown in Table 10.5, the sample mean of this share is extremely high (74.5 per cent), so that most of the sample affiliates may have a higher share than the cut-off.[8] On the other hand, the share of exports to China and the experience on the use of other FTAs (dummy for use of other FTAs in exporting) have significantly positive coefficients. The former result shows the

TABLE 10.5
Basic Statistics

	Obs	Mean	Std. Dev.	Min	Max
FTA Use	461	0.269	0.444	0	1
Export	1,700	0.271	0.445	0	1
Share of originating inputs	1,700	0.745	0.228	0.01	1
Share of labour inputs	1,700	0.169	0.135	0	1
Share of originating materials	1,700	0.361	0.246	0	1
Share of local inputs	1,700	0.254	0.229	0	1
Share of imports from China	1,700	0.046	0.110	0	1
Share of imports from ASEAN	1,700	0.061	0.131	0	1
Share of other inputs	1,700	0.215	0.170	0	1
Share of exports to China	1,700	0.028	0.096	0	1
Dummy for use of other FTAs in exporting	1,700	0.301	0.459	0	1
A log of Employees	1,700	5.452	1.518	1.099	10.4
A log of Export Costs	1,700	6.404	0.161	6.075	7.7
Dummy (1 for positive exports to third countries)	1,700	0.635	0.481	0	1

significant role of export magnitude while the latter result may indicate that some components of administrative costs for FTA use are common across FTAs. As is inconsistent with our expectation, the coefficient for the number of employees in affiliates is negatively significant.

Next, we estimate our Heckman probit model, namely both export and FTA equations. The results are reported in column (II) of Table 10.6. We can find the significant result in Rho, indicating the existence of selection bias in the estimates of the FTA equation. Therefore, the estimation for the Heckman model is preferred to that for the simple probit model. The coefficients for both excluded variables are

TABLE 10.6
Significant Factors in Export and FTA Utilization

	(I)	(II)	
	FTA	Export	FTA
Share of originating inputs	0.583	−0.287*	0.304
	[0.478]	[0.161]	[0.390]
Share of exports to China	1.032**		0.929**
	[0.514]		[0.424]
Dummy for use of other FTAs in exporting	2.518***	0.251***	2.277***
	[0.240]	[0.079]	[0.296]
A log of Employees	−0.126*	0.215***	0.011
	[0.073]	[0.028]	[0.069]
A log of Export Costs		−2.679*	
		[1.446]	
Dummy (1 for positive exports to third countries)		0.729***	
		[0.084]	
Rho			0.717
			[0.194]
Chi-squared statistics			5.10**
Number of observations	445		1,700
Log pseudolikelihood	−139.06		−964.60

Notes: 1. In column (I), we employ the probit estimation technique while the Heckman estimation technique is employed in column (II).
2. ***, **, and * represent significance at the 1 per cent, 5 per cent, and 10 per cent statistical levels, respectively.
3. In the parenthesis is the robust standard error.
4. In all specifications, export country, industry, and year fixed effects are included.

significantly estimated. In the FTA equation, we can see similar results to column (I), although the coefficient for the number of employees is insignificant. Namely, while the coefficient for the share of originating inputs is insignificant, the share of exports to China and the experience on the use of other FTAs have significantly positive coefficients. These results may indicate that difficulty in ROO compliance is not a major reason for not utilizing FTA schemes. Rather, the magnitude of benefits from utilizing those matters compensate for doing cumbersome works for COOs.

Table 10.7 reports the results in industry fixed effects and export country fixed effects in the FTA equation of the above Heckman

TABLE 10.7
Results in Industry Dummy and Export Country Dummy

	Coef.	Significance
Industry Dummy (Base: Chemical)		
Food	−0.78	*
Textile	−0.63	
Apparel	−1.40	**
Wood	−0.24	
Furniture	−0.97	
Plastic	−0.91	**
Rubber	−0.78	
Pottery	0.26	
Ferrous metal	−1.83	***
Non-ferrous metal	−0.87	**
Metal products	−1.22	***
General machinery	−1.41	***
Electric machinery	−0.83	**
Transport equipment	−0.90	***
Precision instruments	−6.37	***
Others	−0.27	
Export Country Dummy (Base: Indonesia)		
Cambodia	−6.49	***
Malaysia	0.11	
Philippines	0.37	
Thailand	0.18	
Vietnam	0.05	

Notes: 1. This table reports estimates for industry and export country dummy variables in column (II) of Table 10.6.

2. ***, **, and * represent significance at the 1 per cent, 5 per cent, and 10 per cent statistical levels, respectively.

estimation. The coefficients for industry dummy variables are measured as the difference with the coefficient for chemical products. No positive coefficients are significant, implying that FTA schemes are most likely to be utilized in chemical products and the industries with insignificant coefficients (e.g., rubber or pottery). We also see the significantly large and negative coefficient in precision instruments, indicating that FTA schemes are least utilized when exporting precision instruments. In general, machinery industries have significantly negative coefficients may be because of the use of processing trade schemes in China.[9] On the other hand, in the case of export country fixed effects, only Cambodia has a significant coefficient, which is negative. Therefore, Japanese affiliates in Cambodia are least likely to utilize FTA schemes probably because of some problems in COOs in Cambodia. One simple example is that the fees for issuance of COOs are extraordinary expensive in Cambodia (US\$50) compared with those in other ASEAN countries (mostly a few U.S. dollars).

These results are qualitatively unchanged even if we further decompose the component of originating inputs. The estimation results are shown in Table 10.8. In column (I), we decompose into the share of labour inputs, share of originating materials, and share of other inputs. In the FTA equation, all these three shares have insignificant coefficients. In column (II), we further decompose the share of originating materials into the share of local inputs, share of imports from China, and share of imports from ASEAN. In this case, we can see a significantly positive coefficient for the share of imports from China in the FTA equation. One possible interpretation is that Japanese affiliates with the higher share of imports from China may import from affiliates in China owned by the same parent and get engaged in intra-firm division of labour.[10] The affiliates conducting such operation will have much knowledge on international business activities including preference utilization. In these columns, the results of the other variables are unchanged compared with those in column (II) of Table 10.6. Namely, the share of exports to China and the experience on the use of other FTAs have significantly positive coefficients.[11]

In sum, in terms of ROO compliance, Japanese affiliates in ASEAN seem to have no difficulty as they have a sufficiently high share of originating inputs. This estimation result is consistent with the aforementioned responses to the questionnaire survey, which show that the major issue in FTA utilization is how to obtain COOs rather than whether or not to comply with ROOs. These results also have implications on the existing theory on ROOs. Most of the theoretical

TABLE 10.8
Decomposition of Originating Inputs

	(I)		(II)	
	Export	FTA	Export	FTA
Share of labour inputs	−0.920***	0.246	−0.883***	0.240
	[0.324]	[0.888]	[0.324]	[0.889]
Share of originating materials	−0.303*	0.247		
	[0.173]	[0.403]		
Share of local inputs			−0.456**	−0.110
			[0.193]	[0.419]
Share of imports from China			0.322	1.755**
			[0.338]	[0.707]
Share of imports from ASEAN			−0.126	0.782
			[0.323]	[0.807]
Share of other inputs	0.079	0.670	0.098	0.693
	[0.246]	[0.576]	[0.245]	[0.582]
Share of exports to China		0.912**		0.735*
		[0.425]		[0.417]
Dummy for use of other FTAs in exporting	0.246***	2.278***	0.251***	2.309***
	[0.079]	[0.308]	[0.079]	[0.315]
A log of Employees	0.207***	0.013	0.206***	−0.005
	[0.029]	[0.069]	[0.029]	[0.068]
A log of Export Costs	−2.722*		−2.732*	
	[1.446]		[1.450]	
Dummy (1 for positive exports to third countries)	0.718***		0.713***	
	[0.084]		[0.085]	
Rho		0.724		0.723
		[0.203]		[0.195]
Chi–squared statistics		4.63**		5.01**
Number of observations		1,700		1,700
Log pseudolikelihood		−960.78		−956.70

Notes: 1. This table reports the estimation results by the Heckman estimation technique.
2. ***, **, and * represent significance at the 1 per cent, 5 per cent, and 10 per cent statistical levels, respectively.
3. In the parenthesis is the robust standard error.
4. In all specifications, export country, industry, and year fixed effects are included.

studies on RTA utilization have examined the compliance to RVC rules (e.g., Krishna 2005) rather than change-in-tariff classification (CTC), which is another type of ROO. However, at least for Japanese affiliates in ASEAN, RVC rules are easy to comply with. Therefore, it might be more interesting or important to theoretically examine firms' RTA utilization in the case of CTC. Also, in the existing theoretical studies, the compliance of ROOs is modelled as a rise of variable costs (e.g., Demidova and Krishna 2008). Our results of significant contributions of export sizes and the experience on preference use may indicate that fixed costs for RTA utilization are much more costly than the rise of variable costs through complying with ROOs.

Finally, we examine the correlation of these elements in the FTA equation with parent's size. We regress parent's size dummy (i.e., one for large size) on each of those. In the case of share variables, we employ a fractional logit estimation technique (Fractional), which is proposed by Papke and Wooldridge (1996) and ensures that the predicted values of the dependent variable are in the unit interval, i.e., [0, 1]. In the cases of binary variables and continuous variables, a probit technique (Probit) and ordinary least square (OLS) method are employed, respectively. The results are presented in Table 10.9 and show that the affiliates by large-sized parents have significantly higher shares of originating inputs, particularly of imports from ASEAN, and of

TABLE 10.9
Correlation with Parent's Size

	Method	Coef.	R.S.D.	Obs.
Share of originating inputs	Fractional	−0.257***	[0.063]	1,700
Share of labour inputs	Fractional	−0.428***	[0.045]	1,700
Share of originating materials	Fractional	0.096*	[0.054]	1,700
Share of local inputs	Fractional	−0.04	[0.061]	1,700
Share of imports from China	Fractional	0.153	[0.129]	1,700
Share of imports from ASEAN	Fractional	0.452***	[0.117]	1,700
Share of other inputs	Fractional	−0.062	[0.052]	1,700
Share of exports to China	Fractional	0.457***	[0.177]	1,700
Dummy for use of other FTAs in exporting	Probit	0.266***	[0.069]	1,698
A log of Employees	OLS	1.188***	[0.065]	1,700

Notes: 1. This table reports the results of regressing on a dummy variable that takes the value one if parent's size is large and zero otherwise.
2. ***, **, and * represent significance at the 1 per cent, 5 per cent, and 10 per cent statistical levels, respectively.
3. In the parenthesis is the robust standard error.
4. In all specifications, export country, industry, and year fixed effects are included.

exports to China. Also, their share of labour inputs is significantly lower. Those affiliates are more likely to have experienced the use of other FTAs and have a larger number of employees. On the other hand, the shares of local inputs, imports from China, and other inputs are not significantly associated with parent's size.

Based on these results, we can derive the following implications on the use of preference schemes in export platform FDI according to parent's size. First, regardless of preference use, SMEs' affiliates are likely to be smaller-sized and thus are less likely to be export platform, i.e., export to third countries. Second, the differences in input structure between large firms and SMEs do not significantly matter in the choice of preference use. Third, affiliates owned by SMEs do not have enough intensity of export to third countries to cover the costs for preference use. Fourth, while experience on the use of other FTAs plays a significant role in reducing the costs for preference use, affiliates by SMEs are less likely to have such experience and thus will face higher barriers to use preferences.

5.   Policy Recommendations

In this chapter, we empirically identified significant firm characteristics in the use of preferences in export platform FDI. Specifically, by employing a unique survey, we investigated the use of ACFTA when Japanese affiliates in ASEAN export to China. Our primary observation is that Japanese affiliates owned by large parents are more likely to use FTA schemes in exporting than those owned by SMEs. Our analysis in this chapter reveals the reasons for this observation and proposes the effective policy measures to encourage affiliates by SMEs to utilize FTA schemes, as summarized in the following.

First, the design of ROOs *per se* does not matter so much. This implication comes from the estimation result of insignificant contribution of originating inputs. The questionnaire survey of Japanese affiliates in ASEAN also shows that the major issue in FTA utilization is how to obtain COOs rather than whether or not to comply with ROOs. In short, Japanese affiliates in ASEAN seem to have no difficulty in ROO compliance as they have a sufficiently high share of originating inputs. As a result, although very unfriendly business rules should not be imposed, the change of ROOs, especially the cut-off level in RVC rules, to the less restrictive ones may not significantly boost FTA utilization by SMEs' affiliates. The introduction of co-equal rules will be enough for firms to easily comply with ROOs although it is another issue whether or not such rules are enough to prevent roundabout trade.

Second, it is effective to enhance affiliates' production and exports. This implication is based on our estimation results of significant contribution of the magnitude of tariff saving (i.e., the share of exports to China) to affiliates' RTA utilization and of the significant difference in its magnitude between affiliates owned by SMEs and large parents. The policy measures to enlarge production and exports will not be limited to specific RTA measures. For example, the development of labour market to supply sufficient labour resources will contribute to enlarging production capacities. Tax reforms such as the reduction of corporate tax rates will also enhance RTA utilization through expanding export sizes at least in the long run.

Third, as is often pointed out in the public, it is important to reduce costs for certifying origin. This importance is at least partly suggested in the significant role of the experience on the use of other RTA schemes. Specifically, it will be helpful to provide tools to easily complete necessary procedures for obtaining COOs. For example, according to Song and Kuno (2015), Customs Agency in Korea developed "FTA-PASS" and distributed it for free. It is a kind of computer software to facilitate firms' administrative works on ROOs. Also, the Korean government has provided various consulting services such as "FTA Call Center 1380". Furthermore, it provides not only services for beginners of RTA utilization but also those for experienced RTA-users. The latter includes consulting services for the preparation for verification. These services will contribute to reducing substantial costs for certifying origin.

APPENDIX 10.1
Sample Distribution by Host Countries

	2012			2013		
	No Export	MFN Exporter	FTA Exporter	No Export	MFN Exporter	FTA Exporter
Indonesia	82	15	7	107	17	6
Cambodia	9	1		13		
Lao PDR	9	1		9	1	
Malaysia	82	22	12	17	4	3
Philippines	43	14	3	53	26	5
Thailand	315	69	31	321	84	36
Vietnam	108	43	9	121	40	12

Source: Survey of Japanese-Affiliated Firms in ASEAN, India, and Oceania in 2012 and 2013.

APPENDIX 10.2
Sample Distribution by Industry

	2012			2013		
	No Export	MFN Exporter	FTA Exporter	No Export	MFN Exporter	FTA Exporter
Food	33	4	3	33	3	3
Textile	9	4	2	6	4	6
Apparel	22	4	1	23	5	1
Wood	9	2	1	5	1	1
Paper	6	1		4	2	
Furniture	4	2		4	1	1
Chemical	40	6	13	34	9	7
Medicine				2		
Plastic	46	8	3	40	17	6
Rubber	7	11		10	10	2
Pottery	11		3	14	1	2
Ferrous metal	36	4	1	33	2	
Non-ferrous metal	15	5	2	18	2	2
Metal products	71	11	2	70	12	2
General machinery	44	8	3	38	11	1
Electric machinery	87	50	11	81	51	8
Transport equipment	122	23	11	120	22	15
Precision instruments	8	4		15	6	
Others	78	18	6	91	13	5

Source: Survey of Japanese-Affiliated Firms in ASEAN, India, and Oceania in 2012 and 2013.

NOTES

1. This research was conducted as part of the Economic Research Institute for ASEAN and East Asia (ERIA) project, "SME Participation in ASEAN and East Asian Regional Economic Integration".

2. These numbers are obtained from the 2010 Survey of Trends in Business Activities of Foreign Affiliates by the Ministry of Economy, Trade and Industry. A similar share of exports to third countries can also be observed in U.S. multinational firms (Ekholm et al. 2007).

3. Specifically, in their paper, "home-country export platform" refers to the situation where MNEs' foreign plant exports to the home market; "third-country export platform" refers to the case where the foreign plant exports only to a third market; and "global export platform" refers to the foreign plant exporting to both home and third markets. Other previous studies have also examined these FDI types (Baltagi et al. 2007; Aw and Lee 2008; Blonigen et al. 2007; Grossman et al. 2006; Yeaple 2003).

4. Kiyota et al. (2008) investigated the determinants of Japanese multinationals' procurement patterns.

5. For more details, see Demidova and Krishna (2008).

6. Joint ventures between Japanese companies in Japan and local companies also follow the FDI definition. Namely, if the share of a Japanese firm is more than or equal to 10 per cent, the firm is defined as a Japanese affiliate. The investment from Japanese overseas headquarters, such as in Singapore, is also defined as Japanese affiliates as long as the share is more than or equal to 10 per cent.

7. Unfortunately, the JETRO survey does not include data on sales value, value-added, intermediate inputs cost, and capital stock. Therefore, we could not compute value-added per worker or the total factor productivity.

8. Also, Japanese affiliates produce multiple products, not only products exported to China but also products for other countries including host countries. Therefore, our variable of originating input share contains various inputs for products not exported to China.

9. The processing trade is a scheme of importing raw materials or intermediate inputs which are further processed to produce exported products. Under this scheme, governments usually offer tariff reduction or tariff exemption. For more details, see Yu and Tian (2012).

10. Due to data limitation, we cannot directly identify whether or not the trade is intra-firm trade or arm's length trade. It is also impossible to identify whether the parent of an affiliate has any affiliates in China or not.

11. In addition, we further decompose local inputs into those by indigenous firms, other Japanese affiliates, and other foreign-owned firms, but found that all of the coefficients for these local inputs are insignificant. The results are available upon request. In addition, one may suggest to estimate this

model by exporting countries. However, perhaps due to a small number of observations, we were not able to obtain the convergence of log-likelihood.

REFERENCES

Aw, Bee Yan and Yi Lee. "Firm Heterogeneity and Location Choice of Taiwanese Multinationals". *Journal of International Economics* 75 (2008): 167–79.

Baldwin, Richard and Toshihiro Okubo. "Networked FDI: Sales and Sourcing Patterns of Japanese Foreign Affiliates". *The World Economy* 37, no. 8 (2014): 1051–80.

Baltagi, Badi H., Peter Egger, and Michael Pfaffermayr. "Estimating Models of Complex FDI: Are There Third-Country Effects?" *Journal of Econometrics* 140 (2007): 260–81.

Blonigen, Bruce, Ronald Davies, Glen Waddella, and Helen Naughton. "FDI in Space: Spatial Autoregressive Relationships in Foreign Direct Investment". *European Economic Review* 51, no. 5 (2007): 1303–25.

Bureau, Jean-Christophe, Raja Chakir, and Jacques Gallezot. "The Utilisation of Trade Preferences for Developing Countries in the Agri-Food Sector". *Journal of Agricultural Economics* 58, no. 2 (2007): 175–98.

Cadot, Olivier, Celine Carrere, Jaime De Melo, and Bolormaa Tumurchudur. "Product-Specific Rules of Origin in EU and US Preferential Trading Arrangements: An Assessment". *World Trade Review* 5, no. 2 (2006): 199–224.

Cherkashin, Ivan, Svetlana Demidova, Hiau Looi Kee, and Kala Krishna. "Firm Heterogeneity and Costly Trade: A New Estimation Strategy and Policy Experiments". *Journal of International Economics* 96, no. 1 (2015): 18–36.

Demidova, Svetlana and Kala Krishna. "Firm Heterogeneity and Firm Behavior with Conditional Policies". *Economics Letters* 98, no. 2 (2008): 122–28.

Ekholm, Karolina, Rikard Forslid, and James Markusen. "Export-Platform Foreign Direct Investment". *Journal of European Economic Association* 5, no. 4 (2007): 776–95.

Francois, Joseph, Bernard Hoekman, and Miriam Manchin. "Preference Erosion and Multilateral Trade Liberalization". *World Bank Economic Review* 20, no. 2 (2006): 197–216.

Grossman, Gene, Elhanan Helpman, and Adam Szeidl. "Optimal Integration Strategies for the Multinational Firm". *Journal of International Economics* 70 (2006): 216–38.

Hakobyan, Shushanik. "Accounting for Underutilization of Trade Preference Programs: U.S. Generalized System of Preferences". *Canadian Journal of Economics* 48, no. 2 (2015): 408–36.

Hayakawa, Kazunobu. "Does Firm Size Matter in Exporting and Using FTA Schemes?" *Journal of International Trade and Economic Development* 24, no. 7 (2015*a*): 883–905.

———. "Impacts of FTA Utilization on Firm Performance". *B.E. Journal of Economic Analysis and Policy* 15, no. 3 (2015*b*): 1325–52.

Hayakawa, Kazunobu and Nuttawut Laksanapanyakul. "Impacts of Common Rules of Origin on FTA Utilization". *International Economics and Economic Policy* 14, no. 1 (2017): 75–90.

Hayakawa, Kazunobu and Toshiyuki Matsuura. "Trade Liberalization in Asia and FDI Strategies in Heterogeneous Firms: Evidence from Japanese Firm-Level Data". *Oxford Economic Papers* 67, no. 2 (2015): 494–513.

———. "Complex Vertical FDI and Firm Heterogeneity: Evidence from East Asia". *Journal of the Japanese and International Economies* 25, no. 3 (2011): 273–89.

Kiyota, Kozo, Toshiyuki Matsuura, Shujiro Urata, and Yuhong Wei. "Reconsidering the Backward Vertical Linkages of Foreign Affiliates: Evidence from Japanese Multinationals". *World Development* 36, no. 8 (2008): 1398–414.

Krishna, Kala. "Understanding Rules of Origin". NBER Working Paper No. 11150 (2005).

Manchin, Miriam. "Preference Utilisation and Tariff Reduction in EU Imports from ACP Countries". *The World Economy* 29, no. 9 (2006): 1243–66.

Papke, Leslie E. and Jeffrey M. Wooldridge. "Econometric Methods for Fractional Response Variables with an Application to 401(k) Plan Participation Rates". *Journal of Applied Econometrics* 11, no. 6 (1996): 619–32.

Song, Joon-Heon and Arata Kuno. "FTA Utilization Promotion Policy in the ROK and the Implications for Japan". ERINA Report No. 126 (2015).

Takahashi, Katsuhide and Shujiro Urata. "On the Use of FTAs by Japanese Firms: Further Evidence". *Business and Politics* 12, no. 1 (2010): 1–15.

Van de Ven, Wynand P.M.M. and Bernard M.S. Van Praag. "The Demand for Deductibles in Private Health Insurance: A Probit Model with Sample Selection". *Journal of Econometrics* 17 (1981): 229–52.

Yeaple, Stephen. "The Complex Integration Strategies of Multinationals and Cross Country Dependencies in the Structure of Foreign Direct Investment". *Journal of International Economics* 60, no. 2 (2003): 293–314.

Yu, Miaojie and Wei Tian. "China's Processing Trade: A Firm-Level Analysis". In *Rebalancing and Sustaining Growth in China*, edited by Huw McKay and Ligang Song. Canberra, ACT: Australian National University E-press, 2012, pp. 111–48.

11

SOUTH KOREAN MULTINATIONAL ENTERPRISES AND VIETNAM SMEs' PARTICIPATION IN GLOBAL PRODUCTION NETWORKS IN THE CONTEXT OF INCREASED ASEAN AND EAST ASIAN REGIONAL ECONOMIC INTEGRATION[1]

Nguyen Ngoc Anh, Nguyen Thi Tuong Anh,
Nguyen Ngoc Minh and Nguyen Thi Phuong Mai

Introduction

During the last decade, Asian countries, especially East and Southeast Asia countries, have witnessed an ever increasing trend of regional integration with the dramatic proliferation of regional free trade agreements (FTAs), both concluded and still in the process of negotiation. This process of regional economic integration has been driven by the mutually reinforcing market forces and trade agreements (regional and preferential). According to data from the Asian Development Bank (ADB), the number of FTAs involving at least one Asian country has almost doubled, from 124 in 2005 to 220 in 2016. In addition, there are 67 FTAs being proposed and pending negotiation.[2] This phenomenon is referred to as the "Asian noodle bowl" with the economies of ASEAN and East Asia becoming increasingly integrated. According to data from ADB, the 16 ASEAN+6 countries (10 ASEAN members plus Australia, PRC, India, Japan, the Republic of Korea and New Zealand) account disproportionately for over 62 per cent of total FTAs (being in effect and in negotiation) of the total 48 ADB member countries/economies in Asia.[3]

The most important market force that drives international trade in recent years is the rise of global production networks operated by multinationals in which firms slice up a production chain into small production stages and then assigning them each to the most cost effective location across borders (ADB 2010; Helpman 2011). Globally operating firms have been taking advantage of these factors to exploit differences in factor prices (i.e. inputs and low-skilled labour) around the world (Blinder 2006; Baldwin-Edwards 2011) and multi-nationals are at the forefront of global production networks taking advantage of reductions of trade barriers, rapid advancements in production technology, and a decrease in transport and communication costs as explained by Athukorala (2013). He explains that firstly "rapid advancements in production technology have enabled the industry to slice up the value chain into finer, 'portable', components" (i.e. modular production technology with "standard fragments"); secondly "technological innovations in communication and transporta-tion have shrunk the distance that once separated the world's nations, and improved speed, efficiency and economy of coordinating geographically dispersed production process", and thirdly the "liberalization policy reforms across the world over the past four decades have considerably removed barriers to trade and foreign direct investment (FDI)".

Although such fragmented production has been argued to be beneficial as it allows economies, especially in Asia thanks to its strong intraregional and international links, and its adeptness at transferring and absorbing new production technologies, to specialize in narrower niches to enter international markets with a more limited range of skills than previously (ADB 2010, p. 62), a major area of concern amongst policymakers has been the extent to which small and medium-sized enterprises (SMEs) are participating and benefitting from regional economic integration. It is a valid concern given that about 95–99 per cent of all firms in the region are SMEs. Furthermore, SMEs are also likely to be more resource-constrained (compared to large firms) to take advantage of the benefits from trade and investment liberalization.

Like other countries in the region, during the last decade, global production networks operated by large multinational enterprises (MNEs) have become increasingly relevant for Vietnam, as the country witnesses more and more global production facilities being set up by MNEs, from lower-skilled sectors like garment and textile to high-technology sectors like electronics. Among other factors, this phenomenon has been partly attributed to the recent proactive engagement of Vietnam through various FTAs like the ASEAN–Korean FTA, Vietnam–EU FTA, the Trans-Pacific Parnership (TPP) and the like.[4] The arrival of many MNEs has helped to integrate the country deeper into the global production networks in various sectors from furniture, garments to electronics. For example, the arrival of the largest electronics giants such as Intel, Nokia, and most notably Korean MNEs such as Samsung and LG together with their first-tier suppliers such as Foxcon, has turned Vietnam into one of the largest electronic production hubs in the global production networks.

Like many other developing countries, the private sector of Vietnam is mostly made up of SMEs which account for more than 90 per cent of all firms. The country shares the same above-mentioned policy concerns, that is, beyond the initial direct effect on the local economy in terms of capital injection and employment creation, the question that a developing country like Vietnam is facing is how to stimulate the diffusion of technology and productivity gains from the FDI sector in general and these global production networks in particular to other parts of the economy. Despite the fact that FDI has been widely perceived as a panacea for developing countries as a way to reduce poverty and kick-start sustainable modern industries, most Vietnamese domestic firms, especially SMEs, cannot yet participate in the global production networks through which Vietnam can improve its technology level. Policies should be implemented to make FDI firms become more connected with the rest of the economy rather than as an "enclave" FDI sector.

This question is particularly relevant in the process of Vietnam's transition from a lower to a higher middle-income country status because despite the potential positive effects of spillovers, the presence of these MNEs and their production networks can also have negative effects on local firms (Damijan et al. 2013). The capital, managerial, technological and know-how advantages of FDI firms enable them to take over the market of domestic firms, forcing them into less efficient scales and less productive activities. Moreover, MNEs which are attracted to a country due to its low labour productivity may contribute to that country's falling into low productivity trap (Seguino 2005). Without appropriate policies the arrival of MNEs could result in the so-called "enclave economy", the benefits of which are confined to an international sector not connected to the wider economy (Gallagher and Zarsky 2007).

Despite their importance, there is currently a lack of systematic and comprehensive research on these issues. This study is an attempt to fill in this gap of the literature. In particular, the chapter seeks to address two related questions:

- Firstly, how regional economic integration (e.g. AEC, FTA) has affected MNEs in their investment decisions and operations?
- Secondly, what is the nature and extent of linkages that MNEs have developed with SMEs in Vietnam (host country), and to the extent possible, how is this relationship shaped by regional economic integration?

To address these inter-related questions, in this chapter, we adopt a case study approach. We focus on Korean MNEs, their investment decisions and operations in Vietnam as the host country in response to the increasing regional integration trend and the linkages with their local Vietnamese SMEs. Vietnam is selected as a country for study because it is part of ASEAN, recently opened up to the world economy and actively engaged in numerous FTAs, including the ASEAN Economic Community (AEC), EU–Vietnam FTA, TPP and many other bilateral agreements. Korean MNEs are selected because Korea is one of the biggest foreign investors in Vietnam. But more importantly, Vietnam has been experiencing a recent wave of inbound FDI from Korean MNEs in both traditional manufacturing sectors like garment and more advanced sectors like electronics. One of the greatest challenges for addressing these questions is data availability. In this study, instead of relying on quantitative data analysis and modelling, we combine descriptive data statistics (both administrative data and survey data) with qualitative data collected from in-depth interviews with both Korean MNEs and their local partners as well as policymakers.

Although we focus largely on the manufacturing sector, we conducted our in-depth interviews mostly with CEOs of firms in two main sectors: electronics and apparel. Apparel is selected because Vietnam has developed a vibrant domestic apparel processing industry during the last 20 years. Vietnam is one of the biggest apparel exporters in the world, ranked 5th after China, Bangladesh, Italy and Germany. Electronics is not a new industry in Vietnam. During the early years of economic reform, there were attempts to jump-start the sector but failed. However, during the last five to seven years, the electronics sector has been experiencing a spectacular export growth thanks to the arrival of many electronics giants, including Korean MNEs. The remainder of the chapter is structured as follows. In the next section, we present our analysis on the first question, and in section three we focus on the linkages between MNEs and SMEs. Section four offers some concluding remarks.

1. Vietnam's Regional Economic Integration and Korean MNEs

1.1. Vietnam–Korean Bilateral Trade and Investment Relations

Vietnam and South Korea have continuously developed a significant bilateral trade and investment relation since Vietnam's opening-up to the global economy and established diplomatic and economic relations with South Korea. According to the latest data, Vietnam–Korea trade grew continuously during the last ten years (see Figure 11.1), with the total trade value reaching US$28.9 billion in 2014. During the period 2005–14, it had a composite average growth rate of 23.7 per cent. Vietnam's import accounted for the major share of this bilateral trade. In 2014, Vietnam's imports from Korea (Rep.) amounted to roughly US$21.7 billion, tripling the export value (US$7.2 billion). In the last ten years, Vietnam's deficit in trade with Korea (Rep.) widened significantly to reach US$14.6 billion in 2014 from only US$2.9 billion in 2005. Looking at the structure of exports and imports between the two countries could reveal the underlying structure and

FIGURE 11.1
Vietnam–South Korea Bilateral Trade Flows (USD billion)

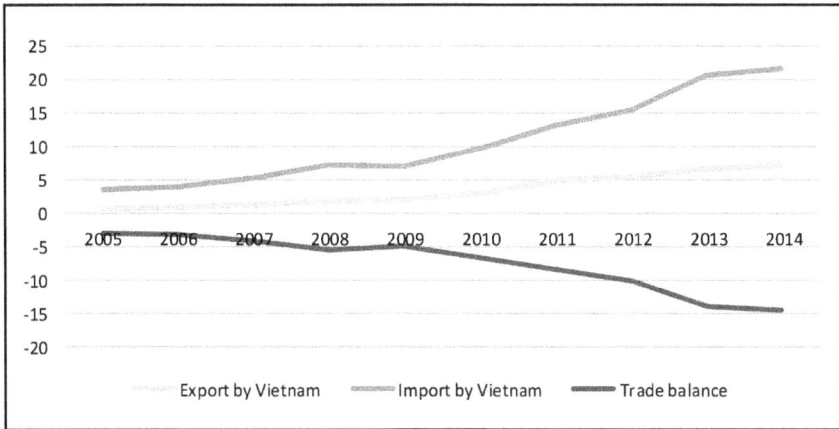

Source: UN Comtrade..

the complementarity. Capital and/or technology-intensive products are imported most by Vietnam. Electrical equipment is imported most by Vietnam from Korea. Its import value at US$5.7 billion, accounted for over one-fourth of total imports from Korea. The other major product groups include textile materials (10.4 per cent) and telecommunications and sound-recording and reproducing equipment (10.1 per cent). Apparel and clothing accessories stood out to be the most important export by Vietnam to the South Korean market. In 2014, these products generated a total revenue of US$2.0 billion, corresponding to a 28.1 per cent share of Vietnam's exports to South Korea.

Vietnam has successfully attracted large volumes of FDI, reaching levels of around US$10–12 billion per year during 2010–15. According to the General Statistics Office, for 2015 there were over 2,000 newly registered FDI inflow projects with total capital of US$15.6 billion, along with another 814 projects expanding their investment to US$7.2 billion by the end of 2015, a year-on-year increase of 12.5 per cent. According to Foreign Investment Administration under the Ministry of Investment Planning of Vietnam, South Korea has become one of the biggest foreign investors in Vietnam (see Table 11.1). Electric and electronics industries are Korea's main investment as well as a number of light industries, such as textile and shoe.

TABLE 11.1
Key Investors in Vietnam (as of February 2016)

TT	Country	Number of Project	Total Registered Capital (US$ million)
1	South Korea	5,058	45,390
2	Japan	2,965	38,860
3	Singapore	1,570	36,050
4	Taiwan	2,491	31,160
5	EU	1,788	24,300
6	British Virgin Islands	632	19,580
7	Hong Kong	992	15,850
8	Malaysia	528	13,660
9	US	791	11,320
10	China	1,336	10,390

Source: Foreign Investment Administration, Ministry of Planning and Investment.

1.2. The Impact of Regional Integration and Investment Decision by Korean MNEs

This section of the chapter aims to explore how regional economic integration has affected the operation of Korean multinational firms and their relationship with both domestic and international SMEs to give a better idea of East Asian regional economic integration in the country. To assess the impact of regional integration on investment decision, ideally, we would like to observe the investment decision made by "similar" firms before and after the so-called regional integration "event". However, we do not have such luxury. Instead, in the context of this study, we rely on some aggregate macro data and qualitative data we obtained from in-depth interviews with Vietnamese policymakers and representatives of MNEs and SMEs in Vietnam.

The FDI inflows from South Korean firms into Vietnam during 2005–15 are presented in Figure 11.2. There are some indications that trade liberalization does have some impact on the inflow of Korean FDI into Vietnam, especially at two important points: The ASEAN–South Korea FTA in 2005 and the Vietnam–South Korea FTA in 2015.

FIGURE 11.2
South Korean FDI Inflows into Vietnam, 2005–15

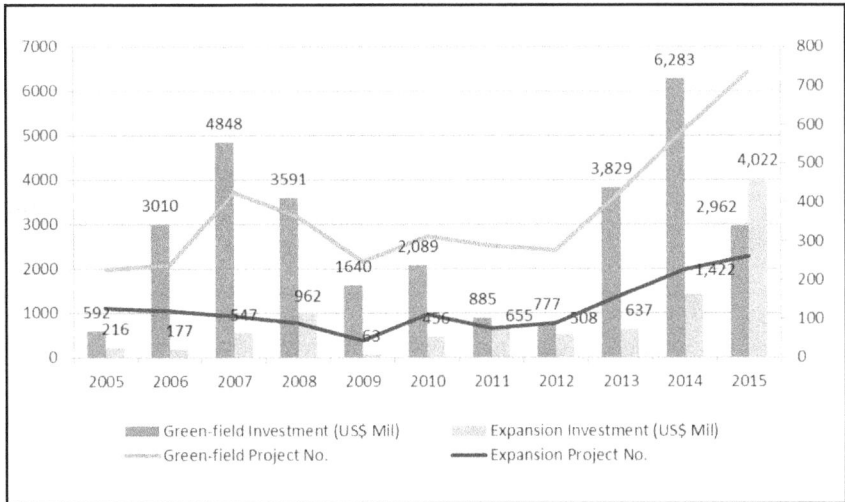

Source: Foreign Investment Administration, Ministry of Planning and Investment.

- First is the sharp increase of Korean FDI inflows (both in terms of investment amount and number of projects) into Vietnam during 2006–8 when the ASEAN–South Korea FTA was concluded (effective in 2007). During this period, there were large investment inflows by MNEs such as the Posco Steel BRVT project in 2006 (worth US$1.13 billion), Keangnam real estate in Hanoi in 2007 (worth US$500 million), Hyosung textile in Danang in 2007 (worth US$368 million), and Inpyung real estate in Hanoi in 2008 (worth US$660 million).
- Second is another even larger increase of Korean FDI inflows in the build-up to the Vietnam–Korea FTA in December 2015 which promises sharp cut on import duties for Vietnam's agricultural products and materials for textile, electric and electronics, and automobile parts from Korea. During this period, there were many mega projects. For example, in 2010 Posco Steel BRVT invested US$700 million; in 2013, LG Electronics invested US$1.5 billion in Hanoi; and Samsung Electronics invested US$1.23 billion in Thai Nguyen. In 2014, Samsung Electronics further invested US$3 billion while Samsung Display invested another US$1 billion in

Bac Ninh which was expanded further to US$3 billion. In 2015, Posco Steel BRVT invested US$1.13 billion.

While such aggregate data is illuminating to some extent, we explore further the linkage between the two by conducting a number of interviews with both policymakers and South Korean investors in Vietnam and their local partners.

We conducted an informal interview with a senior policymaker from a FDI-relevant agency in the Ministry of Planning and Investment. This official believes that regional integration has an important impact on MNEs' decisions on investment in Vietnam and suggests that there would be strong FDI inflow in such sectors as electronics, distribution, wholesale and retail, real estate, tourism, food and food processing, textile, and agriculture. This official also holds the view that the expansion of Korean transnational corporations (TNCs) such as Samsung, Doosan, LG, Posco, Taekwang, Hyosung, and Kumho has led to significant increase of their satellite Korean SMEs due to the follow-the-leader effect. For example, in the case of Samsung, not only they have constructed their electronic and electronics plants, but also expressed interest in Vietnamese retail market. Korean retailer Emart, which is owned by Samsung's relatives, entered Vietnam with an investment of US$60 million and is expected to be operational by the end of 2015 or early 2016 (Production Service Vietnam 2015).

Previous surveys and anecdotal evidence on the factors that influence investors' decision to invest in Vietnam are abundant. Besides citing an abundant and young labour force as an important factor, foreign investors often cite Vietnam's geographical position near global supply chains, the growing consumer market, expected improvements in the business climate upon completion of the TPP, and relative political and economic stability. Investors are also showing an increasing desire to diversify their manufacturing base in Asia away from China as a reason they opted to invest in operations in Vietnam. This phenomenon is highly due to Chinese economic development plan that has moved up the value chain in manufacturing. Instead of China, Vietnam takes a call to action on the "China plus one" model and successfully invites foreign investment using the advantage of its abundant human resources. However, evidence on the impact of regional integration through such agreements like Vietnam–

South Korea FTA, or ASEAN–Korea FTA on the decision of Korean MNEs are scant. To explore this issue, we conducted a number of interviews with Korean invested firms in Vietnam as well as their local partners.

There are mixed evidence on the impact of regional integration in MNEs' investment decisions and the picture is quite complex. In this section, we focus on the garment sector. We interview two Korean garment firms in Vietnam, a medium-size and a large one.[5] In the interview with the medium-size Korean-invested garment company with around 400–500 employees established in 2005 in Vietnam, the manager suggests that in theory they would benefit from the zero duty rate provided in the Vietnam–Korea FTA. However, getting such preferential treatment is difficult as it is not easy to obtain the certificate of origin for exports from Vietnam as the country still relies too much on imports of materials from China. Similarly, the manager is quite cautious of the prospect of the TPP. While they have been watching the development of the TPP, they are worried about the actual implementation as there are strict requirements such as the yarn-forward criteria, thus rendering garments produced in Vietnam not eligible for preferential treatment in TPP. Despite the initial not-so-positive assessment toward Vietnam–Korea FTA and the TPP, the manager reveals that they are exploring possibilities to invest in new product lines that could take advantage of the FTA and TPP. For example, they are considering production of higher quality products that could use materials of Vietnamese origin. The larger firm has been investing in Vietnam for a relatively long time, since 2002, and expanded its operation in 2009 with a total workforce of 8,000 employees. According to the manager of this garment company, Korean enterprises are investing in Vietnam due to Vietnam's abundant labour force and tax incentives. On top of that the recent Vietnam–Korea FTA would be an important factor attracting Korean investors to Vietnam. The TPP is also assessed positively as 99 per cent of the company's export is to the U.S. market. The company, besides having two large factories in the north of Vietnam, has just opened a new company based in Ho Chi Minh city (south of Vietnam) in the expectation that new orders are coming and they would be able to handle these new orders by themselves rather than through the headquarter in Korea.

2. Vietnamese SMEs' Integration into the Korean MNEs' Global Production Networks

To address the second research question, in this section, we explore the state of Vietnamese SMEs' participation in regional trade, production networks, and investment activities. In doing so, we also explore the enabling factors and obstacles to SME participation in regional trade, production networks, and investment activities.

2.1. An Overview of Vietnamese SMEs' Participation in Global Production Networks

Although the concept of participating in global production networks is intuitively clear, operationalizing this concept and measuring it is not so easy. As a proxy for participating in global production networks, we rely on a number of operational measures: exporting, importing, supplying to FDI firms, and subcontracting for other firms. In this study we use two data sources:

(i) The Survey of Small and Medium Scale Manufacturing Enterprises (SMEs) in Vietnam from 2009 to 2013 conducted consistently by the Ministry of Labour, Invalid and Social Affairs (MOLISA) and the Stockholm School of Economics (hereafter the MOLISA SMEs survey);

(ii) The Survey of Small and Medium Scale Manufacturing Enterprises (SMEs) commissioned by ERIA and conducted by DEPOCEN (hereafter the ERIA survey).

The former survey is conducted every two years in ten provinces of Vietnam and provides information on about 2,500 firms in 12 industries each year, focusing on SMEs in Vietnam. The latter is a special survey commissioned by ERIA to look specifically at the participation of Vietnamese SMEs in three sectors.

As indicated in Table 11.2, the level of participation of Vietnamese SMEs in global production networks in general is very limited. The percentage of SME exporting firms is very small, according to the MOLISA survey data, although there is a small increase from 5.8 per cent in 2009 to 6.4 per cent in 2013. Similarly, the number of importing firms is small, at about 3.5 per cent of the total number of firms. The

TABLE 11.2
Vietnamese SMEs' Participation in Global Production Networks

	Sample Size	Exporting		Supplier to FDI Firms		Importing		Import from ASEAN		Subcontract	
		No.	%	No.	%	No.	%	No.	%	No.	%
2009	2,659	155	5.8%	130	4.9%	92	3.5%	32	1.2%	—	—
2011	2,552	100	3.9%	132	5.2%	84	3.3%	37	1.4%	—	—
2013	2,533	163	6.4%	119	4.7%	92	3.6%	37	1.5%	—	—
2015	208	77	37.0%	—	—	71	34.1%	14	6.7%	88	42.3%

Source: MOLISA SMEs survey 2009, 2011, 2013; and ERIA survey, SME Participation in ASEAN and East Asian Regional Economic Integration 2015.

number of firms importing from ASEAN countries is even smaller, staying at just about 1 per cent. Interestingly, in comparison with figures on importing and exporting, there are about 5 per cent of firms who are suppliers to FDI firms in Vietnam. The ERIA survey provides much higher figures on these aspects. This is because the sectors covered in the survey are export-oriented sectors of Vietnam such as wood processing and garment. The overall conclusion from these surveys is that the participation of Vietnamese SMEs in global production networks in general is still limited. However, for sectors that are more export-oriented, the level of participation is much higher. This finding is somewhat consistent with previous study on ASEAN by Wignaraja (2012) who reported that the larger firms are playing bigger roles than SMEs in global production networks. However, the number reported in the SME survey is even lower than that reported by Wignaraja (2012), which could be explained by the nature of the sample. Still the number reported in the ERIA survey is more comparable with Wignaraja (2012). Comparing between ASEAN countries, he reported a higher participation rate in more advanced countries like Thailand and Malaysia and lower rates in such countries like Vietnam, Philippines and Indonesia. This is also consistent with popular opinion that firms in Vietnam are not yet ready to joint global production networks.[6]

2.2. Participation in Global Production Networks in the Traditional Apparel Sector

2.2.1. Overview of the sector

The apparel sector is one of the key sectors for Vietnam and has long been considered an important light industry for the country. The Ministry of Industry and Trade approved the Master Plan for the Development of Vietnam's Textile and Garment Industry until 2020, with an orientation to 2030 in Decision No. 3218/QD-BCT dated 11 April 2014. This official document specified the industry development perspectives and objectives, the product development orientation and the regional planning. According to *Statistical Yearbook of Vietnam 2014*, the industry consists mainly of SMEs with nearly 85 per cent of the total 5,167 enterprises having less than 300 employees, a threshold commonly used to distinguish medium from small enterprises. The sector employs more than 2.5 million workers and accounts for about 25 per cent of the labour in the industrial sector in Vietnam.

Along with phones and mobile devices, apparel is the major export sector. The sector's export value reached US\$20.1 billion in 2014, 16.7 per cent higher than in 2013, with a composite average growth

TABLE 11.3
Top Ten Largest Exporters of Apparel Worldwide, 2014

Rank	Exporter	Value (USD billion)	Share (%)	Growth (%)
1	China	191.4	39.1	5
2	Bangladesh	24.6	5	4.6
3	Italy	23	4.7	6
4	Germany	20.1	4.1	7.3
5	**Vietnam**	**20.1**	**4.1**	**16.7**
6	India	19.9	4.1	3.7
7	Hong Kong	19.4	4	−6.4
8	Turkey	18	3.7	8
9	Spain	12.4	2.5	9
10	France	10.9	2.2	4.4

Source: UN Comtrade and Depocen.

rate of 17.3 per cent over the period 2010–14, resulting in positive gains in global market share. Consistent with findings from the ERIA survey (see above), the last two decades have witnessed rapid and active participation of Vietnam apparel firms in global value chains. In 2014, Vietnam became the fifth largest exporter of apparel worldwide thanks to its gaining global market share and continued high growth rates.[7]

An important point to note is that Vietnam's apparel export depends on foreign traders who play a very important role as intermediaries in the apparel supply chain of Vietnam garment producers. These traders are generally from Hong Kong, Taiwan and South Korea with whom top leaders of global retailers/brands from the European Union, Japan and the United States, and their own international top brands rely to develop their supplier networks in Vietnam in order to reduce transaction cost of contracting and sourcing from much smaller Vietnamese garment factories although recently these top global retailers/brands have established contacts with larger Vietnamese firms.

According to the Vietnam Textile and Apparel Association (VITAS), the cut-make-trim (CMT) model which yields the lowest value added is still a dominant mode of production/business in Vietnam with about 85 per cent of the enterprises using this model as their primary businesses in 2013.[8] Most of Vietnam's apparel enterprises only act as the subcontractors by performing the outsourcing contracts for the mass merchant retailers, specialty retailers, brand marketers and brand manufacturers. The orders are normally accompanied by the product design and specifications. As a result of this CMT, despite the high level of Vietnam's participation in these global value chains, the benefit of participation has been questioned. In addition, competing at the lower cost segment (i.e. cheap labour and low value added segment) of the highly fragmented global apparel value chain drives down the margin of the Vietnamese SMEs, at the same time strengthen the buyers' power as they have more options to consider in order to select the most appropriate partners. Another weakness of apparel production in Vietnam is the fact that the sector relies heavily on imported fabric materials (mostly from China), especially in the production of apparel for export. The value of fabrics imported was estimated at US$9.4 billion in 2014, of which US$4.7 billion was for Chinese fabrics. South Korea was the second largest supplier with a 19.5 per cent share, followed by Japan (5.9 per cent).

The fragmentation makes the apparel sector become highly competitive both globally and within Vietnam. As the international buyers source their products worldwide, competition occurs not only among the exporting companies from Vietnam, but also between Vietnamese companies and those from other countries, including Bangladesh, Cambodia, China, Indonesia, Pakistan, etc. as well as multinational manufacturers. In 2013, there were over 5,000 apparel enterprises in Vietnam, nearly 5,000 garment factories in Bangladesh and more than 15,000 in China (OECD Observer). Although it does not mean that all of these companies are capable of integrating into the international trade or global production networks, these figures show a great deal of how numerous the apparel exporters worldwide are, and how competitive the sector is. In Vietnam, for example, the individual shares of the leading exporters were less than 2 per cent of Vietnam's garment industry in 2014, such as Viet Tien (1.85 per cent), Tinh Loi (1.36 per cent), Hansae Vietnam (1.16 per cent) and HANESBRAND Vietnam (1.06 per cent), implying a large number of apparel exporters and fierce competition.

2.2.2. Participation in Korean apparel production network

There are evidence that it is possible for Vietnamese apparel SMEs to integrate into apparel global production networks with and through Korean MNEs. These global chains may either be led by a Korean MNE or sourced through a Korean MNE. Our interview with a medium-sized Vietnamese apparel processing Kien Giang company suggests that the company may be able to supply directly to orders placed by international MNEs, including Korean MNEs. However, it is not always possible to link up with these global production networks. There are at least two issues.

First is the nature of the apparel production network and the capacity of SMEs. Typically in the global market, the larger MNEs prefer to source from a few, but large manufacturers in order to avoid the unnecessary time and transaction costs. The desirable vendors must be able to offer consistent quality, reliable delivery, short lead times, large-scale production, flexibility, competitive prices, full package services and social compliance. The implication is that in order to directly work with the global buyers, the suppliers need to be operating at a large scale and with sufficient management skills so as to be capable of completely fulfilling their obligations.[9]

For the smaller SMEs, on their own, they would not be able to deliver on large orders. Their strategy is to form an informal network of smaller garment processing factories in such a way that they could together deliver the large orders/assignments and share the risk of having to invest into production lines that may only operate part of the time. This informal network could serve the smaller factories to a certain extent for some time, but at the same time put a cap on their growth and inherently become a trap for these SMEs. Without serious investments in production capacity, the smaller factories would not be able to secure regular and frequent orders for their operations. Many enterprises act as the subcontractors to the larger national manufacturers by carrying out solely the CMT activities and finishing services. In this case, the contracts are often only short term or seasonal, and the manufacturers operate on an order-by-order basis. The entry barriers to this segment are evaluated to be low as it requires only few investment and low labour skills while it is quite easy for the buyers to switch from one manufacturer to another. There are evidence that SMEs could learn from and perform some higher value-added stages such as design and reverse-engineering for MNEs, but they do not value these activities yet. For example, Kien Giang company could perform certain stages of designing and cutting for its MNE clients, but the company do not see this as moving up the value chain as the "benefit" of doing so is too small for the company.

The second issue relates to the investment strategy of MNEs in Vietnam. Different from other MNEs from the U.S. or European or truly global MNEs which only source their products from Vietnamese garment factories and rarely from their own factories in the host country, these Korean MNEs are investing in Vietnam and setting up their own production facilities to take advantage of cheap labour. Our interviews with a number of Korean FDI apparel MNEs in Vietnam suggest that in a number of cases there is virtually no linkage with the apparel sector in the host country. For example, Shinwon Ebenenzer, a Korean apparel MNE, invested in Vietnam to set up its garment factory since 2002 and employs a dozen thousands of workers. The company receives orders from the parent company in Korea to produce for GAP, Old Navy, and TJ Max, and imports materials (almost 100 per cent from China and Korea) and exports all of its production. The contribution to local economy is mostly through employment generation.

For the apparel sector it is also difficult to connect with medium-sized Korean firms to be part of the global production networks. An example is Vietnam Kumyang, a Korean FDI firm in Vietnam, which invested in Vietnam since 2005. The company has until now created limited connections with the local economy, except for employing workers and mid-level management. The company imports 100 per cent of its materials from China and produces for orders from larger MNEs in which the terms and conditions of processing contracts already specify the source of materials. The strategy of Vietnam Kumyang is to take advantage of cheap labour, like Shinwon, and it has basically no interest in working with local Vietnamese firms, hence little connections with them.

The two cases above illustrate an important point — the investment strategy of MNEs when investing in the host country is critically important. These two companies invest in Vietnam to produce for orders from larger MNEs and take advantage of cheap labour. These companies do not create any connection with local firms, very little spillover effects and in many cases compete with local firms. It is also these types of FDI firms that will compete further with Vietnamese firms, both large and SMEs, when the Trans-Pacific Partnership (TPP) come into force[10] with the customs duties on the textiles and apparel exported by Vietnam and other TPP parties and vice versa will be eliminated either immediately or over longer timeframes.[11] Contrary to our expectations that such FTAs would be beneficial to SMEs, it has been argued that AEC and TPP would benefit the larger firms and FDI firms rather than general and smaller firms like SMEs. With the ever reduction of tariff toward zero rate, there is a corresponding increasing trend of FDI inflows into Vietnam. Theoretically it would create more opportunities for Vietnam SMEs. However, in reality due to the lack of capacity the larger MNEs from Korea (and Taiwan) would "import" the whole value chains, i.e. from providing inputs, components to processing in Vietnam so that they would be qualified as having Vietnam's origin to benefit from such trade agreements. As a result, smaller SMEs would be driven out of the value chain due to their lower capacity and higher competition with an ever decreasing margin (processing fee would be on the decrease). In addition, thanks to their size and hence economy of scale, it is typically the larger firms which would benefit from the agreements, i.e. meeting the stricter and more stringent requirement of the agreements. Our interviews with these

Korean FDI firms suggest that there would be more competition for Vietnamese SMEs. For example, Shinwon has just established a Shinwon company in Ho Chi Minh City in order to seek orders from Vietnam, rather than through its parent in Korea. It is also very unlikely that Shinwon would change its production mode in Vietnam, i.e. shifting toward connecting with garment processing SMEs.

2.3. Participation in Global Production Networks in the Advanced Electronics Sector

2.3.1. An update on the sector

Since 2011, electronics has overtaken textile as the top sector in terms of export value (see Figure 11.3).[12] The spectacular growth during the last few years that Vietnam's electronics sector has experienced is especially due to the arrival of large electronics MNEs, many of whom are Korean MNEs such as Samsung and LG among many others, which establish their production hubs in Vietnam, partly in response to the rising wages in China and partly due to their China plus one strategy, i.e. large firms are moving to Vietnam in order to reduce their production costs, while at the same time still locate near to their markets and reduce their dependency on specific countries or suppliers. According to the General Statistics Office, from 2007–11, the total number of firms in the sector increased 69 per cent from 305 firms to 516 firms, and the number of jobs created in the sector has soared more than two times, from more than 78,000 to nearly 170,000. According to Vietnam Electronic and Informatics Association, by 2012, out of the 500 electronics enterprises, one third are foreign firms. The electronics sector now employs about 500,000 employees.

With the increased electronics FDI inflows, it has been highly expected that Vietnam would soon be able to integrate into the electronics global production networks with both the export and import of electronics increasing. At the moment it can be said that the global production networks start to take root in Vietnam with the presence of world leading electronics firms who are operating in all tiers of the electronics supply chain such as Intel which produces semiconductor components, Foxconn and Compal, which function as electronics manufacturing service (EMS) providers and original design manufacturers (ODMs) respectively, and Samsung, LG, Nokia and Canon, which are original equipment manufacturers (OEMs), but also do final

FIGURE 11.3
Vietnam's Key Exports: Electronics a Rising Sector (USD million)

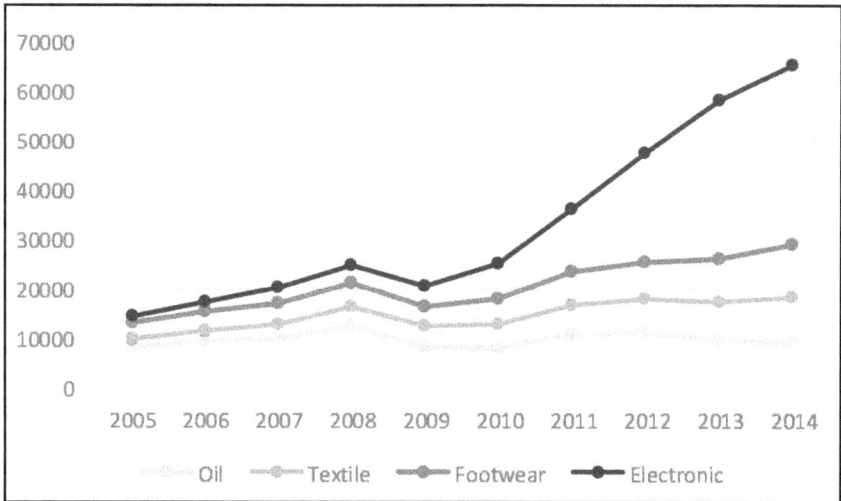

Source: UN Comtrade.

assembly and customization.[13] The recent arrival of electronics FDI firms in Vietnam can be attributed to the efforts by the government to lure these hi-tech companies to Vietnam with the hope that their arrival would bring about employment, capital, and spillover effects for industrial upgrading by local firms in Vietnam. At this stage, we would like to address the question whether Vietnamese local electronics firms could integrate into the electronics global production networks. Given the current status quo policy regime, local SME firms in general would find it hard to integrate into the value chain and the process is not automatic.

Despite its spectacular growth, the domestic/local value added of these ever increasing exports and imports is very low due to limited participation of local firms in the production value chain and the labour cost accounts for a very small fraction (as low as only 1–2 per cent) of the total value for certain MNEs in Vietnam.[14] Almost all of the experts we interviewed share the view that such spectacular growth was due to FDI companies like Samsung, Canon, Nokia and LG while Vietnamese local electronics companies make up less than 20 per cent of the domestic market and nearly 5 per cent of the export turnover.

2.3.2. Participation in Korean Electronics Production Network

Integrating in global electronics production networks, including Korean MNE-led networks, has been proven to be difficult for Vietnamese electronics firms. It is rare to find Vietnamese electronics firms which are able to become direct suppliers to electronic giants. In this section, we attempt to answer the question: Can Vietnamese firms, especially SMEs, establish a supplier–client relationship with large MNEs like Samsung? Our interviews with both FDI and domestic electronics firms indicate that there may be isolated cases where direct link is possible, however, this is the exception rather the norm. There are a number of reasons for this.

First, the nature of the electronics sector is characterized by (i) both capital and technologically intensive; (ii) modular production and stringent technical requirements (high quality, large volume, just-in-time delivery); and (iii) high competition and low margin. As local Vietnamese firms which are often small and have only limited capacity (both financially and technically), they are unable to adopt modular production to compete on low margin to integrate into global value chains led by large MNEs. At the moment, even if the leading electronic companies investing in Vietnam would like to source inputs from local firms to decrease production cost, the limitation in production capacity of domestic firms mainly prevent this process. Samsung Electronics Vietnam has only seven Vietnamese partners in its 93 suppliers, and these Vietnamese firms only provide packaging and printing services while other suppliers are mainly companies from South Korea or other ASEAN countries, or FDI firms in Vietnam.[15] It has been reported that under pressure from the government, Samsung Vietnam has been reaching out to Vietnamese SMEs offering training and coaching to assist SMEs to qualify as Samsung suppliers but so far the results have been minimal because like other MNEs, Samsung is operating an open and competitive tendering procedure to select the most competitive and capable suppliers based on price, quality and time delivery. On the part of the local Vietnamese private firms, they would have little incentive to invest in technological capability to meet the standards imposed by these MNEs unless the government has concrete policies and actions. First, working in manufacturing and being suppliers to these MNEs is not easy and due to the potential intensive competition, the margin is generally low, discouraging firms away from manufacturing including electronics. Second, working with MNEs, taking on more tasks/jobs and moving up the value chain involved extra-proportional risk which the government should be willing to compensate for.

Secondly, like most modern manufacturing industries, the global electronics sector has a tiered production structure,[16] under which the brand manufacturer is designated as an OEM. The second tier is the contract manufacturer. These are either ODMs that design the products to meet the OEMs' requirements or EMS providers that manufacture according to the designs provided by the OEM. The third tier is the producer of components that supply inputs to the contract manufacturers. The fourth tier is the producer of the basic materials used to produce the components.

Due to its tiered structure, it would be extremely difficult for Vietnamese SMEs to participate, integrate and move up the value chain and become first-tier suppliers to Korean MNEs. For example, in the case of Samsung which has invested heavily in Vietnam. Despite optimistic speculations that the arrival of the firm in itself presents an important opportunity for local Vietnamese firms to integrate into the global production networks, to move up the value chain and upgrade its industrial capability, out of nearly 100 suppliers for Samsung in Thai Nguyen there are only seven local Vietnamese firms which are suppliers of packaging and logistics (non-core electronic businesses).[17] The remaining suppliers are Korean and FDI firms.[18] At the moment Vietnamese-owned firms, most of whom are SMEs, are not "qualified" as they are unable to meet the high technical standards required by Samsung. In response to government initiatives to connect potential Vietnamese suppliers with Samsung, the company provides a list of 170 parts and components it would like to source from Vietnam. Vietnamese firms, however, are unable to produce a single component, even a screwdriver, that meets the technical standard, be delivered on time and at a competitive price. It is therefore most likely that Vietnamese firms would only be able to supply to first-tier and second-tier suppliers of Samsung. What may be needed now are the specific and nuance incentives and policies to induce local Vietnamese firms to upgrade. However, all electronic enterprises, including those firms with 40–50 years of experience, are unable to produce the simplest components such as battery charger, USB cable, etc. Since 2015, the managers of Samsung found out that the target of having half of the 170 providers of Samsung be Vietnamese firms by the end of the year is difficult to accomplish.[19]

In addition, for global production networks like electronics, both the inbound and outbound supply chains are managed globally. Inputs are also sourced and delivered globally, using the parent company's distribution network and thus subject to the same standards and requirements. The local managers in Vietnam would have little say in sourcing decision from Vietnam. The fact that Vietnamese firms at the moment could not meet these standards could also be an excuse for large MNEs to source from outside of Vietnam or from the traditional suppliers.

Thirdly, the "follow-the-leader effect" would lead to the creation of the whole supply chain in Vietnam by MNEs and their FDI suppliers. Due to the tiered structure when the MNEs (leaders) invest in Vietnam, they attract their followers ("follow-the-leader effect") — their suppliers to build factories in Vietnam, creating a whole value chain for the original MNEs at the exclusion of local SMEs. These suppliers will import parts to be assembled into components that are then delivered to their clients' factories. It is likely that over time they will increase the amount of locally-produced parts they use. Eventually the brand manufacturers may procure components from local producers. This is a positive scenario. But another scenario is also possible — that is the follow-the-leader effect by MNEs' suppliers may pre-empt and crowd out investment by local Vietnamese firms.

Seoul Metal (SM) is a good case to demonstrate the "follow-the-leader effect" whereby smaller firms follow the lead MNEs in investing overseas. While the follower firms may help fill in the vacuum of missing supporting industries in the local economy, they limit the potential for the development of local SMEs to integrate into the global production networks. Established in Vietnam in 2008 with an initial capital of US$9.6 million, SM produces screwdrivers of various types for mobile phones and other electronic products, with production facilities in Korea, China, Philippines, Indonesia and Vietnam. Since Samsung increased its investment in Vietnam, so did SM. Currently, SM employs 100 Vietnamese workers and 34 Korean employees. Its customers include Samsung (60 per cent of total production) and others like Brothers, Nissei, and Panasonic (40 per cent). Due to the fact that the parent company SM in Korea is a long-time supplier to Samsung, its original intention to invest in Vietnam is to supply to Samsung, hence "follow-the-leader" effect. The main reason SM invests in Vietnam is to follow Samsung. They could relocate their production factory to other countries with ease. There is no linkage with local Vietnamese firms. SM has only one subcontractor (for coating, painting and galvanizing the screwdrivers) and this subcontractor is also a Korean FDI firm.[20] The two share the same production premise. Before moving to Vietnam, SM and this subcontractor have already been doing business with each other. When investing in Vietnam, SM do not need to look for local Vietnamese contractors. According to SM, the reason they do not choose Vietnamese contractors is because they are afraid that local Vietnamese firms are not capable of delivering on a large scale and within stringent timeline. The production would require intensive investment in technology, capital, and machinery, especially specialized equipment. For example, in the case of Samsung, the procurement section will ask for quotations (valid for a limited period of time) from various suppliers for supplies of certain technical specifications, with a given volume and delivery time. In addition to meeting the delivery time and the capacity to supply on a large quantity, suppliers will have to compete by driving down their prices which is only possible if producing on a large scale.

Similar to the apparel sector, there are Korean FDI electronics companies that invest in Vietnam just to take advantage of the country's cheap labour cost and incentives offered by the government,[21] but develop little connection with the local firms. For example, Crucial Tech is a Korean firm with production facilities in Korea (producing software and chips), China (mobi phone cover and touch pad) and Vietnam (assembly). The factory in Vietnam mainly assembles fingerprint identification touch pad for mobile phones for such customers like RIM, Fujitsu, and Sky. The company exports 100 per cent of its production, 50 per cent back to the parent company and 50 per cent directly to customers. It employs about 100 employees, mostly women, and about ten so-called R&D staff. The company has little linkage with local firms, it imports virtually 100 per cent of its inputs for production — mainly assembly in Vietnam to take advantage of the cheap and skillful workers. It only uses logistics services and some non-electronics materials (e.g. glue) for its production. This case illustrates that though Vietnam can obtain a certain volume of record high-tech exports, the value added to the local economy is very much limited except for a small number of jobs created at the expense of tax incentives.

The only case of the 4P company that has been able to become a supplier to LG is an exception. In the case of the 4P company,[22] it was established in 2001 by two entrepreneurs, both of whom previously worked as employees for LG Vietnam. Having worked for LG for many years, they decided to leave and establish 4P company with the intention of becoming a TV-component supplier of LG, which is now its biggest customer. As early as 2001 when first starting up the business, the 4P owners invested as much as US$1.8 million. After 13 years in operation, 4P has become the leading Vietnamese electronic manufacturer and has been experiencing technological upgrading thanks in part to the knowledge transfer from LG.[23] However, the focus is still on assembly manufacturing rather than producing chips and components, which is a very capital and technological intensive business and the company has not yet planned to move into that area. Linkages from 4P to other companies are quite limited and there is also little spillover from 4P to the rest of the sector. The company only uses carton boxes from domestic suppliers while main components are imported from China, Korea, Taiwan, Indonesia and Malaysia.

On its own MNEs have little incentive to transfer technology to local suppliers (who might potentially become their competitors), but at the same time, in order for their suppliers to be able to meet their "specific" requirements, some transfer of technology and/or industrial upgrading must happen for 4P to be able to meet MNEs' requirements. 4P has been able to upgrade by (i) learning directly from these MNEs on specific requirements — usually training will be provided by MNEs; and (ii) using external consultants and training its own staff for general technological capability — 4P sends their technical taff to Korea for technology transfer purposes and recruit foreign technicians when the company introduces new machines and technology. The company also has a technical process in place to meet the stringent requirements by MNEs by having an extensive testing system.

2.4. Integration by Working with Medium-sized Korean Firms

The discussion thus far focuses on the two key sectors and the linkages with Korean MNEs. Evidence so far tends to suggest that integrating into global production networks by directly engaging with MNEs would be out of reach for most Vietnamese SMEs. It seems that the way forward for Vietnamese SMEs is to work with small and medium firms which are more tenable for Vietnamese firms' capacity. In this section, we present a case of "successful cooperation" between a Korean FDI firm and a local manufacturing SME, in which we observe a number of types of industrial upgrading: (i) product upgrading, i.e. the 0.5mm steel tube that meets the requirements of Samsung was introduced; (ii) process upgrading with new equipment being tested and adapted into a new production process suitable for the company's own production technical requirements; and (iii) functional upgrading within the same value chain with the local company being able to assume more and more tasks from the Korea partner. The case is also selected to highlight a number compatibility issues between the two which simply do not exist in the relationship between Vietnamese SMEs and large MNEs. The Korean FDI firm in our analysis is Ys Tech company (YT) which is a small and medium FDI firm with an investment capital of US$5 million and the Vietnamese SME firm is Eco Vietnam (EV) which was established in 2010 with a small investment capital of VND 3 billion (equivalent to US$200,000).

Investing in Vietnam, YT's plan was to become a Samsung supplier. However even for a Korea-origin company, it was not easy to meet Samsung's requirements. The company only secured its first contract with Samsung in 2012, supplying three key components namely tubes, carbon brush, and motor, among which the most technically challenging is the tube. The company faced with a dilemma: importing tubes from China proves unprofitable but producing tubes in Vietnam at a lower cost than China imports was unfeasible due to the lack of competent suppliers. The strategy adopted was to import from China while searching for local partners. On the other hand, EV was making no profits, mainly producing domestic appliances such as clothes hangers, and cupboards. In 2012, EV decided to move into the so-called supporting industry with an aim to linking up with international partners. After four years of looking for the right partners, YT chose EV as a potential partner so that they could collaborate and transfer the necessary vacuum cleaner tube production technology. After years of intensive technical collaboration, EV is finally able to meet the technical requirements not only by YT but also by Samsung — that is to produce tubes of 0.5 mm thickness.

On their part, being a smaller FDI investor in Vietnam, YT always has the incentive to work and interact with local partners in order to find "innovative" ways to do things (i.e. doing whatever it takes). YT has had a hard time finding partners in Vietnam, as Vietnamese firms are not keen to acquire skills and technology as the returns from doing so in manufacturing where the margin is very low may not be enough to compensate for the risks involved.[24] YT does not only create jobs for the local labour force like other foreign-invested enterprises but more importantly, it transfers technology to EV, sets up a partnership with EV, and then makes EV a second-tier supplier for Samsung, acting as a bridge between a Vietnamese supplier (EV) and Samsung. This has pushed this Vietnamese firm to actively participate in the global production networks. On their part, EV has a number of "right conditions" to make things happen. First the founder of EV used to be a manager of a Japanese firm in Vietnam which gave him exposure to technology and management skills (Kaisen or 5S) and experience. Secondly, the company made a strategic decision to enter the supporting industry, and hence later, successful built a partnership with YT. The cooperation, the transfer of technology and the functional upgrading are possible because it is beneficial to the two companies: produce products of better quality and cost-saving (reduced damage caused to final products when transporting in intermediate forms).

3. Conclusion

This chapter attempts to investigate the significance of regional integration for SMEs of developing countries to integrate into global value chains. As a case study, this chapter looks at Korean MNEs investing in Vietnam, especially in the garment and electronics sectors. The chapter addresses two related questions. Firstly, how MNEs are affected by regional integration in their investment decisions. And secondly, how these Korean MNEs establish linkages with local SMEs.

Recent regional integration does have strong impact on the investment decision of MNEs, although it is not the single important factor and certainly not the most important factor. Korean MNEs, especially, choose Vietnam for its cheap labour, political stability, and government incentives. Secondly, integration into global production networks/ value chains is not a simple task and should not be taken for granted for SMEs in developing countries. Working in a global production network requires firms involved not only to be highly competitive in terms of price and technical requirements, but also be able to deliver in large volumes on a very stringent time schedule. It is the highly competitive nature of the business and the relatively low margin that makes integration by SMEs difficult.

From the local firms' perspective, doing business within the global production networks is a tough task (competitive, low margin, capital intensive, higher requirements). There should be policies to compensate for those firms willing to take risks in integrating into global production networks. This is important even for firms to upgrade within the value chain. Taking more tasks (upgrading) involves more risk (for example, when garment firms take on the role of procurement, they have to bear credit risk, which is the risk of loss resulting from the customers' failure to accept the final goods and make payment after the garment firms have expended the money to purchase materials, produce and deliver the goods to them). Without government support, it would be difficult for them to take on more tasks, especially for SMEs.

In order to develop the SME sector, additional efforts by policy-makers are required to encourage integration into the global production networks. A lesson could be learnt from China's experience in developing its electronics sector (Chen 2014). In China, while the government of Suzhou selectively works with large scale leading MNEs and provides them with priorities and incentives, the government in Shenzhen opts for smaller scale FDI. The end result is that Chinese domestic firms face variable markets whereby those in Suzhou are stuck in the race to the bottom on costs, while their counterparts in Shenzhen develop their capacity and climb up the value chain. As pointed out by Lin Chen (2014), by partnering with large MNEs, the government in Suzhou and MNEs create a "supply gap" between these global MNEs and the domestic firms. This gap encourages MNEs to adopt a "group-offshoring" strategy — bringing the whole value chain within the country. This would further create the power disparity between the leading MNEs and local firms — squeezing local firms into the bottom of the value chain. In contrast, by first working with smaller FDI firms, the government in Shenzhen facilitates the upgrading of local firms. Our case studies above also point to a similar story: local firms could supply and move up the value chain by working with smaller FDI firms. Attracting large FDI firms such as Samsung and Nokia would surely be a policy target. However, simply attracting large FDI into Vietnam may not guarantee the technological upgrading of local Vietnamese firms. It would require additional policy design and efforts to make sure that upgrading happens.

NOTES

1. Acknowledgement: This chapter is prepared within the framework of the project: SME Participation in ASEAN and East Asian Regional Economic Integration managed by Economic Research Institute for ASEAN and East Asia (ERIA). The authors would like to thank Cassey Lee, Dionisius A. Narjoko, Sothea Oum and other reviewers for their helpful comments. The authors would also like to thank representatives from companies who agreed to be interviewed by our team. The usual disclaimer applies. The views expressed in this chapter are those of the authors and do not necessarily reflect the views or policies of the institutions that the authors are associated with.
2. The lists of the Free Trade Agreements engaged into by any of the 48 ADB member countries/economies in Asia and the Pacific with another country or an economic bloc within or outside the region can be found at <https://aric.adb.org/fta>.
3. <https://aric.adb.org/fta-trends-by-country>.
4. Developing countries may try to develop particular niche location advantages in order to attract production blocs, rather than attempt the more difficult task of country-wide fundamental improvement of the investment climate. With fragmentation, it would be much easier for less developed countries (LDCs) to start industrializing than in the past by attracting some pieces of production blocks.
5. Vietnam Kumyang in Vinh Phuc (medium) and Shinwon Ebenezer in Bac Ninh (large). Ideally we would like to interview newly established FDI firms in Vietnam. However arranging interviews with these new firms proved difficult. Instead, we rely on interviewing these two firms, and asked for

their opinions on the impacts of regional integration on other firms and the sector.

6. *Viet Nam News*, "VN Not Ready to Join Global Value Chains", 11 December 2014, available at <http://vietnamnews.vn/economy/263874/vn-not-ready-to-join-global-value-chains.html>.

7. This may be in part attributable to rising labour costs, strengthening environmental regulations in China and appreciating RMB, which all have led to the shifting of orders by the world's leading importers, including the European Union, the United States and Japan from China to other Asian developing countries, such as Bangladesh, Vietnam and Cambodia. Many Chinese and Hong Kong apparel manufacturers also relocated their low value-added activities to these countries while focusing on the more sophisticated and higher value-added activities or urgent orders.

8. Other methods generating higher value added accounted for only the remaining modest share (15 per cent), including Original Equipment Manufacturing/Freight on Board (OEM/FOB), Original Design Manufacturing (ODM) and Original Brand Manufacturing (OBM). Vietnamese companies undertaking OBM usually distribute their products solely in the domestic market.

9. The larger Vietnamese suppliers, such as members of Vinatex group, would be able to engage with MNEs.

10. In the context of the year 2015, when Trans-Pacific Partnership agreement (TPP) (with 12 members: New Zealand, Australia, Canada, Mexico, Japan, Malaysia, Brunei, Vietnam, Singapore, Peru, Chile and the United States) was expected to be signed and approved by country members in February 2016 and come into force in 2018. However, due to President Trump's decision about US's withdrawal from TPP, TPP was replaced by CPTPP with 11 members: New Zealand, Australia, Canada, Mexico, Japan, Malaysia, Brunei, Singapore, Peru, Chile and Vietnam (without the United States).

11. Currently, according to Vinatex, the average rates of import taxes on the textiles and apparel are 12.4–20.0 per cent in the United States, and 9.2–9.4 per cent in the European Union, which are the two largest markets worldwide. These agreements, therefore, make the exporters located in Vietnam become more attractive to the importers than those in other countries, including China, Bangladesh, India and Cambodia. To benefit from preferential access, these products are nonetheless required to strictly meet the rules of origin. The heavy reliance on the input materials imported from China might therefore deter many Vietnam's enterprises from utilizing these agreements. The TPP provides a separate chapter (Chapter 4) concerning this industry with flexible articles related to the rules of origin. In particular, the short supply list allows 194 types of fabrics, yarns and fibres to be sourced from non-TPP countries, and used in the apparel production in the TPP region without losing duty preference.

12. There was an earlier period that the sector experienced significant development. It was during the 1990s, when the economic reform led to the arrival and return of foreign investors. Among the first to arrive were Japanese electronics investors and this was followed by Korean investors. This period was characterized by a large number of joint ventures between FDI electronics firms and domestic firms. Electronics products (assembled from imported parts and components mostly by joint ventures) were even exported to non-traditional markets outside the former social union countries. In the domestic market, such names as Viettronic Dong Da and Viettronic Tan Binh were popular for consumer electronics products and competed successfully against second-hand imports from Japan. By the end of the 1990s, the electronics industry had over 100 factories assembling consumer electronics products. Despite its success during these earlier years, the sector suffered a number of limitations and weaknesses for a variety of reasons that may hinder the long-term development of Vietnam domestic electronics firms and this only came to the fore when Vietnam joined the World Trade Organization. They include: (i) lack of technological upgrading; (ii) being trapped in the low-productivity labour intensive processing/assembling jobs; (iii) being excluded from global production networks. The local Vietnamese electronics sector has had to pay a dear price for this. Today, most of these joint venture factories are either out of business, diversifying into other sectors, or trying to survive by taking on processing contracts for the workers. Their roles are getting smaller in the electronics sector of Vietnam.

13. Taiwan's Foxconn Group on 28 August 2013 opened two hi-tech factories with a combined investment of US$80 million in the northern province of Bac Ninh. The two factories, built on 1.1 hectares of land in the Que Vo Industrial Zone, manufacture hi-tech products such as cameras, computers and electronic appliances. Foxconn CEO Try Guo said the two above-mentioned projects are just the start of the Group's ambitious Vietnam investment strategy that will eventually mushroom to over US$5 billion and make Foxconn the largest foreign investor in the second fastest-growing economy in Asia. The other big investors include: Brother Vietnam (Japan), US$25 million, December 2012; Nidec Seimitsu (Japan), US$40 million, July 2012; SOC Vietnam (Japan), US$62.5 million, November 2012; JBL (USA), US$100 million, June 2012; Terumo BCT (USA, Japan), US$94 million, May 2012; Kyocera (Japan), US$320 million by 2013, October 2012; Hitech BSE (South Korea), US$30 million, April 2013; Fuji Xerox (Japan), US$120 million, November 2013; Nokia (Finland), US$300 million, early 2013; Samsung Electronics (South Korea), US$2.2 billion by 2020, November 2012; Samsung Display (South Korea), US$1 billion by 2020, March 2014; Laird (British), US$10 million by 2015, January 2014; Nokia, US$220 million, May 2014 (moving a large number of production lines from factories in China, Hungary and Mexico to Vietnam).

14. Despite the huge export revenue, the local added value is low which is typical in any global production network. For example, the iphone supply chain where value added for China is about US$8 out of US$500 price tag. See <http://skhdt.bacninh.gov.vn/Index.aspx?item=19&item=18&ba=19&new=304&giai-phap-nang-cao-gia-tri-gia-tang-trong-xuat-khau-hang-hoa-cua-cac-doanh-nghiep-fdi-tren-dia-ban-tinh-bac-ninh.html>.

15. For example, Intel has only 18 Vietnamese partners among hundreds of companies providing materials and components for its production. See "Thoi co cho công nghiep ho tro", *Báo Nguoi Lao Đong Online*, 11 September 2014, available at <http://nld.com.vn/kinh-te/thoi-co-cho-cong-nghiep-ho-tro-20140911222258601.htm>; "Electronics Industry in Dead Throes, VN has to Start Again from Scratch", *VietNamNet*, 8 October 2012, available at <http://english.vietnamnet.vn/fms/special-reports/49741/electronics-industry-in-dead-throes--vn-has-to-start-again-from-scratch.html> or "Electronics Sector in Need of Support", *Viet Nam News*, 3 May 2014, available at <http://vietnamnews.vn/economy/254345/electronics-sector-in-need-of-support.html>.

16. At the top is the brand manufacturer (producer-led production network like Samsung) or retailer (retailer-led production network like Nike), which distributes the branded products to consumers.

17. VN Express, "Tuyen doanh nghiep làm oc vít, sac pin cho Samsung", 11 September 2014, available at <http://kinhdoanh.vnexpress.net/tin-tuc/doanh-nghiep/tuyen-doanh-nghiep-lam-oc-vit-sac-pin-cho-samsung-3078103.html>.

18. Samsung attracts a lot of media attention and the arrival of the conglomerate has sparked a lot of hot debates concerning the failure of the supporting industry and the strategy for Vietnamese firms to become suppliers to Samsung as the company keeps investing in large projects in Vietnam with total investment reaching US$11.2 billion. Samsung built its first electronics factory in Bac Ninh in 2008 and started its operation in 2009. In 2013, Samsung Electronics opened another plant in Thai Nguyen and in 2015, two more plants were opened. Up to 2018, Samsung has invested US$17.3 billion in eight factories and one research and development centre in Vietnam (*Reuters* 2018). An investment project to set up Samsung Display in Bac Ninh was approved in 2014 and Samsung CE Complex in Hi-tech Park Ho Chi Minh City was licensed on 1 October 2014. According to Mr Shim Won Hwan, President of Samsung Vietnam Group, Vietnam is becoming the largest Samsung production hub. "Samsung tro thành nhà đau tu nuoc ngoài lon nhat tai Viet Nam", Vietq.vn, 12 November 2014, available at <http://vietq.vn/nha-dau-tu-nuoc-ngoai-lon-nhat-viet-nam-la-samsung-d45610.html>.

19. See <http://www.thanhniennews.com/business/vietnam to lose fdi due to ailing-support-industries-24245.html>. For Intel, product samples from

domestic firms are very good but when they come to actual business and have to produce a mass quantity, their qualities and deliveries are not consistent.

20. Like Crucial Tech, this company, indeed, purchases some materials from local firms such as protective gears, clothing and some chemicals. However, for its main production and components like steel, cooper, and others, it either imports or purchases from other Korean firms.

21. The company was awarded the High-Tech certificate by the Ministry of Science and Technology and is eligible for an extended tax exemption at zero per cent.

22. The company has been able to supply to other MNEs, not just to the one that they once worked for and gradually integrate into the global production networks. A very interesting development is that when we visited the company in 2015, there were signs that 4P may also become a supplier to Canon and second-tier supplier to Samsung. However, under pressure by LG, the company has focused its production for LG only. Interestingly, when LG invested US$600 million in Hai Phong industrial park, the 4P company also invested US$80 million in the same location to improve its production capacity and maintain close proximity to LG.

23. The company is now investing in a US$80 million factory in Haiphong to supply for LG. In their agreement with LG, 4P will invest in machinery and equipment, while LG will provide the land rent-free, which will later be a factor in the price of products supplied to LG. The company is investing in Haiphong to produce car electronics for LG.

24. The key reason for YT to choose EV is the risk-taking entrepreneurship of the Vietnamese partner. YT has provided technical support to EV for a year so the two firms could produce products that can meet the technical requirements and at a competitive cost/price.

REFERENCES

Anwar, Sajid and Lan Phi Nguyen. "Foreign Direct Investment and Trade: The Case of Vietnam". *Research in International Business and Finance* 25, no. 1 (2011): 39–52.

Arnold, Jens M. and Beata S. Javorcik. "Gifted Kids or Pushy Parents? Foreign Direct Investment and Plant Productivity in Indonesia". *Journal of International Economics* 79, no. 1 (2009): 42–53.

Asian Development Bank (ADB). *Asian Development Outlook 2010*. Manila: ADB, 2010.

Athukorala, Prema-chandra. "How India Fits into Global Production Sharing: Experience, Prospects and Policy Options". Working Paper No. 2013/13, Arndt-Corden Department of Economics, Crawford School of Public Policy, AUN College of Asia and the Pacific, 2013.

Athukorala, Prema-chandra and Tran Quang Tien. "Foreign Direct Investment in Industrial Transition: The Experience of Vietnam". *Journal of the Asia Pacific Economy* 17, no. 3 (2012): 446–63.

Baldwin-Edwards, Martin. "Labour Immigration and Labour Markets in the GCC Countries: National Patterns and Trend". Kuwait Program on Development Government and Globalization in the Gulf States, Paper No 15, London School of Economics, London, 2011.

Blinder, Alan S. "Offshoring: The Next Industrial Revolution?" *Foreign Affair* 85 (2006): 113–28.

Chen, Lin. "Varieties of Global Capital and the Paradox of local Upgrading in China". *Politics and Society* (2014): 1–30.

Chen, Zhihong, Ying Ge, and Huiwen Lai. "Foreign Direct Investment and Wage Inequality: Evidence from China". *World Development* 39 (2011): 1322–32.

Clark, Don P., Jannett Highfill, Jonas de Oliveira Campino, and Scheherazade Rehman. "FDI, Technology Spillovers, Growth, and Income Inequality: A Selective Survey". *Global Economy Journal* 11, no. 2 (2011).

Damijan, Joze P., Matija Rojec, Boris Majcen, and Mark Knell. "Impact of Firm Heterogeneity on Direct and Spillover Effects of FDI: Micro-Evidence from Ten Transition Countries". *Journal of Comparative Economics* 41, no. 3 (2013): 895–922.

Driffeld, Nigel and Sourafel Girma. "Regional Foreign Direct Investment and Wage Spillovers: Plant Level Evidence from the UK Electronics Industry". *Oxford Bulletin of Economics and Statistics* 65 (2003): 453–74.

Feliciano, Z. and R. Lipsey. "Foreign Ownership, Wages, and Wage Changes in U.S. Industries, 1987–92". *Contemporary Economic Policy* 24 (2006): 74–91.

Fukase, Emiko. "Foreign Wage Premium, Gender and Education: Insights from Vietnam Household Surveys". *The World Economy* 37, no. 6 (2014): 834–55.

Gallagher, Kevin P. and Lyuba Zarsky. *The Enclave Economy: Foreign Investment and Sustainable Development in Mexico's Silicon Valley*. Cambridge, MA: MIT Press, 2007.

Hanson, Gordon H. "Should Countries Promote Foreign Direct Investment?" UNCTAD G-24 Discussion Paper Series No. 9 (2001).

Harrison, Ann E., Inessa Love, and Margaret S. McMillan. "Global Capital Flows and Financing Constraints". *Journal of Development Economics* 75, no. 1 (2004): 269–301.

Helpman, Elhanan. *Understanding Global Trade*. Cambridge, Mass: Harvard University Press, 2011.

Hoang, Pham Thien. "Assessment of FDI Spillover Effects for the Case of Vietnam: A Survey of Micro-data Analyses". In *Deepening East Asian*

Economic Integration, edited by Jenny Corbett and So Umezaki. ERIA Research Project Report 2008-1. Jakarta: Economic Research Institute for ASEAN and East Asia (ERIA), 2009, pp. 473–95.

Hoi, Le Quoc and Richard Pomfret. "Foreign Direct Investment and Wage Spillovers in Vietnam Evidence from Firm Level Data". *ASEAN Economic Bulletin* 27, no. 2 (2010): 159–72.

Jaumotte, Florence, Subir Lall, and Chris Papageorgiou. "Rising Income Inequality: Technology, or Trade and Financial Globalization". *IMF Economic Review* 61, no. 2 (2013): 271–309.

Jude, Cristina and Gregory Levieuge. "Growth Effect of FDI in Developing Economies: The Role of Institutional Quality". MPRA Paper No. 49321 (2013).

Khan, Mushtaq H. "Learning, Technology Acquisition and Governance Challenges in Developing Countries". Research Paper Series on Governance for Growth. London: School of Oriental and African Studies, University of London, 2010.

Kimura, Fukunari and Ayako Obashi. "Production Networks in East Asia: What We Know So Far". ADBI Working Paper 320. Tokyo: Asian Development Bank Institute, 2011. Available at <https://www.adb.org/sites/default/files/publication/156175/adbi-wp320.pdf>.

La Porta, Rafael and Andrei Shleifer. "Informality and Development". Mimeo, Harvard University, 2013. Available at <http://scholar.harvard.edu/files/shleifer/files/informality_may27_abstract.pdf>.

Lipsey, Robert E. and Fredrik Sjöholm. "FDI and Growth in East Asia: Lessons for Indonesia". IFN Working Paper No. 852 (2010).

Machikita, Tomohiro and Yasushi Ueki. "Impact of Production Linkages on Industrial Upgrading in ASEAN, the People's Republic of China, and India: Organizational Evidence of a Global Supply Chain". ADBI Working Paper 399. Tokyo: Asian Development Bank Institute, 2012. Available at <https://www.adb.org/sites/default/files/publication/156254/adbi-wp399.pdf>.

Meyer, Klaus E. and Nguyen Hung Vo. "Foreign Investment Strategies and Sub-national Institutions in Emerging Markets: Evidence from Vietnam". *Journal of Management Studies* 42, no. 1 (January 2005).

Mirza, Hafiz and Axele Giroud. "Regionalization, Foreign Direct Investment and Poverty Reduction: Lessons from Vietnam in ASEAN". *Journal of the Asia Pacific Economy* 9, no. 2 (2004): 223–48.

Morrissey, Oliver and Manop Udomkerdmongkol. "Governance, Private Investment and Foreign Direct Investment in Developing Countries". *World Development* 40, no. 3 (2012): 437–45.

Nguyen, Anh Ngoc, Nguyen Thang, Le Dang Trung, Ngoc Quang Pham, Chuc Dinh Nguyen, and Nhat Duc Nguyen. "Foreign Direct Investment in Viet Nam: Is There Any Evidence of Technological Spillover Effect". Development and Policies Research Center (DEPOCEN) Working Papers No. 18 (2008).

Nguyen, Trung Kien. "Wage Differentials between Foreign Invested and Domestic Enterprises in the Manufacturing: Evidence from Vietnam". Asia-Pacific Economic Association's Conference 2014, Bangkok, Thailand, 2014.

Phan, Thanh and Ji Young Jeong. "Potential Economic Impacts of the Vietnam–Korea Free Trade Agreement on Vietnam". *East Asian Economic Review* 20, no. 1 (2016): 67–90.

Production Service Vietnam. "'Vietnam Business News': The Economic Mirror Indochina's". Newsletter, 2015. Available at <http://produktionsservice-vietnam.com/archiv/5-2015%20PSV%20Newsletter.pdf>.

Ramondo, Natalia. "Foreign Plants and Industry Productivity: Evidence from Chile". *The Scandinavian Journal of Economics* 111, no. 4 (2009): 789–809.

Reuters. "Samsung Electronics to Expand Production in Vietnam", 20 April 2018. Available at <https://www.reuters.com/article/us-samsung-elec-vietnam/samsung-electronics-to-expand-production-in-vietnam-idUSKBN1HR1SD>.

Ronald, MacDonald and Muhammad Tariq Majeed. "Distributional and Poverty Consequences of Globalization: A Dynamic Comparative Analysis for Developing Countries". UK: Business School – Economics, University of Glasgow, 2010.

Salonen, Heini. "Registered FDI from South Korea to Vietnam 2001–2013". Third Meeting of the Asia-Pacific Foreign Direct Investment (FDI) Network for Least Developed and Landlocked Developing Countries UNCC, Bangkok, Thailand, 2013.

Schaumburg-Müller, Henrik. "Rise and Fall of Foreign Direct Investment in Vietnam and its Impact on Local Manufacturing Upgrading". *The European Journal of Development Research* 15, no. 2 (2003): 44–66.

Seguino, Stephanie. "Is More Mobility Good? Firm Mobility and the Low Wage–Low Productivity Trap". Working Paper No. 423, The Levy Economics Institute, 2005. Available at <http://www.levyinstitute.org/pubs/wp_423.pdf>.

Thanh, Vo Tri and Nguyen Anh Duong. "Revisiting Exports and Foreign Direct Investment in Vietnam". *Asian Economic Policy Review* 6, no. 1 (2011): 112–31.

Thorbecke, Willem and Nimesh Salike. "Foreign Direct Investment in East Asia". Policy Discussion Papers 13-P-003, Research Institute of Economy, Trade and Industry (RIETI), 2013.

Tran, Thi Anh Dao and Dinh Thi Thanh Binh. "FDI and Growth in Vietnam: A Critical Survey". *Journal of Economics and Development* 15, no. 3 (December 2013): 91–116.

Tran, Van Tho. "FDI and Economic Development: The Case of Vietnam". In *Multinationals and Economic Growth in East Asia*, edited by Shujiro Urata, Chia Siow Yue and Fukunari Kimura. London: Routledge, 2006, pp. 393–422.

UNIDO and MPI. *Viet Nam Industrial Investment Report 2011: Understanding the Impact of Foreign Direct Investment on Industrial Development*. United Nation Industrial Development Organisation (UNIDO) and Ministry of Planning and Investment (MPI) Vietnam, 2012.

Van Reenen, John and Linda Yueh. "Why Has China Grown So Fast? The Role of International Technology Transfer". University of Oxford Department of Economics Working Paper 592 (2012): 1–24.

Vo, Thanh Tri and Anh Duong Nguyen. "Experiences of Vietnam in FDI Promotion: Some Lessons for Myanmar". In *Economic Reforms in Myanmar: Pathways and Prospects*, edited by Hank Lim and Yasuhiro Yamada. BRC Research Report No. 10, Bangkok Research Center, IDE-JETRO, Bangkok, Thailand, 2012.

Von Luebke, Christian. "The Political Economy of Local Governance: Findings from an Indonesian Field Study". *Bulletin of Indonesian Economic Studies* 45, no. 2 (2009): 201–30.

Wignaraja, Ganeshan. "Engaging Small and Medium Enterprises in Production Networks: Firm-level Analysis of Five ASEAN Economies". ADBI Working Paper Series No. 361. Tokyo: Asian Development Bank Institute, 2012.

Wignaraja, Ganeshan, Jens Krüger, and Anna Mae Tuazon. "Production Networks, Profits, and Innovative Activity: Evidence from Malaysia and Thailand". ADBI Working Paper 406. Tokyo: Asian Development Bank Institute, 2013.

12

THE EVOLUTION OF TAIWAN'S ECONOMIC LINKS WITH ASEAN

Shin-Horng Chen, Pei-Chang Wen and Meng-Chun Liu

1. Introduction

As neighbouring countries, economic relationships between ASEAN and Taiwan have been intensified primarily through de facto economic integration of trade and investment, instead of de jure integration, such as free trade agreements (FTAs). Not until in 2013 when Taiwan signed its FTA with Singapore (known as ASTEP) — its very first trade agreement ever with an ASEAN member. However, long before that, trade and direct investment between the two sides have intertwined to enhance mutual economic relationships. Particularly, it was direct investment in ASEAN made by numerous Taiwanese SMEs starting from the mid-1980s that triggered and pushed forward this economic integration (CIER 1995). In Taiwan, many tend to refer to this integration as the "investment-induced trade". However, it can involve a process of "deep integration" (WTO 2011; Baldwin 2013*a*, p. 26) in a cross-border manner.

In addition, global value chains (GVCs) (Gereffi and Frederick 2010; Gereffi, Humphrey and Sturgeon 2005; Gereffi and Memedovic 2003) and otherwise known as global production networks (GPNs) (Chen 2002; Coe et al. 2004; Ernst 2005, 2006; Sturgeon and Lee 2005; UNCTAD 2005) are keys to such integration. It is well-documented that in East Asia, SMEs have made significant contribution to de facto regional economic integration via their participation in GVCs and/or GPNs (ESCAP 2009; Lim and Kimura 2009; Harvie 2010; Chen 2002; OECD 2007), which in turn has become an important source of national economic growth. A typical example at issue refers to the GPNs, led by a few brand marketers in ICT (information and communications technology) hardware and software (Chen 2002; Yang and Coe 2009), involving such countries as Taiwan, Malaysia, Thailand, China, India and the Philippines. Furthermore, the WTO (2011) and a few scholars (Baldwin 2013a, 2013b; Low 2013) have suggested that GVCs/GPNs and FTAs often lead to "deep integration", through intertwining relationships among trade, investment, service and intellectual property; a phenomenon termed the "trade-investment-service-intellectual property (IP) nexus" (Baldwin 2013a, p. 26).

Set against the above context, this study sets out to examine the evolution of Taiwan's economic links with ASEAN. Indeed, GVCs/GPNs are major elements underlying the economic links between ASEAN and Taiwan. To discuss this issue, we examine the macro data of direct investment and bilateral trade, from the Taiwanese perspective. To capture the essence of the "trade-investment-service-IP nexus", we conduct a case study on the textile and apparel industry, which evolved with the GVC led by brand marketers in advanced countries to cement economic linkages between Taiwan and several parts of ASEAN. However, in climbing the ladder of economic development, Taiwan sets out to develop new industries in a way different from the catch-up manner, bringing about new patterns of engagement with a few ASEAN members.

2. An Overview of the Bilateral Trade and Direct Investment

Globalization as an accelerating trend has been shaped by political, economic and technological forces, with its key drivers including policy liberalization, accelerating technological change, increasing mobility of capital and demands of increasing competition (ESCAP 2009). It is well-documented that globalization is transforming the nature and location and hence networking of international production, trade and investment (see for example, Baldwin 2006; Dicken 2007; Lim and Kimura 2009; Chen 2002). In production terms, outsourcing and offshoring by multinational corporations (MNCs) have brought about prevailing cross-border production schemes of GVCs and/or GPNs, in which various stages of a manufacturing process are undertaken at different geographic locations where they can be carried out most efficiently (UNCTAD 2005). This has resulted in increased task- and/or product-related specialization by firms in the production of goods and services, leading to substantial growth in intra-industry and intra-product trade, rather than just traditional trade in final goods (ESCAP 2009). In other words, the locus of globalization has shifted from sectors to stages of production (Baldwin 2013a), leading to bourgeoning trade in intermediate goods and vertical specialization industrialization among countries (Milberg, Jiang and Gereffi 2013). While GPNs are widely seen in many industries, ranging from ICT (hardware and services), automotive, food, to garment sectors, their openness to external suppliers depends on a few factors, such as modularity of product architecture involved (Fujimoto 2008; Ulrich 1995; Sturgeon, van Biesebroeck, and Gereffi 2008) and the dominant power of the key suppliers. More recently, such cross-border networking has been extended from the manufacturing function to services and even design and R&D activities (Chen et al. 2013), increasingly involving latecomers in the Asia Pacific. As a result, different layers of industrial players within GVCs are required to closely interact with one another for innovation, giving rise to global innovation networks (GINs) (Chen 2004; Ernst 2006).

Against this backdrop, even though international trade has been a universal phenomenon for the Asian-Pacific region and the globe, the intensified economic links between ASEAN and Taiwan have had much to do with Taiwan's outward investment in ASEAN, leading to de facto economic integration between the two sides.

Taiwan's outward investment started from the mid-1980s due to substantial appreciation of the national currency (New Taiwan Dollar) and rising labour cost at home. At the beginning, Southeast Asia was the major destination for Taiwan's outward investment, led by SMEs in labour-intensive traditional sectors and then the electronics industry (CIER 1995). Further momentum was gained as the government promoted "South-bound Policy" before the Asian financial crisis in 1997. From 1990s onwards, China has overtaken the Southeast Asian countries as the leading host country for Taiwan's outward investment, with China's share of Taiwan's outward investment reaching 60–70 per cent in the second half of 2000s. Taking 2008 as an example, Taiwan's approved outward investment amounted approximately to US$15.16 billion, with 70.53 per cent (US$10.69 billion) being directed to China. However, in the years after 2012, there has been a resumed interest for Taiwanese firms to invest in ASEAN mainly because many of the Taiwanese firms in China are facing bottlenecks along with the trend of the structural change of the Chinese economy.

As shown in Table 12.1, Taiwanese firms' investments in ASEAN mainly go to Thailand, Malaysia, Indonesia, Singapore, and Vietnam, all registering more than US$10 billion by historical total. In particular, after 2007, Vietnam has become a host spot for Taiwan's outward investment to ASEAN. Up to September 2015, Taiwanese firms' investment in Vietnam totalled US$34.55 billion, making Vietnam Taiwan's leading host country in the region, followed by Indonesia (US$17.05 billion) and Thailand (US$13.99 billion). Taiwanese investment in Vietnam is related mainly to the textile and apparel, footwear, and food processing industries, while in the case of Indonesia, the major sectors are furniture and textile industries (see Table 12.2).

Along with the intensified links via direct investment, ASEAN has been an important partner to Taiwan in terms of international trade. Taiwan's export to ASEAN as a whole has been on a rising trend, particularly after 2010. As shown in Figure 12.1, Taiwan's export to ASEAN increased from US$14.9 billion in 2001 to US$57.2 billion in 2014, with an annual growth rate of more than 15 per cent for the last five years. As a result, ASEAN has become the second largest export market for Taiwan, compared to fourth in 2001 and accounting for 18.45 per cent of Taiwan's total export (see also Table 12.3). Table 12.4 shows the statistics on Taiwan's export to the individual ASEAN members, over the period 2001–15. Of note is the fact that for Taiwan, while Singapore has been the leading export market in the region, Vietnam has overtaken the Philippines, Thailand, and Malaysia to

TABLE 12.1
Taiwan's Outward Investment to ASEAN

(Unit: USD million; %)

Year	Thailand Cases	Thailand Value	Thailand %	Malaysia Cases	Malaysia Value	Malaysia %	Philippines Cases	Philippines Value	Philippines %	Indonesia Cases	Indonesia Value	Indonesia %
~1990	786	2,879.95	30.25	784	3,937.52	41.36	506	490.11	5.15	170	2,002.88	21.04
1991~1995	364	3,370.20	18.80	628	3,922.61	21.89	233	239.25	1.33	238	5,031.43	28.07
1996~2000	403	4,101.61	23.15	374	1,365.53	7.71	85	252.72	1.43	477	5,739.84	32.40
2001~2005	258	1,246.64	13.13	358	749.29	7.89	95	350.27	3.69	252	486.83	5.13
2006	63	284.30	13.33	70	110.48	5.18	27	38.05	1.78	27	218.62	10.25
2007	49	247.75	6.15	41	118.79	2.95	28	444.84	11.04	31	51.40	1.28
2008	47	222.81	1.78	32	256.07	2.05	18	28.95	0.23	46	306.23	2.45
2009	32	155.56	7.42	32	209.38	9.99	8	4.67	0.22	47	118.43	5.65
2010	39	139.57	5.83	41	407.76	17.03	21	33.38	1.39	58	85.40	3.57
2011	40	197.94	8.68	23	439.87	19.30	23	74.10	3.25	94	530.80	23.29
2012	58	376.20	6.43	13	56.08	0.96	2	58.54	1.00	75	487.00	8.32
2013	41	230.30	15.69	18	39.94	2.72	10	70.57	4.81	90	306.53	20.89
2014	42	101.10	3.81	30	197.74	7.46	11	67.49	2.55	95	1565.42	59.04
2015 (1–9)	46	439.00	28.27	16	106.37	6.85	13	30.48	1.96	41	116.27	7.49
Total	2,268	13,992.93	15.28	2,460	11,917.43	13.01	1,080	2,183.42	2.38	1,741	17,047.08	18.61

Year	Singapore Cases	Singapore Value	Singapore %	Vietnam Cases	Vietnam Value	Vietnam %	Cambodia Cases	Cambodia Value	Cambodia %	Total Cases	Total Value
~1990	45	70.30	0.74	9	140.49	1.48	0	0.00	0.00	2,300	9,521.25
1991~1995	75	223.18	1.25	514	5,125.44	28.60	16	10.74	0.06	2,068	17,922.85
1996~2000	196	1,097.52	6.20	838	4,740.21	26.76	152	416.78	2.35	2,525	17,714.21
2001~2005	102	1,350.39	14.22	845	5,214.43	54.92	25	97.35	1.03	1,935	9,495.20
2006	18	806.30	37.81	135	623.86	29.26	15	50.75	2.38	355	2,132.36
2007	9	1,194.11	29.63	216	1933.81	47.98	13	39.94	0.99	387	4,030.64
2008	14	697.63	5.59	166	10954.86	87.72	8	21.45	0.17	331	12,488.00
2009	6	36.70	1.75	89	1544.71	73.68	6	27.16	1.30	220	2,096.61
2010	8	32.70	1.37	116	1603.94	66.98	18	91.83	3.83	301	2,394.58
2011	12	448.59	19.68	69	506.15	22.20	22	82.09	3.60	283	2,279.54
2012	19	4,498.66	76.87	60	278.73	4.76	23	97.23	1.66	250	5,852.44
2013	10	158.29	10.79	75	576.63	39.30	16	85.17	5.80	260	1,467.43
2014	17	136.77	5.16	101	553.79	20.89	7	29.12	1.10	303	2,651.43
2015 (1–9)	11	75.03	4.83	88	757.59	48.78	9	28.25	1.82	224	1,552.99
Total	542	10,826.17	11.82	3,321	34,554.64	37.72	330	1,077.86	1.18	11,742	91,599.53

Source: Compiled by CIER (2013), based on WTA database.

TABLE 12.2
Major Sectors of Taiwan's Direct Investment in the ASEAN Members

Country	Ranking of Foreign Investment	Major Sectors	Note
Vietnam	2	Textile & apparel, footwear, food processing	Secondary to Japan
Thailand	3	Electrical & electronic appliances, chemical, textile	Secondary to Japan and USA
Malaysia	4	Electrical & electronic appliances, non-metal materials, paper	Secondary to Japan, USA, and Singapore
Philippines	8	Electrical & electronic appliances, trade, food processing	
Cambodia	8	Real estate, agriculture	
Indonesia	9	Furniture, textile	
Singapore	N/A	Electrical & electronic appliances, petrochemical	
Myanmar	N/A	Agriculture, optical instruments, food processing, construction materials	
Laos	N/A	Furniture, apparel	

Source: Compiled by CIER.

FIGURE 12.1
Taiwan's Export to ASEAN, 2001–15

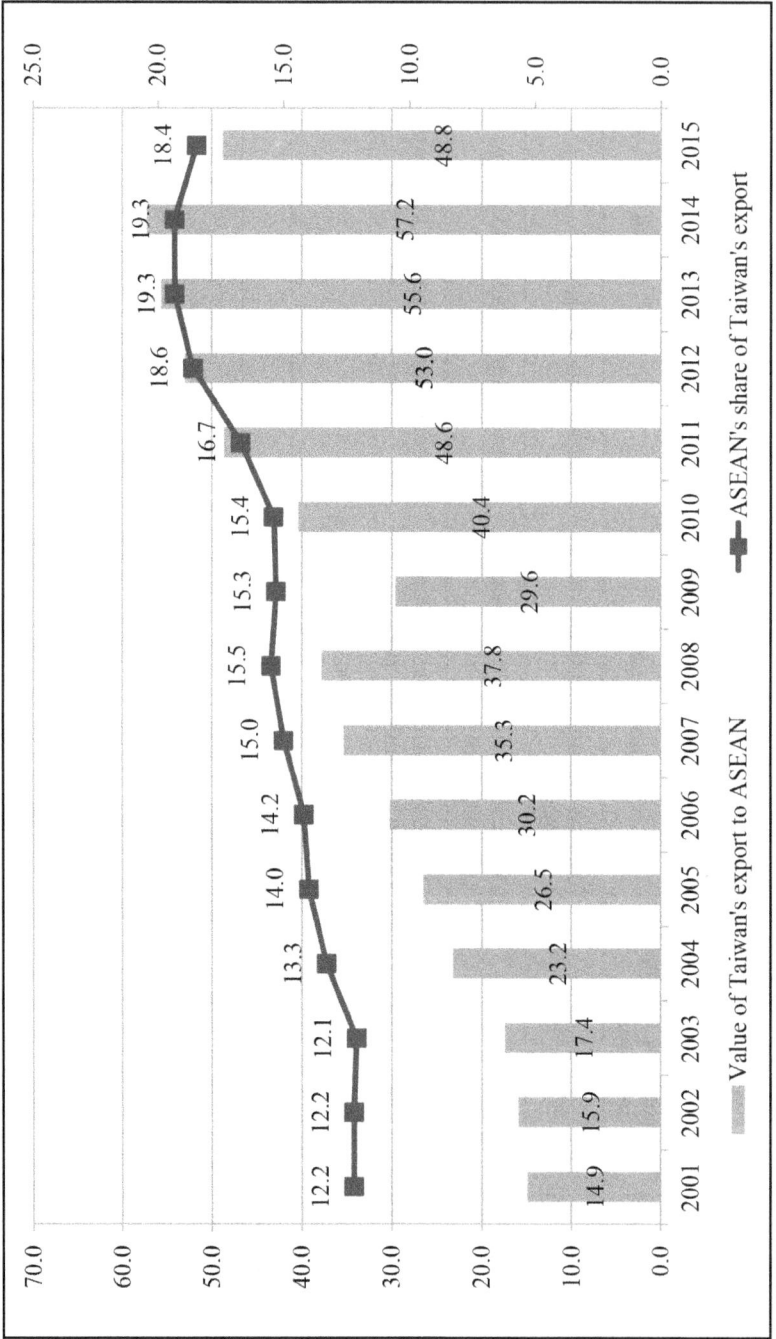

Source: Compiled by CIER (2016), based on database of Bureau of Foreign Trade, MOEA of Taiwan.

TABLE 12.3
Taiwan's Export to Different Parts of the World, 2001–15

(Unit: USD million; %)

Country	2001			2006			2012			2015		
	Ranking	Value	%	Ranking	Value	%	Ranking	Value	%	Ranking	Value	%
Global		122,865.88	100		213,164.33	100		284,182.57	100		264,323.75	100
China (including HK)	1	31,709.58	25.81	1	81,923.04	38.43	1	109,920.99	38.68	1	100,807.78	38.14
ASEAN10	4	14,955.21	12.17	3	30,264.10	14.20	2	52,974.31	18.64	2	48,767.31	18.45
USA	2	27,654.85	22.51	2	31,428.03	14.74	3	31,815.64	11.20	3	32,987.26	12.48
EU28	3	19,077.25	15.53	4	24,442.38	11.47	4	25,523.99	8.98	4	22,899.63	8.66
Japan	5	12,759.16	10.38	5	15,606.63	7.32	5	17,060.38	6.00	5	16,925.22	6.40

Change in Taiwan's Export Share

Country	01~06	06~12	01~12	12~15	01~15
Global	—	—	—	—	—
China (including HK)	12.62	0.25	12.87	–0.54	12.33
ASEAN10	2.03	4.44	6.47	–0.19	6.28
USA	–7.76	–3.55	–11.31	1.28	–10.03
EU28	–4.06	–2.48	–6.55	–0.32	–6.86
Japan	–3.06	–1.32	–4.38	0.40	–3.98

Source: Compiled by CIER (2016), based on database of Bureau of Foreign Trade, MOEA of Taiwan.

TABLE 12.4
Taiwan's Export to the ASEAN Members, 2001–15

(Unit: USD million; %)

Country	2001			2006			2012			2015		
	Ranking	Value	%	Ranking	Value	%	Ranking	Value	%	Ranking	Value	%
ASEAN		14,955.21	100.00		30,264.10	100.00		52,974.31	100.00		48,767.31	100.00
Singapore	1	4,051.26	27.09	1	8,844.10	29.22	1	19,035.35	35.93	1	16,419.72	33.67
Vietnam	5	1,726.77	11.55	3	4,786.37	15.82	2	8,069.75	15.23	2	9,127.42	18.72
Philippines	3	2,148.58	14.37	5	4,396.06	14.53	3	7,367.15	13.91	4	6,903.24	14.16
Thailand	4	2,125.58	14.21	4	4,465.67	14.76	4	6,401.43	12.08	5	5,467.41	11.21
Malaysia	2	3,061.35	20.47	2	4,807.50	15.89	5	6,290.38	11.87	3	6,948.16	14.25
Indonesia	6	1,474.56	9.86	6	2,478.07	8.19	6	4,982.55	9.41	6	2,988.44	6.13
Cambodia	7	182.67	1.22	7	402.67	1.33	7	647.34	1.22	7	673.37	1.38
Myanmar	8	170.63	1.14	8	67.53	0.22	8	144.06	0.27	8	212.82	0.44
Brunei	9	11.48	0.08	9	13.61	0.04	9	33.30	0.06	9	23.65	0.05
Laos	10	2.33	0.02	10	2.51	0.01	10	2.98	0.01	10	3.06	0.01

Country	Change in Taiwan's Export Share				
	01–06	06–12	01–12	12–15	01–15
ASEAN	—	—	—	—	—
Singapore	2.13	6.71	8.84	-2.26	6.58
Vietnam	4.27	-0.58	3.69	3.48	7.17
Philippines	0.16	-0.62	-0.46	0.25	-0.21
Thailand	0.54	-2.67	-2.13	-0.87	-3.00
Malaysia	-4.58	-4.01	-8.60	2.37	-6.22
Indonesia	-1.67	1.22	-0.45	-3.28	-3.73
Cambodia	0.11	-0.11	0.00	0.16	0.16
Myanmar	-0.92	0.05	-0.87	0.16	-0.70
Brunei	-0.03	0.02	-0.01	-0.01	-0.03
Laos	-0.01	0.00	-0.01	0.00	-0.01

Source: Compiled by CIER (2016), based on database of Bureau of Foreign Trade, MOEA of Taiwan.

become Taiwan's second largest export market in ASEAN. This arguably has much to do with investment-induced trade within the framework of GPN/GIN; an issue to be elaborated on below.

Taiwan's import from ASEAN is also on an upward trend, except for the years 2009 and 2015 due to global economic plummet. Compared to US$16.0 billion in 2001, ASEAN's export to Taiwan totalled US$32.8 billion in 2011 and US$34.1 billion in 2014 respectively. ASEAN as a whole accounted for 12.5 per cent of Taiwan's import in 2014, becoming the third largest source of Taiwan's import, secondary only to China and Japan (see Figure 12.2 and Table 12.5). Table 12.6 shows the statistics on Taiwan's import from the individual ASEAN members, over the period 2001–15. Generally speaking, for Taiwan's import from the region, Singapore, Malaysia, Indonesia, and Thailand have been the major sources. In particular, Taiwan's import from Singapore increased from US$3.37 billion in 2001 to US$7.11 billion in 2015. In fact, Singapore is the only country in the region that has signed an FTA with Taiwan. This also resulted in a bourgeoning export from Taiwan to Singapore, from US$8.84 billion in 2006 to US$19.04 billion in 2012 (see Table 12.4). In addition, Vietnam has gained significance in Taiwan's import share, by increasing its export to Taiwan from US$419.04 million in 2001 to US$2.51 billion in 2015 (see Table 12.6).

FIGURE 12.2
Taiwan's Import from ASEAN, 2001–15

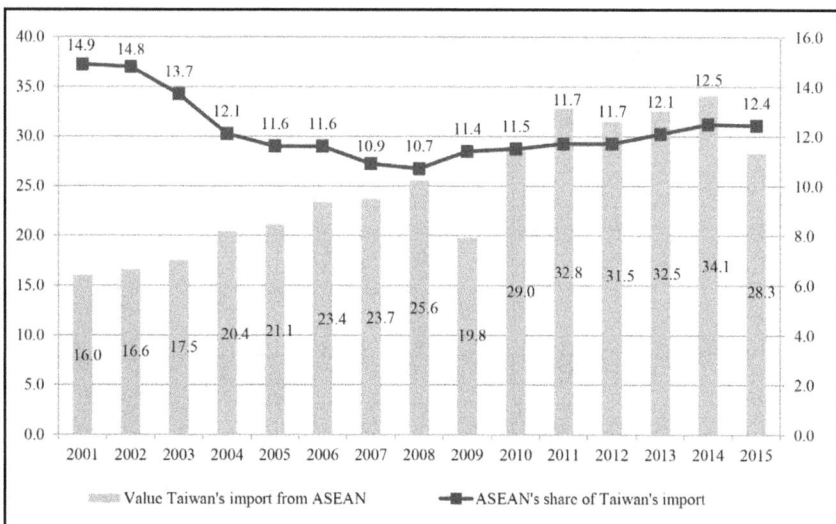

Source: Compiled by CIER (2016), based on database of Bureau of Foreign Trade, MOEA of Taiwan.

TABLE 12.5
Taiwan's Import from Different Parts of the World, 2001—15

(Unit: USD million; %)

Country	2001			2006			2012			2015			Change in Taiwan's Import Share			
	Ranking	Value	%	Ranking	Value	%	Ranking	Value	%	Ranking	Value	%	01~06	06~12	01~12	12~15	01~15
Global		107,232.43	100		201,592.99	100		269,588.90	100		227,813.46	100	—	—	—	—	—
Japan	1	25,847.74	24.10	1	46,202.92	22.92	1	47,513.89	17.62	2	38,700.19	16.99	−1.19	−5.29	−6.48	−0.64	−7.12
China (including HK)	5	7,749.09	7.23	2	26,168.69	12.98	2	43,289.88	16.06	1	45,618.33	20.02	5.75	3.08	8.83	3.97	12.80
ASEAN10	3	15,998.27	14.92	3	23,302.24	11.56	3	31,432.22	11.66	3	28,322.80	12.43	−3.36	0.10	−3.26	0.77	−2.49
USA	2	18,228.85	17.00	4	22,498.33	11.16	4	23,462.21	8.70	4	26,409.46	11.59	−5.84	−2.46	−8.30	2.89	−5.41
EU28	4	13,166.65	12.28	5	17,727.14	8.79	5	22,375.82	8.30	5	22,754.31	9.99	−3.49	−0.49	−3.98	1.69	−2.29

Source: Compiled by CIER (2016), based on database of Bureau of Foreign Trade, MOEA of Taiwan.

TABLE 12.6

Taiwan's Import from the ASEAN Members, 2001–15

(Unit: USD million; %)

Country	2001			2006			2012			2015			Change in Taiwan's Import Share				
	Ranking	Value	%	Ranking	Value	%	Ranking	Value	%	Ranking	Value	%	01~06	06~12	01~12	12~15	01~15
ASEAN		15,998.27	100		23,302.24	100		31,432.22	100		28,322.80	100	—	—	—	—	—
Singapore	2	3,367.10	21.05	3	5,081.79	21.81	1	8,086.02	25.73	1	7,110.60	25.11	0.76	3.92	4.68	-0.62	4.06
Malaysia	1	4,213.67	26.34	1	6,023.59	25.85	2	7,819.20	24.88	2	6,515.62	23.00	-0.49	-0.97	-1.46	-1.87	-3.33
Indonesia	4	2,523.36	15.77	2	5,198.72	22.31	3	7,318.45	23.28	3	5,929.10	20.93	6.54	0.97	7.51	-2.35	5.16
Thailand	5	2,180.90	13.63	4	3,297.89	14.15	4	3,681.02	11.71	4	3,935.91	13.90	0.52	-2.44	-1.92	2.19	0.26
Vietnam	6	419.04	2.62	6	841.38	3.61	5	2,265.07	7.21	5	2,514.11	8.88	0.99	3.60	4.59	1.67	6.26
Philippines	3	3,250.41	20.32	5	2,762.21	11.85	6	2,095.39	6.67	6	1,834.72	6.48	-8.46	-5.19	-13.65	-0.19	-13.84
Myanmar	7	28.95	0.18	7	48.81	0.21	7	76.26	0.24	9	53.35	0.19	0.03	0.03	0.06	-0.05	0.01
Cambodia	8	10.52	0.07	9	6.22	0.03	8	45.53	0.14	8	66.43	0.23	-0.04	0.12	0.08	0.09	0.17
Brunei	10	0.15	0.00	10	2.09	0.01	9	37.43	0.12	7	348.76	1.23	0.01	0.11	0.12	1.11	1.23
Laos	9	4.17	0.03	8	39.52	0.17	10	7.84	0.02	10	14.17	0.05	0.14	-0.14	0.00	0.03	0.02

Source: Compiled by CIER (2016), based on database of Bureau of Foreign Trade, MOEA of Taiwan.

Through bilateral trade, Taiwan has enjoyed a substantial trade surplus against ASEAN, reaching US$21.45 billion in 2012. Of note is the fact that more than 70 per cent of the trade value between the two sides is related to intermediate goods; a typical feature of intraregional trade under the framework of GPN/GIN.

3. The Case of the Textile and Apparel Industry

Despite its stereotype image of being labour-intensive, the textile and apparel industry has nowadays become a technology- and knowledge-based sector due to growing importance of fashion and synthetic fibre. More importantly, alongside with some other sectors, such as the ICT industry, it is a sector with distinct features of GVCs and/or GPNs (Gereffi and Frederick 2010; Gereffi et al. 2005; Gereffi and Memedovic 2003). Driven by international buyers, particularly brand marketers of apparels, and international institutional arrangements, such as quota restrictions and preferential tariffs, the industry is currently governed at the global scale. In production terms, outsourcing and offshoring by leading buyers and garment contractors have brought about prevailing cross-border production schemes of GVCs and/or GPNs, in which various stages of a manufacturing process are undertaken at different geographic locations where they can be carried out most efficiently (UNCTAD 2005). This has resulted in increased task- and/or product-related specialization by firms in the production of goods and services, leading to substantial growth in intra-industry and intra-product trade, rather than just traditional trade in final goods (ESCAP 2009). It is against this background that the textile and apparel industry in Taiwan has co-evolved its counterparts in ASEAN as well as elsewhere, leading to de facto economic integration between the two sides.

As shown in Table 12.7, the textile and apparel industry generates handsome trade surplus for Taiwan. With US$10.8 billion of export value in 2015, Taiwan enjoyed some US$7.35 billion of trade surplus in the industry, accounting for 14.26 per cent of the country's balance of trade in goods. Both China and Vietnam are major export markets and sources of import for Taiwan.

In addition, there are notable structural changes of Taiwan's export in the textile and apparel industry over time (see Table 12.8). While in 1990, apparel was an important item of export for the Taiwanese industry (31 per cent), the industrial chain of weaving (and knitting) becomes the core of the domestic operation in Taiwan, accounting for

TABLE 12.7
A Snapshot of Taiwan's Trade in the Textile and Apparel Industry, 2015

(Unit: USD billion)

Item of Trade	Value		%
Value of Export	10.8		3.9%
Major Export Market	China	2.14	19.8%
	Vietnam	2.05	19.0%
Value of Import	3.46		1.2%
Major Source of Import	China	1.5	43.5%
	Vietnam	0.37	10.6%
Balance of Trade	7.35 (Taiwan's manufacturing sector as a whole generated trade surplus of US$51.54 billion in 2015.)		

Source: Compiled by Taiwan Textile Research Institute.

TABLE 12.8
Structural Changes of Taiwan's Export in the Textile and Apparel Industry

(Unit: USD billion)

Item	1990		1995		2000		2005		2010		2015	
	Value	%	Value	%	Value	%	Value	%	Value	%	Value	%
Fiber	0.603	6	1.002	6	0.954	6	1.147	10	1.170	10	0.878	8
Yarn	1.55	15	2.63	17	1.805	12	2.269	19	2.246	20	1.604	15
Weaving	4.362	42	8.767	57	9.443	62	6.767	57	6.722	59	7.321	68
Apparel	3.163	31	2.349	15	2.637	17	1.319	11	0.783	7	0.650	6
Miscellaneous	0.579	6	0.785	5	0.43	3	0.337	3	0.380	3	0.351	3
Total	10.287	100	15.502	100	15.268	100	11.839	100	11.301	100	10.804	100

Source: Compiled by Taiwan Textile Research Institute.

68 per cent of Taiwan's export in the textile and apparel industry in 2015. Also, fibre and yarn maintain their fair share in Taiwan's export. Underlying this structural change is industrial upgrading towards upstream value chain within Taiwan and the industry's outreach via direct investment by numerous garment factories (CIER 1995). Some of them have grown from SMEs to become vertically integrated garment contractors, with extensive international operations. Notable cases at issue are Nien Hsing, Makalot Industrial Co. Ltd., and Eclat Textile. All of these firms are not well-known household names, but they play

an important role in the GPNs by the leading brand marketers in the industry, especially regarding functional textiles, such as Gore-Tex.

Figure 12.3 highlights international division of labour in the textile and apparel industry since the 1990s, from the perspective of the value chain. Taiwan's textile and apparel industry was developed in a manner of trade-led industrialization, making the country an important exporter by mastering the dynamics of buyer-driven value chains. In this process, Taiwan moved from mere assembly of imported inputs to a domestically integrated cluster, via developing own upstream petrochemical and synthetic fibre industries, and full-package supplier of OEM/ODM (original equipment manufacturing/original design manufacturing) (Gereffi and Memedovic 2003). Afterwards, international institutional arrangements, such as trade restrictions of quota and preferential tariffs, and outsourcing strategy adopted by the leading buyers prompted the Taiwanese firms to go global, particularly China and ASEAN, via direct investments, bringing about functional integration between internationally dispersed activities and value chains (Gereffi and Frederick 2010).

Nowadays, in terms of production, garment factories tend to be located in countries with cost advantages and eligibility for preferential tariffs, such as China, ASEAN, and East Europe, resulting in part from direct investments made by some other countries, like Taiwan, South Korea, and Japan. Particularly, Vietnam has benefitted from its membership of the TPP (Trans-Pacific Partnership) so that a number of Taiwanese textile and apparel firms have moved their production facilities to the country. There is also a trend for Taiwanese firms to increasingly adopt local sourcing and localization in the host countries. On the other hand, Taiwan and some other countries alike either move upwards to master the dyeing, weaving and yarn spinning value chains or downwards to become branded manufacturers. In the Taiwanese case, the industry has turned primarily into OEM/ODM subcontractors by coordinating the multi-layered sourcing networks for the global marketers. In addition, Taiwan enjoys advantages on functional textiles for garments, partly because of its sound base in synthetic fibres and strong relationships with brand marketers of outdoor fashion, such as Under Armour, Nike, and Adidas. With the dynamics of buyer-driven value chains, the Taiwanese textile and apparel industry is on the track of industrial upgrading both at home and in the host countries (see also Figure 12.4).

FIGURE 12.3

International Division of Labour in the Textile and Apparel Industry Since 1990s: A Value Chain's Perspective

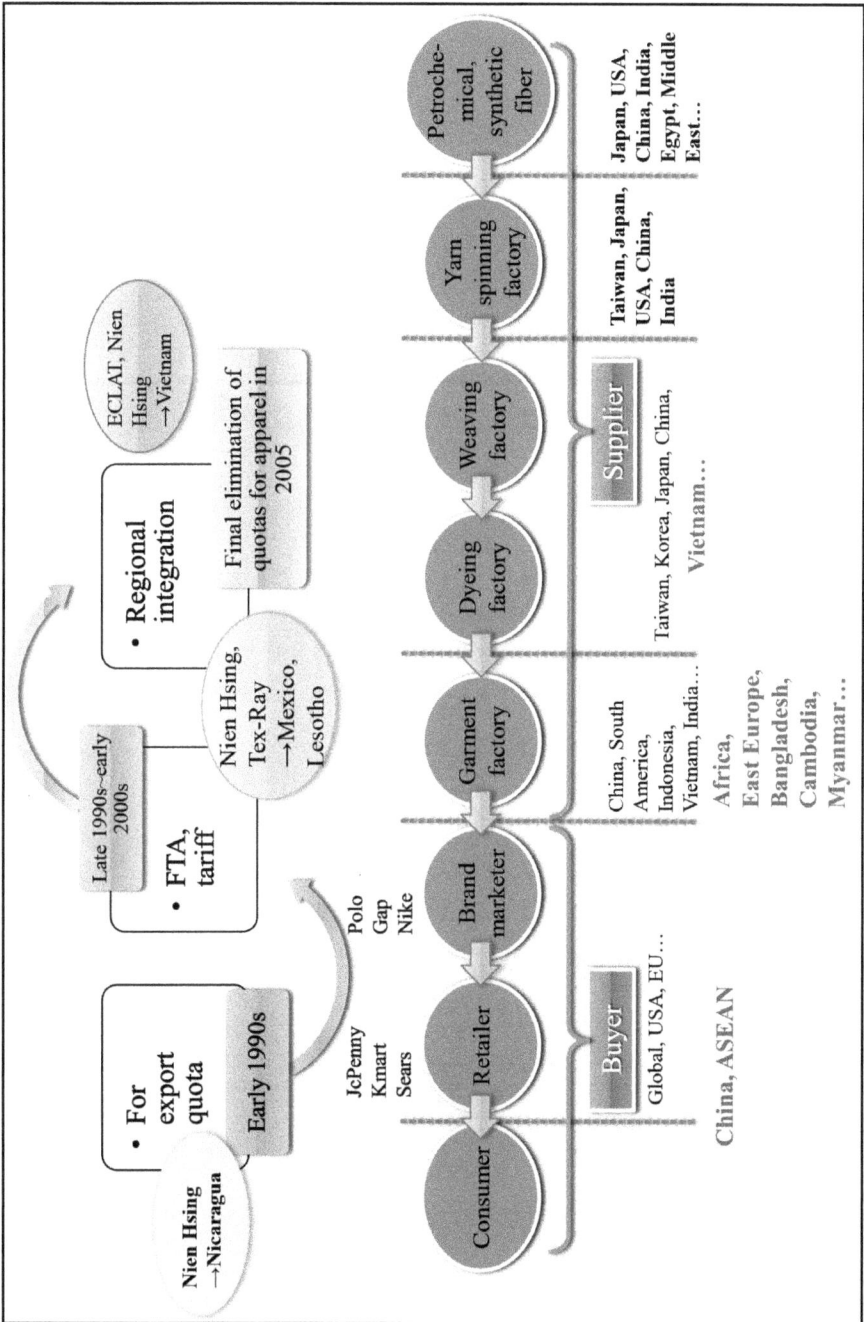

Source: Compiled by Taiwan Textile Research Institute.

FIGURE 12.4

Taiwan's Textile and Apparel Industry and Its Relationships with the Global Value Chains

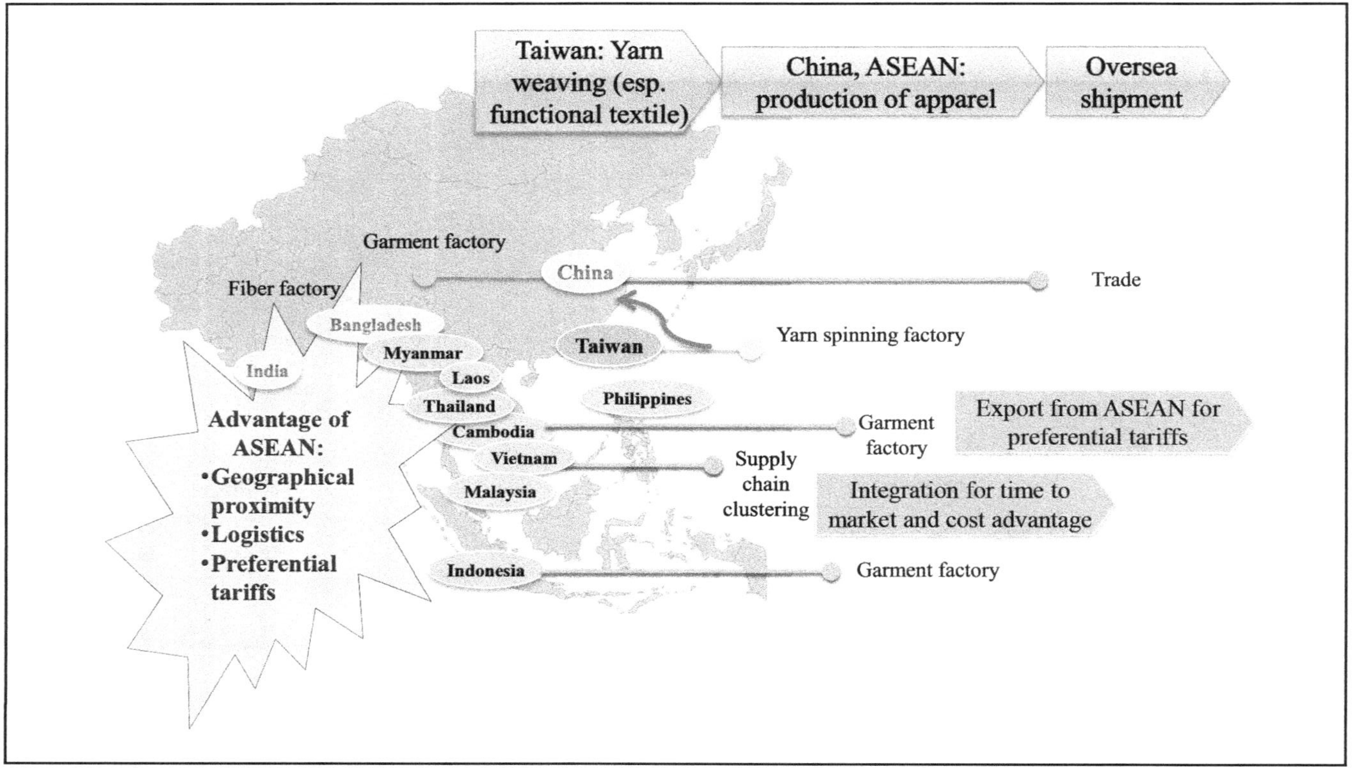

Source: Compiled by Taiwan Textile Research Institute.

In discussing the essence of "deep integration" and preferential trade agreements, the WTO (2011) has thrown out the term the "trade-investment-service-IP nexus" (see also Baldwin 2013*a*, p. 26) to call for a holistic approach to the new trade-FDI reality (Baldwin 2013*b*). In Professor Richard Baldwin's (2013*b*) words:

> The spread of regional supply chain created a richer, more complex, more interconnected set of cross-border flows — especially linkages between trade and FDI. This changed nature of trade transformed policy-making globally, first by creating new supply and new demand for deeper disciplines, and second by creating a bond among various strands of policy-making — some of which were always viewed as international, but many of which are traditionally viewed as domestic policy issues. (p. 26) Today's trade is radically more complex, and this demands more complex, more holistic policies that underpin international flows in goods, services, investment and IP. (p. 28)

Table 12.9 provides a holistic view on the trade-investment-service-IP nexus for the textile and apparel industry from the Taiwanese perspective. With this holistic view, one may better comprehend the economic links between ASEAN and Taiwan than just the view of investment-induced trade. Some of the important linkages involved are listed below.

(1) Trade-investment linkages: The strategy of outsourcing and order-based production adopted by major brand marketers has greatly rationalized their global supply chain, requiring Taiwan's textile and apparel firms to participate in R&D, cross-border supply-chain management, and logistics operations, by forming a fast-response global production and logistics network. In addition, due to the Taiwanese firms' outreach, ASEAN (and China) have become major offshore production sites for the Taiwanese industry, which in turn have fuelled ASEAN's growing significance in the manufacturing and export of apparel products. This has resulted in task- and/or product-related specialization in trade and production between Taiwan and ASEAN.

(2) IP (R&D)-trade-investment linkages: The majority of Taiwanese textile and apparel OEM/ODM vendors nowadays tend to conduct R&D, product design and pilot run mainly in Taiwan, while leaving their mass production jobs to be undertaken at their overseas plants, leading to the delinking of R&D

TABLE 12.9

The "Trade-Investment-Service-IP Nexus" of the Textile and Apparel Industry: A Taiwanese Perspective

Basic configuration of the GPN/GVC	Leading brand marketers & retailers (e.g. Adidas, Nike, the North Face, Columbia, Under Armor, Patagonia...)	←→ Taiwanese OEM/ODM manufacturers and converters	←→ Offshore operations (esp. in ASEAN and China for garments) of the Taiwanese firms
Trade	• Outsourcing and OEM/ODM subcontracting by the brand marketers	• Export of fiber and cloths (esp. functional textile) to offshore plants for making garments • Investment-induced trade between Taiwan and ASEAN (and China)	• China and ASEAN becoming major exporters of garments • Local sales in China by the brand marketers
Investment	• Functions of procurement, collaborative R&D located in Taiwan	• Direct investment and offshore relocation to China and ASEAN	• Increasing local sourcing and localization in the host countries
Service	• Co-creating the configuration of the global value chains with the OEM/ODM subcontractors	• Logistics and supply chain management services performed by the Taiwanese firms for OEM/ODM contracts; namely services in the global value chains	• Increasing localization of part of the headquarters' functions

| IP and R&D | • Marketing, channels, brand names, fashion
• Specifications for new cloths | • Devoted to component technologies (fiber, cloths), post-architectural design & design-to-order
• Delinking of R&D and manufacturing in some cases for Taiwan
• R&D on the pathway and platforms led by the architectural design set by the global keynote firms (e.g. Du Pont for the formula and process technology of functional textile) | • Increasing localization of manufacturing-related R&D in China and ASEAN |

Source: The authors.

and manufacturing in a cross-border manner (Chen 2004; Liu and Chen 2012; Sturgeon 2000). With this hollowing-out of their manufacturing operations in Taiwan, shifting them towards ASEAN and elsewhere, it has become necessary for them to increasingly rely on their subsidiaries in ASEAN for manufacturing-related R&D. On the other hand, Taiwan has managed to capitalize on its first-tier supplier advantage to attract a few global keynote firms to establish functions of procurement and collaborative R&D in Taiwan.

(3) Trade-service-IP (R&D) linkages: Part of brand marketers' innovation offshoring has taken the form of farming out to layers of specialized suppliers. As a result, the brand marketers tend to focus their R&D mainly on product concept initiation and product architecture, thus delegate part of their post-architectural R&D functions to their Taiwanese ODM suppliers, giving rise to offshore collaboration and inter-organizational concurrent development. On the other hand, the R&D routines on the part of the Taiwanese players tend to follow the dominant design and architectural standards set by the players in the advanced countries. For example Du Pont sits at the driver's seat for the formula and process technology of functional textiles. In addition, outsourcing by the brand marketers has involved logistics and aftersales services performed by the Taiwanese OEM/ODM subcontractors, partly because of the feature of modular product architecture (Chen et al. 2013).

4. Cases of an Emerging Pattern

There is no doubt that GVCs/GPNs are major elements underlying the economic links between ASEAN and Taiwan, but new linkages are developing as Taiwan searches for new directions of economic and industrial transformation. For one thing, because of overwhelming concentration of domestic production and export of intermediate goods, Taiwan is promoting innovation and export of total solution. This sets a departure from Taiwan's primary approach to industrial development via vertical disintegration and linking up with the GVC/GPN. Below two cases are presented to show how Taiwan approaches ASEAN with a new collaborative relationship.

(1) Electrical Vehicles and Solution for the Philippines

Taiwan is by no means a strong player in the mainstream automotive industry. The industry in Taiwan has actually been dominated by foreign car makers, especially Japanese ones, with strong control over their product architectures and supply chains. Not until recent years has a newly home-grown brand, Luxgen, brought about seemingly promising breakthrough with domestic root. Meanwhile, the commercialization of electric vehicles (EVs) at a pilot but notable scale, which has resulted from the marriage of electronics and automotive technologies and that of innovative business models and technologies, has brought about a window of opportunity for some of the Taiwanese industrial players to penetrate into this emerging sector. Admittedly, it is too early to judge their success, but their race to a new territory shows different developmental paths for Taiwan.

Of note is an unorthodox approach by some of the Taiwanese players to venture into EV business. For example, Noveltek, an electric-powered material handling equipment maker, provides total solutions for the electrification of diesel-powered flat-bed trucks (off road) used within a large-sized fruit and vegetable wholesale market. Before this electrification project, the diesel-powered flat-bed trucks generated serious pollution and noises, endangering the health of people working for the wholesale market. The electrification of those atypical and niche vehicles means that "powered by electricity" offers a broader perspective of sustainable and "good-enough innovation" (Chen, Wen and Tai 2013; Gadiesh, Leung and Vestring 2007; Brandt and Thun 2010) beyond the typical commercial value creation set by the forerunners, such as Tesla. With its participation in this project, Teco, an industrial motor maker in Taiwan, has won a contract to provide motor solutions for the electrification of e-trikes and e-jeepneys used in the Philippines. Jeepneys are the most common form of public transport throughout the many islands of the Philippines. In the greater Manila area alone, there are estimated to be about three hundred thousand jeepneys on the road. For two years to come, by establishing an assembly plant in the Philippines, Teco is to deliver one thousand e-jeepneys annually plus complementary fleet management solutions to the City of Manila. In other words, what Teco intends to explore is a market at the bottom of the pyramid (BOP) (Prahalad 2005), overlooked by the forerunners of EV makers.

(2) *Electronic Toll Collection (ETC) Solution for Freeways for Vietnam and Some Other ASEAN Countries*

National freeways in Taiwan are toll ways. With a build-operation-transfer (BOT) project, conducted by Far Eastern Electronic Toll Collection Co. (FETC), the billing system has transferred from manual tolling (via flat-rate toll stations) to nowadays all electronic, multi-lane free flow tolling on all national freeways in the country. As a result, Taiwan is the first country in the world to transfer from flat-rate toll stations to distance-based pay-as-you-go tolling system on all of its freeways. Up to April 2014, with a penetration rate of more than 90 per cent (out of 7.1 million vehicles in Taiwan) and tolling accuracy rate as high as 99.9999 per cent, Taiwan also has the longest ETC freeway mileage in the world.

Initially, FETC adopted an infrared-based solution with an over-the-top box inside vehicles and flat-rate manual/electronic hybrid toll stations for the freeway tolling. It failed to meet the competent authority's demanding requirements of high penetration rate, partly because the over-the-top box was relatively expensive. In addition, the government intended to implement distance-based toll collection system. The company then developed an indigenous RFID-based solution, which combined electronic toll collection and technologies of computer and communication. On 30 December 2013, the old flat-rate manual/electronic hybrid toll stations were replaced by the distance-based pay-as-you-go electronic toll collection on all of Taiwan's major freeways. This system not only can expand toll collecting capacity, shorten toll collecting time, reduce air pollution, but also increase convenience and safety for freeway users. In short, the goal of reaching equity by "pay-as-you-go" can be reached by this distance-based electronic toll collecting system. Within two years, the penetration rate of the RFID tolling soared from less than 15 per cent to more than 90 per cent.

Of note is the fact that FETC's RFID-based tolling system can be applied in broader manners than just national freeway tolling. Since the system has a penetration rate as high as more than 90 per cent in Taiwan, for example, FETC has turned it into access control and a billing and monitoring system for private parking lots. Big data collected through the ETC system also serves the innovative need of telematics, vehicle tracking and so on. In a sense, it comes to resemble a platform for internet of vehicles and innovation of smart city.

More importantly, the total solution is being exported to Vietnam and some other ASEAN countries. In light of Taiwan's success in the ETC deployment, the Vietnamese government approached FETC for collaboration. By teaming up with a local partner, TASCO, FETC, supported by a Taiwanese consortium, is working on pilot sites in Vietnam. In addition, according to FETC, its collaborative deals with Malaysia, Indonesia, and the Philippines are underway.

Both cases show a different pattern from Taiwan's existing ways of linking up with ASEAN in economic terms. While GVCs/GPNs are key to the economic links between ASEAN and Taiwan, both cases demonstrate that international collaboration can serve as a means to forge ahead together, for both Taiwan and ASEAN partners. While the societal need in Taiwan facilitated the formation of the total solutions in a couple of sectors, adaption to the ASEAN market via local partnership provides a fertile ground for the Taiwanese players to enhance their capabilities and for social development in ASEAN. In particular, even though Taiwan is by no means a strong player in the mainstream automotive industry, a few of the Taiwanese EV players are trying to offer good-enough electrification solutions to a niche market at home and in a less advanced market in the Philippines.

5. Conclusions

Globalization of production has been changing the competitive environment in both international markets and at home for firms around the globe. Many firms in the world have indeed awakened to the realization that although they are not in the export marketplace, they are nonetheless in the international marketplace, thanks to globalization and the underlying de facto cross-border economic integration. Likewise, institutional arrangements for de jure economic integration (for example FTAs) have increasingly involved many aspects other than the perspective and regime of trade and investment. Against the above backdrop, the "trade-investment-service-IP nexus" has become an important concept to the understanding of the process of "deep integration". Baldwin (2013a, p. 25) goes further to argue: before the second unbundling, the political economy of trade liberalization was "I'll open my market if you open yours." After the second unbundling, the political economy was mostly unilateral: "I'll open my borders and adopt pro-nexus reforms to attract factories and jobs." The intensified economic relationships between Taiwan and ASEAN exemplify the above views. In such an economic integration process, SMEs in ASEAN can become part of the GVCs/GPNs to tap the international market.

However, without denying the importance of Asian countries' participation in GVCs/GPNs to tap the international market (ESCAP 2009), we would like to draw attention to some qualifications. First of all, GVCs/GPNs vary in their degree of openness to external suppliers. For those sectors featured by integral (versus modular) product architecture, their GVCs tend to be closed (Fujimoto 2006; Ulrich 1995). Even serving GVCs with an open network can mean competing in a crowded market. Secondly, it is essential for firms in the region to continuously upgrade their capabilities along the value chain in order to secure their positions within the GVCs, especially in those sectors with technological dynamics. This may require governmental policy to anchor the flagship firms of the GVCs and to strengthen the local industrial base and industrial linkages along the value chains/supply chains (Chen and Wen 2013). Thirdly, there would be a reverse trend of offshoring activities by MNCs from the advanced countries, especially taking into account the fact that the United States has turned to the strategy of "re-industrialization" (President's Council of Advisors on Science and Technology 2011).

It is therefore essential for Asian countries to exploit intra-regional market together via unleashing own market potentials. In doing so, there could be limitations of traditional macro fiscal and liberalization policies in the emerging market. On the other hand, from the perspective of BOP and "good enough" innovation, this can be done through the creation of a massive market space which used to be underserved or underexplored in the emerging markets. The two cases presented above suggest that international technical collaboration between Taiwan and ASEAN can serve as a means for both sides to forge ahead together. While the societal need in Taiwan facilitated the formation of the total solutions in a couple of sectors, adaption to the ASEAN market via local partnership provides a fertile ground for the Taiwanese players to enhance their capabilities and for social development in ASEAN. In his way, Taiwan intends to approach ASEAN members with new partnerships.

REFERENCES

Baldwin, Richard. "Global Supply Chains: Why They Emerged, Why They Matter, and Where They Are Going". In *Global Value Chain in a Changing World*, edited by Deborah K. Elms and Patrick Low. Geneva: World Trade Organization, 2013*a*.

―――. "A Holistic Approach to the New Trade-FDI Reality". In *Foreign Direct Investment as a Key Driver for Trade, Growth and Prosperity: The Case for a Multilateral Agreement on Investment*. Geneva: World Economic Forum, 2013*b*.

―――. "Multilateralising Regionalism: Spaghetti Bowls as Building Blocs on the Path to Global Free Trade". *The World Economy* 29, no. 11 (2006): 1451–518.

Brandt, Loren and Eric Thun. "The Fight for the Middle: Upgrading, Competition, and Industrial Development in China". *World Development* 38, no. 11 (2010): 1555–74.

Chen, Shin Horng. "Taiwanese IT Firms' Offshore R&D in China and the Connection with the Global Innovation Network". *Research Policy* 33, no. 2 (2004): 337–49.

―――. "Global Production Networks and Information Technology: The Case of Taiwan". *Industry and Innovation* 9, no. 3 (2002): 249–65.

Chen, Shin Horng and Pei-Chang Wen. "A Longitudinal View on Global Production Network, Trade and Economic Integration". Paper presented at Conference on Trade and Development Symposium at the Ninth WTO Ministerial Conference, Bali, Indonesia, 3–5 December 2013.

Chen, Shin Horng, Pei-Chang Wen, and Chih-Yen Tai. "China's Good-Enough Innovation: Shanzhai Handsets and Shanzhai Economy". In *The Economic Geography of the IT Industry in the Asia Pacific Region*, edited by Philip Cooke, Glen Searle and Kevin O'Connor. London and New York: Routledge, 2013.

Chen, Shin Horng, Pei-Chang Wen, Pei-Ju Yu, and Chih-Kai Yang. "The Servitization of Taiwan's ICT Manufacturing and its Industrial Upgrading". In *Servitization, IT-ization and Innovation Models*, edited by Kaushalesh Lal, Hitoshi Hirakawa, Norio Tokumaru and Sampa Paul. London and New York: Routledge, 2013.

Christensen, Clayton M. *The Innovator's Dilemma*. New York: Harper Paperbacks, 2003.

Christensen, Clayton M., Thomas Craig, and Stuart Hart. "The Great Disruption". *Foreign Affairs* 80, no. 2 (2001): 80–95.

Chung-Hua Institution for Economic Research (CIER). *Taiwan's Small and Medium-Sized Firms' Direct Investment in Southeast Asia*. Taipei: CIER, 1995.

Coe, Neil M., Martin Hess, Henry Wai-chung Yeung, Peter Dicken, and Jeffrey Henderson. "Globalizing Regional Development: A Global Production

Networks Perspective". *Transactions of the Institute of British Geographers* 29, no. 4 (2004): 468–84.

Dicken, Peter. *Global Shift: Mapping the Changing Contours of the World Economy.* 5th ed. London: The Guilford Press, 2007.

Economic and Social Commission for Asia and the Pacific (ESCAP). *Globalization of Production and the Competitiveness of Small and Medium-sized Enterprises in Asia and the Pacific: Trends and Prospects.* Bangkok: ESCAP, United Nations, 2009.

Ernst, Dieter. *Innovation Offshoring: Asia's Emerging Role in Global Innovation Networks.* East-West Center Special Reports No. 10. Honolulu: East-West Center, 2006.

———. "Pathways to Innovation in Asia's Leading Electronics-Exporting Countries: A Framework for Exploring Drivers and Policy Implications". *International Journal of Technology Management* 29, no. 1/2 (2005): 6–20.

Fujimoto, Takahiro. "Architecture-based Comparative Advantage in Japan and Asia". In *Manufacturing Systems and Technologies for the New Frontier*, edited by Mamoru Mitsuishi, Kanji Ueda, and Fumihiko Kimura. London: Springer, 2008, pp. 7–10.

———. "Architecture-based Comparative Advantage in Japan and Asia". In *Industrialization of Developing Countries: Analysis by Japanese Economics*, edited by Kenichi Ohno and Takahiro Fujimoto. Tokyo: National Graduate Institute of Policy Studies, 2006, pp. 1–10.

Gadiesh, Orit, Philip Leung, and Till Vestring. "The Battle for China's Good-Enough Market". *Harvard Business Review* 85, no. 9 (2007): 81–89.

Gereffi, Gary, John Humphrey, and Timothy Sturgeon. "The Governance of Global Value Chains". *Review of International Political Economy* 12, no. 1 (2005): 78–104.

Gereffi, Gary and Olga Memedovic. *The Global Apparel Value Chain: What Prospects for Upgrading by Developing Countries.* Vienna: United Nations Industrial Development Organization (UNIDO), 2003.

Gereffi, Gary and Stacey Frederick. "The Global Apparel Value Chain, Trade and the Crisis: Challenges and Opportunities for Developing Countries". World Bank Policy Research Working Paper No. 5281 (2010).

Harvie, Charles. "East Asian Production Networks: The Role and Contribution of SMEs". *International Journal of Business and Development Studies* 2, no. 1 (2010): 27–62.

Lemoine, Francoise and Deniz Unal-Kesenci. "Assembly Trade and Technology Transfer: The Case of China". *World Development* 32, no. 5 (2004): 829–50.

Lim, Hank and Fukunari Kimura. *The Internationalisation of SMEs in Regional and Global Value Chains.* Latin America/Caribbean and Asia/Pacific Economics and Business Association, 2009.

Liu, Meng-chun and Shin Horng Chen. "MNCs' Offshore R&D Networks in Host Country's Regional Innovation System: The Case of Taiwan-based Firms in China". *Research Policy* 41, no. 6 (2012): 1107–20.

Low, Patrick. "The Role of Services". In *Global Value Chains in a Changing World*, edited by Deborah K. Elms and Patrick Low. Geneva: World Trade Organization, 2013.

Milberg, William, Xiao Jiang, and Gary Gereffi. "Industrial Policy in an Era of Vertically Specialized Industrialization". Paper presented at the workshop on 'Governance in a GVC World', Duke University, Durham NC, 11–13 April 2013.

Organisation for Economic Co-operation and Development (OECD). *Enhancing the Role of SMEs in Global Value Chains*. Background report for the OECD Global Conference, Tokyo, 31 May and 1 June 2007.

Prahalad, C.K. *The Fortune at the Bottom of the Pyramid*. Philadelphia: Wharton School Publishing, 2005.

President's Council of Advisors on Science and Technology. *Report to the President on Ensuring American Leadership in Advanced Manufacturing*. Washington, D.C.: Executive Office of the President, 2011.

Sturgeon, Timothy J. "Turn-key Production Networks: The Organizational De-Linking of Production from Innovation". In *New Product Development and Production Networks*, edited by Ulrich Jürgens. Berlin: Springer-Verlag, 2000.

Sturgeon, Timothy J. and Ji-Ren Lee. "Industry Co-Evolution: A Comparison of Taiwan and North American Electronics Contract Manufacturers". In *Global Taiwan: Building Competitive Strengths in a New International Economy*, edited by Suzanne Berger and Richard K. Lester. New York, NY: M.E. Sharpe, Inc., 2005.

Sturgeon, Timothy J., Johannes van Biesebroeck, and Gary Gereffi. "Value Chains, Networks and Clusters: Reframing the Global Automotive Industry". *Journal of Economic Geography* 8 (2008): 297–321.

Ulrich, Karl. "The Role of Product Architecture in the Manufacturing Firm". *Research Policy* 24, no. 3 (1995): 419–40.

United Nations Conference on Trade and Development (UNCTAD). *World Investment Report 2005: Transnational Corporations and Internationalization of R&D*. Geneva: UNCTAD, 2005.

World Trade Organization (WTO). *The WTO and Reciprocal Preferential Trading Agreements*. World Trade Report. Geneva: WTO, 2011.

Yang, Daniel You-ren and Neil M. Coe. "The Governance of Global Production Networks and Regional Development: A Case Study of Taiwanese PC Production Networks". *Growth and Change* 40, no. 1 (2009): 30–53.

13

CHINESE MULTINATIONAL FIRMS IN SOUTHEAST ASIA
A Study of Chery in Malaysia[1]

Zhang Miao

1. Introduction

The economic rise of China has generated substantial impact on the globe. Its economic influence following market reforms has had wide ranging ramifications as Chinese firms have become integrated into global production networks as suppliers initially, and since the beginning of 2000, Chinese multi-national corporations (MNCs)[2] have gradually expanded to initiate regional and global production networks (Zhang and Rasiah 2015; Rasiah, Zhang and Kong 2013). While China's miraculous growth has been largely stimulated by economic reforms since 1978 and its insertion into the World Trade Organization (WTO) in 2001, economic slowdown from the global financial crisis (that was triggered by the implosion of the United States economy) drove the government not only to invest domestically on infrastructure but also to encourage national firms to invest abroad. Following the launch of the "Going-out" policy, Chinese

MNCs started to strategize by seeking market opportunities abroad. While the acquisition of the computer division of International Business Machines (IBM) preceded the global financial crisis of 2007–8, acquisitions accelerated after the crisis. The previously Swedish-owned Volvo was among the acquisitions that took place since the crisis. Also, China's outward investment has shown an evolving pathway shifting from capital and resource-intensive industries (including resource-seeking and infrastructure), to market-seeking and technology-intensive industries (especially in transport and telecommunication equipment manufacturing).

Despite forays into Africa and Central Asia, China's FDI has expanded most in the Association of Southeast Asian Nations (ASEAN). Home to around 600 million people in 2015, ASEAN has attracted global attention as an important frontier for growth. ASEAN's US$2,460 billion economy, coupled with its fairly good infrastructure, stability and business-friendly environment, has attracted global MNCs to locate in the region. The implementation of ASEAN–China Free Trade Agreement (ACFTA) and the ASEAN Economic Community (AEC) by 2015 has further added to prospects of cross-border flows of investment between China and ASEAN.

While China–ASEAN economic relations is becoming increasingly integrated, a major focus of researchers and policymakers has been on understanding the motives for Chinese investment in Malaysia, and how such investment is impacting on host-site economies. While the extant literature has extensively discussed the bilateral trade and investment activities (including the importance of MNCs as a mechanism to organize cross-border economic exchanges and activities), little analytical work exists on the specific motives of Chinese investment and its impact abroad. Much of the existing works have focused on spillover effects that are mechanistically estimated using quantitative methods and without a focus on its actual externality effects. Some works have focused on outward investment and overseas merger and acquisition activities but only on the macro-economic indicators (e.g. Athreye and Kapur 2009; Gu and Reed 2012). Some Chinese MNC investment abroad have detailed the motives under the broad category of emerging economies (Rasiah, Gemmeltoft and Yang 2010), but more examples are necessary to construct a reasonably consistent account. An extension of such research into ASEAN can offer new insights since Chinese MNCs have expanded their operations into its member countries since 2000.

Hence, this study aims to examine a case study of the Chinese automobile manufacturer, Chery. The purpose is to analyse the factors that drew the firm to Malaysia, and the economic impact the firm has had so far in the host-country. In doing so, the chapter seeks to add to the scarce stock of works that detailed the motives and impacts of Chinese MNCs abroad. The analytic framework we use to examine these two objectives focus on institutions, namely, (1) national policy to encourage Chinese outward foreign direct investment in the region, and (2) the influence of regional trading agreements. Using in-depth case study of Chery, we aim to provide a profound understanding of how Chinese MNCs have responded to take advantage of the emerging opportunities and challenges in the ASEAN region. The rest of this chapter is organized as follows. After the introduction, sections 2 and 3 discuss the theory and methodology used in the study. Section 4 evaluates the institutional factors underlying the development of China–ASEAN trade and investment. Section 5 analyses the interaction between the two in the relocation of Chery to Malaysia. Section 6 presents the conclusions.

2. Theoretical Considerations

This section seeks to expound the critical concepts, review the main theories, and establish direction for the empirical examination of Chinese MNCs in ASEAN. In doing so we focus on Chinese MNCs in the manufacturing sector. This is important as Rasiah, Gemmeltoft and Yang (2010) have shown the motive of resource seeking often does not follow conventional wisdom. The Australian gold mining company that got contracts in Indonesia (Irian Jaya), the American firms that obtained copper mining contracts in Congo (Katanga) and the Chinese oil mining companies that obtained oil mining contracts in Sudan and Angola went to political risky countries with poor infrastructure through special guarantees for host-governments. Unlike such mineral companies where highly capital-intensive firms could operate with minimal problems from local populations, manufacturing operations in small national markets will require political stability, trainable labour force and good infrastructure.

Since the industrial focus on ASEAN has strongly related to the appropriation of market opportunities from a wide regional market, two groups of theories have emerged to, directly or indirectly, explain how connecting with regional production networks offer opportunities to participate in global value chains. The salient reasons for industrial firms to move abroad still share the then radical exposition of Hymer (1975) who departed from mainstream economic views to argue that firms become MNCs to take advantage of size and reach, and host-site benefits. This argument was expanded by Dunning (1975) who lucidly detailed all possible influences on production internalization decisions to ownership, location, and internalization (OLI) factors. He referred these concepts to what is famously known since as the eclectic theory of MNCs as advantages accruing to ownership-specific advantages, location-specific advantages and internalization-specific advantages. The first two are obvious while the third refers to factors that related to scarce and confidential assets that MNCs seek to retain internally, such as intellectual property rights and management skills. While Lall, Birkinshaw, Buckley, Casson and Rugman have broached these issues to draw implications for host-sites, only a few scholars have approached this topic from strictly host-site considerations to explain the relocation process arguing that some host-governments do introduce and proactively strategize to attract MNCs (e.g. Rasiah 2004).

Neo-Marxist approaches argue that FDI outflows are directed at extending valorization, i.e. to cast the exploitation net to appropriate absolute surplus value from labour (Wallerstein 1974; Frobel, Heinrichs and Kreye 1980). The consequences of such outflows are either underdevelopment or marginal accumulation at host-sites (periphery). The least developed countries of Africa are often cited as examples of how FDI has underdeveloped these economies (Rodney 1981). While Lall (2001) came out with the same conclusion despite not using a Marxist analysis, he offered host-governments the alternative of engendering national capabilities to appropriate gains from FDI inflows.

Production fragmentation internationally is taken as a major channel through which production is separated through arms-length market transactions or internationalized through a transnational division of labour (Helleiner 1973; Gereffi 2000). There is empirical evidence corroborating that outsourcing and transnationalization of operation has offered developing countries great chance in participating in global production sharing (Ando and Kimura 2005; Athukorala and Yamashita 2006). This discourse is further testified by Rasiah (1993) who argues that connecting in global value chains offers firms in developing sites the opportunity to enhance technological capacity and to compete internationally.

While it is the dynamics of evolving production networks and labour division that defines the room for technological upgrading in such account, institutions, both market and non-market, and at both host-sites and home-sites are essential in the emergence and expansion of global production networks. A well-developed and coordinated institutional setting helps drive the co-evolution of cross-border industrial organization by stimulating knowledge sharing and networking. It is a blend of markets, government policy, preferential financial and trade measures that are instrumental in providing the fillip for firms to evolve. Integration into global markets and value chains provides scale, scope and competition for firms to learn, adapt and innovate, so that technological and productivity synergies diffuse through entire economies (Rasiah 2006).

Figure 13.1 presents the analytic framework of this study. The economic environment that influences the relocation of MNCs abroad is conditioned by institutions in both home and host countries with governments as key players. While institutional support from home-country in this article was defined as a supporting mechanism that connects basic and high tech infrastructure and promotes cohesion and integration through trade and FDI to stimulate firm-level insertion into global production network, host-site policy environment has to ensure that insertion into global network will not only help indigenous firms to grow but also enhance the competitiveness of the national economy eventually (Casson 1995). Therefore, a smooth cooperation between economic agents from different countries/regions requires continuous calibration and adjustment. Explicit coordination and power asymmetry is also essential for the institutions by both sides to be completely compatible. The coordinated institutions governing the economic conduct of the agents have direct bearing on firms' relation to their production partners. In this study, we will focus on the interactions between MNCs and SMEs from the perspective of (1) market access and network sharing; (2) technology spillovers; and (3) human capital development. Since Chery only

FIGURE 13.1
Analytic Framework

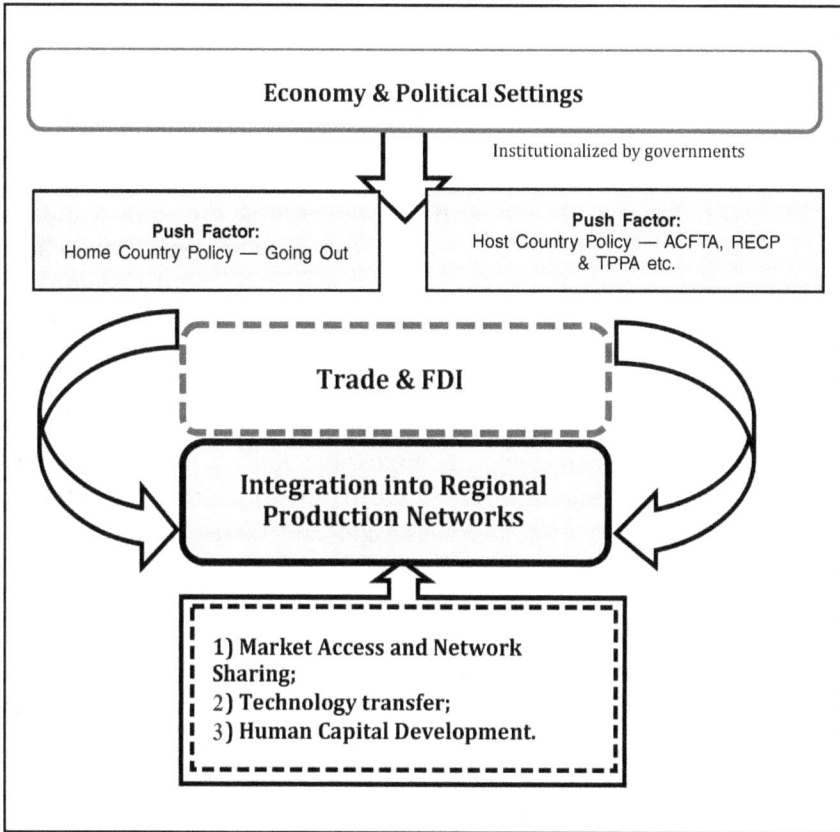

Source: The author.

relocated to Malaysia in 2008, it will be too soon to analyse its conduct and impact in the host-country. Instead, this study evaluates the factors that drove Chery to relocate subsidiary operations to Malaysia.

3. Methodology

We adopt a mix-mode of research. Complemented by descriptive and quantitative analysis, qualitative evidence was collected from interview and secondary sources, such as government documentaries and firms' master plans. The use of qualitative and quantitative techniques enables the appropriation of benefits of both approaches in research, which offers greater latitude to the results and analysis than simply the use of only one of them. By leveraging on the strengths of both approaches, corroborative results from mixed methodologies strengthen the robustness of research.

An in-depth case study was used as the prime qualitative research in this work due to its strength in interpreting the opportunities and obstacles facing the firms in participating in regional production networks. The opportunities and hurdles on ground need case-to-case analysis which by no means be easily generalized and articulated by simply confining the analysis to quantified data. By using contextual analysis of typical events in certain policy environments, case study is appropriate in situations where separation of analysis on firms' choices from certain social phenomenon is impossible. Only a discussion of an analysis of the institutional players' behaviour in specific institutional framework can the analysis becomes valid and robust in its virtue.

While the qualitative information is drawn largely from primary sources from interviews, observations and official documents, concrete quantitative data is extracted from secondary sources including government reports and established databases. Specifically, trade data are collected from Comtrade database, Aseanstates, and China Statistical Yearbook. The analysis of investment is based on the data from the China Global Investment Tracker. Out of 598 Chinese mega investment projects[3] all over the world, 66 projects in ASEAN from 2005 to 2014 were taken for analysis. Despite the evolvement of the local partners, 100 per cent of the projects have Chinese MNCs as major shareholders (over 50 per cent ownership), and hence this database can be a good proxy to indicate MNCs' investments in the region.

After a general contextual analysis of China–ASEAN investment, a detailed analysis is focused on the Chinese carmaker, Chery in Malaysia. We chose to focus on just one industry because all industries are different (Nelson 2008). Hence, apart from its expanding international reach in the region, Chery in Malaysia becomes especially relevant as the Chinese economy is shifting from labour-intensive to high-value added production activities, following a rapid rise in wages in Coastal China.

4.   Chinese FDI in ASEAN

4.1. Regional Distribution

Chinese interest in Southeast Asia is not just limited to trade. The past two years have seen a boost in FDI in the region, making use of its large foreign exchange reserves and seeking to reduce its domestic overcapacity. The fact that most MNCs have state background has given them access to cheap credit from state-controlled banks for overseas expansion. In addition, the highest enterprise savings rate in the world that China keeps further propelled cross-border expansion (Morck, Yeung and Zhao 2008). Although Chinese investment in ASEAN still remains relatively low with limited economic scale,[4] it has shown a robust growth in the past few years. FDI flow to ASEAN has recorded a 61 per cent average annual growth from US$157 million in 2005 to US$7,267 million in 2013 (see Table 13.1). Growing capital inflow raised the FDI stock from US$1.2 billion in 2005 to US$35 billion in 2013, achieving a promising average growth of 51 per cent annually.

Among the ten ASEAN member states, Singapore remains the hottest destination for Chinese outward FDI. Its share in ASEAN in attracting Chinese outward FDI grew from 25 per cent in 2005 to the highest 51 per cent in 2008. Albeit a slight decline to 41 per cent in 2013, the city-state is still far way ahead of the rest of the countries in the region as the No. 1 recipient of Chinese investment from 2005 to 2013 (see Figure 13.2). Indonesia maintains in a relatively stable position to receive Chinese investment as indicated by its share which averaged around 11 per cent throughout the period. While Malaysia becomes less attractive to Chinese investors as its share dropped from 15 per cent in 2005 to 4 per cent in 2013, Myanmar slowly rises absorbing 13 per cent of Chinese FDI in the region in 2013 from a very low level of 2 per cent in 2005. Myanmar has recorded an impressive average annual growth of 10 per cent during the period.

Huge internal varies outline the needs to distinguish regional giant with the rest of the players in the region. Singapore and Indonesia are still the major destinations for Chinese investment, accounting for half (49 per cent) of the total investment flow to ASEAN in 2013. With a small economy, Brunei records a high growth rate of 113 per cent over the period, although the investment still remains very low at US$8.5 million in 2013. Overall, Chinese outward FDI net flow

TABLE 13.1
China's Outward FDI Flows, 2005–13 (USD million)

Country/Region	2005	2006	2007	2008	2009	2010	2011	2012	2013	Average Annual Growth Rate
Brunei	0.02	—	1.18	1.82	5.81	16.53	20.11	0.99	8.52	113.15%
Cambodia	5.15	9.81	64.45	204.64	215.83	466.51	566.02	559.66	499.33	77.14%
Indonesia	11.84	56.94	99.09	173.98	226.09	201.31	592.19	1,361.29	1,563.38	84.11%
Lao PDR	20.58	48.04	154.35	87	203.24	313.55	458.52	808.82	781.48	57.56%
Malaysia	56.72	7.51	-32.82	34.43	53.78	163.54	95.13	199.04	616.38	34.75%
Myanmar	11.54	12.64	92.31	232.53	376.7	875.61	217.82	748.96	475.33	59.17%
Philippines	4.51	9.3	4.5	33.69	40.24	244.09	267.19	74.9	54.4	36.51%
Singapore	20.33	132.15	397.73	1,550.95	1,414.25	1,118.50	3,268.96	1,518.75	2,032.67	77.82%
Thailand	4.77	15.84	76.41	45.47	49.77	699.87	230.11	478.6	755.19	88.34%
Vietnam	20.77	43.52	110.88	119.84	112.39	305.13	189.19	349.43	480.5	48.09%
ASEAN	157.71	335.75	968.08	2,484.35	2,698.10	4,404.64	5,905.24	6,100.44	7,267.18	61.41%

Source: Statistical Bulletin of China's Outward Foreign Direct Investment (2013).

FIGURE 13.2
China's Outward FDI Stock in ASEAN by Country, 2013 (USD million)

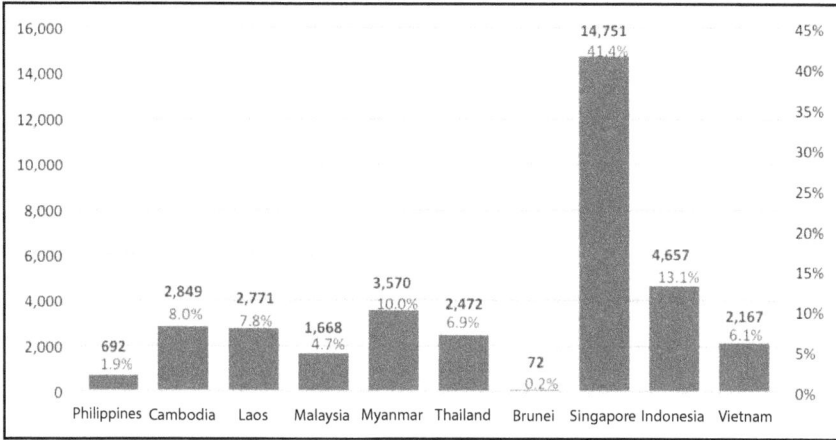

Source: Statistical Bulletin of China's Outward Foreign Direct Investment (2013).

into ASEAN increases rapidly with all the member states recording a two-digit average growth annually during 2005 to 2013.

Compared to inward FDI, outward investment has just started the engine. Those less developed provinces in China have siphoned partial capital from those going abroad. National campaigns such as "West's Great Development" and "The Rise of Central" have made central and western China more attractive than ASEAN in attracting investment. Although Chinese MNCs have made their step to the ASEAN market, China's transition from an FDI recipient to investor needs a while to become an international capital exporter, like the United States and Japan. Meanwhile, uneven distribution of outward investment widely exists between provinces of China. Richer coastal urban provinces and municipalities in the eastern region report much larger investment stocks aboard than those in the central and western regions. The internal heterogeneity has made the economic cooperation between China and ASEAN challenging. Hence, divergent local policies towards outward FDI are starting to become apparent. The variations in economic structure and socio-economic development level among eastern, central and western China and among different ASEAN countries, on the one hand, require great attention for policies to be carefully formulated to meet different demands for local specialty to be well respected.

4.2.2. Industrial Distribution

The analysis of this section is based on the data of 70 mega projects[5] with Chinese investment in the ASEAN region. The total investment of the 70 projects is US$40,570 million, taking up 90.4 per cent of the total Chinese FDI stock in ASEAN by 2014 (US$44,869 million). The fact that the 70 Chinese investors are MNCs again reinforces the fact that MNCs have taken the lead in investing in ASEAN.

By disaggregating the investment by sector, we found that Chinese MNCs' investments are largely concentrated in energy- and metal-related sector where the two sectors take up two-thirds of the total investments from 2005 to 2014 (see Table 13.2). The results in ASEAN have not been much different from the past literature based on other economies (Kolstad and Wiig 2009) as ASEAN is rich in natural resources such as iron ore and petroleum. Investing in natural and energy resources is considered hedging against future increases in commodity prices, though large-scale resource investment may make some in developed nations nervous. Following the energy sector (32.3 per cent) and metal-related industry (31.8 per cent), lucrative real estate business becomes increasingly appealing to Chinese investors, attracting the third largest investment (US$8,370 million) in ASEAN by 2014. Ranking as the fourth largest sector, transport equipment

TABLE 13.2
China's Investments* in ASEAN by Sector, until 2014 (USD million)

Sector	Value	Share in Total
Energy	13,120	32.34%
Basic metals manufacturing	12,910	31.82%
Real estate	8,370	20.63%
Transport sector^	3,130	7.72%
Technology product and services	990	2.44%
Finance	530	1.31%
Others	1,520	3.75%
Total	40,570	100%

Notes: * Only those projects valued above US$100 million.
        ^ Including aircraft lending and shipping.
Source: The China Global Investment Tracker (2014).

manufacturing has received US$3,130 million investment accounting for 7.7 per cent of the total investment by 2014. In general, except for the real estate sector, Chinese MNCs' FDI in ASEAN has shown a strong tendency to the heavy industries.

China's investment in the manufacturing sector has totalled US$14,460 by 2014, taking up 35.6 per cent of total investment in the ASEAN region (see Table 13.3). The majority of investment in manufacturing went to those sectors where China has comparative advantages, such as metal and transport equipment manufacturing. Among all the manufacturing activities, metal manufacturing accounts for the absolute majority (89 per cent) of total investment in ASEAN's manufacturing. Following metals fabrication, transport equipment manufacturing sector attracted 5.7 per cent of the total investment in manufacturing. In a nutshell, Chinese investments in ASEAN's manufacturing are featured by heavy industrial products, such as steel and copper making, whereas the manufacture of light industrial products only takes up approximately 5 per cent of total investment by 2014.

TABLE 13.3
Accumulated Investments in the Manufacturing Sector:
China to ASEAN, 2005–14 (USD million)

Sector	Value	Share in Total Investment
Metals	12,910	89.28%
Transport equipment*	820	5.67%
Textiles	420	3%
Paper and paper product	200	1.38%
Chemicals and chemical products	110	0.76%
Total	14,460	100%

Note: * Excluding shipping and aircraft lending.
Source: The China Global Investment Tracker (2014).

Notably, the low investment level of textile and paper products manufacturing is possibly caused by the absence of data on small-scale investment which the current database does not include. Due to the fact that light industry is not capital-intensive in nature (e.g. metal fabrication and energy industry), the sample has limited coverage on the investment in manufacturing light industrial products. Despite this shortcoming, the analysis using 70 mega projects investment provides considerable insights on MNCs' investment in ASEAN, as the strong capital capacity of most MNCs have made their investment large-scale in nature.

Over half (53 per cent) of Chinese MNCs in ASEAN reported local partnerships. Developing market where the Chinese investors have to face challenges in understanding different policies, consumption behaviour and socio-cultural background, Chinese MNCs inclined to collaborate with local partners to overcome the difficulties in understanding local culture and market condition. While they continued to forge joint ventures (some to establish wholly-owned overseas entities though), Chinese MNC managers turned increasingly to launch local businesses through mergers and acquisitions (M&A) because these offered quicker access to dealership networks and local markets. The strategy of having a local partner helps MNCs to adapt to the local environment quickly by not only managing good relationship with the government and the media, but also to quickly integrate with the local community. Among these, collaboration with host-country SMEs provides a feasible solution by engaging local buyers and suppliers. While the analysis on macro-economic aggregate data may not reflect such interaction between Chinese MNCs and local SMEs, we will illustrate how the collaboration works by the case study analysis in the following section.

5.   Policy Support behind China–ASEAN Economic Integration

While China's push to encourage national firms to invest abroad has been strongly influenced by efforts to access natural resources (especially oil and gas), the market seeking motive has become increasingly important as China's firms expand their production operations not only to sell in national markets but also to access preferential trading arrangements to export to other foreign markets. While such outward investment is mostly orchestrated by MNCs, changes in institutions have quickened outflows by both state-controlled and private enterprises. Continued reforms since 1978 have gradually transformed the government's role from a centrally-controlled directive which focuses on regulatory functions to socially coordinate the evolution of private enterprises within a capital economy. In doing so, emphasis has been placed on building favourable institutions, including preferential policies and meso-organizations, to facilitate the growth of market instruments and to check their undue negative consequences. Therefore, this section discusses the policy environment, including (1) national policy initiative, and (2) regional trade agreements affecting Chinese MNCs' participation in ASEAN's production network. We will also discuss the role of meso-organizations in promoting collaboration and interaction between Chinese MNCs and ASEAN's national firms.

5.1. China's Initiatives Toward Going Global: "Going-out" Policy

Since being a recipient of FDI in 1978, the Chinese government chose to balance outward and inward FDI by encouraging domestic companies to think global and invest overseas. The fact that MNCs that invest abroad are predominantly state-owned has made MNCs pilots in expanding their international businesses. Since the state retains majority of the power and appoints the executives, the investment decision is more political oriented, rather than just profit maximization (Kolstad and Wiig 2009). While the government's policy stance moves away from dependence on a massive trade surplus and capital inflows, China is engaging in an increasingly active investment diplomacy to promote "going global". Outlined by former President Jiang Zemin at the 16th National Party Congress in 2001, "Going-out" strategy was designed to "bring a number of strong multinational enterprises and brand names" to the international arena. It was subsequently defined as a national strategy in the "Eleventh Five-Year Plan" (2006–10). Except for being driven by national pride, "Going-out" policy is also an attempt to steer surplus capital away from speculative investments in real estate and the stock market, as well as to ease growing pressure on the Renminbi to appreciate.

The "Going-out" policy is undergoing a major revamp. While it starts as a simple concept at the beginning, the policy has evolved into a comprehensive policy system which is composed of a series of preferential measures to encourage Chinese firms to go out. The "Going-out" policy system is designed to: (1) reduce red-tape; (2) relax foreign capital control; (3) provide tax and financial support; and (4) improve public service (see Table 13.4). While a great number

TABLE 13.4
Policy Support Framework: China's "Going-out" Policy

Objective		Time	Government Departments	Laws & Regulations	Incentives and Measures
Reduce Red-tape		July 2004	National Development and Reform Commission, Ministry of Commerce and local government	<The decision to reform investment institutions>	The old approval system to invest overseas was fundamentally transformed into simply a register system where the state approval is not necessary for investors to invest overseas.
		March 2009	Ministry of Commerce	<Procedures for the administration of the offshore investment>	Lowered the administrative threshold of offshore greenfield investment; simplified registration procedure
		March 2002	Ministry of Public Security, Ministry of Foreign Affairs, Ministry of Foreign Trade and Economic Cooperation	<Procedures for the administration of foreign contract workers>	Further standardize and simplify the approval procedure for contract labour
Relax Capital Control		2004–6	State Administration of Foreign Exchange	<The notification on the issues on MNCs' internal administration and management of foreign capital>	Allow domestic self-reserved foreign capital to be mortgaged as commercial loans to offshore MNC companies; Abolish 1) the censorship of foreign capital source and 2) quota of purchasing foreign currency
Tax and Financial Policy Support	Special government fund	2007	Ministry of Commerce, Ministry of Finance, People's Bank of China	<Opinions to encourage and guide non-state sector for outward investment and collaboration>	Give 1) special discounted interested rate and 2) special fund for overseas business development to on-state enterprises and SMEs which have offshore operation of manufacturing and trade.
	Industrial investment fund	Since 1998	China Development Bank	Jointly develop China–ASEAN SME Investment Fund where the capital is raised through private equity.	
	Credit support	Oct. 2004 and 2005	National Development and Reform Commission, Ex-im Bank of China	<The notification to give credit support to those overseas investment projects> and other three.	Establish "special loan for offshore investment" every year and give discounted interest rate to the fund raiser;
		August 2005			Ease policy control of financing guarantee for overseas capital raising.
	Insurance support	2001	State Council	Establish China Export & Credit Insurance Corporation	
		2005	Ministry of Commerce	<The notification on supporting SMEs to develop overseas business by using exclusive preferential measures on export credit insurance>	

TABLE 13.4 (*continued*)

Objective		Time	Government Departments	Laws & Regulations	Incentives and Measures
Improve Public Service	Market information provision		Ministry of Commerce	Regularly publish investment reports, providing firms with consultancy such as <National trade and investment environment report>	
	Talent cultivation and training			Organize on-job training for MNCs' management (mostly done by research institutes and universities)	
	Safeguard overseas safety and interest			Establish bilateral trade commission to project Chinese overseas investment, facilitate trade and investment by signing FTAs and inter-governmental agreements, set up contingency plan for emergent incidents.	

Source: Summarized by the author.

of measures has been taken to streamline and decentralize FDI administration and strengthen enforcement, the emphasis of "Going-out" policy is increasingly shifted to risk reduction rather than merely on various forms of encouragement. To avoid excessive interventionism, the key policy slogan has been phrased as "government guides, firms make decision".

While the measures facilitated Chinese companies' expansion around the globe, their bold acquisitions have often been marred by vast inefficiencies and corruption. Hence, the "Going-out" policy is now revamped to shift from reckless expansion toward a more focused approach around exporting Chinese equipment and higher value goods and services. Exporting high value added products like high-speed railways and automobiles promotes China's image abroad and showcases its newfound competitiveness. To achieve these goals, China will need its MNCs to become more strategic, competitive, and efficient. While reformers have tried to increase MNCs' efficiency by emphasizing economic goals, Xi administration gave its "Going-out" champions the political objective of westward expansion along the "One Belt One Road". In accord with the strategy, MNC managers may have to juggle between striving for efficiency on the one hand and pressured to take on less profitable but strategically important contracts on the other. However, investments and products from the Chinese economy will only become more consequential globally, making it crucial to grasp and engage with this change.

5.2. Regional Trade Agreement

5.2.1. The evolution of Regional Trade Agreement— legal protection

The economic ties between ASEAN and China were further promoted to a higher level with the signing of the Framework Agreement on Comprehensive Economic Cooperation between ASEAN and China on 4 November 2002 in Phnom Penh, Cambodia. The policy environment facing China–ASEAN bilateral trade is featured in a series of preferential agreements signed by each party. This largest free trade area in terms of population and third largest in terms of nominal GDP will allow all members to enjoy more favourable trade and investment treatment than the WTO can offer. Similar to the "Going-out" policy which started as a single concept, ACFTA evolves into a comprehensive policy framework by consolidating several regional trade agreements through: (1) progressive elimination of tariffs and non-tariff barriers; (2) progressive liberalization of trade in services and investments; (3) strengthening trade facilitation measures; and (4) economic cooperation in areas of common interest. The completion of a legal system governing ACFTA can be summarized into three phrases:

a. **Phase 1 (2002 to 2010)**: Initial establishment with preliminary tariff reduction. The phase begins with the signing of the Framework Agreement on China–ASEAN Comprehensive Economic Cooperation on November 2002 and ends with the removal of 93 per cent of the tariffs on Chinese products on January 2010.

b. **Phase 2 (2011 to 2015)**: Full establishment of ACFTA, which is marked by tariff removal on most trading products between China and CLMV (Cambodia, Laos, Myanmar and Vietnam) countries, and the further opening-up of trade and investment market.

c. **Phase 3 (2016 and after)**: Consolidation of ACFTA. Comprehensive corporation with full implementation of promised preferential policy.

As the first free trade agreement (FTA) of China, ACFTA framework has undergone continuous evolvement into the current form with five major legal pillars (see Table 13.5). Notably, except for the five pillar documents, the comprehensive corporatization of ACFTA legal system

TABLE 13.5
ACFTA Legal Framework, 2002–9

No.	Time	Document	Function and Content
1	November 2002	Framework Agreement on China–ASEAN Comprehensive Economic Cooperation	• Mark the official launch of ACFTA • Define the cooperation field, including trade of goods and services, investment, economic cooperation
2	November 2004	Agreement on Trade in Goods of China–ASEAN FTA	• Different tariff reduction policies between normal products and sensitive products • Reinforce tariff reduction of 7,000 items: reduce to 0 by 2010, except for sensitive products • Country-of-origin rule: based on value-added principal (origin if VA <= 40%); format of certificate of origin (Form E) differs from WTO format
3	November 2004	Agreement on Dispute Settlement Mechanism between ASEAN and the People's Republic of China	• Designed based on WTO principal and taken ACFTA's specialty into consideration • Procedure for dispute settlement through negotiation, mediation and conciliation, and arbitration
4	January 2007	Agreement on Trade in Services of China–ASEAN FTA	• China's new market open-up: allow ASEAN sole proprietorship in five fields of construction, environment protection,transportation, and sports commercial service. • ASEAN countries vary in offering preferential policy, but all have reduced market entry threshold (more favourable than WTO's policy) to encourage Chinese participation in ASEAN.
5	August 2009	Agreement on Investment of China–ASEAN FTA	• Mark the completion of ACFTA legal procedure • Define 27 important items e.g. national treatment and most-favoured-nation treatment • Highlight institutional support to form a new investment platform • Ensure the completion of ACFTA on time and help economic recovery after crisis

Source: Compiled by the author.

is complemented by the legal aspects in the specific fields, for example, *The Memorandum of Understanding on Agriculture Cooperation* for agriculture cooperation. Both parties have agreed to strengthen the cooperation and collaboration in wider areas such as telecommunication, human resource and cross-border development of Pan-Mekong River Delta. As the ACFTA policy system is a complicated policy network involving regional agreements as well as those signed with individual countries, we would not extensively discuss the policy itself, except for the major policy framework.

With the ASEAN bloc including the Asian Tigers of Indonesia, Malaysia, the Philippines, Singapore, Thailand and Vietnam, together with smaller regional players such as Brunei, Cambodia, Laos and Myanmar, this single FTA is reshaping how China and ASEAN manufacturing develops. Many China commentators have been focusing on the increasing labour costs in China, and noting how many China-based businesses are now struggling in the face of rising wages. The ASEAN agreement offers an alternative by allowing companies to reposition manufacturing to other low cost areas of Asia, taking advantage of the lower costs and yet still be able to service the China market via the duty free imports permitted under the FTA.

Among the ACFTA ordinances, tax reduction is of huge significance to China as this includes Vietnam, which has gradually become an alternative destination to China for low value manufacturing. With Vietnamese wages currently at about a third of those in South China, manufacturing capacity for products ultimately destined for the Chinese market is increasingly finding its way to Vietnam. Knowledge of what products can now be manufactured externally from China and at lower costs yet imported into the country duty free is a strategic and economic issue for many manufacturers.

The legal system of ACFTA is set to be multilateral. In addition to the principal regional agreement, country-to-country agreement has left room for the special needs of particular country in certain areas to be well captured. For example, agriculture cooperation between China and Vietnam has been promoted upon entering the memorandum of understanding in agricultural cooperation on 22 April 2013. In addition, under the governance of ACFTA principle, China–Singapore FTA was established in 2008 with preferential policies on various aspects of trade, such as trade remedies, rules of origin, dispute settlement and custom producers. With the effect of China–

Singapore FTA, Singapore has removed all the tariffs on Chinese products since January 2009, and China has promised to reduce the tariffs of 97.1 per cent of the products from Singapore.

Similarly, China's fiscal decentralization after economic reforms has given local government discretion and motivation to deal with ASEAN and the individual ASEAN countries actively. This is especially true for Southwestern provinces, such as Yunnan, Guangxi and Guizhou, which are highly active in building trade and cultural relations with ASEAN. Sharing border with ASEAN along the Great Mekong River, Southwest provinces expressed stronger initiatives by developing local institutions and meso-organizations to nurture relationships with ASEAN. A number of universities and academic institutions, such as China–ASEAN Center and China–ASEAN Research Institute of Guangxi University, and business collaboration mechanism, such as China–ASEAN Expo, are hosted by these three provinces as an endeavour to tie up the linkage between China and Southeast Asia.

With the further opening-up for the new ASEAN member states, legal documents of ACFTA are undergoing changes simultaneously. The complexities in international legal and economic environment require a close look at the latest legal and regulatory amendments so that the firms could take advantage of the most favourable policy to develop in ASEAN market. With this due, Chinese government should continue its efforts to improve institutional infrastructure to facilitate market information so that Chinese firms can be well informed.

5.2.2. Connect to the World through ACFTA

China has upgraded its trade capacity and investment condition through ASEAN's participation in Regional Comprehensive Economic Partnership (RCEP, also known as ASEAN+6). Formally launched in November 2012 at the ASEAN Summit in Cambodia, RCEP aims to help ASEAN be more integrated with regional key players of China, Japan, Korea, India, Australia and New Zealand. Chinese participation in RCEP has not only helped Chinese firms significantly enlarge potential market in ASEAN countries, but also connect them to a larger global market with preferential policies and tariff reduction. Furthermore, the participation of Singapore, Brunei, Malaysia and Vietnam in U.S.-led Trans-Pacific Partnership (TPP) helps Chinese MNCs in the region connect with countries, such as the United States, Canada and Mexico, making ASEAN's investment environment more attractive (see Figure 13.3).

FIGURE 13.3
ASEAN's FTA Network

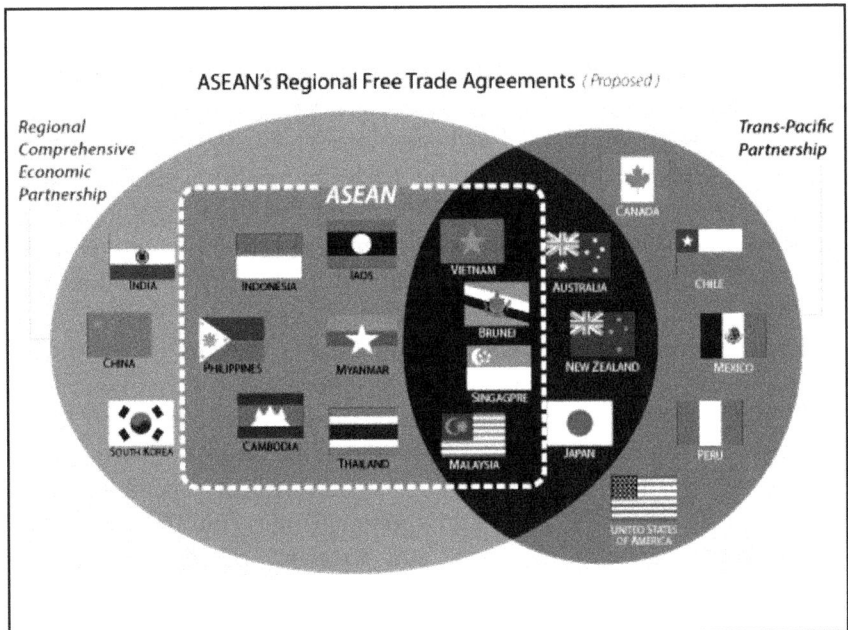

Source: Compiled by the author.

Indeed, the combination of ACFTA, RCEP and TPP has made ASEAN a strategic region for Chinese MNCs to invest. By shifting production to ASEAN, Chinese firms are able to enjoy the preferential trade and investment policy exclusive to ASEAN which they will not enjoy if the production is only limited to the domestic market. While, in the short run, the removal of trade barriers helps Chinese firms enhance competitiveness through cost reduction, in the long run, the free flow of labour and capital over the region will help China in globalizing its production network. Truly, there are still uncertainties before ASEAN+6 and TPP can take final shape. Still, participating in ASEAN provides China with greater chances in negotiating institutional rules in the fields of labour and employment, environment governance, intellectual property protection, government purchase, competition policy and industrial policy.

5.2.3. Impact on Automotive Industry

Being intensively value-added and highly technological in nature, automotive products have to face rigorous export duty to enter the ASEAN market. The fact that automotive products are listed as sensitive products by ASEAN has, to some extent, limited the positive effect of ACFTA in mobilizing resources in the global market. Hence, Chinese MNCs have to face strict control on vehicles import to ASEAN. By 2010, tariff rate for whole-vehicle import was maintained above 28 per cent and vehicle body and bottom remained above 15 per cent. Therefore, ACFTA has placed only partially stimulation effect on bilateral trade and investment activities especially when the tariff rate of sensitive products is unlikely to be further reduced in the foreseeable future.

However, the varieties in industrial policy and market condition of ASEAN countries have provided Chinese automotive MNCs space to strategize business development plans. The exclusion of automotive products from sensitive products list in some countries has offered Chinese carmakers a niche market to address specific needs of the segmented market. For example, China–Malaysia automotive trade value reached US$152 million in 2005, most of which are automotive parts and components. While special purpose vehicles (e.g. snow-field vehicle and golf cart) and most car components (e.g. chassis, engine, brake pad and gearbox) were excluded from Malaysia's list of sensitive products, Chinese access to these market segments becomes much easier as the lowered trade tariff helped Chinese firms significantly reduce production cost.

Higher tariff rates imposed on complete car imports than parts and components have suggested that host-country governments encourage investments on Knocked-Down (KD) factory over simply importing finished products to ASEAN. Additionally, a tax rate of lower than 5 per cent for intra-ASEAN exchange has helped Chinese MNCs significantly reduce cost to access other member states by assembling vehicles in the ASEAN region. Based on the rules of origin, a product with at least 40 per cent of the value accumulatively added inside ASEAN has the right to enjoy preferential trade policy. This has provided strong motivation for Chinese MNCs to establish production base in ASEAN as a hub to access other ASEAN countries, as well as those in TPP and RCEP schemes. We will use a case study in the next section to discuss Chinese MNCs' participation in ASEAN with a focus on the interaction with the host country's SMEs in production and investment activities.

6. Case Study

After the general analysis of the macro-economic environment, this section elaborates the interaction of Chinese MNCs with local SMEs at the micro-economic level. As a major automobile manufacturer in China, Chery Automobile Co. Ltd. (hereafter as Chery) demonstrates strength in exploring overseas market. Bloomfield (1978) argued that the automotive industry of any country that originally does not produce vehicles will go through four stages where (1) import of Completely Built-Up (CBU); to (2) assembly of Completely Knocked-Down (CKD); to reach a level of (3) assembly of CKD with certain percentage of locally produced parts (local content) before the country could finally (4) produce fully local manufactured (FLM) units. Chery's development trajectory in ASEAN has typically reinforced this path, providing a good example of the coordination and collaboration between Chinese MNCs and its counterparty in Malaysia.

Chery is a Chinese automobile manufacturing company head-quartered in Wuhu, Anhui Province, China. It was founded by the government of China in 1997 as a state-owned enterprise (SOE). With its principal product being passenger cars, Chery was ranked as the tenth-largest China-based automaker in 2012 (590,000 units). Since the firm's establishment, Chery has demonstrated strong attempt to upgrading its technological capability. Besides owning its own production lines (e.g. plants for completed car, plants for engine and plants for gearbox), Chery also has its own R&D facilities (e.g. Chery Automobile Engineering Research Institute and Automobile Planning and Design Institute). It has a total of 23,000 staff and total assets of over RMB22 billion yuan in 2012, producing 650,000 completed vehicles and key parts and components, such as engines and gearboxes.

Encouraged by China's "Going-out" policy, Chery became China's first carmaker to export finished vehicles, CKD and engines to foreign countries. The export to Syria in 2001 is the company's first overseas venture. Later, Chery expanded its international reach by massively investing in overseas production facilities. In 2003, Chery became the first foreign firm operating automotive production facilities in Iran. By 2005, Chery cars have been widely found in many countries/regions, such as Russia, Egypt, Indonesia and Malaysia.

Chery's journey to ASEAN began in 2008 via a joint venture with Alado Corporation Sendirian Berhad, a privately held firm owned by a prominent ethnic Chinese businessman, Tan Sri Cam Soh Thiam Hong. Tan Sri Cam Soh, an industrial veteran in the alloy wheel business for more than 21 years, is adept in utilizing its business prowess in the automobile industry to formalize a business arrangement with Chery. As a subsidiary of Chery Automobile Co. Ltd., Chery Alado Malaysia (hereafter as Alado) was officially established in May 2008 through an initial 50:50 partnership to export, assemble and distribute CBU and CKD cars. By taking advantage of Alado's sales network, Chery has successfully become the biggest Chinese car seller in Malaysia with more than 50 direct sales outlets and authorized dealers by 2009. Starting by initially importing fully assembled (CBU) Chery QQ cars, Chery Alado extended the business further to assemble QQ cars and B14 minivans by using Chery technology and parts/ components. Chery Alado then sold 20 per cent of its share to Lembaga Tabung Angkatan Tentera (LTAT) or the Armed Forces Fund Board (a government-linked corporation) for the latter to take in charge of distributing CBU units across the country in 2009.

The cooperation mode is designed such that Chery provides technological support and critical components and Alado is fully in charge of assembling and distribution. To handle the manufacturing and assembly, Alado entered a business arrangement with Oriental Assemblers Sdn. Bhd., a Malaysian vehicle manufacturer and assembler. Based in Johor Bahru, Oriental Assemblers was incorporated in 1967 as a subsidiary of Oriental Holdings Bhd. Having decades-long experience in manufacturing and assembling auto products since 1967, Oriental Assemblers is tasked to assemble two Chery car models, namely Eastar MPV and Tiggo SUV through the strategic alliance with Alado. Oriental Assembler, also manufacturing and selling auto parts and equipment, such as engines and transmissions in the local market, currently employs over 200 employees. Having three major plants of welding, painting and assembly respectively, Oriental Assemblers' production increases from 716 Chery cars in 2008 to 2,526 vehicles in 2009.

Except for the attractive trade agreement of ACFTA, Chery's choice of Malaysia as the entry point to the entire ASEAN market is largely motivated by Tan Sri Cam Soh's initiative to bring Chery into Malaysia. It was Alado that made the first move to approach Chery several times before the deal was finally realized.[6] After the initial 50:50 joint venture with Alado in 2008, Chery's (or rather the Chinese government's) intention to have a government-to-government link brought the subsequent joining of LTAT in 2009. Rather than choosing Thailand which has relatively sound infrastructure and supplier network in automobile industry, Chery's choice of Malaysia seems to show that it is more interested in relatively friendly political–business environment and strategic partnership. Therefore, it is not surprising to observe a weak direct interaction with local suppliers but a strong dependency on their local partners. Indeed, compared to the technology and critical parts that can be easily imported from China with relatively low tariff by ACFTA, local distribution and sales network are the major components of Chery's business strategy. It reinforces the research by Lim (2015) that Chinese MNCs seemed to be at ease with the political economy of Malaysia, in particular when the government-linked LTAT and the influential ethnic Chinese businessman Tan Sir Cam Soh are the major shareholders (Michel and Beuret 2009; Lim 2015). Its experience in navigating a set of complex state–society relations in China has enabled a quick adaption to Malaysia with its unique set of complicated political–business nexus and associated patron–client networks. This is also consistent with Kolstad and Wiig's argument that, differing from FDI from other countries, Chinese FDI outflows tend to be more attracted to developing countries where institutional settings are not necessarily well established than those which are are very well governed (Kolstad and Wiig 2009).

Chery aims to make Malaysia its right-hand drive production hub. It is highly motivated not only by the friendly investment environment under ACFTA framework, but it also intends to take advantage of ASEAN's position in RCEP and TPP as bridges to the global market. Due to ACFTA, Chery parts and components are able to enter the market with low tariff. Meanwhile, the ASEAN Free Trade Area (AFTA) offers Chery zero tariff to export in CKD form to other ASEAN countries. With the first stage investment of a total of US$12 million (RM38.5 million), Chery Alado is looking to export local manufactured automobiles to different markets in Southeast Asian countries. Its CKD factory in Malaysia reflects Chery's global vision to tap other markets such as Indonesia by making Malaysia as a production base. Chery's decision is based on two major factors. One, based on ASEAN Trade in Goods Agreement (ATIGA), Malaysia, as an ASEAN member state, enjoys zero per cent tariff when exporting locally-assembled automobiles to other ASEAN states (see Table 13.6). Two, Malaysia is expected to record total production volume of 1.35 million motor vehicles by 2020 (Malaysia Automotive Association 2014). It has attracted Chery to establish its regional base in Malaysia. Chery's President Yin Tongyao confirmed this point by stating that: "Malaysia is the largest passenger car market in ASEAN and also an important link (for Chery) to other ASEAN countries" (Ministry of Foreign Affairs of the People's Republic of China 2008).

TABLE 13.6
Duties and Local Taxes for Automobiles in Malaysia, 2015

Engine Capacity	Import Duty				Local Taxes	
	CBU		CKD		CBU	CKD
	MFN	ATIGA	MFN	ATIGA	Excise Duties	Sale Tax
<1800	30%	0%	10%	0%	75%	10%
1800–1999	30%	0%	10%	0%	80%	10%
2000–2499	30%	0%	10%	0%	90%	10%
Above 2500	30%	0%	10%	0%	105%	10%

Note: CBU: Complete Built-up; CKD: Completed Knocked-down; MFN: Most Favoured Nation; ATIGA: ASEAN Trade in Goods Agreement.
Source: Compiled by the author (2015).

The managing director of Chery Alado, Paul Ng, recapped the company's strategy in ASEAN by noting:

> To capture ASEAN market, Chery came to Malaysia in 2008 with a clear vision to establish our own factory. We have been waiting for

the policy on emission caps to be further relaxed. Chery intends to invest RM300 million for a Chery CKD factory with annual production capacity of 200,000 units in the coming five years. Actually, we had identified a location for the plant while awaiting government approval. To further develop ASEAN market, we also aim to increase 40 to 50 authorized distributors in ASEAN, which highly possibly starts from Vietnam and Indonesia.

To enjoy the trade preferential policy within the ASEAN region, Chery Alado has to achieve a minimum 40 per cent localization rate based on ACFTA's rules of origin, which indicates that no less than 40 per cent of a product's total value has to, accumulatively or aggregately, be created within the ASEAN region. However, all Chery parts and components are imported from China, although it reported an impressive daily turnover of more than 6 million in ringgit in the Malaysia market. To comply with this regulation, the required 40 per cent value has to be added in the form of labour and capital. Hence, we observed very little interaction between Chery and local suppliers. While supplier network is featured by a two-way interaction, customization, and real-time mutual upgrading of technology and quality control, there is barely any knowledge flow from MNCs to the local firms. Therefore, evidenced by the case of Chinese car maker Chery, Chinese MNCs' presence in Malaysia has turned out to be market-seeking, rather than extensive involvement in regional production network, to increase firms' competitive advantage.

Unlike the early days of export-led growth in Southeast Asia in the 1980s when Japanese and European firms provided engineering help to indigenous firms in meeting precise design specifications, Chery in Malaysia did not report any large-scale assignment of technicians to suppliers' plants to assist in setting up large volume production and quality control procedures. Formal collaborative exchanges on technology and skills occur mostly from the China headquarters to the joint-ventured partner Alado on a contract basis. As there is seldom direct interaction between Chery and the local suppliers, there is no large-scale collective learning in the process of production collaboration. In addition, Oriental Assemblers, as a well-established auto producer in the local market, has had its own regular supplier even before Chery's entry in the region. Given the partner's familiarities in the local market and the rules of origin, Chery expressed that the cost of importing the parts and components from China is still lower than having them from a local supplier. The fact that Chinese firms rely more extensively on their partner firm's business network reflects President Yin Tongyao's comments that "key partnership is very important as it offers the resources and expertise to improve Chery's quality" (Ministry of Foreign Affairs of the People's Republic of China 2008).

In addition, networking links among innovative companies and public institutions, such as industry research laboratories and universities, are found to be very little. Also, on-the-job training tends to be very limited for Chinese investments in the region. It was reported that only three engineers are assigned from the headquarters to Oriental Assemblers to assist in assembly and quality control every year on average. In this case, the finding by Belderbos (2001) that market-seeking FDI in developing countries facilitates more linkages than investment for other purposes found no evidence in Malaysia.

Chery's experience in Malaysia suggests that Chinese MNCs did not fully integrate into local production networks as their interaction with local suppliers barely exists. If there is any, they are mostly managed by local partners. ASEAN expects Chinese investment to renew their capital stock, create employment, and to some extent, stimulate domestic competition. However, the experience that traditional developed economies (e.g. Japan and some European countries) provided engineering help to indigenous firms to meet precise design specifications receives no accordance from Chinese investors in automobile assembling in Malaysia. That Chinese MNCs receive limited generation of linkages and spillovers in the region is not due to sparse and poorly qualified supplier networks, but rather to the company's strategy of relying on their key partner and the partner's existing production network. This finding could be further identified by Chery Alado's recent attempt in seeking partnership with the biggest national carmaker Proton for future development.

Nevertheless, despite Alado's efforts to raise localization rate to 60 per cent, car sales in Malaysia have turned out to be less impressive compared with other countries due to a series of national policy restriction and domestic constraints. Compared to millions of sales in China, Chery Alado has only sold 3,000 units in 2012, which is a slight increase from 2,251 units in 2011. The accumulative sales from 2008 reached no more than 14,000 units by 2015, which is really small compared to competitors such as Toyota and Honda in the market (Interview 2016). Although Chery targets at the non-sedan car sector where the advantages of national carmakers Proton and Perodua are likely to continue as long as local protectionism exists, domestic sales quota, where only 40 per cent of the Malaysia-assembled cars could be sold to the local market while the remaining 60 per cent have to be exported, is still the main hurdle ahead of Chery Alado's further development. According to its managing director, Paul Ng, although the current capacity for each model could be as high as 20,000 units annually, but with only 4,000 units to be sold in Malaysia, the company has to re-calibrate its regional policy to comply with government regulations. While sales network has yet been fully established in other ASEAN countries, Chery is facing great challenges in selling its cars to other countries in Southeast Asia, although the regional tariff policy is very attractive. The domestic consumption quota, argued by others as protectionism over national carmakers, has somehow becomes a barrier limiting beneficiary impact of foreign investment to the local economy.

The challenges facing Chery Alado are more than just sales quota. The manufacturing license is only given to companies which produce cars with engine capacity over 1,800cc as a way to protect national carmakers Proton and Perodua over their position in the compact car segment. Being competitive in low-cost carmaking, Chery has no option but to produce cars with engine capacity of above 1.8 litres. Although local automotive analysts foresee the government will announce new incentives to attract FDI to Energy Efficient Vehicles (EEV) production, "until the NAP [National Auto Policy] becomes friendlier, then only Chery can give Malaysian consumers more choices. Right now, we can only offer them limited choices", Paul Ng further elaborates. With all these restrictions, Chery is now actively working to re-strategize the company's policy by establishing partnership with the biggest national carmaker Proton to seek possibilities for future development in Malaysia and other countries in Southeast Asia.

7. Conclusion

As the economies of ASEAN and China become increasingly integrated, a major concern has been the extent to which local SMEs participate and benefit from such regional economic integration. This chapter aims to examine the nature of Chinese MNCs' engagement with local SMEs and how such interactions are affected by regional and preferential trade agreements in Southeast Asia. Through a push and pull factor analysis, we found that the arrival of Chinese MNCs in the region is highly motivated by the national "Going-out" policy (push factor) and attracted by preferential arrangements such as ACFTA and AFTA (pull factor). This chapter has highlighted the importance of policy initiatives launched by the Chinese government and regional trade agreements in bringing Chinese MNCs into ASEAN, either by conventional trade activities or emerging trend of outward investment.

By analysing the experience of Chinese car manufacturer Chery in Malaysia, we found that its strategy in the region is more featured by market-seeking, rather than extensive involvement in regional production network. While the Chinese government's "Going-out" policy encourages state-owned Chery to venture to Malaysia, it is also largely attracted by Malaysia's advantages in a number of trade agreements, such as AFTA, RCEP and TPP, where foreign firms are able to enjoy reduced barriers in localizing their businesses in ASEAN. Given the fact that most of the key parts and components are supplied by China, local SMEs hardly benefit from collaborating with Chinese MNCs. Little evidence shows extensive production collaboration established between Chinese MNCs and local SMEs. Chery's business strategy of relying on their local partners in making and distributing cars led to little interaction with local suppliers.

Unlike the experience demonstrated by Japanese and European firms in the 1980s in providing large-scale engineering help to indigenous firms in meeting precise design specifications, it seems that Chinese MNCs at this stage have not established extensive production collaboration with local suppliers in developing technology and setting up large volume production and quality control procedures. Rare evidence on collaborative research and product development in host-country shows limited linkages and spillovers effect created by Chinese MNCs. However, it would be too early to conclude that Chery would not evolve in the future, as the experiences from leading players in automotive industry, such as Toyota and Hyundai, seem to suggest that it takes a longer period in Malaysia to establish a sound production network and well-connected supplier–buyer relations (Jomo and Wee 2014). Chery's choice of Malaysia, rather than Thailand which has relatively sound infrastructure and supplier network in automobile industry, suggests Chery's priority in seeking relatively friendly political–business environment and strategic partnership, rather than a sound production network. Therefore, it is not surprising to observe weak interaction with local suppliers but strong ties with local partners.

Although regional trade agreements, such as ACFTA, play an unparalleled role in bringing Chinese MNCs to ASEAN, these MNCs are still facing substantial local protectionism (e.g. manufacturing license and sales quota) in launching mass production locally. In light of the strict policies imposed by NAP, further liberalization of the local auto market would lead to the formation of a sound production network whereby local producers would be given opportunities to participate and benefit from collaboration with MNCs. In that case, foreign MNCs have to source parts and components locally to keep the cost low as simply importing these materials would be impossible to meet the requirements of large-scale production. Meanwhile, policy support in the home country should be extended further from simply encouraging "going-out" to providing comprehensive services in order to enhance the collective bargaining power of Chinese MNCs in the host country. The endeavour should also be extended to establish intermediary organizations and information platforms to enhance mutual understanding, as institutional coordination between government policies and micro-economic agents is essential to support both parties for mutual benefits.

NOTES

1. This research is funded by the Economic Research Institute for ASEAN and East Asia (ERIA) and ISEAS – Yusof Ishak Institute. The author would like to thank Fukunari Kimura, Sothea Oum, Dionisius A. Narjoko, Cassey Lee, Kevin Hewison and Rajah Raisah for their careful review

and helpful comments. The author is responsible for all errors and interpretations.

2. Multinational corporation is defined in this study as a business organization whose business activities are located in more than two countries, where the company is incorporated in the home country and has branches or subsidiaries in other host-countries (Dunning 1975).

3. The mega project refers to those with investment over US$100 million.

4. Compared to other major investors, China still remains a latecomer in investing in ASEAN. With a total investment of US$8,869 million flowing to ASEAN in 2014, China apparently has a long way ahead to compete with other leading investors in the region, such as the European Union (US$29,268 million), Japan (US$13,381 million) and the United States (US$13,042 million).

5. Mega projects refer to those projects with investment of above US$100 million.

6. Interview done in Chery international headquarters in Kuala Lumpur, 29 February 2016.

REFERENCES

Ando, Mitsuyo and Fukunari Kimura. "The Formation of International Production and Distribution Networks in East Asia". *International Trade in East Asia, NBER-East Asia Seminar on Economics* 14 (2005): 177–216.

Athreye, Suma and Sandeep Kapur. "The Internationalization of Chinese and Indian Firms: Trends, Motivations and Strategy". Birkbeck Working Paper in Economics and Finance (2009).

Athukorala, Prema-chandra and Nobuaki Yamashita. "Production Fragmentation and Trade Integration: East Asia in a Global Context". *The North American Journal of Economics and Finance* 17, no. 3 (2006): 233–56.

Belderbos, Rene. "Overseas Innovations by Japanese Firms: An Analysis of Patent and Subsidiary Data". *Research Policy* 30 (2001): 313–32.

Bloomfield, Gerald. *The World Automotive Industry*. North Pomfret: David & Charles, 1978.

Casson, Mark C. *The Organization of International Business*. Cheltenham: Edward Elgar, 1995.

Dunning, John H. *Economic Analysis and the Multinational Enterprise*. New York: Praeger, 1975.

Frobel, Folker, Jurgen Heinrichs, and Otto Kreye. *The New International Division of Labour: Structural Unemployment in Industrialised Countries and Industrialisation in Developing Countries*. Cambridge: Cambridge University Press, 1980.

Gereffi, Gary. "The Transformation of the North American Apparel Industry: Is NAFTA a Curse or a Blessing?" *Integration and Trade* 4, no. 11 (2000): 47–95.

Gu, Lulu and W. Robert Reed. "Chinese Overseas M&A Performance and the Go Global Policy". *Economics of Transition* 21, no. 1 (2012): 157–92.

Helleiner, Gerald K. "Manufactured Exports from Less Developed Countries and Multinational Firms". *The Economic Journal* 83, no. 329 (1973): 21–47.

Hymer, Stephen. "The Multinational Corporation and the Law of Uneven Development". In *International Firms and Modern Imperialism: Selected Readings*, edited by Hugo Radice. Harmondsworth: Penguin, 1975.

Interviews, Chery technical adviser, Kuala Lumpur, 23 March 2016; general manager, Chery franchise workshop, Shah Alam, 25 February 2016.

Jomo, Kwame S. and Wee Chong Hui. *Malaysia@50: Economic Development, Distribution, Disparities*. Kuala Lumpur: SIRD, 2014.

Kolstad, Ivar and Arne Wiig. "What Determines Chinese Outward FDI?" Chr. Michelsen Institute (CMI) Working Paper (2009).

Lall, Sanyaja. *Competitiveness, Technology and Skills*. Cheltenham: Edward Elgar, 2001.

Lim Guanie. "China's Investments in Malaysia: Choosing the 'Right' Partners". *International Journal of China Studies* 6, no. 1 (2015): 1–30.

Malaysia Automotive Association. "National Automotive Policy (NAP) 2014", 2014. Available at <http://www.maa.org.my/pdf/NAP_2014_policy.pdf> (accessed 31 January 2016).

Michel, Serge and Michel Beuret. *China Safari: On the Trail of Beijing's Expansion in Africa*. New York: Nation Books, 2009.

Ministry of Foreign Affairs of the People's Republic of China. 中国驻马来西亚大使程永华出席奇瑞汽车和马来西亚 ALADO 公司合资建厂签约仪式 [The Ambassador of China, P.R.C. in Malaysia Attended the Joint Venture Agreement Signing Ceremony between Chery and Alado]. 2008. Available at <http://www.mfa.gov.cn/chn//pds/gjhdq/gjhdqzz/lhg_14/zwbd/t438341.htm>.

Morck, Randall, Bernard Yeung, and Minyuan Zhao. "Perspectives on China's Outward Foreign Direct Investment". *Journal of International Business Studies* 39, no. 3 (2008): 337–50.

Nelson, Richard. "Economic Development from the Perspective of Evolutionary Economic Theory". *Oxford Development Studies* 36, no. 1 (2008): 9–21.

Rasiah, Rajah. "Electronics in Malaysia: Export Expansion But Slow Technical Change". In *The How and the Why of Technology Development in Developing*

Economies, edited by Vandana Chandra. Washington, D.C.: World Bank, 2006, pp. 127–62.

————. "Technological Capabilities in East and Southeast Asian Electronics Firms: Does Network Strength Matter?" *Oxford Development Studies* 32, no. 3 (2004): 433–54.

————. "Competition and Governance: Work in Malaysia's Textile and Garment Industries". *Journal of Contemporary Asia* 23, no. 1 (1993): 3–23.

Rasiah, Rajah, Peter Gammeltoft and Jiang Yang. "Home Government Policies and Outward Foreign Direct Investment from Emerging Economies: Lessons from Asia". *International Journal of Emerging Markets* 5, no. 3 (2010): 333–57.

Rasiah, Rajah, Zhang Miao, and Kong Xin Xin. "Can China's Miraculous Growth Continue?" *Journal of Contemporary Asia* 43, no. 2 (2013): 295–313.

Rodney, Walter. *How Europe Underdeveloped Africa*. Washington D.C.: Howard University Press, 1981.

Wallerstein, Immanuel. "Dependence in an Interdependent World: The Limited Possibilities of Transformation within the Capitalist World Economy". *African Studies Review* 17, no. 1 (1974): 1–26.

Zhang Miao and Rajah Rasiah. "Globalization, Industrialization and Labour Markets in China". *Journal of the Asia Pacific Economy* 20, no. 1 (2015): 14–41.

INDEX

A

Access, Certainty, Efficiency (ACE), 151

Advanced Science and Technology Institute (ASTI), 294

Agensi Inovasi Malaysia (AIM), 151

agricultural sector
Cambodia, 9, 10
Laos, 104
Myanmar, 171, 185, 196
Philippines, 289
Vietnam, 450, 521

apparel manufacturing sector
impact of AEC on SMEs, 20
Myanmar, 200, 203, 205, 208, 223, 229, 237, 241–43, 266, 273
SMEs' awareness of, 18, 20
South Korea, 529–30, 536
Taiwan, 551, 553, 562–70
utilization rate of FTAs, 24
Vietnam, 518, 526–28

Armed Forces Fund Board, 601

Article IV Consultation (Myanmar), 172

ASEAN+6, 598. *See also* Regional Comprehensive Economic Partnership (RCEP)

ASEAN–Australia–New Zealand FTA, 299, 373

ASEAN–China Free Trade Agreement (ACFTA), 115
connect to the world through, 597–98
economic relations, 579
Japanese affiliates, 492, 496, 499, 500, 502
legal framework (2002–9), 594–96

ASEAN–China Free Trade Area (ACFTA), 255

ASEAN–China FTA, 159, 299, 321, 373

ASEAN Comprehensive Economic Partnership, 188

ASEAN Economic Community (AEC), 1, 4, 34, 36, 109–13, 174, 201, 287, 298, 316, 350, 437
affected businesses, 111, 317–21, 472
ASEAN SMEs Policy Blueprint, 74–75
awareness and impacts, 20, 22–24, 75–76, 316–17, 333, 351, 468–71
business relations with firms, 73
China, 579
customs procedure, 320

export activity and perceptions on
  impact, 337
exporting/importing activities, 74
export tariffs/duties, 319
firm characteristics and perceptions
  on impact, 342–43
firm size and perceptions on
  impact, 335
FTA use and perceptions on
  impact, 338
hiring of foreign workers and
  perceptions on impact, 340
implementation, 112
import tariffs/duties, 319
key changes affecting businesses,
  76–78
micro, small and medium
  enterprises, 91–93
Myanmar
  awareness and perceptions of,
    247–58
  standards regulation, 250
new products and perceptions on
  impact, 341
risk preference and perceptions on
  impact, 339
standards of regulation, 320, 321
ASEAN economic integration, SME
  participation in, 301–5
ASEAN Free Trade Area (AFTA),
  109–13, 154, 602
awareness, 109–13
overall effects of, 112
ASEAN Free Trade Area–Common
  Effective Preferential Tariff
  (AFTA–CEPT) scheme, 298
ASEAN–India FTA, 299, 373
ASEAN IPR SME helpdesk, 153
ASEAN–Japan Framework
  Agreement for Comprehensive
  Economic Partnership
  (AJFACEP), 115

ASEAN–Japan Free Trade Area
  (AJFTA), 159, 255, 299, 321
ASEAN–Korea FTA, 159, 299, 321, 516
ASEAN Policy Blueprint for SME
  Development (APBSD), 317
ASEANSALES, 158, 160, 162, 163
ASEAN SMEs Policy Blueprint, 74–75
ASEAN–South Korea Free Trade
  Agreement (ASKFTA), 115, 373,
  520, 521
ASEAN Strategic Action Plan SME
  Development (2010–2015), 34
ASEAN Trade in Goods Agreement
  (ATIGA), 299, 321, 603
Asian Development Bank (ADB), 362,
  515
Asian financial crisis (1997), 44, 103,
  358, 373, 382, 553
"Asian noodle bowl", 515
Association of Banks in Malaysia, 149
Association of Southeast Asian
  Nations (ASEAN), 171, 264–266
China, 581, 585–90, 596–98, 600–4,
  609n3
FTA network, 596–97
Indonesia, 36, 41–42, 50, 52, 53,
  73–78, 81, 89
Japanese affiliates in, 497, 498, 500,
  501, 505, 507, 508
Myanmar
  ASEAN Economic Community,
    250–52
  awareness and knowledge,
    264–66
  blueprint for SME development,
    247–48
  business relations, 238–40
  customs procedures, 250
  East Asian investment in
    Myanmar, 190–94
  East Asian trade (see East Asian
    trade, Myanmar)

economic integration, 252–53
export products to, 184
exports (*see* exports, Myanmar)
foreign direct investment, 190–93
Free Trade Agreements, 188–90
harmonization, 250
imports (*see* imports, Myanmar)
international trade, 233
standards regulation, 250
trade with, 178–82
production networks, 36
relations with other firms in, 18–20
SME policy index, 52
SMEs' awareness of, 18
Australia
ASEAN FTA with Myanmar, 188
gold mining company, 580
Myanmar investments from, 232
small business, 438
SMEs, 436, 438
Australian Bureau of Statistics (ABS),
438
automotive industry
China, 599–600
Japan, 104
South Korea, 104
Taiwan, 571
average value, of SMEs, 367, 479

B
Banking and Financial Institutions
Act 1989 (BAFIA), 149
bank loans. *See also* finance
medium-sized firms, 218
Myanmar firms, 220
Basic Survey of Japanese Business
Structure and Activities, 497
Bay of Bengal Initiative for Multi-
Sectoral Technical and Economic
Cooperation (BIMSTEC), 188
bilateral exports, Myanmar, 183
Brand Promotion Grant (BPG), 154

broadband penetration, Malaysia, 153
Bureau of Export Trade Promotion
(BETP), 294
Bureau of Small and Medium
Enterprises Development
(BSMED), 293
Bursa Malaysia, 151
Business Assistance Facility (BAF),
Laos, 109
business development services (BDS),
15, 50, 108, 148
business environment
Indonesia, 36
Malaysia, 148
Myanmar, 257, 261
Thailand, 382
Business Forum, Myanmar, 265
business relations
ASEAN, 18–20, 73, 78, 81, 238–40,
415, 417
Indonesia, 78, 79, 81
Business Start-up Fund (BSF), 148

C
Cambodia
"absorptive capacity", investments
in, 31
agricultural sector, 9, 10
characteristics of SMEs and
development policy, 12–15
demand for tourism, 11
economy, 9–11
educational attainment of labour
market, 30
education system, 30
employment, 13
export markets, 11, 12, 20, 29–30
foreign direct investment, 11
imports and exports with East Asia
and ASEAN, 20, 21, 29
industrial development policy, 13,
15, 30, 31

investment, 12, 30
large firms, 13
manufacturing, 9, 13, 15
micro firms, 12
productivity, 30
public–private partnership, 30
Rectangular Strategy Phase III, 12
SME participation in regional
    integration survey
  characteristics of SMEs'
    utilization of FTAs, 25–29
  characteristics of surveyed SMEs,
    16–18
  FTAs' utilization by SMEs, 24–25
  impact of AEC on SMEs, 20,
    22–24
  reasons for not using FTAs, 25
  relations with other firms in
    ASEAN, 18–20
  sample distribution by size and
    industry, 16
  SMEs awareness on ASEAN, 18
  SME promotion policy, 15
  technical and vocational education
    and training, 30
  trade share, 11
Cavite, Laguna, Batangas, Rizal and
    Quezon (CALABARZON), 301
Center for International Trade
    Expositions and Missions
    (CITEM), 294
Central Bank of Malaysia, 149
Central Bank of Myanmar (CBM),
    173, 174
Central Coordinating Agency, 147
Central Department of Small and
    Medium Enterprises, 198, 205
Central Department of SME
    Development, 264–65
Central Statistics Office (CSO), 197
Centre for Industrial Studies (CSIL),
    453

certificate of origin (COO), 90, 288,
    299, 324, 352–53, 353n2, 496, 501,
    505, 508, 509
change-in-tariff classification (CTC),
    506, 507
Chery Alado Malaysia, 601–6
Chery Automobile Co. Ltd., 580, 584,
    600–8, 609n6
Chery Automobile Engineering
    Research Institute, 600
Chery Automobile Planning and
    Design Institute, 600
Chery QQ cars, 601
China
  Chery Automobile Co. Ltd., 580,
    584, 600–8, 609n6
  economic integration, 590–600
  economic rise of, 578
  export market, 183, 185
  FDI in ASEAN, 585–90
  "Going-out" policy, 591–93, 600
  industrial distribution, 588–90
  investments in ASEAN, 588–89
  macroeconomic conditions, 496–97
  mega project, 588, 609n3
  multi-national corporations, 580,
    584, 588–90, 600–2, 604–5
  outward FDI, 585–87
  regional distribution, 585–87
  regional trade agreement, 594–600
  theoretical considerations, 580–83
  trade data, 584
China–ASEAN
  bilateral trade, 594
  economic integration, 590–600
  investment, 584
China–ASEAN Center, 597
China–ASEAN Expo, 597
China–ASEAN Research Institute of
    Guangxi University, 597
China Global Investment Tracker, 584
"China plus one" model, 522

China–Singapore FTA, 596–97
China Statistical Yearbook, 584
Coastal China, 584
commercialization, of electric vehicles
    (EVs), 571
Common Effective Preferential Tariff
    (CEPT), 112
Companies Commission of Malaysia,
    149
Completely Built-Up (CBU), 600, 601
Completely Knocked-Down (CKD),
    600, 602, 603
Comprehensive and Progressive
    Agreement for Trans-Pacific
    Partnership (CPTPP), 447
convertible notes, 148
corruption
    Chinese companies, 593
    in Thai government agencies, 382
country of origin
    foreign inputs sources, 245–46
    Laos imports by, 127
    Myanmar, 193, 246
country's economy, SMEs role of,
    194–96
Credit Bureau of Malaysia, 149
Credit Guarantee Corporation
    Malaysia Berhad (CGC), 149
credit guarantee schemes
    Malaysia, 149
    Myanmar, 269, 272
cross-border networking, 552
Crucial Tech, 536, 545n20
Cut-Make-Pack (CMP) production
    model, 205, 237
cut-make-trim (CMT) model, 527

D
"deep integration", 550, 551, 567, 573
Department of Science and
    Technology (DOST), 293, 294
Department of SME (DSME), 108

Department of SME Development,
    265, 268
Department of Trade and Industry
    (DTI), 293, 294, 344
Design Center of the Philippines
    (DCP), 294
DEval. *See* German Institute for
    Development Evaluation
    (DEval)
developing countries, 195, 226,
    229–31, 353n4, 436, 539–40, 541n4
digital networks, 148
Directorate of Industrial Supervision
    and Inspection (DISI), 198
Directorate of Investment and
    Company Administration
    (DICA), 191
domestic market
    Myanmar, 205, 212, 246
    Philippines, 317, 319, 326
    Thailand, 379, 381, 386
    Vietnam, 450, 469, 475–77, 543n12
domestic sales, 326, 350
    Indonesia, 75, 81
    Myanmar, 256
    Philippines, 317, 319

E
East Asia
    relations with other firms in, 18–20
    SMEs, 436
East Asian trade, Myanmar, 182–88
economic growth
    Laos, 97, 100
    Myanmar, 171, 173, 266
    Philippines, 289–92
    Vietnam, 435, 448
economic integration
    Association of Southeast Asian
        Nations, 252, 253
    China, 590–600
    Myanmar, 258, 261

economic liberalization policy,
Vietnam, 443
economic performance, of SMEs, 298
Eco Vietnam (EV), 538–39, 545n24
electric vehicles (EVs),
commercialization of, 571
electronic components firms, 155–56,
163, 167
electronics manufacturing service
(EMS), 531
Emart, 522
employment
Cambodia, 13
of foreign staff in Myanmar,
224–28
Malaysia, 143–45
Philippines, 298, 310–11
Thailand SMEs, 355, 357, 364–66
"enclave economy", 517
energy efficient vehicles (EEV), 606
engineers and technicians in the
workforce (ET), 158–63, 165
Enterprise Law, Vietnam, 439, 444
enterprises development plans, Laos,
97
enterprises' exports, Laos, 118–26
entrepreneurship education, in
Indonesia, 53
entrepreneurship skills, Thailand
SMEs, 381
2015 ERIA–ISEAS SME Survey, 359,
387
Europe
jobs by SMEs, 436
Myanmar re-engaging with, 176
Everything But Arms (EBA), 20, 29,
188
evidence-based policy-making,
Myanmar, 263–64
export duties, Vietnam, 472
Export-Import Bank of Malaysia
Berhad (EXIM Bank), 154

exports
Cambodia, 11–12, 20, 21, 29–30
Indonesia, 74, 78, 84
Japan, 492, 500, 501, 503, 504
Laos, 101–2, 128
Myanmar, 176–81, 183–85, 241–43,
274, 275, 282n13
Philippines, 317, 319, 324
Thailand, 355, 357–58, 362, 367,
372–77, 379, 384–87, 420–22,
425–30
Vietnam, 454
external trade system, Laos, 101

F
family businesses, 301, 305
Indonesia, 59
Myanmar, 223
Far Eastern Electronic Toll Collection
Co. (FETC), 572–73
female workers in workforce (Fema),
158, 160–63
finance
Indonesia, 53
Malaysia, 149–51
Myanmar, 218–20
Philippines, 288
Thailand, 378
firm respondents, characteristics of,
344
firm sizes (FS), 36, 125, 155, 158, 160,
334, 346, 351, 384–85, 463, 478
firm's technological capability, 26
First SME Promotion Plan (2002–6),
Thailand SMEs, 382–83, 431n8
fiscal deficit, Myanmar, 173–74
"follow-the-leader effect", 535
food and beverage industry, Vietnam
advanced facilities, 451
consumption per capita, 450
human resources, 451
production efficiency, 451

return on equity, 450
return on total assets, 450
revenue of, 449–50
food manufacturing sector
  Myanmar, 208, 210, 212, 223, 232,
    236, 243, 266
  Philippines, 289
foreign companies
  Myanmar, 210, 211, 230, 266
  Thailand, 385
foreign direct investment (FDI), 270,
  287, 292, 353
  Cambodia, 11
  China, 581, 602, 605
    industrial distribution, 588–90
    policy, 591
    regional distribution, 585–87
  conceptual foundations, 229–31
  export platform, 492–94, 500, 508,
    511n3
  intra- and extra-ASEAN, 190–92,
    194
  Japanese affiliates, 497, 511n6
  Laos, 102–4
  in Myanmar, 193, 231–32
  Vietnam, 516, 519, 530
foreign engineers and technicians,
  Myanmar, 226–28
foreign-invested enterprises (FIEs)
  Myanmar, 211–12, 281n11
  Vietnam, 442
Foreign Investment Law, 270
foreign investors
  Laos, 103
  Myanmar, 228, 231
foreign managers, Myanmar, 225–28,
  266
foreign markets
  competition in, 317, 319, 326
  Myanmar, 248, 250, 256
foreign ownership, 281n11, 348, 386,
  478, 480

business relations, Myanmar,
  238–39
Indonesia, 79
Thailand SMEs, 429
foreign staff, Myanmar, 225–28
form of limited companies (FEL), 124
Foxconn Group, 543n13
fragmentation theory, 477
fragmented production, 515
free-trade agreement (FTA), 1, 4, 322,
  350, 446, 514–15, 541n2
  ASEAN, 188–89
  awareness and knowledge, 264–66,
    473
  characteristics of FTA users, 326–31
  characteristics of SMEs' utilization
    of, 25–29
  China, 594, 596, 598
  determinants of, 344–48
  on domestic sales, 324
  on export sales, 326
  foreign ownership, 348
  impact on businesses, 256–57,
    324–26
  Indonesia, 79–83, 86, 87, 90
  influences, 472, 474–75
  innovation expenditure, 331
  Laos, 114–18
  multinational companies, 348
  Myanmar's, 188–89, 256
  non-use of, 324
  in Philippines, 288, 298–300
  schemes, 493, 495, 496, 500–5, 507,
    508
  significant factors in export, 503
  and trade preference schemes
    report, 253, 255
  training expenditures, 331
  use of, 253–54, 472
  utilization, 24–25, 321–24, 472,
    474–75
frugal innovation, SMEs, 195

FTA-PASS software, 509
FTA-PASS, South Korea, 509
fully local manufactured (FLM) units, 600
functional upgrading, 538

G
garment sector, Myanmar, 237
Generalized System of Preferences (GSP), 188, 190, 255, 321, 353n4
German Institute for Development Evaluation (DEval), 199, 206, 208, 224, 234
global export platform, 511n3
Global Financial Crisis (GFC), 360
global innovation networks (GINs), 552
globalization, 551, 552, 573
global production networks (GPNs), 4, 515, 516, 551, 552, 562, 574
  China, 182, 184
  Indonesia SMEs, 35–36
  Vietnamese SMEs' participation in, 524–25
    advanced electronics sector, 531–32
    Korean apparel production network, 528–31
    Korean electronics production network, 533–37
    traditional apparel sector, 526–28
    working with medium-sized Korean firms, 538–39
global value chains (GVCs), 229–31, 287–89, 298, 551, 552, 562, 574, 581, 582
"Going-out" policy in China, 591–93, 600
government assistance, Thailand SMEs, 386
government regulation, Thailand SMEs, 382

Government's Social Assistance Program, 50
government support and assistance, 288, 348, 352
Green Lane Incentive, 152
Green Lane Policy, 147

H
harmonized system (HS), 493
heterogeneity, Myanmar SMEs, 202–5
high technology firms, Malaysia, 148
home-country export platform, 511n3
host country, sample distribution by, 510
human resource development
  Myanmar, 266–67
  Thailand SMEs, 381
Human Resources Development Fund (HRDF), 154

I
import costs, Philippines, 317, 324
import duties, Vietnam, 472
imports
  Cambodia, 20, 21, 29
  Indonesia, 74, 78, 85
  Laos, 102, 127
  Myanmar, 176–81, 185–87, 274, 276
  Taiwan, 559–61
import tariffs/duties, ASEAN Economic Community, 319
Income Tax Order 2009, 150
incubators, in Malaysia, 151
individual enterprise form (FEI), 124
Indonesia
  academic qualifications of workers, 35, 68
  ASEAN Economic Community, 73–78, 89–90
  distribution
    of sales, 61, 63
    of survey sample, 54–55

economic development, 36
employment profile, 65–66
exporting/importing activities
    FTAs utilization *vs.*, 74, 78
government support, 87–88
innovation activities and
    expenditure (2012–14), 68–69
international market expansion, 51
internet-related services, 72–73
micro, small and medium
    enterprises, 37–44
overall sales and destination, 61–62
policy recommendations, 90
process innovation (2012–14), 70–71
product innovation (2012–14),
    70–71
production and input
    characteristics, 63, 64
profile of survey sample, 56–59
regional integration, 78–82
sales distribution and product type,
    59–60
SME development, 34, 35, 44
SME policies in, 44–54
    ASEAN index, 52
    initiatives in 1969–2000, 45–46
    initiatives in 2008, 47–49
    Law No. 1/2013, 44
    Law No. 9/1995, 44
    Law No. 20/2008, 44
    Law No. 23/2014, 44
    Law No. 39 /2014, 49
survey of SMEs in, 35
training expenditure, 68
workforce and salaries (2014), 65,
    67
Indonesia Export Funding Agency,
    49
Indonesian Trade Promotion Centre
    (ITPC), 51
Industrial Development Policy,
    Cambodia, 13, 15

Industrial Master Plan in Malaysia,
    151
Industrial Technology Development
    Institute (ITDI), 294
informal sector, in Myanmar, 206–7,
    261
information and communications
    technologies (ICT), 26, 265
    firm size, ownership and industry,
        212, 214
    percentage of, 212, 213
    usage of SMEs, 271–72
    usage score, 215
information kiosk, 148
information technology (IT), Thailand
    SMEs, 380
in-house R&D (IHRD), 158–64, 166,
    167, 313–14
InnoCERT programme, 151
1-InnoCert programme, 152
innovation
    Malaysia, 151–55
    Myanmar, 211–18
    Thailand SMEs, 380–81, 430n7
innovation expenditure, FTA users,
    331
Institute of Labour Science and Social
    Affairs (ILSSA), 442
intellectual property (IP), 153
intellectual property rights (IPRs),
    153
International Business Machines
    (IBM), 579
international economic transactions,
    Myanmar, 173, 190
internationalization, 377, 436–37, 445
International Monetary Fund (IMF),
    172–74
international trade, 229, 230, 515
    Laos, 101, 116–18
    Myanmar, 232–38
    Taiwan, 552, 553

Thailand, 358
Vietnam, 467
International Trade Centre (ITC),
    453
internet services
    Indonesia, 72
    Philippines, 314, 315
"investment-induced trade", Taiwan,
    550
investment liberalization, Philippines,
    298
investment policy, Laos, 102–4

J
Japan
    affiliate in ASEAN, 498–99
    basic statistics, 502
    data issues, 497–501
    decomposition of originating
        inputs, 505–6
    empirical results, 502–8
    empirical specification, 495–97
    excluded variables, 497
    export, 492, 500, 501, 503, 504
    export platform FDI, 492–94, 500,
        508, 511n3
    export to China, 493, 496, 502, 505,
        511n8
    foreign direct investment, 494, 497
    FTA schemes, 493, 495–96, 500–5,
        507, 508
    Japan External Trade Organization
        survey, 492
    policy recommendations, 508–9
    sample distribution by, 510
    SMEs, 493, 500, 508
Japanese-affiliated firms, 492, 511n6
Japan External Trade Organization
    (JETRO) survey, 492, 497–98,
    511n7
Japan's Small and Medium-sized
    Enterprise (SME) Basic Law, 493

K
Kien Giang company, 528
Knocked-Down (KD) factory, 599

L
labour market
    Cambodia, 30
    Japan, 509
    Malaysia, 155
    Myanmar, 221, 252, 266
    Thailand SMEs, 381
labour productivity, 26, 348, 478, 480,
    485
labour turnover, Myanmar, 269
Laos
    AEC implementation in 2015, 133
    awareness of AEC/AFTA and
        impact, 109–13, 126
    awareness of WTO and impact,
        113–14, 126
    Business Assistance Facility, 106
    capital inflows, 103
    definition of SMEs, 105
    "Dutch disease", 97, 118
    economic growth, 97–98, 100
    enterprises development plans,
        97
    expected impacts of AEC, 132
    exports, 101–2
        by commodity, 128
        by country, 128
        enterprises', 118–26
    external and internal constraints of
        enterprises, 107
    external trade system, 101
    FDI, 139n1
        by sector, 131
        sources inflows, 130
    FDI Law 1988, 102
    foreign investors, 103
    free-trade agreement, 114–18, 126
    heavy manufacturing, 102

impacts
  of AFTA, 134
  of WTO, 135
imports, 102
  by commodity, 127
  by country of origin, 127
inequality, 100
investment policy and FDI
    characteristics, 102–4
large enterprises, 111
macroeconomic situation, 99
national goal of, 100
natural resources, 104, 118
New Economic Mechanism, 98
New Market Mechanism, 108
participation in regional economic
    integration, 98
poverty, 98, 100
preferential tariff utilization,
    114–18, 126
registered capital and number of
    projects, 129
"resources curse", 97
savings rate, 100
SME Development Plan (2016–
    2020), 108
SME Promotion and Development
    Fund, 108
SMEs by activities, 106
SMEs' characteristics and
    challenges, 106–7
SMEs' contribution, 106
SMEs' development policy, 108–9
SMEs exporting using the logit
    model, 119–23
Trade Development Facility Project,
    109
trade expansion, 101
trade policy and trade
    characteristics, 100–2
Lao–Viet Free Trade Agreement
    (LVFTA), 115

large enterprises (LEs)
  Indonesia, 39, 54, 59, 63, 65, 70, 74,
    76, 78
  Laos, 111
  Malaysia, 145
  Myanmar, 196, 198, 226, 232,
    248–49, 256, 260
  Philippine, 301, 305, 350
    domestic market, competition
      in, 319
    domestic sales, 319, 350
    export sales, 319
    foreign market, competition in,
      319
    foreign workers, 313
    free trade agreements, 324
    import and export tariffs, 321
    mean sales, 305
    new and improved products, 314
    part-time workers, 313
    plant and machine operators,
      313
    production costs, 310
  Thailand, 357, 358, 367
large firms, 4, 13, 20, 36, 37
  Laos, 115
  Malaysia, 152, 157, 158
  Myanmar, 217, 226, 243–45
  Philippines, 297
  Thailand, 390
  Vietnam, 484, 531
leasing companies, Malaysia, 149–50
least developed country (LDC), 188,
    190, 261, 541n4
legal status of Myanmar companies,
    210
Lembaga Pembiayaan Ekspor
    Indonesia (LPEI), 49, 51
Lembaga Tabung Angkatan Tentera
    (LTAT), 601, 602
less developed countries (LDCs),
    541n4

LG Vietnam, 537, 545n22
liberalization policy, 515
limited liability companies, Vietnam,
    445, 455, 483
linear probability model (LPM), 420
locally owned enterprises, 301
logit model, 119, 136–38
low-cost labour in Vietnam, 448

M
macroeconomic context, Myanmar,
    170–76
macroeconomic indicators, Myanmar,
    171
main marketing channel, 234–35
Malaysia
    broadband penetration, 153
    connectivity and coordination,
        147–48
    data, 155–59
    duties and local taxes for
        automobiles, 603
    economic development, 143, 147
    electronic components firms,
        155–56, 158
    employment, 144–45
    entrepreneurial education in, 155
    finance, 149–51
    gross domestic product, 144–45
    incubators in, 151
    Industrial Master Plan, 151
    innovation technology
        development, 151–52
    institutional support, 146–47
    intellectual property, 153
    large enterprises in, 145
    legal framework of, 149
    methodology, 155–59
    national electronic components
        firms, 155–56, 158, 162
    national standard development
        agency, 153

regional trading agreements,
    157–60, 162–65
SME policies, 146–55
SMEs role in, 143–46
technology, 151–55
used digital networks, 148
value-added share of, 144–45
Malaysia Debt Venture Berhad, 153
Malaysia External Trade
    Development Corporation
    (MATRADE), 152, 153
Malaysian Exchange of Securities
    Dealing and Automated
    Quotation (MESDAQ)
    listing requirements of, 151
Malaysian Intellectual Property
    Organisation (MyIPO), 153
Malaysian Technology Development
    Corporation (MTDC), 148
Malaysia Productivity Corporation
    (MPC), 148
manufacturing industry, 298
    Cambodia, 13
    China, 580
    gross domestic product, in
        Philippine, 301
    Japan, 497
    Malaysia, 146
    in Myanmar, 201
    in Philippines, 289, 290, 296–98, 301
    total manufacturing value added,
        Philippine, 301
    Vietnam, 534
Market Development Grant (MDG),
    153, 154
marketing. *See also* online marketing
    in Indonesia, 45, 48, 49
    online services, Indonesia, 73
    Thailand SMEs, 379
market-oriented economic system,
    Myanmar, 170, 171
market penetration of SMEs, 445

mean sales, 305
  large enterprises, 305
medium and large enterprises, 109,
    206, 297, 395
medium enterprises, 297, 301, 438
  Indonesia, 37, 39, 44, 54
  Laos, 105
  Myanmar, 211
  Philippines, 292, 301
  Thailand, 364, 367
membership of industry, 455, 483,
    484
*The Memorandum of Understanding on
    Agriculture Cooperation*, 596
Metals Industry Research and
    Development Center (MIRDC),
    294
micro enterprises, 292, 430n3, 438
  Indonesia, 37, 39, 41
  Myanmar, 196, 198, 234
  Philippines, 297
micro entrepreneurs, Malaysia, 149
microfinance, 149
micro firms
  Cambodia, 12–13
  Indonesia, 39
  Vietnam, 469, 472
micro, small and medium enterprises
    (MSMEs), 37
  across ASEAN, 91–93
  development programmes, 293
  Indonesia
    ASEAN, 91–93
    contribution to employment,
        39–40
    definition, 37
    distribution of SMEs across
        ASEAN, 41, 43, 44
    economy contribution, 37–38,
        41–42
    employee productivity, 41
    employment growth in, 39

enterprise establishment growth
    (2008–14), 39–40
  gross domestic product, 37–39
  Law, 44
  Philippine SME, 292–96
Ministry of Commerce (MoC), 281n8
Ministry of Cooperatives, 198
Ministry of Cooperatives and SMEs
    (MoCSME), 50
Ministry of Economy, Trade and
    Industry (METI) survey, 497–98,
    511n2
Ministry of Foreign Affairs of the
    People's Republic of China 2008,
    603, 605
Ministry of Human Resources
    (MOHR), 154
Ministry of Industry (MoI), 197, 265,
    268, 269
Ministry of Industry and Commerce
    (MIoC), 108
Ministry of Labour, Employment and
    Social Security (MOLES), 278
Ministry of Labour, Invalids and
    Social Affairs (MOLISA), 442
Ministry of Science and Technology,
    268
Ministry of Trade, 54
most favoured nation (MFN), 493
  rates, 495
  schemes, 495
MSC Malaysia Intellectual Property
    Grant Scheme, 153
MSME Development Plan, 293
multinational corporations (MNCs),
    2, 4, 5, 348, 353n1, 609n2
  Chery Automobile Co. Ltd., 580,
      584, 600–5
  China, 580, 584, 588–90, 600–2,
      604–5
  eclectic theory of, 581
  Japan, 491, 492, 494, 511n3

Malaysia, 143, 152
offshoring and outsourcing, 552
production networks, 287
Vietnam, 516–17
Myanmar
  access to finance, 218–20
  age, ownership and legal status of,
    208–11
  apparel manufacturing sector, 200,
    203, 205, 208, 223, 229, 266,
    273
  ASEAN (*see* Association of
    Southeast Asian Nations
    (ASEAN))
  business population survey, 201,
    262
  business relations, 238–39
  data collection, 263–64
  development in SME, 195
  economic policy, 258
  economic system, 170, 175
  economy, 171–72, 175
  encourage firm registration and
    formalization, 261–63
  evidence-based policy-making,
    263–64
  exports (*see* exports, Myanmar)
  external trade, 176
  fiscal deficit, 173–74
  food manufacturing sector, 208,
    210, 212, 223, 232, 236, 243,
    266
  foreign direct investment, 190–94,
    229–32
  foreign investors, 228
  FTAs, 264–66
  garment sector, 237
  global value chains, 229–31
  government support by firm size,
    258–60
  gross domestic product, 171–74,
    178

  historical and macroeconomic
    context, 170–76
  human resource development,
    266–67
  ICT usage of SMEs, 271–72
  imports (*see* imports, Myanmar)
  informal sector in, 206–7
  Information and Communications
    Technologies, 212–14
  information sources, 175
  innovation and use of technology,
    211–18
  international economic
    transactions, 173
  international trade, 232–38
  intra-ASEAN exports, 182
  legal status of companies, 210
  macroeconomic indicators, 171
  major export destinations, 241–42
  policy implications, 258–73
  preferential market access, 188–90
  regional trade and production
    networks, 238–47
  registration levels firms, 206–7
  SME Law, 196, 197, 202, 272, 281n6
  SMEs, 174–75, 229–31
  survey methodology, 277–80
  technology and investment,
    267–71
  trade, 229–31
  trade agreements, 175, 188–90
  trade performance, 176–78
  trade with ASEAN, 178–82
  workforce characteristics, 220–29
Myanmar Citizens Investment Law,
  270
Myanmar Companies Act, 270
Myanmar Garment Manufacturers
  Association (MGMA), 200, 205,
  210, 277, 278, 281n8
Myanmar Insurance Company, 269,
  272

Myanmar Investment Commission (MIC), 190, 191, 270
Myanmar Investment Law, 270
Myanmar Kyat, 174
Myanmar Times, 198

N
National Auto Policy (NAP), 606
National Capital Region (NCR), 301
national electronic components firms, Malaysia, 155, 156, 158, 162
National Growth and Poverty Eradication Strategy (NGPES), 100
National Human Resources Centre, 154
National League for Democracy (NLD), 174
National Mark of Malaysian Brand, 153
National Medium Development Plan, 50
National Party Congress in 2001, 591
National SME Development Council (NSDC), 146
    policy-driven approach, 147
National Socio-Economic Development Plan (2011–15), 108
Negosyo Centers, 293
New Economic Mechanism (NEM), 98, 101, 102
new industrial policy, Philippines, 290
New Light of Myanmar, The, 198, 199, 207
non-parametric one-way ANOVA test, 158, 160
nonstate SMEs, Vietnam, 442
Noveltek, 571
"Nut-Cracker Effect", 358, 377

O
OECD–UMFCCI–UNESCAP survey, 199, 207, 208, 215, 220, 221
Office of Small and Medium Enterprises Promotion (OSMEP), 358, 364, 377
Office of the Board of Investment of Thailand, 362
offshoring and outsourcing, multinational corporations, 552
"One Belt One Road", 593
"One Pager Business Census 2013–2014", 198, 199, 220
One Referral Centre (ORC), 147–48
online marketing, 314
    Indonesia, 72
    Myanmar, 213
    Philippine, 314, 315
    Thailand, 412, 414
open trade policy, Philippines, 298
optimistic firms, 332, 349
Organisation for Economic Co-operation and Development (OECD), 199, 358, 377
Oriental Assemblers Sdn. Bhd., 601, 604, 605
Oriental Holdings Bhd., 601
original design manufacturers (ODMs), 531, 534
original equipment manufacturers (OEMs), 531
outsourcing R&D activities, 313–14
ownership, location, and internalization (OLI), 581

P
Pan-Mekong River Delta, 596
participating *vs.* non-participating enterprises, 479
4P company, 537
Perodua, 606
pessimistic firms, 332, 349

Philippine Council for Agriculture,
Aquatic and Natural Resources
Research and Development
(PCAARRD), 294
Philippine Council for Industry,
Energy and Emerging
Technology Research and
Development (PCIEERD), 294
Philippine Economic Zone Authority,
324, 331
Philippines
bilateral partnerships, 299
Bureau of Small and Medium
Enterprises Development, 293
Center for International Trade
Expositions and Missions, 294
chemical and chemical products,
290
Department of Science and
Technology, 293, 294
Department of Trade and Industry,
293, 294
distribution by manufacturing
sector, 302
economic growth performance, 289
economy accounting, 348
electrical machinery and apparatus,
290
electrical vehicles and solution
from Taiwan, 571
employment, 292, 295, 296, 301,
310–11
establishments by industry, 295,
301, 305
firm characteristics, 305–15
food manufacturing, 289
foreign workers, 313
free trade agreements, 288, 298–300
furniture and fixtures, 289, 290
industry growth, 290
innovation activities, 312, 313
internet services, 314, 315

investment liberalization, 298
manufacturing enterprises and
employees, 297
manufacturing industry, 289, 301
manufacturing structure and
growth performance, 291
mean sales, 305
new industrial policy, 290
open trade policy, 298
process innovation, 313, 314
product innovation, 313
production activities, 308–9
production costs, 310
profile of the sample firms, 303–4
R&D activities, 313–14
regional and preferential trade
agreements, 298–300
sales distribution, 306–7
SME growth and development, 288
substantial trade, 298
tariff profile by FTA, 300
Philippines–Japan FTA, 298–99
Philippine Statistics Authority, 298
Philippine Trade Training Center
(PTTC), 294
policies and programmes, for SME
development, 292–94
poverty
Laos, 98, 100
Myanmar, 194
preferential tariff utilization (PTU),
Laos, 114–18, 126
Champassack, 114–15
Khammouane, 115
Savannakhet, 115
Vientiane Capital, 115
Private Industrial Enterprise Law,
198
private sector, 12
Cambodia, 30
Laos, 105, 108
Myanmar, 170, 172, 198, 261, 269

Thailand, 355
Vietnam, 436, 516
process innovation, 313, 314
process upgrading, 538
product innovation, 313, 483
production activities, 308–9
production costs, 310
  large enterprises, 310
  Vietnam SMEs, 461
production networks
  Laos SMEs, 98, 101
  Myanmar's SMEs, 238–47
  participation in, 4, 12, 35, 288
  Philippine SMEs, 288–89, 353
  Thailand, 378, 427
  Vietnam, 446, 476–85
product upgrading, 538
profits, 319, 324
Proton, 606
public–private partnership (PPP),
  Cambodia, 30
Pusat Layanan Usaha Terpadu (PLUT),
  50

R
raw materials, 18, 65, 253, 294, 310,
  461
R&D activities, 313–14
Regional Comprehensive Economic
  Partnership (RCEP), 299, 597,
  598
regional economic integration, 247–58
  advantage of, 247
  in ASEAN and East Asia, 289
  Indonesia, 78–82
  SME participation in, 289
regional production networks. *See*
  global production networks
regional trade agreements (RTAs),
  509
  automotive industry impact,
  599–600

bilateral rates, 493
connect to the World through
  ACFTA, 597–98
legal protection, 594–97
Malaysia, 157–60, 162–65
multilateral rates, 493
Myanmar's SMEs, 238–47
regional value content (RVC) rules,
  493, 499, 502, 506, 507
registered firms, Myanmar, 261–63
Regulatory Review Department, 148
Republic Act 9178 Barangay Micro
  Business Enterprises Act (2002),
  293
Republic Act 10644 Go Negosyo Act
  (2015), 293
Republic Act 6977 Magna Carta for
  Small Enterprises (1991), 292
research and development (R&D),
  215, 218
  Indonesia, 70
  Philippine electronics industry,
  386
  programmes, 294
respondent firms, 349, 351
RFID-based tolling system, 572
rights of land use, Laos, 102–3
"The Rise of Central", 587
rules of origin (ROO), 80, 255, 299,
  352–53, 353n2, 493, 496, 500, 501,
  504–9

S
salaries and wages
  Indonesian SMEs, 65
  Philippine SMEs, 310
  Vietnam SMEs, 461, 463, 465
sales (XS), 158–60, 162–66
sales distribution, 306–7
Samsung Electronics Vietnam, 533–35,
  544n18
"Saturday Talks", 265

savings rate
    China, 585
    Laos, 100
sectoral distribution, Myanmar SMEs,
    205–6
Securities Commission of Malaysia,
    150
Seoul Metal (SM), 535–36
Shinwon company, 531
Shinwon Ebenezer, 529
Singapore
    Chinese investment in, 585
    exports from Malaysia to, 183
    exports to ASEAN, 178
    as foreign investors in Myanmar,
        231
    FTA with Taiwan, 559
    MSMEs, 92
    per capita ASEAN exports and
        imports, 180
    SME employment, 195
    SMEs sales turnover, 37
    Taiwan's import from, 559
    tariffs on Chinese products, 597
single proprietorships, 301
skilled labour
    Myanmar, 221, 252–53, 266, 267
    Thailand, 377
    Vietnam, 443
Small and Medium Enterprise (SME)
    Promotion Law, 108
Small and Medium Industrial
    Development Bank (SMIDB), 269
small and medium industries (SMIs),
    198, 205
small and medium-sized enterprises
    (SMEs)
    ASEAN blueprint for, 247–48
    characteristics, 202–5
    definition, 196–97, 272
    development in Myanmar, 195
    disadvantages, 1

Law, 196–97
    registries and surveys, 197–202
    role of, 194–96
small business credit (KUR), 53
small enterprises, 301
    Indonesia, 37, 54
    Laos, 105
Small Scale Industries Department
    (SSID), 198
SME Competitiveness Rating for
    Enhancement (SCORE), 152
SME Corporation Malaysia (SME
    Corp.), 146, 148
    One Referral Centre, 147
    programmes, 147, 152
    SIRIM, 153
SME development programmes, 146
SME Info Portal, 148, 152
SME Promotion and Development
    Fund, Laos, 108
SME Promotion and Development
    Office (SMEPDO), 105, 108
SME Roving Academy, 293
SME Toolkit Kiosk, 148
"South-bound Policy", Taiwan, 553
South Korea
    FDI inflows into Vietnam, 520–21
    FTA-PASS, 509
    Vietnam–Korean bilateral trade,
        518–19
    Vietnam–Korean investment
        relations, 518–19
special economic zones (SEZs), 268,
    428
Standards and Industrial Research
    Institute of Malaysia (SIRIM), 153
start-up costs, 429
state-owned enterprises (SOEs), 600
    Indonesia, 61
    Vietnam, 442, 458, 461, 485n1
Statistical Package for Social Sciences
    (SPSS), 157

Statistical Yearbook of Vietnam 2014,
526
Statistics Act, 497
Strategic Action Plan for ASEAN
SME Development (SAPASD),
317
strategic businesses, 148
sub-manufacturing sectors, Thailand
SMEs, 387–88, 390, 399, 402, 404,
408, 414
subsidiary companies, Indonesia, 61
substantial trade, Philippines, 298
supply chain, 454

T
Taiwan
bilateral trade, 551, 562
direct investment in ASEAN, 550,
555
economic links with ASEAN, 573
electrical vehicles and solution for
Philippines, 571
electronic toll collection (ETC)
solution for freeways
for Vietnam, 572–73
export
to ASEAN, 553, 556
to different parts of world
(2001–15), 557
to the individual ASEAN
members, 553, 558
FTA with Singapore, 550, 559
import
from ASEAN, 559
from different parts of the world
(2001–15), 559, 560
from the individual ASEAN
members, 559, 561
"investment-induced trade", 550
investment in Vietnam, 553
outward investment to ASEAN,
552–54

"South-bound Policy", 553
textile and apparel industry
export, 562, 563
international division of labour
since 1990s, 564, 565
production, 564
relationships with the global
value chains, 566
trade-investment-service-IP
nexus, 567–69
trade surplus, 562, 563
"trade-investment-service- IP
nexus", 551
tariff margin, 495
tax exemptions, 150
technical and vocational education
and training (TVET), 30, 267
technology
innovations, 515
Malaysia, 151–55
technology commercialisation
platform, and inclusive
innovation, 152
Teco, 571
textile and garment industry, Vietnam
abundant and cheap labour, 448
anti-dumping lawsuits, 448
cutting–making–trimming
production modality, 448
economy growth, 448
exports, 446–47
human resource policies, 449
investment projects, 449
low-quality legal documents, 448
supporting industries, 448
Thailand–Australia FTA, 373
Thailand–Peru FTA, 373
Thailand SMEs, 358
academic qualification of the
founder or family relative,
395–97
affected by AEC, 416, 418–19

aggregate, 360–62
business relations, 414–17
contribution of GDP, 367, 368–71
contribution of manufacturing,
      355–57
cooperation and integration, 378
definition of, 359–60
domestic market, 379
employment, 355, 357, 364–66
entrepreneurial activity and
      ownership, 429
exporting and non-exporting
      enterprises, 398
export products, 182–83
exports (*see* exports)
family business, 393–94
finance, 378
First SME Promotion Plan (2002–6),
      382–83, 431n8
foreign ownership, 429
goods and services, 408, 409
government assistance, 386
government regulation, 382
gross domestic product, 355,
      357–58
human resource development,
      381
information technology, 380
in-house and outsourced
      production, 399–402
in-house R&D and outsourcing
      R&D, 404, 405
innovation and technology, 380–81,
      408, 410–11
intense competition, 373, 377
international competition, 377
internet-related services, 408,
      412–14
investments, 428
key issues facing, 377–78
labour force, 381
large enterprises, 357, 358

machinery, equipment, software
      and external knowledge, 404,
      406–8
manufacture of rubber and plastic
      products, 387–414
manufacturing, 358, 360, 362
marketing, 379
merchandise trade value, 376
number and percentage of
      manufacturing firms, 389
ownership of the parent company,
      393–94
ownership type, 391–92
policy environment, 382–84
policy implications, 426–29
probit and logit models
      for aggregate manufacturing
            firms, 422–23
      large manufacturing firms, 424
      small manufacturing firms, 425
quality and production, 428
regional and urban–rural inequity,
      428
retail sector, 360, 362
Second SME Promotion Plan
      (2007–11), 384
by sector, 362–63
service sector, 360, 362
by size, 361
submanufacturing sectors, 387–88,
      390, 399, 402, 404, 408, 414
trade balance, 373
trade deficit, 373, 376
wholesale sector, 360
worker training and hired foreign
      workers, 402–4
workforce, 428
Thailand–South Korea FTA, 373
Thai National Economic and Social
      Plan, 380
third country export platform,
      511n3

trade agreements, Myanmar, 229–31, 247–58
Trade and Investment Framework Agreement (TIFA), 188
trade characteristics, Laos, 100–2
Trade Development Facility Project (TDF-2), 109
"trade-investment-service-IP nexus", Taiwan, 551, 568–69, 573
  IP (R&D)-trade-investment linkages, 567, 570
  trade-investment linkages, 567
  trade-service-IP (R&D) linkages, 570
trade policy, Laos, 100–2
trade share, Cambodia, 11
training expenditure in payroll (TEP), 158–60, 162–65
training expenditures, 331
training programmes, SMEs, 152
Trans-Pacific Parnership (TPP), 299, 516, 523, 530, 542n10, 597–98

U
UK Companies Act of 1989, 438
unaware or uninformed firms, 332, 349
Union of Myanmar Federation of Chambers of Commerce and Industry (UMFCCI), 199
United Kingdom
  Myanmar trade linkages with, 176
  SMEs, 438
  Vietnam's textiles exports to, 447
United Nations Development Programme (UNDP), 198, 199, 220, 281n7
United Nations Economic and Social Commission for Asia and the Pacific (UNESCAP), 195
United States
  SMEs, 436, 437

University of Copenhagen (Denmark), 442

V
value added growth
  Malaysia SMEs, 144–45
variables, definition of, 345
venture capital corporations (VCCs), 150
venture capital funds, 150
venture capital markets, 429
Venture Capital Tax Incentives Guidelines, 150
Vietnam
  abundant labour force, 523, 536
  apparel processing industry, 518
  capital injection, 516
  development of SMEs, 442
  economic liberalization policy, 443
  electronics FDI inflows, 531
  electronics sector, 518
  electronic toll collection (ETC) solution for freeways from Taiwan, 572–73
  employment creation, 516
  financial access to SMEs, 446
  food and beverage industry, 449–51
  foreign direct investment, 516, 519, 530
  foreign-invested enterprises, 442
  government policies to develop SMEs, 444–46, 485
  human resource development for SMEs, 445
  impact of regional integration and investment decision by Korean MNEs, 520–23
  import from Korea, 518
  investment strategy of MNEs, 529–30
  key exports, 532
  key investors in, 520

limited liability companies, 455
multinational enterprises, 516–17
non-state SMEs, 442
participation in global production
    networks
    advanced electronics sector,
        531–32
    Korean apparel production
        network, 528–31
    Korean electronics production
        network, 533–37
    traditional apparel sector, 526–28
regulation on stamp of enterprises,
    445
share of SMEs in total number of
    enterprises, 439
SME definition, 437–38
SMEs by ownership, 442
SMEs in, 436, 439–44
SMEs' participation
    in global production networks,
        524–26
    in production networks, 476–83
SMEs vs. large enterprises
    employment, 441
    state budget contribution, 444
state-owned enterprises, 442
survey on SMEs' participation, in
        regional economic integration
    AEC affecting businesses, 472
    awareness of AEC and impacts,
        468–71
    education, 465
    employment, 463
    human resources, 463–65
    innovation activities, 465–66
    international trade participation,
        467–68
    production activities, 461–63
    R&D activities, 465
    regional and national levels,
        475–76

sales activities, 458–61
    sample characteristics, 454–58
    utilization of FTAs and
        influences, 472–75
Taiwanese firms' investment in, 553
tax incentives, 523, 536
textile and garment industry,
    446–49
textiles exports to United Kingdom,
    447
timer industry, 453
total revenue by SMEs, 442, 443
Vietnam–Korean bilateral trade,
    518–19
Vietnam–Korean investment
    relations, 518–19
wood processing industry, 451–54
working with medium-sized
    Korean firms, 538–39
Vietnam Development Bank (VDB),
    446
Vietnam Electronic and Informatics
    Association, 531
Vietnam–EU FTA, 516
Vietnam–Korean bilateral trade,
    518–19
Vietnam–Korean investment
    relations, 518–19
Vietnam Kumyang, 530
Vietnam–South Korea FTA, 520, 523
Vietnam Textile and Apparel
    Association (VITAS), 447, 527
Vinatex group, 542n11

W
weak performance, of SMEs, 298
West's Great Development, 587
White Paper on International
    Economy and Trade 2014, 491
wood processing industry, Vietnam
    abundant and cheap labour, 453
    exporting markets, 452–53

export turnover, 451
groups, 451–52
investment, 452
low added value, 453
low labour productivity, 453
outsourcing, 453
workforce, 452
worker training, Myanmar, 224
workforce, 30
educational level of, 30
Indonesian SME, 67
Myanmar, 196, 220–29
Philippine SME, 313
Thailand's SME, 381
training of, 30
Vietnam SMEs, 449
World Association of Industrial and
Technological Organisations
(WAITRO), 153
World Bank, 139n2, 195, 248, 438,
485n1, 498

World Bank and Department of
Statistics, 100
World Bank's Doing Business survey,
53, 220, 262
World Bank's Enterprise Survey, 199,
206, 208, 210–12, 218, 221, 224,
234, 236, 238
World Development Indicators
(WDI), 178
World Trade Organization (WTO),
109–10, 446, 551, 567, 578, 594
awareness and impact, 113–14
overall effects of, 113

Y
Yangon City Development Committee
(YCDC), 198
Yangon Region, 200, 273, 277, 278
Ys Tech company (YT), 538–39,
545n24

www.ingramcontent.com/pod-product-compliance
Lightning Source LLC
Chambersburg PA
CBHW060416220326
41598CB00021BA/2193